STUDIES IN CONNOISSEURSHIP

烟開蘭葉香風暖
岸夾桃花錦浪生
李青蓮鸚鵡洲句清湘老
人濟時亦拓出引興

Tao-chi, *Landscapes, Vegetables, and Flowers*, leaf C, "River Bank of Peach Blossoms"

STUDIES IN CONNOISSEURSHIP

Chinese Paintings from the
Arthur M. Sackler Collections
in New York, Princeton
and Washington, D.C.

MARILYN AND SHEN FU

EXHIBITION VENUES

The Art Museum, Princeton University, Princeton, NJ:
December 8, 1973–February 3, 1974
The Cleveland Museum of Art, Cleveland, OH: July 10–September 2, 1974
The Los Angeles County Museum of Art, Los Angeles, CA:
September 15–November 3, 1974
The Philbrook Art Center, Tulsa, OK: January 9–February 22, 1976
The Metropolitan Museum of Art, New York, NY: May 13–September 7, 1976
The Fogg Art Museum, Harvard University, Cambridge, MA:
February 15–March 31, 1977
The Denver Art Museum, Denver, CO: June 15–July 31, 1977
The Krannert Art Museum, University of Illinois, Champaign, IL:
August 15–September 31, 1977
Fort Lauderdale Museum of the Arts, Fort Lauderdale, FL:
October 15–December 1, 1977
Ackland Art Center, University of North Carolina, Chapel Hill, NC:
December 15, 1977–January 30, 1978
Memorial Art Gallery, University of Rochester, Rochester, NY:
February 15–March 31, 1978
The Winnipeg Art Gallery, Winnipeg, Manitoba, Canada: April 15–May 31, 1978
The Detroit Institute of Art, Detroit, MI: June 20–July 30, 1978
The Fine Arts Gallery of San Diego, San Diego, CA: August 11–October 1, 1978
Beaumont Art Museum, Beaumont, TX: October 13–November 30, 1978
The Witte Museum, San Antonio Museum Association, San Antonio, TX:
December 15, 1978–January 30, 1979
Elvehjem Art Center, University of Wisconsin, Madison WI:
February 15–March 13, 1979
Kimbell Art Museum, Fort Worth, TX: April 17–June 3, 1979
Minneapolis Institute of Arts, Minneapolis, MN: June 15–July 31, 1979
Helen Foreman Spencer Museum of Art, University of Kansas, Lawrence, KS:
August 26–October 7, 1979
The Israel Museum, Jerusalem, Israel: February 26–May 4, 1980
The National Gallery of Ireland, Dublin, Ireland: July 3–October 1, 1980
The Edinburgh Festival, Talbott Rice Art Centre, Scotland:
August 10–September 4, 1984
The Fitzwilliam Museum, Cambridge University, England:
April 11-June 29, 1986

Designed by Crimilda Pontes
Produced by Finn Typographic Service
and the Meriden Gravure Company

The reprint of this catalogue has been made possible through a grant
from the Arthur M. Sackler Foundation, Washington, D.C.

Library of Congress Catalogue Card Number: 73-77442
ISBN: 0-691-03892-9

Distributed by the Arthur M. Sackler Foundation, Washington, D.C.

可樂藏畫研究

壬子秋 天約傅申

TO OUR PARENTS

Contents

Foreword by Arthur M. Sackler   ix

Preface by Wen C. Fong   xi

Acknowledgments   xiii

Catalogue Entries   xv

I. Geography: The "Eye Area" in Chinese Painting   1

Map of the "Eye Area," 2. Lake T'ai, 5. Sung-chiang, 6. Su-chou, 7. Two Loyalist Painters, 9. Huang-shan, Anhwei, 9. Hang-chou and Nanking, 10. Yang-chou, 10. Shanghai, 11. The Influence of Imperial Collecting on the Painters of the Eye Area: The Ch'ien-lung Emperor, 11.

II. Issues in Connoisseurship   15

In Search of the "Right Number" and the "Right Place," 16. "Understanding the Music" and "Eating with One's Ears," 17. The Ideal Art Historian and Connoisseur of Chinese Art, 18. The Methodological Paradox, 19. Aspects of Quality, 20. Problems of Period Style and the Formulation of Method, 21. A Note on the "Importance" of a Work of Art, 22. The True Connoisseur and the Great Forger, 20. The Place of Forgeries in Art History, 23. Criteria for Authenticity, 23.

III. Case Studies in Connoisseurship   27

(1) Three Versions of the Same Composition, Two Forged, One Genuine, 28. (2) Two Versions of the Same Composition, One Genuine, One Forged, 29. (3) Two Versions of a Similar Subject, Both Genuine, 29. (4) A Case of Mistaken Authorship, 30. (5) Identification through a Correctly Deciphered Seal, 30. (6) The *Ku-pen*, or "Only Extant Work," 30. (7) Identification through Calligraphy, 30. (8) Typical Identity, 31. (9) Unusual Identity, 31. (10) Early Identity, 32. (11) Late Identity, 32. (12) Altered Identity, 32. (13) Forged Identity, 33. (14) Three Copies of the Same Composition, Two *Mala Fide*, One *Bona Fide*, 32.

IV. Tao-chi   35

Tao-chi's Life, 36. Tao-chi's Calligraphy, 40. Tao-chi's Painting, 45. Tao-chi's Art Theories, 51. Calligraphy as a Basis for Authentication, 59.

V. Catalogue of the Sackler Collection   71

Bibliography   343

Chinese and Japanese Names and Terms   349

Index   373

Foreword

My interest in the arts of China has its roots in the art-historical studies that paralleled my education in the medical sciences many years ago. I went on to become immersed in the philosophy and practice of medical research, and my perspectives as a collector reflect this lifetime interest in the philosophy of science and the history of man. For me, a pre-eminent function of collecting has been the reconstruction of civilizations, of different cultures, and this goal can only be achieved through scholarly studies. In collecting, as in the sciences, when a large enough corpus of material has been gathered, a representative as well as a true reconstruction of the past can be attempted. In such a total historical reconstruction, it is vital that study materials as well as masterpieces be preserved, and the life work of other collectors is, of course, vital in this regard.

When I came to the field of Chinese art in the 1950's, many of the earlier opportunities to develop collections of ceramics and bronzes were gone. However, there was comparatively little interest in Chinese painting, and this, ironically, at the very point in time when, through the vicissitudes of history, many privately owned treasures were becoming available. We undertook to maintain as complete entities a number of outstanding collections of Chinese art throughout the world that were threatened with dispersal, and we also supported and encouraged conservation studies, research, archeological endeavors, and university symposia, in accordance with the art-historical and archeological goals outlined above.

Amateurs are highly sensitive to the problems of authenticity and forgery, and exposure to Chinese painting, in which the aesthetic so often finds its ultimate expression, increases one's sensitivity to the subtleties of all Chinese art while making him distrustful of his competence to understand and appreciate fully the experience it offers. If there be any one field of art that places the most rigorous demands upon the amateur, it is, I believe, the connoisseurship of Chinese painting and calligraphy. Accordingly, for some years we limited our collection to such clearly authenticated material as frescoes. In the mid 1960's, after years of search, we acquired what is probably the jewel of our collections, the Ch'u silk manuscript, the earliest document of its kind in existence, dating from the sixth century B.C.

In 1967, however, we heard of the efforts of The Art Museum of Princeton University to acquire a group of Chinese ritual bronzes. Because of their cost, there had been talk among collectors of a "wild purchase." We went to Princeton to see for ourselves. One glance at the bronzes that Professor Wen Fong wanted for Princeton convinced us that it would be a privilege to assist in their acquisition. Even more important than those priceless objects was the remarkable phenomenon in progress at the university itself. A new generation of scholars was cross-fertilizing the historic connoisseurship of China with the art-historical studies of the West. There could be no mistaking the infectious enthusiasm and pride that pervaded Wen Fong's department. We decided to participate in this exciting adventure, and most, if not all, of the paintings in our collection were acquired over the next two years under Professor Fong's guidance. Pleasures shared are pleasures doubled: thus almost our entire collection of Chinese painting is now "in residence," so to speak, with the scholars and visitors in Princeton, while friends of all cultures share other works at The Metropolitan Museum of Art and at Columbia University.

With a few exceptions, the paintings that are the subject of this exhibition came from three major sources: Frank Caro (nos. *I–V, VIII, X, XIII, XXXVI–XLI*), Chang Ta-ch'ien (nos. *XII, XVII, XX, XXII–XXV, XXVII, XXIX–XXXIV*), and, later, the Richard Bryant Hobart collection (nos. *VI, VII, XIV–XVI*). Other paintings came from Taiwan (*IX, XI, XIX*), Hong Kong (*XXVIII*), Japan (*XXVI*), and England (*XVIII*). The collection could not have been assembled without the care and patience of Frank Caro and Professor Chang Ta-ch'ien.

People often ask a collector what his favorite object is. Our favorites among the paintings are the albums, especially no. *XXV*, eight leaves of flowers by Tao-chi, that leading individualist master of the late seventeenth century. One marvels at these inspired creations and can scarcely believe that two and a half centuries separate Tao-chi's flowers and Mondrian's chrysanthemums. Special thanks, therefore, are due Marilyn and Shen C. Y. Fu, the authors of the text of this catalogue, for through their eyes we have come to see ever more clearly the significance not only of the collection as a whole but of the painting and calligraphy of Tao-chi in particular. They have shown us Chinese painting for the first time, as it were. To them and to Professor Wen Fong, our congratulations for a major contribution to the study and appreciation of Chinese painting.

Arthur M. Sackler, M.D.

New York, New York
May, 1973

Preface

While Western scholarship has made significant contributions to the study of Chinese archaic bronzes, jades, and ceramics, it has had less success thus far with Chinese painting and calligraphy, the twin fine arts of traditional China. The difficulties encountered in the latter field are not only linguistic and technical but also cultural and philosophical; they involve different artistic sensibilities and attitudes toward authentication, as well as different notions of creativity and artistic value. Ernst Gombrich, in his book *Art and Illusion*, writes that "the language in which we [in the West] discuss pictures differs so radically from the critical terminology of the Far East that all attempts to translate from one into the other are frustrated."[1] Insofar as the modern art historian shares the scientist's faith in the community and unity of knowledge, he must believe that different ways of seeing and thinking can be understood and described. Yet there are times when it seems almost impossible to discuss a single Chinese painting without first becoming immersed in that heritage.

The Chinese view the art of painting in terms of a series of continuing stylistic traditions. Since artists continued to work in earlier styles while new ones were evolving, it has been the rule rather than the exception—especially since the Yüan period (late thirteenth century)—for Chinese painters to work in a variety of styles or idioms. This fact alone suggests that, although there may be great diversity among the works of a single master at a given time because of the practice of imitating and copying earlier models, works produced in different periods but couched in the same idiom may indeed be hard to distinguish from one another.

In the last thirty years the most powerful Western contribution to the study of Chinese art has been the development of stylistic analysis, which attempts to see a logical formal development behind even the most bewildering visual phenomena. The belief that morphological analysis of successive visual positions in history (or "period styles") can provide an independent clue for dating has served as a useful corrective to a picture of random growth, or endless repetition, through copying and imitation. Yet an anonymous history of visual structures can easily become a pointless or even misleading exercise when it fails to explain, or to be explained by, specific paintings and art-historical contexts. No theoretical stylistic categories thus far devised have been able to deal adequately with the full complexities of later Chinese painting.

In a recent special issue devoted to Chinese landscape painting, the editor of *The Burlington Magazine*, applauding the interest in Chinese painting in the Western world since World War II, and in the United States in particular, points out three advantages of this interest: "Firstly, sinology expanded at a spectacular rate and many of its leading authorities had made extended visits to China. Secondly, a number of both Chinese and Japanese connoisseurs visited, and in some cases moved to, the United States, providing an essential fund of experience. . . . Thirdly, this experience has met with the formidable sophistications of Western Art History."[2] To this list may be added a fourth advantage, the massive acquisition of first-rate Chinese paintings in recent years by Western public and private collectors. These fine and exciting objects, though not always fully understood at first, have formed the bases of important exhibitions that have whetted the appetite of the viewing public and have animated academic discussions. Each juxtaposition of the actual paintings in this way answers certain questions while posing others.

Such object-oriented studies—as opposed to the systematic and theoretical speculations developed in the West—build and expand from specific facts: rather than moving within a closed system and from the general to the specific, they proceed in an open-ended fashion, going from fact to fact, and then reach out to construct some general observations. If we start with the assumption that no attribution of a Chinese painting should be accepted blindly, then each new painting becomes a "discovery," which, once properly understood, itself forms the basis for further discoveries. Reflecting on the landscape exhibition held at the Cleveland Museum of Art in 1954, Sherman Lee wrote that "surprisingly, even with the most diversified scholarly painters, a homogeneity of style, or touch, is ultimately revealed, and on a visual basis."[3] This "revelation" is the intuitive and pragmatic response of a connoisseur; it is mercifully free from the academic need to translate from one set of critical terminology into the other, as Professor Gombrich put it.

The Arthur M. Sackler collection of Chinese paintings includes masterpieces from the fourteenth to the twentieth centuries, selected from many sources. Its unique strength, however, lies in a group of fifteen important works of painting and calligraphy by Tao-chi (or Shih-t'ao, 1641–ca. 1710), a Ming loyalist, half-Taoist, half-Buddhist, a wild "mountain man" (*shan-jen*) and the leading individualist master of the early Ch'ing period. The earliest work is from an album dated 1677–78 and the latest a major album of twelve landscapes dated 1707. These fifteen objects—seven scrolls (cat. nos. *XVII, XVIII, XXIV, XXVII, XXIX, XXXI,* and *XXXII*) and eight albums (cat. nos. *XX, XXII, XXIII, XXV, XXVI, XXX, XXXIII,* and *XXXIV*), comprising seventy-three individual leaves—demonstrate the full stylistic range of Tao-chi's landscape, figure, and flower and fruit painting and of his calligraphy. They now constitute the largest body of authenticated works by this leading seventeenth-century Chinese painter. The Sackler collection also contains a forgery album of six landscape leaves in Tao-chi's style (*XXXV*), as well as copies (*XIX, XXI,* and *XXVIII*) of three Tao-chi works in the collection (*XVIII, XX, XXVII*).

With the single exception of *XXVI*, an album of ten landscapes and one leaf of calligraphy dated 1701, which came from the late Sumitomo Kanichi collection in Kyoto, all the works by Tao-chi in the Sackler collection belonged to the famous contemporary Chinese painter and collector Chang Yüan, better known as Chang Dai-chien (properly romanized as Chang Ta-ch'ien), a man who, in reputation and deed, should be regarded as the greatest living authority on Tao-chi. The neglect of Tao-chi's art in official circles during the Ch'ing period is indicated by the fact that the Ch'ing imperial collection (now preserved in the National Palace Museum in Taiwan) includes only half of a Tao-chi work, a painting of bamboo and rocks done in collaboration with Wang Yüan-ch'i, the great orthodox master, and dedicated to the Manchu noble Po-erh-tu. With the downfall of the Manchu Ch'ing dynasty in the early decades of this century, the study of the lives and works of the Ming loyalists of the early Ch'ing period suddenly became fashionable among a group of scholarly Ch'ing loyalists. The two best known of the group are Li Jui-ch'ing (or Ch'ing Tao-jen) and Tseng Hsi, Chang Ta-ch'ien's teachers. They not only wore their hair long and affected the life styles of the early Ch'ing hermit-scholars but, rejecting the rigid orthodox style of late Ch'ing painting, cultivated a taste for the bold brush styles of Tao-chi, Chu Ta, and other early Ch'ing individualist masters.

Two important works by Tao-chi that came from Chang Ta-ch'ien's collection originally belonged to Master Li Jui-ch'ing: Tao-chi's *Letter to Pa-ta shan-jen* of about 1698–99 (*XXIII*) and the album *Flowers and Figures,* dated 1695 (*XX*). These works were the true "teachers" of Master Li's circle of friends and followers; by studying and copying them, they learned to become not only painters and calligraphers but connoisseurs and collectors as well. While Tao-chi's œuvre was being studied and reconstructed by Master Li and his colleagues, his paintings (and works attributed to him) were attracting a devoted following in China and also in Japan. Some, like Nagahara Oriharu, a collector living in Manchuria in the late 1920's, became unwitting victims of the hoaxes (or were they merely studio exercises?) perpetrated by Master Li's circle of inspired followers. In recent years Chang Ta-ch'ien has admitted to having made the famous Nagahara version of Tao-chi's letter to Chu Ta "as a joke." The replica of Tao-chi's *Flowers and Figures* album, according to Mr. Chang, was made by Master Li's younger brother, Li Jui-ch'i (*XXI*).

When the inevitable reaction to these "jokes" set in, Tao-chi's real identity became thoroughly muddled. For some thirty years Chinese, Japanese, and Western assumptions about his chronology were influenced by the deliberately manipulated evidence in the Nagahara (Chang Ta-ch'ien) forgery, so that the majority of scholars placed his birthdate around 1630 instead of 1641. When the original letter by Tao-chi was finally publicly exhibited at the University of Michigan Art Museum in 1967, fear was expressed here and abroad that a third version—or perhaps several more—might exist. The Michigan exhibition, organized by Richard Edwards with the able assistance of Wu T'ung and others, was a great pioneering venture: it showed forty-eight objects, including most of the best-known Tao-chi works outside China. In spite of one extreme view at the time that there were only three authentic Tao-chis in the world, all in the famous Sumitomo collection in Japan, the Michigan exhibition cleared the air of mystery and suspicion. It convincingly demonstrated that the art of Tao-chi, seemingly the most elusive of all Chinese painting problems, could be discussed intelligently and grasped by competent art historians. Professor Edwards' broad and catholic choice of objects has proved, in retrospect, both courageous and wise.

In the following catalogue, prepared by Marilyn and Shen Fu, the authors demonstrate, in a clear and intelligible way, how each attribution was arrived at. A member of the research staff of the National Palace Museum in Taiwan, Shen has spent the past four years studying at Princeton under a grant from the JDR 3rd Fund. During this time he has won the respect and admiration of his teachers and colleagues alike as an impeccable connoisseur and a scholar of great independence of mind and intellectual honesty. His wife Marilyn is American-born and also received her training at Princeton. Together they have produced this monumental work, combining the best of the Western and Chinese approaches to the subject.

I cannot close without a brief but heartfelt word of thanks to Dr. and Mrs. Arthur Sackler, without whose loyal and understanding support the project represented by this catalogue could never have come into being. In view of the difficult and controversial nature of Chinese painting as a whole, and of the Tao-chi problem in particular, Dr. Sackler's willingness to support so risky a venture was especially valuable. Although Chinese painting makes up a small part of his total collection, the present volume represents, we believe, a useful and important contribution in our field.

Wen C. Fong, *Chairman*
Department of Art and Archaeology
Princeton University

NOTES

1. E. H. Gombrich, *Art and Illusion* (Princeton, N.J., 1960), p. 150.
2. "The Post-War Interest in Chinese Painting," *The Burlington Magazine,* vol. 114 (1972), p. 282.
3. "Some Problems in Ming and Ch'ing Landscape Painting," *Ars Orientalis,* vol. 2 (1957), p. 472.

Acknowledgments

This catalogue has grown in size and scope beyond all expectations. The paintings were initially selected and the research and writing begun in the summer of 1969, when it was conceived of as a small handbook to introduce the Sackler paintings now in residence at Princeton, similar to those which were planned for the Sackler jades, sculpture, and bronzes. The manuscript on paintings gained momentum as the other projects fell by the wayside, however, and season after season the exhibition of the Sackler paintings was postponed to accommodate the writing and editing and the addition of new paintings. The catalogue now includes six works purchased by The Metropolitan Museum of Art from the Sackler Fund (*VI, VII, XIV, XV, XVI*, and *XXII*). These were added at the last stages of publication, so that little mention of these paintings will be found in the introductory chapters. To keep the text to a manageable length, discussion of these objects will be published elsewhere, and we apologize for the resultant imbalance of treatment.

The reader should be warned that many of the topics touched upon in Part I deserve or have already received specialized study in their proper fields of the East Asian discipline, to which this survey can contribute in only the most general way. Parts II and III explore certain aspects of the methodology of art history and connoisseurship not discussed in Part V, the catalogue itself. We have not attempted to give historical definitions of style or period, although we hope that the procedures followed in the entries indicate the presence of a working model for such a set of definitions, nor do we offer a systematic exposition of the history of Chinese painting or of traditional Chinese connoisseurship. These topics are beyond the scope of a catalogue. The range and excellence of the Sackler Tao-chi paintings justify the disproportionate length of the discussion devoted to him in Part IV, and the stress is on facets of his work which we believe previous scholars have not yet fully explored, such as his relationship to antiquity and the analysis of his calligraphic style, which offer new areas for further study.

Many readers will find our translations of texts and poetry inadequate—a fault of almost all catalogues so far—and for this we ask their indulgence. We are not literary critics, poets, or even students of literature: we have tried to render what is relevant to the paintings in correct and relatively readable English. In this effort we acknowledge the aid of T'ang Hai-t'ao of Columbia University and others, but none of these friends were able to examine all the renderings, and we alone are responsible for whatever errors and misinterpretations there may be. We had hoped to romanize the more cursive poems, colophons, and inscriptions and to provide a proper index, but technical difficulties and printers' schedules made it impossible to do so.

The goodwill of our colleagues in the Department of Chinese and Japanese Art helped carry us through this project. We owe a special debt to David Sensabaugh, who read various early drafts of text and catalogue entries with care. James and Lucy Lo, old friends of Chang Ta-ch'ien from their Tun-huang days, acted as liaison for us on several matters, and Mrs. Lo executed the Chinese characters of the text. The calligraphy of the dedication page and glossary-index was executed by the author, Shen C. Y. Fu. Professor James T. C. Liu kindly read Part I and made several valuable suggestions. We thank Maxwell Hearn, Jean Schmitt, and the staffs of The Metropolitan Museum of Art, and of The Art Museum, Princeton, especially Virginia Wageman and Jean MacLachlan for their expert coordination of the production of this book. Our editor, Jean Owen, from the very beginning dealt with the project with objectivity and humor and transformed our rough manuscript into a book, and Crimilda Pontes gave us its beautiful design.

Mr. Porter McCray, of The JDR 3rd Fund, was also instrumental in making this book possible, as the fund provided four years of grants-in-aid which enabled Shen to take a leave of absence from the National Palace Museum, Taipei, to enter the Ph.D. program at Princeton. We thank also the American Oriental Society, which awarded Marilyn the Louise Hackney Memorial Fellowship, and Chiang Fu-ts'ung, director of the National Palace Museum, who allowed Shen this period to further his studies at Princeton.

Deepest thanks are reserved for our teachers, Professors Wen Fong and Shūjirō Shimada. Shimada, writing in the early fifties, helped to publish the famous Sumitomo collection, one album of which was acquired by Dr. Sackler. Fong's definitive article on Tao-chi's *Letter to Pa-ta*, now in the Sackler collection (see cat. no. *XXIII*), helped to put Tao-chi studies on a sounder critical foundation; he had the wisdom to encourage the study of replicas and forgeries as a valid and necessary part of the history of Chinese painting. Without his leadership neither the collection itself nor this catalogue would have materialized.

Finally, our thanks must go to those collectors and institutions who have allowed us to reproduce works from their collections, and most of all to Dr. and Mrs. Sackler, art lovers *par excellence*. They have always focused on quality and, as collectors on a grand scale, were willing to support a book of this size with complete reproductions of the highest quality. If this volume is a contribution to the field, it is largely because of the Sacklers' feeling for the significant.

M. Fu
S. Fu

August, 1972

Catalogue Entries

NOTE: *The hyphen following some artists' dates indicates a death date that has not been verified.*

I. Ma Wan (ca. 1310–1378–), *Spring Landscape*, dated 1343. Hanging scroll. Ink and color on paper. The Art Museum, Princeton University (L319.66). *page 72*

II. Wen Cheng-ming (1470–1559), *Chrysanthemum, Bamboo, and Rock*, dated by accompanying inscription during or before autumn, 1535. Hanging scroll. Ink on paper. The Art Museum, Princeton University (L27.70). 82

III. Hsü Chen-ch'ing (1479–1511) and others and Ch'iu Ying (ca. 1494–1552–), *A Donkey for Mr. Chu: Soliciting Pledges for Its Purchase*, undated. Handscroll. Ink on paper. The Art Museum, Princeton University (L320.66). 86

IV. Ch'ien Ku (1508–1578–), *Scholar under Banana Plant*, dated autumn, 1578. Folding fan mounted as album leaf. Ink and light color on paper. The Art Museum, Princeton University (68-219). 96

V. Ch'eng Chia-sui (1565–1643), *Pavilion in an Autumn Grove*, dated early winter, 1630. Hanging scroll. Ink on paper. The Art Museum, Princeton University (L299.72). 98

VI. Sheng Mao-yeh (fl. ca. 1615–ca. 1640), *Landscapes after T'ang Poems*. Album of six leaves. Ink and light color on silk. The Metropolitan Museum of Art, New York (69.242.1-6). 102

VII. Lan Ying (1585–1664–), *Landscapes after Sung and Yüan Masters*, dated in the period January 30–March 29, 1642. Album of twelve leaves. Ink and occasional color on paper. The Metropolitan Museum of Art, New York (1970.2.2a-l). 106

VIII. Lan Ying (1585–1664–), *Landscape in the Style of Huang Kung-wang*, dated winter, 1650. Folding fan mounted as album leaf. Ink and color on gold-flecked paper. The Art Museum, Princeton University (68-220). 111

IX. Lan Ying (1585–1664–), *Bird on a Willow Branch*, dated in the period October 16–November 13, 1659. Hanging scroll. Ink and light color on paper. The Art Museum, Princeton University (66-246). 114

X. Wan Shou-ch'i (1603–1652), *Landscapes, Flowers, and Calligraphy*, dated early May, 1650. Album of eighteen leaves. Ink on paper. The Art Museum, Princeton University (68-206). 118

XI. Chang Chi-su (fl. ca. 1620?–1670), *Snow-Capped Peaks*, probably executed ca. 1660. Hanging scroll. Ink and color on paper. The Art Museum, Princeton University (67-1). 134

XII. Hung-jen (1610–1664), *Feng River Landscapes*, dated spring, 1660. Album of ten leaves. Ink on paper. The Art Museum, Princeton University (L36.67). *page 140*

XIII. Cha Shih-piao (1615–1698), *River Landscape in Rain*, dated in the period May 11–June 10, 1687. Hanging scroll. Ink on paper. The Art Museum, Princeton University (L300.72). 152

XIV. Cha Shih-piao (1615–1698), *Old Man Boating on a River*, probably executed ca. 1690. Hanging scroll. Ink on paper. The Metropolitan Museum of Art, New York (69.242.7). 156

XV. Fan Ch'i (1616–1694–), *Landscapes*, dated in the period October 9–November 6, 1646. Album of eight leaves. Ink and color on paper. The Metropolitan Museum of Art, New York (69.242.8-15). 158

XVI. Kung Hsien (ca. 1618–1689), *Landscapes*, probably executed ca. 1688. Album of six leaves. Ink on paper. The Metropolitan Museum of Art, New York (69.242.16-21). 164

XVII. Tao-chi (1641–ca. 1710), *The Echo*, executed in the period December 24, 1677–January 23, 1678. Album leaf mounted as hanging scroll. Ink on paper. The Art Museum, Princeton University (67-20). 168

XVIII. Tao-chi (1641–ca. 1710), *Searching for Plum Blossoms: Poems and Painting*, dated in the period March 5–April 3, 1685. Handscroll. Ink and slight color on paper. The Art Museum, Princeton University (67-3). 174

XIX. Artist unknown, modern copy of Tao-chi's *Searching for Plum Blossoms: Poems and Painting*, probably executed ca. 1950. Handscroll. Ink and light color on paper. The Art Museum, Princeton University (68-174). 180

XX. Tao-chi (1641–ca. 1710), *Flowers and Figures*, probably executed shortly before 1695. Album of eight leaves. Ink and occasional color on paper. The Art Museum, Princeton University (67-16). 186

XXI. Li Jui-ch'i (ca. 1870–ca. 1940), copy of Tao-chi's *Flowers and Figures*, probably executed ca. 1920. Album of eight leaves. Ink and occasional color on paper. The Art Museum, Princeton University (68-193). 202

XXII. Tao-chi (1641–ca. 1710), *Landscapes, Vegetables, and Flowers*, probably executed ca. 1697. Album of twelve leaves. Ink and occasional color on paper. The Metropolitan Museum of Art, New York (1972.122.a-l). 204

XXIII. Tao-chi (1641–ca. 1710), *Letter to Pa-ta shan-jen*, probably executed ca. 1698–99. Album of six leaves. Ink on paper. The Art Museum, Princeton University (68-204). 210

XXIV. Tao-chi (1641–ca. 1710), *Thousand-Character "Eulogy of a Great Man,"* probably executed ca. 1698. Handscroll. Ink on paper. The Art Museum, Princeton University (L38.67). *page 225*

XXV. Tao-chi (1641–ca. 1710), *Album of Flowers and Portrait of Tao-chi,* probably executed ca. 1698. Album of nine leaves. Ink and color on paper. The Art Museum, Princeton University (L312.70). 232

XXVI. Tao-chi (1641–ca. 1710), *Album of Landscapes,* dated in the period March 3–April 7, 1701. Album of eleven leaves. Ink and slight color on paper. The Art Museum, Princeton University (67-2). 244

XXVII. Tao-chi (1641–ca. 1710), *After Shen Chou's Bronze Peacock Inkslab,* probably executed ca. 1698–1703. Hanging scroll. Ink and light color on paper. The Art Museum, Princeton University (67-21). 256

XXVIII. Artist unknown, modern copy of Shen Chou's *Bronze Peacock Inkslab,* dated summer, 1500. Hanging scroll. Ink on paper. The Art Museum, Princeton University (L245.70). 260

XXIX. Tao-chi (1641–ca. 1710), *Orchid, Bamboo, and Rock,* probably executed ca. 1700. Hanging scroll. Ink on paper. The Art Museum, Princeton University (L12.67). 264

XXX. Tao-chi (1641–ca. 1710), *Lo-Fu Mountains: Calligraphy and Painting,* probably executed 1701–5. Album of eight leaves. Ink and color on paper. The Art Museum, Princeton University (67-17). 268

XXXI. Tao-chi (1641–ca. 1710), *Bamboo, Vegetables, and Fruit,* dated September 18, 1705. Hanging scroll. Ink and light color on paper. The Art Museum, Princeton University (67-22). 280

XXXII. Tao-chi (1641–ca. 1710) and Chiang Chi (fl. 1706–1742–), *Landscape and Portrait of Hung Cheng-chih,* dated winter, 1706. Handscroll. Ink and color on paper. The Art Museum, Princeton University (L13.67). 284

XXXIII. Tao-chi (1641–ca. 1710), *Plum Branches: Poems and Painting,* probably executed ca. 1705–7. Album of eight leaves. Ink on paper. The Art Museum, Princeton University (67-15). *page 294*

XXXIV. Tao-chi (1641–ca. 1710), *Reminiscences of Nanking,* dated September 10, 1707. Album of twelve leaves. Ink and color on paper. The Art Museum, Princeton University (L14.67). 302

XXXV. Chang Ta-ch'ien (born 1899), *Tao-chi Landscapes,* probably executed ca. 1920. Album of six leaves. Ink and color on paper. The Art Museum, Princeton University (68-201). 314

XXXVI. Hua Yen (1682–1765–), *Cloudsea at Mt. T'ai,* dated September 14, 1730. Hanging scroll. Ink on paper. The Art Museum, Princeton University (69-75). 322

XXXVII. Hung-li (1711–1799; the Ch'ien-lung Emperor, Ch'ing Kao-tsung, reigned 1736–1796), *Eight Fragrant Summer Flowers,* dated intercalary summer, 1759. Handscroll. Ink on sized paper. The Art Museum, Princeton University (68-225). 328

XXXVIII. Ch'ien Tu (1763–1844), *Contemplating Poetry by a Snowy River,* dated autumn, 1816. Folding fan mounted as album leaf. Ink and light color on paper. The Art Museum, Princeton University (68-221). 334

XXXIX. Wang Hsüeh-hao (1754–1832), *Landscape after Wang Fu,* dated summer, 1831. Folding fan mounted as album leaf. Ink on paper. The Art Museum, Princeton University (68-222). 336

XL. Ch'en Chao (ca. 1835–1884–), *Landscape,* probably executed ca. 1865–70. Folding fan mounted as album leaf. Ink and light color on silk. The Art Museum, Princeton University (68-223). 338

XLI. Ku Yün (1835–1896), *Landscape at Dusk,* undated. Folding fan mounted as album leaf. Ink and light color on gold-flecked paper. The Art Museum, Princeton University (68-224). 340

I. Geography: The "Eye Area" in Chinese Painting

CHEN-CHIANG 鎮江
Ta Ch'ung-kuang* 笪重光

CHIA-HSING 嘉興
Hsiang Yüan-pien* 項元汴
Li Jih-hua* 李日華
Pei Ch'iung* 貝瓊
Sheng Mou 盛懋
Tung Chi-ch'ang 董其昌
Wang Kai* 王槩
Wu Chen* 吳鎮

CHIA-TING 嘉定
Ch'eng Chia-sui 陳嘉燧
Li Liu-fang 李流芳

CHIA-SHAN 嘉善
Yao Shou* 姚綬

CH'ANG-SHU 常熟
Huang Kung-wang* 黃公望
Wang Hui* 王翬
Wu Li* 吳歷

FU-CHOU 撫州
(LIN-CH'ÜAN 臨川)
Li Jui-ch'i* 李瑞奇
Li Jui-ch'ing* 李瑞清
Ma Wan 馬琬

HANG-CHOU 杭州
(YÜ-HANG 餘杭, LIN-AN 臨安)
Chao Meng-fu 趙孟頫
Che School 浙派
Chin Nung* 金農
Ch'en Hung-shou 陳洪綬
Ch'ien Tu* 錢杜
Hsien-yü Shu 鮮于樞
Huang Kung-wang 黃公望
Hung-jen 弘仁
Lan Ying* 藍瑛
Ma Wan 馬琬
Sheng Mou 盛懋
Southern Sung
Painting Academy 南宋畫院
Tao-chi 道濟
Wang Meng 王蒙
Wen Jih-kuan 溫日觀
Wu Chen 吳鎮

HSIU-NING 休寧
Cha Shih-piao* 查士標
Ch'eng Chia-sui* 陳嘉燧
Hung-jen* 弘仁
Tai Pen-hsiao* 戴本孝
Ting Yün-p'eng* 丁雲鵬
Wang Chih-jui* 汪之瑞

HUAI-YIN 淮陰
Wan Shou-ch'i* 萬壽祺

HSÜAN-CH'ENG 宣城
Hung-jen 弘仁
Mei Ch'ing* 梅清
Mei Keng* 梅庚
Tao-chi 道濟

K'UN-SHAN 崑山
Chu Te-jun 朱德潤
Hsia Ch'ang* 夏昶
Ku Ying* 顧瑛

LU-SHAN 廬山
Hung-jen 弘仁
Tao-chi 道濟

NAN-CH'ANG 南昌
Chu Ta* 朱耷

NANKING 南京
(CHIANG-NING 江寧)
(CHIN-LING 金陵)
(CH'IN-HUAI 秦淮)
Chang Feng* 張風
Ch'en Shu 陳舒
Chou Liang-kung 周亮工
Ch'eng Cheng-k'uei 程正揆
Ch'ien Ch'ien-i 錢謙益
Eight Chin-ling Masters 金陵八家
Fan Ch'i* 樊圻
Kung Hsien* 龔賢
K'un-ts'an 髡殘
Hung-jen 弘仁
Ma Wan* 馬琬
Southern T'ang
Painting Academy 南唐畫院
Tai Pen-hsiao 戴本孝
Tao-chi 道濟
Tung-Chü School 董巨派
Wang Kai 王槩
Wu Pin 吳彬

SHANGHAI 上海
Chang Ta-ch'ien 張大千
Li Jui-ch'i 李瑞奇
Li Jui-ch'ing 李瑞清
Tseng Hsi 曾熙

SHAN-YIN 山陰
(SHAO-HSING 紹興)
Hsü Wei 徐渭

SHE 歙
(HUI-CHOU 徽州, HSIN-AN 新安)
Ch'eng Sui* 程邃
Hung-jen* 弘仁
Li Liu-fang* 李流芳
Lo P'in* 羅聘
Sun I* 孫逸
Wang Shih-shen* 汪士慎
Yao Sung* 姚宋

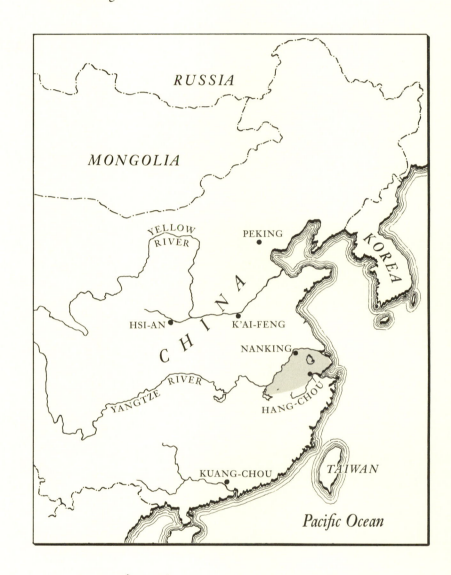

MAPS OF THE "EYE AREA" IN CHINESE PAINTING
The small map below shows the "eye area" in China. The larger map at the right is an enlarged detail of the "eye area."

LIST OF IMPORTANT CITIES AND MAJOR PAINTERS
The list at left and below represents cities important in Chinese painting, followed by names of painters active in those cities to indicate density of representation. Parentheses indicate alternate names for cities. An asterisk indicates a painter's native city. Italics indicate painters represented in the Catalogue.

SU-CHOU 蘇州
(P'ING-CHIANG 平江)
(WU-HSIEN 吳縣)
Chang Seng-yu* 張僧繇
Chang Ta-ch'ien 張大千
Chao Yüan* 趙原
Cheng Ssu-hsiao 鄭思肖
Chiang Shih-chieh 姜實節
Chu Te-jun 朱德潤
Chu Ts'un-li* 朱存理
Ch'en Wei-yün 陳惟允
Ch'ien Ku* 錢穀
Ch'iu Ying* 仇英
Huang Kung-wang 黃公望
Hsü Chen-ch'ing* 徐禎卿
Hsü Pen 徐賁
Ku Yün* 顧澐
Liu Chüeh* 劉珏

Lu Kuang* 陸廣
Lu T'an-wei* 陸探微
P'u-ming 普明
Shen Chou* 沈周
Tu Ch'iung* 杜瓊
T'ang Yin* 唐寅
Wan Shou-ch'i* 萬壽祺
Wen Cheng-ming* 文徵明

SUNG-CHIANG 松江
(HUA-T'ING 華亭)
(YÜN-CHIEN 雲間)
Chang Chung* 張中
Ch'en Chi-ju* 陳繼儒
Ho Liang-chün* 何良俊
Huang Kung-wang 黃公望
Jen Jen-fa* 任仁發
Ku Cheng-i* 顧正誼

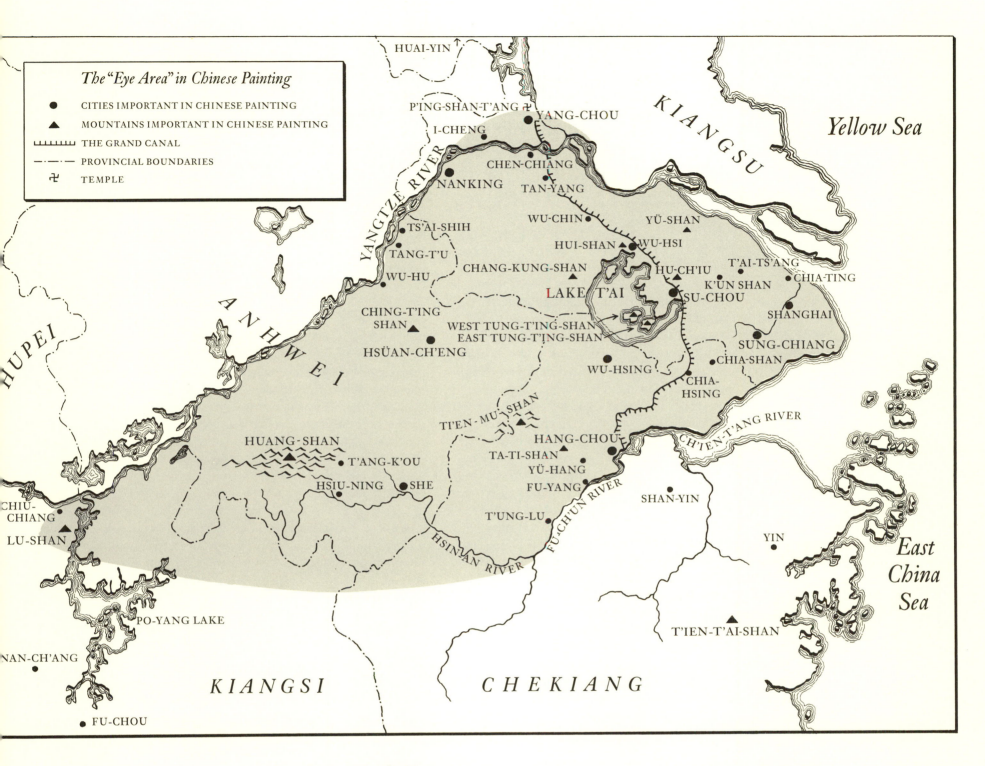

The "Eye Area" in Chinese Painting

● CITIES IMPORTANT IN CHINESE PAINTING
▲ MOUNTAINS IMPORTANT IN CHINESE PAINTING
⊥⊥⊥ THE GRAND CANAL
–·–·– PROVINCIAL BOUNDARIES
卍 TEMPLE

HUAI-YIN

KIANGSU

Yellow Sea

P'ING-SHAN-T'ANG 卍 YANG-CHOU
I-CHENG
CHEN-CHIANG
NANKING   TAN-YANG
WU-CHIN   YÜ-SHAN ▲
TS'AI-SHIH   HUI-SHAN ▲ WU-HSI
TANG-T'U   CHANG-KUNG-SHAN HU-CH'IU ▲ T'AI-TS'ANG
WU-HU   LAKE T'AI   SU-CHOU   K'UN SHAN   CHIA-TING
CHING-T'ING   SHANGHAI
SHAN ▲   WEST TUNG-T'ING-SHAN
         EAST TUNG-T'ING-SHAN   SUNG-CHIANG
HSÜAN-CH'ENG   WU-HSING   CHIA-SHAN
                                          CHIA-HSING

YANGTZE RIVER

ANHWEI

HUPEI

TI'EN-MU-SHAN ▲
HUANG-SHAN ▲   HANG-CHOU
         T'ANG-K'OU   TA-TI-SHAN ▲
HSIU-NING ● SHE   YÜ-HANG
                     FU-YANG   SHAN-YIN
         T'UNG-LU
CHIU-
CHIANG
LU-SHAN ▲   YIN

HSINAN RIVER   FU-CH'UN RIVER   CH'IEN-T'ANG RIVER

East
China
Sea

PO-YANG LAKE

NAN-CH'ANG

T'IEN-T'AI-SHAN ▲

KIANGSI   CHEKIANG

FU-CHOU

Ku Lu* 顧 祿
Ma Wan 馬 琬
Mo Shih-lung* 莫是龍
P'u-ming* 普明
Sun K'o-hung* 孫克弘
Tung Ch'i-ch'ang* 董其昌
Ts'ao Chih-po* 曹知白
Wen Jih-kuan* 溫日觀
Yang Wei-chen* 楊維楨

T'AI-TS'ANG 太倉
Wang Chien* 王鑑
Wang Hsüeh-hao* 王學浩
Wang Shih-min* 王時敏
Wang Yüan-ch'i* 王原祁

TAN-YANG 丹陽
Chiang Shao-shu* 姜紹書

T'IEN-T'AI-SHAN 天台山
K'o Chiu-ssu* 柯九思
Wei Chiu-ting* 衛九鼎

WU-CHIN 武進
(CH'ANG-CHOU 常州)
Chao Yüan 趙原
Wu Chen 吳鎮
Yün Shou-p'ing* 惲壽平

WU-HSI 無錫
Ku K'ai-chih* 顧愷之
Ni Tsan* 倪瓚
Wang Fu* 王紱

WU-HSING 吳興
(HU-CHOU 湖州)
Chao Meng-fu* 趙孟頫
Chao Yung* 趙雍

Chiang Shen 江參
Ch'ien Hsüan* 錢選
T'ang Ti* 唐棣
Ts'ao Pu-hsing* 曹不興
Wang Meng* 王蒙
Yen Wen-kuei* 燕文貴

WU-HU 蕪湖
Hsiao Yün-ts'ung* 蕭雲從
Huang Yüeh* 黃鉞
Hung-jen 弘仁
Sun I 孫逸
T'ang Hsüan-i 湯玄翼
Yao Sung 姚宋

YANG-CHOU 揚州
(CHIANG-TU 江都)
(KUANG-LING 廣陵)
(WEI-YANG 維揚)
An Ch'i 安岐

Cha Shih-piao* 查士標
Cheng Hsieh* 鄭燮
Chin Nung 金農
Ch'en Chao 陳炤
Ch'eng Sui 程邃
Hua Yen 華喦
Huang Shen 黃慎
Kao Hsiang* 高翔
Ku An* 顧安
K'ung Shang-jen 孔尚任
Lan Ying 藍瑛
Li Fang-ying 李流芳
Li Shan* 李鱓
Lo P'in 羅聘
Tao-chi 道濟
Wang Hui 王翬
Wang Shih-shen 汪士慎
Wu Hsi-tsai 吳熙載

The geographic area centered around Lake T'ai, at the juncture of the modern provincial boundaries of Kiangsu, Chekiang, and Anhwei, was a key region from which the mainstream of important painters, calligraphers, and poets of China's Great Tradition arose.[1] On the map it is shaped like a human eye, and the comparison is apt because in Chinese criticism of poetry the concept of *shih-yen* ("eye of the poem") denotes the crucial word upon which the meaning and expression of the whole poem turns, while in criticism of art the same concept has been extended to calligraphy.[2] Here some geographic and art-historical implications of the term will be explored.

The "eye area" designation reflects the traditional association of famous people with specific places and illustrates the interaction of human energies and potentials with the social, cultural, and material foundations of the culture. One part of the area is well known in Chinese history as Chiang-nan, or the Yangtze Delta: since the middle of the tenth century it has been the most agriculturally fertile, economically rich, and culturally advanced region in China. Only recently, however, has the area around Mt. Huang (Huang-shan) been recognized and credited with artistic importance. The creative individuals which this region fostered have earned it a position equal to other artistic centers in Chiang-nan.

To continue the metaphor, Lake T'ai (T'ai-hu), which covers southern Kiangsu and northern Chekiang, forms the "pupil" or focal area of the eye. The "lid" follows the Yangtze from its mouth as it winds westward and passes through Yang-chou, the northernmost city of the eye area, then Nanking, and on to Wu-hu and Hsüan-ch'eng, in Anhwei, where it terminates, for our purposes, near Mt. Lu (Lu-shan) in Kiangsi. From there the lower lid of the eye curves east toward the sea, passing south of Mt. Huang along the Hsin-an River, near the present-day cities of Hsiu-ning and She-hsien, northwest to Hang-chou in Chekiang, where it meets the Ch'ien-t'ang River and flows into the sea. The eye area thus follows three natural river boundaries, and it includes the major artery of the Grand Canal and the nearby cities which branch off from that system. Most of the area is wealthy, fertile, highly populated, and culturally stable; it includes the prefectures designated as modern Su-chou and Sung-chiang and their surrounding towns.

The area can be further subdivided into three sectors, east, west, and central, according to the distinctive local terrain and scenery of each. This variation in the natural landscape has exerted a broad influence on the style and subject matter of Chinese landscape painting. Lake T'ai, which forms the focal point of the eastern sector, has long been known for its scenic beauty. Studded with lakes and rivers, Lake T'ai's marshes, sloping mountains, and tranquil waters dominate the works of painters who traveled or lived in this region. The western sector of the eye is centered around Mt. Huang, a place of extraordinary views, strange ancient pines, and breathtaking rock formations; soaring peaks, old pines, and majestic vistas are major themes in the works of the Mt. Huang painters. The central sector of the eye lies on an axis from Nanking in the north to Hang-chou in the south, and its landscape forms a hybrid of eastern and western terrains. This dumbbell-shaped region is filled with both high mountains and serene waters; thus local scenery of this generic type (*shan-shui*, "mountains and waters") is typical of the works of painters who settled in or wandered through it.

The scenic atmosphere and physical terrain of a native region leave an indelible impress on the mind and feelings of the Chinese painter. No matter how intellectual the orientation of his personal vision, his sojourns with nature, however occasional, constitute a vital source of creativity and an aspect of spiritual discipline. Through the cumulative effects of regions familiar to him—of nature in the large, like mountain scenery, and in the small, like garden landscapes and rockery—he builds up his store of images. These forms energize the spiritually inert brush conventions and formal schemata learned in his traditional training.

The relationship of the Chinese painter to place is less diffuse than his relationship to landscape, if we think of "place" as the city, in the broad sense—the dominant nerve center of a district or prefecture. It is important to remember that the cultural level of the city and its larger political designation was very much dominated by the historical associations of its past. The achievements of its cultural heroes, its historical sites and personages, provided the basis for Confucian thinking and action, as well as the standard of artistic excellence by which the creative individual measured himself. Then too, the Chinese city differed from that of the West in that the cultural activities which occupied the artist were at first not confined solely to the physical area of the "city" itself. Many artists may well have divided their time equally between the metropolis and the cultivated rusticity of a country villa. It is also important to remember that the web of canals and streams of this region encouraged artists to travel beyond their native towns—indeed, most of these painters are known to have wandered from place to place (it would be interesting to plot the routes which each painter or poet covered in his lifetime, so that this study and the eye area map could be expanded beyond this exploratory level). The importance of such mobility lies in the influence which these artists and their works exerted on lesser-known painters and on the region itself in the course of their travels. The implications of an "urban-rural continuum" for the activities of the scholar-painter are applicable only to a varying degree, however, for the painters in our study. By the Ming, and very much so by the Ch'ing, the surge of urban patronage from the emergent merchant class proved an overwhelming attraction, and painters began to center their activities almost entirely within the city. Thus the call of the countryside as a source of inner renewal appears to have become less dominant in their thinking.

The majority of the artists with whom we are concerned lived from the mid-fourteenth century, in the late Yüan dynasty, to the modern period. They were from the educated class; some were officeholders, some "professional" painters with a scholarly bent, some Ming loyalists (*i-min*) living into the Ch'ing dynasty, many of whom turned to the Buddhist faith for protection and as a silent protest against Manchu domination. Their level of education and intellectual cultivation afforded them some part of the privileges of the elite, whether or not they owned land or held formal office. For the most part, they were members of the leisure class, in the broad sense, and were both the producers and consumers of art.

For such men the stimulation of contacts with other scholar-painters and of visits to private collections of antiquities, paintings, and calligraphy, which tended to be more easily accessible and numerous in the urban community, was great and helped to maintain a high standard of aesthetic judgment among this elite. Private gardens in the city were also an important measure of culture and appealed to the scholar. Initially, gardens were meant to simulate on a reduced scale the larger feeling of nature in the wild through the meticulous selection and spontaneous arrangement of rocks and trees. As land in the city was usually flat and streamless, unusual rocks were transported (at great expense), earth was dug out and piled up to form slopes, and the holes left were filled with water to form "natural" ponds. The city garden was an "earthwork." In Chiang-nan, unlike the garden estates of the north, these "earthworks" were not only more intimate in scale but also well integrated into the natural surroundings. In Hang-chou, for example, the famed West Lake was crowned by many peaks, and the gardens of the Ch'an Buddhist temples, well known in the Sung for their serenity and seclusion, were nestled among these hills. These temple gardens were designed to harmonize the architecture of man with nature, employing art discreetly to beautify the landscape. Thus the natural terrain of the original setting greatly influenced the shaping of its gardens. In the later city gardens, whereas, as noted above, land was both level and precious, the earlier taste for creating "miniature mountains" (chia-shan) developed into a fashion and stimulated gardeners to appropriate unusual rocks from nearby lakes, primarily Lake T'ai, for that purpose on a much larger scale than previously (see also below, "Su-chou").

Because of the high level of culture which characterized each of the cities or prefectures in the eye area, the numbers of degree-holders and aspirants to degrees and office were also high. Indeed, such prefectures as Sung-chiang, Su-chou, and Nanking at various times later in Chinese history were ranked highest in the country in numbers of chin-shih degree-holders alone. However, as in any competitive system, not all candidates could succeed, nor, once they had done so, could they be sustained within the system. Those who failed to find employment in the bureaucracy were often forced to make their living by falling back on their talents as teachers, essayists, fortunetellers, poets, storytellers, transcribers, and, of course, painters. This was already the case in the Sung; by that time, because of the broader base and superior educational level created by the dissemination of culture through printed books, sharp competition had arisen among degree candidates. Thus there were always a large number of intellectuals at varying stages of their careers in residence in the various cities and prefectures. A significant number of these talented poets and calligraphers were encouraged by the prevailing amateur ethic to try their hands at painting as an extension of their aesthetic interests. In doing so, they were following the unimpeachable precedent of the "founders" and foremost practitioners of literati art theory, Su Shih (1036–1101), Huang T'ing-chien (1045–1105), Mi Fu (1051–1107), and others. Generally speaking, then, unemployed and retired scholars formed the ranks from which the increasing numbers of painters in the literati tradition since the Sung were drawn.

THE CITIES of major artistic influence in the eastern sector of the "eye" seem to radiate outward from Lake T'ai. Two important cities, Wu-hsi and Su-chou (which became the center for the Wu school of painting), lie along the Grand Canal; I-hsing and Wu-hsing border the lake on the opposite side. On the outer circle to the north and east lie Wu-chin, Ch'ang-shu, K'un-shan, Chia-hsing, Sung-chiang, Chia-ting, and, finally, Shanghai, along the coast.

These cities were all important centers of economic and cultural activity, known for rice, tea, cotton, and silk products. They counted among their inhabitants the greatest painters of the orthodox tradition, including the Four Great Masters of the Yüan (Wu Chen, Huang Kung-wang, Wang Meng, and Ni Tsan), the Four Masters of the Ming (Shen Chou, Wen Cheng-ming, Ch'iu Ying, and T'ang

Yin), and the Six Great Masters of the Ch'ing (Wang Chien, Wang Shih-min, Wang Hui, Wang Yüan-ch'i, Wu Li, and Yün Shou-p'ing). Given such formidable artistic personalities, the Lake T'ai region can be called, in our metaphor, the very pupil of the eye area, the central focus of the geographical and artistic picture.

Huang-shan figures relatively late in the history of this sector, but the late Ming and early Ch'ing painters associated with the mountainous scenery of the region are major personalities in the history of Chinese painting. Artists such as Mei Ch'ing, Hung-jen, Cha Shih-piao, and, most significant, Tao-chi all spent formative periods of their life near the mountains or in such nearby cities as Hsiu-ning and She-hsien to the south, or Hsüan-ch'eng to the north. This sector also includes, in the southwest, the city of Nan-ch'ang, home of Chu Ta.

The artistic importance of the cities in the central sector reaches far back in Chinese history. For our purposes, Nanking's cultural roots extend back at least to the Three Kingdoms and Eastern Chin periods, when it functioned as capital for those dynasties. On such foundations artistic activity flowered in the Southern T'ang period (937–975) of the Five Dynasties, when the city became the center of the Tung Yüan and Chü-jan painting traditions. In the late Ming and early Ch'ing, Nanking again sheltered an important group of Individualist painters (such as Wu Pin, Kung Hsien, K'un-ts'an, and Tao-chi) whose heterogeneous styles had a seminal influence. Hang-chou rose to prominence as the seat of both political and cultural power in the Five Dynasties as the capital of the Wu-yüeh kingdom and later in the Southern Sung, where it was the center of academic painting. In the early and middle Ming there was a minor resurgence of imperial artistic patronage, and Hang-chou became the center for the regional school designated as the "Che" (for Chekiang) school.

LAKE T'AI

Chao Meng-fu, The Four Yüan Masters, Ma Wan

Generally speaking, the eye area as a whole has produced important literary and artistic figures since the Three Kingdoms period. When the Eastern Chin court fled south to escape the encroachments of the Northern Wei barbarians, entire households and a large number of persons of education, talent, and wealth fled with it. Poets like Lu Chi, painters like Ts'ao P'u-hsing and Ku K'ai-chih, Lu T'an-wei, Hsieh Ho, and Chang Seng-yu, and the calligrapher Wang Hsi-chih were among those whose reputations as artistic heroes helped to establish the south as a new area of culture.

By the early seventh century, in the Sui dynasty, the Lake T'ai area's economic and cultural impact was such that the emperor Yang, in part to speed the passage of grain tribute and in part to mollify southern opinion and to solicit military resources, ordered the completion of the Grand Canal,[3] thereby establishing closer relations between north and south. Communications and transportation developed to such an extent that the southern Chiang-nan region soon rivaled the northern capitals in importance. In the T'ang dynasty painters like Chang Tsao and calligraphers like Chang Hsü and Sun Ch'ien-li contributed their measure of fame to the area.

In the Five Dynasties period the eastern sector of the eye was divided politically into the Southern T'ang and the Wu-yüeh kingdoms. While barbarian incursions and internal warfare ravaged the countryside in the north, this region, and the kingdom of Shu (Szechuan), were relatively peaceful for several decades and continued their economic and cultural advancement. The T'ang Emperor Hsüan-tsung (712–756), fleeing from the rebel uprising of An Lu-shan, re-established his court in the kingdom of Shu, which became an artistic mecca, but the level of artistic activity in the eye area soon challenged that of Shu. According to literary records, painting in Szechuan reached an unparalleled height of sophistication in the mid-T'ang through the late T'ang and Five Dynasties, but by the tenth century, when the empire was reunited in the Sung and artists migrated to the capital at Pien-ching, Szechuan's importance as an artistic center had declined, despite the presence of such painters as Huang Ch'üan.

The eye area prospered for several reasons. In the Southern T'ang period (937–975) Emperor Li Yü's artistic taste and interests encouraged such painters as Chou Wen-chü, Hsü Hsi, Tung Yüan, and Chü-jan. Later, when his empire fell to the Sung and Li Yü was summoned north by the Emperor T'ai-tsu, the painter Chü-jan followed him and was known to have executed murals in the capital. Artistically, there seems to have been no transplantation of the southern Tung-Chü landscape style to the north, for most artists of the Northern Sung preferred the more monumental and rocky scenery of their own environment. It was not until the Yüan dynasty, when the Tung-Chü tradition was thrust to the fore, that it emerged as one of the mainstreams in Chinese landscape painting.

In the Southern Sung, as the capital first moved south to Yang-chou, then later to Hang-chou, artists from north and south were attracted to the eye area. The painting style of the north was transplanted to the southern climate, producing the Southern Sung academic painting style of courtly elegance and intimacy. This style superseded the native Tung-Chü landscape style of the Yangtze region and flourished into the Yüan dynasty and middle Ming period before its eclipse by the Ming literati tradition. In the early Yüan, the Tung-Chü school again emerged, revived by the key painter and calligrapher Chao Meng-fu (1254–1322). When Mongol domination forced a change in the regular pattern of political advancement for the educated, many adopted the verbal and pictorial arts as one means of expressing the distress and humiliation of foreign rule and the futility of political careers. The Tung-Chü style of painting, with its emphasis on the scholar's discipline, calligraphy, became an archetypal ideal. Its simplicity of form and mild, unpretentious style seems to have suited the expressive needs of the Yüan scholar-painters, and the southern tradition once more flourished in its own heartland. The importance of the Tung-Chü school in later Chinese painting cannot be overestimated. In formal mode and aesthetic ideal, it provided later painters with a continual source of artistic renewal.

Chao Meng-fu is the seminal figure in this reassertion of southern ideals, and his own biography, artistic circle, and interests reflect these crucial changes. His activity centered around Hu-chou (Wu-hsing), southwest of Lake T'ai, which indicates the shift of painting activities within the eye area from the court at Hang-chou to Lake T'ai. The Lake T'ai region became the representative regional direction of Yüan painting. Two of Chao's paintings depict East and West Tung-t'ing-shan, a small island and peninsula in Lake T'ai and two of its famous sites. Ma Wan's (ca. 1310–1378-) *Spring Landscape* (see cat. no. I), dated 1343 in the mid-Yüan, almost twenty years after Chao's death, reveals a strong stylistic affinity with Chao's landscape art. Chao's circle of relatives, rivals, and friends included his older contemporary Ch'ien Hsüan (ca. 1235–1300), the northern calligrapher Hsien-yü Shu (1257–1302), Chao's son Chao Yung (1289–ca. 1360), his grandson Chao Lin (fl. 1350), and his maternal grandson Wang Meng (1308–1385). Other painters who flourished near Lake T'ai were Huang Kung-wang (1269–1354), at Ch'ang-shu; Ni Tsan (1301–1374), near Wu-hsi; Ch'en Ju-yen (fl. ca. 1340–1370), at Su-chou; Wu Chen (1280–1354), at Chia-hsing; and Ts'ao Chih-po (1272–1355), at Sung-chiang.

The important influence which geographical mobility exerted on artistic styles and their perpetuation and dissemination, mentioned earlier, can be illustrated by the local impact which some of the Yüan masters had in certain regions. For example, Chao Meng-fu and Huang Kung-wang must have left some influence in Hang-chou and Sung-chiang and, stylistically, aspects of Wu Chen's style display a merging of elements from both Chao and Huang. Ma Wan is a minor painter whose style contains a hybrid of features which he may have derived from some of the painters in his various places of residence. He himself may also have had some local influence over later painters in areas like Lake T'ai, where he traveled, and Fu-chou, Kiangsi, where he served as prefect, although his style was not distinctive enough to attract a following rivaling that of the Four Yüan Masters. Such an important collector as Ho Liang-chün (ca. 1531–1573) in his *Ssu-yu-chia hua-lun* praises not only the Four Yüan Masters but also some of the secondary, transitional painters of the late Yüan as possessing a high degree of subtlety. Ho took particular interest in collecting works by the Four Yüan Masters and must also have sought out paintings by Ma. Later painters from Sung-chiang were influenced by Ma: Wang Chien (1598–1677) is known to have painted landscapes in his style.

Other painters whose artistic activity carried over into the early Ming and who were also praised by Ho Liang-chün were Hsü Pen (fl. ca. 1370–1380), Lu Kuang (fl. ca. 1350), and Chao Yüan (fl. ca. 1360–1372). These men were working in Su-chou, and, artistically transitional painters like Ma, their importance in art history lies in their extension of the literati styles and ideals of Chao Meng-fu and the Four Yüan Masters into the early Ming.

SUNG-CHIANG

Ma Wan, Yang Wei-chen, Tung Ch'i-ch'ang

Economic and agricultural advances (mainly in cotton textile production) in the region of Sung-chiang (or Yün-chien, and including Hua-t'ing) had helped it become a major nucleus for artists and intellectuals by the Yüan period.[4] The intellectual and material wealth of the region was reflected in the proliferation of bibliophiles, printers, connoisseurs, collectors, and artists. During the late Yüan, Ts'ao Chih-po's estate, the Wa-ying-hsüan in Sung-chiang, was one of several exclusive and famous gathering places for literati. Ku Ying's (1310–1369) Yü-shan ts'ao-t'ang in K'un-shan and Ni Tsan's Ch'ing-mi-ko in Wu-hsi were the two other such estates well known in their time. The studio of another Yüan scholar, the Chih-chih-t'ang of Hsia Shih-tse (fl. ca. 1320–1355), is also associated with thirteenth- and fourteenth-century artistic notables. Chao Meng-fu is known to have written a pediment stone (*pien-e*) for Hsia, and in 1350, when Huang Kung-wang inscribed his memorable handscroll *Dwelling in the Fu-ch'un Mountains*, it was done at Hsia's studio.

Other prominent literati such as Kao K'o-kung (1248–1310), Ni Tsan, Wang Meng, Ma Wan, and Yang Wei-chen (1296–1370) are known to have stopped in Sung-chiang on their travels. The artistic interests which they encouraged and the prestige which they gave the region gradually formed the basis for the growth of a tradition whose adherents were natives of the area. The most influential of these was Tung Ch'i-ch'ang (1555–1636), although there were other important artist-intellectuals in residence before Tung, such as the connoisseur Ho Liang-chün, the painter-collector Sun K'o-hung (1533–1611; see cat. no. VIII), Tung Ch'i-ch'ang's elder contemporary Mo Shih-lung (ca. 1539–1587), Tung's painting teacher Ku Cheng-i (fl. 1575–1584), and the bibliophile Ch'en Chi-ju (1538–1639). Their presence in the Sung-chiang region linked it with the artistic traditions of the Yüan and Ming and helped prepare the way for Tung's genius.

Although there are no paintings by Tung Ch'i-ch'ang in the Sackler collection, his presence is felt strongly in the work of his artistic circle. Later painters could not resist the powerful artistic forces which this intellectual and painter generated. Yet it is interesting to note how little of his influence can be seen among his immediate contemporaries and how much more susceptible he was than some of his colleagues to the atmosphere to which they were all exposed. His artistic and intellectual ambitions and receptiveness set him apart from his friends, such as Mo Shih-lung. Tung turned his interests and contacts with older collectors and painters to his own use; his spirit is exemplified in his exhortation "to travel ten thousand miles and to read ten thousand books." His historical orientation and systematically gathered collection of antique works enabled him to penetrate the transcendental sources of transmission from master to master. From the Four Yüan Masters he went back to the Five Dynasties' Tung Yüan and Chü-jan, and finally to Wang Wei of the T'ang, to create his syncretic concept of chi-ta-ch'eng (the "great synthesis").

In the dynamics of art history, Tung Ch'i-ch'ang's position was like Chao Meng-fu's in the Yüan: both men helped direct the random impulses of the moment into new fields of exploration. This energy drawn from the past revitalized Tung's talented contemporaries and younger associates active in T'ai-ts'ang (Lou-tung), and those with artistic genius are known to posterity as the Six Masters of the Ch'ing: Wang Shih-min (1592–1680), Wang Chien (1598–1677), Wang Hui (1632–1717), Wang Yüan-ch'i (1642–1715), Wu Li (1632–1718), and Yün Shou-p'ing (1633–1690). Yet at the time Tung was just one of a group of talented artist-intellectuals known as the Sung-chiang (Yün-chien) school, or the Nine Friends of Painting. This second group included Ch'eng Chia-sui (1565–1643), Wang Shih-min, Li Liu-fang (1575–1629), Yang Wen-ts'ung (1597–1645), Pien Wen-yü (fl. ca. 1622–1671), Chang Hsüeh-tseng (fl. 1633–1656), and Shao Mi (fl. ca. 1626–1662). By seniority alone Tung was preeminently the leader, but in each of these masters we catch only a fleeting glimpse of his ultimate influence, illustrating how diverse currents in painting were at the time.

Of these Nine Friends, one painter seems to exemplify the late Ming scholar-artist whose work hints at the direction which the Six Masters took. The relatively little-known Ch'eng Chia-sui (see cat. no. V) was ten years younger than Tung, but Tung is known to have praised his paintings, which were rarities and eagerly sought after even in Ch'eng's lifetime. It is evident that the Nine Friends represent a group whose high level of cultivation ensured a strong

artistic individualism. Many aspects of their styles, which at the time were inconsistently demonstrated or only hinted at in their paintings, were developed on a more distinctive level by Ch'ing painters, some of whom were also outside the orthodoxy as defined by Tung. Thus the heterogeneity of the late Ming could provide the multiple skeins of formal and expressive modes which could be woven at will by painters of such temperaments and background as Tao-chi or Wang Hui.

SU-CHOU

Shen Chou, Wen Cheng-ming, and the Genres of Bamboo, Flowers, Vegetables, and Animals

Su-chou (Wu-hsien, including Wu-hsi) had once been chosen as dynastic capital, but its political significance had been superseded in importance by its commerce and trade.[5] A variegated economy and such products as silk, silk textiles, and rice were drawn from the fertile countryside around the city, and by the Sung it had become the wealthiest region in Chiang-nan and in the whole country. Later, in the Yüan, it was a magnet for intellectuals and artists, frequently those with Sung loyalist sentiments, and also became the seat of Chang Shih-ch'eng's rebel government. By the middle Ming an influential literati painting movement had grown up there, known as the "Wu" school. Its spiritual founders were Shen Chou (1427–1509) and Wen Cheng-ming (1470–1559; see cat. no. II), who represented a new breed of scholar-recluse (although Wen did hold office for a time). Along with the transitional painters mentioned in connection with Ma Wan, there were also masters a generation or so younger than Shen Chou from nearby areas who form a bridge from the great Yüan masters to the early Ming—men such as Wang Fu (1362–1416) of Wu-hsi, Yao Shou (1423–1495) of Chia-shan (east of Chia-hsing), and Hsia Ch'ang (1388–1470) of K'un-shan. Within Shen Chou's own large family there are some links with the Yüan. His grandfather, Shen Ch'eng (fl. ca. 1380–1450), was a painter, and Shen Ch'eng's two sons, Shen Chen (1400–1482) and Shen Heng (1409–1477)—the father of Shen Chou—were also painters. They studied with Ch'en Chi (fla. ca. 1370–1450), the son of Ch'en Ju-yen (fl. ca. 1340–1370) and with Tu Ch'iung (1396–1474). Ch'en Chi, a specialist in bamboo, also taught Hsia Ch'ang. Thus the stylistic bonds of these early Ming masters were quite close. Shen Chou himself was influenced directly by his father and uncle and by Tu Ch'iung and Liu Chüeh (1410–1472), the latter related by marriage to the Shen family.

In terms of subject matter, Shen Chou's and Wen Cheng-ming's contributions were most important in landscape, but their taste for lighter subjects, such as animals, fruits, flowers, bamboo, and vegetables, can be linked with earlier traditions. For example, ink bamboo was given impetus in the Yüan by Chao Meng-fu and Wu Chen, among others; Wang Fu and Hsia Ch'ang later continued the style, as did Wen Cheng-ming and T'ang Yin. Flowers and birds in the monochrome ink wash style of the Yüan were painted by Ch'en Lin, Wang Yüan, and Chang Chung. The early Ming painter Yao Shou is known to have expanded the genre to include vegetables. In all likelihood, he learned such methods from Wu Chen, although no such works by Wu are extant today. Paintings by the monk Mu-ch'i (d. ca. 1285) are traditionally said to have provided the earliest prototype for this free and expressive style, but it seems that the Ming masters were major pivotal figures, passing on the tradition to Ch'en Shun and Hsü Wei. Only with their impetus could the genre have reached its peak in the late Ming and early Ch'ing with the masters Tao-chi and Chu Ta. Tao-chi's own activities in Yang-chou exerted a deep and lasting local influence on painters of that metropolis, who came to be known as the "eccentrics." The genre continued to the modern period, flourishing in the works of such painters as Chao Chih-ch'ien (1829–1884), Wu Ch'ang-shih (1844–1927), and finally the great Ch'i Pai-shih (1861–1957). From this outline, one realizes that such ostensibly "minor" works as Wen Cheng-ming's *Chrysanthemum, Bamboo, and Rock* (cat. no. *II*) and Tao-chi's various bamboo and vegetable subjects (*XX, XXIX,* and *XXXI*) are significant links in a noble lineage.

Ch'iu Ying and the Tradition of Figure Painting

Of the four major masters of the Ming dynasty, Shen Chou, Wen Cheng-ming, T'ang Yin (1470–1523), and Ch'iu Ying (ca. 1494–1552-), Ch'iu was the youngest and most versatile stylistically. His handscroll in the Sackler collection (*III*) is executed in one of his antique figure methods, the "plain-drawing" (*pai-miao*) style modeled after the Sung master Li Kung-lin (1049–ca. 1105). It is a small work in size, but its high quality affords a rare glimpse into Ch'iu Ying's true potential as a draftsman. The regard of contemporary literati and critics for Ch'iu as a figure painter, despite his status as a professional, was ultimately based on the refinement of his work.

By the late Ming, figure painting in general seems to have suffered a decline; in the "plain-drawing" style in particular, only Ch'en Hung-shou (1598–1652) and Ts'ui Tzu-chung (died 1644), and perhaps Ting Yün-p'eng (ca. 1560–ca. 1638), maintained a high level of taste and individuality of visualization. Wan Shou-ch'i (1603–1652; see *X*) is also known to have executed figures, primarily of women, but the extant examples are slim-shouldered and listless, a manner which was still popular in the Ch'ing. Most painters came to adopt the fine-line, heavily colored "palace style" and, later, some Western shading techniques. Chiang Chi (fl. before 1706–1742-), whose treatise *Ch'uan-shen mi-yao* spells out in quite explicit terms the art of portraiture as it was known in the late Ming, also provides us an insight into its subtler psychological aspects and describes some innovative techniques. The portrait of Hung Cheng-chih (executed jointly with a landscape by Tao-chi) in the Sackler collection (*XXXII*) is probably by Chiang. It illustrates the methods he records and indicates his relationship with the earlier well-known portraitist Tseng Ching (1568–1650). The late Ch'ing seems to have produced pale and effete representatives of this art and mainly in the "palace style." By contrast, the Ch'iu Ying handscroll in outline style constitutes both a high point and a final flourish of this revered tradition.

Ch'ien Ku and Some Members of the "Wen" School

Ch'ien Ku (1508–after 1578; see *IV*) was a talented though secondary painter from Su-chou who studied under Wen Cheng-ming. Like Ma Wan, Ch'ien performed the vital though less conspicuous role of relay or transmitter of a stylistic tradition whose central impulse was expressed a generation or so before him. Such other late Ming painters as Chang Fu (1546–1631) and Ch'en Huan (fl. ca.

1605–1615) came from Wen's stylistic circle, and Chü Chieh (1531–1585; see *XXXVIII*) was considered an outstanding exponent of his style. Ch'ien Ku's life is interesting for the resourcefulness he showed in taking advantage of his cultural milieu. From a poor family, he is known to have supported and educated himself by copying by hand volumes from Su-chou's renowned private libraries. He, like Chu Ts'un-li (1444–1513; see *III*), who was a contemporary of Shen Chou and a close friend of T'ang Yin and Wen Cheng-ming, ranked among the many avid bibliophiles of Su-chou.

While not an innovator, Ch'ien's stylistic range and artistic temperament are worthy of attention, and he counts as one of the finer representatives of the Wen school. He seems also to have had his own limited sphere of influence, as Chang Fu is said to be a direct follower of his. The colored fan *Scholar under Banana Plant* (*IV*) has a clarity and charm of vision which is comparable to any of the minor works of his mentor Wen Cheng-ming or of Shen Chou. Ch'ien occasionally depicts subjects of narrative interest, but they were firmly in the tradition of scholar painting and not meant to be archaistic in style. The antiquarianism which was in vogue in Su-chou did not seem to affect the painters of the Wen school: Ch'ien's style bears none of the stylized archaistic features of contemporaries elsewhere (especially in Nanking), who may have been influenced by folk art or the revival of past styles. On the contrary, his artistic intentions, like those of the Wen school in general, were quite straightforward (despite the occasional choice of antique subject), and his work is refreshing and memorable for this very freedom from mannerism.

Ch'ien Tu (1763–1844; see *XXXVIII*) was a painter active mainly in Hang-chou, but the influence of the Wen school is immediately apparent in his art. He extends the links over two centuries, from Wen himself. While Ch'ien Tu was also able to assimilate certain stylistic features from other masters, such as Yün Shou-p'ing, his work has a slightly enervated lyricism which afflicted much of late Ch'ing painting. It seems that Wen Cheng-ming's style embodied a certain classic refinement of expression and offered a range of stylistic formulas which were easily adapted by painters of less forceful artistic personality. In this process of perpetuation lies much of the art-historical interest of the Wen idioms and lineage.

The Tradition of Private Gardens

One of Su-chou's advantages in being near Lake T'ai was the development of private gardens. The garden became a source of pleasure both directly and through its representation in painting. The Lake T'ai area was known for its magnificent rocks, which came from Western Mt. Tung-t'ing (Hsi Tung-t'ing-shan). Their strange and marvelous shapes were produced by the action of the water of the lake, wearing away the softer parts of the stone to reveal its natural skeleton, with its contorted and pierced silhouette. These rocks, called generically *t'ai-hu* stones, became one of the distinguishing characteristics of the Chinese garden, especially of the Chiang-nan area. Nearby cities like Su-chou were famed for their landscaping, not only for their arrangements or groves of these stones but also for their unusual flora and imaginative architecture. Thus the garden became a popular subject for literati painters and, later, professional ones also, as such scenes were associated with the refinement and ideal cultivated life of the scholar. All of the important cities—Hang-chou, Yang-chou, Nanking—contained the exclusive, secluded gardens of the gentleman. Since the southern population was denser than that of the north (whose gardens were also renowned in their day), the Chiang-nan gardens were more intimate and less spacious. There man's artfulness was felt in the smallest area or detail.

There seems to be little specialized garden literature before the Yüan period, although by the Sung connoisseurs such as Mi Fu (1051–1107) and Tu Wan (fl. ca. 1125–1130) had already become specialists in the genre of rockery. One of Su-chou's most famous gardens in the late Yüan was the Shih-tzu-lin, "Lion Grove," composed primarily of choice specimens of *t'ai-hu* stones which resembled crouching lions. It was founded by the monk Wei-tse as part of a temple complex, and famous scholars from the vicinity were said to have helped in the design—men like Ni Tsan, Chao Yüan, Hsü Pen, and Chu Te-jun. The painters Ni Tsan and Chao Yüan are known to have depicted this garden in handscroll form.

The name *t'ai-hu* could also be extended to the category of garden as well, for, by the Ming, views of gardens invariably included the highly prized stone. It became a classic theme for Wu school painters, whether meticulously described on silk with color or more freely, with ink and occasional color on paper. Such depictions were often sketch-like in intention and included local garden scenery, as well as such famous Su-chou spots as Hu-chiu, "Tiger Hill." Ch'iu Ying became known for both styles, and his particular "palace style" of color on silk established its own line of followers which continued into the Ch'ing. For example, Ch'ien Tu, whose vision was well suited to depicting the intricacies of the garden, reveals such an influence. In the Ming the elaborate garden estates (where man's artistry became ever more visible) came to constitute a special theme, especially in album format. Wen Cheng-ming was associated with the Cho-cheng-yüan, "Garden of the Unsuccessful Politician," which he depicted in several different versions. In the late Ming, painters like Sun K'o-hung (1532–1610) of Sung-chiang and Chang Hung (1557–1668) produced some extended and charming scenes of famous gardens throughout Su-chou, while Wu Pin (ca. 1598–1626) recorded his impressions of garden estates in Nanking.[6]

TWO LOYALIST PAINTERS

Wan Shou-ch'i and Kung Hsien

The fall of the Ming dynasty did not produce any fundamental stylistic change in the landscape art of the orthodox school, but the change was more than a political one for those loyalists who were born in and served under the Ming. The fragmentation of an empire must have deeply shocked these intensely emotional gentlemen, for their individualism found expression in highly stylized, schematic, and often mannered forms with a strongly personal and introspective flavor. This manner was seen not only in figure painting, such as that of Ch'en Hung-shou, the leading loyalist painter of figures, and others, but in landscapes, especially the dense and atmospheric masses and occasionally skeletal creations of the master Kung Hsien (ca. 1618–1689; see *XVI*), who was active in Nanking.

Wan Shou-ch'i (1603–1652), whose paintings are rare and little known in the West, was an important intellectual and one of the few loyalist painters who actively participated in anti-Ch'ing activities. At the time of the Ming collapse he became a Buddhist monk and

sought refuge in Huai-yin, north of Yang-chou. He is also known to have lived in Su-chou and Nanking. Wan Shou-ch'i's painting style and total expression are cast in Ni Tsan's mold. His works reveal a man who could submit himself to the strictest self-discipline, but not without imagination and philosophical profundity. The extensive colophons by a later appreciator of Wan's album *Landscapes, Flowers, and Calligraphy* (*X*) very much corroborate the artistic temperament suggested in his style.

HUANG-SHAN, ANHWEI

Hung-jen, Cha Shih-piao, Tao-chi

Since the T'ang and Sung dynasties, Anhwei had been the empire's leading producer of the scholar's writing tools—the brush, ink, inkstone, and paper—known as the "four treasures of the scholar's studio" (*wen-fang ssu-pao*). The Hsieh district in Anhwei produced a type of stone which became renowned for its use as inkstone, the majestic pines of Mt. Huang provided the soot to be pressed into ink-sticks, and the city of Hsüan-ch'eng made superb brushes and paper (hence the generic name for *hsüan* paper). In the tenth century of the Southern T'ang period of the Five Dynasties, the scholar's instruments produced in this region were unexcelled elsewhere, and the mutual influence of crafts and consumers provided a favorable background for artistic activities which finally blossomed in the late Ming.[7]

As noted earlier, Mt. Huang appears quite late as a subject in Chinese painting in general and in that of the eye area in particular.[8] Its altitude, topography, and terrain discouraged climbing and the extensive building of dwellings. After the Buddhist monk P'u-men chose Mt. Huang as the site for the Ssu-kuang-ssu ("Temple of Merciful Brilliance") in 1606, more roads were carved into the mountainside. As the remote and wonderful views of Mt. Huang were thus made more easily accessible, a larger number of poets and painters began to frequent the temple and savor the landscape. By the middle of the seventeenth century other temples (mainly of the Ch'an sect) attracted traveling scholars as retreats for meditation, and Mt. Huang and the rest of Anhwei emerged quite suddenly into painting history. Eventually, because of the number and quality of the painters the area fostered, one could speak of a Huang-shan school in the geographical sense. Tao-chi, for example (see Part IV of this volume), along with Mei Ch'ing (1623–1697), Mei Keng (fl. ca. 1681–ca. 1706), Ting Yün-p'eng (ca. 1560–ca. 1638), Cha Shih-piao (1615–1698), Hung-jen (1610–1664), Yao Sung (1647–1721), and others, spent his formative years near Huang-shan or in the vicinity. Tao-chi is known to have joined an informal painting society there composed of lesser-known poets and painters. It was among individuals like these and under the spiritual leadership of elders like Hung-jen that the Huang-shan school of painting rose in stature. Local interest in the mountain is indicated by the proliferation of illustrations to local gazetteers of Huang-shan which were designed by famous painters like Hung-jen, Sun I, and others for woodblock printing.

Hung-jen (*XII*) and Cha Shih-piao (*XIV*) have traditionally been associated with Sun I (fl. ca. 1640–1655) and Wang Chih-jui (fl. ca. 1650–1655); they have been picturesquely named the Four Masters of Hai-yang (*Hai* ["sea"] being a special term for Mt.

Huang, which was divided into different sectors called seas, and *yang* indicating south of the mountain). The works of Sun I and Wang Chih-jui are extremely rare, but those of Cha and Hung-jen are more numerous (see the catalogue, entries *XI* and *XII*). Hung-jen succeeded in transforming the physical terrain of the mountain into an enduring archetype, so that when we imagine Huang-shan in our minds it is invariably as envisioned by his brush. The roots of his style lie basically in the configuration of the mountain itself, but his characteristic generalized schemata can also be seen in Sun I's hand and in less marked form in an Anhwei painter seven years his senior, Hsiao Yün-ts'ung (1596–1673). Wan Shou-ch'i (1603–1652) is also related stylistically to Hung-jen although there is no evidence of their having known each other. Further research on the precise stylistic connection between these several painters is needed and should prove fascinating.

Concurrently, She-hsien, or Hui-chou, the region slightly southeast of Mt. Huang, emerged as a city of cultural significance. Economically it was not known for any particular product, but the fortunes amassed by astute businessmen elsewhere in the empire (primarily around Lake T'ai) enabled a generous patronage and the formation of notable collections of art. Owners of estates near the Hsin-an River belt would also be included among these "long-distance merchants." Wu T'ing, a contemporary and friend of Tung Ch'i-ch'ang, was such a patron and collector. Tung observed that many works from his own collection had passed into Wu T'ing's hands. In addition, Hui-chou, like Su-chou and Wu-hsi, had become known as a leading center for the carving and printing of books. This commercial activity was encouraged and sustained by the educated class, who, on different levels, were both its consumers and its producers.

HANG-CHOU AND NANKING

Lan Ying, Fan Ch'i, Chang Chi-su, Tao-chi

Lan Ying (1585–1664-) has traditionally been considered one of the last proponents of the "Che" school of painting because of his origins and activity in the Hang-chou region of Chekiang,[9] but closer examination of the Che school at the end of the Ming reveals that the distinction between it and the Wu school was far from clear. Painters classified as its members were gradually assimilating many of the Wu idioms and aspiring to share the growing prestige of the latter. Viewed chronologically, the Che and Wu school traditions were not simultaneous developments. At its height, the Che school, as led by Tai Chin (1388–1462), developed a generation or so earlier than the Wu. When the second- and third-generation followers of the Che school (such as Wu Wei [1459–1508], Chang Lu [1464–1538], Chiang Sung, and Chu Tuan [fl. ca. 1518]) appeared, the major masters of the Wu school, Shen Chou (1427–1509) and Wen Cheng-ming (1470–1559), were just reaching the height of their achievement and influence. The Che artists were strongly influenced by Tai Chin's derivations from the Ma Yüan-Hsia Kuei styles of the Southern Sung Hang-chou court, but they were not necessarily from Chekiang. Lan Ying, for example, was from Hang-chou, Chekiang, and has long been classified as a Che school master, but his painting style and social contacts differed from those of the Che school painters, and there is evidence of his friendship with prominent scholars and collectors of the Wu school and with Tung Ch'i-ch'ang and his circle.

In Lan Ying's twelve-leaf album dated 1642, *Landscapes after Sung and Yüan Masters (VII)*, we find in the inscriptions and stylistic idioms references to nearly all the ancients whom Tung Ch'i-ch'ang recommended in the construction of his orthodox line. Thus this album, like other imitations of his after ancient masters, provides evidence of his ambiguous social position as painter and documents his attempt at a broad assimilation of the styles fashionable among scholar-painters of his day.

While the Wu school was in an advanced stage of artistic activity, both Nanking and the western sector of the eye area had been developing as artistic nuclei. Nanking in the late Ming and early Ch'ing was a ferment of political and intellectual activity (as exemplified by the *Fu-she* movement), and it was also the location of the tomb of the Ming founder.[10] It attracted scores of talented poets and painters, a large majority of whom became Ming loyalists in the Ch'ing. Some of the painters who were active in Nanking at this time were Ch'en Hung-shou, K'un-ts'an (1612–ca. 1686), Ch'eng Cheng-k'uei (fl. ca. 1630–ca. 1674), Kung Hsien (ca. 1618–1689; *XVI*), Ch'en Shu (fl. ca. 1649–ca. 1687), Tai Pen-hsiao (1621–1691), and, later, a distant relative of one of the Ming princes, Chu Jo-chi, known as the monk-painter Tao-chi.

Fan Ch'i (1616–1694-; *XV*) and Wu Pin (ca. 1573–1625) were also active in Nanking at a time when the activities of the Jesuit priest Matteo Ricci (1552–1610) were a topic of conversation among the literati. Western prints, oil paintings, and murals are known to have reached Nan-ch'ang, Nanking, and Peking, where the Jesuits preached. We may be sure that any painter with a modicum of curiosity would have sought a glimpse of these unusual pictures. Without any conscious intention of imitation or copying, painters could well have added the new images to their visual store, however fleeting or superficial the initial contact may have been. In Fan Ch'i's work, for example, such influences are hard to dismiss.

The style of Chang Chi-su (fl. ca. 1620?–1670), a hitherto unknown painter, links him to several of the masters associated with these regional centers. Chang, author of the monumental *Snow-Capped Peaks* in the Sackler collection (*XI*), was born in Shansi, far from the eye area, but his art derives from that fountainhead. His landscape forms in particular contain a trace of willful fantasy reminiscent of Wu Pin, his brushwork is rooted in Lan Ying's manner, and a degree of realism in concept and depiction relate him to such early Ch'ing masters as Fan Ch'i. We hope that other works by this painter will be uncovered, as the quality of the Sackler work indicates that he is worthy of our attention. Interestingly enough, Chang Chi-su's native Shansi had also become a center of "long-distance mercantilism" by the late Ming and early Ch'ing and came to rival Yang-chou and Hui-chou (Anhwei) in the accumulation of wealth derived from sources outside the province.

YANG-CHOU

Lan Ying, Tao-chi, Hua Yen, Ch'en Chao, Ku Yün

The situation of artists and patrons in Yang-chou is typical of some of the artistic changes that occurred in eighteenth-century China. The proliferation of wealth and culture made possible by the complex functions and exchanges of the city created a whole new class of consumers for art, which was no longer limited to the scholar elite. Historically, in the north-south interregional transport of commodities the city occupied a vital position on the Yangtze River.[11] Ever since the opening of the Grand Canal in the seventh century Yang-chou's importance as a strategic military and commercial center had grown. For example, the Liang-huai region controlled the entire salt trade of the country, and local merchants accumulated vast fortunes through marketing and distribution of this staple. The "new rich" were willing and eager to acquire the traditional upper-class manifestations of wealth. They sought all kinds of aesthetic pleasures, among these paintings and calligraphy, and their taste and level of appreciation had a direct influence on the quality, subject matter, size, and, to a certain degree, style of the paintings produced for them. The new painting was not in the traditional literati taste: it was colorful, striking, non-intellectual, and often facile in execution. Simpler subjects like birds, flowers, bamboo, and vegetables gained in popularity. A merging of different aesthetic values occurred, for the patrons encouraged a new breed of painter, who, in turn, was still dependent upon the endorsement of the literati for his credentials. These painters were often ambiguously styled "professional amateurs" or "amateur professionals."

Lan Ying worked in Yang-chou as well as Hang-chou, and his position exemplifies the ambiguous status of the amateur professional. The sheer volume and range of his output qualify him as a professional, yet he also rubbed shoulders with literati and gentlemen painters. In him the "amateur ideal" is blended with the changing aspirations of the professional. His album of landscapes (*VII*) was inscribed at the historic P'ing-shan-t'ang, a site founded in the Sung dynasty by Ou-yang Hsiu (1007–1072), which remained famous up to the Ch'ing, when it was visited twice by the K'ang-hsi Emperor on his Southern Tours.

Equally celebrated in Yang-chou were the gardens attributed to Tao-chi. The most famous was the Wan-shih-yuan ("Garden of Ten Thousand Stones"), which was later destroyed. The P'ien-shih-shan-fang ("Sliver of Stone Retreat") was less famous but is still intact and is considered the earliest extant rock garden in Yang-chou. A sizeable majority of Tao-chi's extant paintings were executed in Yang-chou, when he was, for all intents and purposes, a professional. Many of them are said to be large in format, revealing the prevalent taste, which was not necessarily suited to his style. On the other hand, his fruit, flower, and bamboo works created a new genre, eagerly received by other artists and patrons. He not only helped broaden the scope of upper-class taste but established a standard which at the outset transcended mere popularity.

Another painter who worked in Yang-chou and represents the well-known and more popular aspect of its metropolitan style was Hua Yen (1682–1765–; *XXXVI*). Unlike the other eight Eccentrics, Hua did not limit himself to a single genre of bamboo, plum, figures, or flowers but painted them all and evolved a highly witty and individual approach. His work shows how fluid the formal traditions could be in the later stages of development, embracing creative mixtures in the right artistic personality.

The market for paintings in Yang-chou continued well into the late Ch'ing, when the city's cultural milieu had become highly complex. Contemporary sources praise conservative painters like Ch'en Chao (ca. 1835–1884?; *XL*) and Ku Yün (1835–1896; *XLI*), indicating how catholic the city's taste had become.

SHANGHAI

Li Jui-ch'ing, Li Jui-ch'i, Chang Ta-ch'ien

Shanghai in many respects mirrors Yang-chou. It was originally considered a part of Sung-chiang prefecture. Situated on the bank of the Huang-p'u River, a tributary at the mouth of the Yangtze, it could be reached directly by steamboat from the sea. From the late Ch'ing, therefore, it mushroomed as one of the great international seaports, and as a center of commerce and trade it soon came to rival Yang-chou. The construction of the railways from Shanghai to Nanking and to Peking (the Tientsin-Pukou line) in the first decade of the twentieth century favored Shanghai's development and was detrimental to Yang-chou, which they bypassed. By the early twentieth century Shanghai had become the empire's newest artistic center.[12]

Shanghai's culture and cosmopolitan vigor attracted painters and emigrés from all over the country. The fate of Tao-chi's painting in art history is intimately tied to Shanghai and to three artist-collectors who were associated with its exclusive artistic circles. Li Jui-ch'ing (1867–1920), an eminent calligrapher, and his brother Li Jui-ch'i (ca. 1870–ca. 1940) were from Kiangsi but lived in Shanghai. Chang Yüan (born 1899), better known as Chang Ta-ch'ien, was Li Jui-ch'ing's pupil. Chang Ta-ch'ien is undoubtedly the one living Chinese collector and painter in the traditional style whose fame is international. In 1919, when he was twenty, he went to Shanghai to study calligraphy with Li Jui-ch'ing. At the time Tao-chi paintings were decidedly in vogue with the new rich of the city. Some of its most impressive collections were owned by Ch'eng Lin-sheng, and the holdings of Chang Tse (born 1883, the elder brother of Chang Ta-ch'ien) can also be counted as significant. Eventually the Tao-chi craze spread to Japan, where the study of his paintings was also enthusiastically undertaken. Such scholars as Aoki Masaru, in his early article published in *Shina-gaku* (1921), and Hashimoto Kansetsu, in *Sekitō* (1926), paved the way for several generations of intense interest in Tao-chi.

It was probably around this time that Chang Ta-ch'ien began to collect Tao-chi works, which, along with his brother's collection, provided the basis for his exemplary replicas. One could interpret this kind of "creativity" as representing both an irresistible impulse and a true love for Tao-chi's paintings: what better tribute than to produce variations of one's own? Indeed, Chang's personal style of painting from this period reveals Tao-chi's strong influence (the authors hope to examine the mutual interaction of these two personalities and their works in a future study; the role which Chang and other painters in Yang-chou and Canton played in the propagation of Tao-chi paintings also merits attention).

THE INFLUENCE OF IMPERIAL COLLECTING ON THE PAINTERS OF THE EYE AREA: THE CH'IEN-LUNG EMPEROR

In the eighteenth century the traditional system of patronage and collecting of paintings and calligraphy underwent some important changes in China. Before and during the Sung period Chinese emperors to a greater or lesser degree encouraged the arts and were without doubt the most influential of patrons, either through their painting academies or their individual pursuit of the arts. Scholar-officials who painted were appreciated and recognized for their contributions, and the lines of communication between court and literati were relatively open and flexible.

In the Yüan, as noted earlier, when political circumstances severely limited the scholar's arena of action and official unemployment allowed him more leisure to pursue the arts, the ranks of amateur painters increased, and painting, poetry, and calligraphy flourished independently of imperial recognition and censorship. With this state of affairs, the literati tradition of painting, which had been gaining ground since the Sung, was finally consolidated into a movement of distinct strength. By the early Ming, however, the temperament of the Emperor himself crippled the free expression of the arts, although there were some attempts to establish court patronage under the Hsüan-tsung Emperor. By the fifteenth and sixteenth centuries the polarity of court-academy and scholar-amateur was acutely felt by the painters themselves. With the Ch'ing and the Hsüan-yeh Emperor, known as K'ang-hsi (reigned 1662–1722), this polarity was less pronounced, or, rather, the two trends merged again. In one respect the merger represented the triumph of the tradition of scholar painting because the painters who had been schooled in the literati traditions of the Yüan and Ming, such as Wang Yüan-ch'i and Wang Hui, were now openly assuming professional status and being endorsed by the court as well.

The scroll *Eight Fragrant Summer Flowers* (*XXXVII*), painted by the Ch'ing Emperor Hung-li, known as Ch'ien-lung (reigned 1736–1796), partially illustrates the change in academic-scholar painting relations, as it reflects the style which the Emperor himself aspired to imitate—"plain-line" drawing with ink. This style, also seen in other paintings of his, can be associated with the literati painting style of the Yüan and Ming. In this respect Ch'ien-lung's paintings differ from those of his other imperial predecessors, such as the Sung Emperor Hui-tsung (reigned 1101–1125) and the Ming Emperor Hsüan-te (reigned 1426–1435). Both also painted flower subjects, but Hui-tsung preferred a style of meticulous outlining filled in with color on silk and Hsüan-te preferred subjects advocated by the Ming academy.

The relation of the K'ang-hsi and Ch'ien-lung emperors to the eye area also had some bearing on the general cultural artistic shifts described. Both K'ang-hsi and Ch'ien-lung conducted six Southern Tours and visited the major cities within the eye area, Nanking, Su-chou, Hang-chou, and Yang-chou. Although their main purpose was political and economic, they were undoubtedly attracted to the culture and artistic activity of the Lake T'ai region. Partially as a result of K'ang-hsi's Southern Tours and his personal interest in art, a Ming prince and individualist like Tao-chi went north to the capital and spent three fruitful years in Peking in the company of educated Manchus.

The Ch'ien-lung Emperor was the greatest imperial collector since the Sung emperor Hui-tsung. The art world was entirely different after he amassed his collection, which directly affected the history of art. The most illuminating illustration of this assertion is that of Tung Ch'i-ch'ang. Tung's theories, which have dominated Chinese painting since his time, were largely formed on the basis of a large number of antique paintings, which he was able to study and collect on a comprehensive scale. In the late Ming, when he was actively engaged in collecting, the field was mainly limited to private persons of wealth. Ultimately, Tung's "great synthesis" generated not only the orthodox tradition but the various developments

of the Ch'ing individualists and eccentrics as well. In the late seventeenth and early eighteenth centuries such first-generation masters of the Ch'ing as Hung-jen, Tao-chi, Lan Ying, and others, who were active before Ch'ien-lung's reign, could see in private collections the same works which had fed Tung's imagination.

All this changed in Ch'ien-lung's time. He summoned thousands of the greatest examples of calligraphy and painting in the empire to his palace, so that none but a privileged few had access to them. The generation of painters which followed the Six Masters had little first-hand knowledge of the works which had nourished their teachers, and the same is true of the Individualists and their followers. Consequently, the artistic range of each subsequent generation grew ever more limited and their painting ideals ever more shortsighted. By the end of the Ch'ing there was no major painter of landscapes in the great tradition. This is not to say that there were no painters of respectable quality and quantity: several post-Ch'ien-lung painters of interest in this catalogue still hold a position in the history of art, such as Wang Hsüeh-hao (1754–1832; *XXXIX*), Ch'ien Tu (1763–1844; *XXXVIII*), Ch'en Chao (ca. 1835–ca.1884?; *XL*), and Ku Yün (1835–1896; *XLI*). But the flame in Tung Ch'i-ch'ang's "lamp of transmission"—the antique painting of the ancients—was to all intents and purposes snuffed out. It was a dire consequence which the Emperor could not have foreseen. The gradual decline of landscape painting cannot, of course, be attributed solely to his act, but in terms of the vital role which the great masterpieces of the past, whether literary, philosophical, or visual, have played as the source of spiritual renewal, his removal of ancient paintings from circulation severely stunted the growth of this tradition at a most vulnerable point in its history.

One last word may be added about one of the painters who flourished almost a century after Ch'ien-lung's reign. Ku Yün was one of the last in the line of painters who affiliated themselves with Tung's orthodox line. Working at the close of the nineteenth century in Yang-chou, Ku's range testifies not only to the strength of his chosen tradition but to the flexibility of its adherents. Like many of the orthodox painters in Yang-chou, Ku admired Tao-chi's paintings and even made close copies of them. One work of this type exists in a book of reproductions after old masters. The painting bears a self-inscription by Ku (see *XLI*, fig. 3), and the style is different enough from Ku's own and close enough to Tao-chi's to pronounce it genuine. It is a most interesting document, for it not only tells us about some of the changes that were occurring in the training of painters in the orthodox tradition—such as copying the works of Tao-chi—but also indicates that by the nineteenth century Tao-chi's paintings were not only sought after by collectors but imitated by painters.

NOTES

See the Bibliography at the end of this volume for full information on sources abbreviated here.

1. Names of provinces, cities, etc., are given according to modern usage unless otherwise specified. The interested reader is referred to the following studies and the bibliographies they contain, which provide general information on many of the regions within the "eye area" (no attempt has been made to give a comprehensive listing here): *Chung-kuo tzu-pen chu-i meng-ya wen-t'i t'ao-lun-hui-chi (Symposium on the Question of Incipient Capitalism in Chinese History)*, 2 vols. (Peking, 1957), of especial interest for articles on the craft industries in China; Fu I-ling, *Ming-tai chiang-nan shih-min ching-chi shih-t'an (An Investigation into the Economy and Population of the Chiang-nan Region in the Ming Period)* (Shanghai, 1957); J. L. Gallagher, *China in the Sixteenth Century: The Journals of Matteo Ricci, 1583–1610* (New York, 1953);

Ho Ping-ti, *Studies on the Population of China*, where the phrase "long-distance mercantilism" is found on pp. 196–97; Ho Ping-ti, *The Ladder of Success in Imperial China: Aspects of Social Mobility, 1368–1911*; Charles O. Hucker, *China: A Critical Bibliography* (Tucson, 1962); James T. C. Liu and Peter Golas, *Change in Sung China* (Lexington, Ky., 1969); Dwight H. Perkins, *Agricultural Development in China: 1368–1968* (Chicago, 1969); Teng Ssu-yü and Knight Biggerstaff, eds., *An Annotated Bibliography of Selected Chinese Reference Works*, 3d ed. (Cambridge, Mass., 1971); K. T. Wu, "Ming Printers and Printing," *Harvard Journal of Asiatic Studies*, vol. 7 (1943), pp. 203–60; Yang Lien-sheng, *Money and Credit in China*.

2. For its literary derivation, see Morohashi Tetsuji, ed., *Dai Kanwa jiten*, vol. 10, 35427/40. For calligraphy specifically, see Huang T'ing-chien, who said that calligraphy without brush method was like a Ch'an aphorism without an "eye" (*Shan-ku t'i-pa*, 7/71).

3. On the Grand Canal, see Chu Ch'i, ed., *Chung-kuo Yün-ho shih-liao hsüan-chi (Materials on the History of the Grand Canal)* (Peking, 1962); Ch'üan Han-sheng, *T'ang-Sung ti-kuo yü Yün-ho (The T'ang-Sung Empires and the Grand Canal)* (Shanghai, 1943); Ray Huang, "The Grand Canal during the Ming Dynasty," Ph.D. diss., University of Michigan, 1964.

4. On the Sung-chiang region, see Chia Ching-yen, "Ming-tai Ching-te-chen-te tz'u-ch'i-yeh ho Sung-chiang-te Mien-chih-yeh" ["On . . . and the Cotton Industry in Sung-chiang"], in Li Kuang-pi, ed., *Ming-Ch'ing shih-lun-ts'ung* (Hupei, 1957), pp. 82–91; Feng Chia-sheng, "Wo-kuo fang-chih-yeh-chia Huang Tao-p'o-te kung-hsien" ("Huang Tao-p'o's Contribution to the Weaving Industry in China"), *Li-shih chiao-hsüeh* (Tien-ching, 1954), vol. 4, pp. 19–22; Nelson I. Wu, "Tung Ch'i-ch'ang: Apathy in Government and Fervor in Art," in A. F. Wright and D. Twitchett, eds., *Confucian Personalities*, pp. 260–93; Shen C. Y. Fu, "A Study of the Authorship of the So-Called 'Hua-Shuo' Painting Treatise."

5. On the Su-chou region, see Richard Edwards, *The Field of Stones*; Richard Edwards, "Pine, Hibiscus and Examination Failures," *University of Michigan Museum of Art Bulletin*, vol. 1, nos. 1–2 (1965–66), pp. 14–28; Kao Chen, *Hua-yüan chih-ch'eng, Su-chou (Su-chou, the City of Gardens)* (Shanghai, 1957); Li Chu-tsing, "The Development of Painting in Soochow during the Yüan Dynasty"; Frederick W. Mote, "The Poet Kao Ch'i (1366–1374)"; Wang Ao, *Ku-su-chih (Gazetteer of Su-chou)*, reprint, preface dated 1506 (Taipei, 1965); *Wu-hsi Chin-k'uei hsien-chih (Gazetteer of Wu-hsi)*, reprint, orig. pub. in Wu-hsi, 1881 (Taipei, 1968).

6. Further information on the Chinese garden tradition is found in Ch'eng Chao-hsiung, *Lun Chung-kuo chih t'ing-yüan (On Chinese Gardens)* (Hong Kong, 1966); William Hung, *Shao-yüan t'u-lu-k'ao (On Mi Wan-chung's Shao Garden)* (Peking, 1933); Edward H. Schafer, *Tu Wan's Stone Catalogue of Cloudy Forest* (Berkeley, Calif., 1961); Mirei Shigemori, *Nihon teien-shi zukan (Historical Album of Japanese Gardens)*, 24 vols. (Tokyo, 1936–39), especially vols. 1–3; Osvald Sirén, *Gardens of China* (New York, 1949); Rolf Stein, "Jardins en miniature d'extrême-Orient: le monde en petit," *Bulletin de l'École Française d'Extrême-Orient*, vol. 42 (1943), pp. 1–104; T'ung Chün, *Chiang-nan yüan-lin-chih* (Peking, 1963); Wango H. C. Weng, *Gardens in Chinese Art* (New York, 1968); Wu Shih-ch'ang, "On the Origin of Chinese Private Gardens," *China Journal of Arts and Sciences*, vol. 23, no. 1 (July, 1935), pp. 17–32.

7. Mu Hsiao-t'ien, *An-hui wen-fang ssu-pao-shih (History of the Treasures of the Scholars' Studio of Anhwei)* (Shanghai, 1962).

8. On Mount Huang and the rise of the Anhwei region, see Ch'en Ting-shan, *Huang-shan* (Taipei, 1957); Fujii Hiroshi, "A Study of the Hsin-an (Hui-chou) Merchants, I–IV," *Tōyō gakuhō*, vol. 36, nos. 1–4 (1953–54), pp. 1–44, 1–31, 65–118, and 115–45, respectively; Hsü Shih-ying, *Huang-shan lan-sheng-chi (Record of a Journey to Huang-shan)* (Shanghai, 1934); Hsü Hung-tsu (1586–1641), *Hsü Hsia-k'o yu-chi (A Record of Hsü Hung-tsu's Travels)*, reprint, orig. pub. 1808 (Taipei, 1965); Li Chi and Chang Chun-shu, *Two Studies in Chinese Literature: Hsü Hsia-k'o and His Huang-shan Travel Diaries* (Ann Arbor, Mich., 1968).

9. On Hang-chou, see Chiang Yün-ch'ing, ed., *Che-chiang hsin-chih (A New Gazetteer of Chekiang)* (Hang-chou, 1935); Huang Yung-ch'üan, ed., *Hang-chou Yüan-tai shih-k'u i-shu (The Art of Buddhist Cave Sculptures in Hang-chou during the Yüan)* (Peking, 1958); Ni Hsi-ying, *Hang-chou* (Shanghai, 1936).

10. On Nanking, see William Atwell, "The *Fu-she* of the Late Ming Period," Paper Delivered at the International Symposium on Late Ming Thought, Lake Como, Italy, 1971; James Cahill, "Wu Pin and His Landscape Paintings"; Chou Hui, ed., *Chin-ling so-shih (Miscellaneous Events of Chin-ling)*, reprint, preface dated 1610 (Peking, 1955); Chu Ch'i, *Chin-ling ku-chi ming-sheng ying-chi (Reproductions of Famous Sites and Relics of Chin-ling)* (Shanghai, 1935); Chu Ch'i, *Chin-ling ku-chi t'u-k'ao (Pictures of Sites and Relics of Chen-ling)* (Shanghai, 1936); Frederick W. Mote, "The Transformation of Nanking," Paper Prepared for the Conference of Urban Society in Traditional China, Portsmouth, N.H., 1968, of interest for his discussion of the concept of the "urban-rural" continuum; Archive Society of Nanking (Nan-ching-shih wen-hsien wei-yüan-hui), eds., *Nan-ching hsiao-chih (Minor Chronicle of Nanking)* (Nanking, 1949); Michael Sullivan, "Some Possible Sources of European Influence on Late Ming and Early Ch'ing Painting"; Wang Huan-piao, ed., *Shou-tu-chih (Gazetteer of the Capital City)*, 2 vols., reprint, orig. pub. 1935 (Taipei, 1966).

11. On Yang-chou, see Ch'en Ts'ung-chou, "Yang-chou P'ien-shih shan-fang," *Wen-wu*, vol. 2 (1962), pp. 18–20; Ho Ping-ti, "The Salt Merchants of Yang-chou: A Study of Commercial Capitalism in Eighteenth Century China"; Li Tou, *Yang-chou hua-fang-lu (A Descriptive Account of Yang-chou's "Decorated Boats")*; Chao Chi-pi, ed., *P'ing-shan-t'ang chih (Gazetteer of P'ing-shan-t'ang)* (Yangchou, preface dated 1765); William Henry Scott, "Yangchow and Its Eight Eccentrics," *Asiatische Studien*, vols. 1–2 (1964), pp. 1–19.

12. On Shanghai, see T'ang Chin, ed., *Hung-chih Shang-hai-chih (Shanghai Gazetteer of the Hung-chih Period)*, reprint, preface by Wang Ao dated 1504 (Shanghai, 1940); *Shang-hai Ch'un-ch'iu* (Shanghai, 1948); *Shang-hai yen-chiu tzu-liao (Research Materials on Shang-hai)* (Shanghai, 1936); *Shang-hai-te ku-shih (Accounts of Shanghai)* (Shanghai, 1963).

II. Issues in Connoisseurship

IN SEARCH OF THE "RIGHT NUMBER" AND THE "RIGHT PLACE"

In the past decade or so, scholars of Chinese painting have attempted to remedy the uncritical and indiscriminate acceptance of traditional attributions of Chinese painting and calligraphy which characterized the earlier stages of its study. They have sought to establish the field on sound art-historical principles by more disciplined methods and more systematic inquiry, especially in regard to stylistic analysis and authentication. Great strides have been made in this direction, but unfortunately, as far as authentication is concerned, enthusiasts have often applied a remedy worse than the disease, and in many minds unquestioning acceptance has been replaced by rampant and contagious doubt. Thus, when confronted with a group of attributed paintings or calligraphy, such scholars may pronounce nine out of ten "forgeries" and relegate them to oblivion, an equally unhealthy state of affairs. Such measures, and consequent countermeasures, have bewildered collectors of Chinese paintings; on the other hand, alert students in the field have benefited from the controversy and are seeking to strike a balance between the two extremes.

Suppose we are faced with a group of Chinese paintings whose authorship, date of execution, provenance, and artistic quality are "unknown" (i.e., unstudied) or are in doubt. Many of them have been traditionally attributed to a single painter, while opinions vary about the rest. We are then asked to select the finest authentic works of the said master and to identify and assemble all the paintings in some kind of order or sequence which will illuminate both the master and the paintings themselves. Furthermore, we are asked to articulate and justify our choices and to undertake any documentary research necessary to substantiate them. The task, then, is to correctly identify the "right number" of works by the supposed master in that group and to restore the other paintings to what we believe to be their "right place" in history.

Identification and authentication of artistic works is usually referred to the connoisseur—the "one who knows," who is a critical judge of art and matters of style—while research and explication are commonly assigned to the historian—the narrator of past events, works of art being the "events." In Chinese art the "narrative" is in large part a reconstruction of authenticated works; its broader goal is a weaving of artistic events into the larger historical tapestry of human events.

The process of "identifying" an art work and attributing it to a given master assumes an understanding of that work which is suggested in the word "identify." In the context of Chinese art and for our purposes, it has two meanings. It connotes a life-enhancing, intuitive projection of our psychic faculties into the work in order to apprehend its form, content, and the "artistic intentions" of its maker or creator as fully as possible, both by research and by intelligent looking. This apprehension is also implied in the word "re-create," which means to re-enact mentally the creative act or processes of its maker—his artistic choices, his ultimate decisions, and even his physical movements, insofar as we are capable of doing so. This order of perception constitutes to a major degree what is known as the transmission of the spirit or content of the work, and it is this experience which may qualify even the viewer who may be neither connoisseur nor historian to externalize his responses and to hazard an opinion as to how "good" the work is and how "original"

is its conception. This level of understanding can probably be attained by any serious student and lover of art, Eastern or Western. As the viewer's interests concentrate on questions of style, aesthetic quality, originality, or attribution, however, he is concerning himself with specific problems which interest the connoisseur. This is our second meaning of the word "identify."

Connoisseurship, in the definition of one classic practitioner, the late Bernard Berenson, is based on the assumption that "perfect identity of [stylistic] characteristics indicates identity of origin. . . . To isolate the characteristics of an artist we take all his works of undoubted authenticity and we proceed to discover those traits that invariably recur in them but not in the works of other masters." [1] The precise identification of these characteristics poses methodological problems which we will take up later. Suffice it to say at this point that a correct identification of a doubtful work through thoughtful consideration and reconsideration of it in the context of the artist's attributed œuvre and of related works helps to establish all such works in a new visual order; this order should further clarify by degree its relationship to other works by other masters and thereby lead to a truer historical conception of the period and of its reconstruction.

With this goal in mind, we can see that those students who have examined and understood—or "identified"—a great number of paintings and formulated a broad conception of individual masters and schools will be best qualified to undertake the task of identification and historical restoration of "unknowns." As identification is based largely on visual acuity, in Chinese art one of the main goals in one's visual training is to equip oneself to distinguish shades of stylistic differences between close identities, for while depth of discernment is important, breadth is also vital. In the authentication of any group of objects ascribed to a particular master, we should be wary of a hit-or-miss approach, a fault almost as grievous as indiscriminate acceptance of traditional labels. To select only the most familiar image of a master's work may seem to be simpler and "safer," but that is not our job. Misattributing a painting often indicates that one's attention has been limited to the single period or painter under immediate consideration: assigning what is in fact a Yüan painting to the Ming means that our knowledge of Ming painting is as inadequate as that of Yüan; identifying a genuine Tao-chi work as by Cha Shih-piao or Chang Ta-ch'ien reveals our ignorance of Cha and Chang as well.

In order to determine the "right number" of a given master's extant works and to restore them to the "right place" in the history of pictures and events, then, we must strive to comprehend as completely as possible the full range of that master's abilities and those of his contemporaries, his predecessors and followers, and those who are of the same and differing artistic traditions. Only studies which radiate and overlap on vertical and horizontal scales of time and space and which are supported by sympathetic inquiry into the weak and strong moments of the masters in question can provide the foundation for a comprehensive account of Chinese painting. Such comprehensiveness may in actuality be unattainable, but we maintain it as a useful working ideal, for a stylistic scale which measures both large and small increments of change in the works of minor and major masters also permits more subtle judgments to be formed on any one problem.

Our task, therefore, is to subject *all* extant works to the same penetrating visual scrutiny, regardless of previous traditional judgments. Only by undergoing this renewed process of evaluation, discrimination, and research can the methods of tradition and history—upon which we must acknowledge our great dependence—be made relevant for the present and for advancing scholarship. In this way, too, the works themselves and the judgments passed upon their "greatness" can be tested by methods which transcend current taste, fashion, or individual opinion:

the art historian cannot make an *a priori* distinction between his approach to a "masterpiece" and his approach to a "mediocre" or "inferior" work of art. . . . But when a "masterpiece" is compared and connected with as many "less important" works of art as turn out, in the course of the investigation, to be comparable and connectable with it, the originality of its invention, the superiority of its composition and technique, and whatever other features make it "great," will automatically become evident—not in spite but because of the fact that the whole group of materials has been subjected to one and the same method of analysis and interpretation.[2]

The fruit of these studies, while initially limited in scope, may eventually help to narrow the gap created by the distances and differences of space and time, cultural heritage and language.[3]

"UNDERSTANDING THE MUSIC" AND "EATING WITH ONE'S EARS"

One day a famous violinist, whose concert appearances were always sold out, thought he would try to find out whether people really listened to his music, so he donned a pair of dark glasses, took up his position on one of the busiest corners of the city, raised his violin, and played. For two or three hours he stood there, while all sorts of people passed him by. Few stopped to listen, and even fewer asked who he was. Most never found out that he was the same man whose name drew record crowds when it was advertised outside the concert hall.[4] The point of this anecdote is essentially the same as that of the well-known Chinese story about the famed lutist Po-ya, who upon the death of his friend Chung Tzu-ch'i broke his lute and never played again because, without his friend, there was no one who could "understand the music" (*chih-yin*).[5] From this phrase came the earliest Chinese term for connoisseur, *chih-yin-che*, "one who understands the music." Both Po-ya and the unnamed violinist were in search of the sensitive listener, the understanding critic—in other words, the true connoisseur.

The judgment of a true connoisseur is based ultimately on his personal experience. He ignores hearsay, which in Chinese is known as "eating with one's ears" (*erh-shih*), and he confronts the work of art itself, alone with his reflections, and carries on a genuine dialogue with it. The modern Chinese term for "connoisseur" is a binome, *chien-shang-chia*, combining the word *chien* ("mirror," or something which reflects and discriminates) with *shang* ("to enjoy," "to appreciate") and *chia* (a verb suffix for "one who"). It is indicative of the deeper meaning of the word that *chien-chia*, "one who discriminates," implies the process of *shang*, enjoyment and appreciation, along with the discriminatory process. The Chinese term *chien-shang*, however, should properly be defined in English only as discrimination on the highest and subtlest levels. The ideal connoisseur of Chinese painting and calligraphy must, like his colleague in Western art, possess an artistic sensibility and a feeling for "style"; he must also be trained in the history and connoisseurship of Chinese

painting as such. His personal cultivation, taste, and artistic sensibilities must be not only more acute but also deeper and more catholic than those of the talented amateur. He must be able to discriminate between similar styles not only when he is dealing with periods of several hundred years but when he is dealing with contemporaries working in the same region and exposed to the same influence. He must be able to tell a work of original artistic intention from a close copy and to sort out original works of inferior rank from superior examples of deception.

The order of intuitive judgment possessed by the ideal connoisseur trained in the Chinese tradition is equivalent to the process of artistic "identification" mentioned earlier. He would have received intensive training in the arts of both calligraphy and painting, so that his understanding was acquired on both the technical and theoretical levels and closely approximated that of the creative artist. Like his Western counterpart, he would seek to understand as accurately as possible the psychological and artistic state of the artist and, particularly in Chinese brush painting, to confirm and recapture the psychic energies and physical vitality infused in the original work by the master.[6]

For the modern student of Chinese art, as for the traditional connoisseur, some actual experience in the techniques of painting and calligraphy is almost mandatory. To know from actual experience the planning that is necessary to compose and execute a picture without mechanical corrections, the sense of timing that must be present when different materials respond under different circumstances, the ways in which different brushes are handled to produce certain effects, the effects of overdrawing—all this knowledge largely determines how much we see and how clearly we understand what we see.[7]

Before art history became an independent discipline, the study of Chinese paintings in China was dominated by the gentleman-scholar, whose own good taste, aesthetic judgment, and private collection of calligraphy and paintings permitted him more contact with and insight into works of art than the ordinary man of letters, who had limited access to collections. The connoisseur of old China was esteemed in his immediate circle and in his class as a whole for his powers of discernment, which he had cultivated in greater depth and breadth than had his educated peers. Today the traditional connoisseur seems to have lost much of his former status and, in fact, has come to be regarded as a tool or technician in some circles.

Such an attitude to a certain extent reflects the proliferation of academic disciplines in the West and the tendency, present even among some art historians, toward overspecialization and aspirations toward applying the "scientific method" to the discipline of art history. However innocent or unconscious such condescension may be, it fails to distinguish the various motives and abilities of those who have been called "connoisseurs." There are as many different kinds of connoisseurs as there are art historians or scientists: there are major and minor antique dealers and collectors of art, calligrapher-painters of limited and of wide renown, those who make art their hobby (like the businessman or scientist) and those who make it their profession (like the art historian); there are self-styled experts, and there are obsessed and life-long devotees. While the general public may consider them all "connoisseurs," it is clear that their abilities vary greatly. We must remember that the job which the connoisseur undertakes makes him neither a technician nor a mystic, neither a high priest-astrologer nor a technical menial. Some connoisseurs acquire their knowledge more or less empirically, others more or less systematically. In the final analysis, what matters is the depth and subtlety of their approach and their ability to enlighten the viewer and illuminate the object.

THE IDEAL ART HISTORIAN
AND CONNOISSEUR OF CHINESE ART

The activities of the modern art historian and connoisseur of Chinese painting and calligraphy as described thus far differ little from those of the art historian and connoisseur of Western or European art. As Panofsky defines the two, the connoisseur "limits his contribution to scholarship to identifying works of art with respect to date, provenance and authorship and to evaluating them with respect to quality and condition."[8] The art historian, with a view to building up a historical conception, engages in archeological research which attempts to reconstruct the artistic intentions or alternatives which faced the maker of the work of art. In doing so, he tries to make adjustments for the inevitable gap in his "cultural equipment" by "learning as much as he possibly can of the circumstances under which the objects of his studies were created."[9] Wen Fong has defined the goal of those engaging in the study of Chinese painting and calligraphy as one of building "a network of geographically and historically related styles into a reliable 'history of styles'."[10] This is the historian's voice speaking. Such a goal can only be achieved by "establishing such 'monuments' one by one," through careful research, and placing each object of dubious attribution in its correct period or in some specific art-historical context.[11] This has been the task of the connoisseur.[12]

If we subscribe to R. G. Collingwood's definition of history as the "re-enactment of past experience" (in contrast with the mere classification and ordering of those events, which is "science"),[13] then the awareness of a history of styles requires sensitivity to what constitutes style. This sensitivity involves the aesthetic re-creation which is a part of the process of "identification," and therefore is as much a part of the historian's equipment as of that of the connoisseur. Thus, ideally at least, in Chinese art the activities of the connoisseur and the art historian, like those of their counterparts in Western art, are indeed interconnected.

When we speak of the history of Chinese painting, as Max Loehr puts it, we are talking about a concept that has been derived primarily from those paintings which have survived and which we know today.[14] Through the mere accidents of history they have become the events of our account. As material objects, of course, they must be apprehended through the vision as well as the intellect,[15] in what Panofsky calls "intuitive esthetic re-creation."[16] It demands that we muster all our sensory probes—both naturally endowed and culturally acquired. By "intuitive" Panofsky means the synthetic, sophisticated intellectual activity which accompanies the visual scrutiny. By "re-creation" he means "apprehending the individuality of a thing by thinking oneself into it, by making its life one's own."[17] Meaning in a work of art, he goes on, "can only be apprehended by re-producing, and thereby, quite literally, 'realizing' the thoughts that are expressed in the books and the artistic conceptions that manifest themselves in the statues."[18] According to this, then, the process of writing history and the apprehension of aesthetic meaning may coincide on a very fundamental level. There-

fore in Chinese art, as in the art of the West, the differences lie not so much in principle as in emphasis and explicitness: "The connoisseur thus might be defined as a laconic art historian, and the art historian as a loquacious connoisseur. In point of fact the best representatives of both types have enormously contributed to what they themselves do not consider their proper business."[19] The qualifier "best representatives of both types" should be stressed because, as pointed out earlier, without any objective way of measuring their abilities[20] we cannot assume that all historians are expert connoisseurs, nor all connoisseurs knowledgeable historians. The ideal art historian-connoisseur is far from a model type. To a great extent, the various spheres of knowledge of those in the West and East who have contributed to the growth of Chinese art studies have charted the course of the field as a whole, and their personal interests suggest its future emphases as well. If the connoisseur-art historian as described in the preceding paragraphs has dealt primarily with formal and aesthetic problems of style and their interconnections in history, the "pure" art historian has concerned himself, for the most part, with the study of monuments authenticated and classified for him by the field archeologist and connoisseur. He has been mainly preoccupied with the historical narrative, and questions of aesthetic expression and the creative process have ranked second.

The historian of Chinese art theory, in contrast, is often most occupied with translating into a Western language selections from the sizable body of critical literature on aesthetics and the theory of art produced by the Chinese. His work is heavily descriptive and is often presented without reference to actual art objects. This approach has depended more heavily on general art history and sinology than on connoisseurship. The value to art history of such accounts and monographs lies in the extent to which their textual interpretations of terms and concepts can corroborate and clarify the visual material. Pure sinological or linguistic knowledge is often insufficient to cope with problems which initially were visual. At any rate, the correct interpretation of the technical terms, artistic phenomena, and psychology of vision found in the literary texts remains a challenge to the translator, whatever his primary discipline may be.

The theorist of art-historical studies, a fourth type of historian, frequently steps into the realm of pure aesthetics; his inquiries draw less on individual objects of art than on art theory and the philosophy of art. He is often interested in large stylistic movements rather than in the specific problems of style involved in authentication and tends to focus on what he believes to be seminal figures and on the inception of artistic inventions. His command of many disciplines allows him this role of critic of the methodology in the field and makes him more interested in formulating a conceptual framework for his observations, but again often without calling upon the evidence of the monuments. In this respect, the connoisseur's findings are of special use to him.

A fifth aspect of Chinese art studies has only recently come to the fore, although it should have been the very foundation of the discipline; this is art history's alliance with cultural history. In recent years overspecialization in the field obscured this fundamental alliance: now attention has turned to it again, mainly as a result of the recent proliferation of historical efforts in the field of East Asian studies generally—institutional, political, economic, geographical, social, intellectual, religious, and so forth. As all humanistic studies focus upon the activities and works of man as they appear under varying historical conditions, we are all in a sense "cultural historians," but the art historian takes as his point of departure the work of art as a concrete expression of the human mind and heart. Inevitably, in the process of investigation, he trespasses on the domains of various specialized historical studies and may find himself, despite his best efforts, sinking into rather deep methodological waters, but he takes courage in the fact that only through such incursions, however problematic, can he contribute in a broad fashion to cultural history.

THE METHODOLOGICAL PARADOX

One of the ultimate goals of the connoisseur is the discrimination of the genuine from the spurious, with its attendant problem of proper identification of artist and date. In terms of the reconstruction of a history of styles (in art history's narrow sense) and the restoration of works of art as a part of human history (in its broader sense), the authentication of individual works as to date, provenance, and authorship and the evaluation of their quality and condition are of vital importance. The very stuff of our inquiry is the works themselves and what they tell us about the human energies and minds which produced them. Their physical presence provides that objective substance which separates the art historian and connoisseur from the art theorist and aesthetician.

Max Loehr raises some provocative questions in this context: "too few originals of pre-Sung times are left to build a history on them, and . . . worse still, we cannot ever be sure that we have to do with originals, whether pre-Sung, Sung or post-Sung in alleged date, because *it is not possible to prove authenticity*."[21] If by proof is meant scientific, independently verifiable evidence or the testimony of an eye witness, then authenticity certainly cannot be proved. Yet Loehr does believe that it can be determined, for he writes, "It is conceivable that we might arrive at a fairly accurate idea of the history of Chinese painting on the basis of copies and imitations, if these are *understood* in their stylistic sequence" (Loehr's italics). Following his reasoning, if it is not possible to prove authenticity, then how is the understanding proper to the constructing of a stylistic sequence achieved? What is more, if one can determine copies and imitations, then clearly one should also be able to determine genuine works.

The questions raised here are not simply ones of field jargon. The authenticity question cannot be separated from the general question of art-historical procedure. The crux of Loehr's formulation, as he himself was aware, is not so much the immediate question of authenticity vs. concepts of style but the whole methodological dilemma facing the historian, that of mastery of both the general and the conceptual vs. the specific and the factual, of the document vs. the object to be documented. Equally relevant are the problems of documentation, the confines of the period under investigation, and the number of works extant and available for investigation. "The case for or against authenticity," says Loehr, "rests on conviction, and for the convincingness of a work, style is the foremost criterion. . . . the historian . . . has to go by style alone until his concepts are sufficiently advanced to enable him to pass on matters of authenticity." In sum, he sees the authenticity question as presenting a "true paradox": without knowledge of styles we cannot judge the authenticity of individual works, and without convictions about authenticity

we cannot form concepts of style.[22] However, the title of Loehr's essay hints at a solution, for it states that these are issues in the history of *Chinese* painting. Although the study of the history of Chinese painting is much briefer than that of the West, there is little indication that the problems mentioned by Loehr are unique to it: historians of Western painting have arrived at solutions to the authenticity problem which can help resolve not only theoretical but methodological questions in Chinese painting as well.

First of all, we must agree that genuine Chinese paintings were at one time produced, and that despite destruction, loss, and debasement through copies and forgeries, some of them still exist. Second, we must agree that it is possible to discriminate between degrees of originality, or primacy of artistic conception (which is not necessarily the same thing, but which has a major bearing on the determination of quality) in each work. Primacy of artistic conception, as has been pointed out by Berenson, Offner, Friedländer, and other connoisseurs of Western art, is one of the foremost measures of authenticity and has very much to do with style—indeed, it forms an inseparable part of the concept of style and the authentic, as we understand these words. The historian cannot reasonably consider style without considering "primacy of conception" and the "authentic" as well.

Loehr is correct in saying that "coming to terms" with a work of art "does not mean a compromise between opposed views or viewers. Rather it means that the right understanding of the work or sequence in question will sooner or later prevail." The question is how this understanding will be achieved, when, as he points out, "it is possible for several critics to arrive at surprisingly contradictory judgments about one and the same work, or sequence of works, or about the meaning of the same evidence."[23] The simpler answer lies in the varying abilities of those several critics to deal with the problem at hand and the embryonic state of our discipline. Disagreement does not mean that everyone is wrong—and even if everyone should be mistaken at a given time, the problem is not necessarily forever insoluble.

The key to this paradox—whether it is seen in terms of style vs. authenticity, facts vs. continuity, or knowledge of the specific vs. the general—lies in the realization that its elements are all part of a total "organic situation."[24] This is not a mechanical assemblage of prefabricated parts into a "finished" product. We are as much interested in the process of building and constituting as we are in the product. It is the process of learning, as much as the possession of knowledge, that concerns us, and each affects the other.[25] As E. Wind has phrased it, in science, just as in history, "every instrument and every document participates in the structure which it is meant to reveal."[26]

Our concepts of style must continually be corrected by confrontations with original works of art which test our intuitive aesthetic reactions; our judgments on the age, quality, and authorship of such works must continually be reviewed on the basis of our notions about style. Each fundamentally changes or subtly alters our understanding of the other. With more astute responses to the formal and expressive manifestations of individual masters and their changes and transformations from masters to pupils, regions to periods, we will be better able to make judgments as to the authenticity of discrete objects. Our notions of style and of authenticity must continually evolve, slowly but surely, so that both concepts, like the halves of an arch, may eventually stand firm.[27]

ASPECTS OF QUALITY

Because it is our understanding of works of art which undergoes change, not the works themselves, the judgment of quality is a key factor. Opinions as to how quality can be isolated and described may vary, but it is generally agreed that a feeling for it is essential in the study of art and particularly in connoisseurship. Berenson said, "The sense of quality is indubitably the most essential equipment of a would-be connoisseur. It is the touchstone of all his laboriously collected documentary and historical evidence."[28]

It is important to remember that by "quality" is meant not only the excellence of a thing but also its sensory aspects, which are vital to the process of "identifying" and "re-creating." In Chinese painting and calligraphy (or any work where the medium of depiction is the oriental brush), "quality," as we are using the word, has more to do with the viewer's sense of visual delight as apprehended through bodily feeling than with the work's technical "excellence." Here we seek to grasp the energies invested in the brushlines, the artist's psychic and physical poise. This transmission is at once physical—as originally projected by the artist—and kinesthetic—as re-created and felt by the viewer. As directed through the brush onto paper, the level of performance and the energy manifested are direct reflections of the artist's psychological makeup and his mental and spiritual prowess, as well as his physical well-being at the precise moment of execution.

In traditional Chinese criticism the notion of *ch'i* (the word means "breath," "spirit," or "vital force," depending on the context) and later the binome *ch'i-yün* would have been used to indicate desirable qualities present in an artistic work. Historically, the use of the term *ch'i* as an aesthetic concept appeared sometime in the second century A.D. in Han dynasty writings about the analysis and criticism of the human personality. It was assimilated into the language of literary criticism and belles-lettres in the Six Dynasties in the third to fifth centuries. Around that time *ch'i* is said to have made its way into criticism of painting. The original concept implied no absolute values but rather a combination of the physiological, spiritual, and intellectual endowments of the literary man. For example, a scholar's *ch'i* could be either "pure" or "turbid," and his literary style would vary accordingly.[29] Only when it was linked with other attributes in the specific context of the art of painting did ambiguities arise. This occurred in the first of the so-called six principles (*liu-fa*) associated with Hsieh Ho, where it appears as *ch'i-yün sheng-tung*, and in this context and that of the entire text, it was unclear whether *ch'i-yün* was a property belonging to the artist, to the natural object to be depicted, or to the expression in the painting. By the eleventh century in the Sung dynasty writing of Kuo Jo-hsü, the concept had become a mysterious, rare, and ineffable quality which, while it was a direct reflection of the artist himself, was found only in a work of art.[30] For our purposes, it is useful to keep in mind *ch'i* in its earliest meanings as a vital physical component of the human personality coloring the form and expression of a man's creative work.

In contemporary jargon the word "kinesthesia" describes the instinctive responses of movement, weight, pressure, tension, balance, and duration which are involved in our reaction to the energy levels manifest in art. This bodily feeling is very much a part of Panofsky's "intuitive esthetic re-creation." Gombrich has suggested the word "tonus" to clarify the notion of *ch'i*,[31] as it denotes the responses of the viewer's muscles, tendons, and joints. Here we are in essence recreating the physical movements of the artist and thereby sensing his mental state and the level of energy with which he was charging the work during its execution.

When the forms in a work of art represent the product of the artist's thought and planning in advance of its actual execution, they are imbued with primal vitality and spontaneity, no matter how derivative the basic technical formulas or initial formal stimulus may have been. What we see has been achieved through triumph and struggle. Such a work, provided that the necessary technical command of brush, ink, and prototypes is also present, differs substantially from the close or so-called line-for-line copy (*lin* or *mo-pen*). The supposedly identical lines, shapes, and basic design are as different to the sensitive eye as a living, growing organism is from a mechanically constructed one. Max Friedländer has said: "The copyist, by contrast to the creative master, takes as his starting point a picture, not life; and is concerned with a vision already realized. . . . Strictly speaking, it is a question of difference of degrees. Even a great and independent painter has not only seen nature but also works of art . . . [but] the truly creative master struggles with the task of projecting on the picture surface the vision which exists in his imagination."[32]

In Chinese painting and calligraphy the idea of an original visualization and its attendant sense of living, energetic growth in the forms is relevant in itself, even without consideration of the historical position and critical importance of the master whose work exhibits these qualities. It may be that the higher the "energy level" of the master—both psychic and physical—the more complex the elements transmitted through the brush tip and the greater the artistic genius. The artist's mental powers, degree of traditional training, extent of self-discipline, and depth of personal cultivation are all at stake during the performance itself. And the master does perform, like a musician or an athlete. Musician, athlete, and artist have all received intensive training directed toward performance; no two performances or games are ever exactly alike, as no two artistic circumstances surrounding a work are ever alike. What sportsman and artist have in common is the goal of perfection and the preoccupation with technique as it bears on performance. Once the fundamental rules are mastered, the performer is free to express himself and to pursue perfection—a mental idea which is ever changing, a spiritual elation which is always elusive. In this sense, then, performance is the display of those qualities which are unique to one's mental and physical endowment and which are the result of a single congruence of place, period, and person.

How can we use these "energy levels" to determine a single artist's range and to reconstruct his corpus? Richard Offner says:

Creative activity operates by a law of reason that the artist's hand is guided fundamentally by the same preferences, the same inevitable choice of what is significant in everything he produces . . . that these are subject to the same organizing tension and speak to us with the same degree of energy. . . . Thus his central character will have to be sought in the energy released by his forms and by the vital tension that holds them together on the one hand, and on the other in the fixed ambit implicit in his works. Besides the various factors that constitute a work of art occur in such number and complexity that their order will not be met with in any other master.[33]

Quality, after all, is a relative thing. Our sense for it, like relative pitch in music, can be developed to a certain extent. Once we have learned the rules of a game or perfected the music of a certain work, we may appreciate another performance of it because we are "insiders" (*chih-yin*). We can also learn to appreciate individual performances of works of art, once we have gone beyond the basic rules and have acquired some depth and subtlety of interpretation and knowledge of what is most difficult. But moving from this state of semi-understanding to that of understanding is a large step. The man starting to climb a mountain may imagine intellectually or on the basis of previous experience what is ahead, but only the experienced climber, who has reached the top, knows the ravines, fissures, or snowdrifts along the route. Like the finest climbers, the best connoisseurs have traveled many miles and over much terrain, but each confrontation, like each trip up the mountain, holds something of the unknown.

The search for quality may be described as a process of psychic preparation—of having the thing constantly on one's mind, one's entire being in a state of acute sensitivity. This state is the basis for the intuitive enlightenment reached when one confronts a work and truly "understands the music." It matters little whether the enlightenment is gradual or sudden. What we are speaking of here is again an organic process. Without work and study, sudden understanding would not be possible. Exposure to many different kinds of paintings of varying degrees of excellence, by both great masters and hacks, is essential, as is a tenacious visual memory and an eye for resemblances and discrete differences. Hence the value of studying copies and all manner of forgeries: having seen what is truly bad, one will know what is good. One should be equipped with both a large structural scale for measuring period styles and a fine ruler of expressive nuances, as well as a comprehensive stock of formal allusions on which to draw. With these tools we will be better able to distinguish a virtuoso performance of a given master from a hasty, mediocre work from that same hand. One's confidence in his own physical responses to the energy levels mentioned above enriches this kind of scale and, we hope, teaches us to evaluate different hands with greater certainty.

PROBLEMS OF PERIOD STYLE
AND THE FORMULATION OF METHOD

While aesthetic re-creation and archeological research on an object or group of objects may be exercised independently of qualitative judgments, the latter play an important role in determining the degree of "possibility" when attempting to assess the range of a particular master or period. Heinrich Wölfflin's statement "not everything is possible at all times" was restated more recently by George Kubler, who notes that ineluctable frontier conditions "confine originality at any moment so that no invention overreaches the potential of its epoch."[34] A great master often pushes the formal and technical possibilities of his time to their limits, but how are we to determine these limits and frontier conditions without the benefit of intensive comparative studies of a significant number of secondary, minor, and anonymous works? Max Friedländer has said: "The study of the lesser masters furthers knowledge of the general level, of the style of the period. We learn to know the starting line of the great masters, and see how it is set off lustrously against the dark background of average activity. . . . the personalities of the great artists, as a result, have been defined more clearly and deci-

sively."[35] Thus the historian cannot limit himself only to those styles which are "new" in their time, for he cannot determine what is new. If he ignores the background of artistic activity provided by the lesser masters, he will not only deprive himself of historical perspective but will be falling into the methodological paradox described earlier.

The research which the art historian undertakes in his study of a given object often obliges him to assess both its authenticity and that of a comparable work or document which may clarify it.[36] This circular reasoning, inherent in historical inquiry, also marks the problems of method in Chinese art history. Wen Fong has shown the importance of utilizing archeologically dated evidence as the structural framework on which to build the historical model of changing styles as one solution to this paradox:

We must study the archaeologically recovered early works for the only remaining evidence of fixed visual positions during the early periods. . . . The significance of such data lies in their indubitable authenticity. Archaeological materials showing early Chinese landscape painting through the late thirteenth century are found from Japan to innermost Asia and these offer a clearly definable stylistic development. . . . Even though these works may not mark the stylistic frontiers of their time, they indicate a set of visual positions that must be taken into account whenever the dating of an attributed work is in question.[37]

This approach represents a significant methodological advance over previous attempts at historical reconstruction and has introduced a greater degree of discipline into the study of the early periods. However, no comparable archeological material exists for works from the fourteenth century and later, such as those in the Sackler collection.[38] Thus, Fong says,

To prove the authenticity of an individual work, we must go beyond structure. . . . historical and literary records, artistic treatises, as well as attributed works which constitute the bulk and essence of the available visual material [relating to the work in question] must necessarily play an even more important role than the archaeological evidence. . . . To prove that one of two attributed works in a stylistic sequence is an original and the other a later imitation or forgery, we must give in order the following evidence: firstly, that the "correct" painting is structurally a work of the period to which it is attributed; secondly, that together with literary and other attributed material, *the painting not only contributes to the understanding of the personal style of the master, but also explains the transmitted image of the master's manner in later periods;* and finally, that the "wrong" painting can be explained and placed in a later period, within the attributed master's stylistic sequence, or tradition.[39]

The soundness of this method cannot be overemphasized. However, it is on Fong's second criterion (in italics) that much of the approach used here builds and expands. A work which "contributes to the understanding of the personal style of the master" and "explains the transmitted image of the master's manner in later periods" could also be an extremely close copy. Such a copy presumably would fulfill the stylistic requirements of our historical reconstruction, but it would give us a distorted image of the master's true powers: "An exact tracing copy may preserve much of the original structure, but it suffers from a lack of spontaneity in execution."[40] This very quality and spontaneity must occupy our attention if we are to distinguish the "hands" of the masters involved.[41] We therefore hope to augment his criteria of period and personal styles so that we can discern the "hands" of the different artistic personalities presented in the case studies in Part III below.

A NOTE ON THE "IMPORTANCE" OF A WORK OF ART

The process of authentication does not determine the importance of a work of art. Even if the task of ascertaining the degree of genuineness or falseness of a work were achieved, the equally challenging one of restoring all extant works to their proper place in art history would entail value judgments on many levels. While assessments of importance may depend upon a subjective interpretation of history, there are at least three questions we may ask in order to approach the problem more objectively.

1. What is the work's *artistic importance?* What are its intrinsic qualities and expressive vitality, as measured by the aesthetic norms contemporary with and proper to the work itself — form, line, brushwork, composition, color, volumes, movement, etc.?

2. What is the work's *art-historical importance?* What is its significance in terms of its innovative or non-innovative style and its effect on other artists, as indicated by imitations, copies, forgeries, etc.? Assessments of this order are still visual and focused on the object, but they extend beyond the given work of art to its involvement with other works, the "perturbations" set off by the "main signal," in Kubler's words.

3. What is the work's *critical importance?* First, how does it appear in commentaries, art criticism, catalogues, etc., contemporary and later, which tell its historical and critical history as seen by observers in direct contact with the artist, the work, and the culture? Second, how is it affected by recent twentieth-century criticism and art-historical studies, whose new methods of discussion and frequent visual reproduction may alter its actual artistic or art-historical importance?

Evaluation of "importance" suggests a movement of ever-larger concentric circles radiating from the given work outward and touching all relevant material. A decision on importance cannot be made on one level without affecting our knowledge of the others in terms of comparative values. The usefulness of evaluating a work in this way can be illustrated. *Travellers in Mountains and Streams (Hsi-shan hsing-lü-t'u)*, now in the National Palace Museum, Taipei,[42] is almost universally acclaimed as one of the few great Sung masterpieces extant and as perhaps the only surviving work by the master painter Fan K'uan. The fact that its authenticity has never been successfully questioned testifies to the critics' agreement as to its artistic importance — the quality of its execution, conception, etc. From the art historian's standpoint, however, it had next to no direct influence, as a painting, on subsequent masters until it reappeared in the so-called *Hsiao-chung hsien-ta* album[43] (now associated with Wang Shih-min) and, later, was copied exactly by Wang Hui from that album.[44] So the influence of Fan K'uan and this particular work on subsequent scholar-painters in the Yüan to late Ming was limited, as was its appearance and that of the painter in critical literature. Because of the dearth of genuine Sung works of quality in the twentieth century it has received much attention in reconstructions of Sung painting, yet in terms of Fan's whole œuvre, it may not have been his most important work artistically.

While objections may be voiced to the foregoing distinctions as creating more confusion than order, they nevertheless have some merit in terms of a working method. The assessment of the artistic importance or quality of a work is justified by the view that its intrinsic qualities formed the individual artist's primary standard.

These standards or norms evolved (whether consciously or unconsciously) out of the artist's technical, critical, and artistic tradition and were a part of his evaluation of his own work. An important aspect of the historian's research is to ascertain these norms as best he can. The artist himself knows the past and the present, but only the historian knows the future as well. He can interpret the significance of an individual visual statement and weigh it against the norms of the artist's own lifetime. The contemporary norm of judgment may or may not concur with history's estimate of "importance" because neither the artist nor his contemporaries can be aware of any subsequent influence. Indeed, the ability to attract a following is, in the view of some historians, material evidence of the stature of an artist or a work.[45] Nevertheless, our attempt to evaluate intrinsic artistic importance (while often not a wholly conscious or intellectual response) is the foundation of the judgment we make in each of our encounters with a work.

THE TRUE CONNOISSEUR AND THE GREAT FORGER

If one must study the inferior as well as the superior to recognize quality, one must know what constitutes a forgery as well as what is genuine. Generally speaking, a forgery is any work of art made with the intention to deceive, i.e., to be passed off as the product of a different hand or different period. The deception may represent only a harmless joke, as in the case of certain scholar-forgers; more commonly, it may be a direct and intentional fraud by a second or third party for monetary gain.[46] Forgeries, or, to use a more neutral term, "copies," may be thought of as malignant entities because of their misrepresentation of period and person, which, if undetected, may seriously distort our understanding of the artistic energies generated by individual artists, of formal innovations, and of the continuities in divergent stylistic trends.

Although their motives differ, the state of mind and the technical preparation of the great forger are similar to those of the ideal connoisseur. The great forger, like an impersonator, seeks to approximate in every formal and expressive detail the line and the shape of the work, the artist's materials, and his attitude. Whether he is aware of it or not, he must penetrate into his subject's psyche to match and even anticipate all his "moves." Beyond making exact copies, he must know the period style or phases of development of his model and the subject matter and poetic inscriptions that would be likely to be within his repertoire. Thus the great forger puts both his mind and hand to work, and in his supreme moments he is both an interpreter and a connoisseur.[47] Of course, the depth and subtlety of his interpretation is the ultimate measure of quality, but breadth — mastery of several masters' styles from several periods of history — also plays a part in our evaluation of his art. Some forgers are limited by their temperament and interests to only a single image of one or two masters. Generally speaking, however, the truly great forger, like the connoisseur, can command many styles from many periods. By contrast, the bulk of spurious works have been perpetrated by ordinary men of limited talents and knowledge.

Forgers are often spoken of collectively as an evil, as greedy professionals with low artistic standards. But the history of Chinese painting and calligraphy reveals another variety, the talented scholar who produces so-called forgeries for amusement, to show off his technical virtuosity. There are several anecdotes about such diversions among famous figures in Chinese art. Their original intent was to deceive, but the deception was not considered unethical, and there was no desire to profit financially from it. For example, Wang Hsien-chih (344–388) felt that he was the equal of his father, Wang Hsi-chih (307?–365), traditionally known as the "calligraphic sage." One day Wang Hsi-chih, after having drunk a quantity of fine wine, blissfully wrote several lines of calligraphy on a nearby wall, as was his inclination at the moment. When he retired, his son erased his father's writing and daringly replaced it with his own rendering, thinking that no one could tell the difference. The next time his father passed the spot, he turned back quickly to look again, then slowly shook his head, saying, "I must have really been drunk to write such poor characters!" Only then did the son realize how far short of his father's achievement he fell—not only in the quality of his writing, but also in his judgment.[48] Another story told by the Ming scholar-painter Shen Chou (1427–1530) concerns the great Sung painter, calligrapher, and connoisseur Mi Fu (1051–1107):

Duke Hsiang [Mi Fu] at the time loved to collect calligraphy by Chin and T'ang masters. Having acquired them, he himself would always copy and make tracings of each kind, going to every length to re-create the appearance of the original. Then he would replace the genuine with his copy in order to confuse people. If someone pointed out the deception, Mi would have a good chuckle. In this way Mi would test his own artistic abilities as well as the understanding of others.[49]

To this day there are still those who accept the products of some of Mi Fu's jests after the old masters as original, but certainly his art cannot be relegated to the same level as that of the professional forger.

The authors of two works in the Sackler collection may be considered in this category of "scholar-forgers," Li Jui-ch'i (ca. 1870–ca. 1940; see XXI) and Chang Ta-ch'ien (born 1899; see XXXV). Both Li and Chang are painter-calligraphers of renown and expert connoisseurs and collectors. Chang Ta-ch'ien's holdings of antique paintings and calligraphy represent one of the last of the important Chinese private collections.[50] As the level of connoisseurship has risen in this country, Chang's activities as a scholar-forger have received more notice, but even apart from this aspect of his work, he has had a notable career as a modern creative painter with roots in the classical Chinese tradition. Whether as a contemporary painter or as a scholar-forger, his style is not limited to the images of one or two painters, nor to the influence of the ancient works he imitates. Rather, like a truly creative forger and connoisseur, he commands the styles of many masters from the eighth to the eighteenth century, both famous artists in the scholar-painter tradition and anonymous craftsmen of religious subjects.

THE PLACE OF FORGERIES IN ART HISTORY

As the activities of the forger are very much a fact of our visual past, we would do well to rid the word of its moralistic and pejorative connotations. The forger himself is an artist, and his output of energy, however devious its purpose, also forms a part of that comprehensive history of artistic energies we are attempting to reconstruct.[51] His works, when they were produced, satisfied a contemporary demand. Once detected, they may tell us much about the artist whose name was attributed to them, along with the social and economic factors leading to their production—properly interpreted, they may indicate the artist's popularity in succeeding generations, his esteem in collectors' eyes, and the impression or impressions of his style extant when a given forgery was made. Such evidence, if it can be gathered, forms a part of the history of the artist. Forgeries, therefore, have a place in art history. As historians, we can use them advantageously. Thus the task of restoring every extant work to its proper place in history must include proper identification and evaluation of forgeries as well. Ideally, our authentication of forgeries would include, just as with genuine works, the period or specific date of execution, possible region, and, ultimately, even the identity of the forger.

CRITERIA FOR AUTHENTICITY

When faced with the authentication of a single work attributed to a given master, we are in essence confronted with assessing the whole body of his attributed works. None of us starts from scratch in this endeavor. Traditional attributions are seldom disregarded with profit, for they may offer insight into some aspect of the history of the painting, and our researches and subsequent confirmation or revision of traditional views in turn will corroborate previous research and build up the corpus of known works of the master.

In seeking "authenticity" we are seeking the individual artistic personality at the core of each of these works, particularly those of the later (post-fourteenth-century) period in Chinese painting, when the individual artistic personality was strikingly manifest. Our notion of artistic individuality in this context is based on two assumptions formulated by connoisseurs of Western art: that "perfect identity of [stylistic] characteristics indicates identity of origin"[52] and that "the divergence between works of [the master's] youth and his maturity, even though it might be considerable, cannot be as great as that between his own and another master's works."[53] These hypotheses are equally valid in the study of Chinese painting.

As noted above, from the Yüan dynasty on, extant paintings attributed to a given master are of sufficient homogeneity and number for us to assemble a credible corpus. We are not confronted with scores of anonymous or unsigned works whose authors' names are lost to history, nor need we investigate a ghost figure or search for his long-deceased masterpieces, as one must do for the majority of Sung and pre-Sung names found in the literary records. For paintings attributed to the Sung and earlier, whether anonymous or attributed, it is the determination of period and date of execution which is crucial, with individual authorship or school tradition less so; for a large number of Yüan and post Yüan attributions, both period and personal style count, as well as the individual "hand" of the master.

In the preliminary steps to authentication, as noted above, one should be aided by all previous attributions, regardless of their credibility or lack of it. Accordingly, we gather together as many of the attributed works as possible, in the original or in reproduction. In confronting each work, certain criteria will help us to fix more accurately its position in relation to others. No order or priority is implied in the following discussion; in actual practice, the criteria function as an organic system. The validity of each is tested against the strength of the others and according to the specific given conditions of each work (e.g., if a work has no literary records or contemporary criticism, no second work attributed to the same master, no seals or inscriptions, etc., then these cannot be considered for purposes of authentication, although their absence is significant in terms of archeological research). The criteria, organized here as three tests of authenticity, may also serve as areas and topics of concentration when archeological research is being done.

1. The *morphological features* of the style of a work, whether painting or calligraphy, should be compatible with what is known of the given master's personal range and period of activity, and these features aid in clarifying to some degree the historical relationship of his style to that of contemporaries, predecessors, sources, and followers, if any.

This criterion functions on the levels of both "motifs" and "form relationships," to use Meyer Schapiro's definition of style,[54] and alerts us to the authenticity of its period, or "historical style," and also to personal or archetypal images, in the case of great masters. Thus a work whose period and personal style have been correctly identified (that is, linked to specified co-ordinates of time and space) should strengthen our current formulation of the history of styles and also reinforce our knowledge of specific developments and major innovations by artistic giants thereafter. Morphology does not necessarily aid in determining the date of execution, however. As Fong has pointed out, unless corroborated by other criteria, a correct identification of period and personal style may still be insufficient evidence for the work's authenticity, in the full sense of the word (e.g., a modern line-for-line tracing copy may fulfill this criterion with ease). The value of this test lies in helping to establish a probable earliest date for the appearance of the morphological features themselves. The term "historical style" implies a recognition of the chronological stages at which period and personal features appeared. In calligraphy, for example, it would denote any of the various historically evolved script types such as *chuan, li, ts'ao, k'ai,* or *hsing,* and the "personal style," like those script types practiced by and associated with their leading exponents in history, e.g., Wang Hsi-chih for *hsing,* Yen Chen-ch'ing (709–785) for *k'ai,* and so forth. It is important to note that we are testing not only the individual work of painting or calligraphy under consideration but also the calligraphic style of any inscriptions or colophons written on the same paper or silk.

2. The *artistic quality* of the execution of a work's pictorial features, primarily the psychic vitality or energy levels of the brushwork, should be congruent with our evaluation of any other authentic work or works by the same hand and be compatible with traditional critical appraisal, if any, and modern assessment of the master's historical position as determined by archeological research.

This test keeps us vigilant for possible discrepancies among individual hands in a close copy of an original or historically correct design and tends to function on the third level of stylistic definition, i.e., "expression." While the morphological features or historical style may offer a more or less accurate reflection of a master's period and personal image, the total expression and artistic quality evinced by the level of execution may be incommensurate with our estimate of him. In such a case, were the work found to be genuine, this estimate would have to be reappraised. In stressing actual execution, this criterion also aids in establishing the latest possible date for the painting itself.

3. *Basic physical properties* (paper, silk, ink, colors, and seal paste used by the artist) should not postdate the determined period of execution, and evidence such as seals, content of inscriptions, colophons, catalogue records, and biographical data should be carefully examined to detect contradictions.

Accurate scientific tests on the physical properties of works of art have yet to be devised, and opinions on these matters can only be considered as provisional. Such judgments gain in relevance, however, as they are founded on a broad range of paintings known to be genuine and when these properties are considered in the light of the work's other features.[55] Again we are faced with a tautological method: a so-called paper specialist's opinion would be valid only if he based his knowledge on authenticated paintings whose dates were verifiable by other means as well. One might also point out that inscriptions and colophons, even when found on genuine paintings, may still contain errors. Both style and content of the inscription must be authenticated and counter-checked for the light they shed on the painting and for the evidence they bring to the theoretical framework. When genuine, collectors' seals are also an invaluable aid in determining a rough date of execution for any work, or at least in setting up its terminal boundaries. Like calligraphy, the study of seals has thus far been neglected in art-historical training. The correct reading, recognition, and authentication of seals should not be considered specialists' work but a basic and indispensable tool of the connoisseur-art historian. Like learning a new language, such work requires intensive training and investigation of a wide range of paintings bearing both early and late seal impressions.[56] Each set of criteria is thus thought of as a flexible system of checks and counter-checks by which to measure and correct our visual analysis of style, whether on the level of period or of personal or individual hand. A decision of authenticity on any one level depends on our knowledge of the whole context.

When we move from the single work to a group attributed to a single master, we would divide them into representative categories. These function as a working aid in defining the master's range; they take into consideration his individual development, as well as his relationship with his period and his impact on later painters:

1. genuine works of quality from the period of attribution with "typical" or "mature" characteristics of the master;

2. genuine works of the period (which may be of varying quality) with characteristics associated with "early" and "late" styles of the master;

3. genuine works of the period of mediocre and poor quality and works with characteristics "untypical" of the master;

4. imitations, copies, and forgeries of the attributed master, which may be contemporary with, close in time to, or somewhat later than his period of activity (in archeological research these may be linked more easily with contemporary historical or critical records than the next group);

5. imitations, copies, and forgeries, etc., of relatively modern or of recent origin.

This preliminary grouping is, of course, a fluid one; its function is to construct a horizontal and vertical framework for our inquiry and to highlight related styles and clusters of formal relations on a contemporary and historical scale. The representation or sequences within any category will, of course, vary according to the extant attributed material of any given master. Group (1) forms the "core," the prime works on which we formulate our criteria of judgment of the remaining sequences. As we desire to reconstruct as full a biography as possible from the extant works, we proceed from the "mature" and "perfect" works to a consideration of groups (2) and (3), and thereby gradually expand the master's corpus.

Although it may not seem apparent at first, group (4) plays an important part in reconstructing and determining the degree of authenticity in the first three groups. The incompatibility of the structural features found here with our general concept of style is often a deciding factor. This group tends to be least homogeneous, and may often display common motifs and compositional similarities with group (1). Authentication of these works is often the most challenging of all. They are distinct from the semi-historical interpretations by known masters "in the style of" or "imitations after," and their importance lies in showing how close contemporaries interpreted the master's style in strict terms. Once these early forgeries are detected and dated by rough period or hand, they may further aid us in dating to a more precise degree other contemporary imitations attributed to other masters. Thus our notion of what is and what is not close to the period style of the given master aids us in determining, by contrast and regrouping, what we may initially consider the more peripheral images of a master's style, i.e., those in groups (2) and (3).

Ideally, the reconstruction of the artistic personality should take place in as many dimensions of artistic production as possible. Among the extant works, genuine and spurious, the mature, youthful, and aged images should appear, as well as those faces adopted and adapted for imtation during the artist's lifetime and thereafter. The "proof" of authenticity, then, emerges from the most rigorous visual biography of this master that we can assemble.

NOTES

1. "The Rudiments of Connoisseurship," in *The Study and Criticism of Italian Art*, pp. 122–24. On the psychoanalytic validity of these levels of "identification," see the interpretation by Ernst Kris in *Psychoanalytic Explorations in Art* (New York, 1952), esp. pp. 54–63.

2. Erwin Panofsky, "The History of Art as a Humanist Discipline," in *Meaning in the Visual Arts*, pp. 18–19.

3. Cf. *ibid.*, pp. 16–17.

4. We are indebted to James Lo, Princeton University, for this anecdote.

5. For the original text see Yang Po-chün, ed., *Lieh-tzu chi-shih* (*Collected Commentaries on the* Lieh-tzu [450–375 B.C.]) (Taipei, 1970), chap. 5, p. 111 (*T'ang-wen-p'ien*); for the full meaning of the phrase, see Tetsuji Morohashi, ed., *Dai Kanwa jiten*, vol. 8, no. 23935.8. See also A. C. Graham, trans., *The Book of Lieh-tzu* (London, 1960), pp. 109–10.

6. Chang Heng (*tzu* Ts'ung-yü, 1915–1963), one of the last of the great Chinese connoisseur-collectors, gives a detailed and systematic account of the requirements for the would-be connoisseur of Chinese painting and calligraphy in "Tsen-yang chien-ting shu-hua" ("The Authentication and Identification of Ancient Paintings and Calligraphy"), pp. 3–23; for Chang's biography, see *ibid.*, vol. 9 (1963), p. 32.

7. In this regard, R. H. van Gulik's *Chinese Pictorial Art as Viewed by the Connoisseur* is most helpful in presenting the history, terminology, and physical aspects of scrolls and their mountings. See also the review of his book by James Cahill in *Journal of the American Oriental Society*, vol. 81, no. 4 (1961), pp. 448–51; and Laurence Sickman's fine introduction to *Chinese Calligraphy and Painting in the Collection of John M. Crawford, Jr.*, pp. 17–28.

8. *Meaning in the Visual Arts*, p. 19.

9. Further clarifying the historian's role, Panofsky says: "Not only will he collect and verify all the available factual information as to medium, condition, age, authorship, destination, etc., but he will also compare the work with others of its class, and will examine such writings as reflect the aesthetic standards of its country and age, in order to achieve a more objective appraisal of its quality. He will read old books on theology or mythology in order to identify its subject matter, and he will further try to determine its historical locus, and to

separate the individual contribution of its maker from that of forerunners and contemporaries. He will study the formal principles which control the rendering of the visible world . . . and thus build up a history of 'motifs.' He will observe the interplay between the influences of literary sources and the effect of self-dependent representational traditions, in order to establish a history of iconographic formulae or 'types.' And he will do his best to familiarize himself with the social, religious and philosophical attitudes of other periods and countries, in order to correct his own subjective feeling for content" (*ibid.*, p. 17).

10. "The Problem of Ch'ien Hsüan," p. 189.

11. *Ibid.*

12. In Western art, according to Panofsky, Richard Offner, in his *A Critical and Historical Corpus of Florentine Painting, 1933–1947*, "developed connoisseurship in the field of Italian Primitives into the closest approximation to an exact science" (*Meaning in the Visual Arts*, p. 326).

13. *The Idea of History*, pp. 7–9, 282ff. Cf. also J. Huizinga, "A Definition of the Concept of History," in Raymond Klibansky and H. J. Paton, eds., *Philosophy and History: Essays Presented to Ernst Cassirer*, where this succinct definition is given: "History is the intellectual form in which a civilization renders account to itself of its past" (p. 9). For the key role played by the investigator as a participant, see note 26 below.

14. Sickman, ed., *Chinese Calligraphy and Painting in the Collection of John M. Crawford, Jr.*, p. 29.

15. Cf. Offner's brief but illuminating observations in *A Critical and Historical Corpus of Florentine Painting*, (sec. 3, vol. 5, pp. 1–4).

16. *Meaning in the Visual Arts*, p. 14.

17. Collingwood, *The Idea of History*, p. 199, referring to Croce's concept of history as the dual apprehension of individual and universal reality.

18. *Meaning in the Visual Arts*, p. 14.

19. *Ibid.*, pp. 19–20.

20. E. H. Gombrich and O. Kurz, in the former's "A Plea for Pluralism," p. 84, have cited the possibility of a test, yet the precise implementation of such an examination does pose difficulties: what are the "independent grounds" by which the answers can be known?

21. "Some Fundamental Issues in the History of Chinese Painting," p. 188.

22. *Ibid.*, pp. 187–88 passim.

23. *Ibid.*, p. 185.

24. Panofsky's usage, after T. M. Greene (*Meaning in the Visual Arts*, p. 9).

25. *Ibid.*, p. 25.

26. Edgar Wind, "Some Points of Contact between History and Natural Science," in *Philosophy and History*, p. 257. He says by way of introduction that "in defiance of the rules of traditional logic, circular arguments are the normal method of producing documentary evidence" (p. 256). Wind states also that participation is very much part of the historian's role, for "the investigator intrudes into the process that he is investigating. This is what the supreme rule of methodology demands. . . . otherwise, there would be no contact with the surrounding world that is to be investigated" (p. 258).

27. See Panofsky, *Meaning in the Visual Arts*, p. 19, where he quotes Leonardo da Vinci and the original Italian source.

28. Berenson, *Italian Art*, pp. 147–48. More recently, Jakob Rosenberg's *On Quality in Art: Criteria of Excellence, Past and Present* has tackled the problem from the more specific (and now standard) point of view of terminology and description, isolating relative characteristics of excellence as discernible in pairs of similar works. His lecture has stimulated two fruitful reviews relevant to Chinese art, one by E. H. Gombrich ("How Do You Know It's Any Good?" *New York Review of Books*, February 1, 1968, pp. 5–7), and one by Wen C. Fong ("A Chinese Album and Its Copy," pp. 74–78).

29. Cf. Ts'ao P'i (reigned 220–226), "Tien-lun Lun-wen": "A man's *ch'i* is the basis of literature [*wen*]. His literary style [*t'i*] depends on whether his *ch'i* is pure or turbid [*ch'ing chuo*]. It is not a quality which can be achieved by force or effort" (given in Hsiao T'ung [501–531], comp., *Wen-hsüan* [Taipei, 1950] [Ch'i-ming shu-chü ed.], 52/719–20). For Han literature see Liu Shao (ca. 196–220), *Jen-wu-chih* (Taipei, 1965) (*SPTK* ed., vol. 97); and John K. Shryock, trans., *The Study of Human Abilities* (New York, 1937). For the Six Dynasties, see Liu Hsieh (465–522), *Wen-hsin tiao-lung*, ed. Fan Wen-lan (Hong Kong, 1960), esp. chaps. "Shen-ssu," "T'i-hsing," and "Feng-ku"; and Vincent Shih, trans., *The Literary Mind and the Carving of Dragons* (New York, 1959).

30. In *T'u-hua chien-wen-chih* (preface dated 1074, *ISTP* ed., vol. 10), 1/28, "Lun ch'i-yün fei-shih." Cf. Alexander C. Soper, trans., *Kuo Jo-hsü's "Experiences in Painting"* (Washington, D.C., 1951), p. 15. The reader should not be misled by the simplicity of the foregoing account. The ancient and modern literature on this fascinating subject is vast, and its philological and aesthetic aspects constitute a separate study, the depth of which can only be suggested here. We are indebted to Professor Shūjirō Shimada for his guidance on this topic.

31. Verbal communication to the authors, Princeton, 1970.

32. *On Art and Connoisseurship*, pp. 234–36. Friedländer's discussion reflects a lifetime of experience as both art historian and connoisseur.

33. *Corpus*, vol. 5, pp. 1–2.

34. See Wölfflin's "law" in *Principles of Art History*, p. 11; Kubler's statement in *The Shape of Time*, p. 65; and Loehr's discussion, "Fundamental Issues," p. 189.

35. *On Art and Connoisseurship*, p. 217. See also James S. Ackerman and Rhys Carpenter, "Style," esp. pp. 181–86.

36. To put it another way: "However we may look at it, the beginning of our investigation always seems to presuppose the end, and the documents which should explain the monuments are just as enigmatic as the monuments themselves" (Panofsky, *Meaning in the Visual Arts*, p. 9).

37. "Towards a Structural Analysis of Chinese Landscape Painting."

38. Actually, "archeological" materials which date from the late thirteenth to the twentieth century do exist (e.g., Yung-lo-kung, Fa-hai-ssu, and other murals dated in the early twentieth century have been published in mainland Chinese periodicals). But then the methodological difficulty is reversed. Many of these examples represent distinct continuous traditions by folk artists or craftsmen who perpetuate the mode of their predecessors by employing relatively fixed schemata and patterns. This method tends to suppress individual stylistic innovations. Here the increments of change would be perceptibly small in comparison with the work of the more independent scholar-painters who would be stressing expressiveness on a more individually creative level and who would also be more closely in touch with the frontiers of stylistic innovation in the metropolitan centers. While it is theoretically possible to date an "unknown" work of later date by means of this kind of archeological evidence, the stylistic divergence in the two traditions would leave too large a discrepancy for such a method to aid us visually. It would be more of an academic exercise to use a Ming-dated mural by an anonymous craftsman to "prove" the structural validity of an attributed painting which clearly manifests the distinct personal traits of an historically well-documented scholar-painter. If a large number of excellent paintings by such a master and other contemporary painters of the same tradition are available, they should be used as evidence. The question in these later works is not so much one of period style, then, but of authorship, as indicated by formal and expressive differences on a personal level, and differences between "hands."

39. "Structural Analysis," pp. 7–9; italics added.

40. *Ibid.*, p. 12, n. 23.

41. See Fong's own study toward this goal, "The Problem of Forgeries in Chinese Painting"; Shen Fu, "Notes on Chiang Shen," "A Preliminary Study to the Extant Works of Chü-jan," and "Two Anonymous Sung Dynasty Paintings and the Lu-shan Landscape: The Problem of Their Stylistic Origins."

42. Illustrated in National Palace Museum, Taipei, *Three Hundred Masterpieces of Chinese Painting*, vol. 2, pl. 64.

43. *Ku-kung shu-hua-lu*, vol. 4, 6/71 (where it is attributed to Tung Ch'i-ch'ang under the title "Inscriptions to Reduced Versions of Paintings Imitating Sung and Yüan Masters"), reproduced in the National Palace Museum archive, no. 1605-32, published by the University of Michigan.

44. *Three Hundred Masterpieces*, vol. 2, pl. 65 (where it is attributed to Fan K'uan).

45. See Ackerman and Carpenter, *Art and Archaeology*, pp. 173–74. "While the ability of a particular work of art to compel a following is not necessarily a sign of its greatness, it can be. Thus historians and critics are justified in pointing to the impact of masterpieces on future generations as material evidence of their stature." Cf. also Professor L. S. Yang's "games theory," in which the stature of a mind can to a certain degree be measured by the extent to which the best possibilities of the "rules" of his invented "game" are not quickly exhausted by subsequent followers.
On norms as limitation, Gombrich says: "one approach to the problem of style is to observe the limitations within which the artist or craftsman works. The style forbids certain moves and recommends others as effective, but the degree of latitude left to the individual within this system varies at least as much as it does in games" ("Style").

46. For a standard definition and illuminating discussion relevant to both Eastern and Western art, see Han Tietze, *Genuine and False: Copies, Imitations, Forgeries*: "What is an art forgery? A painting, sculpture, or any product of artistic character may be called a forgery if it has been made with the intention of passing it off as the work of a different hand or of a different period" (pp. 9ff.).

47. On this same point but from a slightly different angle Gombrich observes: "It is true that this achievement of the successful forger also suggests that the understanding of style is not beyond the reach of the intuitively minded and that the great connoisseur who is pitted against the forger has at least as much chance as has his opponent" ("Style").

48. This anecdote is related in various sources, the most lively being Sun Kuo-t'ing (649–688) in his *Shu-p'u* (dated 687), the original manuscript of which is still extant. See *Ku-kung fa-shu* (Taipei, 1961), vol. 2, p. 5, for the text; also *Shoseki meihin sōkan*, vol. 25; Chu Chien-hsin, *Sun Kuo-t'ing Shu-p'u tsuan-cheng* (Shanghai, 1963), pp. 13–14.

49. Shen Chou's colophon (dated 1506) appears at the end of one of Mi Fu's finest extant works, *Calligraphy on Szechuan Silk* (dated 1088), *Ku-kung shu-hua-lu*, vol. 1, 1/58–59; this scroll is reproduced in *Chinese Art Treasures*, no. 117.

50. Part of Chang Ta-ch'ien's collection is recorded in *Ta-feng-t'ang shu-hua-lu* and is illustrated in *Ta-feng-t'ang ming-chi*.

51. Cf. Van Gulik, *Pictorial Art*, especially pp. 396–99; Fong, "Forgeries" and the bibliography cited there on p. 95, n. 4.

52. Berenson, *Italian Art*, p. 122.

53. Offner, *Corpus*, vol. 5, p. 2: "the various factors that constitute a work of art occur in such number and complexity that their order will not be met with in any other master.... This means simply that from the time a painter creates out of an organic and purposeful impulse, the terms by which he expresses himself will always agree."

54. "Style," in *Anthropology Today*, pp. 287–312.

55. On this last criterion of basic physical properties, inscriptions, colophons, catalogue records, and so forth, see also the more detailed discussion in Chang Heng, "Tsen-yang chien-ting shu-hua," esp. pp. 6–11.

56. As an extension of our research on Sung and Yüan calligraphy, we are undertaking a study of early seals which should augment the work done by Contag and Wang.

III. Case Studies in Connoisseurship

Fourteen studies of paintings found in this catalogue are summarized here. They are meant to illustrate some of the possible situations which may confront the connoisseur and to illustrate the methods employed in the analysis described in the individual entries. We hope that they may, like cases in judicial literature, provide the student and connoisseur with some precedents to guide him in the future. The studies include genuine works of which a single version is extant and works for which a second and even a third version are known. When there are two or three extant versions, it is possible that one (or even two) of them may be genuine, but it is equally possible that all three may be replicas—that the original is no longer extant (or is unpublished) and is unknown to the investigator. One cannot be sure that the "best one" among such a group is the genuine one: quality is foremost, but it alone is an inadequate measure. In principle, each version should undergo the same scrutiny in terms of period, school, personal style, and possible hand of the attributed master. The "best" of the extant versions, while meeting all of these criteria, may still not be "authentic"—it may lack that vital energizing spark which marks an original composition.

There is also the possibility that two versions of a given painting may be genuine. A master may have been particularly pleased with a certain work, decided to keep it for himself, and then executed another, or one very similar to the first, for his client. The second version is seldom an exact duplicate, but many elements may be close enough to the first to arouse our suspicions.

With only one extant version, the process of stylistic comparison still remains the same. If its style can be related to at least one other firm monument of the period and fits our notion of the master's personal style, direct comparison with the accepted body of his works can follow. The advantage of having replicas of a single composition is that they affirm one's memory or visual stock for the range of quality. However good one's memory may be, nothing substitutes for the work's being at hand. Moreover, another inferior or more superior version may sharpen our insight by virtue of contrast.

In terms of personal style, paintings which are most difficult to assess are those which extend beyond the established "common image." Works of a master's best-known style are frequently products of his maturity, while those produced in his youth or old age often offer an unfamiliar image. In the latter cases the homogeneous visualization to which we may be accustomed in his mature works may be disrupted by embryonic, bizarre, or experimental aspects of form. These may signal artistic youthfulness; or a certain redundancy of form bordering on self-imitation may indicate approaching old age or a weakening of physical vitality. We must learn to differentiate lapses of vigor reflecting stages of growth well within the artist's structural and qualitative repertoire from thoroughly counterfeit visualizations. The extremes of a master's style frequently pose great difficulties of authentication and dating, and may occasionally become the target for the forger's brush.[1]

Thus, here as elsewhere, the connoisseur must outwit the forger in his understanding of an individual painter's range and the limitations and possibilities of his period. As art historians it is primarily on the basis of these peripheral and most difficult works that we extend our knowledge of the creative potential inherent in personal and period styles. Acceptance of renegade works into the corpus of an artist, when supported by archeological research, takes not only rare acumen but also courage on the part of the connoisseur, for

many factors other than art-historical and artistic ones may weigh against such a decision.

There is also the problem of the *ku-pen, unica*, or "only extant work" (known at the time) attributed to a particular master.[2] Works of calligraphy or painting of this kind are usually connected with relatively obscure names in art history. In terms of method, one should approach a *ku-pen* as if it were a forgery. Psychologically, an interesting game is often played here. As a rule, forgeries of obscure artists are infrequent because there is little market (with the exception of the rare knowledgeable buyer) on which to draw. Collectors may therefore strive to acquire a so-called *ku-pen*, on the assumption that it is most certainly genuine. But the astute forger, always one step ahead of the innocent collector, may turn this situation to his own account: he will daringly fabricate a complete artistic personality—with attendant inscriptions, colophons and seals, etc.—fulfilling perfectly the *ku-pen* criteria. In these instances one cannot draw on one's knowledge of personal style but must rely on firm notions of successive period styles, on the internal consistency of the work (such as signature, content of inscriptions, dates, seals, etc.), and, often more important, on its stylistic relationship with known contemporaries, forerunners and followers, and plausible teachers and models, along with geographical factors—one's knowledge of the centers of activity and influence, region or city, in which this unknown master has been placed.

The fourteen examples which follow suggest various kinds of problems in authenticity. Specific solutions to problems of dating, more detailed explanations of the logical steps taken, and illustrations of related works will be found within the individual catalogue entries.

1. THREE VERSIONS OF THE SAME COMPOSITION, TWO FORGED, ONE GENUINE

Tao-chi, *Searching for Plum Blossoms: Poems and Painting*

Prior to acquisition by Dr. Sackler, two versions of this subject were known, the one considered for purchase (see *XVIII*) and a second version (see *XIX*, fig. 1) published in *Sekitō* in 1926. Upon comparison of the two it was clear that the one available for purchase was far superior to the other in quality and that it could confidently be considered a genuine work, fitting well into our knowledge of Tao-chi's style. The calligraphic and pictorial style, place of execution, and literary content were all consistent with the 1685 date and reinforce all we know about Tao-chi.

After the painting was acquired for the collection, it was learned that yet another version of the same composition was in a Taipei collection (see *XIX*). If we had not been confident of the authenticity of the Sackler painting, the appearance of a third version could have been disturbing, but as its authenticity and stylistic significance had been thoroughly studied, its genuineness could not be loosely challenged no matter how many other replicas appeared. Unless we discovered, by the same method of inquiry, that Tao-chi could have painted a second version of the work (unlikely because of its length and style), we could be certain that all other versions were also copies after the original (or after other close copies of the original unknown to us).

In the case of the second and third versions, blatant errors in the transcription of the poems do in fact provide objective evidence of their secondary nature. Since the third version was available for purchase, it was acquired for the collection to enrich study of the original. The two copies are widely spaced in time, the second probably executed in the late nineteenth century, while the third may have been done quite recently as an exercise by a beginner. We are reserving our opinion on the modern copyist's hand and only identify regional characteristics in the hand of the earlier one.

Tao-chi, *The Lo-Fu Mountains: Calligraphy and Painting*

The problems raised by this album are more complicated than those presented by the composition described above. The Sackler collection has only four leaves of the original twelve (*XXX*); neither these leaves nor the rest of the album had been published prior to acquisition. The other two extant versions known to us were published in 1953 and 1955, respectively, and are complete in twelve leaves *XXX*, figs. 1–3, 5–12). They are in collections in Hakone, Japan, and Cologne, Germany. The paper used in the four Sackler painting leaves is of an unsized, highly absorbent texture which on initial viewing creates superficially different effects of line and wash from the genuine works thus far encountered. After extensive comparison of the images and calligraphy with those of other Tao-chi originals, however, we became convinced of their prime quality. This decision was much influenced by the integrity and close correlation of the images with the content of the narrative.

The paintings of the Hakone and Cologne versions are free renderings, but they give themselves away by great lapses of fidelity in the pictorial detail illustrating the text. The problem of distinguishing the quality of the calligraphy leaves was more subtle, and challenged our methods of description. The copyist of the painting leaves, who can be identified and at one time had the Sackler leaves in his possession, could have further complicated the matter by exchanging the genuine leaves of painting and calligraphy for the spurious creating a true mixture of "pearls and fisheyes," but both the calligraphy and the paintings are untampered with in the Sackler version.

2. TWO VERSIONS OF THE SAME COMPOSITION, ONE GENUINE, ONE FORGED

Tao-chi, *Flowers and Figures*

The version of this album illustrated in the catalogue (*XXI*) is an exact copy of the Tao-chi original (*XX*). The copyist has been identified by Chang Ta-chien as the younger brother of his teacher. An identification of this nature by one of the leading Tao-chi specialists extends our knowledge of one more of the members of Tao-chi's imitative audience.

In a line-for-line copy of this kind, we must focus on a limited range of the pictorial vocabulary, the brushwork alone—ink lines, washes, and their interaction—because the composition is identical with the original. Indeed, the limited number of compositional elements in this particular album reduces the usefulness of period style, school influences, etc., which occasionally may aid in revealing the approximate date of execution. If, for example, the original did not exist, we could take the spatial inventions, subject matter, and content of the poetry as quite accurate reflections of the original, as they corroborate our previous knowledge of this aspect of Tao-chi's activity. But our previous study of his methods should have warned us of the expressive differences in vitality, modulation, richness, and spontaneity of brushwork, control and blending of ink and washes, and so on. In this case, the adjudged discrepancies of purely pictorial qualities constitute the telling difference.

Chang Ta-Ch'ien's eyewitness testimony (which is recorded on the label of the outer folio of the copy [*XXI*, fig. 1]) causes us to reflect on his role as a connoisseur as well as his abilities as a forger. Although amusements such as his still remain one of the stumbling blocks to Tao-chi connoisseurship, Chang's certification of this work allows us to clear one stone from the pathway.

Tao-chi, *Letter to Pa-ta shan-jen*

Here the copy after Tao-chi (*XXIII*, fig. 8) is a free "interpretive" variation introducing differences of content and form. The validity of one work could not be accepted without discrediting the other. Wen Fong has offered detailed arguments in support of the authenticity of the Chang-Sackler *Letter to Pa-ta* against a version in a Japanese collection. Although related articles by A. Soper, H. Kohara, and Hsü Fu-kuan have clarified some points, in other areas they have only confused the issue. Therefore it was still necessary to present further evidence for the authenticity of the Sackler letter and the spuriousness of the Japanese version.

While content (and, to a lesser extent, style) was the important criterion in Fong's defense of the letter, we have focused mainly on calligraphic style and habits of letter-writing format. As it happens, the forger in question overlooked an important custom found in all of Tao-chi's genuine letters.[3] In our discussion, certain morphological features of brushwork found in examples of Tao-chi's genuine works were isolated as they appear in the Sackler work, but not in the Japanese copy. Furthermore, aspects of the forger's personal writing style are shown to be present in the copy, but not in the original letter. In the course of our inquiry, a separate comparative study of Tao-chi's several calligraphic styles, as well as those of the copyist, was made. A condensed version may be found in *XXIII*.

Hung-jen, *Feng River Landscapes*

In this case the second version of Hung-jen's album (*XII*, pp. 150–51, n. 26) appears as a record in a catalogue. The colophon on the last leaf and the description of each of the separate leaves appear to be similar, but the second version bears different collectors' seals and is rendered in ink and color. We have not seen this second version and do not know whether it is still extant. We believe the Sackler version to be genuine from comparison of calligraphy, painting, and seals with other accepted works of Hung-jen. As to the question of whether Hung-jen could have executed two albums—one with color and one without—of the same subjects and with the same inscription, it is improbable because of the range, variety, and number of leaves. Thus, given the authenticity of this album, the version recorded in the catalogue is suspect.

3. TWO VERSIONS OF A SIMILAR SUBJECT, BOTH GENUINE

Tao-chi, *Bamboo, Vegetables, and Fruit*

The subject matter and poetic inscription of *Bamboo, Vegetables, and Fruit* (*XXXI*) are similar, although not identical, to another work ascribed to Tao-chi in a New York collection. There are three possibilities: one is genuine and the other a copy, both are copies, or both are genuine. The fact that both works are similar but not identical in image, dedication, and format and that seals, signature, and painting quality are comparable (though still differing in tone and relative success) made a decision extremely difficult.

After comparison of calligraphy and painting with other genuine Tao-chi works of similar subject matter and after much weighing of the hypothetical possibilities and circumstances which may have faced the artist in the process, we came to the decision that both works are genuine. The relative simplicity of the subject matter supports the likelihood that the artist repeated the same subject, theme, and even poetic inspiration, and it also allows the conjecture that they could have been finished on the same day. Conversely, two large landscapes, or albums of landscapes, for example, which bear the same date, inscription, and composition would hardly suggest this conclusion, as their complexity would tend to preclude duplication within such a short time span.

4. A CASE OF MISTAKEN AUTHORSHIP

Chang Chi-su, *Snow-Capped Peaks*

This large snow scene (*XI*) bears no signature and only one barely legible seal. The painting underwent a series of tentative attributions ranging from "anonymous" to Tai Chin (1388–1462) (which attribution appears on a superscription above the painting), to Wu Pin (fl. ca. 1568–1621), which was the attribution given when it was selected for this catalogue. Although the work does reflect some of the exaggerated features of the late Ming artist Wu Pin, more intensive study of period features and specific influences suggested that its style was post-Lan Ying (1585–1664-), with some early Ch'ing features. Research into the archeological aspect of the painting led to an identification of the seal, then of the painter's name and his brief biography. Thus Chang Chi-su's name was brought to light. His period of activity coincides happily with our estimation of his style. In this case literary biography and stylistic analysis helped place this painting in a more accurate historical position.

5. IDENTIFICATION THROUGH A CORRECTLY DECIPHERED SEAL

Chang Chi-su, *Snow-Capped Peaks*

The stylistic and historical analysis of this painting, it should be noted, did not lead us to the painter's name. Only the correct reading of the seal and recognition that it was a painter's and not a collector's or appreciator's seal led to the linking of Chang's name with it.

6. THE *KU-PEN*, OR "ONLY EXTANT WORK"

The problem of the *ku-pen* and its detection was discussed in the introduction to these case studies. A judgment of such a work is inevitably provisional, as it awaits further research and the possible discovery of other works bearing the same author's genuine signature and seal or, given an "anonymous" *ku-pen*, a second work stylistically consistent with the first. (Of course, a second work with

the same attribution which is stylistically incompatible with the first will require additional study.) We have here two examples of how the problem can be approached.

Chang Chi-su, *Snow-Capped Peaks*

Apart from the problems of attribution mentioned above, the Chang Chi-su snow scene is also an example of a *ku-pen*. Our analysis of style agreed with what little is known of Chang's biography and region of activity. In addition, the general history of the work appears completely honest; for example, the earliest attribution (preserved on the superscription) links it with the Ming painter Tai Chin and further mentions that it "captured the spirit of Sung masters," but no attempt was made to add a false signature or seal of a Sung or better-known later master, or a series of spurious seals of well-known collectors.

Ch'en Chao, *Landscape*

According to available records, Ch'en Chao gained local fame in Yang-chou, but no paintings by or attributed to him, other than this Sackler fan, are known to us. In this respect, this landscape (*XL*) remains a *ku-pen* until other works of Ch'en are discovered. The criteria for authenticity here again lie in its corroboration of what is known of his biography and painting activities, combined with a general appraisal of its painting and calligraphic style.

The landscape style of this fan is strongly derivative of the Four Wangs and their tradition but is generally looser and less monumental in conception. The personal element of the painter is almost completely submerged, and someone who overlooks the modest inscription and signature could almost mistake it for a work of the major orthodox Ch'ing masters or their better-known followers. Nevertheless, as with Chang's snow scene, no attempt was made by a subsequent dealer or collector to deface the relatively little-known signature of Ch'en Chao or replace it with a more fetching name.

All in all, the style of the calligraphy and the signature and content of the inscription are straightforward and of a quality which accords with what is known of Ch'en's artistic circumstances, period, and region.

7. IDENTIFICATION THROUGH CALLIGRAPHY

The presence of calligraphy in the form of a signature, inscription, or colophon on the same silk or paper as the painting itself can often provide crucial evidence. It may also establish a terminal date of execution. In many instances, a positive judgment on the content and authorship of the calligraphy may decide the case in favor of the authenticity of a work which has been damaged or retouched, which is unusual in style for its attribution, or which is a *ku-pen*.

The use of calligraphy which is physically joined to a painting to aid in its authentication is common in the study of Eastern painting, but highly unusual in that of the West. The writing which occasionally appears on Western drawings is often too brief to allow the kind of positive and extensive comparison of "graphological features" permissible in Eastern—Chinese, Japanese, and Korean—art. The importance and reliability of positive identification of a hand in calligraphy are stressed here because of relative neglect on the part of art historians in recent years. Two items in the Sackler catalogue will demonstrate this point.

Inscriptions on Ma Wan's *Spring Landscape*

Two inscriptions appear on this landscape (*I*) of the late Yüan master Ma Wan (ca. 1310–1378), dated 1343, one by a certain Kung Chin (fl. ca. 1340–1370?), another by the well-known scholar, calligrapher, and poet Yang Wei-chen (1296–1370). While no other specimen of Kung Chin's calligraphy was available, his late Yüan style could be verified by comparisons with the works of contemporaries. Positive identification of Yang's inscription as representing his early style could be made from the abundant examples of his distinctive hand. Moreover, Yang's role as Ma Wan's teacher of classics gave the work an additional significance.

The presence of the fine calligraphy enabled verification of the fourteenth-century date on two levels: the calligraphic and the pictorial. The style and format of the painting can be shown to be a typical product of Yüan scholar painting in the Lake T'ai area. Moreover, Ma Wan's own signature and the execution of the landscape (despite some surface damage and subsequent retouching in the foreground mass) compare favorably with the other firm monuments of his limited œuvre. Our confidence in the accompanying calligraphy is such that, were no other Ma Wan works extant to provide a personal stylistic context, we could affirm the authenticity of the period and the execution on the basis of the inscriptions alone.

Colophon on Tao-chi's *Landscape and Portrait of Hung Cheng-chih*

A colophon by the early Ch'ing painter and calligrapher Chiang Shih-chieh (1647–1709) appears on this handscroll by Tao-chi (*XXXII*, detail). Tao-chi's own inscription at the beginning of the painting states that the work was completed in the winter of 1706; on the same sheet of paper as the painting three colophons follow, the last of which is Chiang Shih-chieh's. Although Chiang's colophon bears no date, it can be dated by the physical context of the preceding and following colophons to before 1709, that is, three years after the execution of the painting.

Chiang Shih-chieh was a slightly younger and lesser-known contemporary of Tao-chi. His own works are calligraphically and stylistically harmonious with this colophon and therefore constitute a homogeneous corpus which provides firm evidence for authenticity.[4] A fine landscape in the Freer (*XXXII*, fig. 3) bears a generous specimen of his calligraphy and allows positive identification of the colophon appearing on the Tao-chi work. In this instance, the calligraphy of a less well-known contemporary makes the likelihood of forgeries in his name remote, and its presence on the handscroll offers evidence of date and authorship which is difficult to refute.

THE FOLLOWING FOUR categories represent "identities" or stages of artistic growth which may confront one in assessing the body of works attributed to a single master, more or less distinct features whose recognition may help to chart the scope of an artist's development. Generally speaking, the largest number of extant works by a given master tend to date from his period of artistic maturity, his "middle years." Works which can be labeled as "typical" in style most frequently date from this period as well. Conversely, works from the early and late periods of artistic development may be fewer in number (for reasons given below). The periodization here does not necessarily refer to an artist's chronological age but to the span of his artistic activity. How it coincides with his chronological age would depend on the individual case.[5]

8. TYPICAL IDENTITY

"Typical" identity denotes a relative stylistic homogeneity abstracted from representative works known to the connoisseur and in the course of time accepted as a reliable yardstick. To a certain extent, it also implies works which are clearly genuine because they exemplify—at a high level of achievement—our image of a given master. Recognition that a work is genuine and of the master's typical style is thus built on a broad acquaintance with both extant works and literary records; it also necessitates experience in judging his qualitative range. Examples of such typical works in the Sackler catalogue are those by Ch'ien Ku (*IV*), Lan Ying (*VII–IX*), Ch'ien Tu (*XXXVIII*), Wang Hsüeh-hao (*XXXIX*), and Ku Yün (*XLI*).

It should be mentioned here that works of typical style are those most often imitated by the unscrupulous. The replicas most difficult to detect in this category are the close or exact copies of fine original works by expert forgers. These copies are often quite faithful, and thus the typical aspect they display in terms of period style, personal morphological characteristics, and so forth, may be devilishly accurate. Our sensitivity to brush vitality and the energy levels charging the forms is consequently of utmost importance.

A copy of typical identity in the Sackler collection is a modern but poor replica of the Ming master Shen Chou's *Bronze Peacock Inkslab* (*XXVIII*). Unfortunately, the original Shen Chou work has not been located, although other copies do exist. From literary records and the evidence of his own renditions of similar subjects, i.e., banana plants, seated figures in a garden setting, etc., we can recognize the underlying composition as a characteristic Shen Chou design. In the course of the copyist's execution, however, the master's idiomatic elements have been exaggerated to such a degree that the reference is too obvious. The hyperactive line and thinly distributed energy alert us to its being of typical style but not of typical quality, and definitely not by the master Shen Chou. On the other hand, Tao-chi's copy of the same composition (*XXVII*) so impresses us with its quality that his own interpretation challenges that of Shen Chou himself, and we are surprised and delighted to find Tao-chi's own "typical" signature admitting the fact.

9. UNUSUAL IDENTITY

The identification of a work of "unusual" style as genuine entails the recognition that it may represent an impulsive or experimental venture or that it may be a close copy of some other master of equally distinctive style. To be authentic, the work must be deemed within the range of possibility associated with the given master's brush style. Our first impression may be one of doubt. We may sense inconsistencies between structure, motif, figure types, or composition and their actual execution. The latter may exhibit features which are characteristic of later periods. Our initial tendency may be to dismiss it as a forgery or pastiche. Such a work actually necessitates prolonged consideration and examination not only of the master's whole range of accepted works and characteristic features, along with biographical details and literary accounts, but also of possible later hands to which the work might be attributed. If we can accept such a work as within the master's range, we may use it as our probe, and it may help to clarify hitherto unexplored aspects of his artistic activities.

A most rewarding example is offered by the Tao-chi replica of Shen Chou's *Bronze Peacock Inkslab* (*XXVII*) mentioned above. Like any copyist worthy of his craft, Tao-chi captures and intensifies the typically Shen Chou characteristics in his interpretive effort but cannot help reflect his own brush habits in the forms. Thus his own artistic taste and sense of moderation temper what in the other copies are gross exaggerations. Once we are aware of Tao-chi's own inscription and make the initial link with his personal style, more and more of his stylistic features become apparent. We can almost extract—like the various elements from a compound in quantitative chemical analysis—the features which were originally Shen Chou's and those which are Tao-chi's.

10. EARLY IDENTITY

To designate a work as "early" places it in the period of initial training and experimentation when the artist's formal vocabulary and expressive visualization are being formed. Authentic works from this stage may often differ radically in style and artistic quality from his mature works and reveal highly derivative characteristics. The connoisseur should also be aware that early works were often produced before the master gained recognition, so that their market value was usually low, and, as a result, they were often neglected, lost, or destroyed. Even after the artist had won some measure of fame—usually in the period of his artistic maturity—these early works may still have been slighted by collectors or even mistaken for forgeries.[6]

Recognition of a work as from an artist's early period therefore requires not only a feeling for quality but, ideally, a clear conception of "how an artist thinks artistically." We must be able to imagine how he would have visualized his subject before the refinements and relatively more fixed vocabulary of ideas and technique of his mature period took hold. During this period many artists may indulge a taste for the bizarre or the unusual, features which help intensify their attempt to develop a personal artistic identity. All the powers of connoisseurship and the fruits of art-historical research we can amass are required in such cases, for, like renegade works of unusual style, early works are often the most challenging and yet the most fascinating we may encounter.

An example of a work from this category is a leaf by Tao-chi, *The Echo* (now mounted as a hanging scroll), from an album of landscapes dated early in 1678 (*XVII*). *The Echo* is the earliest Tao-chi work in an American collection. When studied in the context of the rest of the album to which it belongs and in the light of the master's mature style, it presents an enticing glimpse of his more familiar images and of the work to come.

11. LATE IDENTITY

Depending on the master, an "old-age style" may offer a more engaging and artistically richer image of the master than his mature works. We may observe trends which, having come to fruition in his maturity, are now further intensified—a simplification or increasing complexity of composition, a coarsening or loosening of brushwork, and so forth. Often a particular physical defect may be used to great artistic advantage, or with painters of superior technical training, one may discover a tendency to self-imitation and a reliance on technical facility to compensate for a depletion of artistic ideas. The appearance of any of these tendencies in a master would reflect characteristics latent in the course of his development.

Thus recognition of works from a master's artistic old age necessitates an equally full knowledge of the formal and expressive traits encountered in his earlier works, with one important qualification: his physical health. Like his mental and spiritual well-being, his physical health during his active years influences the level of his artistic production and performance. Just as a strong or weak pulse may indicate one's basic constitution and the condition of one's heart, the energy level charging the forms functions as one of the important criteria by which one may assess quality and distinguish authorship. For example, a master such as Wen Cheng-ming enjoyed good health throughout his life and well up to his death at the age of ninety. We can therefore expect of him a more or less consistent standard despite the various changes in style which were still taking place late in his career. But judgment of the works of masters whom we know to have suffered illness or some malfunction in old age requires a certain degree of judiciousness, as it does for masters whose biographies are less well studied. In authentication, therefore, we should not be too eager to dismiss works which could conceivably have been painted in a master's advanced, or early, artistic years. However, excessive caution in this regard can make us the victim of the "advanced age" or "tender age" fallacy in reverse—i.e., the delusion that such works are categorically acceptable. It is preferable to keep an open mind about such cases until we have attained a more advanced stage of study.

An exemplary work of "late identity" is Tao-chi's 1707 *Reminiscences of Nanking* (*XXXIV*). The album contains the latest dated Tao-chi landscapes known to us. The different scenes are characterized by a simplification and a coarsening in the brushwork which are the culmination of gradual changes seen in his earlier works. More important, these characteristics function as vehicles to distill the expressive effects which he sought. The twelve leaves are striking testimonials that although his technical meticulousness wavered in his latest works, his imaginative power did not. On the contrary, this album, as well as the 1706 *Landscape and Portrait* (*XXXII*), shows an increased interest in the use of a single pictorial idea to integrate the scene. A heightened unity of artistic purpose permeates each leaf, and the saturated colors and monochromatic reduction further intensify this effect.

12. ALTERED IDENTITY

Included in this category are works in album, handscroll, or hanging scroll format which originally were part of a set and have been cropped or split apart (in the case of works executed on laminated paper of two layers). The cropping may have been an expedient because of physical damage to the edges of the work or for a less innocent reason: the splitting of a work, whether by layers or into sections, may have been done to gain several for the price of one.

An additional flourish in such operations may be the erasure or addition of signature and seals. The physical nature of albums makes them frequent prey to such practices. Moreover, the cost of remounting is not incurred, although the finer mountings of original works have been attached to copies.

Authentication of works which we suspect have been tampered with in this way is straightforward only in the case of an artist whose style, standards of performance, and range of patronage are relatively consistent. Works of a master whose range is broad and equivocal require greater perseverance. Often we can only abandon our research for the moment and hope that the other parts of the work may surface on the market or may be published, in which case we must recognize their identical origins.

Tao-chi is one of the most protean of artists. When viewing one or two of his album leaves apart from the whole, we may doubt their authenticity, although, if seen in context, they would be entirely acceptable. *The Echo (XVII)* falls into this category. When we first encountered the landscape, it was in its present format, mounted as a hanging scroll. Our preliminary judgment was that it was an early work, perhaps before the artist's Nanking period, and that it was originally an album leaf. We were impressed with the lyrical and imaginative quality of its vision and the dry, flowing brushwork. In the summer of 1970 we saw on display, at the fine exhibit of Ming and Ch'ing paintings held in the Hong Kong City Hall Museum, an album of nine leaves dated 1678. The quality of the execution, the somewhat tentative writing style, the seals, the paper and its dimensions, as well as the subject matter—illustrations to poems by Su Shih—all matched. *The Echo* settled very nicely into this group. Moreover, with one of the leaves dated 1678, our earlier conjectures could be made more explicit.

13. FORGED IDENTITY

Recognition of "forged identity" entails knowledge of the complete range of identities of the master in question, so that we may conclude with a reasonable degree of certainty that master so-and-so could not have painted in such a manner. At the same time, we must be able to sense the discrepancy in visualization and to postulate a rough period of execution, answering such questions as whether it is a contemporary copy, a copy of a century or so later, or modern. In any case, judgment is based not only on knowledge of quality and of period styles but on recognition of the individual features of great masters. These mark the stylistic peaks which leave an indelible influence on the works of lesser painters working in the same or nearby regions, and they constitute the data from which we derive a concept of "period" style. Thus if the hand is unknown, we may say "this must be post-Shen Chou" or "around the time of Wang Hui," and so forth. The real position and time of execution of the work may most likely correspond to the latest features present in its style.

Examples of works in this category which are blatant in their deception—highly unsuccessful forgeries—are *XIX* and *XXVIII*, which are by unknown authors of recent times, and *XXXV*, by a well-known author still living. Detection was facilitated by discovery in each case of the original from which the three copies departed in varying degrees. But quality, and the fact that none of these works were close copies of the original, gave us more clues to the possible date of execution.

With a line-for-line replica of an original, such as *XXI*, it is difficult to estimate more than a rough period of execution because the copyist has less freedom in which to assert his personal style. The more liberties a copyist takes with the original, the more he reveals his own artistic preferences and time of execution. In being less servile to his model, he allows his own visualization to take command, albeit surreptitiously. We must remember that, as Friedländer has pointed out, the copyist has before him not a mental vision bursting with living and unpredictable forces, which he must arrest and realize on paper, but a finished, static design which needs only calculation and concentrated effort for its completion. He can seldom avoid misinterpretations of form or line, for "the master who . . . realizes his own vision has taken in much more than he notes down— what he gives is an excerpt, a shorthand note, an abbreviation. . . . The copyist has before his eyes the result of a visual action in which he takes no part. A tiny projection or twist of the original line has a cause which the copyist does not know, a significance of which he is ignorant."[7]

In this catalogue, *XXXV*, a free variation by Chang Ta-ch'ien on works by Tao-chi, is of special interest to us because of the merging of personae which has taken place. Chang's own signed works are well documented and published. We can map a range from early to late and see the development of his own personal style. Such knowledge in this case aided recognition of his copies. Moreover, the two hundred years that have passed since the original master's lifetime have witnessed artistic movements of international consequence. Thus even Chang, a painter trained in traditional Chinese style, could not avoid absorbing these revolutionary trends, revealing, inadvertently, that he is very much a child of his time.

14. THREE COPIES OF THE SAME COMPOSITION, TWO *MALA FIDE*, ONE *BONA FIDE*

Catalogue entries *XXVII* and *XXVIII* are both copies after an original Shen Chou painting whose present whereabouts are unknown. A third version is now in a Hong Kong collection and is known to the authors only through reproduction. These three versions are all executed on paper. A fourth version, known only by a record in a nineteenth-century catalogue, is executed on silk. *XXVIII* is entirely spurious, a poor copy, probably of modern origin. We can say with a high degree of certainty that the Hong Kong version is of similar quality and possibly of similar origin. Both are signed "Shen Chou" and are *mala fide* copies.

Catalogue entry *XXVII* bears the same inscriptions and signature, but it is an earlier copy and of high quality. It contains an additional inscription by Tao-chi, which he signed "Tao-chi, inscribed again." The fine quality of both inscription and image testify that this is a *bona fide* copy. The number of copies of a given work, whether *bona fide* or *mala fide*, could be infinite. Each must be subjected to the same archeological study.

NOTES

1. See R. H. van Gulik, *Chinese Pictorial Arts as Viewed by the Connoisseur*, p. 31, where the reader is warned of the "old-age fallacy" in regard to inscriptions and colophons; the same warning may be extended to paintings.

2. Cf. *ibid.*, where the *unica* is mentioned in relation to rubbings of calligraphy.

3. The element of circularity implied in the method is nullified by our prior authentication of the letters to be used as evidence. These were scrutinized for authenticity of content and style and constitute a separate study too lengthy for inclusion in *XXIII*.

4. E.g., Freer Gallery of Art, acc. no. 58.9; *Shinchō shoga fu*, pl. 31; *Great Chinese Painters of the Ming and Ch'ing Dynasties*, nos. 72 and 73, in the collection of J. P. Dubosc.

5. E.g., T'ang Yin's (1470–1523) "early" period would be set in his twenties, as he died at fifty-four, while the "early period" of the recent painter, Wu Ch'ang-shih (1844–1927) would be after his fiftieth year, for he commenced painting late in his career.

6. An interesting case in calligraphy in which the artist himself has authenticated an example of his early work is related in an inscription by Chao Meng-fu (1254–1322), which he wrote on his transcription to Chiang K'uei's *Lan-t'ing-k'ao*. His comment, dated 1309, is recorded on the reverse side of the writing. Chao says that this transcription was executed twenty years ago (ca. 1289, at age thirty-five) at someone's request; it was made at a time when the weather was windy and dusty and not conducive to good writing. He continues, "Recently I feel I have made some progress. For that reason, those who see this [early transcription] all think it is a forgery. How could they ever understand that in that instance there was a discrepancy of age and that the difference between the favorable and unfavorable in circumstances was also great!" (*Ku-kung shu-hua-lu*, vol. 1, 1/82–85).

7. Max J. Friedländer, *On Art and Connoisseurship*, p. 240.

IV. Tao-chi

Tao-chi was born in 1641 in Kuei-lin, Kwangsi Province, quite far from the artistic centers of the "eye area" in which he eventually settled and became famous.[1] His original family name was Chu, and he counted himself as the eleventh descendant of one of the imperial Ming princes, Chu Shou-ch'ien, the grandnephew of the Ming founder and the first prince (posthumously) of Ching-chiang.[2] Chu Shou-ch'ien's son was Chu Tsan-i, "Tsan" being the first character in the pedigree which designated the names of the prince's descendants. Tao-chi's name was Jo-chi, the "Jo" being the tenth character in the pedigree, and, according to one of his own late seals, *Tsan-chih Shih-shih-sun, A-ch'ang*, he counted himself the tenth lineal descendant of Tsan-i.

"Ch'ing-hsiang" was used frequently in Tao-chi's signature and seals; the name refers to the Hsiang River, which had its source in Kwangsi and passed through Ch'üan-hsien near the place of his birth. In 1645 Tao-chi's father, Chu Heng-chia, was defeated in his *chien-kuo* claim to the throne. Nanking, the Ming capital, had already fallen to the rebels, and in an autobiographical manuscript written by one of Tao-chi's pupils (Yüan Tun; cf. *XXXII*), we learn that the child Tao-chi was entrusted to a family servant, with whom he escaped from Kuei-lin. Tao-chi probably lived in Ch'üan-chou for a while. There he soon entered the Buddhist faith for safety[3] and adopted the Buddhist names Tao-chi, Yüan-chi, and Ch'ao-chi. His *tzu* or style name was Shih-t'ao ("Stone Waves"), the name by which he is commonly known to the Chinese (in Japanese, Sekitō); some of his *hao* or sobriquets were K'u-kua ho-shang ("Friar Bitter Melon"), Ch'ing-hsiang lao-jen ("Old Man of Ch'ing-hsiang"), Hsia-tsun-che ("Blind Abbot"), and later Ta-ti-tzu ("Purified One"), Ch'ing-hsiang Ch'en-jen, and Hsiu-jen ("The Useless").

Tao-chi spent his early years in the charge of an older brother monk, Ho-t'ao,[4] with whom, in the next few decades, he wandered throughout the Chiang-nan area (the modern provinces of Anhwei, Kiangsu, and Chekiang, the latter two regions of which were most active Buddhist centers at the time). From the 1650's to the 1670's, the young monk traveled some of the most memorable artistic routes in China's natural landscape: the area of the Hsiao and Hsiang rivers and Lake Tung-t'ing, in Hunan, as well as Mt. Lu in Kiangsi and Mt. Huang in Anhwei.

Little is known about Tao-chi's religious life. In a self-inscription on one of his earliest dated works, the 1667 *Sixteen Lohans* handscroll (fig. 1), he refers to himself as the "grandson of Min" and the "son of Yüeh." Yüeh is the priest Lü-an Pen-yüeh, who was the disciple of Mu-ch'en Tao-min (1596–1674), a well-known Ch'an master of the Lin-ch'i sect. Tao-chi probably studied Ch'an with Lü-an in Sung-chiang when the latter returned from Peking in 1662.[5]

Hsüan-ch'eng, Anhwei: late 1660's to 1680

Sometime in the late 1660's Tao-chi is known to have settled at several monasteries located near Hsüan-ch'eng at Mt. Ching-t'ing, Anhwei,[6] where he remained for more than a decade. The Anhwei years include much travel in Hsüan-ch'eng and its environs, and they are some of the most important in terms of his artistic development. He made a second trip to Huang-shan (Mt. Huang) in 1668–1669,[7] which laid the groundwork for some of his greatest works.

In this period Tao-chi met Mei Ch'ing (1623–1697), the Hsüan-ch'eng poet-painter, and forged a close artistic and personal friend-

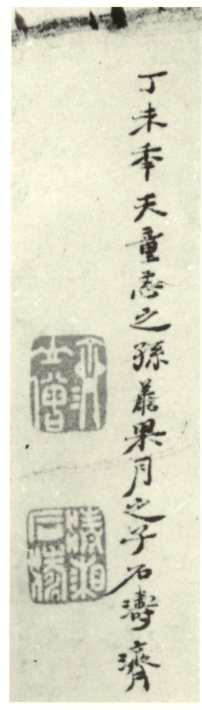

1. Tao-chi, *Sixteen Lohans*, dated 1667, detail of self-inscription. Handscroll. Ink on paper. Collection unknown.

ship with him. It was undoubtedly through Mei Ch'ing that he became acquainted with the works of the great Anhwei masters Hung-jen (1610–1663), Ch'eng Sui (1605–1691), Cha Shih-piao (1615–1698), Mei Keng (fl. 1681–1706), Ch'en Shu (fl. 1649–1687), and others. Together with other less well-known poets and painters of Anhwei, they formed an informal painting society.[8] Other side trips took him to Yang-chou in 1673, to Chiu-feng (Sung-chiang) in 1675, and to Chung-shan, east of Nanking, in 1678.[9]

The Hsüan-ch'eng period is important for two reasons. In these thirty-odd years of immersion in the landscape, he "stored up the scenic wonders in his breast" and "traveled the ten thousand miles" which were the source of his transformations of his own immediate artistic heritage and the weight of tradition. In the eyes of later critics, these transformations made him the equal of such late Ming and early Ch'ing giants as Tung Ch'i-ch'ang (1555–1636) and Wang Hui (1632–1712). His contact with the Anhwei masters and those sympathetic to their new expressive vision formed the basis of his own art and taste. He was born artistically into their world: his first exposure to and link with tradition was through their eyes, and his later transmutations were built on the artistic ground they had cultivated.

Nanking, Kiangsu: 1680–1686

At the invitation of a fellow monk, Tao-chi and Ho-t'ao moved south of Nanking to the Ch'ang-kan temple (also known as the Pao-en temple in the Ming and Ch'ing periods). In the Nanking period we first encounter the name I-chih-ko ("the One-Branch Studio"), where Tao-chi spent the next six years. Much of the information on this period of his life comes from the handscroll dated 1685, *Searching for Plum Blossoms* (*XVIII*).

An important event of this period was Tao-chi's meeting with the K'ang-hsi Emperor late in 1684. The emperor was conducting the first of his Southern Tours, and in Nanking he visited the imperial Ming tombs and called at the Pao-en temple.[10] During this time Tao-chi maintained his contacts with contemporary painters and their works: Mei Ch'ing visited him at the temple, and painters such as K'un-ts'an (1612–1686), Tai Pen-hsiao (1621–1691), and Wang Kai (1679–1705) were among his acquaintances.[11] However, the Nanking years were essentially ones of seclusion and contemplation, in which Tao-chi mustered his intellectual and spiritual resources after his decades of roaming.

Yang-chou, Kiangsu: 1687–1689

In the spring of 1687, Tao-chi went to Yang-chou, the great commercial metropolis, and entered the world of society. He was introduced by the poet Cho Erh-k'an to the playwright K'ung Shang-jen. At his garden estate, the Mi-yüan, K'ung held a poetic gathering: among his guests were some of the greatest poets and painters active at the time. There Tao-chi met artists like Kung Hsien and Cha Shih-piao. This exchange of conversation and ideas must have made a lasting impression on him.[12]

In the fall of 1687, Tao-chi wrote an important poem describing his Nanking life, "Shen-p'ing hsing" ("The Course of My Life"), in which he says he dreamt of visiting the capital, as he had received an invitation to do so from old friends.[13] Sometime in 1689 he met a gentleman who was to exert a tremendous influence on him, the Manchu Po-erh-tu (Bordu, *tzu* Wen-t'ing, died 1701–). Po had accompanied the K'ang-hsi Emperor on the second of his Southern Tours in March of that year and had met Tao-chi at the P'ing-shan-t'ang.[14] His position as an imperial clansmen (he was the great-grandson of the Ch'ing founder, Nurhaci) may have stimulated an amateur interest in the arts, but he seems also to have been a painter and collector of taste and discrimination.[15] Late in 1689, perhaps as a result of the encouragement of his new-found friend, Tao-chi traveled north to Peking, where he spent the next three significant years.

Peking, Hopei: 1689–1692

Artistically Tao-chi's trip north and his association with the Manchu were important turning points. He made many acquaintances in varying social and bureaucratic positions whose penchant for art made them likely patrons, and he could also view the great private collections of antique paintings which were still intact in the capital. He recorded his reaction to these works in his colophons to his paintings and in several copies of antique works, of which he executed many specimens for Po-erh-tu over the years. In the fall of 1692 Tao-chi returned south by way of the Grand Canal. Some of his scenic impressions were recorded later in a work dated 1696, the long and important handscroll *Sketches of Calligraphy and Painting by Ch'ing-hsiang*.[16]

The Peking stay not only stimulated Tao-chi's interest in the works of the past but also aroused more self-awareness and profounder understanding of his own artistic and spiritual goals. His colophons from paintings after this period reveal subtle changes of attitude and a deeper confidence in his own vision. In addition, the northern sojourn also established his position as a painter. Henceforth his involvement in the social circle of paintings, patrons, and pupils was to be an ever-widening one.[17] (See below, "Tao-chi in Peking," for further discussion of paintings from this period.)

Yang-chou: 1693–ca. 1710

With the expansion of Tao-chi's social world came an increase in pupils (cf. *XXXII*) as well as artistic commitments. The subject matter in his repertory grew, as did his artistic production as a whole. Two significant personal events occurred during the earlier half of his Yang-chou residence which also make it convenient to discuss his artistic chronology in terms of two periods, from 1693 to about 1697, and from about 1697 to about 1710. These events were Tao-chi's renunciation of Buddhism and his reconciliation with his imperial heritage.

Sometime between 1696 and 1697, Tao-chi severed his monastic vows and built a studio in Yang-chou which he called Ta-ti-t'ang. The words "Ta-ti" appear more frequently in the signatures and seals of works dated after these years, as do the names Jo-chi and Ta-pen-t'ang (cf. *XXXIV*). "Ta-ti" means "great cleansing" or "purification." The mountain by that name west of Hang-chou had been one of the important centers of Taoism since the Sung and Yüan dynasties.[18] Tao-chi offers no extended explanations as to why he adopted this new cognomen, but inscriptions and colophons suggest a change in his life which he wanted others to recognize.[19] The "purification" seems to imply not only a spiritual cleansing of past sins in a religious sense but also an absolving of his former fears and retreat into Buddhism to avoid persecution as a member of the Ming line. Such a change included abandoning the external signs of his faith, such as his monk's robe and shaven head.[20]

Judging from the scanty but diverse comments in his poems, letters, seals, and signatures, it appears that Tao-chi realized that Ming restoration was unlikely quite late in his Yang-chou years, at a time which closely coincides with his break with Buddhism. Written with a slight tone of self-mockery, his late letters indicate that any sentiment he may once have had about the loss of Ming glory had been dissipated.[21] Moreover, by signing and sealing his works with his palace name, Jo-chi, and by using Ta-pen-t'ang, the palace which belonged to the Ming imperial household, Tao-chi seems to have freed himself from the contradictions of his past. Names and phrases related to his abandonment of Buddhism and acceptance of his heritage appear repeatedly in his seals and signatures, such as Ta-ti-t'ang and Ta-ti ts'ao-t'ang; in the early 1700's other studio names such as Ch'ing-lien ts'ao-ko and Keng-hsin ts'ao-t'ang also appear with his signatures.

From Amateur to Professional

Tao-chi's change in status from monk to commoner meant providing for himself the necessities of daily existence which had heretofore been supplied by the monastery. With no other financial resources, no income from family, he had in fact become a professional painter. To be sure, his gradual secularization as a painter and teacher helped to make the final move into the world somewhat easier. By "professional painter" is meant one who is dependent upon the sale of his paintings as a sole means of income. Craftsmen, teachers of painting, and painters in attendance at court or in the Imperial Academy fall in this category. Traditionally, the Chinese painter of professional status had not been respected by his contemporaries and critics because of the Confucian stigma attached to the materialism which professionalism entailed, and because the post-Sung increase in scholar-painting helped to establish the amateur ethic as a measure of the quality of a man and his work. Moreover, critics and consumers of art were scholars who were naturally predisposed toward painters of literati status and thus tended to slight painters with professional connections. There were a few exceptions: Wu Chen (1280–1354), Ch'iu Ying (ca. 1499–1552), and T'ang Yin (1470–1523), for example, were highly respected masters.

Changes in critical standards reflect changes in social attitudes, and by the time of the Ch'ing dynasty "professional painter" was no longer a pejorative term. The situation of a master such as Wang Hui, who garnered imperial favor, a wealthy clientele, and the esteem of scholars, might be described as one of both professional and institutionalized orthodoxy.[22] Tao-chi's brand of individualism had not yet become institutionalized or fashionable, as it was when taken up by his followers in the mid-eighteenth century. Even though the public had begun to value the professional painter a century earlier, Tao-chi still considered some aspects of that position demeaning. In one of his later letters, there is a note of loneliness and desperation: "My entire life and fate rests in this brush of mine!"[23] Another such admission appears on the last leaf of the 1701 Album of Landscapes (XXVI), in which he expresses his anxiety at letting professionalism "become his downfall." In fact, his Yang-chou followers ultimately allowed the reification of their artistic values to limit the scope of their achievement in a way in which Tao-chi resisted to the end.

Apart from the nature of professionalism itself, one might ask whether this change in status affected his art, in terms of subject matter, format, or style, and whether success and the development of a clientele required him to employ "help" in the form of a workshop team or "substitute" painters. It is evident that Tao-chi's flexibility was challenged to unusual degrees in this period, and some of his late letters indicate that he was often physically unable and spiritually unwilling to meet the demands of his profession. For example, he loved to paint on fine old paper: in his inscriptions he often mentions Sung lo-wen, ch'eng-hsin-t'ang, or "palace" papers.[24] But he could not always afford this luxury. Cultivating a clientele also meant overlooking personal dislikes, such as painting on silk, which he loathed, or executing large hanging scrolls in a series, a format which had become popular with wealthy metropolitan patrons. The

number of his extant works in a large format are few; the enormous 1693–94 Panoramic Vista, in twelve scrolls,[25] gives us an idea of the tremendous physical demands of such an undertaking. As his health weakened, the execution of such gigantic works was a great physical and emotional strain. Moreover, he was sensitive to their decorative nature. In one letter he apologizes to a client that his style is not suitable for decorative screens, but he accepts the commission because he needs the money. In other letters he discusses fees or laments his ill health; he complains that his energies and mental powers are failing because of old age and that he often cannot stand the strain of stretching the large panels over frames or climbing up and down footladders to execute them.[26] The tone and content of such letters offer a glimpse of the human side of the man which his poetry and painting often disguise. In spite of these hardships, Tao-chi in his late years was still able to maintain the core of self-esteem vital to any artist. In some cases he may even have attained new heights of originality because of practical necessities which forced him to draw on less familiar aspects of his talent. Our awareness of these details may permit a more just assessment of the painting of his late period, when these demands may have affected artistic quality.

The question of a "workshop" parallels in general terms the relationship between the master painter and his apprentices in Western painting. The Chinese term tai-pi (literally, "substitute brush"[27]) refers to a work executed by an agent at the request of the master. The latter invariably acknowledges this substitution without condescension by endorsing the work with his own signature and an inscription. Generally this takes place when a painter is too busy to comply with all the requests made of him. He may choose a gifted and compliant pupil or friend, a person, as one would expect, whose style bears some resemblance to his own. Scholar-painters of established fame might employ these substitutes or agents,[28] but it was a more common practice among professional painters. Rather than relinquish a profitable commission, the professional would hire others. We have no objective means of measuring the extent of Tao-chi's clientele; from his letters it seems extensive enough to have supported him. At any rate, there is no indication that he ever employed a substitute hand. If on rare occasions he did refuse a commission, it was because of old age and poor health, not because of any overwhelming demand for his work.

Tao-chi's Dates

In 1959 Wen Fong determined Tao-chi's birth date as 1641 by using the authenticated Letter to Pa-ta written by Tao-chi (see XXIII).[29] He refuted two other theories of Tao-chi's birth date, 1630 and 1636, proposed by earlier scholars. Since that article a major supporting document was published in 1961, the Keng-ch'en ch'u-yeh shih-kao ("Manuscript of Poems Written on the Eve of the Last Day of the Lunar Month in the Cyclical Year keng-ch'en"), dated in correspondence to February 7, 1701.[30] This manuscript (fig. 2), now in Shanghai, contains Tao-chi's own statement that he was sixty at the time (see line 2 of the manuscript), thus establishing 1641 as his year of birth.

The 1641 theory, however, does not easily explain the relationship between Tao-chi and the older scholar Ch'ien Ch'ien-i (1582–1664).[31] To some this dilemma has cast a shadow on the authenticity of the Letter to Pa-ta and the 1701 Manuscript of Poems. We firmly believe that these two works are reliable and that their authenticity can be demonstrated.

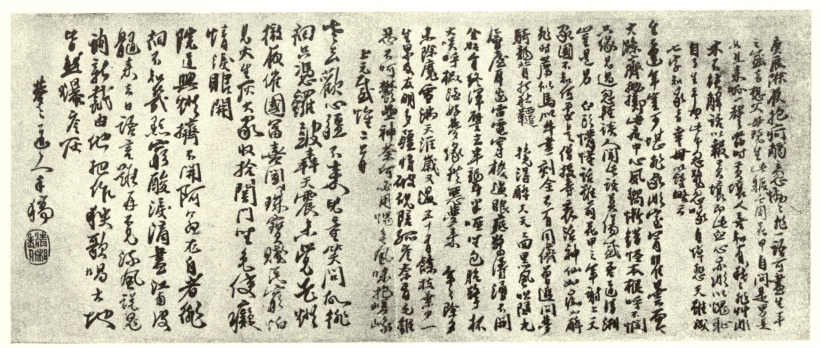

2. Tao-chi, *Manuscript of Poems* (*Keng-ch'en ch'u-yeh shih-kao*), dated in accordance with 1701. Ink on paper. Shanghai Museum. (See also *XXIII*, fig. 14.)

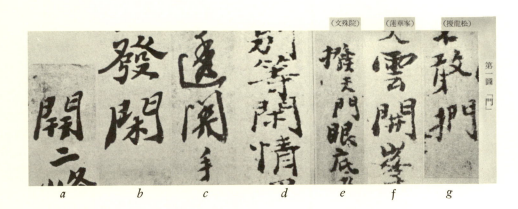

a   b   c   d   e   f   g

3. Tao-chi, details of self-inscriptions: *a–c, Waterfall at Mt. Lu*, ca. 1697; *d, Huang-shan* handscroll, dated 1699; *e–g, Eight Views of Huang-shan*, ca. 1683. Sumitomo collection. From Yonezawa Yoshiho, "Shohō-jo kara mita Sekitō ga no kijun-saku."

The 1641 proposal does not stand or fall on any single proof, but is the considered result of evidence gathered from many sources which themselves have undergone authentication. In *XXIII*, Tao-chi's *Letter to Pa-ta*, we demonstrate that the Sackler letter was executed by the same hand as the self-inscriptions found on three prime works in the Sumitomo collection, and by the same comparative method we show that the Nagahara version of the *Letter* is from a well-known forger's hand. In doing this, we have built and expanded on the method and findings of two studies: Fong's analyses (1959 and 1967)[32] and Yonezawa Yoshiho's essay (1968),[33] which compares the inscriptions from the three important Sumitomo works.

The three works—the album *Eight Views of Huang-shan*, the hanging scroll *Waterfall at Mt. Lu*, and the 1699 handscroll *View of Huangshan* (fig. 3)—are almost "universally accepted" as genuine.[34] Yonezawa has taken the laudatory step of showing that the calligraphy (and, by implication, the paintings) of these three are by the same hand, that of Tao-chi. With this link between calligraphy and painting established, it is imperative that this core of accepted works be further augmented. In the study of Tao-chi's calligraphy which appears at the end of this discussion (see pp. 59–67), we expand on Yonezawa's work by a similar comparative analysis of extracts from some thirty prime monuments in order to demonstrate by this means that they are by Tao-chi. The examples chosen are not inclusive.

Even among the three "universally accepted" works from the Sumitomo collection, discrepancies of script, date, and quality of execution exist as reminders that authenticity is not equivalent to uniformity.

Tao-chi's death date is not known. From an inscription dated 1720 by one of his students, we know that he was already dead by that time.[35] The date of about 1710 which we use is based upon the latest dated works of whose authenticity we are certain. Such a work is a ten-leaf *Album of Flowers*,[36] two leaves of which are dated by the artist as *ting-ch'iu shih-yüeh* (autumn, tenth lunar month of the cyclical year *ting-*[?]). Because the second cyclical character was omitted on Tao-chi's inscription, the date may be interpreted either as autumn, in the period October 25–November 23, 1707 (*ting-hai*), or autumn, 1717 (*ting-yu*). We know of no authentic paintings or poems with a date later than that corresponding to November, 1707. Paintings of his dated 1706 and 1707 do exist; two are reproduced in Part V as entries *XXXII* and *XXXIV*. On the basis of his artistic production, the hiatus after 1707 suggests that Tao-chi may have died soon after, in 1708 or thereabouts. The style of the *Ting-ch'iu Album of Flowers* is consistent with Tao-chi's performance of ca. 1706–1707, and we believe that the album could not have been painted as late as 1717. Given the absence of other authentic works after that date, we tentatively conclude that he must have died sometime after November of 1707 but before 1720, when his pupil Hung

Cheng-chih wrote his colophon (see *XXXII*). Thus the dates 1641–ca. 1710 are a shorthand for the more cumbersome implication "after 1708, but before 1720."

Other literary evidence has been cited in previous studies for a death date closer to the 1720 terminus. The reliability of such evidence can only be tested by internal consistency and our knowledge of other facts which have been corroborated by stylistic evidence; without such tests these literary references can only be used with reservation. We offer here a summary of the evidence presented by earlier studies; each is followed by our opinion of its reliability.

1. A painting treatise titled *Hua-p'u*, close in content and organization to Tao-chi's *Hua-yü-lu* but simpler in language, was said to have been published in 1710 (*keng-yin*).[37] It contains a preface by a certain Hu Ch'i, signed in that year. The text of the treatise is printed in a style of calligraphy close to Tao-chi's, implying that he himself handwrote the text from which the blocks were carved. Two of Tao-chi's seals are also reprinted in the opening pages. Hu Ch'i's preface is also written in a style close to Tao-chi's, suggesting that Tao-chi may have transcribed the content of Hu's remarks. If the latter is true, Tao-chi may have still been alive in 1710. The reliability of the *Hua-p'u* has been questioned recently,[38] but without concrete evidence of a conclusive and independent nature to the contrary, we cannot say that the entire work is a complete fabrication.

2. The *Ting-ch'iu Album of Flowers* does present the possibility that Tao-chi may have painted a work as late as 1717. As noted, however, we believe the style to be consistent with works of a decade earlier.

3. A handscroll of fruits, flowers, and rocks on silk[39] is dated *chia-wu ch'iu, chiu-yüeh ehr-shih yu-liu-jih* (November 2, 1714) (*XXIII*, fig. 17). We believe this entire work to be a forgery. The calligraphy and the painting are unconvincing stylistically, so that even its accuracy as a copy cannot be confirmed.

4. The mainland scholar Yü Chien-hua, in his *Shih-t'ao nien-piao*, mentions a self-inscription by Tao-chi to a work painted in Wu-ch'eng, Anhwei, with the cyclical date *chi-hai wu-yüeh* (June 18–July 16, 1719). Cheng Cho-lu has correctly interpreted the date as 1719,[40] as it refers to a friend of the painter Hung-jen who was still living. Unfortunately, there is no way of checking the authenticity of the painting from which this reference is taken. We must also doubt the likelihood that Tao-chi made the long trip to Anhwei in his late years.

5. A poem recorded in Tao-chi's *Ta-ti-tzu t'i-hua shih-pa* is dated autumn of the year 1717 (*ting-yu ch'iu*).[41] We believe the poem to be a forgery because its signature states that the poem and painting were executed at his studio in Nanking, I-chih-ko, and it is signed "Ta-ti-tzu, Shih-t'ao, the mountain monk." It is unlikely that Tao-chi signed Ta-ti-tzu (a post-1697 name, indicating his return to secular life) in combination with "*seng*" ("monk"). Moreover, he is not known to have ever returned to his studio in Nanking after he left it in the spring of 1687.[42]

6. Hung Cheng-chih's 1720 colophon to Tao-chi's painting (see *XXXII*) we believe to be reliable as literary evidence, even though Tao-chi's painting and Hung's colophon are not available in the original for examination. The tone of Hung's inscription implies that Tao-chi had been dead for several years; this interpretation makes the 1719 and perhaps even the 1717 death dates unlikely.

Tao-chi and Antiquity

Previous studies of Tao-chi have tended to stress his role as an artist who broke through the stultifying hold of tradition at a crucial time in the history of Chinese painting. This aspect of his achievement is valid both as a historical and a critical judgment, but it is incomplete because it fails to account for the formative influence which that very tradition exerted on the development of Tao-chi's art. No matter how radical or revolutionary a painter's or theorist's contribution, he is still the product of his age and of the traditions into which he was born and trained. The following pages focus on

three aspects of Tao-chi's relationship with antiquity—his calligraphy, painting, and art theories. We do not wish to overstress his relationship with antiquity or to distort the art-historical assessments presented by other scholars; we hope simply to offer a closer examination of his art in relation to the past.

TAO-CHI'S CALLIGRAPHY

Calligraphy is a fitting point of departure for this examination of Tao-chi's art because the extraordinary range of his script styles and his calligraphic innovations illuminate his painting, his art theories, and his attitudes toward the past. His relationship with the calligraphy of the past was two-fold: he emulated the personal styles of several great masters, and he revived archaic script types. In his emulation and absorption of past styles, he was merely following the pattern established by calligraphers past and present. More unusual was his revival of major ancient scripts, a phenomenon in part stimulated by certain contemporary trends. He was able to assimilate and transform these scripts into a working and flexible basis for an extensive calligraphic repertory while still maintaining a pronounced stylistic identity—this was a significant and individual achievement. He was master of all the major historical scripts then current, and he practiced them at a time when most painters and calligraphers were writing in only one script, or at most two. Because of his broad command of archaic scripts and styles of great masters, Tao-chi's attainments as a calligrapher closely rival his distinction as a painter.

TAO-CHI'S ATTITUDE toward the achievement of past masters is revealed in the last lines of a self-inscription to one of his paintings: "I think of Li Po and recall Chung Yu. Together, unexcelled in all three [poetry, calligraphy, and painting], who ranks with us?"[43] By regarding himself the equal of Li Po (699–762), the romantic T'ang poet-hero, and Chung Yu (151–230), the Wei master of the "small-standard" script, Tao-chi was not making a hollow boast. On the contrary, he regarded these and other ancients as the measure of his creative growth and as living guides to his aspirations. Most significant, he felt he was their equal because he had experienced a spiritual correspondence (*shen-hui*) with them.

He studied and imitated Chung Yu's strong and unpretentious style with great diligence and developed his own interpretation of Chung's script, which counts among his finest achievements. But in the realm of calligraphy Chung Yu's distinctive personal style was just one of several which he mastered: those of Ch'u Sui-liang (596–658), Su Shih (1036–1101), Huang T'ing-chien (1045–1105), Ni Tsan (1301–1374), and Shen Chou (1427–1509) were also imitated with enthusiasm and success.

Tao-chi's emulation of past calligraphers and ancient scripts was guided by study and by a feeling for quality. In an inscription to a collection of antique rubbings in his possession, he reveals his awareness of the importance of the excellence of one's models and stresses the necessity of collecting fine originals of ancient prototypes for study purposes: "Calligraphers ought to collect specimens of [*Ch'un-hua*] *ko-t'ieh*, for if one wants to comprehend [calligraphy in general] one must investigate its origins in the past. But forgeries (i.e., recut versions) may be confused with the genuine. To distin-

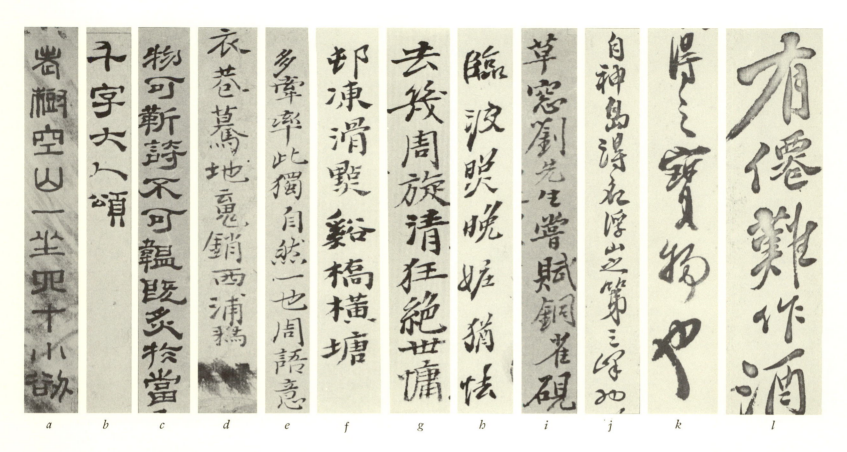

a   b   c   d   e   f   g   h   i   j   k   l

4. Tao-chi's four historical scripts and personal variations (not to scale): *a*, "seal" script, *Sketches of Calligraphy and Painting by Ch'ing-hsiang*, dated 1696; *b*, "clerical" script, *Thousand-Character "Eulogy of a Great Man,"* ca. 1698; *c*, "clerical" script, *After Shen Chou's Bronze Peacock Inkslab*, ca. 1698–1703; *d*, "regular" script after Chung Yu, *Searching for Plum Blossoms*, dated 1685; *e*, "regular" script after Ni Tsan, *Thousand-Character "Eulogy of a Great Man,"* ca. 1698; *f*, "regular" script after Chung Yu, *Plum Branches*, ca. 1705–7; *g*, "regular" script after Ni Tsan, *Plum Branches*, ca. 1705–7; *h*, "regular" script after Huang T'ing-chien, *Flowers and Figures*, dated 1695; *i*, "regular" script after Shen Chou, *After Shen Chou's Bronze Peacock Inkslab*, ca. 1698–1703; *j*, "running" script, *Lo-Fu Mountains*, ca. 1701–5; *k*, "running" script, *Letter to Pa-ta shan-jen*, ca. 1698–99; *l*, "running" script, *Bamboo, Vegetables, and Fruit*, dated 1705.

guish the forgery from the genuine may seem relatively easy, but among the genuine, there are still degrees of superiority and inferiority. . . . I have seen more than ten versions of *ko-t'ieh* and this is quite a good one."[44] A letter to a friend is accompanied by a gift of an antique rubbing from his collection: "This specimen is one which I have collected and appreciated all my life. Nowadays there are so many things which people cannot know [about good calligraphy]. Among the ancient methods, this is the 'real face' [*chen-mien-mu*]. Please receive and keep it, so I will still have a chance to look at it."[45]

Though there is no way to evaluate the quality of the works Tao-chi mentions, it is evident that he had acquired a standard of quality in which he had confidence, and this was important in the development of his aesthetic taste. It was no doubt fostered in his early years in Hsüan-cheng and Nanking and sharpened and broadened as a result of his trip to Peking and later in Yangchou, where he came to know more collectors and artists. By establishing his artistic sensibility on a firm foundation of classic models available through these contacts, Tao-chi's training in fact differed little from that of the scholar of orthodox background.

Tao-chi revived and practiced all the scripts current in the late Ming and early Ch'ing and even improvised several new variations of his own. His personal range covered four historical script types (fig. 4): *chuan-shu*, "seal" script, which he used occasionally for the titles of paintings but most often for his own stone seals, which he carved himself;[46] *li-shu*, "clerical" (also known as "official" or

"chancery") script of the *T'ang-li* variety; *k'ai-shu*, "regular" (also known as "model," "block," or "standard") script, which he wrote in several forms, one after Chung Yu, others modeled after the two T'ang and Yüan dynasty masters, Ch'u Sui-liang and Ni Tsan; and *hsing-ts'ao*, a mixture of "running" and "cursive" scripts which characterizes his freehand manner and also includes related derivations from *li* or *k'ai-shu*. To these four a fifth non-historical or miscellaneous category can be added, which would include any of the above scripts in "slender" or "plump" modes, in addition to his variations on the styles of other masters.

"Seal" script had evolved its fundamental forms by the second millennium B.C. and was in prominent use as a commemorative script until the Chou to early Ch'in dynasties, from 1000 to 200 B.C. The form of "seal" Tao-chi wrote, however, was actually closer to the Han interpretation revived for usage on seals from 200 B.C. to 200 A.D. The essential shape of Han "seal" style (in contrast to its historical prototype) is more rectangular, with the strokes tending to conform more closely to the imaginary square which encloses the form.[47]

The title inscription to the 1696 *Sketches of Calligraphy and Painting by Ch'ing-hsiang* (fig. 4a) shows the severe, static symmetry of each character drawn in place by round, tense, unmodulated strokes. Tao-chi's sense of intervalic spacing and modular balance was exercised to the utmost in this script, whether in strict vertical columns, as here, or in his seals. In the latter his sensitivity to linear design and solid-void relationships was concentrated in the small space of a square, rectangle, or oval. Characters carved on the face of a seal could be elongated or shortened according to necessity; one could stress rectangularity and angles or ellipses and curves, depending on the shape of the stone and the basic form of the characters. Whereas the written "seal" script demanded an even, unvarying stroke and strict adherence to the rectangle and its fixed proportion, the carved seal allowed greater creative freedom within the strictures of the script type. It was probably for this reason that Tao-chi carved his "seal" script more often than he wrote it; examples of his brush-written "seal" style are relatively rare.

Historically the "clerical" script is associated with the Han dynasty from about 200 B.C. to 200 A.D. It retains the rectangular configuration of the "seal" type, but the significant difference lies in its beautifully modulated strokes. The full potential of the pointed brush is utilized: it sweeps from one end (usually the left or top part) of the stroke, thinning in its path and then splaying forth with a concentrated pressure to create an arching, "wave-like" form with flaring or tapered ends. Several different styles of "clerical" script were already practiced in the Han: an earlier type was closer to the "seal" in composition and stroke form; a later one, the *pa-fen* style, was squatter in composition and more attenuated, with greater contrast of thicks and thins in a single stroke. Dynamic asymmetry and graceful sweep are more characteristic of the *pa-fen*. The late Ming masters revived the "clerical" form practiced during the T'ang dynasty, *T'ang-li*, and Tao-chi followed this prototype.[48]

The ca. 1698 *Eulogy of a Great Man* and the ca. 1698–1703 *After Shen Chou's Bronze Peacock Inkslab* (fig. 4b–c) both bear title inscriptions in Tao-chi's "clerical" script, the five characters of the *Eulogy* title representing one of his most poised and elegant examples of the type. A powerful inner tension and dynamism charges each of the strokes and lends a centripetal energy to the total configuration (see *XXIV, detail*). The strokes are crisp and firm. Despite the difference in script style, the fine stroke formations which appear in both the "seal" example (4a) and the *Eulogy* indicate the same hand: the pointed heads of the strokes are sharp and well-formed, the rounded ends reveal a fine sense of articulation and control, and the lines and spaces are in balanced proportion. The example in fig. 4c is larger in actual scale and was written with a blunt painting brush, so that the strokes appear coarser, but the same control of round and pointed stroke ends, of intervalic spacing, and of restrained movement found in *b* also characterize *c*.

"Clerical" script best suited Tao-chi's temperament; it expressed his generous personality and his love of variety, and it became his most memorable ancient script. His fundamental orientation in this script invariably structured the significant brush movements of his other scripts, whether a formal "regular" or a casual "running." He loved the continual rhythmic modulation of the stroke; the flaring motion of the horizontals and diagonals had an exuberance and expansiveness which invited subtle expressive changes. His practice of this movement was a habitual, subconscious muscular response. It resembled an up-and-down, circumambulating movement of the brush propelled by numerous, small, complex motions in the muscles of the fingers, hand, and arm. These motions and their habitual rhythm were cultivated over years of training and produced the constantly fluctuating thick and thin strokes which underlie all of his varying script styles (except the "seal"), and they became his basic graphological feature. This is a vital point which distinguishes

Tao-chi's hand from that of his imitators. Copyists have inevitably cultivated different basic habits and script forms, making their renderings different not only in quality of execution and artistic interpretation but in personal habits of form.

The development of *k'ai* "regular" script reached its characteristic forms soon after the Han, and achieved some stature by the third and fourth centuries A.D., when the names of outstanding individual masters began to illuminate calligraphic history. Tao-chi evidently modeled his "small regular" script after one of the founding masters of the Wei period, Chung Yu. The Wei master's style is today highly problematical because specimens of his writing survive only in the form of rubbings made at a later date. Tao-chi probably had access only to Ming examples through the *Ko-t'ieh* collection he mentions, as the Ming period witnessed a revival of Chung Yu's style among many scholars. Despite these drawbacks, however, Tao-chi was quite clear about the aesthetic virtues of Chung Yu's style: simplicity, unpretentiousness, a flavor of the antique.[49] He had a superb command of the Chung Yu idiom, whatever his specific model or source. The inscriptions on his early works, dated in the late 1660's and 1670's, and especially his *Searching for Plum Blossoms* (fig. 4d, *XVIII*), have the superior calligraphic qualities of internal tension, outward restraint, and archaic simplicity. The seemingly idiosyncratic forms of the blunt, brief strokes and oar-like diagonals arranged in a squat composition in fact compare well with some specimens of brush writing on wooden slips contemporary with and slightly later than Chung Yu which archeologists have recovered (see fig 1).

As a script type, the "regular" style has marked differences from the two types just discussed in both composition and stroke method: the size of the characters (e.g., fig. 4d–i) varies more freely than in "clerical;" the vertical and horizontal configuration of the individual graph is not confined as strictly to an imaginary square, the strokes are executed more consistently with the very tip of the brush, and there is an increased articulation and definition of the individual stroke form. The pace and pressure of the brush are more uniform, with a tendency to roundness rather than flatness, and greater attention is given to the turning of corners and to the formation of hooks and diagonals. This concentration on structural articulation gives the script a more three-dimensional quality.

Tao-chi's poetic inscription to his ca. 1705–7 *Plum Branches* album (fig. 4f) shows his "old-age" variation on the same Chung Yu type. With the passage of twenty years and a difference in paper and brush (a blunt painting brush as opposed to a writing brush), a general process of simplification has occurred (see fig. 4d–f). Although the horizontal and vertical strokes are thicker and more incisive, the articulation of the hooks and turns, the basic squat configuration, and the disposition of the horizontals and dots in relation to one another all show the same feeling for significant form found in his earlier works. The inscription to *Plum Branches* is slightly looser in composition than in *Plum Blossoms*, indicating a lapse in physical vigor which accords with its late date.

Within the "regular" script category Tao-chi's second most frequent choice was modeled after the T'ang master Ch'u Sui-liang and the Yüan painter Ni Tsan (cf. *XXIV*). Both masters' styles are outwardly elegant and graceful, with longer, thinner, and shapelier forms distinguished by accents at the beginning and end of each stroke. Tao-chi's ca. 1700 *Eulogy* (fig. 4e) has the wiry resilience, lilting rhythm, and full, spacious disposition of the strokes which characterize his interpretation of this script. Another inscription from the ca. 1705–7 *Plum Branches* album (fig. 4g) shows the "plump" variation of this style as it appears in Tao-chi's late years.

Ni Tsan's influence on Tao-chi was not an isolated phenomenon: it was part of a revived interest in the Yüan painter's art among painters of the "eye area" in the late Ming and early Ch'ing. A contemporary and friend of Tao-chi's was Chiang Shih-chieh (1647–1709), whose calligraphy appears on his *Landscape and Portrait of Hung Cheng-chih*, dated 1706 (*XXXII*). Chiang's script style shows the same formal influence of Ni Tsan, but a comparison of his writing (*XXXII*, fig. 4) with that of Tao-chi reveals the more expansive artistic personality of the latter. Chiang's feeling for form is tighter; his brushstrokes tend either to shrink toward the central axis or to extend impulsively beyond the rectangular form. These traits are coupled with a sudden thickening at the ends of the strokes which may be linked to an influence from *chang-ts'ao* "draft-cursive" script. The differences between the two calligraphic hands are instinctive, and this contrast facilitates recognition of Tao-chi's underlying grasp of form and its various expressions through different scripts.

In the evolution of calligraphic form the "small regular" script developed by Chung Yu and his contemporaries played a formative role in the early development from the "clerical" to the more classic "regular" script of the T'ang by instilling a greater perfection of its structure. The Chung Yu-type forms still retain a degree of "official" brush movements, as compared to the eighth- and ninth-century "regular" script, which had by then emancipated itself from earlier brushwork to emphasize a more monumental aspect suitable to commemorative steles; yet it is significant that the T'ang master Ch'u Sui-liang effected an extraordinary revival of the style by combining the graceful "clerical" brush method with the more balanced symmetry of the T'ang "regular" script.[50] It is doubly significant that it was Ch'u's "regular" style as envisioned by Ni Tsan (also a Ch'u proponent) which Tao-chi adapted. Thus to him the "clerical" and "regular" scripts were closely related both formally and historically.

Within the "regular" script category, Tao-chi's adaptations of the scripts of earlier masters constitute one of his great achievements as a calligrapher. His grasp of the essential characteristics of their styles was broad and true. Although he recognized certain individual prototypes, his actual range was not fixed, but mercurial. One can easily identify his renderings in the Shen Chou, Huang T'ing-chien, or Su Shih styles, but they are doubly memorable for the spontaneous and often unpredictable mixture of traits which he selects to combine or to emphasize in any one work. Fig. 4h, from the ca. 1695 *Flowers and Figures* album, contains some *hsing-k'ai* traits in the Huang T'ing-chien manner, but they are combined almost capriciously with the flatter, tremulous brushwork of "clerical" style. A pronounced upward slant of the horizontal axis, a narrow and elongated total shape, and wavering, tremulous strokes generally characterize the Sung master's style.[51] These traits are also visible in fig. 4i, which is Tao-chi's imitation after Shen Chou, who in turn was imitating Huang T'ing-chien.[52] But in fig. 4h we see that Tao-chi has combined these elements with "official"-style brushwork, emphasizing the flat, flaring movement found in the diagonal, vertical, and hook strokes and exaggerating their verticality. The example in fig. 4i is worthy of attention because it reveals the tenuous equilibrium struck between the Ming master's traits and his own. In addition to these examples, the Fong *Small Album* contains an unusually rich

spectrum of derived and hybrid forms within one work, showing Tao-chi's unparalleled ability to vary his formal styles according to shifts of mood.

Tao-chi's "running" script could be called his everyday writing style. Basically, the script integrates in one brush movement the strokes which would be executed by separate movements in "regular" script, giving the forms a fluency and a greater outward dynamism. Like his other scripts, this type also oscillates between the two extremes of "slender" and "plump," depending upon the brush and the writer's mood. The ca. 1701–5 *Lo-Fu Mountains* album (fig. 4j) exhibits small "running" script in a slender mode. It revels in the fine movements of the brushtip and the crisp inner articulation, which resemble "muscle" and "joints." Fig. 4k and *l* are examples of large "running" style in the "plump" mode. The characters are broader and weightier; the strokes are rounder, and the tip of the brush is less prominent than in the "thin" mode. Despite the discrepancy in size and the even more simplified movements of *k* as compared with *j*, one can recognize the script as issuing from the same hand. The forms shown in fig. 4l also bear elements of Su Shih.

Tao-chi's emulation of one other calligrapher is worthy of mention — the T'ang master Yen Chen-ch'ing (*hao* Lu-kung, 709–785).[53] His stylistic references to this major calligrapher's art lie primarily in the realm of pure brush method and in emulation of the master's energy level, rather than in any formal configuration. Tao-chi selects the most characteristic forms associated with Yen's calligraphy, and he draws the blunt and decisive lines with an upright brush and a firmly centered tip. It is surprising that Tao-chi adapted this incisive brush attack in his paintings and not in his calligraphy. Such brushwork appears in the 1701 *Album of Landscapes* (*XXVI*) and the 1700 *Peking Album*, among others. He testifies to this derivation in one of the leaves by announcing, "this is like Lu-kung's calligraphy method!" (fig. 5). His understanding of Yen's approach to form, like his other derivations from past masters, was culled from a broad rather than specific acquaintance with Yen's style. He made his adaptations with great freedom, yet in an intuitive and most essential way, never failing to catch the master's spiritual energy. It was this, and not archeological reconstruction of form, which constituted his spiritual correspondence with antiquity and placed his summary of the past on such an unshakable aesthetic foundation.

The actual sources of Tao-chi's "running" style are difficult to specify; he so thoroughly assimilated his original models that we see only his strongly personal image. It does not bear any of the formal mannerisms associated with the styles of currently prevailing masters (as did, for example, the contemporaries of Wen Cheng-ming in the mid-Ming or Tung Ch'i-ch'ang in the late Ming and early Ch'ing). This independence from the dominant artistic personality of the period links him with the sense of artistic individuality attained by the Sung masters[54] and constitutes another of Tao-chi's great achievements.

LIKE THE CONTEMPORARY developments in painting, calligraphy in the late Ming showed an exciting formal diversity, which had coalesced into a set of more or less dominant trends by the early Ch'ing. By that time Tung Ch'i-ch'ang's influence could be seen clearly in calligraphy as well as painting in the work of the group of painter-calligraphers who aligned themselves with his orthodoxy, and even in some who did not. There were also calligraphers who had cultivated distinct personal styles independent of the major

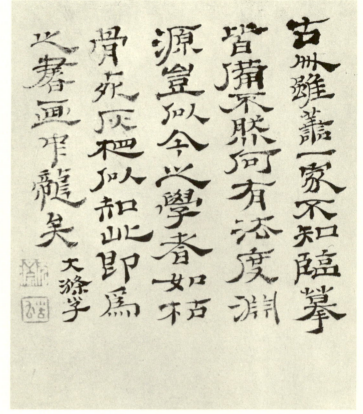

5. Tao-chi, *1700 Peking Album*, "Landscape Using Yen Chen-ch'ing's Brush Method," detail. Album leaf. Ink on paper. Palace Museum, Peking.

6. Tao-chi, *Twelve-Leaf Album of Landscapes*, dated 1703, detail of self-inscription to leaf F. Ink on paper. Museum of Fine Arts, Boston.

7. Tao-chi, *Ten-Leaf Album of Landscapes*, dated 1682, leaf E. Ink on paper. Ta-feng-t'ang collection.

8. Tao-chi, *Ten Thousand Ugly Inkblots*, dated 1685, detail of self-inscription. Handscroll. Ink on paper. Su-chou Museum.

contemporary influences, either Tung in the late Ming or Wen Cheng-ming in the mid-Ming. It is important to recall that few masters of either sphere wrote in purely archaic styles. Whether as calligraphers or painters, the majority of these masters wrote in one script type, or at most two: usually a "small regular" and a "running." When they sought variations, the changes were largely of size and degree of cursiveness, not of script type. Most of the great calligraphers of the Ming and early Ch'ing fall into this category: Chu Yün-ming (1460–1526), who usually wrote in "small regular" (after Chung Yu) or "large cursive"; Ch'en Shun (1483–1544), who wrote mainly in "cursive"; Wang Ch'ung (1494–1533), who was an exponent of "small regular" and "cursive"; Ni Yüan-lu (1593–1644), who wrote exclusively in "running"; and Chang Jui-t'u (1570–1640?), Huang Tao-chou (1585–1646), Wang To (1592–1652), and Fu Shan (1607–1684), all of whom wrote primarily in a monumental or "small regular" and "cursive-running" script.[55]

The regional painters of the late Ming, several of whom form Tao-chi's artistic ancestry in painting, were even less versatile than the preceding group and much less so than Tao-chi himself. Hsü Wei (1521–1593), Ch'en Hung-shou (1559–1652), Cha Shih-piao (1615–1698), Mei Ch'ing (1623–1697), K'un-ts'an (1612–ca. 1686), Hung-jen (1610–1663), Kung Hsien (ca. 1618–1689), and even the mid-Ch'ing Yang-chou painters would also fall into the "one script" category. Two notable exceptions are Wen Cheng-ming (1470–1559), who wrote in the same four historical scripts as did Tao-chi,[56] and Wang Shih-min (1592–1680), who mainly practiced the conservative "running" script after Tung Ch'i-ch'ang (as did the other three Wangs) but who was also known for his monumental "clerical."[57] Some late Ming painters like Wu Pin (ca. 1568–1626), Shao Mi (fl. ca. 1620–1640), and Lan Ying (1585–ca. 1664) did occasionally inscribe the titles of their paintings in "seal" or "clerical" scripts,[58] but these were exceptions in a generally one-script vocabulary, and they did not gain a reputation for this kind of writing.

A trait which Tao-chi has in common with these calligraphers, whatever their range, is that their revival of ancient scripts was not strictly historical or based on archeological principles, as it would be among calligraphers of the later Ch'ing;[59] rather, different scripts were practiced more as a blending of the specific brushwork of an older script with the writer's own freehand manner. Tao-chi, in particular, was interested mainly in capturing the general spirit of "clerical" script. This does not imply that his forms were incorrect, only that he did not necessarily imitate a specific source and, if he did do so, transformed it so that it was not immediately identifiable.

Tao-chi's range of calligraphy types and brush styles underwent what appear to be radical changes, yet an underlying consistency of structure and stroke formation stemming from his basic mental habits and technical discipline is discernible and was retained through the three decades of his dated works. His calligraphic breadth parallels the stylistic wealth of his paintings. Moreover, in the context of the development of late Ming and early Ch'ing calligraphy, the richly synthetic nature of his calligraphy and his departures from his immediate predecessors and contemporaries are of historical significance. His stylistic scope was motivated by his intense interest in diverse forms of expression and in protean change itself, preferences which underlie the variety of expressive modes found in his painting. (A more detailed discussion and analysis of his calligraphy, illustrated with prime specimens from his hand, is found on pp. 59–67 below.)

TAO-CHI'S PAINTING

The relationship of Tao-chi's painting to antiquity can be studied through his comments on the ancients in self-inscriptions on extant and recorded paintings, through his free interpretations "after" (fang) certain ancient masters, and through his extant and recorded copies after old paintings. His comments quoted here were chosen to illuminate his extant paintings and to reconstruct his artistic ideas as they bear on works known to us today. (On pp. 55–58, "Tao-chi's Art Theories," some of his artistic concepts are discussed in a more theoretical vein.)

TAO-CHI'S IDEAS ON COPYING (lin-mo) are clearly stated on an inscription on leaf F of the 1703 Boston album (fig. 6): "The ancients were masters of one style; nevertheless, their copying encompassed many styles. Otherwise, how could they have fathomed the sources of various principles [fa-tu]? They could never be considered like the present-day scholars whose works are like dried bones and dying ashes, lacking variety and depth. To comprehend this idea in all its ramifications is to attain the state of the dragon [supreme height] in painting."[60] Tao-chi was not averse to the traditional process of close copying from many different sources as a means of acquiring technical training. Although the specific models for his learning experience are unknown, it is more than likely that his earliest knowledge of painting, like that of his calligraphy, was acquired in the traditional manner by copying and that initially it was strongly influenced by the prevailing styles of the late Ming and early Ch'ing and by contemporary versions of ancient works. It has not been sufficiently recognized that such individualist painters as Mei Ch'ing, Kung Hsien, K'un-ts'an, and Chu Ta[61] were familiar with ancient models. Several statements dated after Tao-chi's 1692 trip to Peking indicate that his acquaintance with old works was broad enough to give him confidence in his own judgment; for example, a colophon dated 1699 written on a work by a contemporary reads: "Nowadays, painters . . . have seldom seen any truly genuine paintings by ancient masters. What they have seen are all forgeries, or if they happen to see any genuine ones, they are unable to understand what they see."[62] This tone of critical disdain echoes that of Tung Ch'i-ch'ang or one of his immediate followers who had studied an impressive number of antique paintings. What is important to note here is that Tao-chi does not repudiate antique paintings or tradition; he is criticizing contemporary painters who are unable to "understand what they see" (k'an-pu-ju), a phrase which in Chinese implies an inability to go beyond the external formal conventions to grasp the spiritual ideal of the old works.

A number of inscriptions on works dated in the early 1680's suggest that Tao-chi's interest in ancient paintings and masters paralleled his artistic growth and that initially his interest in them was less that of a connoisseur than that of a painter. For example, a revealing inscription is found on one leaf of a ten-leaf album dated 1682 (fig. 7):

> It may look like Tung Yüan, but it isn't Tung,
> It may seem like Mi Fu, but it isn't Mi.
> The rain passes over the autumn mountains,
>   creating a brilliance as though the world were washed clean.
> Nothing but "coming out," nothing but "going in"—
> All it is is an essential turning and twisting of my brush.[63]

Tao-chi's "imitations" after the ancients were never a sacrifice of self-image; they represented a realization of self through the renunciation of the enslaving concept of "resemblance" (*ssu*), in the sense of a fixed, conventional image of an ancient style. We might say that this "self-realization" occurred in the midst of arresting that image between "resemblance and non-resemblance" (*shih-fei chih-chien*).[64] The method employed was as natural to him as the passing rain washing clean the mountains: it consisted of nothing more than a "going in" (*tan-ju*) and a "coming out" (*tan-ch'u*)—a penetration of those forces which motivated the minds and spirits of the ancients as a consequence of a total immersion in and subsequent liberation from the bonds of external resemblance.

In these early works of the 1670's and 1680's, one can sense a tension generated from this striving for independence from the specific formal modes of his heritage. This tension manifests itself in a high degree of stylization and contrast of line with mass and of lines with suffused washes. The occasional exaggeration, as in his Hsüan-ch'eng albums, the 1685 handscrolls, and other works, has been interpreted as defiant and rebellious. Yet other works of this period suggest that the force of the artistic drive was less a rebellion against the past and its formal strictures than a struggle with and exploration of the self and the emerging artistic energies which he was compelled to control. Occasionally these forces released themselves in the bizarre shapes and textures which we associate with his Anhwei and Nanking works. Tao-chi did not attempt to obliterate the past, nor did he wish to deny it; on the contrary, he struggled with it and overcame its potentially oppressive hold (to which lesser painters succumbed) by understanding it, absorbing it, and using the true sources of its wealth for his own creative purposes.

Another painting from his Nanking period, the 1685 *Ten Thousand Ugly Inkblots* (fig. 8 and *XVIII*, fig. 2),[65] bears an inscription which offers us further insight into the painter's link with antiquity:

Ten thousand ugly ink dots to scare Mi Fu to death!
Some fibers of soft traces to make Tung Yüan roll over laughing!
From afar the perspective doesn't work—it lacks a landscape's winding ways.
Close up the details are all confused—you can barely make out a few simple cottages.
Once and for all cut off the "heart's eye" from conventional molds,
Just as the immortal who rides the wind has freed his divine spirit from the bounds of flesh and bones!

The traditional ink dots (*mi-tien*) of Mi Fu and the "hemp-fiber" strokes (*p'i-ma ts'un*) of Tung Yüan are here given pictorial definition in distilled form. The conventional and, by Tao-chi's time, classic but outworn modes by which these two tenth- and eleventh-century painters had come to be known function here for Tao-chi as visual stimulants: the idea of ink dots and linear *ts'un* is recast in such a way that they become all the more expressive of elemental artistic forces. Tao-chi unabashedly flaunts those hallowed motifs of Mi dots and Tung hemp fibers and exhorts himself to free the "eye of his heart" (*hsin-yen*) from fixed formulas to call forth that divine spirit—the forces of nature communicated to man—not by abandoning those formulas but by employing them to his design with a technical freedom which transcends the ordinary expression to which they had been limited. Dots and lines receive a new definition in this context, and there is decidedly a negation of conventional space and perspective in the seemingly incoherent scattering and piling of forms and the absence of a fixed ground line. Tao-chi regards Tung and Mi as real, incarnated beings to be addressed as living persons: "Dots to repel you and lines to make you laugh." The tone is defiant and challenging, but full of pride and a touch of self-mockery as well.

In the Nanking years, it becomes evident that Tao-chi is working with both the tools of his art and the conceptual means by which to achieve and to clarify his artistic identity. These essentials are not only the brush, ink, paper, and colors but also form, line, texture, and the traditional brush formulas and schematic types associated with certain major masters and subjects. In this phase, he is stretching these basic ingredients to the limits of his artistic sensibility and technical prowess. Only by reaching out for extreme solutions to the fundamental problems of artistic creation, by experimenting, succeeding, failing, and then turning around to laugh at himself and his results, could he plumb the depths of his creative identity.

The inscriptions of this period tend to be longer and begin to show a greater self-awareness and interest in a more critical discussion of artistic value. Tao-chi was aware of the differences between the methods of past masters, seen not from an art-historical viewpoint, or even in terms of masters or schools, but as pictorial identities removed from the stream of time and available for qualification and transformation. Thus Mi dots and Tung Yüan hemp-fiber strokes, as well as the traditional approaches to certain subjects like plum branches, could all become the basis for purposeful stylistic departure, compositional innovation, and derision. Tao-chi had played with lines and dots before; there was nothing new in his pictorial schema as such. What was new was the elation he derived from his awareness of his links with and deviations from the masters whose names had long been associated with these forms.

An *Album of Landscapes in Six Leaves*,[66] probably from the mid-1690's, bears inscriptions which relate the album to the work of such ancient masters as Chou Wen-chü of the Five Dynasties, Chang Chih-ho of the T'ang, Li Tsung-ch'eng and Fan K'uan of the Northern Sung, and Chang Seng-yu of the Liang. Little is asked of the viewer other than the nominal recognition of these masters, for the styles depicted are cast in Tao-chi's mold. However, these inscriptions indicate that he had some kind of pictorial association with these names and that he was familiar on a general level with the writings of art critics, either antique or slightly earlier than he, who had discussed such painters. In each work, for example, he names the painter and identifies the specific brush methods used. By his time, the names in themselves came to represent no more than attempts of critics to describe technical methods or aesthetic ideas which, like Mi "dots" or Tung Yüan "hemp fibers," had become almost synonymous with the masters themselves. Tao-chi refers to Chou's "thin and resilient" method (*shou-ying-fa*), Chang's "vista of mist and waves" (*yen-po-ching*), Li's "graded ink" method (*p'o-mo-fa*, literally, "broken ink"), Fan's "brush concepts" (*pi-i*), and Chang Seng-yu's "boneless" method (*mo-ku-fa*). In these excursions, he again illustrates his idea of "resemblance through non-resemblance." For example, he says that he used Chou's "thin and resilient" method (fig. 9), a linear approach which had been associated traditionally with Chou's near-legendary landscapes and figures. Tao-chi adapts the "thinness" and the "resilience" in a fundamental sense but introduces compositional innovations. Crispness and clarity prevail, with an unusual handling of space: two kinds of distances are presented, one focused down on the garden wall (set close to the picture plane to give the scene with its open cottage and seated scholar a sense of intimacy) and another focused up toward the luxuriant growth of tall and elegant trees (the different ranks of their height accentuated

9. Tao-chi, *Landscape after Chou Wen-chü*, ca. 1695, leaf A. Album of six leaves. Ink on paper. Collection unknown.

10. Tao-chi, *Landscape after Fan K'uan*, ca. 1695, leaf E. Album of six leaves. Ink on paper. Collection unknown.

by the distant mountains, which are lower than the treetops).

The literary reference to Fan K'uan's "brush concepts" (fig. 10) is too vague to trace. The significant expression of the landscape is remarkably close to the Sung, however, in its feeling of solidity and monumentality. Foreground, middle ground, and distant mountains are well-articulated. There is a strong sense of progression from the repoussoir-like boulders, to the well-placed cottages with scholars chatting, to the horizontal screen of mixed trees and the narrow path leading up into the mountains. The brushwork of this leaf is close in precision, tightness, and weight to the 1694 Los Angeles album and the 1696 *Sketches of Calligraphy and Painting by Ch'ing-hsiang* scroll, resemblances which help to date this album at about 1695.

Tao-chi's concept of "resemblance through non-resemblance" did not represent a haphazard aspect of his self-knowledge or a lack of ability to capture the likeness of physical forms. In his copy after Shen Chou (e.g., *XXVII* and others) he catches an astonishing likeness in both painting and calligraphy, testifying to a technical facility which he never allowed to become his master, even in his last years. Apart from direct copies after old masters, works in the Ni Tsan mode recur throughout his career. Tao-chi disavowed any intentional resemblance to Ni Tsan in several of his poems. One such disavowal is found on a painting dated 1702 (fig. 11):

My poetic feeling and painting methods are both quite innocent.
With pine and bamboo sparsely scattered, the meaning is
*   naturally deep.*
As joy approaches, the painting is finished, and
*   autumn thoughts grow distant,*
Then they all say again, "It looks like Ni Yün-lin![67]

Tao-chi wished the similarity between his work and the Yüan master's to be read as more than mere formal resemblance; he sought a deeper spiritual correspondence of expressive ideals and poetic vision. If this was his concept of *fang* ("to imitate"), it certainly differed in practice, if not in principle, from the orthodox masters. Thus Tao-chi showed little sustained interest in authenticity of a particular work or in the fidelity of an image or technique to a specific model. The works of the masters, like the natural landscape, constituted his inspirational wellspring and were but another means to achieve the *hsing* ("elation") which lay at the root of his expression.

Tao-chi's epilogue to his self-inscription on *Waterfall at Mt. Lu* (fig. 12) suggests the psychology operating in his appeal to ancient names. He mentions the paintings of Kuo Hsi, which he undoubtedly saw in Peking, and reiterates the notion that painting should represent a penetration of nature, not a mere repetition of form:

It has been said that "Kuo Ho-yang's painting was schooled in the Li Ch'eng method, and that he was able to capture clouds and vapor appearing and disappearing, and the stance of peaks and hills receding and emerging. He walked alone in his time. In his early years, his works were of fine and consummate skill; in his later years, he wielded the brush with increased virility and power."

In my lifetime I have seen over ten of Kuo Hsi's paintings, all of which were praised by most people. I alone had nothing to say, for I saw nothing which achieved a breakthrough with the "eye of the hand" [*t'ou-kuan shou-yen*].

Now I recall my earlier travels and, taking Li Po's poem, "A Song of Lu-shan: For the Censor Lu Hsü-chou," I have used my own method in combination with the Kuo Hsi styles I have seen so far. One may as well view this work as by Kuo Hsi, rather than relying on those from the past.[68]

Tao-chi was challenged, not overawed, by the works of the past;

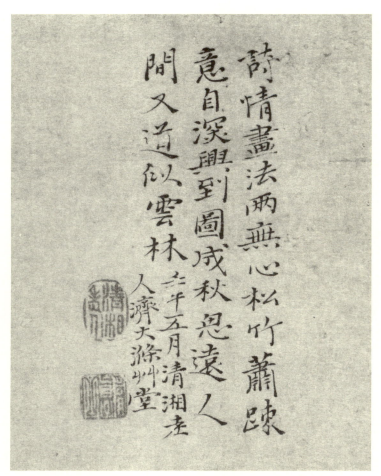

11. Tao-chi, *Landscape in Ni Tsan Style*, dated 1702, detail of self-inscription. Hanging scroll. Ink on paper. Ta-feng-t'ang collection.

13. Po-erh-tu, *Landscape with Self-Inscription*. Album leaf. Ink on paper. Collection unknown.

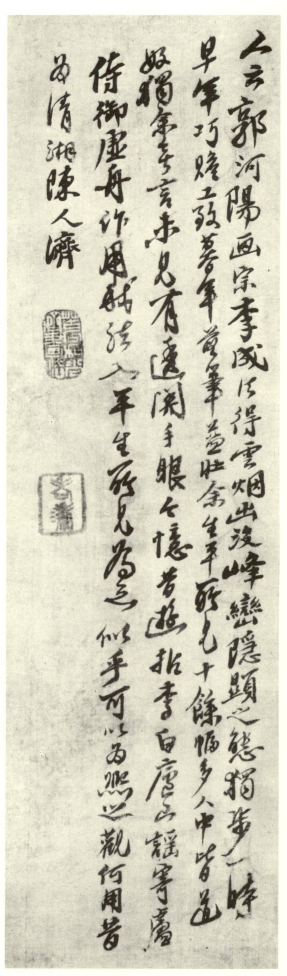

12. Tao-chi, *Waterfall at Mt. Lu*, ca. 1697, detail of self-inscription. Hanging scroll. Ink and color on silk. Sumitomo collection.

he placed himself on an equal footing with past masters and even felt that he could surpass them. His critical standard was not influenced by generations of praise, past conventions, or modes of seeing: he used his own eyes, and his assessment was based on his own understanding. He had eyes, ears, and a mind just as the ancients did, and was standing on the same creative plateau and was heir to the same powerful energies which fed his predecessors. In this lies the source of his "individuality." With a vision which fed directly on nature, he had utter confidence in his method (*wo-fa*). What he sought in painting, and what he felt the works of Kuo Hsi (or the ancients) which he had seen did not possess, was a pictorial revelation of the inner content of nature which broke through the surface of the work to the heart of the viewer.

Tao-chi in Peking

During Tao-chi's stay in Peking from late 1689 to the autumn of 1692, one important event was his friendship with the Manchu official Po-erh-tu, as noted earlier. Po was Tao-chi's "contact" in the capital and can be counted among his few understanding friends and contemporary admirers of his art. Tao-chi executed a number of close copies of works by well-known figure painters in Po's collection, such as *Hundred Beauties Competing in Loveliness*, by the Ming painter Ch'iu Ying, and *One Hundred Beauties*, by the T'ang painter Chou Fang. These titles sound enticing because there are few figure paintings by Tao-chi extant. Po apparently liked the version of the Ch'iu Ying so much that in 1701, when he sent the painting to be remounted in Yang-chou, he asked Tao-chi for a second inscription. In that inscription Tao-chi mentions having seen figure paintings by Chou Fang, Chao Meng-fu, and Ch'iu Ying in Po's collection, all of which he has greatly admired, and modestly apologizes for his own meager ability in figure painting. He seems also to have made copies of Sung tapestry designs in Po's collection.

Through Po's good offices Tao-chi was able to see some of the important private collections in Peking. One of the better known of these was that of Keng Chao-chung (1640–1686), whose major holdings of old paintings were apparently still intact in the early 1690's, although Keng had died a few years earlier. Tao-chi may also have viewed something of Chou Liang-kung's (1612–1672) possessions through the introduction of mutual friends, although there are no known references to such a fact.[69]

Po's painting style, while untutored in the traditional sense, bears the marks of cultivation and scholarly taste. A leaf from an album of landscapes[70] (fig. 13) shows him to be fluent in the literati style prevalent among late Ming and early Ch'ing painters like Li Liu-fang (1575–1629) and Ch'eng Chia-sui (1565–1643; see *V*). It has some of the directness and charm of Tao-chi and resembles his compositions in the slight diagonal balance and the use of layered washes to unify the parts.

Of the few surviving works Tao-chi is known to have executed for Po, one of his finest is a large hanging scroll, *Banana Plant in Rain*,[71] which bears a poetic inscription by the Manchu (fig. 14). Po's calligraphy, like his painting style, shows flair, restraint, and sensitivity, although it cannot be considered that of a master. Po's writing here agrees stylistically with his inscription on the landscape album and corroborates Tao-chi's execution of the painting. The painting is not dated, but the signature ("Ch'ing-hsiang Ch'en-jen, Ta-ti-tzu") and style place the work in Tao-chi's late Yang-chou

years. The marvelously wet feeling of the ink, its controlled blotches and suffusions, are close to the 1700 *Autumn Melon and Praying Mantis*, while the generously stroked bamboo leaves are closer to his mid-1700 depictions, such as *Bamboo, Vegetables, and Fruit* (XXXI). The date of the work is likely to be about 1700. Tao-chi's grading of the ink for the bamboo leaves is consistent with his desire to build complexities of form in space: broad, wet layers ranging from pale to dark are strengthened by carefree but structural delineation of veins. This visualization resembles his spatial layering of mountain peaks. The work forms a fitting complement in the "wet" style to the "dry" banana plant depictions in the ca. 1695 *Flowers and Figures* album (XX) and the ca. 1698 *Album of Flowers* (XXV).

Po-erh-tu was a friend to Tao-chi in more ways than as patron and confidant. His residence must have been the much-represented site of literary and artistic gatherings of those residing in the capital or from other cities in the empire who were the occasional guests of patrons of the arts. Through Po's influence and broad contacts we have two paintings of unusual significance: Tao-chi's collaborative works, each executed with the greatest painters of the day and chief exponents of orthodox painting, Wang Hui (1632–1717) (fig. 15) and Wang Yüan-ch'i (1642–1715) (fig. 16). We have no conclusive evidence that the painters met personally to execute the works, but it was surely Po's personality as catalyst which made them possible.[72] The three artists undoubtedly knew each other's paintings by reputation, through the collections of others, or through Po-erh-tu himself. Wang Yüan-ch'i said of Tao-chi: "I cannot know all of the painters in the country, but south of the Yangtze, one must recommend Shih-t'ao as the greatest. He has achieved aspects which both Shih-ku [Wang Hui] and I cannot attain."[73] This well-known statement may reflect Po-erh-tu's enthusiasm for Tao-chi as much as Wang Yüan-ch'i's astute eye. Po seems to have possessed an artistic foresight and a catholic taste unmatched by other collectors of his period. Furthermore, Wang Yüan-ch'i's comment did help to plant the seeds of appreciation for Tao-chi by later orthodox masters, such as two nineteenth-century painters in this collection, Ch'en Chao (1835–1884–; see XL) and Ku Yün (1835–1896; see XLI).

The painting done with Wang Hui contains a single strong stalk of bamboo with clumps of orchids scattered at three progressive levels. The feeling is spare and serene, with the paler tonalities of ink setting the mood. According to Tao-chi's inscription in the upper left, Po-erh-tu asked him to paint a work of this subject, leaving space for a "prominent painter" (*kao-jen*) to fill in the rock. Tao-chi first worked out the composition by placing the orchids in discreet positions which would allow his collaborator some freedom. He modestly describes his part as unfinished and "awaiting the adding of the eye," or significant expression (*tien-ching*). From this account it seems that he did not execute the painting in Wang Hui's presence. Indeed, it was not necessarily customary for collaborative efforts to be executed in succession, or even very close in time.

In the work executed with Wang Yüan-ch'i, dark thickets of bamboo are blown furiously by the wind. The feeling is of restlessness, and there is an auditory dimension of rustling leaves. Other than a few words of modest apology, Tao-chi gives no clue as to the circumstance of the execution. Of the two, *Bamboo in Wind* seems to be a more harmonious blending of styles of the collaborators. Tao-chi's three clumps of orchids are staggered in diagonal progression from dark to pale ink, and Wang Yüan-ch'i has extended this suggestion by emphasizing three stages of the ground plane. The rocky

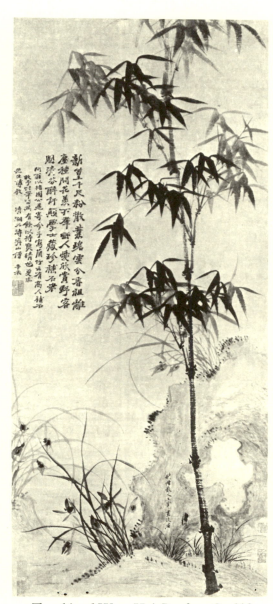

14. Tao-chi, *Banana Plant in Rain*, ca. 1700, with inscription by Po-erh-tu at bottom. Hanging scroll. Ink on paper. Ta-feng-t'ang collection.

15. Tao-chi and Wang Hui, *Bamboo, Orchid, and Rock*, dated 1691. Hanging scroll. Ink on paper. Tsi-lo-lou collection, Hong Kong.

16. Tao-chi and Wang Yüan-ch'i, *Bamboo in Wind*, dated 1691. Hanging scroll. Ink on paper. National Palace Museum, Taipei.

slopes and the bulky foreground boulders added by Wang reinforce the impression of density, substance, free movement, and depth in space. Wang Yüan-ch'i seems to have given much thought to the work. The fluffy, dry textures of the rocks are executed with quick lively movements of the brush; these compare well with Wang's dated works of the 1690's, before his style assumed the heavier, rod-like brushline of his works after 1700.[74]

By comparison, Wang Hui's contribution seems flatter, more screen-like, but we must concede its subtle conception. The horizon line of the rocky slope is lower and confined to a few undulations; this lower ground serves to unify the orchids and their direction in space. The base of the pierced rock is set on two levels of slope to meet the third clump of flowers. In the Wang Yüan-ch'i work the stalks grow upright with the leaves in motion; here the leaves are at rest, and the stalk and orchid slant in opposing directions. Wang Hui conceived of the rock, which leans to the right, as a balance to this tilting axis. One might have expected him to use a coarser brush and a freer conception to blend with the bamboo, but basically the *hsieh-i* spontaneous execution was not suited to his style. His dated works of the 1690's reveal a still supple brush and a preference for

the finer, more meticulous mode of Wang Meng suggested here, with its modeling strokes like "unravelled hemp."[75]

The difference in the artistic temperaments and brush habits of the two Wangs is certainly evident in this comparison and even in the signatures. Wang Yüan-ch'i signed his signature in the upper left corner with a simple "Lu-t'ai completed the slope and rocks," while Wang Hui identified his contribution in an even more modest manner on the base of the rock in small characters, "Ching-yen san-jen, Wang Hui, painted the slope and rock." Although the painting with Wang Yüan-ch'i is more striking for its crisp line and potential movement, the work with Wang Hui is a more serene and thoughtful arrangement of forms. Neither of these paintings can be considered as mature works of Tao-chi, but they are his earliest dated paintings extant in this genre. His bamboo improved with old age. The 1693–94 *Panoramic Vista*,[76] in twelve large panels of bamboo, flowers, and banana plants, is his early masterpiece in these genres and reveals the complexity and imaginative control which he could exert over this and related subjects, all of which culminates in the works of the late 1690's and early 1700's (e.g., *XX*, leaf B, *XXII*, leaf D, *XXIX*, and *XXXI*).

Bamboo and orchids were minor subjects for Tao-chi in comparison to his landscapes, but his style was not without influence. Cheng Hsieh (*tzu* Pan-ch'iao, 1693–1765), one of the Yang-chou Eccentrics, based his fame and style entirely on these two subjects as derived from Tao-chi. He once said: "I have tried with all my might to emulate [*fang*] Shih-t'ao. Slashing, smearing, lunging, dabbing—but whatever I do with my brush, I am still hemmed in by my own methods and cannot step beyond method [*fa*]. Alas, there is no way to match Master Shih."[77] Although Cheng was indebted to Tao-chi, he made his contribution to the history of ink bamboo by expanding certain of Tao-chi's minor stylistic preferences to suit his own temperament. A hanging scroll dated 1757 (fig. 17)[78] shows how he explored the flat, screen-like potential of rows of bamboo stalks. Indeed, stalks alone and their varying disposition in space seem to constitute his primary interest. His bamboo leaves are straighter and more angular than Tao-chi's, and he seems much less interested in tonal contrasts of ink. Cheng's integration of poetry and the calligraphic element in bamboo is another significant aspect of his style. The writing is thoroughly integrated into the design of the stalks, so that the columns or blocks of script form an inseparable part of the weight and balance of the spaces.

Despite Tao-chi's concentration on landscape, his output in minor genres was still sizeable and accounts for much of his influence on the later Yang-chou painters. In his late years (see *XXIX, XXXI,* and their related text figures) he attained the state of self-knowledge described in the Confucian maxim: "at seventy I could follow my heart's desire without transgression."[79] In artistic terms this meant that hand and heart worked in accord to realize his vision and that in a few strokes he could infuse bamboo and orchid with a spirit which could not be matched by his followers.

It was not until the nineteenth century that collectors and critics in other artistic centers and of more traditional artistic views recognized the merit of Tao-chi's works. Wang Yüan-ch'i was the first of his generation to institute such a trend. While he was undoubtedly speaking of the intuitive element in Tao-chi's works when he praised him in the comment quoted above, Tao-chi's possession of only that element would not have earned him such respect. The quotation implies that Wang was using the same yardstick of quality to measure Tao-chi's achievement by which he and Wang Hui measured their own. Thus it would seem that, by implication, he was recognizing Tao-chi's roots in the past and in the classic tradition out of which the Four Wangs themselves grew. These roots gave Tao-chi's paintings, as well as those of the Four Wangs, a power and grandeur generally lacking in those who repudiated that tradition.

TAO-CHI'S ART THEORIES

Tao-chi's greatness lies not only in his painting and calligraphy but also in his art theory. Several recent studies responding to the unprecedented nature of his treatise, the *Hua-yü-lu,* have examined the intricacies of its content from what is primarily a philosophical point of view.[80] These admirable dissertations are basically a-historical in orientation and give minor attention to Tao-chi's relationship to his contemporaries and to artistic tradition.[81] However, Tao-chi's art and theory very much reflect his era and the stage of development of art theory proper. The *Hua-yü-lu,* which puts equal stress on the spiritual and technical aspects of art, betrays its background

17. Cheng Hsieh, *Bamboo,* dated 1757. Hanging scroll. Ink on paper. Collection unknown.

in the late Ming and early Ch'ing, when both dimensions were believed to be attainable by means of rules and formulas.[82] As might be expected from these comments, the approach here is to supply what we felt has been lacking in Tao-chi studies thus far. We view Tao-chi primarily as a painter and theorist of painting (and not as a philosopher) and therefore draw not only on the contents of the *Hua-yü-lu* but on self-inscriptions, recorded colophons, and visual material as well. What follows is far from complete, but we believe it suggests a useful direction for more extensive studies.

The documentation available on Tao-chi's monastic life is so meager that one can only guess at the depth of his religious and philosophic thought through examining its influence on his art. His affiliations with the Lin-ch'i sect of Ch'an and his interest in Taoism are expressed profoundly in his paintings. He seems to have had no pretensions to the practice of Ch'an itself. As he once said, "I don't know how to explain Ch'an, and I don't expect alms; I merely sell landscapes which I have done at my leisure."[83] The metaphysical dimension in his art theories and his ideas about antiquity and the natural world seems to have been the product of the central role played by art in his life. One would also expect that his views about nature and man would be in tune with late Ming and early Ch'ing thought, for he was very much a product of his times, but that these views would be cultivated for their value to his activities as a painter. If we seek out his "mind" in his theories, then, it is very much the artistic mind and eye as an inseparable unit of perception which will best act as our key.

Tao-chi and Tung Ch'i-ch'ang

A statement frequently quoted as representative of Tao-chi's extreme individualism and defiance of tradition is this: "The beards and eyebrows of the ancients cannot grow on my face, nor can their lungs and bowels be placed in my body. I vent my own lungs and bowels and display my own beard and eyebrows" (*HYL*, 3, "Pien-hua").[84] By contrast, Tung Ch'i-ch'ang's position as fountainhead of orthodoxy and synthesizer of the past is often summed up in his comment, "painters ought to take the ancients as their teachers."[85] Limitation of our knowledge of Tao-chi's and Tung Ch'i-ch'ang's theories to statements of this nature would lead to an exaggeration of their respective positions in the "individualist" and "orthodox" modes—a labeling of Tao-chi as a renegade who tried to sever all ties with the past and Tung Ch'i-ch'ang as a slavish imitator of ancient works.

If we go beyond such summary statements we find, for example, that it was not Tung Ch'i-ch'ang's ultimate aim merely to imitate the ancients; on the contrary, he sought a spiritual correspondence (*shen-hui*) with their minds through a process of metamorphosis or "fermentation" of the principles and methods which they had developed (*wen-jang ku-fa*).[86] The concept of metamorphosis or transformation (*pien*) of one's models was a fundamental and explicitly stated thesis of Tung's: "Those who study the ancients and cannot transform them may just as well be considered trash" (*li-tu-chien-wu*; literally, "garbage outside the fence").[87] Transformation meant a form of self-realization in which the vital forces motivating past models were assimilated and, in the process, one's own artistic cultivation raised to the level wherein it reflected, as in a mirror, that of the ancients.

Inherent in this transformation was the spiritual discipline which accompanies calligraphic training. In the traditional emulation of a calligraphic model, the student sought, through successive periods of technical application and through intuitive understanding, to free himself from close imitation of the form and to reflect the inner spirit and psychic energies of the master. This spiritual equivalence constituted a form of communion with the past which eventually freed the student from the established artistic forms and also nurtured an increased level of self-knowledge on his part. Thus for Tung Ch'i-ch'ang the process of transformation was based on a summary of historical styles involving both form and spirit and on a mastery of the principles of nature. As he said, "To maintain methods [of the past] without transformation is equivalent to being a slave of calligraphy" (*shou-fa pu-pien, chi-wei shu-chia-nu-erh*).[88] As a means of self-realization, however, it was limited by the will and artistic gifts of its practitioner. Spiritual correspondence meant attainment of a realm of psychic freedom in which the forms created with brush and ink are uniquely one's own, for only the spirit of "he who has established his own style can be transmitted" (*ch'i-k'o ch'uan-che tzu-ch'eng i-chia*). "Copying and imitating are quite easy; it is spiritual communication which is difficult to transmit" (*lin-mo tsui-i, shen-hui nan-ch'uan*).[89] Thus while imitation of the

great masters of the past was historical in its orientation, the quest for spiritual correspondence in essence was a-historical because its goal was the uniting of one's mind with that of the ancients to become their spiritual contemporary.

The issues of imitation, transformation, spiritual correspondence, and individual style which were so potent in Tung's generation and which figure so prominently in his thought were by no means dead when Tao-chi was beginning his career. The frequency and seriousness with which he mentions them indicate not only that he was very much influenced by Tung (whether he was aware of it or not, for he seems not to have mentioned Tung's name) but also that they were aesthetic concerns of fundamental importance to an artist attempting to come to terms with his tradition.

Little material dated before the 1680's is available to trace the emergence of the theoretical dimension in Tao-chi's art. However, by 1682, and especially in the decade of the 1690's, the conflict between his awareness of himself as an individual and the accumulated burden of tradition was voiced in increasingly verbal and polemical form. For example, the last leaf of the 1691 *Album of Landscapes* in the Sakuragi collection contains one of the most penetrating analyses of his artistic position found on an extant work.[90] Similar ideas are expressed here and there in other self-inscriptions and colophons (both recorded and found on extant works). The *Hua-yü-lu* presents them in a more synthetic and systematic form.

As can be seen from the previous quotations in the discussion of Tao-chi's calligraphy and painting, his attitude toward the past and to copying was one of creative challenge. He wrote on leaf F of the 1703 album in the Boston Museum, "The ancients were masters of one style; nevertheless, their copying encompassed many styles; otherwise how could they have fathomed the sources of various principles?" The goal was "to transcend antiquity in its concrete manifestation" (*chü-ku i-hua*); the past served only to "break ground for the present" (*chieh-ku k'ai-chin*; *HYL* 3, "Pien-hua"). The implication of "transcendence" (*hua*) was more crucial for him than that of mere "change" or "transformation" (*pien*). He conceived of the past in these terms but also in terms of the master-slave analogy which Tung Ch'i-ch'ang had also used. Transcendence meant mastery of all principles of creation, liberating one to establish one's own method (i.e., *liao-fa*). Thus in the *Hua-yü-lu* the second crucial chapter after that of his fundamental *i-hua* is that of *liao-fa*: "To master and be freed of any fixed method." Without this mastery, one is merely in the employ of someone (*shih-wo wei-mou-chia-i*; *HYL* 3, "Pien-hua"), which to Tao-chi was equivalent to being a slave or eating someone's "leftover stew" (*ts'an-keng*). With a command of the past and the present, one can attain that state of artistic freedom and self-knowledge which means that one has "established one's own style" (*ch'uan-chu ku-chin, tzu-ch'eng i-chia*; *HYL* 7, "Yin-yün").

Tao-chi and His Contemporaries

In the late Ming and early Ch'ing new forms of pictorial expression began to spring up alongside the orthodox styles, creating a climate of great artistic diversity. In a long self-inscription on a leaf from the 1694 Los Angeles album (fig. 18), Tao-chi bears witness to many of these new developments:

Those who enter through the ordinary gate to reach the *Tao* of painting are nothing special [literally, "not family treasures"]. But to achieve resounding fame for a time—isn't that difficult to accomplish? For example, the lofty antiquity [*kao-ku*] of the works of gentlemen like Pai-t'u [K'un-ts'an, 1612–ca. 1686], Ch'ing-hsi [Ch'eng Cheng-k'uei, fl. ca. 1630–ca. 1688], and Tao-shan [Ch'en Shu, fl. ca. 1649–ca. 1687]; the pure elusiveness [*ch'ing-i*] of Mei-ho [Cha Shih-piao, 1615–1698] and Chien-chiang [Hung-jen, 1610–1663]; the parched leanness [*kan-shou*] of Kou-tao-jen [Ch'eng Sui, fl. ca. 1650–1691]; the drenched moistness [*lin-li*] and rare antiquity [*ch'i-ku*] of Pa-ta shan-jen [1626–ca. 1705] from Nan-ch'ang; or the untrammeled expressiveness [*hao-fang*] of Mei [Ch'ing] Ch'ü-shan [1623–1697] and [his brother, Mei Keng] Hsüeh-p'ing-tzu [fl. ca. 1681–1706]. Of a generation these were all the ones who understood [*chieh-jen*]! Only I cannot comprehend the idea of painting. Therefore my works are empty and hollow, dull and mute like this.

This passage contains at least three notable points. First, nearly all the painters mentioned by Tao-chi in this inscription are older contemporaries, and he shows an unusual measure of critical generosity toward them. This respect is more than the polite deference ordinarily given one's seniors, and it reflects his genuine admiration of their artistic accomplishments and personal character. Tao-chi is known to have had some direct contact either with them or with their works at some time when he was in Hsüan-ch'eng and Nanking. Second, in this inscription Tao-chi actually names the artistic personalities whom he admired and who guided him. Such information is rare in his extant work. Equally unusual is the deprecation of his own talent, an admission which underlines his admiration of these masters. Third, the critical phraseology which he uses here focuses on the expressive qualities *kao-ku*, *ch'ing-i*, *kan-shou*, *lin-li*, and *hao-fang*. *Kao-ku*, *ch'ing-i*, and *hao-fang* are terms from traditional poetics which had found their way into painting criticism,[91] but *lin-li* and *kan-shou* in this context pertain strictly to brushwork and describe the formal and expressive effects of the ink proper.

What is of special interest to the historian of art theory is that such effects are ranked alongside the classic appraisals *kao-ku*, *ch'ing-i*, and *hao-fang*. The admiration of the "parched" and "lean"

is especially significant, for its appearance as an ideal in art criticism is entirely new. Its stylistic validity was first asserted visually in the works of the Anhwei painters, some of whom are mentioned by Tao-chi, and although he applies it only to Ch'eng Sui (see *XVII*, fig. 3), he could also have mentioned Tai Pen-hsiao (1621–1691; see *XVII*, fig. 2) and Ch'en Shu (fig. 19). Moreover, *kan-shou* was one of the pictorial and poetic qualities particularly marked in Tao-chi's early style, indicating his fundamental formal kinship with the Anhwei group. His style can also be related to the works of late Ming painters in other regions such as Nanking or even the Wu area. Cha Shih-piao (cf. *XIV*), whom Tao-chi praises for "pure elusiveness," and Ch'en Shu both flourished around Nanking, and another master working in that area with whom he may have been sympathetic in temperament is Hu Yü-k'un. Even some of the freer and more imaginative aspects of Shao Mi's work prefigure Tao-chi.[92] Other than the knowledgeable ones mentioned in the inscription, however, formal resemblances in his work to these other painters probably reflect the interconnection of period style, as there is no evidence that he ever saw the work of Hu or Shao.

One other concept which must be stressed is *lin-li*, which implies not merely saturation or moistness but a drenched, dripping-wet feeling of the ink. Tao-chi praises Chu Ta in this regard. *Lin-li* also characterizes his own remarkable expressiveness in ink and color washes, which, along with *kan-shou*, became prominent in his late Yang-chou style. Tao-chi's contemporaries also mention Hsü Wei (1521–1593) as his spiritual equal (see *XX*, colophon to leaf B). In their transcendence of particular schools or traditions and in their free exploration of the possibilities of wet ink as a describer of form, the works of Hsü and Chu well define the *lin-li* concept. Their stylistic breakthrough, however, was achieved by the force of genius, as the technique of wet descriptive wash was basic to many painters. Tao-chi drew upon the precedents set by their expressive freedom and formal ink innovations as much as he did the approaches of the Anhwei and Nanking masters.

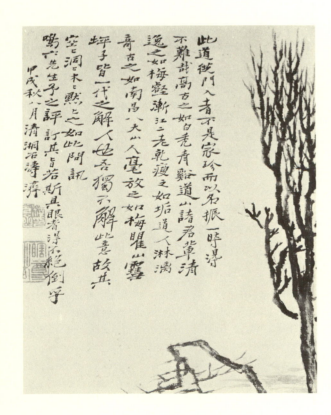

18 (*left*). Tao-chi, *Old Trees for Ming-liu*, dated 1694, detail of leaf E. Album of eight leaves. Ink on paper. Los Angeles County Museum of Art.

19 (*above*). Ch'en Shu (fl. ca. 1649–ca. 1687), *Old Tree by Waterfall*, leaf B. Album of three leaves. Ink on paper. Collection unknown.

During this period, technical and stylistic innovations such as these were gradually inducing changes in critical attitudes and aesthetic tastes. The descriptive vocabulary of critics and artists reflected these trends. Those changes which became part of the prevailing visual and critical framework were no doubt dismissed as marginal and extreme by many conservatives of the day, but Tao-chi accepted and expanded upon them, just as he absorbed and adapted technical and expressive modes of the older contemporaries mentioned above. For example, the qualities of "drenched moistness" and "parched leanness," "lofty antiquity" and "pure elusiveness" are all present in his own works. This breadth was to provide the essential substance of his later works. By synthesizing those expressive qualities he admired from many masters and schools, he indeed transcended those whom he praised.

Tao-chi elsewhere is unremitting in his criticism of modern as well as ancient painters. He judged the works of others by the same aesthetic criteria which he maintained for himself, and criticism directed at others was very much self-criticism as well. Praise of the kind showered on the painters named in this album inscription is therefore not only rare but of great interest for the insight into his own standards which it provides.

His judgments of his contemporaries are consistent with those of ancient masters. For example, in an inscription from an album dated 1682 (fig. 20) he attacks the early Ch'ing painters from Yün-chien (i.e., Hua-t'ing or Sung-chiang): "The brushwork must be parched

20. Tao-chi, *Village among Green Willows*, dated 1682, leaf C. Album of ten leaves. Ink on paper. Ta-feng-t'ang collection.

[*k'u*] in order to be refined. If the brushwork is too wet [*shih*, "slick"], it borders on vulgarity. Nowadays the handling of brush and ink of the Yün-chien [painters] all has this fault." [93] It is notable that Tao-chi made this statement at a time when his own style was characterized by the dry scrubbed brushline. As indicated above, the targets of his criticism were not the late Ming painters of that region, among them Tung Ch'i-ch'ang, but those early Ch'ing followers who had developed and exaggerated but one aspect of Tung's style.

Another attack on the parochialism of painters from other regions is found in an inscription dated 1699:

Nowadays it doesn't matter whether the painters are from the "san-Wu" area [Lake T'ai] or from the "Liang-Che" area [East and West Chekiang]; from Chiang-Ch'u [Kiangsi and Hunan], Kwangtung, or Kwangsi; the areas around Nan-tu-Ch'in-huai [Nanking], Hui-[chou], Hsüan [ch'eng] [Huang-shan], or the Huai-hai [Yang-chou] belt. After a while painters from these places will settle into the vulgar habits [*hsi-ch'i*] of their respective regions. This is because they seldom have seen many truly genuine paintings by ancient masters. What they have seen are all forgeries, or if they happen to see any genuine ones, they are unable to understand what they see. [94]

The phrase *hsi-ch'i*, meaning vulgar or of bad habits, is a pejorative term which one finds frequently in Tung Ch'i-ch'ang's writings as well. The connotation in Tao-chi's inscription is linked to "after a while," implying that it is the followers falling into formalized ruts who are at fault. Of historical interest is Tao-chi's informative listing of what he considered the various centers of painting in the early Ch'ing. Presumably, these were the modern painters (*chin t'ien-hsia hua-shih*) who are being accused here (as they were later, in his 1703 landscape album in Boston) of "imitating the footprints" rather than the "heart" of their models (see fig. 22 below).

Tao-chi's assault on contemporary painters became vehement in the following inscription, in which he describes what he believes to be the sources of creative power:

Nowadays those who dabble with brush and ink invariably have never set their eyes on famous mountains or great rivers; they have never lived in a lonely cottage deep in the mountains, stepped more than a hundred *li* beyond the city gates, or sat quietly in a room for more than half a year. Their friends are rowdy and excessive drinkers, and they buy brand-new antiques. The "eye" of the understanding of all principles [*tao-yen*] is not clear to them, so how can they detect undisciplined and vulgar habits? If they comment on a work of their contemporaries, saying, "This is the brushwork of so-and-so's school," it is like a blind man reporting to another blind man or an ugly woman harping on the ugliness of another ugly woman. That is called appreciation and connoisseurship! [95]

This inscription, dated 1691, was probably written during Tao-chi's stay in Peking. He criticizes the painters for their superficial attitudes toward the past, which constitutes their own heritage, and their insensitivity toward the natural world, which forms their immediate sensory environment. He understood traversing mountains and streams as a broadening of the inner horizon. The same principle was articulated by Tung Ch'i-ch'ang: "to walk ten thousand miles and to read ten thousand books" (*hsing wan-li-lu, tu wan-chüan-shu*). [96] For Tao-chi the appreciation of antiquities represented an attempt to enter the minds of the ancients and to apprehend their formal creative principles. Here the idea of *tao-yen* is a key one. Like other phrases involving the concept of *yen* ("eye," e.g., *hsin-yen shou-yen*), it denotes the intuitive mind and its ability to cut through external, concrete appearances to the inner core and nature of all things.[97]

Tao-chi's Art Theories and Antiquity

Tung Ch'i-ch'ang was quoted earlier as saying, "painters ought to follow the ancients as their teachers." The complete text reads: "to advance further one ought to follow nature as one's teacher; as rising at dawn to view the vision of changing clouds and mists—this can be drawn into the tip of one's brush."[98] Tung professed to draw strength from nature, and in this respect his thought coincides with Tao-chi's. In the "mountains and rivers" chapter of the *Hua-yü-lu* (*HYL* 8, "Shan-ch'uan") we find: "mountains and rivers compel me to speak for them: the mountains and rivers are transformed [*t'uo-t'ai*] through me, and I am transformed through them. Therefore I design my paintings around all the extraordinary peaks which I have sought out."

Despite these ostensible similarities in the views of the two artists toward nature, however, we must recognize two important underlying differences. Tung Ch'i-ch'ang's views of nature were derived from his exhaustive studies of antiquity: he was not only an art collector of stature but also a historian. We might say that Tung's thought was based in history and was liberated by nature. He saw the natural landscape in terms of the paintings and the historical modes established by the ancient masters. "I once sailed on Lake Tung-t'ing," he wrote: "when I opened the canopy of my boat and looked far beyond, the scene was just like one of the ink plays of the Mi family method."[99] Tao-chi would say, "when the spirit of the rivers and mountains meets with my spirit, both their images are transfigured into one, so that in the end, everything leads back to Ta-ti [Tao-chi]" (*HYL* 8, "Shan-ch'uan"). In contrast with Tung, then, Tao-chi's artistic thought was based in nature and was liberated by antiquity. Tao-chi did not see nature through the stylistic lens of an ancient master; his experience of it was direct, intuitive, and undeniably mystical. He submitted his whole being to and identified himself with the forces of nature (*shan-ch'uan t'uo-t'ai yü-wo*) and therefore felt able "to speak for them." No intermediary in the form of an ancient mode was needed.

This merging of the painter's consciousness with the depicted object was not only a source of Tao-chi's creative power but was part of his psychic state during the creative act of painting. In literary sources this attitude can be traced back at least to the Sung, when we find Su Shih observing Wen T'ung painting and recording Wen's experience in this well-known poem:

> When Yü-k'o painted bamboo,
> He saw bamboo only, never people. . . .
> He himself became bamboo,
> Putting out fresh growth endlessly.[100]

For Tao-chi and Tung Ch'i-chang, like the great masters before them, the creative act was a form of self-realization. Their writings reveal their preoccupation with artistic concerns, with the clarity of mind, elation, and intuitive understanding achieved during the aesthetic experience. Yet the major artistic goals of both masters were still framed within the aesthetic values of the established artistic tradition and focused on issues which trace back to the T'ang and Sung. Transformation of one's models, for example, was a crucial issue and

was related to the requisite qualification for greatness—achievement of one's own stylistic identity. In the past this was invariably achieved through a process of synthesizing and reconstructing past models. For example, the phrase "to establish one's own style" (*tzu-ch'eng i-chia*) implies a high degree of self-awareness and a form of individualism. As such, it recurs conspicuously in the writings of the great masters within this tradition. Although this sense of self or individualism did not become widespread in Chinese thought until the sixteenth and seventeenth centuries,[101] it was fundamental to the creative integrity of earlier artists as members of an elite. For, in a sense, this individualism presupposes that the painter, poet, or calligrapher asserts stylistic qualities which set him apart from his predecessors and contemporaries. While the sense of urgency in Tao-chi's individualism was in part a function of late Ming humanism, the view of artistic identity he held still had much in common with the formulations of the T'ang and Sung masters. Basically, the sense of being challenged to rise above one's tradition to create a unique and memorable style was a necessary response to the renewal of the tradition. It was therefore not exclusive to any one generation of artists but was the right of each artist who was to achieve stature.

This sense of self was especially prominent in the writings of the Sung literati. Huang T'ing-chien (1045–1105) once said, "follow someone else in one's designs and one will always be after someone; but to establish one's own style—that is the ultimately true goal," and again, "to achieve one's own individual style is not in the least regrettable."[102] Compare this statement with one by Mi Fu (1051–1107): "By following and imitating others, one can only become a man of the past. To achieve one's own individual style—that is the ultimately true goal."[103] Su Shih (1036–1101), the elder of these great Sung masters, described Ou-yang Hsiu's (1007–1072) calligraphy as "a script which is fresh and gracious and which achieves its own style."[104]

The painter Kuo Hsi (fl. ca. 1060–1075), in his treatise on landscape, *Lin-ch'üan kao-chih*, went a step farther in pointing out that this philosophy was found in a specific social class and breed of man: "High officials and prominent scholars do not limit [their training to] one master. [For that reason] they have achieved their own individual style."[105] Probably the earliest articulation of this idea by a painter was that of the Five Dynasties painter Ching Hao: "I have distilled the merits of both masters and thereby have achieved a single unique style."[106]

On this subject Tao-chi quotes an even earlier master, the Six Dynasties calligrapher Chang Jung. An inscription dated 1686 is found on a work executed earlier in Hsüan-ch'eng (fig. 21): "In painting, there are the Northern and Southern Schools, and in calligraphy, the methods of the two Wangs. Chang Jung once said: 'I don't regret not having the methods of the two Wangs, but regret the two Wangs not having my method.' Now if it is asked, did I learn from the Northern or the Southern School, or did they learn from me? Holding my belly laughing, I would reply: I naturally use my own methods [*wo-tzu-yung wo-fa*]."[107] Tao-chi's reply, "I use my own methods," parallels the meaning of *tzu-ch'eng i-chia*. He adopted Chang's phrase as a kind of slogan, quoting the words more than once and using it to reinforce his not really unprecedented *wo-fa* ("my methods"). Chang Jung's reference to the Two Wangs had been well known since the Sung dynasty and even at that time may have come to represent a kind of individualists' credo. Su Shih also quotes it in praise of Huang T'ing-chien's calligraphy in "cursive" style.[108]

The figure contains Chinese calligraphic inscriptions.

21. Tao-chi, *View of Huang-shan*, dated 1667: (*top left*) self-inscription dated 1687; (*top right*) undated inscription by T'ang Yen-sheng (fl. ca. 1650–1670); (*center*) self-inscription dated 1686. Hanging scroll. Ink on paper. Collection unknown.

The statement by Tao-chi with which this discussion opened occurs significantly in "Transformations," chapter 3 of the *Hua-yü-lu*, and reveals his unshakeable conviction:

I am what I am because I have an existence of my own. The beards and eyebrows of the ancients cannot grow on my face, nor can their lungs and bowels be placed in my body. I vent my own lungs and bowels and display my own beard and eyebrows. Though on occasion my painting may happen to resemble that of so-and-so, it is he who resembles me, and not I who willfully imitate his style. It is naturally so! When indeed have I ever studied past masters and not transformed them!

The awareness of self through the attainment of a unique style has been present in individual calligraphers and painters ever since their awareness of *fa* ("method") itself, long before its tardy recognition by critics.

The concept of *tzu-ch'eng i-chia* can be considered as a summation of the personal crises of an artist during a good part of his formative period, for implicit in the phrase is the sense of internal struggle and process which gives a sense of depth and substance to the artistic personality. In Tao-chi's case, his indomitable sense of self was nourished by the rising current of individualism in late Ming thinkers which, joining forces with his basic orientation, further reinforced these effects on his development. What seems new in the Ming is the sense of the urgency of this quest for self-knowledge. The leader of the anti-revivalist Kung-an literary movement, Yüan Hung-tao (1568–1610), who was also a friend of Tung Ch'i-ch'ang, demonstrated this unwavering sense of ego in his statement, "My face can't resemble your face; how then could it resemble the faces of the ancients?"[109] An earlier freethinker, Li Chih (1527–1602), the central figure in the *k'uang-ch'an* ("wild Ch'an") movement who also was greatly admired by Tung Ch'i-ch'ang, wrote: "Heaven gave life to man and each by nature has his own contribution [*i-jen chih-yung*]. He need not wait to receive something from Confucius to be complete. If he had to receive something from Confucius to be complete, then several thousand ages ago when there was no Confucius was there no one who could be considered complete?"[110] This tension between the present and the past was acutely felt by Tao-chi. He describes it as a kind of yoke, enslaving those who fail to assert their own freedom. In an important inscription dated 1703 (fig. 22) he says: "Before the ancients established method, we don't know what method they pursued. After man established method, they didn't allow modern man to proceed beyond ancient methods. Therefore hundreds and thousands of years later modern man has not been allowed to distinguish himself."[111]

If the works of the ancients could leave the historical continuum and become a part of the present and if the natural world could become a part of one's artistic sensibilities, then from these outer circles of awareness one's search for the self ultimately withdrew to the innermost vital transforming agent—the heart or mind (*hsin*). While there are occasional references to *li* (inherent principles or rationality), by far the predominant concept in Tao-chi's art theories is that of *hsin*: it meant both the rational and the affective capacities (*ch'ing*, feelings or emotions, is mentioned less often). He says quite simply, "As to painting, it is an expression of the heart." This fundamental declaration is found in the first chapter, "I-hua," of the *Hua-yü-lu*. Thus Tao-chi's metaphysical orientation was monistic, and his basic attitude reflected the current "doctrine of the mind" (*wei-hsin-lun*).

This monistic orientation as an ideology can be traced to the Sung

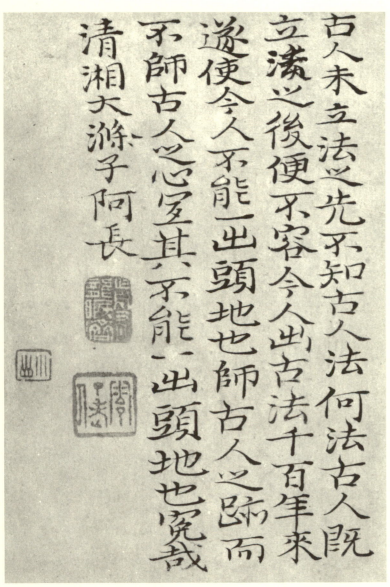

古人未立法之先不知古人法何法古人既
立法之後便不容令人出古法千百年来
遂使令人不能一出頭地也師古人之跡而
不師古人之心宜其不能一出頭地也冤哉
清湘大滌子阿長

22. Tao-chi, *Twelve-Leaf Album of Landscapes*, dated 1703, leaf I, detail of self-inscription. Ink and color on paper. Museum of Fine Arts, Boston.

thinkers Lu Hsiang-shan (1139–1192) and Ch'eng Hao (1032–1085), but as an expression of their literary culture and basic cultivation scholars much earlier than the Sung had engaged in such activities as poetry and calligraphy, which stimulated penetrating and prolonged contact with other great minds and with nature. Such activities led to contemplation of the natural forces and principles inherent in the perceptual world and to reflection on the role of the mind in the creative process. This analytic tendency was no doubt encouraged by their interest in Ch'an Buddhism. By the Sung, painting could rank as one of the creative activities of scholars, and an interest in the mind reflected an introspection which was already basic to the aesthetic tradition. Painters also had an opportunity to formulate their own expression of the role of mind in the creative process, and in this sense they parallel other thinkers, but the value of their pronouncements lies in their articulation of the role of the mind in its relationship to the painting process itself.

In this context Tao-chi's analysis should not come as a surprise: "the painting is the recipient of the ink, the ink of the brush, the brush of the wrist, and the wrist of the heart" (*HYL* 4, "Tsun-shou"). This, in essence, is an amplification of Huang T'ing-chien's observation that "the mind directs the wrist, and the wrist operates the brush."[112] Hence apart from its immediate intellectual origins in

the late Ming and the towering influence of Wang Yang-ming and the followers of the T'ai-chou school, the role of mind had been a central issue in the writings of painters and calligraphers before Tao-chi's day. They too were interested in the psychological implications of their own activity and had begun to develop their own historical tradition of thought on the subject. Keen observers of nature and of their own minds, painters were bound to notice the mechanics of perception quite early in their quest for self-knowledge. Their statements may seem to us clumsily formulated and less systematically pursued than those of writers whose speculations fall in the realm of pure theory, but we may recognize in them a lively interest in the processes of perception and its relation to their creative life. For example, Shen Chou (1427–1509) said: "The memorable aspects of landscape are grasped by the eye and lodged in the recesses of the mind [*hsin*]. Yet what is given form by brush and ink is nothing but my elation [*hsing*]."[113] He also felt that painting was a manifestation of the inner workings of the mind. Here the feelings (heart) and the intellect (mind) are important dual connotations of *hsin*. His *hsing* is in harmony with Tao-chi's *t'ao-yung yü-wo* (*HYL* 3, "Pien-hua"), his state of joy while painting: "Employing brush and ink to write out the myriad things of heaven and earth makes my heart feel joyous."

The late Yüan painter Wang Lü (1332–1383-) anticipated Shen Chou's analysis of the perceptual process in a preface to a lengthy album painting of forty-two leaves depicting the scenery of Mt. Hua, in which he said: "I learn from my mind [*shih-hsin*], my mind learns from my eyes [*shih-mu*], and my eyes learn from Mt. Hua."[114] This description accords so well with Tao-chi's experience of scenic natural sites, especially those of Mt. Huang, that he could almost have said: "I learn from my heart, my heart learns from my eyes, and my eyes learn from Mt. Huang." The idea of learning from the mind or heart goes back directly to the Sung scholars Su Shih, Mi Fu, and even to such a marginal scholar-painter as Fan K'uan. A contemporary Sung record contains this account: "at first he [Fan K'uan] studied Li Ch'eng; then, after having been enlightened, he sighed and reflected, 'there has never been an instance when the ancients did not select their method from the world of objects [or nature], so instead of taking man as my teacher, I'd rather learn from nature. [But if a further choice could be made], instead of learning from nature, I'd rather learn from my own heart.'"[115]

Mi Fu, however, advanced from mere preference to the establishment of levels of superiority and, in so doing, focused on the more complex issue of subject matter and its relation to inner spirit, as opposed to external likeness, which also interested Su Shih. Mi said: "Likeness of subjects such as oxen, horses, and human beings can be gotten by imitation [*mo*]. But landscape painting cannot be achieved [by this method]. Landscape [painting] is a creation of the mind [*hsin-chiang*] and is intrinsically a superior art."[116] Unlike Fan's subjective statement, Mi's is a critical one. Besides pointing out the issue of "form-likeness" and "spirit-resonance," he reminds us that painting is an intellectual activity and a form of self-cultivation. He implies that the act of painting landscape is an inner experience and that, in addition to choice of subject matter, its success or failure depends on the artist's degree of personal cultivation. A contemporary of Mi's, Chao Pu-chih (1053–1110), inscribed a colophon to one of Tung Yüan's paintings with a similar thought: "thus we know that formerly the men of wisdom learned from their minds [*shih-hsin*] and did not tread in the path of [physical] likeness."[117] Tao-chi's own statement on this subject, again found on leaf I of the Boston album, is quite explicit: "They [modern painters] follow in the footsteps of the ancients, rather than learning from their hearts. No wonder they cannot achieve any distinction." In other words, he was reiterating the famous rule of the T'ang master Chang Tsao: "Externally learn from nature [*wai shih tsao-hua*]. Internally grasp its origin in the heart [*chung te hsin-yüan*]." [118] Thus the concepts of "individuality" and "mind" had their own history in the theory and practice of painters and calligraphers, and this history extended as far back as the T'ang.

Tao-chi's link with tradition also involves the relationship between calligraphy and painting, and his understanding agrees with the pronouncements of several great masters who had achieved distinction in both arts. In a record of one of his inscriptions, we find the statement: "the ancients said: in painting one ought to employ the *ts'ao* [cursive] and *li* [clerical] scripts as methods of execution. Trees [may be painted] like twisted iron rods and mountains as if drawing in the sand. To eliminate completely the sweet vulgarity of common models—that is the scholarly spirit [*shih-ch'i*]." [119] This passage is clearly derived from the following statement by Tung Ch'i-ch'ang: "when the scholar executes a painting, he ought to employ the [calligraphic] methods of the *ts'ao, li,* and *ch'i-tzu* scripts. Trees [may be painted] like twisted iron rods, and mountains as if drawing in the sand. To eliminate completely the sweet vulgarity of common models—that is the scholarly spirit." [120]

Another idea Tung stressed in his theory of scholar painting which was adopted by Tao-chi in his writings is that calligraphy is the foundation of painting and that their common origin is all-important. Tung said: "he who excels in calligraphy should excel in painting; and he who excels in painting ought also to excel in calligraphy, for actually the two are one and the same!" [121] Tao-chi devotes a chapter of the *Hua-yü-lu*, "The Equal Mastery of Calligraphy," to these concepts. He says that "calligraphy and painting are different in form, but in achievement, they are one" (*tzu-yü-hua-che, ch'i-chu liang-tuan, ch'i kung i-t'i*; *HYL* 17, "Chien-tzu").

He then articulates the specific ways in which he has combined the practices of calligraphy and painting: "The ancients combined the 'eight principles' [of calligraphy] with the 'six principles' [of painting] to create methods of painting. Therefore my brush outlines are sometimes like 'running' script, 'standard', or 'seal' scripts, sometimes like 'cursive', 'clerical', or other methods." [122] He was not only aware of the diversity of his painting and writing styles but consciously sought such variety. His calligraphic and painting styles reveal his mercurial range and metamorphic abilities and show that his formulations were living principles based on experience.

Painters before Tao-chi and Tung Ch'i-ch'ang had long been aware of the nature and implications of the common origin of writing and painting. In the Yüan, Huang Kung-wang's *Hsieh Shan-shui-chüeh* (*The Secrets of Landscape Painting*) noted, "in painting landscapes one's methods respond to the needs of the moment. . . . The same holds true in writing: practice makes perfect." [123] Earlier Chao Meng-fu (1254–1322) had actively extended calligraphic theory and practice to painting and thereby set the course of Yüan painting: "Executing bamboo involves the same methods as the 'eight principles' of calligraphy. . . . To follow this is to know that the principles of calligraphy and painting were originally the same." [124] Kuo Hsi, in the chapter "Secrets of Painting" of his *Lin-ch'uan kao-chih*, well understood the unity of the two disciplines: "The methods of calligraphy . . . are precisely the same as the theory

of brushwork in painting. For this reason most people say that those who excel in calligraphy invariably excel in painting. This is because, in both cases the brushwork requires a nimble wrist" (i.e., the wrist is turned and the brush moves without restraint). [125] The importance of the nimble wrist is not only that it is lifted off the paper but that its action is spontaneously controlled. Power and control issue not only from the arm and shoulder but often from the soles of the feet and involve the painter's entire stance. Tao-chi devoted another chapter (*HYL* 6, "Yün-wan"), "On Wrist Motion," to this concept.

In the *Hua-yü-lu*, Tao-chi's lengthy discussion of technique (chs. 5 through 14) constitutes about half of his total treatise and reflects the sixteenth- and seventeenth-century interest in the mastery of technical principles as means to achieve the spiritual in a work, an approach unthinkable in the Sung. In the Yüan such interests surface unsystematically and survive only in such fragments as Huang Kung-wang's notes. By the Ming and the Ch'ing the increase in critical and technical treatises on art by painters and scholars reveals the intensity of interest that could culminate in such a figure as Tung Ch'i-ch'ang.

Tao-chi's "Great Synthesis"

One can see that Tao-chi's theories on art are firmly in the mainstream of the scholar-painting tradition. This tradition has its own history, and many of its concepts did not necessarily coincide chronologically with the intellectual currents of the time. Much of it arose out of primarily artistic and aesthetic concerns which were later given authority through the personality of Tung Ch'i-ch'ang, who figures prominently as the most immediate influence on Tao-chi's art theory. However, poets and painters like Su Shih and Kuo Hsi were close spiritual compatriots of Tao-chi, and their ideas on the creative process and the intuitive mind, among many others, also found their way into his thought. This mainstream and the intellectual trends of the time intensified Tao-chi's intuitionist tendencies and his search for artistic identity, developing in him the sense of independence which made him as much a product of the intellectual scene as the artistic one. The phrase "the great synthesis" aptly describes the complexity of Tao-chi's development and links him not only to the other great painter, calligrapher, and theorist of his age Tung Ch'i-ch'ang but also those who worked out Tung's theories in more concrete artistic terms. The challenge of history and nature was met most fundamentally by Wang Hui, whose sober intellect encompassed the works of the ancients in a studiously inspired manner. He epitomized the master whose magnificent paintings were the result of having read the "ten thousand books" by which he grasped the spirit of the ancients. Tao-chi, on the other hand, answered the dual challenge of history and nature by having first traveled the "ten thousand miles." He absorbed both, and took the middle way. His assimilation and subsequent transcendence of the modes of the ancients were built on intuitive knowledge derived from natural forces. His forms differ from Tung's and Wang's because they are shaped not primarily by the intellect, by ancient modes of viewing nature, or even by the discipline of calligraphy, but primarily by feeling. His landscapes represent scenes which he had traversed, in real life or in dreams. Flowers, bamboo, and vegetables were subjects encountered in daily life which reflect his basic humor and joyousness. For Tao-chi nature was ultimately qualified by feelings rather than formulas.

CALLIGRAPHY AS A BASIS FOR AUTHENTICATION

Authentication of calligraphy means discriminating the genuineness not only of an individual work of calligraphy but also of calligraphy which is physically a part of a painting, such as a painter's inscription or signature, an inscription or colophon of a close contemporary (see *XXXII*), and so forth. Four problems in authentication are common: a genuine painting with a genuine signature, a forged painting with a forged signature, a genuine painting with a forged signature, and a forged painting with a genuine signature.

The first two situations are most frequent in Tao-chi's work. In the third case ("adding legs to a snake"), a painting of an anonymous or less well-known master has acquired a spurious signature or inscription of a more illustrious master. In the fourth case, often a *tai-pi* situation, a genuine signature or inscription is added to a work executed by an agent with the consent of the master involved. Thus far there is no indication that Tao-chi employed a substitute to execute his works. Just as a genuine inscription and signature place a painting in a more favorable light, doubtful calligraphy makes it suspect. On the other hand, we may believe a certain work to be genuine but may be unable to find comparable pictorial material to support this belief (i.e., the subject matter or its treatment may be unprecedented, the materials, style, or technique unusual, and so forth). If an inscription (preferably a long one) and signature are present, they may be compared with other genuine calligraphic works by the same master's hand, and we are given more facts with which to settle the question.

An artist's calligraphic style tends to be more stable than his painting style. A master may imitate any number of different artists in varying modes in both painting and calligraphy, but the calligraphic formulas tend to be fewer. The main purpose of writing is the recognition of graphic signs and the communication of meaning, and Chinese characters have necessarily evolved a more or less fixed sequence of strokes and composition for one script or any one sign. Therefore in the written script the total number of graphs and possible combinations of component parts is stable, whereas in landscape painting, for example, compositions and individual elements are limited only by the size of the categories of generic types, and the sequence of execution or combination and composition of individual trees or rocks are fixed primarily by the traditions prevailing in any one period. In writing, habits of daily utility and temperament encourage a certain repertory of forms based on instinctive muscular responses in the arm and hand. Although attempts can be made to alter or disguise the forms, successful alteration requires a prolonged period of practice and intense mental concentration. Even then, unless the "new" forms have become thoroughly assimilated into the original repertory, consistency can be maintained for only a limited length of time. (There are, of course, various degrees of "similarity," but this is not of direct concern here.) When the responses have been absorbed on the subconscious level, the forms created will, for the most part, be those "typical" or characteristic of the writer.

The formal levels or modes of an author's derivations and allusions are discernible to an eye versed in the distinguishing characteristics of the basic script types and different modes in various periods. The process of imitation and that of recognition are based to some extent on the psychology of caricature, so that the simpler the reduction and the more salient the characteristics the more vivid the recognition. Tao-chi, for example, loved to vary both his painting and writing styles, but his calligraphic allusions—not of script type but of personal mode—are more straightforward than those of his painting. Stylistic constants in calligraphy are more readily identifiable because of the established repertory of scripts, the prescribed structure of any one character, and the nature of the single brushline—a situation which differs from the more complex interrelationship and integration of a multitude of different brushstrokes and elements in a landscape. A large proportion of the graphs and their component parts are repeated in any two or more separate works by the same author (this is not necessarily the case in landscapes or figure paintings), and seldom is a calligraphic passage so brief as to contain no characters in common with the available comparative material; if it is, one can turn to graphs of related form and structure. Moreover, the repetition and specified stroke order and configuration of each character within any one script type result in a greater uniformity and more frequent recurrence of stylistic idiosyncrasies than can usually be found in the same master's painting. This recurrence of basic forms in writing has been identified as the artist's "graphology."

Authentication is therefore founded on the assumption that calligraphic forms (just as in painting) are limited in their degree of variation within an artist's lifetime and that the forms of one master will demonstrate a greater morphological affinity to each other than to a second mind or hand. What we look for in any two specimens is not the mechanical duplication of form but the underlying tendencies constituting this morphology. Our observations must be supplemented by knowledge of, and ability to recognize, distinguishing characteristics of the historical script in question, its periodic and regional distinctions, as well as possible influences and any subsequent interpretations which the writer has adopted.

Analysis of a Specimen

One initially examines a single passage in terms of its overall composition and its relationship to the painting design, the format of the writing itself, and the spacing between columns and between characters within the column and the phrasing and rhythms in the use of ink. One then focuses on the single graph—the components which determine its form, and then the interrelationships between it and others: the axis, slant, and overall direction of the characters, their individual configuration and posture, and the prevalence of angles or curves. One's attention ultimately settles on the single brushline, tracing the writer's tendencies in the formation and sequence of the individual stroke and scrutinizing the hooks, diagonals, and the articulation or "bones" and "joints" of the distinguishing parts, such as the commencement or "head" and the finish or "tail." On each level of analysis one distinguishes between the characteristics which may adhere to the script type and those which represent the epochal and individual styles. Within these distinctions the stance, the axial tendency, and the articulation of individual strokes tell us most about the personal morphology. Equally important and foremost in the initial perusal of a passage is an awareness of the artistic energy infusing the lines. Any form can be duplicated mechanically by a second hand; it is ultimately the vitality of the stroke, the phrasing and ink saturation, the tension level, and the consistency with our working standard which distinguish degrees of excellence and allow identification of the writer.

The discussion below implements this approach and supplements the studies found in the catalogue entries by detailed visual comparisons of some thirty specimens of Tao-chi's calligraphy. Twenty-eight sequences of individual characters have been extracted from these thirty works, each of which has been authenticated. They represent a condensation of an extensive network of similar comparisons which we have undertaken in our study of the Sackler works. Characters with the same lexical components, whether a phonetic or semantic radical, have been isolated and placed in related series and in rough chronological order according to our dating. As similar characters could not be found in each work, each sequence contains a varying representation. (See diagram, pp. 63–67.)

The Calligraphy Diagram

In order to read the diagram correctly, the characters of a single sequence are isolated and in each the similarities in compositional structure as well as the brushwork of the individual strokes are assessed. Because of the difference of script type and expressive intent, we must focus on the most fundamental morphological similarities. We must not seek out mechanically repetitive likeness but rather habits of instinctive muscular response which condition the pace, pressure, pauses, and stresses in any one stroke and its interrelationship with others. These works span three decades, from 1677 to 1707, and thus not only the differences in historical scripts but their intermediary variations, the differences of materials, the circumstances of execution, and the physical health of the master must be taken into account, any of which may affect the subtle formation of any one stroke. In spite of all these variables, however, the underlying consistency of the infrastructure of these characters reveals their single authorship.

The diagram can be used in several ways apart from its immediate purpose here. It can act as a general standard for assessing Tao-chi's calligraphy by means of lexical components; although not meant to be all-inclusive, it can help to expand Tao-chi's corpus by presenting a body of firmly authenticated works with which other attributed works may be compared; and, most important, the sequences can test our knowledge of Tao-chi. Skeptics may scan the different sequences and test their own recognition of works they believe to be genuine. Likewise, they can see whether they are able to spot works which to them are suspicious. If they cannot do so, they would be well advised to re-examine the bases of their doubts. Picking out a detail from a large group of unknowns in this way can be a fairly accurate test of one's knowledge of a particular work and should stimulate interest in returning to the works in question for further consideration.

The individual works are identified by lower-case italic letters. The sequences read from left to right in rough chronological order. Characters in vertical order and identified by a single letter are all from the same work; thus in sequence II*j* the four characters above *j* can all be found in the same work; the smaller subscripts under *j* have been added merely for easy description.

In sequence II, for example (the "gate" radical), *b*, *j*, and *n*, three works in the Sumitomo collection, formed the basis of Yonezawa's demonstration. Can *b*, *j*, and *n* be from the same hand? Focusing on the outer configuration, we notice that the right side of the "gate" is higher than the left and that its horizontal axis slants upward to the right. Moreover, the left downward stroke is shorter than the right;

the right-hand "gate" is drawn with a distinctive movement of the brush: as the tip extends upward to the right to form the corner, it bears down with increased pressure and creates a bulge which indicates inner articulation and small internal brush movements. As it proceeds downward, it makes a slight indentation to the left, then swings back to the right, as if struggling against a force pulling it in both directions, but with a greater pull to the right. The hook, which extends below the left side of the "gate," can be horizontal in its final flourish (forming a 90-degree angle), or can swing upward with less inhibited energy (at a 45-degree angle). In either case the outer configuration of the character resembles a trapezoid with wider sides at the right: , as if the brush were being drawn toward the upper right and the lower right simultaneously in the course of forming of the character. The tension which governs this shape can be extreme in its distortion of the form, as in j_1 (*bottom*) or j_2; it can be self-contained and hardly apparent, as in *b* or *n*. Moreover, in j_1 (*top*) (which is in "running" script, with the upper "boxes" of the "gate" simplified to a few undulations), the right side is relatively straight in its downward course, as it is in j_2 (*top*), seemingly differing from j_1 (*bottom*) and j_2 (*bottom*). What links the characters from the three Sumitomo works is the same asymmetrical stance (with the left side shorter and lower than the right) and the same tension toward the upper right, which causes the horizontal axis to slant strongly upward and the downward stroke to splay vigorously in a recoiling energy. Also within the context of a single work, like *b* or *j*, several degrees of tension and resultant changes in form are manifest. Subtle variations are found within the most "standard" of works.

The formation and articulation which we have just described are not prescribed forms of the standard "gate" character; they represent Tao-chi's personal interpretations of the "regular" and "running" scripts beyond the fixed lexical form. These formal differences are significant because they constitute the basic morphology governing his execution of any character of related form.

If we turn to the other examples in sequence II and look for the same features of outer configuration and tension, we find corroboration of the same hand and mind. The energy in II*c* is highly consistent, for example (much more consistent than in *b*), and the "gate" formations are straighter and even more alert, yet the same tendency toward an upward-slanting axis and downward-swerving hooks is apparent; *c* (*top*) and *c* (*bottom*) have the same kind of small articulating bulge in the upper right corner, while a tremulous line in *c* (*middle*) testifies to the inner strength and poise which characterize this dated example. In terms of discipline, *c* is close to *b*, placing their dates in logical proximity; they also have the same tremulous mannerism found in *n*; *d* is closer to *b* (*bottom*) in its strong upward slant and exaggerated curve at the upper right; *e* (*top and bottom*) and *f* (*bottom*) are close to the plumpness of *b* (*bottom*); in these three the leftward stroke expands in its descent and terminates with a blunt, round emphasis. This plumpness is echoed in the right side, where the stroke gradually expands to offset the thickness on the left side. *F* (*top*) affects a different personal style with consciously exaggerated undulations; nevertheless, its distinguishing configuration (which stands slightly askew, as if pulled from the upper right by an invisible force) strongly resembles that of *j* (*bottom*). Examples *g*, *h*, and *i* are all closely dated works, and their stylistic similarity corroborates the dating. Their outer configuration is like *b*, *c*, and *n* in being less strongly slanted and slimmer in stroke emphasis.

K_1 and k_2 resemble b, c, d, and g in their balanced form and are further distinguished by particularly precise and well-formed strokes, especially notable in the left terminal strokes with their emphatic knots, in the turning strokes of the corners, which are extremely well articulated, and in the perfection and control of the hook strokes. As demonstrated in the three Sumitomo works, no two hooks are precisely the same: they may be long and sharp, brief and restrained, and even internalized wthout a final release. Yet they circumscribe a range of similarity. In the k examples, the brush has taken particular care to complete the whole sequence of fine movements which create the rounded, firm, and pliant hooks and corners. The verticals of k, which are particularly thin and tensile in feeling, contrast handsomely with the sinewy emphasis of the terminations and hooks. This is one of the finest examples of Tao-chi's writing in this mode, and in perfection of strokes and aesthetic vitality it exceeds the best examples in the Sumitomo group.

The discrepancy between k and j, therefore, becomes all the more meaningful when viewed in the light of one man's range of performance and energy level: j, m, and o appear slightly flaccid in contrast to the k examples. But the differences are due mainly to changes in expressive intention which accompany a change in script type. They are written in a freehand "running" script which is more casual and much less attentive to the articulation of internal structure than is the "regular" (j_2 even bears vestiges of "clerical" script in the left-hand stroke, which, instead of ending in a blunt form, expands and terminates in a point). In these examples of "running" script the structural components are more loosely conceived and the energy is released with less concentraton, whch allows the hairs of the brush to splay more easily, producing flatter, more protracted verticals and hooks. Thus the strokes of m, o, p, and cc seem flatter, and their outer configuration tends to be taller, as in j_1 (*top*). Examples r, t, x, y, and z exemplify the "thin" versions of Tao-chi's writing in his old age, while u, x_2, and z_2 exemplify the "plump." The forms are less distorted and the horizontal axis more perpendicular, but they have the same strong asymmetrical balance and firm, incisive articulation of the hooks and corners.

Two general structural categories within this sequence can be noted: a broad, generous configuration wider than it is tall (in which the "boxes" of the "gate" are separated by at least one "box" unit), and a more elongated structure taller than it is wide (in which the space between the "boxes" is less than a unit). The latter appears more consistently in Tao-chi's "running" style, where a certain simplification, speed, and conciseness of expression are in order. Hence in j_1 (*top*), m, o, q, and cc, we see that preciseness of articulation was sacrificed to fluidity and speed of transcription. The differences in function and intent account in part for the difference in overall structure.

The broader, more generous configuration belongs to Tao-chi's more precise renderings in "clerical" or "regular" styles: n, one of the Sumitomo works, contains the broadest, most expansive example (apart from o_2 [*bottom*], which bears a "heart" radical, making it an extreme demonstration of one of Tao-chi's tendencies, yet it is authentic, as is an extremely slender example (p [*top*])). These two, n and p (*top*), represent the polar types of the two tendencies.

E ACH OF THE TWENTY-EIGHT sequences that appear at the end of this section demonstrates a different aspect of Tao-chi's morphol-ogy. A detailed description of each cannot be given here, but some salient points can be mentioned.

In sequence I, the *pu* negation can be squat, with the first horizontal stroke elongated and stressed (as in "regular" or "clerical" scripts); it can be taller, with the horizontal stroke shortened and connected to the diagonal stroke to the left (as in a, e, m, o, q, x, z, aa, and bb). This diagonal is invariably short, with the last stroke simplified to a brief comma-shaped dot.

In sequence III, *ch'ang*, Tao-chi's feeling for asymmetry balances the first four strokes to the far right, while the bottom frame juts far to the left and right.

In sequence IV, the *k'o* phonetic, the horizontal stroke tends to slant sharply to the upper right, increasing in thickness at the same time; the general configuration is low and squat.

Sequence V presents two forms of the phonetic *chin*, in "regular" and in the shortened "cursive" form. Two points distinguish Tao-chi's "regular" form: the right diagonal *na* stroke may move in three arched waves (as in g_1 [*bottom*], k, n, p, x, and z_1), or it may be relatively straight and restrained (the two forms may often be found in the same work); and in the lower half of the graph he uses an individual variation derived from the "clerical" script, as in t (in the conventional form the two bottom strokes are usually joined into one). The shorter sequence (g, j, o, q) is the abbreviated form of the same graph. Tao-chi's personal variation consists of stressing the horizontals and joining the strokes in a series of angles in which the last movement ends horizontally.

Sequence VI, the "heart" (*hsin*), is distinguished, in Tao-chi's hand, by the frequent joining of the last two strokes, which invariably swerve upward with great vigor. Example b is the more conventional way to write the character, while f, v, and z represent extremes of his personal interpretation.

Sequence VII, "to fly" (*fei*), again divides into the squarer and taller categories: a, b, c, g, and r in "regular" script contain an extra horizontal stroke and more precise articulation; the remaining characters, in "running," appear taller and more simplified in form but still maintain the articulation of the corners and hooks, as well as controlled fluctuations of the stroke thickness.

Sequence VIII, the first person (*wo*), is distinguished primarily by Tao-chi's brief second stroke (the horizontal) which barely reaches the right diagonal hook of the *ko* radical; when the strokes are linked in "running" form (g, j, o, x, bb), the character tends to split in two.

Sequence IX, "to accomplish" (*ch'eng*), is similar to sequence V in the formation of the two interior third and fourth strokes, which often form a horizontal and vertical dot. The right diagonal hook, as in sequence VIII, is also quite vigorous and well-formed in its final flourish.

Sequence X, the *shih* phonetic, bears a characteristic which Tao-chi derived from "clerical" script; the upper right sign forms the graph for "large" over "inch" (instead of the more common form of two horizontals and a vertical).

Sequence XI, the *ch'ing* phonetic, also derives from Tao-chi's familiarity with "clerical" script, in that the bottom portion ("moon") often contains three horizontals, with the verticals touching the upper horizontal.

Sequence XII concentrates on *tzu* (the right half of the character), which has a tendency to slant upward with a strongly elongated horizontal extending far to the right.

Sequence XIII, the *wu* negative, is written by Tao-chi in two ways: the first stroke can either be a dot over a horizontal (as in *b, e, h, i, k, r,* and *u*), or the customary two parallel short strokes. Otherwise, the four dots, whether separate or connected, invariably end with the last stroke forming an emphatic downward comma (cf. sequence I also).

Sequence XIV concentrates on the right-hand "knife" radical. Tao-chi invariably shortens the second-to-the-last stroke from the usual vertical (as in *b* [*left*]) to a short crescent which is continuous with the last stroke. Moreover, the crescent is placed very high, and the last stroke ends either in a downward slash (as in *e, p, r,* or *z*) or in a well-formed hook.

Sequence XV should be compared with XVII, XXIII, and XXVII. All four show the same tendency to begin the large rightward hook with a slight depression; the writer thins it slightly in its course, then increases the pressure, raising the line to the right with great vitality to form the generous curve which dominates the proportions of the graph. XVII and the "bird" of XXVII are distinguished by the four dots extending outward far to the left. The "bird" is also written in a more archaic form in which the "head" resembles a "boat" (as in *a, c, g, j, l, q, r, x,* and *z* [*bottom*]).

Sequences XVI and XXII are distinguished by their unusually squat configuration and the formation of the hook; the hook does not extend beyond the upper half.

Sequence XVIII, "to paint" (*hua*), is also related to XXIV, where the last stroke tends to form a strong vertical with a slight hook. The horizontal strokes of the *ch'u* character in XXIV are stacked like trays, one into the other (as in *b* through *i*) rather than one over the other (as in *m*), which is the more conventional form.

Sequence XIX is notable for the three right diagonals: the second begins below the first, and the last begins to the far right of the first and extends to the far left, as if enclosing the whole form.

Sequence XX, "former" (*ch'ien*), shows both the "regular" form, which is low and square, and the "running" form (*b, m, o*), which, while linking and simplifying the different strokes, stretches the entire character vertically. Note also the vigorous last hook which tends to enclose the form.

Sequence XXI concentrates on the radical "to see" (*chien*), in "running" script; in this type the separate strokes are simplified and linked into one stroke movement. A character with several continuous linkages like this exemplifies Tao-chi's habitual round brush fluctuations and the circular motion in his fingers and hand. The stroke linkages and changes of direction form his characteristic loops, and the hooks recoil in energetic curves or occasionally with slight angles (as in *j*). It is notable that the vigor of these hooks is closely related to that of the preceding hooks of sequence XX (cf. also the analysis of the phrase *hsien-sheng* in entry *XXIII*).

Sequence XXV, "yellow" (*huang*), again shows Tao-chi's preference for a "clerical" derivation of a character, but written primarily with "regular" brushwork. Example *e* shows his interpretation of pure clerical brushwork and composition; it is especially squat and characterized by an additional horizontal stroke which provides a strong lateral balance to the character; also, the center vertical stroke often touches the horizontal above it. The last two dots are related in symmetry and position to the next sequence.

Sequence XXVI again contains two characters similar in form. Tao-chi's notable idiosyncrasy, apart from the unusually squat shape, is found in the last two strokes, which diverge sharply and extend beyond the weight of the upper mass, echoing each other in direction and articulation.

The last sequence, XXVIII, "wind" (*feng*), shows Tao-chi's tendency to place the inner strokes quite low, leaving a generous pocket of space below the roof of the outer frame (as seen in *e, j, k,* and *x* especially); this formation accentuates the low, squat stance of the character and gives it a personal and slightly eccentric flavor.

23. Tao-chi's calligraphy, twenty-eight comparisons arranged in rough chronological order (*circa* dating is the authors'): *a*, December 24, 1677–January 23, 1687, *The Echo* and *Album Depicting the Poems of Su Shih*; *b*, ca. 1683, *Eight Views of Huang-shan*; *c*, March 5–April 3, 1685, *Searching for Plum Blossoms*; *d*, winter, 1693, *View from Yü-hang*; *e*, ca. 1695, Fong *Small Album*; *f*, 1695, *Flowers and Figures*; *g*, June 29–July 29, 1696, *Sketches of Calligraphy and Painting by Ch'ing-hsiang*; *h*, spring, 1697, *Spring on the Min River*; *i*, winter, 1697, *Landscape after Ni Tsan*; *j*, ca. 1697, *Waterfall at Mt. Lu*; *k*, ca. 1698, *Thousand-Character "Eulogy of a Great Man"*; *l*, summer, 1698, *Inscription to Chu Ta's Ta-ti ts'ao-t'ang-t'u*; *m*, ca. 1698–99, *Letter to Pa-ta shan-jen*; *n*, August 25–September 22, 1699, *Huang-shan*; *o*, February 7, 1701, *Manuscript of Poems*; *p*, March 3–April 7, 1701, *Album of Landscapes*; *q*, ca. 1701–5, *Lo-Fu Mountains*; *r*, ca. 1703, *Sketches after Su Tung-p'o's Poems*; *s*, ca. 1703, *Peach-Blossom Spring*; *t*, ca. 1698–1703, *After Shen Chou's Bronze Peacock Inkslab*; *u*, summer, 1705, *Wan-li's Porcelain Handle Brush*; *v*, September 18, 1705, *Bamboo, Vegetables, and Fruit*; *w*, September, 1705, *Loquats and Melon*; *x*, ca. 1705–7, *Plum Branches*; *y*, winter, 1706, *Landscape and Portrait of Hung Cheng-chih*; *z*, September 10, 1707, *Reminiscences of Nanking*; *aa*, n.d., letter to I-weng; *bb*, n.d., letter to T'ui-weng (*lien-jih*); *cc*, n.d., letter to Shen-lao; *dd*, n.d., letter (*tso-wan*).

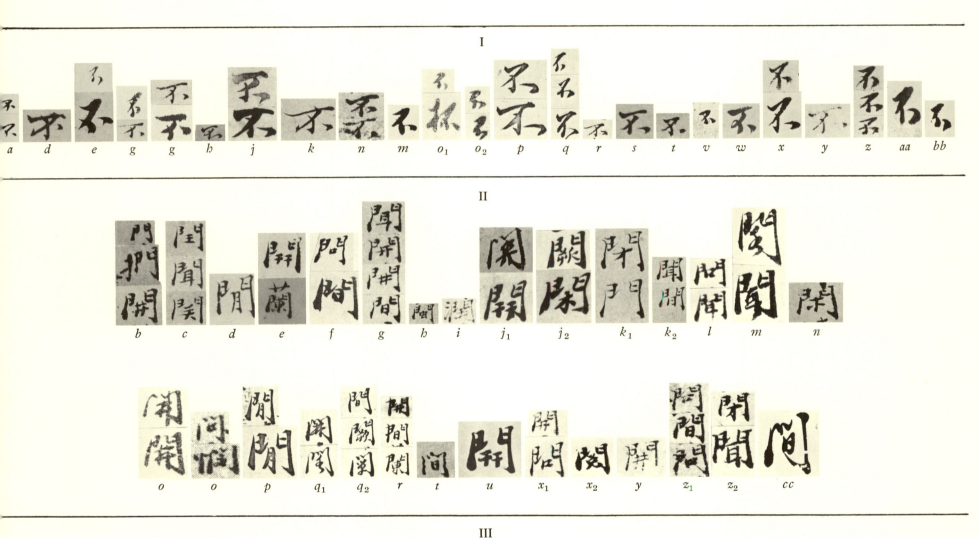

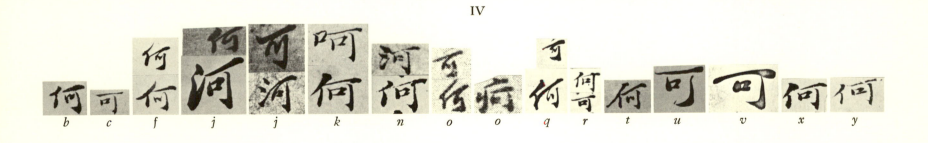

V

| c | g$_1$ | g | h | j | k | n | p | r | t | x | y | z$_1$ | z$_2$ | | g | g | j | o | q |

VI

| b | f | g | j | k | k | l | n | o | r | s | v | w | x | y | z |

VII

| a | b | c | e | g | j | l | m | q | r | z |

VIII

| b | b | d | f | g | j | j | l | o | q | r | t | x | x | x | y | bb |

IX

| b | f | g | j | j | k | n | n | o | q | r | x | aa |

X

| b | e | e | f | g | k | l | q | r | s | x | x | y | z | z |

XI

b c g g h j k n o r s u v w x y

XII

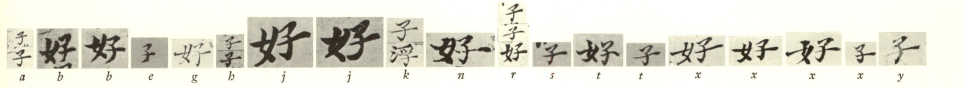

a b b e g h j j k n r s t t x x x x y

XIII

b c e e e e g h i j k l n p r r u x x x

XIV

b b b b c e e e j j k n n n p r r x z

XV

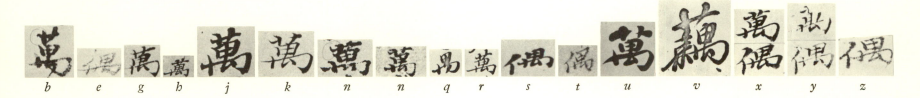

b e e g h j k n n q r s t u v x y z

XVI

b c e h j k n q x x

c   *e*   *g*   *h*   *j*   *k*   *r*   *x*   *y*

a   *a*   *f*   *i*   *j*   *l*   *m*   *p*   *z*

c   *c*   *j*   *j*   *k*   *k*   *y*

b   *b*   *j*   *k*   *n*   *m*   *o*

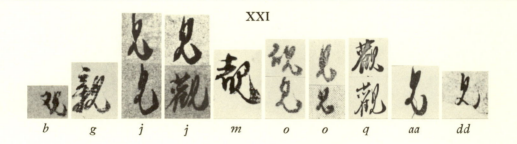

b   *g*   *j*   *j*   *m*   *o*   *o*   *q*   *aa*   *dd*

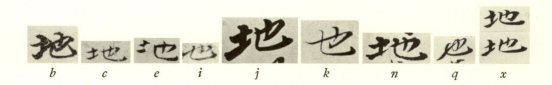

b   *c*   *e*   *i*   *j*   *k*   *n*   *q*   *x*

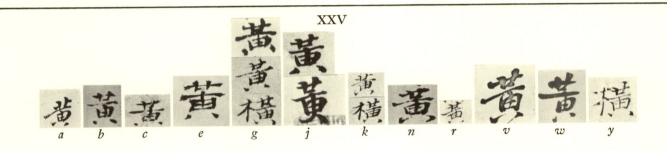

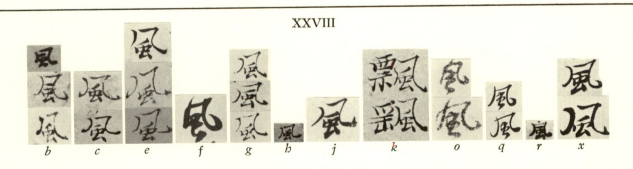

XXIII

NOTES

See the Bibliography at the end of this volume for full information on sources abbreviated here.

1. The main sources for this résumé are Fu Pao-shih, *Shih-t'ao shang-jen nien-p'u*; Wen Fong, "A Letter from Shih-t'ao to Pa-ta shan-jen and the Problem of Shih-t'ao's Chronology"; Cheng Cho-lu, *Shih-t'ao yen-chiu*; Cheng Wei, "Lun Shih-t'ao sheng-huo, hsing-ching, ssu-hsiang ti-pien chi i-shu ch'eng-chiu"; *PTC*; and Chou Ju-hsi, "Tao-chi," from the Ming Biographical History Project.

2. The title commemorates the successful defense in Kiangsi of the Ming founder, Chu Yüan-chang, by Shou-ch'ien's father, Wen-cheng. Both he and Shou-ch'ien were nephews and grandnephews of the Ming founder and were brought up under his close protection. The Ching-chiang prince was enfeoffed in Kuei-lin, Kwangsi, in 1370, and at that time a quatrain in twenty characters was designated as the *p'ai-hang*, or lineal pedigree, for the names of the princes and their male descendants. See Cheng Cho-lu, *Shih-t'ao yen-chiu*, pp. 3–5.

3. *Ibid.*, pp. 5–6. For Yüan Tun's account, see *Ch'ing-hsiang lao-jen t'i-chi fu-lu* (appended colophons), in *Hua-yüan pi-chi*, p. 17; Yüan's colophon is dated 1758.

4. For Ho-t'ao, see Cheng Cho-lu, *Shih-t'ao yen-chiu*, pp. 9–10.

5. *Ibid.*, pp. 8–9.

6. *Ibid.*, p. 11.

7. According to Shūjirō Shimada in *Niseki Hachidai* (Oiso, 1956), p. 5, and summarized by Richard Edwards in "Tao-chi, the Painter," *PTC*, pp. 31–32. See also Kohara Hironobu, "Sekitō to Kōzan hasshō gasatsu," an essay accompanying a portfolio of color reproductions of the Sumitomo *Eight Views of Huang-shan* album and the most recent and thorough study of the literary evidence related to the album.

8. For Mei Ch'ing, the painting society, and several related poems and inscriptions, see Cheng Cho-lu, *Shih-t'ao yen-chiu*, pp. 13–15.

9. Cf. Wu T'ung, "Tao-chi, a Chronology," pp. 56–57, under those years.

10. Cheng Cho-lu, *Shih-t'ao yen-chiu*, p. 23.

11. *Ibid.*, pp. 17–21, 25.

12. Tao-chi inscribed one of Kung Hsien's early paintings; see *ibid.*, p. 23, for the list of the guests and a poem by K'ung describing his favorable impression of Tao-chi.

13. *Ibid.*, pp. 23–25.

14. *Ibid.*, pp. 25–27.

15. A leaf from an album by Po is illustrated in *Min Shin no kaiga*, pl. 91. For Po-erh-tu, see also Cheng Cho-lu, *Shih-t'ao yen-chiu*, p. 28, and Jonathan Spence, "Tao-chi, an Historical Introduction," pp. 19–20; for Po's lineage, see Fang Chao-ying's essay on Nurhaci in Arthur W. Hummel, ed., *Eminent Chinese of the Ch'ing Period*, pp. 594–99, 934.

16. Published as *Ch'ing-hsiang shu-hua-kao-chüan* in fifteen sections with appended commentary by Hsü Pang-ta.

17. Cheng Cho-lu, *Shih-t'ao yen-chiu*, pp. 34–35.

18. For its importance in the Yüan, see Wai-kam Ho, "The Recluse and the I-min," in Sherman Lee and Wai-kam Ho, *Chinese Art under the Mongols*, p. 95.

19. Visual evidence for this change appears in several sources. We summarize the extant materials here: in the 1696 *Sketches of Calligraphy and Painting by Ch'ing-hsiang* (sec. 9) Tao-chi still refers to himself as a monk, but in the 1697 inscription on Chu Ta's painting *Narcissus* (see *XXIII*, fig. 12), he already mentions Ta-ti-t'ang; in the ca. 1698–99 *Letter to Pa-ta* he clarifies his situation to Pa-ta in these words: "Please do not refer to me as a monk, for I am a man who wears a hat and keeps his hair, and who purifies [*ti*] everything from here on" (translated by Wen Fong). Cf. also the perceptive discussion by Cheng Wei, "Lun Shih-t'ao sheng-huo," p. 48.

20. Cheng Wei, "Lun Shih-t'ao sheng-huo," p. 48.

21. *Ibid.*, pp. 45–47.

22. The phrase is borrowed from Davida Fineman's essay, "The Yang-chou Eccentric School: Institutionalized Unorthodoxy," in Martie Young, ed., *The Eccentric Painters of China*, pp. 8–12.

23. Cheng Wei, "Lun Shih-t'ao sheng-huo," p. 47.

24. *Ibid.*, p. 47; also Fu Pao-shih, *Shih-t'ao shang-jen nien-p'u*, pp. 67, 81, 85, 89, 91, 95.

25. Reproduced in National Palace Museum, Taipei, *Special Exhibition of Paintings from the Ming and Ch'ing Dynasties*, cat. no. 50, pl. 36, pp. 28–30.

26. Cheng Wei, "Lun Shih-t'ao sheng-huo," pp. 47–48.

27. The term is sometimes rendered misleadingly as "ghost painter."

28. One of the best-known cases is that of Tung Ch'i-ch'ang. His heavy responsibilities as a prominent official, historian, scholar, and art connoisseur left him little extra time to respond to the many purely social requests for paintings and calligraphy, and he is known to have added his signature to paintings which he had requested others to execute for him. Chao Tso and Shen Shih-ch'ung are two artists who have been named in this substitute capacity. This fact, plus the abundant number of forgeries made both during Tung's lifetime and thereafter, compounds the problem of authenticating works by his "hand." Thus the stylistic aspect of any *tai-pi* assertion must be researched from several angles.

29. See "A Letter from Shih-t'ao to Pa-ta shan-jen and the Problem of Shih-t'ao's Chronology"; research on the problem of Tao-chi's birth year is summarized on pp. 22–53. A bibliography on the letter may be found in *XXIII*.

30. The manuscript is also known as *Meng-meng tao-jen shou-kao*, according to Tao-chi's signature. First published in *Hua-p'u* and in Cheng Wei, "Lun Shih-t'ao sheng-huo," no. 12, p. 50 (figs. 1–2).

31. To quote Fong, "in the collected works of the famous late Ming scholar Ch'ien Ch'ien-i [i.e., *Mu-chai yu-hsüeh-chi, SPTK* ed., 4/6–7], there is a group of fourteen poems which were dated 1651 and were dedicated to a priest named Shih-t'ao. The postscript attached to these poems reads in part as follows: "Shih-t'ao k'ai-shih [a polite title for bodhisattvas as well as accomplished priests] brought from Lu-shan a letter from Po-yu [Hsiao Shih-wei, 1585–1651]. On his return, I wrote fourteen quatrains to bid him goodbye . . . . [In the year of] *hsin-mao* [1651], the third moon, Meng-sou, your brother, Ch'ien-i, respectfully presented them" ("A Letter from Shih-t'ao to Pa-ta shan-jen," pp. 31–32). The problem is whether the Shih-t'ao mentioned here, who was seemingly a friend of two such older and accomplished scholars as Ch'ien and Hsiao, can be identified with the painter Shih-t'ao.

Fong has suggested the possibility that the Shih-t'ao referred to in Ch'ien's letter may be another monk of the same name. Cheng Wu-min's investigation of such a possibility has proved negative however. Cf. "Shih-t'ao shu-chi pa," p. 171. Wu T'ung, in his excellent "Tao-chi, a Chronology," has presented the most plausible arguments so far in support of the "letter-bearing Shih-t'ao" being one and the same person as the painter, Tao-chi; see pp. 53–55.

32. "A Letter from Shih-t'ao to Pa-ta shan-jen" and "Reply to Professor Soper's Comments on Tao-chi's Letter to Chu Ta."

33. "Shohō-jo kara mita Sekitō ga no kijun-saku."

34. Reported by Richard Edwards as representative of the opinions at the 1967 symposium discussion in Michigan; see "Postscript to an Exhibition," p. 261.

35. The inscription is by Hung Cheng-chih (1674–1731–) and is found on a landscape handscroll dated 1686 by Tao-chi which Hung had acquired. Both are recorded in *T'ing-fan-lou shu-hua-chi hsü, ISTP* ed., vol. 20, 1/651. See *XXXII* for further discussion of Hung.

36. Published in *Shih-t'ao hua-chi*, nos. 53–58; *PTC*, cat. no. 43, pp. 182–86; and *The Selected Painting and Calligraphy of Shih-t'ao*, vol. 4, no. 96. Wen Fong mentions the album as dated 1707 (*ting-hai*) and as being in the C. C. Wang collection; see "A Letter from Shih-t'ao to Pa-ta shan-jen," p. 48, no. 16.

37. Published in Shanghai in 1962. See also n. 30 above.

38. Notably Kohara Hironobu, "On a New Version of Shih-t'ao's *Hua-yü-lu*."

39. Sumitomo collection, published in *Sō Gen Min Shin meiga taikan*, vol. 2, no. 225; details are found in *Min-matsu san oshō*, nos. 10 and 11, and in *Un Nanden to Sekitō*, nos. 13 and 15.

40. As quoted in Cheng Cho-lu, *Shih-t'ao yen-chiu*, p. 40.

41. 1/11, titled "Shao-shui ch'ui-lun."

42. Cf. *PTC*, p. 57, under the year 1687.

43. *Ta-ti-tzu t'i-hua-shih-pa*, 2/50.

44. *Ibid.*, 4/85–86. "Ko-t'ieh" seems to be a clear reference to the collection of rubbings of works collected and reproduced by imperial order in the Ch'un-hua era by Emperor Sung T'ai-tsung, hence the name *Ch'un-hua ko-t'ieh* (*Calligraphy from the Ch'un-hua Hall*). The compilation of ten volumes (*chüan*) was completed in 992. It was the first large-scale attempt in the Sung to reproduce and compile handwritten specimens (*t'ieh*) of the calligraphy of the ancient masters. Included in the collection were examples of *hsiao-k'ai, hsing*, and *chang-ts'ao*, with an occasional appearance of *chuan*. The compilation purported to represent the work of masters from the pre-Han, Han, Wei, Chin, Sui, and T'ang dynasties. Chung Yu was included in the second volume; three full volumes were devoted to the then extant examples of Wang Hsi-chih and two to his son Wang Hsien-chih. This choice and emphasis are some indication of the taste of the period. An inferior version recut from the original *Ch'un-hua ko-t'ieh* set of rubbings was already in circulation by the late Northern Sung, and the original choice of specimens had been sharply criticized by several Sung scholars, most notably Mi Fu and Huang Po-ssu. No complete set of the original rubbings exists today; a complete version recut in the late Ming (1627) is extant and was reproduced in facsimile recently as *Jun-ka kaku-jō*, giving us an idea of the range and possible quality of the original selection. See also Wang Shu, *Ch'un-hua mi-ko fa-t'ieh k'ao-cheng*.

45. Cheng Wei, "Lun Shih-t'ao sheng-huo," p. 47.

46. Cf. Cheng Cho-lu, *Shih-t'ao yen-chiu*, pp. 70–71 and fig. 23. Sasaki Kozo's "Tao-chi, Seals," pp. 63–70, supersedes the Contag and Wang listing in *Seals*, pp. 425–28, 708, and identifies 113 different seals; the Sackler works contain two

unlisted seals for a total of 115. Tao-chi did not necessarily carve them all him-self, and he may have had several versions of the same impression; such identifi-cation and authentication would constitute a separate study.

47. For examples of Han seal impressions in "seal" script, see *Shodō zenshū*, ser. 2, vol. 2, pls. 17–23, and rubbings from various media, pls. 42–67.

48. For examples of *T'ang-li*, see "Ta-chih ch'an-shih" stele transcribed by Shih Wei-tse, dated 736, pls. 72–73, and the "Shih-t'ai Hsiao-ching" transcribed by the T'ang emperor Hsüan-tsung, dated 745, pls. 76–79, in Nishikawa Yasushi, ed., *Seian hirin*. The latter is also reproduced and discussed by Ecke in *Chinese Calligraphy*, cat. no. 14.

49. For a historical and critical review of the extant attributions to Chung Yu, see the essay in *Shodō zenshū*, vol. 3, pp. 5–6, 24–32. This volume also con-tains a selection of examples of brushwriting on wooden slips and paper frag-ments excavated from Lou-lan and dated from A.D. 263 to 310 which may serve as valuable comparisons in the reconstruction of the style of this and other early masters.

50. See Ch'u's "San-tsang sheng-chiao-hsü" stele, dated 653, in *Seian hirin*, pls. 53–56.

51. For an example of Huang T'ing-chien's *hsing-k'ai*, see *Shodō zenshū*, vol. 15, pls. 58–61. One of the authors (S. F.) is undertaking a study of Huang's calligraphy.

52. For Shen Chou's calligraphy, see *ibid.*, vol. 17, pls. 58–59.

53. For Yen Chen-ch'ing's calligraphy, see *ibid.*, vol. 10, pls. 12–65, pp. 10–13.

54. Also noted of Tao-chi by Ecke in *Chinese Calligraphy*, cat. no. 83.

55. For examples of their works, see *Shodō zenshū*, vols. 17, 21.

56. *Ibid.*, vol. 17, pls. 76–92.

57. Cf. Roderick Whitfield, *In Pursuit of Antiquity*, frontispiece and p. 131.

58. Cf. James Cahill, ed., *The Restless Landscape*, pp. 73, 108–9, 136–37.

59. For a recent study of the *Han-hsüeh* movement in the Ch'ing dynasty and especially its relation to "seal" script, see Lothar Ledderhose, *Die Siegelschrift (Chuan-shu) in der Ch'ingzeit*, esp. pp. 57–64.

60. Cf. Museum of Fine Arts, Boston, *Portfolio of Chinese Paintings in the Museum*, pl. 134, p. 24 (leaf F); our translation is modified from theirs. The inscriptions on the Boston album contain many of Tao-chi's central ideas on the ancients, only a few of which we cite here.

61. For example, an album of landscapes in *Mei Ch'ü-shan hua-chi*, pls. 21–26, are "imitations" (*fang*) after Shen Chou, Kao K'o-kung, Ching Hao, Kuan Tung, Wu Chen, Liu Sung-nien, and Chao Meng-fu. Kung Hsien's similarities to and differences from the ancients have been pointed out by Marc F. Wilson in *Kung Hsien: Theorist and Technician in Painting*, pp. 16–24; Kung's views on the ancients are known through extant works, especially the self-inscriptions to the landscape album and handscroll in the Nelson-Atkins collection; see Wilson, *ibid.*, cat. nos. 8–9, and the album in the Wen Fong collection, cat. no. 10. The inscriptions in the latter are translated in Ecke, *Chinese Calligraphy*, cat. no. 80. For Chu Ta, see *XXXVI*, where his calligraphy is discussed in this context.

62. Quoted in Fu Pao-shih, *Shih-t'ao shang-jen nien-p'u*, p. 85.

63. Cf. *Ta-feng-t'ang ming-chi*, vol. 2, pl. 26.

64. Cf. *XVIII*, where this idea is discussed in relation to his execution of plum blossoms.

65. *Sekitō meiga fu*, pl. 1; the painting is now in the Su-chou Museum. We are grateful to Maria Solange-Macias for her aid in the English rendering of the inscription, modified after a draft by Wen Fong. For the Buddhist term *hsin-yen*, see, for example, Morohashi Tetsuji, ed., *Dai Kanwa jiten*, vol. 4, 10295/57.

66. *Shih-t'ao hua-chi*, pls. 44–49.

67. *Ta-feng-t'ang ming-chi*, vol. 2, pl. 5.

68. *Min-matsu san oshō*, pls. 5 and 8. Cf. Edwards, "Tao-chi, the Painter," p. 23; our interpretation of the text differs slightly.

69. For the preceding, see Cheng Cho-lu, *Shih-t'ao yen-chiu*, pp. 27–30; Fu Pao-shih, *Shih-t'ao shang-jen nien-p'u*, pp. 86, 93–94; and Spence, "Tao-chi, an Historical Introduction," pp. 17–20.

70. *Min Shin no kaiga*, pl. 91.

71. *A Garland of Chinese Paintings*, vol. 4, pl. 25.

72. For the work with Wang Hui, see *The Selected Painting and Calligraphy of Shih-t'ao*, vol. 1, pl. 9; for the work with Wang Yüan-ch'i, see National Pal-ace Museum, Taipei, *Three Hundred Masterpieces*, vol. 6, pl. 289.

73. Cheng Cho-lu, *Shih-t'ao yen-chiu*, p. 73.

74. E.g., as in his 1694 *Summer Landscapes* or his after-1693 *Autumn Colors on Mt. Hua*; see National Palace Museum, Taipei, *Three Hundred Master-pieces*, vol. 3, pls. 275–76. For a brief study of Wang's stylistic development and working methods, see Chiang Chao-shen, "Wang Yüan-ch'i: Notes on a Special Exhibition."

75. E.g., in his 1692 handscroll *Mountain Hermitage on a Clearing Autumn Day*; see Whitfield, *In Pursuit of Antiquity*, cat. no. 19, pp. 147–49.

76. Reproduced in *A Garland of Chinese Paintings*, vol. 4, pl. 27.

77. *Pan-ch'iao t'i-pa*, p. 128.

78. Reproduced from *Min Shin no kaiga*, pl. 131; see also Ecke, *Chinese Cal-ligraphy*, fig. 18, and *Shodō zenshū*, 2d ser., vol. 21, pp. 100–101, for two other fine examples of Cheng's work.

79. From *Lun-yü*, 2/4; see also James Legge, *The Chinese Classics: The Con-fucian Analects* (rpt. Taipei, 1966), vol. 1, pp. 146–47; Arthur Waley, *The Ana-lects of Confucius* (London, 1938), p. 88.

80. Cf. Chiang I-han, "K'u-kua ho-shang Hua-yü-lu" *yen chiu*, pp. 397–546; also Chou Ju-hsi, "In Quest of the Primordial Line: The Genesis and Content of Tao-chi's *Hua-yü-lu*."

81. See Pierre Ryckmans, "Les 'Propos sur la Peinture' de Shi-t'ao: Traduc-tion et Commentaire," which offers the most complete explication of the *Hua-yü-lu* text in a Western language. A preliminary article of that title (accom-panied by four illustrations) was first published in *Arts Asiatiques* in 1966. We are indebted to David Sensabaugh for this reference. Unfortunately, the bulk of our study was too near completion to utilize M. Ryckmans' researches fully. We are gratified to see, however, that he has pursued his inquiries with a broader base of aesthetics and history in mind and that many of our interpreta-tions of the text coincide with his.

82. For the intellectual and cultural background on this subject and its rela-tion to art and literary theory, see Wai-kam Ho's brilliant paper, "Tung Ch'i-ch'ang's New Orthodoxy and the Southern School Theory." See also Wen Fong, "Tung Ch'i-ch'ang and the Orthodox Theory of Painting"; and Mae Anna Quan Pang, "Late Ming Painting Theory," in Cahill, ed., *The Restless Landscape*, pp. 22–28.

83. Cheng Cho-lu, *Shih-t'ao yen-chiu*, p. 31; translation from Wu T'ung, "Tao-chi, a Chronology," p. 60. It is quite likely that this statement was made during his Yang-chou years, however, so it may not necessarily speak for any initial enthusiasm or deep involvement in the Buddhist faith.

84. Quotations from the *Hua-yü-lu* will be cited by chapter in the text as *HYL*. We have used the edition of Yü An-lan, *Hua-lun ts'ung-k'an*, vol. 1, pp. 146–59. See Chou Ju-hsi, "Tao-chi, a Note on His Writings," *PTC*, p. 71, and Ryckmans, "Les 'Propos sur la Peinture,'" pp. 197–98, for a complete bibliog-raphy of sources in Chinese and Western languages.

85. From *Tung Hua-t'ing shu-hua-lu*, p. 44.

86. As found in Tung's "T'i T'ang-Sung-Yüan ming-jen chen-chi-hua," in *Jung-t'ai pieh-chi*, vol. 4 (1/9a), p. 1703.

87. From "Hua-chih," in *Jung-t'ai pieh-chi* (6/19b), p. 2126.

88. From *Jung-t'ai pieh-chi* (4/49a), p. 1941.

89. From *Hua-ch'an-shih sui-pi*, p.44.

90. Reproduced in *Sekitō meiga fu*, also a facsimile edition printed in Japan with brocade covers, no date. This last leaf is reproduced in Victoria Contag, *Zwei Meister chinesischer Landschaftsmalerei*, pl. 17. A free copy is published in *The Selected Painting and Calligraphy of Shih-t'ao*, vol. 3, pl. 86.

91. These terms or "modes" were originally set forth in poetic form; cf. Ssu-k'ung T'u (837–908), *Erh-shih-ssu shih-p'in (The Twenty-four Modes of Poetry)*, in Ho Wen-huan, ed., *Li-tai shih-hua* (preface dated 1770; Taipei, 1956), vol. 1, pp. 24–27; an English rendering by Yang Hsien-yi and Gladys Yang, "The Twenty-four Modes of Poetry," appeared in *Chinese Literature*, vol. 7 (1963), pp. 65–77. Tao-chi's *ch'ing-i* is close to Ssu-k'ung's *p'iao-i*.

92. Cf. two exemplary works of Hu and Shao in the recent Berkeley exhi-bition (Cahill, ed., *The Restless Landscape*, cat. nos. 59, 19, and 20 especially) from the Ching Yüan Chai, Seattle Art Museum, and University of Michigan Museum of Art collections, respectively.

93. *Ta-feng-t'ang* collection, *Ta-feng-t'ang ming-chi*, vol. 2, pl. 25. Tao-chi unfortunately does not specify which followers of the Yün-chien school he had in mind.

94. *Ta-ti-tzu t'i-hua-shih-pa*, 4/85.

95. *T'ing-fan-lou shu-hua-chi*, *hsü*, 2/652.

96. From "Hua-chih," *Jung-t'ai pieh-chi* (6/4a), p. 2097.

97. The terms are Buddhist. Cf. Morohashi Tetsuji, ed., *Dai Kanwu jiten*, vol. 11, 39010/79, where the Lankavatara sutra is quoted. See also Wai-kam Ho, "Tung Ch'i-ch'ang's New Orthodoxy and the Southern School Theory," for the wider ramifications of these concepts in connection with literary and art theory.

98. "Hua-chih," *Jung-t'ai pieh-chi*, p. 2107.

99. *Ibid.*, 6/3a, p. 2093.

100. Translation from Burton Watson, *Su Tung-p'o: Selections from a Sung Dynasty Poet* (New York, 1965), p. 107. Cf. *Chi-chu fen-lei Tung-p'o hsien-sheng shih*, vol. 2, 11/226, "Shu Chao Pu-chih so-ts'ang Yü-k'o hua-chu," the first of three poems.

101. Cf. W. T. de Bary, "Individualism and Humanitarianism in Late Ming Thought," in *Self and Society in Ming Thought*, pp. 145–248; see also his intro-duction to the same volume, pp. 1–28. Max Loehr, in his "The Question of Indi-vidualism in Chinese Art," discusses the concept from a slightly different point of view.

102. *Shan-ku t'i-pa*, 5/51, "Pa Ch'ang-shan-kung shu."

103. From Mi's *Pao-chin ying-kuang-chi.*

104. Tung-p'o t'i-pa, 4/87, "T'i Ou-yang t'ieh."

105. P. 7.

106. As quoted by Kuo Jo-hsü in *T'u-hua chien-wen-chih*, 2/61–62.

107. This major statement appears in several sources, the most reliable of which we believe to be the inscription dated 1686 (see fig. 21), which states that the painting on which it is inscribed was completed in 1667 (center inscription). Tao-chi inscribed the work again in 1697 (top left); and there is also an important undated colophon by T'ang Hsüan-i (*tzu* Yen-sheng), a friend of Hung-jen, which is consistent with the style and quality of T'ang's numerous other colophons found on Hung-jen's works (cf. *XII*). Although Tao-chi's painting is available to us only in this reproduction, the painting and calligraphic style and quality seem consistent with the other accepted works of the Hsüan-ch'eng period. Moreover, the content of this 1686 inscription is in harmony with the critical thought which appears in Tao-chi's Nanking years. The visual evidence of the painting allows a closer comparison with other reliable works than is possible with literary sources whose authenticity cannot be verified by other means. Tao-chi's statement also appears in *Ta-ti-tzu t'i-hua-shih-pa*, 1/20, and in *Shih-t'ao hua-chi*, pl. 2, an undated painting which needs further study.

108. *Tung-p'o t'i-pa*, 4/90, "Pa Shan-ku ts'ao-shu."

109. As quoted by Kuo Shao-yü, *Chung-kuo wen-hsüeh p'i-p'ing-shih*, p. 274.

110. Li Chih, *Fen-shu* (ca. 1600; rpt. Peking, 1961), p. 16, "Ta Keng chung-ch'eng."

111. Cf. *Portfolio of Chinese Paintings in the Museum*, pl. 137, p. 24, for a slightly different rendering in English.

112. *Shan-ku t'i-pa*, 4/34, "T'i Feng-pen fa-t'ieh."

113. Yü Chien-hua, ed., *Chung-kuo hua-lun lei-pien*, vol. 2, p. 707, "Shih-t'ien lun shan-shui," as extracted from *Shu-hua hui-k'ao.*

114. As recorded by Chu Ts'un-li, *T'ieh-wang shan-hu shu-hua-p'in*, vol. 16, 6/22.

115. As recorded in *Hsüan-ho hua-p'u*, 11/291.

116. Yü Chien-hua, ed., *Chung-kuo hua-lun lei-pien*, vol. 2, p. 653, "Lun shan-shui," as extracted from Mi's *Hua-shih.*

117. *Wu-chiu t'i-pa*, p. 12.

118. As quoted in *Li-tai ming-hua-chi* (traditionally dated 847), *ISTP* ed., vol. 8, 10/318.

119. From *Ch'ing-hsiang lao-jen t'i-chi*, p. 1.

120. From "Hua-chih," in *Jung-t'ai pieh-chi* (6/3a), p. 2093. The wording of Tao-chi's passage is too close to that of Tung Ch-i'ch'ang to postulate an independent origin. Elsewhere we have noted that Tao-chi mentioned the Northern and Southern schools of painting; here is further evidence of the wide dissemination of Tung's influence. For an investigation of several aspects of this problem, see Shen C. Y. Fu, "A Study of the Authorship of the So-Called 'Hua-shuo' Painting Treatise."

121. From *Hua-ch'an-shih sui-pi*, p. 43.

122. From *T'ing-fan-lou shu-hua-chi*, 4/368, "Ta-ti-tzu shan-shui hua-hui-shan ts'e."

123. From Yü An-lan, ed., *Hua-lun ts'ung-k'an*, vol. 1, p. 57.

124. From Yü Chien-hua, ed., *Chung-kuo hua-lun lei-pien*, vol. 2, p. 1063, as extracted from *Yü-feng-ch'ing shu-hua t'i-pa-chi.*

125. From Yü An-lan, ed., *Hua-lun ts'ung-k'an*, vol. 1, pp. 26–27.

V. Catalogue of the Sackler Collection

I MA WAN (ca. 1310–1378-)

Born Nanking, active Sung-chiang, Kiangsu, and Fu-chou, Kiangsi

Spring Landscape (*Ch'un-shan lou-ch'uan-t'u*)

The Art Museum, Princeton University (L319.66).

Hanging scroll. Ink and color on paper, watermarked with fine vertical striations. 83.2 x 27.5 cm.

DATED: December 12, 1343 (*Chih-cheng san-tsai, tung-chung erh-shih-wu-jih*).

SIGNATURE OF THE ARTIST: Wen-pi (as part of a three-line inscription).

INSCRIPTION BY THE ARTIST: on left edge of painting in three lines of free "regular" script dedicated to Liu Pen-chung (unidentified).

SEALS OF THE ARTIST: *Ma Wan chang* (intaglio, square) and *Wen-pi* (relief, large square) after inscription.

INSCRIPTIONS (two, on the same paper):
Yang Wei-chen (1296–1370) upper right corner, a seven-character quatrain in four lines of "running" script, accompanied by two seals and a third half-seal (identified in discussion below):

> *On the peaks red pavilions unite with the clouds,*
> *Below the mountains the Yangtze waves meet the heavens.*
> *Waiting until the spring waters of the Peach Blossom overflow,*
> *The beautiful one sits in the tall-masted boat high in the sky.*

Kung Chin (fl. ca. 1340–1370?) upper left corner, a seven-character quatrain in three lines of "draft-cursive" script; no seals:

> *In the tall-masted boat sailing east from Han-yang [Wu-ch'ang, Hupei],*
> *On the riverbanks the green mountains press toward me.*
> *Tonight I want to rest my boat at Niu-tu [Ts'ai-shih cliffs, Anhwei],*
> *To burn the [magical] rhinoceros horn and gaze at the rising tide.*

COLLECTORS' SEALS:
Hsiang Yüan-pien (1525–1590), *Shen-p'in* (relief, double seal in two squares; Contag and Wang, *Seals*, no. 21, p. 610) top left edge of painting, *Tzu-sun yung-pao* (intaglio, square; Contag and Wang, *Seals*, no. 18, p. 610) upper left side of painting, *Hsiang Yüan-pien yin* (relief, square; Contag and Wang, *Seals*, no. 71, p. 700) upper left edge of painting, *Mo-lin mi-wan* (relief, square; Contag and Wang, *Seals*, no. 25, p. 611) upper left edge of painting, *T'ui-mi* (relief, double-gourd shape; Contag and Wang, *Seals*, no. 22, p. 610) lower right edge of painting.
Chang Heng (1915–1963), *Chang Heng ssu-yin* (intaglio, square) lower right corner of painting; *Yün-hui-chai yin* (intaglio, square) and *Chan-te-yü-chi k'uai-jan tzu-tsu* (relief, square), both on mounting silk, lower right corner.
Owner unidentified, *Chen-ts'ang* (relief, double-gourd shape) and *Chang-shih chi-ts'ang shu-hua chih-chang* (relief, tall rectangle), both on lower left corner of painting; these two seals may belong to Chang Heng but, unlike his, are poorly carved and probably belong to another Mr. Chang.

CONDITION: fair; there is insect damage and moderate abrasion over the surface of the paper, especially the lower half. At some time in the remounting process the cracks and damaged areas were filled in (notably in the waves and parts of the reeds in the foreground). A slightly dull surface in the houses and parts of the foreground rocks suggests overpainting with ink and color wash (i.e., flat washes of red in the houses and dark umber in the rocks). The brushwork and condition of the ink in the distant mountains and calligraphy are original and have not been visibly retouched.

PROVENANCE: Frank Caro, New York.

PUBLISHED: Cheng Chen-to, ed., *Yün-hui-chai-ts'ang T'ang-Sung-i-lai ming-hua-chi* (*Paintings in the Collection of Chang Heng*), vol. 1, pl. 50 (illustrated); Hsü Pang-ta, *Li-tai liu-ch'uan shu-hua tso-p'in pien-nien-piao*, pp. 36, 254.

MA WAN (*tzu* Wen-pi, *hao* Lu-tun-sheng) is typical of a host of scholar-painters from the late Yüan. The works of these transitional painters provide a link between the styles of the major masters of the early Yüan and those of the Ming. Ma Wan was born into the Yüan,

but he preferred the life of a recluse to serving the Mongol court.[1] Little is known of his life and of the precise ideological basis for his retreat, but his reputation as a scholar was sufficiently widespread during the Yüan that, after the founding of the Ming, the Hung-wu emperor summoned him to serve as a prefect in Kiangsi Province. For the greater part of his life he was disengaged from politics, however, and had the leisure necessary for self-cultivation and expression in the arts. A native of Nanking, he lived later in Hua-t'ing (Sung-chiang, Kiangsu). His associations with other more illustrious literary figures, such as Yang Wei-chen (1296–1370) and Pei Ch'iung (1317/18–1378?), have helped us to establish his approximate birth and death dates and a few salient aspects of his career (for more detailed discussion, see below).

Ma Wan's genuine extant works are few. His most celebrated and best painting is the 1366 *Spring Hills after Rain* in the National Palace Museum, Taipei (figs. 2, 4).[2] *Spring Landscape* is stylistically consistent with this work, and its 1343 date makes it both the earliest and the only genuine work of Ma Wan's in a Western collection. The two inscriptions on the painting are also of Yüan origin, and they strengthen the painting's artistic value as well as corroborating its authenticity. Yang Wei-chen's inscription, in particular, enhances the historical and literary content of the painting, as it documents his relationship as Ma's teacher and also offers a rare example of his own early calligraphic style.

A tall, vertical format is given spatial definition by two triangular masses separated by generous stretches of water. Space also occupies the immediate foreground, in which a triangular mass extends from the left, composed of ovoid-shaped boulders through which is cut a path and bridge to the edge of the water. Two riders on horseback approach the bridge on their way to the buildings at the top of the hill, which overlook a broad view of the lake. Two boats catch the strong spring breeze; they are positioned on a slant to indicate a continuity of the water surface. This continuity is achieved by a network of waves drawn in undulations across the entire surface of the water. In the far distance, slightly above the center of the picture, the second triangular mass projects from the right. On the foreshortened horizon a flat screen of peaks in blue wash and a range of mountains is indicated by several decisive horizontal strokes, representing the receding shoreline.

The hills and boulders are modeled by long strokes firmly drawn with a brush held upright, producing the round linear texture called *p'i-ma ts'un* ("hemp-fiber wrinkles"). Umber washes combined with plump "moss-dot" accents lend a sense of bulk and pattern to the rock forms. Two groves of trees, each differentiated by its foliage pattern and hue, frame the pathway and the two riders. Figures and horses are drawn with great animation (the gentleman on the left is riding sidesaddle in order better to talk with his companion); they are conceived in a scale proportionate to the trees, bridge, and houses. Thick growths of water reeds, drawn with a fine tensile line in a fanning direction, line the foreground banks and provide a transition from rocks to water. The atmosphere is clear. All the forms are strongly and densely defined with the contouring done in round, firm lines. This kind of depiction and the two-part composition, with its generous proportion of water to land masses, are general indications of a Yüan period style. A typical Yüan view of nature, it reflects the influence of the Lake T'ai scenery on the painters of that region.

Two inscriptions occupy the upper third of the narrow format, left blank by the painter for that purpose. He has executed the work for a friend, whose name is noted specifically in his inscription. This stress on literary value and specific dedication in a painting gained prominence in the Yüan period and remained an integral part of the literati tradition in painting.[3]

洞庭波兮山崚嶪川弓濟
兮不可以沙兮蘭為舟兮
桂為檝渺渺予懷兮綠一
葉
三湘七澤香難分兮恍
見潑風葭景紛誰識
王孫多意緒月明波
吟弔湘君

王昂

1. Chao Meng-fu, *East Tung-t'ing Mountain*, ca. 1290's. Hanging scroll. Ink and light color on silk. Shanghai Museum.

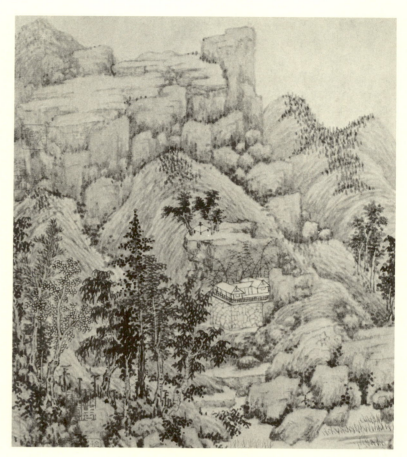

2. Ma Wan, *Spring Hills after Rain*, dated 1366, detail of left section. Handscroll. Ink on paper. National Palace Museum, Taipei.

3. Wu Chen, *Hermit Fisherman at Tung-t'ing*, dated 1341, detail of upper half. Hanging scroll. Ink on paper. National Palace Museum, Taipei.

MA WAN'S STYLE represents a merging of those of several great masters of the early Yüan who were active in the Lake T'ai region and who have been recognized in traditional and modern criticism as having laid the foundation for scholar painting. Chao Meng-fu (1254–1322) is one of the key figures in this development, and his stylistic explorations relate directly to Ma Wan's. For example, Chao's *East Tung-t'ing Mountain* (fig. 1) was probably executed in the late 1290's, some fifty years earlier than *Spring Landscape*. Compositionally, *East Tung-t'ing* represents an important solution in vertical format to the problems of continuity and spatial definition which are found in Chao's historic 1296 *Autumn Colors on the Ch'iao and Hua Mountains*, and it provides a significant transition to his 1302 *Water Village*.[4] A comparison of *Spring Landscape* with *East Tung-t'ing* reveals some of the sources of Ma's conception of brushwork and composition and at the same time illustrates Chao's seminal position in relation to painters of Ma's generation.

In *East Tung-t'ing* volumetric emphasis is concentrated in the middle-ground mass, while the extension of land in the foreground and background, including some high faraway mountains, roughly indicates three distances. A fine net of crosshatching stretches over the water surface and links the masses, reinforcing the diminution of scale. Trees are arranged in groups which fan outward. The slopes are modeled compactly in round linear strokes and punctuated by small round moss dots in the mountain crevices. All forms are clearly and distinctly defined; the scale of elements is consistent as the forms recede in depth, the proportion of land to water is approximately half, and the artist's self-inscription dominates the upper third of the composition.

Similar principles of proportion, brushwork, and form are found in Ma Wan's work. In *Spring Landscape* the volumetric weight is reversed, with the solid mass placed in the foreground. Such a change harks back to earlier Southern Sung "one-corner" compositions, but with decided differences. This kind of two-part design could have resulted in a compositional split, as the eye's field of vision does not necessarily encompass the land mass in the distance. The Southern Sung masters solved that difficulty by the liberal use of ink washes to indicate mist, so that the eye intuitively linked the forms. Chao Meng-fu's role in redirecting Yüan painting was to reject the use of wash and the mist-concealing and somewhat arbitrary juxtaposition of masses of the Southern Sung in favor of a lucid and structurally clearer design. All landscape elements are in clear view, nothing is concealed by spatially ambiguous mist; on the contrary, all elements are graded by size and ink tones to reinforce the viewer's understanding of spatial depth. Ma Wan solved the problems of continuity and spatial definition posed by Chao in similar ways. He employed two pictorial devices: linear linking of the masses and a method of directed foci. The undulating network of waves is the same device which artists before Chao had used (see, for example, the tenth-century painter Chao Kan's *Early Snow on the River*[5]), but he refines and integrates the formula into the composition to a higher degree. By this means, physically disparate objects are linked, and the illusion of a continuous ground plane is achieved. He reinforces this sense of continuity even further by the deft placement of the few elements of the landscape. Directed focal points lead the eye in a zig-zag motion up the picture plane and into depth. Starting from the two riders approaching the bridge, the eye moves diagonally up the path to the houses on the promontory and jumps across to the two boats, which slant in such a way as to preserve the angle of direction and lead the eye to the distant mountains on the slightly sloping horizon. The three distances—near, middle, and far—which appear more distinctly in Chao's *East Tung-t'ing* scroll, have been condensed to two in Ma's work, with the boats functioning as a vestige of this tripartite conception. The rational clarity of the whole design is also seen in the minor motifs, in the way the two boats—dark shapes against the white paper—echo the two riders on the path, who appear as white against the dark foliage. This minor device of "motif mirroring" employing negative and positive values also draws the two parts of the composition together, just as the two grounds are unified by the tension implied in the slanting forces. There is thus a coherent structural conception underlying this deceptively simple composition, as even our cursory analysis reveals.

The theoretical framework in which this idea of pictorial unification developed historically has been cogently presented recently as a phase in the "structural morphology" of Chinese landscape painting.[6] Two pictorial ideas—the conquest of illusion and the control of space—can be isolated as a basis for this analysis: they can be identified as pictorial inventions in the formal development of landscape painting. The refinements in the development of form which relate to *Spring Landscape* and to Yüan painting in general can be traced from the Five Dynasties and Northern Sung. In works which can be dated to these periods, one observes the artist's interest in compartmental spacing of frontal masses in three stages in the picture plane—foreground, middle ground, and background. The grounds are more or less distinct and are unified by intuitive devices of mist and scale, as well as by single spatial themes of height, depth, or breadth. By the Southern Sung and early Yüan, the disparate concepts of controlling pictorial space by mist, by scale, and by volumetric mass had gradually been integrated, and, as we see in Chao Meng-fu's works, there is less interest in the description of three separate grounds or even in the presentation of a single compositional theme. Rather, there is a preference for merging and unifying several classic themes and motifs established earlier, and thus we see height, depth, and breadth depicted within a single hanging scroll format.

In the Yüan, along with this compositional integration went a view of the brushline as a more direct means of conveying the psychic and emotional intention of the artist. Scholar-painters bolstered and made the structural conception more expressive through calligraphic discipline, which was seen as the technical and expressive basis of pictorial description. The term *hsieh-i*, "to write out ideas and feelings," was basic to the aesthetic outlook of these masters. With this attitude went an interest in reviving the modal statements on nature from works by the great masters of the past. Certain views of nature and specific modes of brushstrokes had come to be associated with certain masters—mainly those of the southern Chiang-nan region such as Tung Yüan, Chü-jan, Mi Fu, and others. Hence the parallel term *ku-i*, "spirit of antiquity," implied both formal and visual allusions to the past, whether in specific motif, brushwork formula, composition, or general feeling. As both expressive ideals and technical approaches, *hsieh-i* and *ku-i* are the two most vital principles of Yüan painting. They were articulated in verbal and pictorial form by Chao Meng-fu and are here extended by Ma Wan.

In this Sackler scroll we can speak of the landscape as having been "written out" because as we view its forms we are conscious of an integrity of brushstroke both as an expressive entity and as a descriptive element. The low, sloping hills, dense, linear, "hemp-fiber" textures, and plump moss dots are Yüan interpretations which clearly allude to the Tung-Chü tradition of landscape art revitalized by Chao almost singlehandedly. A comparison of the trees and slopes in *Spring Landscape* with the foreground clump of trees in Chao's *Autumn Colors* and *East Tung-t'ing* reveals the extent to which Ma was influenced by Chao's formulas for describing specific form. In the hills, Ma's texture strokes are dense and tightly conceived (see the detail); in the trees, the trunks and the bark are lightly textured by long strokes, and the oval knots and joints are dimpled and left in relief. An upright tree in the center is flanked by two bowing and arching ones, each distinctly foliated by a different pattern of brush-strokes. A glance at Ma's 1366 handscroll *Spring Hills after Rain* (figs. 2, 4) reveals the same visualization of form in the trees and in the compact massing of the hills and rocks. Also notable is the conception of the distant mountain range, which, in both scrolls, consists of a firm undulation in wash on the horizon. Bold horizontal strokes also line the edges of the banks and the receding surface of the water, providing a transition from the water to the land masses.

4. Ma Wan, *Spring Hills after Rain*, detail of central section.

Ma Wan's style did not develop directly from the single influence of Chao Meng-fu; on the contrary, it is also rooted in that of two masters whose careers followed Chao's, Wu Chen and Huang Kung-wang. Wu Chen's *Hermit Fisherman at Tung-t'ing*, dated 1341 (fig. 3), reveals Wu's own derivation from Chao Meng-fu and the Tung-Chü concept of rolling earthen mounds and thick foliage. Wu's artistic temperament is more vigorous and expansive, however. His texture strokes convey a sense of drama and sweep; the larger forms spread and flow, and the smaller ones cohere with great intensity. His two-part composition and rendering of the reeds, as well as his looser concept of foliage, are other sources of Ma's design. Huang Kung-wang's influence (see his 1350 *Dwelling in the Fu-ch'un Mountains*) is less specific, but the fact that he was active in Sung-chiang, where Ma lived, as well as in Ch'ang-shu, is of significance. Wu Chen worked in nearby Chia-hsing. The proximity of these neighboring towns almost ensures the rapid interchange of stylistic ideas: in fact, the similarity between the styles of Ma Wan and Chao Meng-fu and Chao Yung, as well as other painters like Wu Chen, Wei Chiu-ting, and Huang Kung-wang, shows the strength of the local tradition which was being fostered at that time in southern Kiangsu and northern Chekiang. It was through such dissemination of the styles of great masters by amateur painters of secondary importance like Ma Wan that the great tradition of Yüan painting was perpetuated into the early Ming. Further study of Ma Wan's other accepted works will reveal those elements which were developed by Ming painters such as Liu Chüeh, Hsieh Chin, and others, especially those in the Su-chou region (see Part I above).

One final point about Ma Wan's style should be noted. In the work of a great master such as Huang Kung-wang, we can sense the effulgent energy and psychic drive which charge each brushstroke and endow the landscape with a monumental grandeur. Huang Kung-wang's years of wandering in the mountains can be read in each line and dot and in his essential feeling for form. It is tempting to call such a successful evocation of nature "naturalism" or even "realism," but what it does convey is a profound and intimate under-standing of nature's benign forces, a viewpoint which characterizes many of the early Yüan painters in general. By contrast, Ma Wan's works present an entirely different artistic personality, as seen in his attention to the fine details of pictorial construction, his preference for compact massing of the mountains, his modeling with shorter, denser strokes, and his conception of foreground trees as small and closely grouped. These formal traits suggest not only a more retiring and introspective nature (perhaps one closer to the more aloof rationality of Chao Meng-fu) but an attitude toward the natural landscape which is more that of the observer in a garden estate than that of the wanderer with his paintbrush amidst hills and valleys. The painters of the late Yüan set a pattern which would predominate in the Ming—painting culled not so much from direct experience with nature as from brush formulas established by their predecessors. By Ma Wan's time, painters were already using methods which were consciously influenced by other painters' styles (as is especially evident in his own, if limited, corpus). In the works of other transitional painters, such as Chao Yüan, Wang Fu, and Ch'en Ju-yen, it is clear that painting in other painters' modes had now found a permanent place in the literati tradition.

MA WAN'S APPROXIMATE birth and death dates have been ascertained through his association with two other late Yüan-early Ming scholars, Yang Wei-chen and Pei Ch'iung (1317/18–1378?). Pei (*tzu* T'ing-chü, from Ch'ung-te, Chekiang), a poet and well-known scholar, was one of the compilers of the Yüan history in the early Hung-wu period. He later held a teaching position in the capital.[7] He wrote the preface to Ma Wan's collected works, *Kuan-yüan-chi*, and to Ma's philological treatise on the correct usage of radicals in Chinese graphs, *P'ien-p'ang pien-cheng*. In addition, three of Pei's colophons to Ma's paintings survive.[8] These materials are the primary sources on Ma Wan's life thus far.

According to Pei's preface to the *Kuan-yüan-chi*, Ma Wan studied the *Ch'un-ch'iu* classics (*Spring and Autumn Annals*) with Yang Wei-chen, who was renowned in Chekiang for his special knowledge of the text. Ma's exact birth date has not been recorded, but, as Yang's student, he would probably have been about half a generation younger (about ten to fifteen years), so that he may have been born ca. 1310. According to this reckoning, the Sackler painting, which is dated 1343, would have been executed relatively early in his career, when he was in his thirties.

In Pei Ch'iung's *Ch'ing-chiang chi* there is an inscription to a painting by Ma Wan titled *Yin-chü-t'u* which tells us that he and Ma were once neighbors in Hua-t'ing (Sung-chiang), and that in 1370, the third year of the Hung-wu period, Ma was summoned by the emperor to serve as prefect of Fu-chou in Kiangsi Province. Two years later, in 1372, Pei Ch'iung was called to the capital to assume the position of instructor (*chu-chiao*) at the National University (*Kuo-tzu-chien*). After that time, Pei and Ma were separated for six years. Later Pei received news of Ma from a friend who came to deliver a poem to him. The friend had just seen Ma and reported that his hair had turned gray but that he was in good health, his vision and hearing still keen. Pei Ch'iung died the next year (1378?), and that is the extent of our knowledge of Ma's activities. We do not know how long he lived after Pei's friend saw him.

THE THOROUGH STUDY of Ma Wan's attributed works that would be necessary to establish his range is beyond the scope of this entry, but we will summarize our findings concerning the five works which we do accept as genuine[9] on the basis of their signatures and seals (fig. 5). Ma's attributed works are in a broad range of styles on different media, silk as well as paper, color as well as monochrome, reflecting the more formalized and catholic modes of the late Yüan.

I, details.

The 1343 Sackler work (see the detail) and the 1366 Palace Museum handscroll (fig. 5d) provide the ground upon which we may build a more complete analysis of his style. Like the materials and intent of the paintings on which they are found, the script types vary with each work, but stylistic affinities in the important stroke movements can be discerned.

The signature on the 1366 Palace Museum scroll (fig. 5d) is separated by an interval of twenty-three years from *Spring Landscape* (see the detail). In addition, it is executed in *chang-ts'ao* ("draft-cursive") script, with the four characters of the title in a strong "regular" style. The two seals are different, but the position of the inscription (on the extreme upper right corner of the handscroll) is as unpretentious as in the Sackler painting (this feature is not found, for example, in the copies listed in n. 9). Ma Wan is known to have modeled his "small regular" style after Yen Chen-ch'ing.[10] The four characters in the 1366 work especially reflect this influence; in *Spring Landscape* it is also seen in the fleshy diagonal and horizontal strokes. The spacing of the characters in each line and of the columns themselves is consistent, as is the tall, rectangular shape of each character and the strong contrast of thicks and thins in a single stroke.

Stylistic links can also be found with the other works by focusing on the first character of the *Spring Landscape* inscription, *chih* 之 (from the Yüan reign date, *chih-cheng*), which is found in the signatures to three of the other four paintings shown here. It is the only cursive character in the inscription and derives from the *chang-ts'ao* type found in the 1366 inscription (fig. 5d). It begins with a generous accent in the horizontal stroke, then curves from left to right in a continuous loop ending in a horizontal with an emphatic hook; the hook is linked immediately to a crescent-shaped comma dot. A second similar character which may be compared is the Wen 文 of Ma Wan's *tzu*, Wen-pi. The two 1349 scrolls and the undated Ex-J. D. Ch'en work (figs. 5a–c) are all quite close in basic configuration and identical in stroke emphasis: the right diagonal *na* stroke extends far to the right with a horizontal completion; furthermore, the same stroke begins with a slight space left between its "head" and the horizontal stroke above it. The second character of Ma's name is written in two ways: in the 1343 and 1366 works the "jade" radical is below the *pi* phonetic; in the others it is written to the left in a more rectangular arrangement. Nonetheless, despite the differences, the significant stroke movements point to execution by the same hand. These stylistic observations are strengthened by the presence of identical seals: *Ma Wan, Wen-pi yin-chang* (relief, large square) is found on the two 1349 scrolls and the undated work; and *Lu-tun-sheng* (intaglio, square) is found on the two 1349 paintings. Several factors must be considered in determining the authenticity of a painting: in this case, the judgments based on pictorial style are strengthened by the examination of calligraphy and seals.

THE INSCRIPTIONS provide further evidence that this is a fourteenth-century painting and an authentic Ma Wan work and have value of their own as documents of Yüan calligraphy. In the upper right-hand corner, the well-known scholar, poet, historian, and calligrapher Yang Wei-chen[11] (1296–1370; *tzu* Lien-fu, *hao* T'ieh-yai, T'ieh-hsin tao-jen, T'ieh-ti tao-jen, from K'uai-chi, Chekiang) has written a quatrain in seven-syllable verse. The poem is followed by the signature "T'ieh-yai," one of Yang's early cognomens. The name dates back to the period before his *chin-shih* degree (1327) when, according to traditional accounts, his father locked the youth up in a studio on Mt. T'ieh-yai for five years to encourage him to prepare for his exams. The other names most commonly seen on his works are those which he adopted after he was fifty.

Yang's calligraphic style is distinctive for its bold, sharp brush-work and strong, angular shapes. It is straightforward and unrestrained, indicative of the scholar's physical and intellectual vigor, in contrast to the other two inscriptions—the mild and modestly shaped characters of Ma Wan on the far left and the regular and contained "clerical-cursive" of Kung Chin. Three distinct calligraphic hands and temperaments are revealed in these inscriptions.

Although undated, this calligraphy is probably from Yang's early period, when he wrote more often in the *hsing* than *ts'ao* script. Relatively even columns, a uniform character size in a tall rectangular configuration, and a strong vertical axis within each character predominate. Yang consistently employs the exposed brushtip at the beginning of each stroke: it cuts squarely into the paper, forming a sharp triangle "head." This form contrasts with the tensile roundness of the remainder of his lines, indicating the active turning and twisting of his brush. Flamboyant angularity and a high degree of tension and release of energy characterize his style.

Most of his dated works were done after 1360, when he was in his sixties. These late monuments show contemporaneous styles of two extremes: one a more regular character size, the other a deliberately impulsive and irregular character shape. An example of the first is his 1365 *Chang-shih T'ung-po Ch'ien-piao*,[12] where the mixture of "running" and "draft-cursive" with the square composition of the latter type prevails. This script is the source of the characteristic splayed diagonal *na* stroke, which forms the distinguishing flat triangle occurring so consistently in Yang's writing. Other than the oblique right and left strokes, the movements of the brush are primarily drawn with the centered tip and stress a vigorous horizontal movement between strokes. This jagged energy constitutes Yang's most basic rhythm. The axis of the individual character tends to sway from side to side. The second style can best be illustrated by the 1360 colophon to Tsou Fu-lei's handscroll of plum, *A Breath of Spring*, in the Freer Gallery.[13] In this scroll, Yang Wei-chen wields the brush in such a way that he is almost painting his characters. He employs abrupt and dynamic changes of size, thickness of stroke, and depth of ink to accent meaning, content, and overall design. The beauty of his composition lies equally in its relentless release of energy and in its pure, abstract forms.

A third undated work which stands stylistically between these two is a hanging scroll, *Yü-tzu-wo-ming* ("Essay on the Den of Selling One's Writings") (fig. 6).[14] The same light and heavy contrasts between characters appear in a line here, but on a less dramatic scale than in the Freer inscription. The combination of "draft-cursive" with "running" and purer "cursive" forms is also visible. Stylistically this work is closest to the inscription found on the Sackler scroll (see the detail). There is a similar tall rectangularity and a general consistency in character size. Structural parallels in the two works may be found by comparing lexically similar characters, such as *t'ien* (天 "Heaven"), *hsia* ("beneath"), and other similar components, such as the horizontals, the hooks, and the manner in which strokes are linked. In them we see the same headstrong movements in the horizontals (with their emphatic opening and closing accents) and the characteristic right-diagonal stroke with its strong arch, often bending at three points in the course of a single brush movement.

Yang's inscription on *Spring Landscape* is probably earlier than that on the *Yü-tzu-wo-ming* and the 1360 and 1365 works. In all likelihood it was written soon after the painting was executed, about 1345. This hypothesis is strengthened by the use of his youthful name, T'ieh-yai, and one of his early seals, *T'ieh-hsin tao-jen* (relief, square), on the upper right edge of the painting, a cognomen which was later superseded by T'ieh-ti tao-jen.[15] The second seal (after his signature), *K'uai-chi Yang Wei-chen yin* (relief, square), is also found on the *Yü-tzu-wo-ming*.

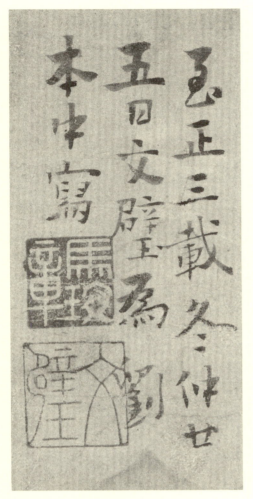

I, detail of signature.

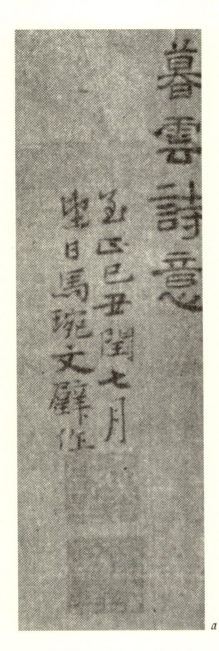

a

b

5. Ma Wan, signatures: *a*, *Evening Clouds*, dated 1349, hanging scroll, ink and color on paper, Shanghai Museum; *b*, *Lonely Retreat among Great Cliffs*, dated 1349, hanging scroll, ink on silk, National Palace Museum, Taipei; *c*, *Autumn Woods*, n.d., detail, Ex-J. D. Ch'en collection; *d*, *Spring Hills after Rain*, dated 1366.

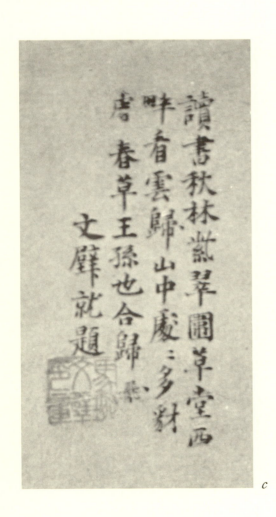

c

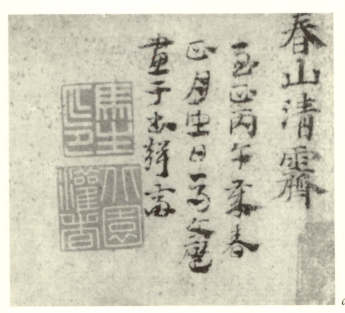

d

IN THE UPPER left corner of *Spring Landscape* there is a seven-syllable poetic quatrain written in three even lines of "draft-cursive" poetic script by a certain Kung Chin (see the beginning of this entry for its text). Little information is available about him. He may be related to the better-known poet and litterateur Kung Hsiu (1266–1331; *tzu* Tzu-ching, from Su-chou), as both names are single characters written with a "jade" radical.

The calligraphy of Kung Chin's inscription falls into the general category of late Yüan and early Ming adaptations of the *chang-ts'ao* script. This script was revived during the late Yüan and was practiced by many scholars, Ma Wan and Yang Wei-chen included. Kung was probably a late Yüan master, as his writing bears few of the looser, more extravagant features and the free linking of characters found in the early Ming development of the *chang-ts'ao*.[16] His writing is a fine example of the late fourteenth-century interpretation of form, which stressed the spatial separation of each character with

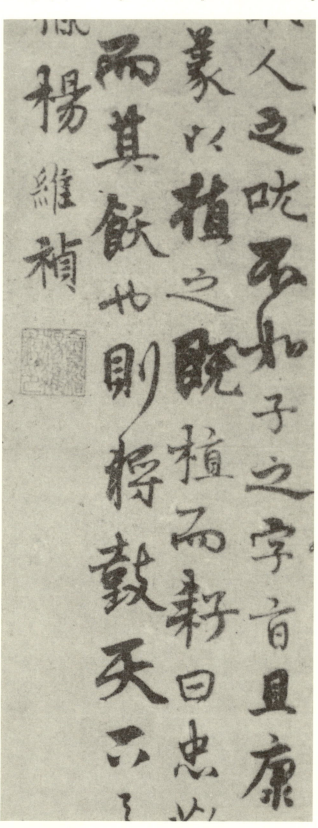

6. Yang Wei-chen, *Essay on the Den of Selling One's Writings* (*Yü-tzu-wo-ming*), detail, n.d. Hanging scroll. Ink on paper. Collection unknown.

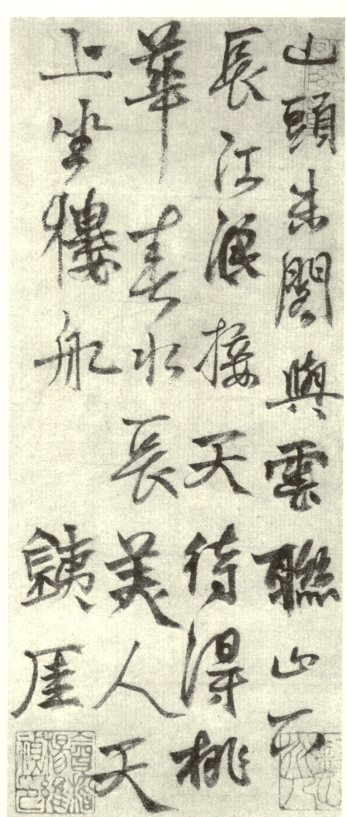

I, detail of inscription.

few exaggerated contrasts between the strokes. The brief and firm diagonals form a pleasing balance with the rounder, more centered tip of the other strokes. Simplicity and a certain restraint characterize Kung's style, which sharply contrasts with the formal eccentricity of Yang Wei-chen's bold hand.

A PAINTING attributed to Ma Wan with the title *Ying-hai-t'u* ("The Ocean") is recorded in several Chinese catalogues, Wang K'o-yü's (fl. 1628–1643) *Shan-hu-wang* and Yü Feng-ch'ing's (ca. 1634) *Shu-hua t'i-pa-chi*.[17] The entries are highly summary; measurements, media, signatures, and full inscriptions are not given, nor is there a description of the work recorded. Both catalogues give the poem written here by Yang Wei-chen, but with one variant character (the twenty-first), a different signature, and no seals. They do not give Ma Wan's inscription or seals or Kung Chin's poem. The question is whether the work they record is *Spring Landscape* or another version.

The traditional criticism of these two catalogues is that many of the colophons listed in Wang K'o-yü's compilation, for example, were not necessarily objects in his collection or even seen by himself. Handwritten copies of his manuscript circulated for almost two hundred years before it was printed in 1916, and that publication was based on a collation of several handwritten versions.[18] Thus, in *Shan-hu-wang*, the margin for error before printing was indeed wide. Pien Yung-yü's *Shih-ku-t'ang shu-hua hui-k'ao* drew in large measure from Wang's catalogue; hence it perpetuates the errors contained therein. As to the *Shu-hua t'i-pa-chi*, the colophons it contains were also copied without regard to authenticity and, as in Wang's case, with no indication as to whether the objects were viewed by Yü Feng-ch'ing personally.

In view of the above criticisms and discrepancies, it seems likely that the versions which both Wang and Yü saw were copies after the present painting or after yet another copy. Perhaps they did see this painting, but in their transcriptions or the later transcriptions and editions of their manuscripts the mistakes now present were introduced. As the landscape and calligraphic inscriptions of *Spring Landscape* are of Yüan origin and of high quality, it is imperative that we honor this visual evidence if it is consistent with other genuine works, especially as such evidence is verifiable in ways which written records cannot be.

NOTES

See the Bibliography at the end of this volume for full information on sources abbreviated here.

1. On this subject see F. W. Mote, "Confucian Eremitism in the Yüan Period"; Wai-kam Ho, "Chinese under the Mongols," especially chap. 4, "The Recluse and the *I-min*," pp. 89–95, and the extensive notes and bibliography following his essays; and Wang Yao, "Lun hsi-ch'i yin-i chih-feng" ("On the Tendency To Long for the Life of a Recluse"), in *Chung-ku wen-jen sheng-huo* (Shanghai, 1951), and the revised version in *Chung-ku wen-hsüeh-shih lun-chi* (*Collected Papers on the History of Medieval Literature*) (Shanghai, 1957), pp. 49–68.

2. Ink on paper, the fifth scroll in a series of eight remarkable landscapes from the Yüan mounted together in a single handscroll. See *Ku-kung shu-hua-lu*, vol. 2, 4/302–5, and the partial reproductions in National Palace Museum, Taipei, *Three Hundred Masterpieces*, vol. 4, pl. 50, vol. 5, pls. 198, 200–202, and in *Chinese Art Treasures*, cat. no. 90.

3. On the interrelationship between poetry, painting, and calligraphy, see Shūjiro Shimada's discussion in *Shodō zenshū*, vol. 17, pp. 28–36.

4. In the National Palace Museum, Taipei, and the Palace Museum, Peking, respectively. For a discussion of these major paintings, see Chu-tsing Li's *Autumn Colors on the Ch'iao and Hua Mountains* and "Stages of Development in Yüan Dynasty Landscape Painting"; Max Loehr's review of Li's first article in *Harvard Journal of Asiatic Studies*, vol. 26 (1965–66), pp. 269–76; and Kiyohiko Munakata's review of it in *Art Bulletin*, vol. 48 (1966), pp. 440–42; see also Richard M. Barnhart, *"Marriage of the Lord of the River": A Lost Landscape by Tung Yüan*.

5. For a discussion of the style and content of this excellent scroll, see John
Hay, "Along the River during Winter's First Snow," pp. 294–304.

6. Most notably by Wen Fong in his "Toward a Structural Analysis of Chinese Landscape Painting"; the seed of the idea appeared in his "The Problem of Ch'ien Hsüan" and "Chinese Painting: A Statement of Method," among other works. See also Barnhart's extension of this approach in *A Lost Landscape*.

7. The biographical information on Pei has been gleaned from the prefaces by Pei Yung dated 1821 and 1827 in Pei Ch'iung's collected works, *Ch'ing-chiang Pei hsien-sheng-chi*, pp. 1–3. For an account of some of the social and institutional shifts that occurred in the change of dynasty from the Yüan to the Ming and its relationship to scholars and the National University, see Ho Ping-ti, *The Ladder of Success in Imperial China: Aspects of Social Mobility, 1368–1911*, pp. 216–17.

8. *Ibid.*, pp. 38–39, 58, 196, and 205 passim. Unfortunately only the titles to Ma Wan's works survive.

9. The selection of the works in Sirén's and Laing's lists is as follows (dates are given first because they are of primary importance in identifying this group of paintings):

Genuine works:

1. 1343 *Spring Landscape* (*Ch'un-shan lou-ch'uan-t'u*), The Art Museum, Princeton University (not in Sirén's or Laing's lists).

2. 1349 (summer, seventh moon) *Lonely Retreat among Great Cliffs* (*Ch'iao-hsiu yu-chü*) (also known as *High-Terraced and Deeply Crevassed Mountains in Snow*), hanging scroll, ink on silk, National Palace Museum, Taipei, see *Ku-kung shu-hua-lu*, 5/246.

3. 1349 (intercalary seventh moon) *Evening Clouds and Poetic Feelings* (*Mu-yün-shih-i*), hanging scroll, ink and color on silk, Shanghai Museum, see *Shanghai po-wu-kuan ts'ang-hua*, pl. 30.

4. N.d. *Autumn Woods* (*Ch'iu-lin chao-yin*), hanging scroll, ink on paper, Ex-J. D. Chen collection, see *Chin-k'uei ts'ang hua-chi*, vol. 1, pl. 23.

5. 1366 *Spring Hills after Rain* (*Ch'un-shan ch'ing-chi*), handscroll, ink on paper, National Palace Museum, see *Ku-kung shu-hua-lu*, 4/302–5.

Problem works (may be close copies; available to the authors only in poor reproduction):

6. N.d. *Fishing Boat by an Autumn Grove* (*Ch'iu-lin tiao-t'ing*), hanging scroll, ink on paper, painted for Chu-hsi wai-shih, with inscription by Tao Tsung-i, National Palace Museum, Taipei, see *Ku-kung shu-hua-lu*, 5/247; possibly a close copy by a Ming painter.

7. N.d. *Secluded Dwelling* (*Yu-chü-t'u*), handscroll in Wang Meng style, ink on paper, collection unknown, see *Kokka*, vol. 492; a copy made around the sixteenth century.

Forgeries (or paintings with forged signatures):

8. N.d. *Travelers in Autumn Mountains* (*Ch'iu-shan hsing-lü*), hanging scroll, ink and color on paper, with inscription by Tung Ch'i-ch'ang, National Palace Museum, Taipei, see *Ku-kung shu-hua-lu*, 5/246; probably after the middle of the Ming.

9. 1328 or 1388 *Landscape in Wang Meng Style* (*Sung-ho kuan-ch'üan*), hanging scroll, ink and color on paper, Palace Museum, Peking; a Ch'ing painting; both dates are wrong, but the composition is notable because it is close to Wang Meng's extant 1367 *Elegant Gathering among Forest and Trees* (*Lin-ch'üan ch'ing-chi*).

10. N.d. *Landscape*, ink on paper, hanging scroll, Cincinnati Art Museum, acc. no. 1948.83; a late Ming painting by a follower of the Wen school.

11. 1360 *High-Wooded Mountains*, see *Chung-kuo ming-hua-chi*, vol. 1, pl. 109; a painting done after the middle of the Ming.

10. As noted by Pei Ch'iung in his preface to Ma Wan's essay on the correct use of radicals, *P'ien-p'ang pien-cheng-hsü*, in *Ch'ing-chiang Pei hsien-sheng-chi*, 7/39. In the same essay Pei states that Ma Wan's painting style resembled that of Tung Yüan.

11. For Yang's biography see Edmund H. Worthy's essay in the Ming Biographical History (publication forthcoming).

12. Reproduced in *Shodō zenshū*, vol. 17, pls. 48–49.

13. For a discussion of the painting, see Archibald Wenley, "A Breath of Spring," pp. 459–69; Thomas Lawton, "Notes on Five Paintings from a Ch'ing Dynasty Collection," pp. 202–3.

14. Ping-teng-ko collection, *Chung-kuo ming-hua-chi*, vol. 1, pl. 113 (illustrated).

15. See Chu Sheng-chai, *Sheng-chai tu-hua-chi* (Hong Kong, n.d.), p. 97, which records a colophon of Yang's dated 1343 signed "T'ieh-hsin tao-jen."

16. Four typical Ming writers of this script were Sung K'o (1327–1387) and his brother Sung Sui (1344–1381) and the Shen brothers, Shen Tu (1357–1434) and Shen Ts'an; for examples of their calligraphy, see *Shodō zenshū*, vol. 17, pls. 52–55; *Ming Sung K'o shu Chi-chiu-chang* (Peking, 1960), and works in the National Palace Museum, Taipei, arch. nos. 5213–15.

17. Wang's catalogue was published in 1916, Yü's in 1911. John C. Ferguson lists two others, *P'ei-wen-chai shu-hua-p'u* and *Shih-ku-t'ang shu-hua-chi* (*Li-tai chu-lu hua-mu*, vol. 2, p. 248); P'ei contains only a title, while *Shih-ku-t'ang* is based on Wang K'o-yü's version but with the entry under Ma Wan's hao, Lu-tun-sheng.

18. Criticism from *Ssu-k'u ch'üan-shu tsung-mu t'i-yao* and Yü Shao-sung's *Shu-hua shu-lu chieh-t'i*, as quoted by Ting Fu-pao, *Ssu-pu tsung-lu i-shu-pien*, vol. 1, pp. 754–55.

II WEN CHENG-MING (1470–1559)

Ch'ang-chou, Kiangsu

Chrysanthemum, Bamboo, and Rock

The Art Museum, Princeton University (L27.70).

Hanging scroll. Ink on paper. 48.0 x 26.5 cm.

DATED: by accompanying inscription during or before autumn, 1535 (*i-wei, ch'iu*).

SIGNATURE OF THE ARTIST: Cheng-ming.

SEALS OF THE ARTIST: *Wen Cheng-ming yin* (intaglio, square), *Heng-shan* (relief, square), both after signature (slightly different seals with the same legend appear in Contag and Wang, *Seals*, pp. 20, 636).

INSCRIPTION: poem in eleven columns, signed Hsü Chin (*chin-shih* degree 1505), dated autumn, 1535 (*i-wei, ch'iu*) (see following discussion).

SEALS OF THE INSCRIBER: *Chia-hui* (relief, square) after signature.

COLLECTORS' SEALS:

Feng Ch'ao-jan (contemporary Shanghai painter), *Ch'ao-jan shin-shang* (intaglio, square) lower right corner.
Ma Chi-tso (contemporary Hong Kong collector), *Chi-tso* (relief, rectangle) lower left corner.
Wu Hu-fan (1894?–ca. 1965, Shanghai collector), *Mei-ching shu-wu pi-chi* (relief, tall rectangle) lower left corner.
Owners unidentified, *Po-yüan shen-ting* (relief, square) lower right corner, probably contemporary; *Ching-chai shin-shang* (intaglio, square) lower right corner, probably Ch'ing dynasty seal.

CONDITION: there are moderate elliptically shaped abrasions in upper and lower sections of the painting—in central area of bamboo stalks and grasses and in inscription, where two characters are illegible (fourth character of line four, first character of line seven); there is a slight 12.5-cm. crease down the center of the paper; no retouching on the painting is apparent.

OUTER LABEL OF PAINTING: inscribed by Wu Hu-fan, undated.

PROVENANCE: Frank Caro, New York.

UNPUBLISHED

WEN CHENG-MING (*tzu* Cheng-chung, *hao* Heng-shan), whose early name was Pi and who later came to be known by one of his other style names, Cheng-ming, was one of the great scholar-painters of the Ming dynasty and a seminal figure of the "Wu school" centered around Su-chou. A gentleman of exemplary character and cultivation, he lived to the ripe age of ninety years and was highly prolific in both painting and calligraphy up to his death, producing works of immense size and power. He is traditionally known as a follower of Shen Chou (1427–1509), but their art-historical relationship is interdependent, and in view of their enormous influence on later generations, critics judge their accomplishments as equal.

Chrysanthemums and bamboo are silhouetted against a garden rock and slope. Reeds, moss dots, and flowers placed on the edges of the forms reveal the artist's predominant structural preference for a radial design, thus stressing the feeling of a flat graphic composition devoid of any atmospheric effects. In terms of Wen Cheng-ming's complete œuvre, this hanging scroll is relatively early and minor in both size and subject, yet its artistic quality adumbrates the fruitful years of his maturity.

This work records an occasion at which the painter and a friend, Hsü Chin,[1] were engaged in tasting tea and savoring the fragrance of chrysanthemum in the cool autumn twilight. In a fashion typical of the connoisseurs of their day, poetry and painting accompanied the event. The long inscription by Hsü Chin is a fourteen-line eulogy in five-character regulated meter. It is executed in a modest and poised "running" (*hsing*) script bearing the elongation and crisp refined turns of Wen Cheng-ming's influence. To the far left appears Wen's own signature in two characters, which is followed by two seals. Verse[2] and image capture the moment:

Open shutters reveal the fading dusk
Solemnly around the courtyard settles chilling frost.
A gentle wind sways the slender bamboo
And rustles vines near the room.

Together we sat in the studio
Leisurely viewing the chrysanthemums blooming in profusion.
Their flowering late makes them all the more aloof and appealing
Leaving a fragrance to charm only the secluded ones.

I tilt the teapot to pour Lu-ya ["dew-sprout"] tea.
We picked it on the south side of the hill and brought it to the
*   foot of the mountain.*
There was the essence of bubbling spring and stones;
Stalks and leaves were cut for their autumn fragrance.
The clay brazier brings the water to the boil
And with one sip—a feeling refreshing as a shower!

> Written in autumn of the year *i-wei* [1535]
> with Mr. Wen as we sat in the Yin-pai studio
> enjoying chrysanthemums and tasting tea.
> [Signed] Hsü Chin.

The painting represents an evocation of the aesthetic pleasure found in the enjoyment of tea and the fragrance of flowers as expressed through the brushwork and perennial motifs favored by the scholar. The compact radial design of this painting was an arrangement Wen Cheng-ming favored in subjects of rocks, bamboo, pine, and flowers and spans the whole of his career. The brushwork is vigorous and quick, with the wrist and arm in lively motion, producing a feeling of dryness in the ink, even in areas where wash is used. This astringent quality is partly the result of the texture of the sized paper and partly of Wen's habitual working speed and manner of grading the ink. He was particularly eager to achieve this soft, fused quality of lineation and the textural contrasts of wet wash with parched ink in works done after the 1530's, and he continued to develop its expressive potential until the end of his career. Such brushwork appears in profound and perfect form in the Nelson Gallery *Cypress and Weathered Rocks* (dated 1550)[3] and in the Cleveland *Old Pine Tree* (undated).[4]

THE DATE OF this work places the execution in Wen Cheng-ming's sixty-sixth year, when he had reached a level of artistic maturity not seen in his earlier works. For example, a painting of similar subject dated 1512 in the Abe collection, Osaka (fig. 1),[5] is recognizably from the same hand. A similar centralized composition consisting of flowers and a rockery are set on a slope. The rock shape, also tapering at its base, is likewise built up with slanting brushstrokes in dry ink forming long concavities. Clusters of grasses, chrysanthemums, and the bamboo executed in the same tripartite *ko*-character form of the leaves are all repeated. In this earlier work, however, the individual elements are less coherently managed. The brush slips and slides with an overstated confidence which is visible also in the calligraphy by the artist written above the painting. The ink tonalities are more uniformly applied, and the wash is used in large, flat areas of the rock, which tends to overpower the rest of the composition. The total expression seems more dynamic than serene. At this stage of development Wen Cheng-ming was not in full command of a "free" style and tended to force his effects. By the 1520's

above left

1. Wen Cheng-ming, *Chrysanthemum, Bamboo, and Rock*, dated 1512. Hanging scroll. Ink on paper. Abe collection, Osaka Municipal Museum.

above right

2. Shen Chou (1427–1509), *Cock and Chrysanthemum*, dated 1509, detail. Hanging scroll. Ink on paper. Abe collection, Osaka Municipal Museum.

left

3. Ch'en Shun (1483–1544), *Chrysanthemum and Pine*, detail. Hanging scroll. Ink on paper. Abe collection, Osaka Municipal Museum.

at least, he had become master of both "free" and "fine" manners.

This work in the Sackler collection represents a refinement of the energies found earlier in the Abe work. More significant, it also reveals Wen Cheng-ming's concept of brushwork and his roots in the Yüan tradition of scholar painting: the modeling in the rocks combines the oblique wash strokes of Wu Chen (1280–1354) and the turning wrist movement of Wang Meng's (1308–1385) twisting linears, coupled with Chao Meng-fu's (1254–1322) idea of dry, porous, "flying-white" textures of the ink. The randomly scored bamboo alludes to Ni Tsan (1301–1374), and the fine linework of the grasses may even recall Chao Meng-chien (1199–1295). The dominant theme unifying these varying stylistic strains is the conception of the scholar-painter's credo articulated by Chao Meng-fu and Ni Tsan, which established calligraphy as the fundamental aesthetic in painting. Its expression fostered the "writing out" of the pictorial idea in painting (*hsieh-i*) rather than the mere imitation of the outward form.

In the execution of the chrysanthemums, Wen Cheng-ming shows his immediate debt to Shen Chou and demonstrates how far the calligraphic emphasis in painting had extended itself. In a work also from the Abe collection, Shen Chou's *Cock and Chrysanthemum* (fig. 2),[6] dated in the year of Shen's death, 1509, the blunt, carefree, but forceful lines still bear a representational intent: the leaves and flowers curl and turn in a space made airier by two butterflies. There is a balance struck, despite the freedom of the brushwork, between the defined shape of the objects and the energies manifested in the forms. In the Sackler work, Wen Cheng-ming has adopted Shen Chou's technique of composing the petals of the flowers by controlled overlapping layers of linear ellipses, but Wen conceives of the chrysanthemums from only one angle and as repeating elements in a larger design. The leaves are rendered almost uniformly in one tone of wash, and they seem to function also as pattern, forming a flat ground of tonal contrast to the flowers, thus intensifying the graphic visualization.

The intensification of the draftsmanlike qualities of depiction and an ever more assertive brush is seen in still a more advanced stage in the work of one of Wen Cheng-ming's pupils, Ch'en Shun (1483–1544). In a painting of a similar subject in the Abe collection (fig. 3),[7] Ch'en's interest lies even less in the modeling of individual forms and more in the action of the brush as it scatters the elements across the surface in directions which activate the blank spaces. He seems to prefer a discontinuity of energy in the lines, a preference which seems to diffuse the compositional forces. These features may constitute significant structural preferences distinguishing Ch'en Shun's mature works from those of Wen Cheng-ming in this genre.

NOTES

1. *Tzu* Tzu-jung, *hao* Yen-hsi, a native of Su-chou. His birth and death dates are not known. His literary works are preserved in his *Hsü Wen-min kung chi* (*Ming-jen chuan-chi tzu-liao so-yin*, p. 471). Hsü Chin and Wen Cheng-ming were quite likely of the same generation, and it is possible that the Yin-pai studio where the painting was executed belonged to Hsü.

2. We are indebted to Mr. T'ang Hai-t'ao and Dr. Lin Shun-fu for their help with the English rendering of this poem.

3. Reproduced in *Handbook of the Collections in the William Rockhill Nelson Gallery of Art and Mary Atkins Museum of Fine Arts* (Kansas City, Mo., 1959), p. 203.

4. Andrew R. and Martha Holden Jennings Fund, acc. no. 64.43, reproduced in *Bulletin of the Cleveland Museum of Art*, vol. 53 (1966), fig. 2, p. 4.

5. Reproduced from *Sōraikan kinshō*, vol. 1, 2/30.

6. *Ibid.*, vol. 2, 2/49.

7. *Ibid.*, 3/56.

III HSÜ CHEN-CH'ING (1479–1511) and others and CH'IU YING (ca. 1494–1552-)

Su-chou, Kiangsu

A Donkey for Mr. Chu: Soliciting Pledges for Its Purchase   (Mu-lü-t'u)

The Art Museum, Princeton University (L320.66).

Handscroll of calligraphy and painting mounted together. Ink on paper. Painting: 26.5 x 70.1 cm.; calligraphy: 26.5 x 104.0 cm.

PAINTING BY CH'IU YING:

UNDATED

SIGNATURE OF THE ARTIST: Ch'iu Ying shih-fu (see discussion of signature at end of entry).

SEAL OF THE ARTIST: Shih-fu (relief, square).

CALLIGRAPHY BY HSÜ CHEN-CH'ING AND OTHERS:

DATED: January 16, 1500 (Hung-chih chi-wei chi-tung-wang hou-i-jih).

SIGNATURE OF THE ESSAYIST: Hsü Chen-ch'ing (after a prose essay in twenty-one lines) in "regular" script.

SIGNATURES OF THE PLEDGERS (ten):

Ch'ien T'ung-ai (1475–1549), one line of "regular" script.
Chu Liang-yü (fl. ca. 1506–1520), one line of "regular" script.
Chu Yün-ming (1460–1526), one line of "regular" script.
Chang Ch'in (fl. ca. 1550), one line of "regular" script.
Shen Pin (fl. ca. 1550), one line of "regular" script.
T'ang Yin (1470–1523), three lines of "regular" script.
Hsing Shen (fl. ca. 1550), one line of "regular" script.
Yeh Chieh (fl. ca. 1550), one line of "regular" script.
Tung Sung (fl. ca. 1550), one line of "regular" script.
Yang Mei (fl. ca. 1550), one line of "regular" script.

COLLECTORS' AND APPRECIATORS' SEALS:

Ch'eng Shang-fu (fl. ca. 1624–1652-) left no seal but is mentioned in Ch'en Chi-ju's 1624 colophon as being the owner at that time.
Tan Hsün (?) (chin-shih degree 1628–1644, from Hua-t'ing, Kiangsu), Chu-hsiang (relief, square) lower right corner of painting and lower right corner of colophon; Chu-hsiang-an (relief, square) lower right corner of painting, lower left corner of calligraphy, and lower left corner of colophon; Chu-hsiang (relief, double seal in two small squares) lower left corner of painting.
Ch'ien T'ien-shu (hao Meng-lu, fl. late seventeenth century), Ch'ien T'ien-shu yin (intaglio, square) lower right corner of frontispiece, third seal from bottom at right edge of painting, second seal from bottom at lower left corner of calligraphy, and lower left corner of colophon; Tseng-ts'ang Ch'ien Meng-lu-chia (relief, tall rectangle) lower left edge of colophon below preceding seal.
Chin Fu-t'ing (fl. eighteenth century?), Chin Fu-t'ing shou-hsien-shih k'ao-ts'ang (relief, tall rectangle) lower left corner of frontispiece, right edge of painting, right edge of calligraphy, and right edge of colophon.
Wu Shang-chung (fl. ca. 1750?), Wu Shang-chung yin (intaglio, square) lower left corner of painting and lower right corner of calligraphy.

Shen Shu-yung (tzu Yün-ch'u, 1832–1873, from Nan-hui, Kiangsu), Shen Yün-ch'u chen-ts'ang-yin (relief, tall rectangle) lower left corner of colophon.
Ching Ch'i-chün (chin-shih degree 1852), Ching-shih (relief, round) right edge of painting, Chien-ch'üan p'ing-sheng p'i-tz'u (relief, large square) left edge of colophon.
Mr. Ts'ao (unidentified), Hsieh-nan Hang-fu Ts'ao-shih kuo-yün-lou chien-ts'ang chin-shih shu-hua-yin (relief, square) third seal from top at right edge of painting, lower left corner of calligraphy, and second seal from bottom at lower right edge of colophon.
Huang Chao (?) (fl. ca. 1850?, a painter from She-hsien, Anhwei), Hsü-t'ang chien-ting (relief, square) lower left corner of colophon at bottom.
Owner unidentified, Hsing-ch'eng chien-ts'ang (relief, square) left edge of calligraphy and right edge of colophon; this seal precedes Lu Hsin-yüan's and is recorded in his catalogue.
Lu Hsin-yüan (1834–1894, a celebrated collector from Kuei-an, Chekiang), Ch'ien-yüan chien-shang (relief, square) lower left corner of frontispiece, lower left corner of painting, lower right corner of calligraphy, and lower right corner of colophon; Ch'ien-yüan shu-hua chih-yin (relief, square), Kuei-an Lu Hsin-yüan, tzu Kang-fu yin (relief, square), and Ts'un-chai yu-ch'eng Ch'ien-yüan (relief, square), all on silk mounting preceding painting; Hu-chou Lu-shih so-ts'ang (intaglio, square) on silk mounting following painting and on silk mounting following first colophon section; a portrait seal (relief, square) on silk mounting following first colophon section.
Chang Chih-wan (?) (1811–1897, a collector and painter from Nan-p'i, Hopei), Tzu-ch'ing so-chien (relief, tall rectangle) lower left corner of colophon.
Li Yen-kua (fl. late nineteenth century?), Wu-ch'eng Li Yen-kua, Ch'ü-chi-fu so-chien so-ts'ang chin-shih shu-hua-chi (intaglio, large tall rectangle) lower left corner of silk mounting following first colophon section.
Miao Ch'üan-sun (?) (1844–1919), Chih-feng shen-ting (relief, square) lower left corner of colophon.

COLOPHONS (five, on paper separate from painting and calligraphy):

Ch'en Chi-ju (tzu Mei-kung, 1558–1639), dated 1624, seven lines of "running" script followed by two seals.
Na Yen (fl. mid-seventeenth century), dated 1652, seven lines of "free regular" script followed by two seals.
Shen Hung-tu (fl. mid-seventeenth century), dated 1652, twenty-eight lines, nine of "regular," nineteen of "running" script.
Yang Shou-ching (1839–1915), dated 1907, three lines (on a separate sheet after Shen Hung-tu) followed by two seals.
Li Pao-hsün (1859–1915), dated 1907.

CONDITION: good, except for six oval mold stains at regular intervals on the upper edge of the painting and calligraphy which become successively smaller toward the inner part of the scroll.

FRONTISPIECE: inscribed by Chu Chih-fan (ca. 1571–1620-) in four large characters of "regular" script (ink on paper, 27.2 x 131.1 cm.) which may be rendered as "Lofty Stature and Unrestrained Generosity" (kao-feng i-yün) (see the detail). [Seals:] Ta-yin chin-men (intaglio, tall rectangle) upper right, Chu Chih-fan yin (intaglio, square) and Chung-yüan tsung-po (intaglio, square) left side.

PROVENANCE: Frank Caro, New York.

PUBLISHED: Wu Hsiu (1765–1827), Ch'ing-hsia-kuan lun-hua chüeh-chü i-pai-shou (Wu's preface dated 1824), pp. 216–17, contains a seven-character quatrain eulogizing the subject, followed by a brief prose record of some of the pledges; Lu Hsin-yüan, Jang-li-kuan kuo-yen-lu (preface dated 1892), 19/3a–5b, records the seals and signature of the painter, the pledgers, and the first three colophons; Kuan Mien-chün, San-ch'iu-ko shu-hua-lu (Kuan's preface dated 1928), pt. 1, p. 46; Tō Sō Gen Min meiga tengo, p. 59 (illustrated as in the Kuan Mien-chün collection); Tō Sō Gen Min meiga taikan (1929 ed.), vol. 2, pl. 279 (painting illustrated); The Pageant of Chinese Painting, pl. 569 (painting illustrated).

Frontispiece by Chu Chih-fan.

THE PAINTING depicts Mr. Chu Ts'un-li[1] (*tzu* Hsing-fu, 1444–1513, from Ch'ang-chou, Kiangsu), a poor but noted poet and bibliophile, receiving the gift of a donkey purchased from funds collected for him by friends. The story which the picture illustrates is told in the calligraphy section, which forms the second major portion of the scroll. The painting is undated, but the calligraphy was written early in 1500, before Ch'iu Ying illustrated the event. A younger contemporary of Chu's, Hsü Chen-ch'ing (1479–1511), wrote the essay to arouse the sympathies of ten other honorable gentlemen, who pledged money and various articles of value toward the purchase of a donkey for Mr. Chu. Among the pledgers were such well-known personalities as T'ang Yin, Chu Yün-ming, and other poets and scholars of local fame active in Su-chou in the late fifteenth to mid-sixteenth century. T'ang Yin, Chu Yün-ming, Hsü Chen-ch'ing, and Wen Cheng-ming (who did not contribute to this gift) were known in their youth as the Four Talents of Su-chou (*Wu-chung ssu-ts'ai-tzu*). The interaction of their different personalities and their amorous escapades subsequently inspired a host of colorful anecdotes and even a play.[2]

The composition of an essay memorializing the plight of a friend, the soliciting and signing of pledges toward the purchase of a donkey for him (especially generous in the case of T'ang Yin, who was himself almost continually in financial straits), and the subsequent illustration of the incident by a later member of the Su-chou circle with its preservation in handscroll form are events which typify the spirit of fellowship in this important circle of Ming literati. The scroll itself further demonstrates the integral role which literature and painting played in illuminating the ordinary events of the lives of these men. Any generous and sincere gesture could become the subject for literary or pictorial expression—and it was often the small, seemingly mundane events which inspired the most memorable works of art among the literati.

Ch'iu Ying is best known for his more colorful and meticulous "palace" manner of rendering landscape and figures. The restrained and classic monochrome style shown here is less familiar, but in terms of his whole œuvre it is qualitatively the finest and most expressive example of his abilities as a figure painter in the *pai-miao* ("plain drawing") style.[3] This scroll displays the descriptive power of pure line when visualized by a master, and it shows Ch'iu's subtle and elegant characterization of figures of different types and stations. It furthermore sets a new standard of excellence for Ming dynasty figure paintings in general, a standard in force until new forms of portraiture would supersede the more antique method found here.

THE TEXT of Hsü Chen-ch'ing's essay (see the detail) reads in part as follows:

> *Mr. Chu Hsing-fu was a white-haired and impoverished scholar....*
> *Of frugal disposition and simple attire, he loved to ride donkeys....*
> *He had nothing but an empty pocket to reach into*
> *And to go home and ask his wife was also useless.*
> *Though my request is clumsy*
> *I count on friends to contribute to this cause....*
> *It's pitiful being poor! Therefore the important thing in friendship*
> * is the sharing of wealth.*
> *To buy a donkey, we must rely on the lofty and wise....*
> *Thus I am depending on your full understanding:*
> *Please don't slight my humble words.*

> Composed by Hsü Chen-ch'ing
> of Tung-hai [Kiangsu]
> on January 16, 1500.

The signatures of the ten pledgers follow:

Ch'ien T'ung-ai, the *hsiu-ts'ai* [degree-holder], presents six ounces [*ch'ien*] of silver [*pai-chin*].

Chu Liang-yü of Hsi-yen [unidentified, probably near Su-chou] presents five ounces of silver [*ying*].

Chu Yün-ming of T'ai-yüan [Shansi Province, the home of his ancestors] presents five ounces [*hsing*] of silver.

Chang Ch'in of Su-wei [unidentified] contributes one picul [*shih*, 133⅓ pounds] of rice or husked grain [*mi*].

Shen Pin of Hsing-ch'eng [Ch'ang-chou, Kiangsu Province] presents one picul of rice.

T'ang Yin, the man from Lu [Shantung Province, the home of his ancestors], offers one set of books in ten volumes of the *Chiao-k'o Sui-shih-tsa*, worth fifteen ounces of silver [*ying, i-liang su-ch'ien*].

Hsing Shen contributes three ounces of silver.

Yeh Chieh contributes three ounces of silver.

Tung Sung, who memorialized the Emperor with an essay on the subject of government, helps by contributing five ounces [*wu-shih-fen*] of silver.

Yang Mei offers one picul of rice.

This calligraphy section alone is a valuable socioeconomic document. The pledges may give us a clue by which to interpret the relative value of objects and commodities in silver currency at that time during the Ming, an aspect of the scroll which deserves further study.

THE PRECISE CIRCUMSTANCES and date of the painting are not clear, but it may be assumed that it was commissioned by a proud collector to illustrate the essay. As Ch'iu Ying is known to have been active for several decades after the date of the essay, the painting may have been executed at a time when the other two key personages in this story, Chu Hsing-fu (1444–1513) and Hsü Chen-ch'ing (1479–1511), were no longer living.[4]

Chu Ts'un-li, the central figure of the painting and the essay, was a man of letters but held no official position. He was noted for seeking out rare and unusual editions of printed texts, as well as painting and calligraphy, and he edited a catalogue of paintings and calligraphy which he had seen, entitled *Shan-hu mu-nan*, among other journals and notebooks. *Shan-hu mu-nan* was one of the earliest private catalogues and was the first to provide more specific details and comment on the works examined.[5] Although Chu was about a generation older than the author of the essay, Hsü Chen-ch'ing, and even some of the pledgers, he apparently had endeared himself to these sophisticated Su-chou gallants.

The scroll also provides us with fine and informal specimens of the calligraphy of the three most famous masters: Chu Yün-ming, at age forty, T'ang Yin, at age thirty, and Hsü Chen-ch'ing, at twenty-one. Hsü was known mainly for his skill as a poet and for his comely appearance rather than for calligraphy. He died at thirty-three, and genuine autographs from his hand are therefore extremely rare.[6] His calligraphy has a regular and serene perfection of the individual strokes and a balanced configuration, which also characterize the "small regular" script of his contemporaries Wen Cheng-ming and Wang Ch'ung (1494–1533), who were celebrated calligraphers. The period influence is a strong distinguishing factor in Hsü's style. His refinement, grace, and restraint were overshadowed, however, by the dash and flair of his friends Chu Yün-ming and T'ang Yin.

IN THE PAINTING two men and a donkey are shown against a plain white ground. A scholar in ordinary dress and cap (therefore not an office-holder) stands at the left with his hands clasped behind his back. His knees are flexed, and he bends slightly at the waist; his

1. Li Kung-lin, *Five Tribute Horses*, dateable to 1090, detail of fifth groom. Handscroll. Ink on paper. Collection unknown.

III, detail.

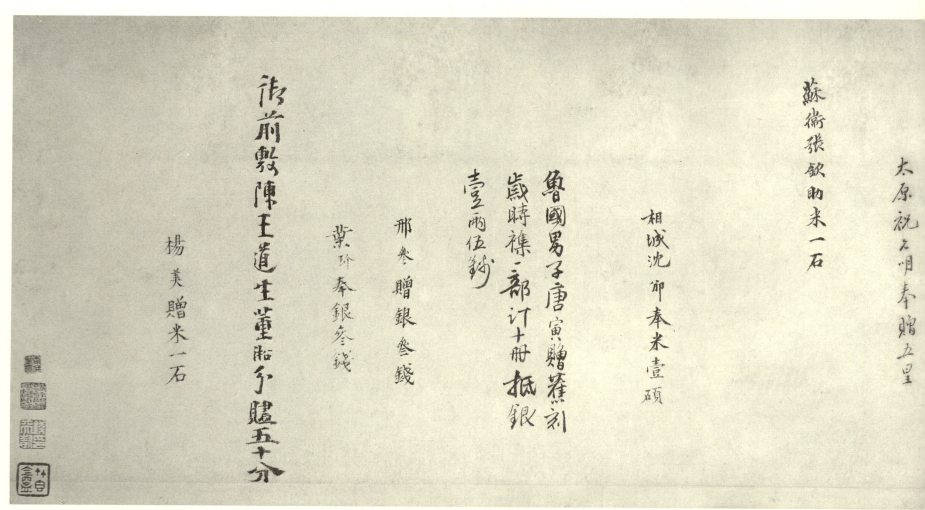

III, detail. The calligraphic essay by Hsü Chen-ch'ing and the signatures of the pledgers.

head is inclined to the right as he looks intently at a servant (or groom) who tugs at the bit of a recalcitrant donkey. We recognize the gentleman on the left as a scholar by his clothing, features, and bearing; he carries himself with the composure of a man of learning. We interpret the second figure as a servant or man of lower station because of his unkempt appearance and his movements. He is attempting to subdue the beast by pulling on the rope; his right hand is stretched out and twisted inward, and he tries to catch his balance on his right foot, while his left one grabs at the air (its big toe curled inward) for leverage. His whole body is tilted and out of control, and this discomfiture is reflected in the expression on his face—eyes narrowed and askew, mouth set, cap ribbon flying.

The donkey, on the other hand, is in full command of himself and performs a star's role. Its form is sharply foreshortened, and the balance of body and legs suggests that its four hooves are firmly planted on the ground. It resists the servant's pull from this rooted position. The momentum of resistance affects its entire being: it swings to the left and its tail responds sympathetically in the same direction. As it relentlessly strains at the taut rope with head lowered, it pulls the man off balance, twisting his arm and hand.

Although blank paper separates the three forms, there is an intense psychological correspondence between them, as in a drama, and this correspondence transforms what might have otherwise been a rather commonplace scene. Ch'iu chose to illustrate Hsü's essay by stressing a kind of "static dynamism"—the scholar stands by in a passive role, his expressive face revealing his concern, while the donkey is at center stage, vigorously contesting for its freedom with the servant. The characterization tells us much of Ch'iu Ying's

and perhaps of the Ming concept of man. Class and social background of scholar and servant have been clearly differentiated, yet each is viewed sympathetically. This degree of humanism is found in more extended form in the works depicting beggars and street characters by Ch'iu Ying's teacher, Chou Ch'en (ca. 1450–ca. 1535),[7] who employed a more jagged and aggressive brushline and a certain amount of caricature to convey the special characteristics of each beggar type. Nonetheless the figures in his depictions are not seen as objects of scorn, ridicule or even pity, but as human beings possessing their own integrity: Ch'iu Ying's depiction of the groom derives both the psychological insight and a certain degree of brush mannerism from his teacher.

Of equal interest is Ch'iu's view of man and beast. In the past, figures of men with animals (primarily horses) had been a classic subject of the scholar-painter. Two of the most impressive works which are still extant and which constitute the mainstays of the tradition out of which Ch'iu's depiction grows are Li Kung-lin's *Five Tribute Horses*[8] and Chao Meng-fu's *Horse and Groom*.[9] In Li Kung-lin's scroll (fig. 1) the figures of the five grooms are differentiated in physical type and personality, but they are idealized and restrained in movement and facial expression. Chao Meng-fu's groom is also subdued in attitude, permitting the brushline and the highly expressive concept of the wind blowing the beard and mane of both groom and horse to dominate the composition. In the Ming, as seen in Ch'iu Ying's scroll, the lower classes are recognized as imperfect and are depicted with a degree of realism and even whimsy which is not found in earlier illustrations of such figures.

Technically Ch'iu Ying achieves such immediacy of effect with

為朱君募買驢疏
稅驂贈友昔者聞之
有馬借人今為上矣
朱君性父
白首窮儒
宴息中林時思放跡
蕭閒布褐自愛騎驢
欲削袁文封曰匡廬處士
深然漢志宓於山谷野人
無裹可探歸空問婦
丐言雖拙仰欲謀朋
老者安之惟仁人為能播惠
傷哉貧也故友道重夫通財
市纏阮籍手
高賢
執鞭何辭於賤子
訪交呂氏行將待卜以賠門
好酒李生會見騰上而過市
庶垂明覽
不鄙譾言
弘治己未季冬望後一日東海徐禎卿撰

秀才錢 同壑奉贈白金六錢

three different brushlines: a modulated one of uneven pressure and speed with slightly angular accents, which is used mainly in the clothing and which is drawn with the brush held slightly obliquely; a continuously fine and supple line of even pressure and slow speed used mainly for the faces; and a brisk, sweeping wash line applied with a broad brush. No underdrawing has been used. The angular accents help to articulate the bulk of the form, but the rhythmic acceleration and pressure of the brush makes them also independently expressive. This is especially notable in the folds of the scholar's robe, which are more swift and continuous than elsewhere and are accented at the angle or outer curvature of the line to suggest volume. In the servant's suit, shorter, briefer lines give a slightly rumpled look, as opposed to the sleekness of the scholar's robe, but the swelling brushstroke, with its greater pressure at a curve or angle and its diminution to an attenuated tip at the end of a line, is an inherent movement of the artist's hand and is found throughout the painting.

Wash has been effectively used in both the figures and especially in the donkey. A few curving arcs applied with a plump, soft brush to slightly dampened paper have lent a soft, furry depth to the animal, while still stressing the purely pictorial texture of the wash. The proportion of the donkey and the streaks of white on its forehead and neck have been spontaneously and felicitously drawn in, allowing the white of the paper to function descriptively. The fine-line details of the hooves, mane, eyes, ears, and nostrils have been quickly and decisively added.

Chu Hsing-fu, the scholar, has been given the traditional generalized depiction proper to a man of learning. Ch'iu Ying excelled at the portrayal of this "type" in his three general categories of figure styles: the monochrome outline or *pai-miao* style without architectural or landscape setting found here, the heavily colored "palace" style on silk with architecture and ladies in attendance, done in a tight, meticulous line,[10] and the slightly colored "garden" style in ink on paper with gentlemen in a minimal landscape setting, executed with a bolder, looser brush.[11] These three styles are more or less clearly distinguishable in Ch'iu's œuvre, and genuine works by him in all three modes are extant. Each style evolved from an earlier classic prototype of figure painting—the "garden" style from Liu Sung-nien or Li T'ang of the Southern Sung and, most immediately, from Ch'iu's teacher, Chou Ch'en; the "palace" style from Chao Po-chü and Po-hsiao of the Southern Sung; and this scroll from the tradition given renewed strength in the Northern Sung by Li Kung-lin in his *Five Tribute Horses* and Chao Meng-fu in the Yüan. Ch'iu Ying may have even drawn directly on a Northern Sung prototype, as can be seen by comparing Li's fifth horse and groom with Ch'iu's scholar.

In the Sung period the distinction in class between scholar and groom is much less pronounced in terms of physical description, and there is a distinct change in the means of depiction—the brushline—which is both visual and tactile. A similar restrained and elongated line has been employed in the robes, except that in Li's depiction the brush moves more slowly, the pressure is more even, and the line is more continually tensile. The Sung brushline is less independent in its movement and direction, and it strives to describe the form while retaining a ductile strength and to subordinate its own freedom to the integrity of the object itself. In this we can read the difference between the Ming and Sung visualizations and the gradual ascendence of the line in its more self-sufficient, calligraphic sense in the Ming. Ch'iu allows the line to gain in speed and pressure from the sheer momentum and sweep of his arm, and the accents and points of emphasis are not necessarily related to the form they describe.

Ch'iu Ying has given the scholar's face a slight frown which suits the human qualities of the incident and his response to both the donkey's and the servant's predicament. The face is rendered according to a canon of proportion which stresses symmetry and harmony of form in the depiction of a scholar type. The whole figure stresses ovals and curves, and the skull is described by a series of smoothly graduated planes from forehead, nose, and cheekbones to chin. The head is in three-quarter view with the cheekbones drawn as arcs; the shape of the nose repeats the slope and finishes with small, narrow nostrils. This noble profile is enhanced by eyes which are wide-set and evenly spaced; they are placed in perfect symmetry in the sockets on each side of the nose bridge. The ears are large, well-formed, and oval, with the hair brushed neatly behind them. The beard is thin but silky, well-combed and tended. His stance is dignified and firm, but betrays his interest in the difficulties of the situation. All of the facial features have been executed in a fine, supple line and subtly graded ink tones. The total appearance is one of refinement and cultivation.

By contrast, the servant embodies the uncouth illiterate who is accustomed to action rather than reflection. The cranium is low and receding; the skull is spherical with sharply projecting planes. The eyes are puffy, close-set, and asymmetrically placed, set in their sockets with arcs above and below the dull slits. The nose is bulbous with exaggerated flaring nostrils; the ear is misshapen and pointed; and the hair and beard are coarse and unruly. The facial exaggerations are continued in the figure, with its awkward, ungainly stance. The servant type's distortion and deviation from an ideal canon of proportion allows him to function like a pivot between the contained moral strength of the scholar and the direct animal instinct of the donkey: he stands, literally, between man and beast, and wavers in between.

The success of this visualization assumes not only a highly acute imaginative power but a degree of technical prowess, usually acquired in the course of an artist's calligraphic training. Ch'iu Ying was not a calligrapher (there are no works or signatures known to be from his hand), yet he excelled in this pure and most difficult of the figure genres. For this reason literati critics esteemed his work despite his professional status. Indeed, in the serenity of the figures and the refinement of the execution, Ch'iu's scroll has no equal among the works of other painters in the Ming, not even the great T'ang Yin.

Ch'iu Ying's signatures (reproduced actual size in the detail) are problematical. As noted above, he was not a calligrapher and is said to have felt his calligraphy inferior, allowing close friends to sign his paintings for him. Therefore the signatures in his works are only a secondary consideration in establishing authenticity. In his better works, however, the signature is usually of a quality commensurate with the painting itself: in this case, the fine brushwork seems to suggest Wen Chia's (1500–1583) hand.[12]

CHU CHIH-FAN'S FRONTISPIECE (see the detail at the beginning of this entry) is written in his well-known "regular" script. The first character, *kao*, has two strokes (the "hook") which have been traced over. The writer himself probably did this after he had writ-

ten the other three characters and when he discovered an imbalance in its proportions, as the other three characters are unretouched and of the same size. This form of retouching occasionally occurs with monumental writing demanding a high degree of symmetry. Chu's style combines the fleshy and monumental features of Yen Chench'ing (709–785) and the slender proportions and dash of Su Shih (1036–1101). Chu Chih-fan was a former ambassador to Korea. His exact dates are not known, but he received his *chin-shih* degree in 1595, and in 1620 he was still known to be active. As he spent much of his life in Korea, many of his works are doubtless to be found there.[13]

CH'EN CHI-JU'S COLOPHON is dated (in the last two lines) June 9, 1624, of the T'ien-ch'i era of the Ming dynasty (*t'ien-ch'i, chia-tzu, ssu-yüeh erh-shih-ssu-jih*). In it he says that he saw the painting at his studio, the Wan-hsien-lu ("Hut of Playful Immortals") on Paishih ("White Stone") mountain. The remainder of the colophon reads:

This scroll describing the gathering of contributions to buy a donkey comes from the hand of the erudite Mr. Hsü [Chen-ch'ing, *po-shih*]. It also has T'ang Chieh-yüan's [Ying's] pledge of books as a deposit for money. It is all a very good story about the great goings-on of the older generation in Su-chou. Ch'eng Shang-fu [the present owner of the scroll] obtained it, and it should be transmitted just as the scroll of calligraphy by Su Tung-p'o [a scroll which records Su Shih's gift of a horse to his student Li Chih] and [which also had] Huang Shan-ku [T'ing-chien's calligraphy appended to it].
[Seals:] *Ch'en Chi-ju yin* (intaglio, square), *Mei-kung* (relief, square).

The second colophon consists of a seven-character narrative poem by Na Yen (fl. mid-seventeenth century), written in spring of 1652 (*jen-ch'en ch'un-jih*), followed by two seals, *Chün-yen chih-yin* (intaglio, square) and *Hsüeh-shang tao-che* (intaglio, square).

The third colophon, by Shen Hung-tu, consists of two lengthy poems in five- and seven-character meter in old narrative verse style. They are dated 1652 and, along with Na Yen's, were written when the scroll was in Ch'eng Shang-fu's collection. The second of Shen's poems reads in part: "T'ang Yin was most extraordinary, as he was equally poor, hence his pledge of books for money was no false pretense. All of it represented the older generation's lofty sense of morality. Thus this painting will endure without perishing and speak for Ch'iu Ying." [Seals:] *Su-an* (intaglio, square) and *Kung-ya-shih* (intaglio, square).

The fourth colophon, by Yang Shou-ching, from I-tu, Hopei,[14] a geographer and prominent official, is dated in March of the year 1907 (*kuang-hsü san-shih-san-nien, erh-yüeh*). Like Ch'en Chi-ju, he recalls an earlier precedent for this scroll, that of a famous scholar and calligrapher whose written note acknowledging a debt became a treasured specimen: "This scroll ought to be enjoyed in company with Wang Ya-i's [Ch'ung's, 1494–1533; a major Ming calligrapher] I.O.U." [Seals:] *Yang Shou-ching yin* (intaglio, square) and *Lin-su lao-jen* (relief, square).

The fifth and final colophon, by Li Pao-hsün (*hao* Meng-ai-fu, 1859–1915, from I-chou, Kweichow[15]), dated December 16, 1907 (no seal). Both Yang Shou-ching and Li Pao-hsün were friends of the great antiquarian and archeologist Tuan Fang (1861–1911).[16]

NOTES

1. Biographical material on the Ming personages in this entry have largely been drawn from the following sources: *Ming-jen chuan-chi tzu-liao so-yin*; the Draft Ming Biographies (where available) and their appended bibliogra-

phies; and Chiang Chao-shen, "A Study of T'ang Yin." The last (in four install-ments) is a brilliant study of the four masters and their circle.

2. The anecdotes have been translated recently by T. C. Lai in *T'ang Yin: Poet and Painter* (Hong Kong, 1971), which includes Chu-tsing Li's study of T'ang Yin from the Draft Ming Biographies and an essay by Chuang Shen. For more detailed information on the circle, see Chiang Chao-shen, "The Life of Wen Cheng-ming and the School of Su-chou Painting in the Middle and Late Ming."

3. As Martie W. Young, in "Ch'ou Ying" (we prefer to retain the more stand-ard romanization of the artist's surname), Draft Ming Biographies, puts it, "in the very distinguished way he practiced his craft, Ch'iu gained the respect of a highly critical audience in Su-chou, and overcame the handicap of inferior status associated with the professional artist."

4. Ch'iu Ying's dates are as determined by Chiang Chao-shen in "A Study of T'ang Yin, II," p. 37; his earliest dated painting is 1509, his latest 1552. Three of the pledgers, Chu Yün-ming, Ch'ien T'ung-ai, and Hsing Shen, also inscribed the colophons to T'ang Yin's fine handscroll *Journey to Nanking (Nan-yu-t'u)* in the Freer Gallery of Art; see Thomas Lawton, "Notes on Five Paintings from a Ch'ing Dynasty Collection," pp. 207–15, fig. 14. The calligraphic styles of all three masters agree in the two scrolls.

5. For a critical discussion of Chu's art catalogues, see Ting Fu-pao, *Ssu-pu tsung-lu i-shu-pien,* vol. 1, pp. 748b–49; and Thomas Lawton, "The Mo-yüan Hui-kuan by An Ch'i," pp. 16 and n. 18, 32.

6. Another example in "running" style is reproduced in *Shoen,* vol. 2 (1938), no. 10, pt. 2.

7. Twelve leaves of an original album of twenty-four are now mounted as a handscroll, *Street Characters,* in ink and color on paper (Honolulu Academy of Arts, acc. no. 2239.1, 1956, gift of Mrs. Carter Galt), illustrated in Gustav Ecke, *Chinese Painting in Hawaii,* vol. 1, p. 297, fig. 97, pl. 36, vol. 3, pl. 60; the other twelve leaves, also mounted as a handscroll, *Beggars and Street Charac-ters,* are in the Cleveland Museum of Art (acc. no. 64.94, John L. Severance Fund), illustrated in *Bulletin of the Cleveland Museum of Art,* vol. 53 (January, 1966), fig. 3a–1. See also Thomas Lawton, "Scholars and Servants." For a discussion of the new humanism which arose in the Ming, see the stimu-lating essays contained in W. T. de Bary, ed., *Self and Society in Ming Thought.*

8. Its present whereabouts are unknown; it is illustrated in *The Pageant of Chinese Painting,* pls. 83–87. This marvelous scroll is Li Kung-lin's finest work. We show here for comparison (fig. 1) the groom accompanying the fifth horse. This fifth section lacks the excellent inscriptions by Huang T'ing-chien which follow each group of horse and groom, and there is a join in the paper separating this final portion from the preceding ones. Nonetheless, judging from the reproduction available to us (a collotype facsimile published in Japan, n.p., n.d.), we believe the last portion to be by the same hand as the preceding sections. For a discussion of this scroll, see Richard M. Barnhart, "Li Kung-lin's Hsiao-ching-t'u," Ph.D. thesis, Princeton University, 1967.

9. Chao Meng-fu's handscroll is in the National Palace Museum, Taipei; it was recently reproduced in Chu-tsing Li's "The Freer Sheep and Goat and Chao Meng-fu's Horse Paintings," pp. 304–5 and fig. 11. The painting is in ink on paper, not silk, as Li states. For a superb example of Chao's figure painting in the *pai-miao* style which is also in this tradition, see his *Imaginary Portrait of Su Tung-p'o,* dated 1301, in the National Palace Museum, Taipei, repro-duced in Chu-ts'ing Li's "Stages of Development in Yüan Dynasty Landscape Painting," frontispiece.

10. E.g., the pair of hanging scrolls in the Chion-in, reproduced in *Min Shin no kaiga,* pls. 73–74.

11. E.g., the hanging scroll *Conversation under Firmiana Trees,* reproduced in the National Palace Museum, Taipei, *Three Hundred Masterpieces,* vol. 6, no. 242.

12. This signature is identical with that found on the two scrolls in the Chion-in collection (cf. *Min Shin no kaiga,* signature section, fig. 47) which can be considered two of Ch'iu Ying's finest works in that genre and are there-fore a standard of quality in terms of the signature found thereon.

13. Another example of Chu's bold hand may be found in *Shodō zenshū,* o.s., vol. 20, p. 237.

14. See Arthur W. Hummel, ed., *Eminent Chinese of the Ch'ing Period,* pp. 484, 782.

15. *Ibid.,* p. 782.

16. *Ibid.,* p. 780.

III, *A Donkey for Mr. Chu (overleaf).*
Scroll reads continuously from right to left, top to bottom.

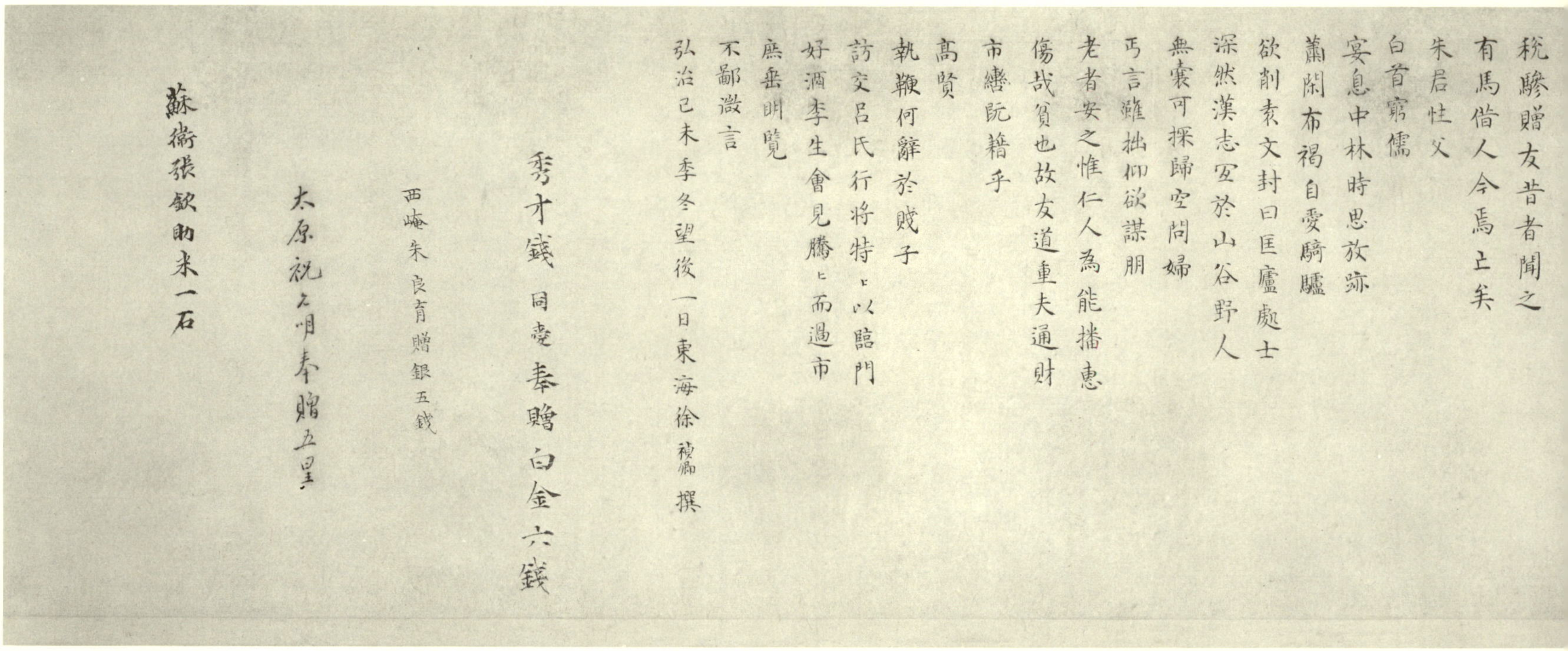

稅駕贈友昔者聞之
有馬借人今焉上矣
朱君性父
白首窮儒
宴息中林時思放跡
蕭閑布褐自愛驕驢
欲削素文封曰匡廬處士
深然漢志宦於山谷野人
無裹可探歸空問婦
丙言雖拙仰欲謀朋
老者安之惟仁人為能播惠
傷哉貨也故友道重夫通財
市纙阮糟手
高賢
執鞭何辭於賤子
訪交呂氏行將特上以賠門
好酒李生會見騰上而過市
庶垂明覽
不鄙譾言
弘治己未季冬望後一日東海徐禎卿撰

秀才襄　同寅　奉贈　白金六錢

西崦朱良育贈銀五錢

太原祝允明奉贈五星

蘇衛張欽昞米一石

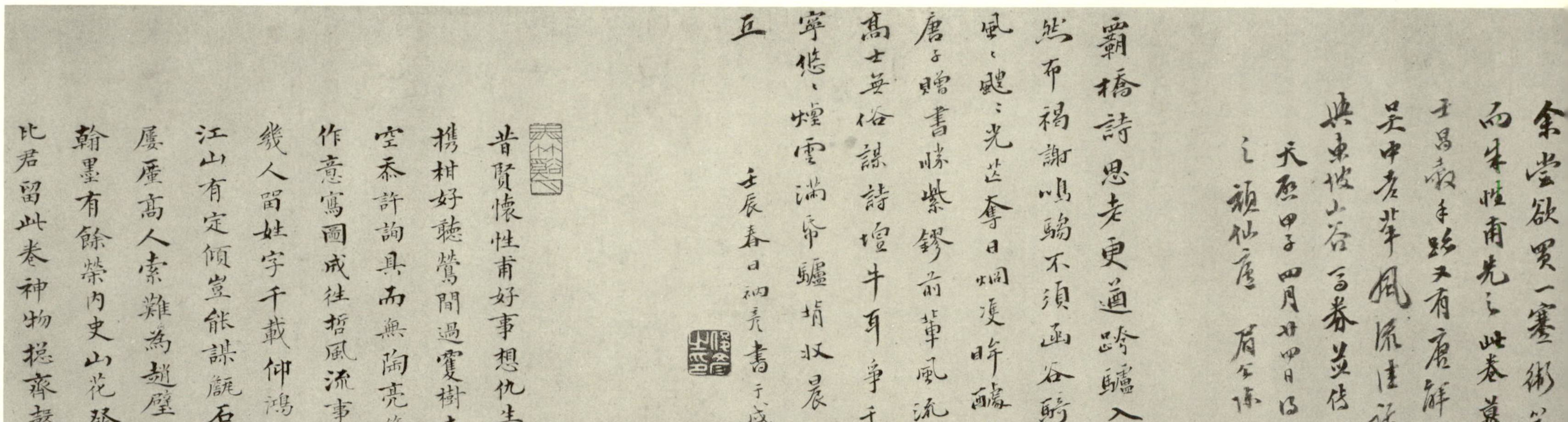

霸橋詩思老更道跨驢入市便清遊蕭
然布褐謝鳴駒不須畫谷騎青牛舊暖搖
風飀飀光芒芒日煙復昨釀金之友娃氏沼
唐子贈書瞇紫鏒前華風流誰為傳尚文
高士蔑俗謀詩壇牛耳爭千妹玲瓏重此圖
寧態煙雲滿帝驢峭奴晨夕把玩老林
壬辰春日兩峯書于戊上乞一枝栖

余嘗欲買一簑衲策蹇九峯中
而朱惟甫先之此卷暮徑跡五徐惟
壬昌敷手跎五有唐解元以贈禎卿時
吳中虛荜風流佳話程名甫得之
興東坡山谷百春苤佳可也
天歷甲子四月廿四日觀來白正山
之頑仙廬　荀全陳從周記

昔賢懷性甫好事想仇生策寒聊當步
攜柑好聽鶯間過寶樹去安入亂山行
空秦許詢具而與陶亮蕭釀錢買飛衛
作意寫圖成往哲風流事追題我華情
幾人罵姓字千載仰鴻名古道誰鷹滅
江山有定傾宣能謀贋石壹重即連城
屢歷高人索難為趙壁輕和嶠無此癖
翰墨有餘榮內史山花發公孫劍器驚
比君留此卷神物提護辟

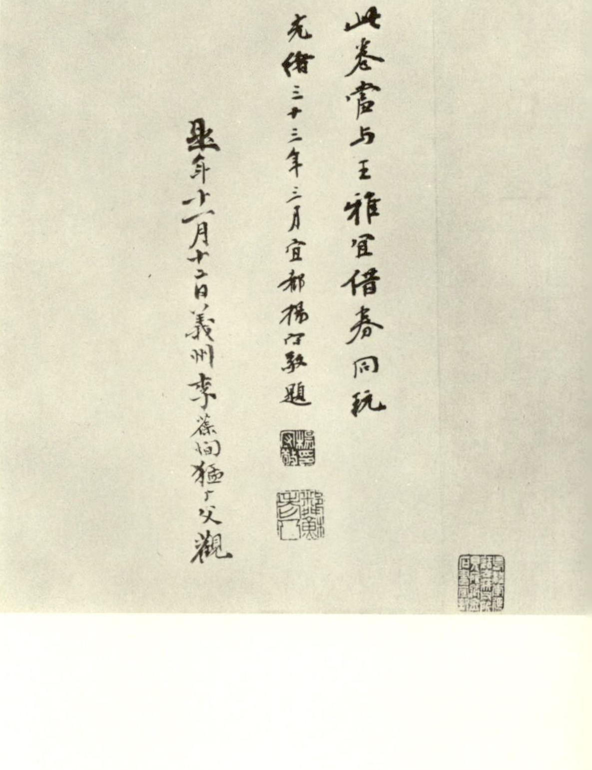

此卷嘗與王雅宜借春同玩
光緒三十三年三月宜都楊守敬題
某年十一月十二日義州李葰田穉又觀

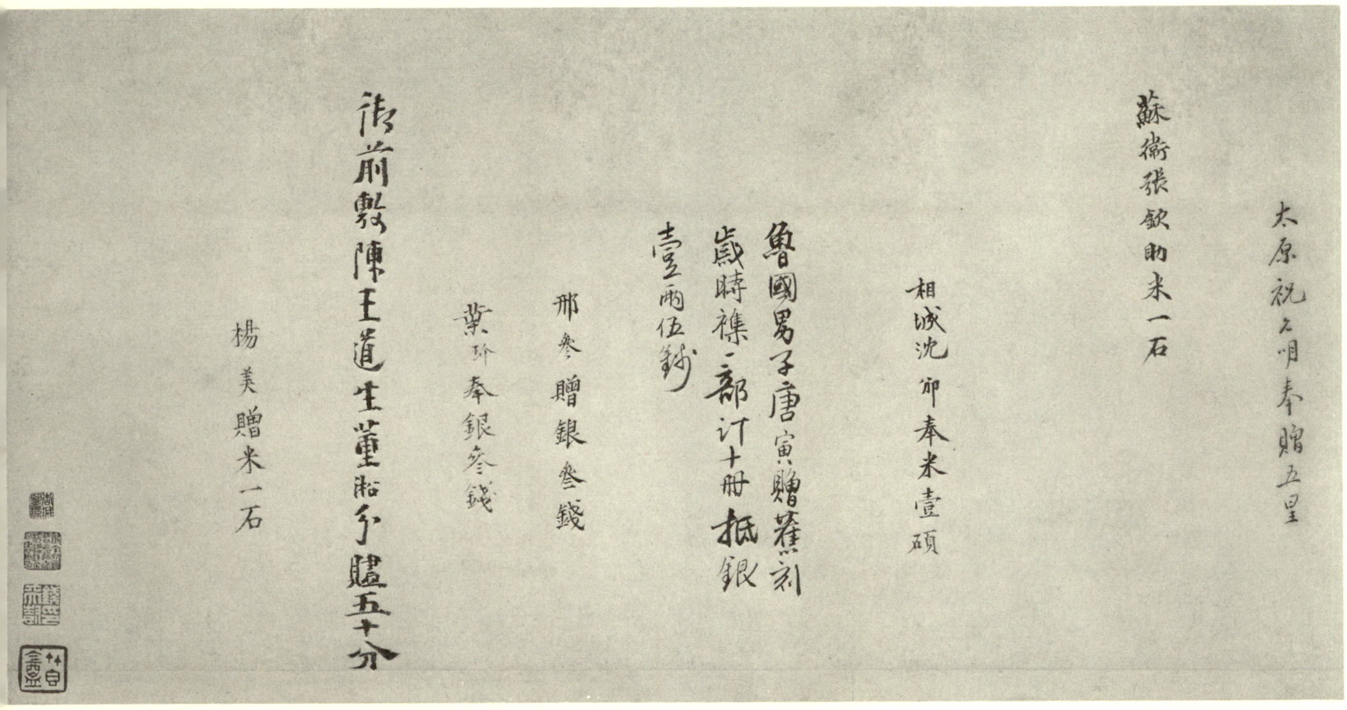

相城沈卯奉米壹碩

蘇衛張欽助米一石

太原祝允明奉贈五星

魯國男子唐寅贈蔡剂
歲時褲一部計十冊抵銀
壹兩伍錢

邢參贈銀參錢

葉玠奉銀參錢

後前軟陳王道生董贴子賠五十分

揚美贈米一石

賢我惟有朱先生先健日逐溪
山行貸無籃與雲不儒愛覽
嘉客徐禎卿一疏手寫謂兩好
催驢代步身為稿不詢朱提
莘賬粟為山一貰求貰成唐
子晨齊家六竇心書抵鋪非福
偽是皆前輩絕高陵圖傳
不朽推仇英程子貰圖與五系
拂々素絹煙霞明陳君見此勤
神砚屢書苦黑膳九紫尚甫
絕廉誶恐割餅無儲粟當子
磬遗亖詩人求品目懸亖好
句寫其礬惜將魚眼生鮫
晴
阮作五言排見雪臘硝挨
焉自发俊贵此影終慚
續點耳
至辰晚春廿六日疏菴沈啟度
題亓記

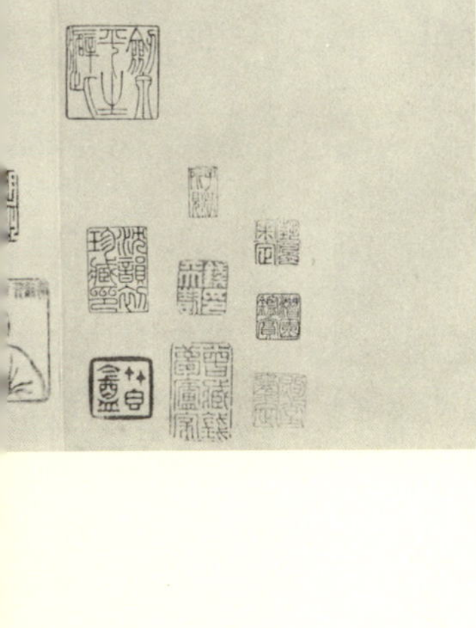

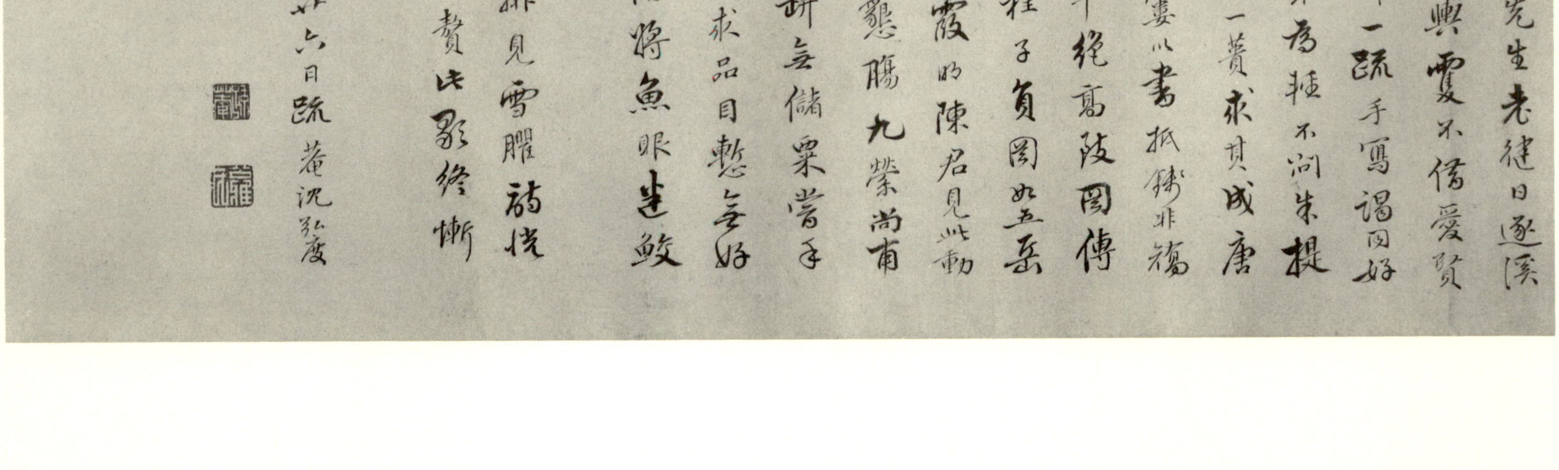

IV CH'IEN KU (1508–1578-)

Ch'ang-chou, Kiangsu

Scholar under Banana Plant

The Art Museum, Princeton University (68-219).

Folding fan mounted as album leaf. Ink and light color on paper. 16.5 x 48.2 cm.

DATED: autumn, 1578 (*wu-yin, ch'iu-jih*).

SIGNATURE OF THE ARTIST: Ch'ien Ku.

SEAL OF THE ARTIST: *Hsüan-ch'ing-shih hua-yin* (intaglio, tall rectangle; Contag and Wang, *Seals*, no. 20, p. 717).

COLLECTORS' SEALS:
Pao Hu-ch'en (*tzu* Tzu-chuang, fl. ca. 1875, a painter, calligrapher, and seal carver from Wu-hsing, Chekiang), *Pao Hu-ch'en ts'ang* (relief, square) lower right corner.
Owners unidentified, *Ch'ien* (relief, trigram and tripod within a square) and *Shang-ch'ih-chai Chi-shih chen-ts'ang* (relief, square), both on lower left corner and probably belonging to the same owner.

CONDITION: fair; there is minor wormhole damage at the base of the fan and slight abrasions over the central and side portions (near the signature); no retouching in these areas is apparent.

PROVENANCE: Frank Caro, New York.

PUBLISHED: *Record of the Art Museum, Princeton University*, vol. 28, no. 2 (1968), p. 94; *Archives of Asian Art*, vol. 23 (1969–70), p. 84.

THIS FAN REPRESENTS Ch'ien Ku's latest dated work. Both the date itself and the quality of the painting extend our knowledge of Ch'ien's activity in his latest years. Arched leaves of a banana plant silhouetted against a large garden stone provide shade for a scholar chanting a favorite verse. Around the curve of bank under a bright flowering tree, a servant crouches over the water's edge to wash his master's inkstone. Gay little fish have gathered nearby, presumably to enact the line, "fish come nibbling at one's fingers when washing the inkstone."[1] Yellow iris and green moss adorn the base of the banana and fruit trees, and clumps of reeds sprout along the banks. The pale coloring captures that often indescribable feeling of the lull between the end of spring and the onset of summer.

TRADITIONAL ACCOUNTS of Ch'ien Ku's (*tzu* Shu-shih) background stress the financial poverty of his childhood and his late education. The straitened circumstances of his youth led to an amusing studio name, Ch'ing-shih ("Rice-Bin Studio"), and seal, *Hsüan-ch'ing-shih hua-yin* ("painting seal of the Empty-Rice-Bin Studio"), which is found on this fan following his signature and date.

Ch'ien Ku's position in art history is overshadowed by that of his mentor, Wen Cheng-ming (1470–1559), but the personal modesty and charm of his vision in this leaf, long appreciated by traditional connoisseurs, are best summed up in the simple entry under his name in *T'u-hui-pao-chien hsü-tsuan*: "He excelled in landscape and figures. His notions of brushwork [*pi-i*] were devoid of vulgarity; therefore those who elevate scholar painting [*shih-pi*] regard him as important."[2]

In terms of the brush conventions, the ink tonalities, pictorial motifs, and subject matter, this work is a typical representative of the Ming dynasty Wu school and owes a major debt to its founders,

Wen Cheng-ming (cf. *II*) and Shen Chou (1427–1509, cf. *XXVIII*). Descriptive details are finely drawn, with the lines tempered and restrained. The brush is primarily held upright to produce thin and pliant contours, as in the waves and drapery folds. The refinement and serenity in the depiction of forms, the lively individuality of the figures, and the purity of the colors reflect Ch'ien's personal style in its full artistic maturity.

Both subject and execution compare favorably with similar representations from Ch'ien's large corpus of paintings. For example, the long handscroll *Gathering at the Orchid Pavilion* in the Earl Morse collection[3] (fig. 1) was painted almost two decades earlier, in 1560, but it bears striking similarities: the rendering of the figures in intimate spatial relationship with the landscape, the compositional viewpoint with its slanting river bank, the relaxed poses of the seated scholars, and the meticulous contouring of the figures and modulated lineation of the flowing robes. The brushwork in the Morse work is slightly drier and, because of the length of the scroll, less attentive to pictorial details. The quality of this fan shows that Ch'ien's lucid and charming style gained in impact with the years.

1. Ch'ien Ku, *Gathering at the Orchid Pavilion*, dated 1560, detail. Handscroll. Ink and light colors on paper. Morse collection, New York.

Recent sources have generally followed the year 1572 (in correspondence with the cyclical date *jen-shen*) given in *Li-tai ming-jen nien-li pei-chuan tsung-piao*[4] as the date of Ch'ien's death. There is reason to believe, however, that the date is wrong. Several genuine late works by Ch'ien show that he lived beyond 1572: the inscription on this fan states, "an autumn day in the year 1578." In the Liaoning Provincial Museum, the Shanghai Museum, and the National Palace Museum, Taipei, fine paintings, inscriptions, and colophons by Ch'ien Ku are dated 1573, 1574, and 1576.[5] Hence Ch'ien's dates should be amended to read "1508–after the autumn of 1578."

NOTES

1. A line from "Su-yü-shih" by the T'ang poet Han Wu (*chin-shih* degree 889).
2. 1/2.
3. See Roderick Whitfield, *In Pursuit of Antiquity*, cat. no. 4, pp. 76–82.
4. P. 313; their source for this death date is not known. The *Ming-shih* (287/*wen-yüan* 3/3b–4a) appends a few brief lines on Ch'ien after the entry on Wen Cheng-ming, with no dates. No dates are given in *Ming-jen chuan-chi tzu-liao so-yin*, p. 880. For a fuller biography, see Thomas Lawton, "Ch'ien Ku," Draft Ming Biographies.
5. *Liao-ning po-wu-kuan ts'ang-hua-chi*, vol. 2, no. 34; *Shanghai po-wu-kuan ts'ang-hua*, pl. 60; and *Ku-kung shu-hua-lu*, 6/172, 5/40, 8/*chien-mu*, and 4/145, respectively. The four works from the National Palace Museum, Taipei, have been examined for authenticity in the original, the others in reproduction. Hsü Pang-ta, in his *Li-tai liu-ch'uan shu-hua tso-p'in pien-nien-piao*, p. 79, lists some ten paintings dated from 1573 to 1578; unfortunately, we have no way of judging their authenticity.

V CH'ENG CHIA-SUI (1565-1643)

Born Hsiu-ning, Anhwei; later active in Hang-chou, Chekiang, and Chia-ting, Kiangsu

Pavilion in an Autumn Grove   (Ch'iu-lin t'ing-tzu)

The Art Museum, Princeton University (L299.72).

Hanging scroll. Ink on paper. 48.1 x 25.8 cm.

DATED: early winter, 1630, of the Ch'ung-chen era (*Ch'ung-chen keng-tzu, ch'u-tung*).

SIGNATURE OF THE ARTIST: Meng-yang.

INSCRIPTION BY THE ARTIST: a quatrain in seven-syllable meter in three lines of small "free-regular" (*hsing-k'ai*) script:

> [*Ni Tsan, hao*] *Yün-lin has not been seen for three hundred years—*
> *Who of mortal bones could become of immortal spirit?*
> *But with some breeze, mist, and sorrowful autumn glow,*
> *We obtain the golden pill [of immortality] right before our eyes.*

> Early winter of 1630 [*keng-wu*]
> in the Ch'ung-chen era, rendered
> playfully by Ch'eng Meng-yang.

SEAL OF THE ARTIST: *Meng-yang* (relief, square; a slightly different seal appears in Contag and Wang, *Seals*, no. 4, p. 374).

COLLECTOR'S SEALS: Chang Ta-ch'ien (born 1899), *Chang Yüan ssu-yin* (intaglio, square) and *Ta-ch'ien fu-chang Ta-chi* (intaglio, square), both on right edge.

CONDITION: fair; there is general foxing over the surface and some wormhole damage; no retouching in these areas is apparent.

PROVENANCE: Frank Caro, New York.

PUBLISHED: Sirén, "Lists," vol. 7, p. 169; *Ta-feng-t'ang ming-chi*, vol. 1, pl. 31.

CH'ENG CHIA-SUI (*tzu* Meng-yang, *hao* Sung-yüan lao-jen, Chieh-an) was a late Ming poet and painter. He was a native of Hsiu-ning, Anhwei, but spent most of his life in Chia-ting, near Shanghai, Kiangsu. Failing in the official exams, he chose to devote himself to poetry and painting and knew many of the cultivated elite of the late Ming, one of whom was the prominent official, poet, and historian Ch'ien Ch'ien-i (1582-1664). Along with the painter Li Liu-fang (1575-1629), Tung Ch'i-ch'ang (1555-1636), Wang Shih-min (1592-1680), Yang Wen-ts'ung (1597-1645), Wang Chien (1598-1677), and others, Ch'eng was counted among the Nine Friends of Painting by the scholar-painter Wu Wei-yeh (1609-1676). Ch'eng was a prolific poet and essayist; several volumes of his poems appeared, and he is also known to have compiled a gazetteer of the Hsing-fu monastery at Mt. P'o in Kiangsu.[1]

Ch'eng Chia-sui is little known in the West, but the true measure of his abilities as a scholar-painter is the esteem he won from the critic Tung Ch'i-ch'ang, who was Ch'eng's senior by ten years. Ch'eng's stylistic position can be interpreted as that of a precursor of the Four Wangs. Only a limited number of his works are extant today; the ones in large format have a freedom and broadness of execution which was also characteristic of other younger contemporaries of his, such as Li Liu-fang and Yang Wen-ts'ung. Ch'eng could also work in a slightly finer style, with an economy of form and a highly imaginative sense of detail, especially in album format. His quality of brushline was one which had a solid basis in calligraphic discipline, but the act of painting was for him a pleasure, and there is little sense of struggle or tension in his forms. In this his

style differs from that of Wan Shou-ch'i (cf. X). Ch'eng's paintings show one direction a man of culture slightly younger than Tung Ch'i-ch'ang might take in the late Ming. His entrance into the orthodox line was too early in its development for his work to display the full fruits of Tung's stylistic redirection, and unlike Tung he left no critical writings to indicate the theoretical basis of his art. In his art and life, however, we see the literati amateur style exemplified.

As STATED IN Ch'eng's poem, *Pavilion in an Autumn Grove* evokes the spirit of the Yüan master Ni Tsan (1301-1374). Compositionally the allusion is obvious: one or two clumps of thin, sparse trees on a foreground slope, one thatched pavilion overlooking the water, a low-lying mountain scattered with black ink dots, and no figures. The painter's poetic rationale is given in the verse—he will capture the spirit of "breeze, mist and sorrowful autumn glow"—but his true visual intentions are felt in the activity of the brush and ink, which transcend the descriptive content of the landscape.

The structure and brushwork tell us how far painting developed in the late Ming from the classic Ni Tsan motifs of the Yüan. In the fourteenth century interest in brushwork and in the description of nature were in equilibrium. By the late Ming, however, gradations of ink and pure surface textures of brushlines interacting as movement and pattern had become the painter's primary concern. Ch'eng's work reveals this interest, coupled with a sense of restraint derived from his own temperament and his calligraphic discipline. In the trees, for example, the brief, blunt strokes in rich graded ink contrast with the long thinner lines of round and oblique strokes in pale and dark tones. The brush is flexible and responsive to change; it twists with light extended movements of the wrist in the areas of the rocky slopes, which in the distant mass are strongly accented by the firm, decisive moss dots. Composition and brushwork are loosely and broadly conceived; the attitude of casual, suggestive execution is as much a reference to Ni Tsan as the landscape motifs themselves.

According to the noted collector Chou Liang-kung (1612-1672), Tung Ch'i-ch'ang considered Ch'eng an important painter. By the early Ch'ing his paintings were already rare, and Chou was only able to obtain a few leaves from an album. Chou quotes one of Tung Ch'i-ch'ang's colophons to a painting by Ch'eng which tells us that forgeries were already being made during Ch'eng's own lifetime: "[Ch'eng Chia-sui, *tzu*] Meng-yang is sparing with his work and doesn't execute paintings easily [upon request]. Truly this painting is rare and precious [*chi-kuang p'ien-yü*] and is not something which can be seen often. Recently there was a painter in the Su-chou area who forged an album of Meng-yang's. He wanted me to inscribe it for him, but I reprimanded him to his face and stalked out. Now I am inscribing this work for Yao-yüan [Chou Liang-kung]. Meng-yang ought to give it his tacit approval."[2] The paucity of extant works in Ch'eng's name would simplify authentication of his works if we were not aware of the great esteem in which he was held and the early existence of forgeries in his name, as indicated in this colophon.

A hanging scroll signed by Ch'eng and dated 1642, also in the Ni Tsan style,[3] bears a poetic quatrain which differs from the Sackler work in only one line. Instead of "With some breeze . . . autumn glow" in the third line, we find "In the cold and far expanses with distant peaks reflected in the river" (according to Sirén). Conceivably the painter could have inscribed two similar poems on two separate paintings, but there is a decided stylistic discrepancy in the two works which makes it doubtful that they were painted by the same hand. The landscape is also in Ni Tsan's mode, but the rocks are heavily built up by sharp, straight strokes, which have a harsh and

不見雲林三百年誰六凡骨換神仙
風烟慘澹秋光淡拾得金井庄眼前
崇禎庚午初冬孟陽戲作

above left

1. Ch'eng Chia-sui, *Landscape in the Style of Ni Tsan*, dated 1627. Hanging scroll. Ink on paper. Collection unknown.

left

2. Ch'eng Chia-sui, *Landscapes after Old Masters*, dated 1640, leaf 8. Album of ten leaves. Ink and occasional color on paper. National Palace Museum, Taipei.

above right

3. Li Liu-fang, *Thin Forest and Distant Mountains*, dated 1625. Hanging scroll. Ink on paper. Collection unknown.

deadening effect. In the trees the dots are mechanically repeated, and the result is visually monotonous. This lapse from the mobile brush action seen in the 1630 work thus differs both in visualization of form and in quality of execution.

On the other hand, an earlier painting dated 1627 and signed by Ch'eng[4] (fig. 1) is comparable in style, quality, and calligraphy. The writing is characterized by the same strong slant and neat and retiring forms. In the painting we see a similar thin, crystalline buildup of rocks, the contrast of moist, dark ink, the play of line and dotted foliage, and the fine, wire-like strokes of the willow leaves. These traits strengthen the links between this 1627 work and the Sackler 1630 painting, but not the 1642 scroll. The definitive evidence which helps us to complete this sequence of Ch'eng's style is an album of landscapes imitating the old masters[5] (fig. 2). This fine work is dated 1640, and the range of styles displayed allows us to confirm the authorship of the Sackler painting.

The 1640 album is an example of Ch'eng's "fine" style. The compositional elements have undergone a reduction of scale and a refinement of form. The rocks are more densely modeled by layers of linear dry and wet strokes. There appears to be a greater interest in the detailed description of foliage through a broader range of linear patterns. Within the scope of the various old masters evoked, the forms remain clean and spare, the expression tranquil and restrained. This linear visualization of form and serenity of mood link the two extreme styles to one master. We see the same flexible brushtip, the same interest in the precise and spare use of rich ink dots for emphasis and contrast, and the same thin willow strands as in *Pavilion in an Autumn Grove*. There is, as well, a quality of linear expression in the album which anticipates some of the calligraphic aspects of the styles of the Four Wangs.[6]

As noted earlier, Ch'eng's style has occasional similarities to that of Li Liu-fang and Yang Wen-ts'ung. Li was a highly productive painter, and although he was ten years younger than Ch'eng and died fourteen years earlier, his fame seems to have eclipsed that of his elder contemporary. A comparison of the two masters' styles[7] (e.g., fig. 3) reveals basically similar structural concepts in both composition and individual forms and may provide visual evidence of Ch'eng's influence on Li, but while Ch'eng stressed the building of form by a thin, tensile line, with very little wash, Li Liu-fang preferred the rounder wet line and developed a dotting method with

wash which was adopted later by Cha Shih-piao (1615–1698; cf. *XIII, XIV*).

Ch'eng's style can also be contrasted with that of Lan Ying (cf. *VII*, leaf H), a painter some twenty years younger. Their landscapes after Ni Tsan may seem superficially similar, but Ch'eng's work not only reveals a more serene temperament but also a willingness to forgo mannerisms and those flicks and turns of the brush which make Lan Ying's work so much livelier on initial comparison. Even their painting signatures show a different temperament and discipline. Ch'eng's is usually a few thoughtfully inscribed lines of small *hsing-k'ai*, in contrast to Lan Ying's conspicuous scrawl. The vast difference in the number of their extant works, or, rather, the facility with which, we know, Lan painted for others, may also have some bearing on the differences in their styles. Lan's late works show the ease and skill acquired in the course of a prolific career. Ch'eng's few works, especially his later paintings, such as *Landscapes after Old Masters* and another album of landscapes and figures dated 1639,[8] show how his restricted output led to a more carefully cultivated manner. Although he earned great respect among his contemporaries as a result, he may have lost art-historical prominence. Nonetheless, with the art historian's renewed interest in the styles of the orthodox school, Ch'eng's role, not as an innovator but as a precursor, may be more fully appreciated.

NOTES

1. For the titles of Ch'eng's other works and additional biographical material, see Fu Pao-shih, *Ming-mo min-tsu i-jen-chuan*, pp. 1–7; Arthur W. Hummel, ed., *Eminent Chinese of the Ch'ing Period*, pp. 113–14; Chou Liang-kung, *Tu-hua-lu* (epilogue dated 1673), pp. 18–19. For Wu Wei-yeh, see Yang Han (1812–1879), *Kuei-shih-chai hua-tu* (n.p., 1940), 5/10.

2. *Tu-hua-lu*, p. 19.

3. Published in Osvald Sirén, *A History of Later Chinese Painting*, vol. 2, pl. 128, and erroneously cited later in his *Chinese Painting: Leading Masters and Principles*, vol. 5, p. 45.

4. Published in *Chung-kuo ming-hua-chi*, vol. 2, pl. 43; collection unknown.

5. Album of ten leaves, ink and color on paper, National Palace Museum, Taipei; published in *Ku-kung shu-hua-lu*, vol. 4, 6/76–77; arch. no. 5820–24, MA38a–j.

6. Cf. the fine album by Wang Chien (1598–1677) of twenty large leaves of landscapes after old masters in ink and color on paper dated 1651 (anonymous loan L232.70, The Art Museum, Princeton University).

7. Published in *Chung-kuo ming-hua-chi*, vol. 2, pl. 45; collection unknown.

8. Album of ten leaves, ink on paper, National Palace Museum, Taipei; published in *Ku-kung shu-hua-lu*, vol. 4, 6/76; arch. no. 5815–19, MA37a–j.

VI SHENG MAO-YEH (fl. ca. 1615–ca. 1640)

Su-chou, Kiangsu

Landscapes after T'ang Poems

The Metropolitan Museum of Art, New York, Purchase,
the Sackler Fund (69.242.1-6).

Album of six leaves. Ink and light color on silk. 28.0 x 32.0 cm.

UNDATED: probably executed ca. 1630–1635.

SIGNATURE OF THE ARTIST: Sheng Mao-yeh (on each leaf).

INSCRIPTIONS BY THE ARTIST: a couplet by different T'ang poets of the
eighth and ninth centuries on each leaf in "running" script.

SEALS OF THE ARTIST: *Yü-hua* (relief, small square) after signature on each
leaf (a slightly different seal with the same legend appears in James Cahill, ed.,
The Restless Landscape, cat. no. 15, p. 66), *Yu-hsin ch'iu-ho* (intaglio, square)
and () () (undecipherable seal in two characters, relief, square) on each leaf in
the two corners opposite the signature.

COLLECTORS' SEALS:

Huang Po-hou (unidentified), *Yü-pei Huang-shih Po-hou chen-ts'ang* (relief,
tall rectangle) on each leaf.
K'ung I (unidentified), *K'ung I shen-ting* (relief, tall rectangle) lower left
edge of leaf C and *K'ung I so-ts'ang* (relief, square) lower left and lower
right edges of leaves E and F, respectively.
Owner unidentified, *Tao-hsiang ts'ao-lu ts'ang-pao* (relief, square) lower right
corner of leaves B and C.

CONDITION: fair; scattered wormhole damage and minor abrasion appear
over the surface of the silk, but there is no apparent retouching.

PROVENANCE: Richard Bryant Hobart collection, Cambridge, Mass.,
through Parke-Bernet Galleries, New York.

PUBLISHED: *The Richard Bryant Hobart Collection of Chinese Ceramics and
Paintings*, pp. 78–79 (leaf C illustrated); *Metropolitan Museum of Art Bulletin*,
n.s., vol. 29 (October 1970), p. 81 (acquisitions list); *Archives of Asian Art*,
vol. 24 (1970–71), p. 113 (acquisitions list); James Cahill, ed., *The Restless
Landscape*, pp. 58 and 68 (leaves A and C exhibited, leaf C illustrated p. 68).

SHENG MAO-YEH, a professional painter who is often classified in
the Wu school line of his native Su-chou, shows in his work a lively
and persistent interest in the shifting and atmospheric effects of
nature—landscapes in mist, rain, and clouds in the twilight and dawn
hours. His brushwork is marked by a reticent control of line,
dominated by a precise and remarkable command of ink tonalities,
whether through wash, stippling, or occasional linear accent.
Through the deft gradations of ink and the layering of forms on a
tilted but continuous ground plane, spatial recession and the diminution of elements in a blurred, vapor-filled atmosphere are evoked.
The dense buildup of fine, meticulously placed strokes reveals
Sheng's primarily descriptive intent, one which ostensibly differs
from that of a scholar-painter such as Cha Shih-piao (cf. *XIII, XIV*)
but which is completely in harmony with the concrete imagery of
the poetic couplets written in his rather restricted and angular hand.
The exploration of the descriptive potentials of ink to suggest different states of atmospheric realism and the effects of light in general
are characteristic features of several late Ming painters of highly
varied stylistic affiliations.

Leaf A, "Trees at Dawn"

Leaf B, "Cloud-Swept Steps"

Leaf C, "Knocking at the Gate in the Moonlight"

Leaf D, "Beyond the Solitary Bamboo Grove"

Leaf E, "Cockcrow by the Fading Moon"

Leaf F, "Fog-Hidden Trees by the Shore"

VII LAN YING (1585–1664-)

Hang-chou, Chekiang; Yang-chou, Kiangsu

Landscapes after Sung and Yüan Masters
(Fang Sung-Yüan shan-shui ts'e)

The Metropolitan Museum of Art, New York, Purchase,
the Sackler Fund (1970.2.2a-l).

Album of twelve leaves. Ink and occasional color on paper. 31.5 x 24.7 cm.

DATED: in the period January 30–March 29, 1642, on leaves A, D, H, K, and L.

SIGNATURE OF THE ARTIST (in "running" script on each leaf): Hsi-hu wai-shih, Lan Ying (leaf A); Lan Ying (leaves B, C, D, F, H, I, J, K, and L); Ying (leaves E and G).

INSCRIPTION BY THE ARTIST: on each leaf.

SEALS OF THE ARTIST (on each leaf):
Ying (intaglio, square; Contag and Wang, *Seals*, no. 14, pp. 721–22) leaves A, B, and I.
Ying (intaglio) and *T'ien-shu* (relief; a double seal in two squares; Contag and Wang, *Seals*, nos. 15–16, pp. 721–22) leaves C, D, G, H, J, and K.
Lan Ying (intaglio) and *T'ien-shu-shih* (intaglio; a double seal in two squares; Contag and Wang, *Seals*, nos. 12–13, pp. 721–22) leaves E, F, and L.

DEDICATION: to Chiang Shao-shu (*tzu* Erh-yu, ca. 1575–ca. 1643), leaves C, F, G, and L.

PLACE OF EXECUTION: P'ing-shan-t'ang, Yang-chou, Kiangsu.

NO COLLECTORS' SEALS OR COLOPHONS

CONDITION: excellent.

PROVENANCE: Richard Bryant Hobart collection, Cambridge, Mass., through Parke-Bernet Galleries, New York.

PUBLISHED: *Ran Denchiku hoko sanzui-satsu* (Kyoto, 1920); Osvald Sirén, "Lists," vol. 7, p. 204; *1000 Jahre Chinesische Malerei*, p. 138; *1000 Years of Chinese Painting*, p. 134; Roger Goepper, *The Essence of Chinese Painting*, pl. 14, pp. 48, 224 (leaf F illustrated in color); Contag and Wang, *Seals*, nos. 12–16, pp. 721–22; *The Richard Bryant Hobart Collection of Chinese Ceramics and Paintings*, no. 263, pp. 70–71 (leaf F illustrated); James Cahill, ed., *The Restless Landscape*, no. 64, pp. 133–34, 137, 167 (leaf J illustrated); *Metropolitan Museum of Art Bulletin*, n.s., vol. 29 (October, 1970), p. 81 (acquisitions list); *Archives of Asian Art*, vol. 25 (1971–72), p. 114.

Sung and Yüan painters whose styles are imitated in this album:
Li Ch'eng (919–967), from Ying-ch'iu, Shantung (leaf A).
Fan K'uan (fl. ca. 990–1030), from Hua-yüan, Shensi (leaf B).
Chao Ling-jang (fl. ca. 1070–1100), of the Sung imperial family (leaf C).
Mi Fu (1051–1107), from Hsiang-yang, Hupei (leaf D).
Kao K'o-kung (1248–1310), from Ta-t'ung, Shansi (leaf E).
Ts'ao Chih-po (1272–1355), from Hua-t'ing, Kiangsu (leaf F).
Huang Kung-wang (1269–1354), from Ch'ang-shu, Kiangsu (leaf G).
Ni Tsan (1301–1374), from Wu-hsi, Kiangsu (leaf H).
Wu Chen (1280–1354), from Chia-hsing, Chekiang (leaf I).
Wang Meng (1308–1385), from Wu-hsing, Chekiang (leaf J).

LAN YING'S LANDSCAPES in the styles of old masters are a major theme in his works. Extant paintings dated in the early 1620's, when he was in his early maturity, reveal that the pictorial idiom of the Sung, Yüan, and even T'ang masters not only provided his technical training but also inspired many of his most expressive works. This album in twelve leaves was painted when Lan Ying was fifty-eight, and thus represents a mature work. According to the inscription on leaf A the album was completed in Yang-chou, Kiangsu, at the historic P'ing-shan-t'ang (see Part I above). It was executed for the scholar and occasional painter Chiang Shao-shu, who is well known as the author of the *Wu-sheng shih-shih* and the *Yün-shih-chai pi-t'an*.

The year 1642 was a productive one for Lan Ying, and the P'ing-shan-t'ang was important because the literary gatherings that he attended there stimulated several of his finest variations after the old masters in album format. Two of these are extant, the one shown here in the Sackler collection and one in the Art Institute of Chicago. The latter album was also dedicated to a scholar-painter, Fang Heng-hsien (ca. 1620–1678). These albums are stylistically similar and demonstrate the range and versatility of Lan Ying's command over the idioms of ancient masters, all of whom were placed by Tung Ch'i-ch'ang in the grand line of the Southern School. In these and other albums dating from the twenties to the fifties Lan Ying reveals a clear knowledge not only of the brush formulas but also of the expressive value of the ancient works available to him for study. Nonetheless, despite Lan's exposure to a certain number of antique works and to the taste of eminent connoisseurs, his imitations after the ancients still differ from those of the orthodox line, remaining primarily late Ming in concept. His shortcomings lie primarily in the realm of brushwork and composition. The large number of paintings he produced encouraged a certain speed and glibness, qualities inevitably judged harshly by critics oriented toward amateur painting of scholar-calligraphers. On another level, Lan's shortcomings may also be partly the result of his motives, or at least those perceptible in his works. Tung Ch'i-ch'ang and the Six Masters sought out and studied the ancients as part of a systematic larger plan of artistic recovery. Lan's imitations, it seems, were not motivated by an inner plan or artistic necessity but by what seemed feasible or fashionable at the time. He occasionally followed his own artistic intuition and in many cases succeeded marvelously in capturing certain moods or coloristic effects. Beyond that, however, he seems to have had little interest in recapturing or ability to restore what was monumental in composition or impact in the models he followed. In the main he tended to rely on the simplest and most expedient arrangements, those which were often a mere repetition of key motifs.

Yet Lan did command a following, and perhaps his ultimate contribution in art-historical terms is his influence, which took several different paths in the Ch'ing. Not only the Lan family (his son, Lan Meng, and his two grandsons, Lan Shen and Lan T'ao) but also contemporaries like Liu Tu (fl. ca. 1636), Chiang Hung (fl. ca. 1674–1690), Ch'en Hung-shou (1598–1652), and Chu Ta (1626–ca. 1705) show his influence in both landscape and in the genres of figures and flowers and birds. In the latter category, Lan provided a formal type which both Chu Ta and Ch'en Hung-shou adapted to a highly expressive degree (cf. *VIII*).

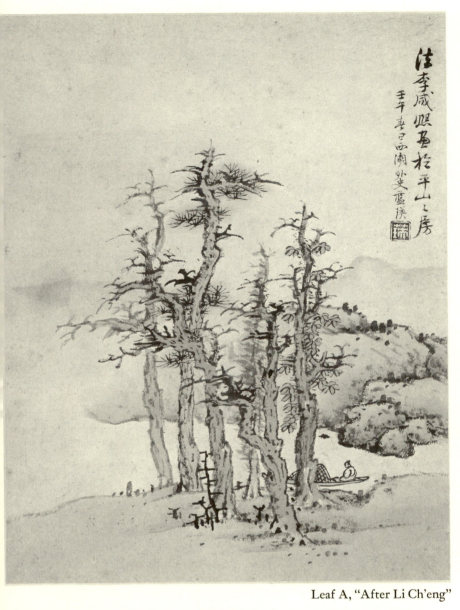

Leaf A, "After Li Ch'eng"

Leaf B, "After Fan K'uan"

Leaf C, "After Chao Ling-jang"

Leaf D, "After Mi Fu"

曹雲西之意水
二南先生社冉正

蘆溪

Leaf F, "After Ts'ao Chih-po"

觀大癡
江山勝覽
卷法以
二南先生
鑒室漠

Leaf G, "After Huang Kung-wang"

壬午春三月
蝶叟金震廣笔

Leaf H, "After Ni Tsan"

觀樗蓊光小畫
遂仿其法蘆溪

Leaf I, "After Wu Chen"

Leaf E, "After Kao K'o-kung" (actual size)

Leaf J, "After Wang Meng"

Leaf K, "Promontory and Stream"

Leaf L, "Cottages by a Stream"

Landscape in the Style of Huang Kung-wang

The Art Museum, Princeton University (68-220).

Folding fan mounted as album leaf. Ink and color on gold-flecked paper. 16.0 x 50.3 cm.

DATED: winter, 1650 (keng-yin, tung-jih).

SIGNATURE OF THE ARTIST: Lan Ying.

INSCRIPTION BY THE ARTIST (in twenty-six characters of "running" script in fourteen brief lines):

Great years as lofty as a mountain. Painted in Ta-ch'ih's [Huang Kung-wang's] method to commemorate the longevity of Chung-weng Lao-tsu-t'ai (unidentified). A winter's day of the year 1650 [keng-yin], Lan Ying.

SEAL OF THE ARTIST: *T'ien-shu* (relief, oval).

COLLECTORS' SEALS:

Yü Jung(?) (a Ch'ing painter of orchid and bamboo from Chia-shan, Chekiang), *Yao-nung p'ing-sheng chen-shang* (relief, tall rectangle) lower right corner.
Owner unidentified, *Chao-(?)-fei ts'ang* (relief, square) lower left corner.

CONDITION: fair; there is slight abrasion over the whole surface of the work and especially in the lower and upper edges; four vertical creases at regular intervals on the paper indicate that the fan may have been folded after being dismantled from its bamboo framework.

PROVENANCE: Frank Caro, New York.

PUBLISHED: *Record of the Art Museum, Princeton University*, vol. 27 (1968), p. 94 (acquisitions list); *Archives of Asian Art*, vol. 22 (1969–70), p. 85 (acquisitions list).

A BRILLIANT "blue-green-style" landscape with the proper inscription has conveniently served the purpose of commemorating the birthday of a friend. In this work Lan Ying's early study of the old masters[1] has enabled him to suggest monumentality within the limited format of a fan. The three-cornered rock forms, the low and slanting plateaus, and the clusters of small houses and pine foliage are formal motifs idiomatic of the Yüan master Huang Kung-wang (1269–1354). But the way the brush delineates the forms—the sharp, angular turns of the rock silhouettes, the layers of flat colored washes substituting as modeling strokes, and the bold, broken outlines of the trees—all spell the late Ming departure from the equilibrium which the Yüan masters struck between descriptive reality and expressive freedom.

Here the integrity of rocks and trees as images from nature is insignificant: their forms function more than ever as vehicles for pure brushwork—in Lan Ying's case, forceful angular brushlines offset by planes of colored washes. Lan was sixty-six when he inscribed this work. In terms of the range of his œuvre, he had reached his mature period by the 1620's, when he was in his forties. The long handscroll in the Seattle Museum of Art, *Landscapes after Four Masters*, dated 1624, is an excellent testament of his convictions at that stage. In this fan Lan's choice of a stubby, worn-out brush was felicitous, for it diminishes that staccato, occasionally sharp and slippery quality which is typical of his brush manner.

Landscapes in the style of Huang Kung-wang were Lan Ying's forte. The mimetic goal of the round, full ideal of brushwork seen in the Yüan master's works helped to temper the tendency of Lan's simplified forms to verge on thinness and to lack a sense of weight. Indeed, in late works such as this one, color assumes an increasingly important role in the modeling of form to suggest greater volume. In another long handscroll in the manner of the Yüan masters, dat-

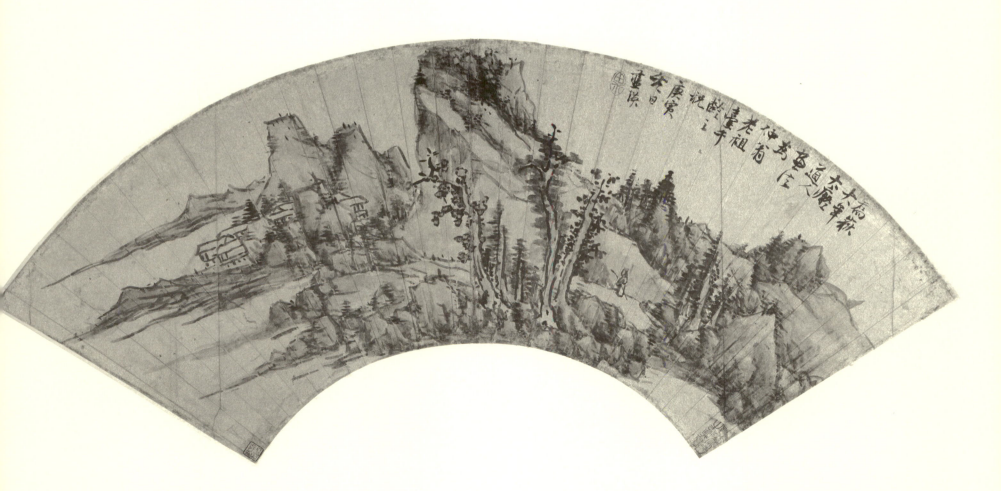

able by style to ca. 1650,[2] large amounts of paper are also left undefined within the outline of a rock or boulder. This order of simplification lends a quality of decorative abstraction to the form. The layers of color which are applied to model the various facets of the rock help to create that highly attractive and shimmering effect of landscape which in this fan is further heightened by the reflections from the gold paper on which it is painted.

AESTHETIC CRITICISM by the early eighteenth century had become more rigid and factional than in the previous century, when the painters concerned were still active. Critical pronouncements came to assume the strength of dogma, and such designations as the Che school,[3] with which Lan Ying was associated because he was a native of Ch'ien-t'ang, Chekiang, came to imply academicism, professionalism, and therefore bad taste. The exposure of critics to the various painters of the seventeenth century was often quite random and limited to only a few paintings of a given master. Such categorical judgments, therefore, often had little to do with a master's specific works or stylistic range but had the character of a general condemnation—a condemnation, in fact, frequently contradicted by many of the critics' own sources. For example, one of the most influential and frequently quoted biographical entries on Lan is by Chang Keng (1685–1760), who says in his *Kuo-ch'ao hua-cheng-lu*:

Lan Ying (*tzu* T'ien-shu, *hao* Tieh-sou) was a native of Ch'ien-t'ang [Chekiang]. In his landscapes he followed the various masters of the Sung and Yüan, and in his late years established his own style, [which featured] precipitous peaks and old trees. He was especially adept at large works. He also painted figures, birds and flowers, and plum and bamboo, which were famous in their time. In painting there is the Che school; it began with Tai Chin and reached its summit with Lan Ying. For that reason connoisseurs do not esteem them.[4]

What is most memorable about this brief entry is Chang's last comment affiliating Lan Ying with the Che school. It is the only "art-historical" statement in the brief account and seems strange in the context of what is otherwise a lackluster description of Lan's command of subject matter. Nonetheless, its influence has outweighed the authority with which it was pronounced. A biographical source such as this may lose such authority when the critic's partialities and knowledge of the paintings of the master in question are made clear and his criticisms are compared with the views of the same work by his contemporaries. Such knowledge may be especially important in the case of an artist like Lan Ying, whose art-historical position is in dispute. It appears that many critics were either not aware of Lan's broad stylistic range or, if they were, had seen only one aspect of this output. Chang Keng reveals in his other biographies of painters a very strong bias toward painting produced by persons of scholarly or bureaucratic status. Had his pronouncement on Lan been understood as a record of prevailing late Ming and early Ch'ing taste, no harm would have been done, but by the eighteenth century so much opprobrium had been attached to the "Che school" designation in painting criticism that a true appreciation of Lan's work was seriously jeopardized. The influence of such shifts in aesthetic standards on later evaluations of both entire periods in art history and of individual painters within those periods, such as Lan Ying, is not yet well understood and merits further study.

Today, a visual examination of Lan Ying's style reveals no similarities to the work of Che school practitioners. In fact, his brushwork differs from theirs in a most fundamental sense. He builds his forms primarily with line and with the centered tip of an upright brush (*chung-feng*). The angular rock forms and outlines he prefers are then modeled with flat washes and dots. Technically the

proponents of the Che school built their reputations on the oblique side stroke or "axe-cut" method, which combines both line and wash in one sweeping movement. As to subject matter, Lan Ying's own inscriptions on paintings seldom mention either the Northern or Che school models.[5] On the contrary, the many albums in the style of old masters which date from the 1620's onward[6] reveal Lan's familiarity with the styles of ancients of both lineages, going far beyond the models of any Che school master to incorporate the Wu school, and therefore revealing further the influence of Tung Ch'i-ch'ang.

Visually, these points cannot be ignored. Moreover, some of the colophons and criticism written by his close contemporaries indicate that he was not associated with the Che school during his own lifetime. In a late Ming-early Ch'ing compilation by Hsü Ch'in, the *Ming-hua-lu*, the view presented of this artist is far more informative:

He painted landscapes which, in his early years, were elegant and moist [*hsiu-jen*]. He copied the works of T'ang, Sung, and Yüan masters, in which every brushstroke recalled antiquity. As to [Huang Kung-wang, *tzu*] Tzu-chiu, he applied his mind to study him with special effort, saying that it was like a calligrapher [learning] *k'ai* ["regular"] script: he must begin with this before he can undertake transformations of other scripts. In his late years his brush grew increasingly mature and powerful. He also excelled in painting figures from life, and his orchid and rocks were particularly exceptional. He lived to over eighty, and those who carried on his methods were particularly numerous: Ch'en Hsüan, Wang Huan, Feng Shih, Ku Hsing, and Hung Tu were among the select ones.[7]

Two points are worth noting in determining the reliability of this account: first, Hsü Ch'in's observation that Lan Ying made a special study of Huang Kung-wang is also mentioned by Lan's contemporaries (see below); second, it seems likely that Hsü Ch'in may actually have known Lan Ying or his pupils because the names which he lists as Lan's followers (beyond those which are entered separately in the *Ming-hua-lu*) are fairly obscure and were probably known only to close contemporaries.

The colophons and self-inscriptions on extant or recorded paintings offer further information on Lan Ying's activities. The Sackler *Landscapes after Sung and Yüan Masters* (*VII*), for example, not only documents Lan's friendship with Chiang Shao-shu, to whom it is dedicated, but also informs us of his visit to the collection of the important connoisseur, painter, and bibliophile Sun K'o-hung some thirty years earlier. The visit must have taken place sometime before 1611, when Sun died. The occasion may have been that mentioned in a self-inscription to a hanging scroll of bamboo dated 1607,[8] in which Lan states that he painted the work for Sun K'o-hung at his studio, the Hsüeh-t'ang. The Chicago album dedicated to Fang Heng-hsien and a third album after old masters, no longer extant but again dated 1642 and painted at the P'ing-shang-t'ang in Yang-chou,[9] also document his contacts with intellectuals of the day.

Lan Ying's emulation of Huang Kung-wang developed over many years of study. Some colophons written by contemporary scholar-painters further illuminate his relationship with the old masters and with contemporary literati and their standards of criticism. In a self-inscription to a landscape handscroll he painted after Huang Kung-wang (*lin Ta-ch'ih shan-shui chüan*) recorded in an early nineteenth-century catalogue, Lan says: "Of all the extant scrolls by Huang Kung-wang, I have had a chance to see more than half of the treasures within the empire. My thirty years of research and study of the master have come to this [i.e., what can be seen in this scroll]. If the Four Yüan Masters could see this scroll of mine, they certainly would allow me to enter their groves."[10] Neither the colophon nor the scroll is dated, but two additional colophons (see below) are dated 1638; these may have been written soon after the execution of the scroll and Lan's own colophon. From their contents we can surmise that Lan began his study of Huang around 1607, which, as noted above, was about the time that he made his excursion to Sun K'o-hung's studio and viewed his collections.

Other colophons on this handscroll are by such eminent scholars as Ch'en Chi-ju (1558–1639) and Fan Yün-lin (1558–1641). From what they say, Lan had good reason to be proud of that particular work. Ch'en says that when he had opened the scroll only a few feet he had the strange feeling that Huang Kung-wang himself had reappeared. Ch'en, who signed the work a year before his death at eighty-one, was a connoisseur of vast experience who had no need to praise the work of a younger painter. The scholar and theorist Fan Yün-lin describes his reaction to the scroll in a similar way. He writes that Lan Ying came to visit him with a landscape scroll in hand, not telling him its author. As soon as Fan opened the scroll he was stunned: when did Huang Kung-wang ever paint such a scroll, he asked—where did this landscape come from? Lan Ying smiled, but did not reply. Only when Fan had reached the end of the scroll and saw Ch'en Ch'i-ju's colophon did he realize that it was painted by Lan himself. The last recorded colophon on the scroll is by another scholar in Tung Ch'i-ch'ang's circle, Yang Wen-ts'ung (1597–1645, also one of the Nine Friends of Painting). Yang states that Lan Ying's imitations after Huang Kung-wang had undergone three stages of transformation; in this scroll he had reached the point at which the brushwork and handling of ink approximated that of the famous *Dwelling in the Fu-ch'un Mountains*—hence it had attained the ultimate.[11]

Such praise could not be idle. While not all of Lan's work necessarily reached such a high level, it is clear that his contemporaries were aware of and appreciated his intensive study of Huang Kung-wang's work. The scroll so highly praised here was executed in Lan's early maturity, when he had already spent some thirty years in training and study of ancient works. As early as the 1620's his close studies of old masters reveal his versatile brush repertoire.

To return to Chang Keng's entry on Lan Ying, in the closing lines Chang observes that in his youth, whenever he heard his elders (in Hsiu-shui, or the modern Chia-hsing, Chekiang) discuss painting and speak of Sung Hsü (1523–ca. 1605) or Lan Ying, it was inevitably in a tone of disdain, yet he finds it unfair to speak of Lan Ying and Sung in the same breath, for he has seen a painting by Sung which certainly puts him in a superior category. This statement is revealing in several ways. First, it indicates that many of Chang Keng's opinions on painters were influenced by the taste of his elders of the late seventeenth-early eighteenth century. Second, it seems that Chang Keng himself would have continued to perpetuate their opinions (in this case, the judgment of Sung Hsü) had he not seen with his own eyes a painting by that master which put them in question. Chang was active for about forty years after Lan Ying died, yet apparently he was not personally acquainted with Lan's work. Such intellectuals as Ch'en Chi-ju, Fan Yün-lin, and Yang Wen-ts'ung *did* know Lan Ying, and their opinion on a specific painting was based on the visual evidence of the work as well as on personal acquaintance with the artist. (Chiang Shao-shu, recipient of the Sackler 1642 album, offers but a brief, one-line entry on Lan Ying in his *Wu-sheng shih-shih*;[12] we have found no colo-

phons by Chiang to other works of Lan's and cannot say what his opinion of him may have been.)

Not all eighteenth-century critics agreed with Chang Keng in dismissing Lan Ying's works, however. The 1642 album of landscapes recorded in the *Hsü-chai ming-hua-lu* bears a colophon dated 1769 which quotes verbatim the contents of the *T'u-hui pao-chien hsü-tsuan* entry on Lan Ying.[13] Nominally this biographical compilation was edited by Lan Ying himself and another painter, Hsieh Pin. As one would expect, the biography contains no negative criticism,[14] but neither does it mention any affiliation with schools or regions. According to this source, Lan Ying seems to have traveled to all the important centers of culture, both north and south. This is significant not only for Lan's own development but also for the influence which he may have exerted in the places through which he passed (this is another aspect of his activity which deserves study). Biographies of this nature must, of course, be used with circumspection. However, of the various later ones, the *Ming-hua-lu* and the *T'u-hui pao-chien hsü-tsuan* appear to be most informative and least biased.

NOTES

1. A process verified in such works as the 1622 album in the National Palace Museum, Taipei, in ink and color on silk, *Ku-kung shu-hua-lu*, vol. 4, 6/91–92, arch. no. MA47a–j, 1648–54; and the 1624 handscroll *Landscapes after Four Masters* in the Seattle Museum of Art (the four masters are Tung Yüan, Huang Kung-wang, Wang Meng, and Wu Chen), in ink and color on paper, acc. no. CH 32.L22.09.1.

2. In the C. C. Wang collection, New York; see James Cahill, ed., *The Restless Landscape*, no. 66, pp. 140, 167.

3. The most recent study on the Che school was undertaken by Suzuki Kei in *Mindai kaigashi no kenkyū: Seppa* (Tokyo, 1968).

4. Pt. 1, pp. 12–13.

5. Lan Ying did on occasion paint works after the styles of painters in the Northern school, e.g., a leaf after Li T'ang in the 1622 National Palace Museum album (see n. 1 above) or the fine landscape after Ma Yüan reproduced in *Kokka*, vol. 539 (October, 1939), but these are relatively few in comparison to those of artists belonging to the Southern lineage.

6. Some key works by Lan in styles after the old masters are the album and handscroll mentioned in n. 1 above; a 1635 twelve-leaf album in ink and color on silk in the National Palace Museum, *Ku-kung shu-hua-lu*, vol. 4, 6/93–94, arch. no. MA48a–l, 1655–65; a 1642 eight-leaf album in ink and color on paper painted for Fang Heng-hsien at the P'ing-shan-t'ang in Yang-chou, Ex-Saito collection, in The Art Institute, Chicago (see *Tōan-zō shōgafu*, vol. 4, no. 34 [1–8]); a 1643 seven-leaf album in ink and color on paper in the National Palace Museum, *Ku-kung shu-hua-lu*, vol. 4, 6/94–95, arch. no. MA49, 5866–72; a 1646 ten-leaf album in ink and color on paper in the collection of C. C. Wang, New York; and a 1655 seven-leaf album in ink and color on paper in the National Palace Museum, *Ku-kung shu-hua-lu*, vol. 4, 6/94–95, arch. no. MA49, 5866–72.

7. 5/63. The date of this compilation is not clear, but on the basis of the painters included and the reference to the Ming emperors by their temple names in the opening pages, the author may be considered to have lived in the Ming. This opinion is confirmed by Professor Shimada.

8. Recorded in P'ang Yüan-chi, *Hsü-chai ming-hua-lu*, vol. 4, p. 60.

9. *Ibid.*, vol. 13, pp. 29b–30a; leaf 6 (after Chao Meng-fu) mentions the city and date, and leaf 8 gives the specific location as the P'ing-shan-t'ang.

10. Recorded in Yang En-shou, *Yen-fu-pien*, vol. 3, pt. 2, 15/36a.

11. For a reconstruction of the ownership and influence of the famous Fu-ch'un handscroll, now in the National Palace Museum, in relation to Wang Hui's 1672 copy in the Freer Gallery of Art, see the exemplary article by Hin-cheung Lovell, "Wang Hui's 'Dwelling in the Fu-ch'un Mountains.'"

12. 4/75.

13. Colophon by Fang Yin (*hao* Ling-ch'iao chu-jen, a native of Kao-yu, Kiangsu), in P'ang Yüan-chi, *Hsü-chai ming-hua-lu*, p. 302.

14. Chap. 2. Notable in the entry is the remark that Lan Ying loved the natural landscape and traveled to Fukien, Chekiang, Hupei, and Hunan in southern China, as well as to Hopei, Shensi, Shansi, and Honan in northern China.

IX LAN YING (1585–1664-)

Bird on a Willow Branch

The Art Museum, Princeton University (66-246).

Hanging scroll. Ink and light color on paper. 164.5 x 53.2 cm.

DATED: in the period October 16–November 13, 1659 (*chi-hai, ch'iu chiu-yüeh*).

SIGNATURE OF THE ARTIST: Lan Ying.

INSCRIPTION BY THE ARTIST: in three lines (see following discussion).

SEALS OF THE ARTIST: *Lan Ying chih-yin* (relief, square), *T'ien-shu* (relief, square), both after signature (Contag and Wang, *Seals,* nos. 20, 19, pp. 721–22).

COLLECTOR'S SEAL: Chang Po-chin (born 1900, Hsing-t'ang, Hopei; former ambassador to Japan from the Republic of China), *Hsing-t'ang Chang-shih Huan-an chien-shang-yin* (relief, square) lower left corner of silk mounting.

CONDITION: fair; there is slight abrasion over the entire surface, with some holes filled in the area of the rock.

PROVENANCE: Chang Po-chin, Taipei.

PUBLISHED: *T'ien-yin-t'ang Collection: One Hundred Masterpieces of Chinese Painting,* no. 66 (illustrated); *Archives of Asian Art,* vol. 21 (1967–68), fig. 42, pp. 87, 101 (illustrated).

INSCRIPTION: an old vertical label in seven characters of "clerical" script is set into the present mounting in the upper right corner:

Lan T'ien-shu hsien-sheng — a genuine work.
Inscribed by an old man of eighty, Tzu-hsiang.
[Seals:] *Chang Hsiung* (intaglio, square), *Chen-yin* (intaglio, square), *Ta-[wu]* (relief, square).

The inscription, written in 1882, is by Chang Hsiung (*tzu* Tzu-hsiang, 1803–1886), who was one of the foremost bird and flower painters of his day in Shanghai.

AN EARNEST LITTLE BIRD perched high on a willow branch squawks over his domain. His setting is a large, pierced garden rock resplendent with bamboo, chrysanthemum, red leaves, and orchids. The colors of the autumn leaves dominate, but, as in his free, effusive brushwork, Lan Ying takes the liberty of combining plants and flowers of several seasons to form a highly attractive work. The forms do not grow out of the ground, as in nature, but are stacked along the right border of the paper, with rock and orchids placed in the very foreground. This device unifies the composition and provides a central focus for the variety of shapes which stretch toward the empty spaces on the left. Lan preferred this arrangement for various subject matters from quite early in his career on into his late years.[1] His inscription in cursive script tells us that the work was painted in his old age: "Painted at the Yü-chao hall, east of the city. [Signed:] Old man of the mountains, Lan Ying, at seventy-five years."

THE DECORATIVE FRESHNESS in the work seems entirely suitable to the lightness of the subject and clearly demonstrates many of Lan Ying's most definitive stylistic traits. Each form is reduced to its most schematic essentials, despite the variety of subjects. The brushwork is highly consistent, and its rhythms echo each other throughout the work. For example, the outline of the rock is done in a coarse, thick line, moving in a series of continuous but abrupt angular movements; the double outline of the tree trunk is executed in similar motions. The few strings of willow leaves are brushed with a bent, linear contour and overlap each other like the orchids, which form a flat screen in the lower foreground. Furthermore, the short, blunter strokes of the bamboo, while executed in a darker ink tonality, nonetheless have the same rhythm as the single outline twigs of the tree on which the bird is perched.

Although *Bird on a Willow Branch* is decidedly a mature work, the landscape elements, the expression of the bird, and the compositional arrangement are seen much earlier, and can be considered stock elements from Lan's repertoire. In a charming fan dated 1637, *Bluejay on a Branch*[2] (fig. 1), the same arrangement is adapted to the fan format. The forms are also placed to one side and extend to the left. The same alert red leaves appear, as does the bird, here slightly less insistent than in the Sackler scroll. Apart from a more masterful command of the larger format and a greater élan and projection of personality in the bird, twenty years hardly seem to separate the two in terms of their basic visualization.

1. Lan Ying, *Bluejay on a Branch,* dated 1637. Folding fan mounted as album leaf. Ink and color on gold paper. Shanghai Museum.

That Lan Ying was not merely a "conservative" painter or an exponent of the Che school, as traditional categories would have it, may again be illustrated by his works in the bird and flower genre. During the Ming dynasty this subject matter was dominated by two groups of painters—the academy school, led by Lin Liang, Lü Chi, and Tai Wen-chin, and the scholar-painters, of whom Shen Chou, Wen Cheng-ming, Lu Chih, Ch'en Shun, and Hsü Wei were the most representative. The former group worked mainly with descriptive line and color on silk and specialized in that one category; the latter group primarily painted landscapes, depicted birds and flowers only occasionally, and stressed the revelation of expressive line and ink on paper based on calligraphic discipline.

Lan Ying has little in common stylistically with the first group. He preferred to work on paper and liked to explore the full range of both ink and color (the latter used more heavily on landscapes) as a foil for his facile and highly demonstrative brushwork. His method of signing a work also emulated literati taste: he did not simply sign a name in "model" or "running" script, which was the customary manner for a professional painter, but scrawled a slightly more personal and specific inscription in running or cursive style. He also frequently adopted the pictorial license of the scholar-painter: he was not restrained by seasonal subjects and, as seen in this scroll, often combined flowers and plants of all climates and seasons in one work.

STYLISTICALLY, Lan Ying's position in the history of Chinese painting can be evaluated more justly by tracing his influence on

two slightly later artists who have since become more celebrated as "individualists" than he. When we closely examine the bird (see the detail) we may think we have seen it before. Its sauciness, its restrained whimsy, and the shape of its double-circled eye remind us of Ch'en Hung-shou (1599–1652) and Chu Ta (1626–ca. 1705). Indeed, Lan Ying's bird provided a formula which both masters adapted with even greater success than Lan's. Two generations or so later Chu Ta's transformation of ordinary forms into distinct personalities as a quality in painting would transcend Lan Ying's. There is no evidence that they ever met (Chu Ta worked in Nan-ch'ang, Kiangsi), but Lan Ying's bird offered a model which Chu's genius expanded upon and intensified[3] (e.g., fig. 2). By distorting the attitude of the bird and exaggerating the placement of the pupil in the eye, the painter encourages the viewer to transfer the human feelings associated with such physical postures to the bird, giving him a "personality." The sense of vitality in the expression is thus achieved by a form of mimicry, as well as by the power inherent in the brushwork itself.

Ch'en Hung-shou, a closer link with Lan Ying, adapted both the bird type and the technique of rendering the branches in ink. In a leaf from an album dated 1645[4] (fig. 3), the bird now assumes a taciturn and enigmatic character. Instead of flattening the eye into an ellipse, as Chu Ta did, Ch'en Hung-shou retains the circle but enlarges both the pupil and the outer rim, so that it now dominates the bird's head. The beak, which also formed a significant aspect of the expression in Chu Ta's bird, is here tightly shut. With these changes of internal proportion, the expression is now concentrated on the huge eye, with its concentric circles emphasized in dry-brush strokes. Again one can almost attribute human qualities to the form, and in this lies the power of both Chu Ta's and Ch'en Hung-shou's transformations of the Lan Ying prototype. Ch'en's brushwork is

IX, detail.

drier and more meticulous than Lan Ying's in the branches. Also characteristic of Ch'en's style is the greater variation of ink tones and the articulation of the forms, as, for example, in the small twigs, which vary in value and saturation, and in the feathers and tail of the bird, which also receive subtle value emphasis.[5]

There is literary as well as stylistic evidence of Lan Ying's influence on Ch'en Hung-shou. In Mao Ch'i-ling's (1623–1716) biography of Ch'en he describes Lan's role as Ch'en's teacher: "At the time there was Lan Ying of Ch'ien-t'ang [Hang-chou, Chekiang], who excelled in birds and flowers. Lien [Ch'en Hung-shou] invited

2. Chu Ta, *Birds*. Album leaf.
Ink on paper. Collection unknown.

3. Ch'en Hung-shou, *Birds and Flowers*, dated 1645. Leaf from an album of ten leaves. Ink and occasional color on paper. National Palace Museum, Taipei.

[Lan] Ying to teach him his methods. Before long he thought little of Ying, and Ying himself felt that Lien surpassed him. . . . Hence toward the end of his [Ying's] life, he stopped painting birds and flowers, saying, 'this is heaven's wish.'"[6] While this verifies the contact between the two painters, it is difficult to tell whether Mao Ch'i-ling's words represent Ch'en's true feelings toward Lan Ying. Mao seems to be allowing himself biographical license in this instance, for Ch'en's collected works, the *Pao-lun-t'ang-chi*, contain three poems dedicated to Lan Ying the tone of which shows no disdain for his mentor. To be sure, Ch'en may have had some youthful pride, but the thirteen-year difference in their ages would still assume a basic deference in Ch'en's attitude toward Lan.[7]

An additional aspect of Mao's comment is unreliable: Lan Ying did not stop painting birds and flowers toward the end of his life. *Bird on a Willow Branch* was executed when he was seventy-five, and although his death date is still not certain, the quality of the execution of this scroll certainly does not suggest defeat or submission to the talents of a younger master.

We will conclude with a work (fig. 4) of subject matter similar to the Sackler painting, but done jointly by Lan and two highly respected gentlemen-painters, Yang Wen-ts'ung (1597–1645) and Chang Hung (1577–1668). Lan executed the bird and the plum branch, Yang Wen-ts'ung painted the rock, and Chang Hung added the camellias. Yang was not only a high official (a magistrate of Nanking) but also one of the Nine Friends of Painting, the exclusive circle which included Tung Ch'i-ch'ang, Ch'eng Chia-sui, Shao Mi, Li Liu-fang, and others. Chang Hung, active mainly in Su-chou, was known as a proponent of Wu school traditions. The composition seems close to Lan's own mode and could well be mistaken as a complete work by him were it not for the discreet signatures of Chang Hung on the far right edge and of Yang Wen-ts'ung on the protruding rock. The painting must have been executed before 1645, when Yang died, and, as the painters were highly mobile, could have been painted in Su-chou, Nanking, or Hang-chou. Lan's collaboration with these two painters not only provides further evidence of his association with intellectual circles in the cities where he worked but also suggests that he exerted a degree of stylistic influence over the younger Yang in works of this genre. In addition it might be noted that Lan Ying's grandson, Lan Shen (son of Lan Meng), quite faithfully perpetuated his grandfather's style in the bird and flower genre, even to the point of maintaining the one-sided vertical composition, the same bird type, and the tree and leaf motifs.[8]

NOTES

1. Cf. a painting of the same subject dated 1634 in *Hua-yüan to-ying*, vol. 1, pl. 48.
2. Published in *Ming-Ch'ing shan-mien hua-hsüan-chi*, pl. 42.
3. Published in *Shina nanga shūsei*.
4. In ten leaves, ink and occasional color on paper, in the National Palace Museum, Taipei; see *Ku-kung shu-hua-lu*, vol. 4, 6/88–89, arch. no. 1637.
5. The degree to which Ch'en's birds, flowers, rocks, and even figures have their source in Lan Ying's types can be further illustrated by Lan's leaf dated 1636 (published in *Ming-Ch'ing shan-mien hua-hsüan-chi*, pl. 43; ink and color on gold paper), which depicts two ladies in a garden. This fan offers one of the early prototypes for Ch'en Hung-shou's lissome ladies. The proportions of the figures are more slender than the then-current "Ch'iu Ying" type; their heads are cast in an elongated oval with full brows and chins, and the features are placed in the center of the oval. The shoulders slant pronouncedly, and the heads incline forward. Beyond that, certain compositional features, such as the use of large rocks as a background screen, can also be seen with varied emphases in Ch'en Hung-shou's works.
6. Quoted in Huang Yung-ch'üan, *Ch'en Hung-shou nien-p'u*, p. 9.
7. *Ibid.*
8. See his hanging scroll in ink and color on silk, published in *Ku-kung po-wu-yüan ts'ang-hua-niao hua-hsüan*, pl. 69.

4. Lan Ying, Yang Wen-ts'ung, and Chang Hung, *Bird, Rock, and Camellias*, ca. 1645. Hanging scroll. Ink on paper. Collection unknown (photo Princeton Photo Archives).

X WAN SHOU-CH'I (1603–1652)

P'eng-ch'eng (Hsü-chou), Kiangsu; later Nanking,
Su-chou, and Huai-yin (Huai-an), Kiangsu

Landscapes, Flowers, and Calligraphy

The Art Museum, Princeton University (68-206).

Album of eighteen leaves: four of landscapes, two of flowers, and twelve of calligraphy (nine single leaves and three double leaves), plus three additional colophon leaves (see below). Ink on paper. Painting: 25.8 x 17.0 cm.; calligraphy: (single leaves) 27.8 x 18.2 cm., (double leaves) 27.8 x 36.4 cm.

DATED: early May, 1650 (*Keng-ch'en, han-shih*), on leaf J.

SIGNATURES OF THE ARTIST (on each leaf):
Shou tao-jen (leaves A, B, G, H, I, J, K, L, and Q).
Hui-shou (leaves C and D).
Nei-ching, Shou (leaves E and F).
Wan Shou (leaf M).
Shou (leaves N and O).
Sha-men, Hui-shou (leaf R).

SEALS OF THE ARTIST (on each leaf, fifteen in all;
none listed in Contag and Wang, *Seals*, p. 413):
Wan-shou (intaglio, tall rectangle) leaf A.
Shou-ch'i (intaglio, double seal of two small squares) leaf B.
Hui-shou (relief, square) leaves C and D.
Shou (relief, single ideogram, oval) leaves E and F.
Wan-shou (intaglio, double seal of two small squares) leaf G.
Shou (relief, round ideogram, oval) leaf H.
Shou-ch'i chih-yin (half-intaglio, half-relief) leaf I.
Wan-shou (relief, square) leaf J.
Ch'en-shou (intaglio, square) leaf K.
Shou-ch'i (relief, square) leaf L.
Shou-ch'i (relief, square) leaf M.
Seng-shou (relief, square) leaf N.
Wan-jo (intaglio, square) leaf O.
Wan-shou (relief, square) leaf P.
Wan-shou (relief, square) leaf Q.
Shou-ch'i (relief, double seal in two squares) leaf R.

COLOPHONS AND LABELS:
Chang Po-ying (*tzu* Shao-p'u, 1871–1926-) wrote the present label on the outer covers (see detail, *right*) and added colophons on the paper mounting which faces each leaf of painting and calligraphy (except P, Q, and R, which are double leaves) and on the last colophon leaf, UU, totaling seventeen inscriptions; Chang obtained this album in Peking in 1925 (see colophon leaf UU).
Unidentified writer, on old outer label, now mounted as an album leaf (see detail, *left*).
Unidentified colophon writer, on three additional leaves, SS, TT, and UU (a double leaf) written before 1925; they contain transcriptions of fourteen biographical sources pertaining to Wan Shou-ch'i.

SEALS OF THE INSCRIBER: Chang Po-ying, after each of his colophons, twenty in all (identified on each leaf).

CONDITION: fair; there is some foxing over the surface of each leaf and mounting paper and slight abrasion on the edges of the calligraphy leaves; the outer label by Chang Po-ying and the brocade cover are in tattered condition.

PROVENANCE: Frank Caro, New York.

PUBLISHED: Lu Hsin-yüan, *Jang-li-kuan kuo-yen-lu* (preface dated 1892), 34/21b–23b; no colophons are recorded.

X, detail: (*left*) outer label from a former mounting by an unidentified writer; (*right*) label on outer cover by Chang Po-ying.

WAN SHOU-CH'I (*tzu* Nien-shao, Jo, Chieh-jo, Nei-ching; *hao* Shou tao-jen) was a prominent poet, painter, and patriot of the late Ming. Of the several loyalist painters known in the West such as Chu Tà, K'un-ts'an, Tao-chi, Ch'en Hung-shou, Kung Hsien, and Hung-jen, whose lives spanned the late Ming and early Ch'ing dynasties, Wan is the least well known, yet he was one of the few who actively resisted the Manchus. Wan received his *chü-jen* degree in 1630 and then spent several years in Nanking and Huai-yin (in northern Kiangsu). He joined the *Fu-she* ("Restoration" or "Regeneration" society), the political-literary organization founded in 1629, whose activities were centered in Nanking and Su-chou. When the Ming capital fell to the Manchus in 1645, Wan was in Su-chou and, along with several friends, led a band of troops in a vain but valiant attempt to resist the invaders. He was captured but released. His reputation as a poet and scholar was apparently known to the Manchu general in command and helped save his life. In 1646 he retired from active life to enter the Buddhist clergy. We can imagine the sentiments of bitterness and frustration which inspired such lines as: "My country's invaders have still not been vanquished, yet I am spared my life. My family has been scattered, and, having achieved nothing, I still have ambition to spare."[1]

Wan retreated to Huai-yin and there built a studio, the Hsi-hsi ts'ao-t'ang ("Thatched Hut of the Western Marsh"), after which his collected works and poetry were titled. He supported himself by farming and by selling his calligraphy, painting, and seal carving. He was quite versatile in these three arts; he wrote in both large and small calligraphy and painted both figures and landscapes and flowers. His seal carving was well known, and he worked in such materials as gold, bronze, and jade as well as stone. Wan was also well versed in herb medicine, and his skills even extended to the art of embroidery.

The content and style of this album reflects what we know of Wan's biography after the 1644–45 catastrophe. He saw himself in a long and venerated tradition of resistance painters caught in transitional political circumstances whose ideals were in conflict with the policy of the rulers. The texts of the poems he chose and the biographies he transcribed in this album, such as those of Kuo T'ai and Chiang Hung (leaves G and H), reflect this identification with earlier worthies. He also found solace in the simplicity of farm life and the eremitic ideal, both as a psychological retreat and as a practical antidote to the futility of government service. These themes (see leaves I, K, M, and N) had been classic subjects of poetry since the time of such personalities as T'ao Ch'ien and Lu Hung, and they surfaced again in the Yüan under the frustrations of Mongol domination. Their extension to the pictorial dimension was especially notable in the works of Ni Tsan. Imitations after Ni Tsan's style recur in many late Ming painters (like Ch'eng Chia-sui [see cat. no. V] and Lan Ying [see cat. no. VII]), but especially sensitive temperaments like Wan Shou-ch'i and Hung-jen (see cat. no. XII) captured Ni Tsan's poetic sentiment, rather than merely his pictorial forms. The change of dynasty deeply affected the lives of these loyalists or "residuals" (i-min), and the ruptures in personality which it brought about can be felt in their art, though not necessarily in the art of other less introverted sensibilities.

It is significant, therefore, that Ni Tsan's formal motifs and aesthetic ideals were outstanding themes in Wan Shou-ch'i's landscapes. As a loyalist, Wan must have felt an ideological affinity with Ni Tsan's own historical circumstance. At the same time the Yüan master's formal ideal, which was emptied of all but the most essential feeling and form, must have seemed to him the most expressive of all possible archetypes. In this sense Wan Shou-ch'i and Hung-jen can be compared, for their attraction to Ni Tsan went beyond mere form. For Wan the spirit constituted the form it embodied—indeed, the compositional themes of the four landscapes in this album are ones which may have been associated with Ni Tsan. They range from "emptiness," as in leaf A, to "fullness," as in leaf B, yet they still reflect certain classical arrangements such as "height" (leaf B), "level distance" (leaves A and D), and "deep distance" (leaf D).

Wan's painting and calligraphic style reveal a man capable of deep thought and of strict self-discipline. There is a large measure of inner, unresolved tension in his forms, a quality which is not apparent at first, but which can be recognized primarily in the deliberate pace and meticulousness with which every dot and line is drawn. His forms are spare and controlled, and they stress a three-dimensional, geometric precision. The sense of a strong intellect and of a personality in complete command is indicated by the absence of ink wash and of any factor which could admit "accidental" effects. All forms are built up by lines in graded ink, mainly pale to medium, and then restrained touches of texture and "shading" are added by rubbing with a dry brush. The darkest accents are saved for moss dots, which are applied with great precision and a perfect sense for position and effect. Wan sought a feeling of formal tension in his designs, placing the volumes at extreme angles, and he gently defies pictorial convention by using traditional motifs in unexpected positions (such as a waterfall or pavilion distorted in shape or placed on the edge of a picture), or calmly alludes to archaistic form by using curved lines where they would ordinarily be straight (as in river banks, bases of rocks, or tree trunks and twigs).

As one turns the pages of the album, one is drawn into each scene by its silence. The ink tones are pale in gradation, the lines faint, though visible. The scale of the forms is small and distant. Nothing is harsh in effect, nor is it soft or relaxed. It may seem surprising that a man of action like Wan Shou-ch'i should produce paintings of such meticulousness and technical restraint. The answer may lie not only in the different concept of the hero and man of action in China but also in Wan's own personality. He seems to have purged himself of all destructive psychological feelings: no aggressive or sharp qualities (huo-ch'i) are asserted in his painting. Neither are they found in his calligraphy, where the same deliberate pace and sense of perfect balance controls the articulation of line and the total expression.

Historically, Wan's calligraphy is related to the ko-t'ieh tradition, referring to calligraphic training acquired through the copying of old rubbings. It was unlikely that he had much opportunity to view antique works in the original; his own writing was probably cultivated in the more usual manner by the study of the great masters through secondary reproduction of originals from carved blocks. Biographical sources cite one of his calligraphic models as Yen Chen-ch'ing, but visually his hand is closer to the later interpretations of other T'ang masters like Ch'u Sui-liang or Ou-yang Hsün, whose styles were also popular at the time. Expressively, Wan's style does display the qualities of a calligrapher who has patterned his writing after the carved interpretations of the old masters, rather than brushwritten specimens. His lack of interest in the potential of ink and its infinite variations supports this view. By contrast, the more daring calligraphy of a master like Tung Ch'i-ch'ang not only reflects differences in personality and artistic sensibilities but also a broad contact with original ink manuscripts (mo-chi), in which subtleties not only of form but of ink could be preserved.

Leaf A: "Misty Willow-Lined Stream and Boat"

SIGNATURE OF THE ARTIST: Shou tao-jen (in "small regular" script).
SEAL OF THE ARTIST: Wan-shou (intaglio, tall rectangle).

The tops of two willow trees are silhouetted in the lower foreground, a taller one to the right, a smaller one to the left. On the far bank, in the upper third of the picture, the silhouette of two slender willows is again repeated, with the taller one placed to the left and the smaller one to the right bending in response. Two thatched cottages and a bridge span the far bank at the left. Their thin shapes are echoed by the boat which skims the waters in the right foreground. Beyond the distant bank the filigree tops of several willows can be discerned through layers of mist, which are indicated by pale, horizontal smudges of dry ink.

The extended lateral expanse and the sparse motifs are significant not only as idiomatic references to the style of Ni Tsan but also, as the inscriber points out, as a possible depiction of the idyllic setting of Wan's own studio, the Thatched Hut of the Western Marsh.

THE COLOPHON on the accompanying leaf, inscribed in six lines by Chang Po-ying, gives the title in four characters of "regular" script, followed by a quatrain in four-syllable verse transcribed in one line:

A few cottages over the water,
Misty trees extending into the haze.
The person of whom I am thinking
Will step out if you call him.

One of the leaves from an album which Tao-jen [Wan Shou-ch'i] gave Hsü [Ping-heng, *tzu*] Chün-p'ing resembles this one. Wan inscribed that leaf as follows: "During the years 1646 [*ping-hsü*] and 1647 [*ting-hai*] Chün-p'ing traveled around Huai-yin [in northern Kiangsu]. I was then a monk at the P'u-yin temple, and my studio, Hsi-hsi ts'ao-t'ang, was located there. Reeds grew in the water, and birds often came to the sandy banks. Fishing boats appeared and disappeared. Chün-p'ing often went walking with his staff and visited my simple cottage." From this account, this scene seems to be the Hsi-hsi ts'ao-t'ang.
[Seals:] *Yün-lung-shan-min* (intaglio, square),
Chang Shao-p'u (relief, square).

Wan Shou-ch'i's friendship with Hsü Ping-heng (1601–1650-, from She-hsien, Anhwei) dates from 1639, when the two met at Huai-yin. They were known to have visited each other in 1640, 1641, and 1645 in Su-chou, when they both fled to Huai-yin. Hsü celebrated his fiftieth birthday in 1650.[2] The album Wan Shou-ch'i executed for Hsü may also have been in Chang's collection, since he quotes Wan's inscription on one of its leaves here.

Leaf B: *"Wintry Forest with Distant Waterfall"*

SIGNATURE OF THE ARTIST: Shou tao-jen (in "small regular" script).
SEAL OF THE ARTIST: *Shou-ch'i* (intaglio, double seal of two small squares).

Flat plateaus arranged in serried layers in the center of the composition create a feeling of height and suggest a certain substantiality of form. A few trees placed here and there in the lower foreground are completely leafless, and the boulders are barren of all foliage except a few touches of moss indicated by dark ink. A small waterfall, placed inconspicuously in the upper right corner of the picture behind the looming central mass, provides the scene with a suggestion of movement.

THE COLOPHON in four lines by Chang Po-ying gives the title in four characters, and continues:

Ni Hung-pao [Yüan-lu, 1593–1644] once said: "Only if it is unassuming can it be aloof. If it is not simple, it is not unusual." Wu Tzu-yüan [Ch'i-yüan, fl. 1665–1669] said: "Using the dry brush to paint is the unspoken secret of Wang Shu-ming [Meng]. It's all in this painting!" [This painting] imitates Ying-ch'iu's [Li Ch'eng's, 919–967] cold wintry forests, and beyond the mountains he painted a distant waterfall. This placement makes the scene especially marvelous!
[Seals:] *Hsin-wei-sheng* (relief, tall rectangle;
seal dated 1871), *Chang-Po-ying yin* (intaglio, square).

Leaf C: *"Wild Pavilion and the Flavor of Bamboo"*

SIGNATURE OF THE ARTIST: Hui-shou (in "small regular" script).
SEAL OF THE ARTIST: *Hui-shou* (relief, square).

Darker ink tones and a broader, blunt brushline lend a slightly more expansive feeling to this leaf. A flat bank with a pavilion proceeds from the middle foreground diagonally in angular steps up the left edge of the picture. The edges of the bank increase in size as they recede in the distance, suggesting a tension between the forms and the blank spaces. On the far bank, which is placed in the upper third of the picture plane, a grove of trees grows on a spit of land drawn straight across the horizon. To the extreme left, a distant plateau zigzags into further depth, continuing the movement of the masses

from the foreground. What is unusual about this composition is the emphasis on the "lightness," or empty space, in the foreground (which is usually "heavy"), in contrast to the "heaviness," or fully described elements, in the distance. This effect is intensified by the contrast between the slanting foreground and the perfectly horizontal baseline of the background.

The artist shows a subtle sense for the nuances of distorted form, as seen in the little pavilion and in the balance of the foreground and distant masses. The texture of the clump of bamboo softens the plainness of the pavilion and the surface of the plateaus. This feeling for pattern is exploited more generously in the upper half of the picture.

A hanging scroll done some four years earlier than this album in the Hashimoto collection (fig. 1) shows the same proto-geometric feeling for form and brush technique, with a more conventional treatment of the masses converging in the foreground plane. The better-known Hashimoto hanging scroll is much larger in format, but the style of the painting, calligraphy, and seals agree. The configuration of the central tree, with the smaller ones bending to each side, is an expansion of the group found in this Sackler leaf. Likewise, the controlled dry modeling of the rocks and the deliberate placement of the moss dots on the edges of forms, as well as the pavilion set to the far right, all indicate Wan's delicate feeling for balance and emphasis.

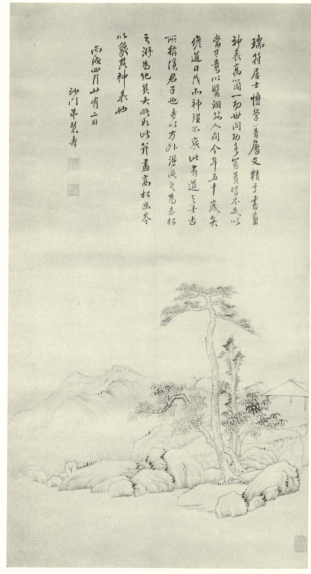

1. Wan Shou-ch'i, *Lofty Pine and Secluded Dwelling*, dated 1646. Hanging scroll. Ink on satin. Hashimoto collection, Osaka.

THE COLOPHON in four lines by Chang Po-ying gives the title in four characters and is followed by:

When Tao-jen [Wan Shou-ch'i] painted, he never said that he was copying this person or imitating that one, but the spirit of this work certainly resembles that of Ni Tsan. He absorbed [the accomplishments of] the ancients and formulated his own personal style. If he had relied [completely] on the earlier masters, he would not have felt it worth his while.

[Seals:] *Shao-p'u* (relief, square),
Chang Po-ying (intaglio, square).

Leaf D: *"Leaning on a Staff in an Autumn Grove"*

SIGNATURE OF THE ARTIST: Hui-shou (in "small regular" script).
SEAL OF THE ARTIST: *Hui-shou* (relief, square).

A cluster of small trees and shrubs growing among some rocks is placed at the lower left base of the picture. Immediately above, a high cliff projects at a precipitous angle from the left. A small stone shrine next to a lone tree is grounded on this strongly slanting promontory. Other boulders continue to rise upward at the far left. On the right side of the picture there is only space and a solitary figure with his back to the viewer. He stands on a low cliff in the right corner and overlooks the horizon and the lone outline of a distant mountain range. The three kinds of foliage which are differentiated in the foreground trees offer a richness which is absent in the rest of the picture. The small figure, drawn in sharp and exacting lineament, sets the scale and spotlights the effect of deep distance which is suggested by the juxtaposition of the projecting cliff and the empty space at the right.

THE COLOPHON in four lines by Chang Po-ying gives the title in four characters and reads:

I once saw a painting by Kuan T'ung like this. The paper [of this painting] is fine and "furry" in feeling. When [Wan] paints, there is an astringent quality to the line, as if the paper were resisting his brush. In painting, the more raw and astringent [the brushline] is, the more sensitive. Whoever paints in a smooth, glib manner is not worthy of having these words spoken to him.

[Seals:] *P'eng-ch'eng Chang-lao*
(intaglio, square),
Ying (relief, tall rectangle).

Leaf E: *"Begonia and Plantain Lily"*

SIGNATURE OF THE ARTIST: Nei-ching, Shou (in "running" script).
SEAL OF THE ARTIST: *Shou* (relief, single ideogram, oval).

The round and pointed petals of the pair of lilies and the large, flat, expansive leaves of the begonia provide a silent dance of lines and shapes. Each outer contour of the brushline begins with a slight emphasis; then an interval of space is left before it commences its next undulation. Wan Shou-ch'i's success, as noted in the perceptive colophon, lies in his "plain and retiring" brushwork. His visualization is devoid of vulgarity, which is an easy pitfall in the depiction of flowers.

THE COLOPHON in two lines by Chang Po-ying reads:

Autumn flowers elegant and pure
Are not stained by even a speck of dust.
Only plain and retiring brushwork such as this
Can be worthy of these flowers.

[Seal:] *Hsiao-lai-ch'in-kuan*
(intaglio, tall rectangle).

Leaf F: *"Camellia and Narcissus"*

SIGNATURE OF THE ARTIST: Nei-ching, Shou (in "running" script).
SEAL OF THE ARTIST: *Shou* (relief, single ideogram, oval).

The long, elliptical leaves of the narcissus extend from the right corner of the picture and provide a stark frame for the single effulgent camellia, placed behind their blooms. The contrast of straight and curved lines is more evident in this painting, especially in the leaves and stems. As in the preceding design, the petals and parts of the leaves have been modeled not by wash but by deft touches of dry ink which have been rubbed onto the desired areas, much like stumping. This technique, which is used also in the landscapes, lends a strong graphic quality to all of the depictions in the album. In addition to the broken contour of the forms, this precise shading suggests that Wan Shou-ch'i's paintings may have been influenced by the exacting medium of woodcuts. Certainly the linear control and frozen stillness of his brushline is consistent with his abilities as a seal carver, and is in fact one of the reasons why his seals are so exemplary.

THE COLOPHON in two lines by Chang Po-ying reads:

[When] Yün [Shou-p'ing, 1633–1690, *tzu*] Nan-t'ien painted this kind of flower, he only used heavy saturations of color without outlines. But Nei-ching [Wan Shou-ch'i] uses only contours. The way each one does it is very different, but they both achieve perfection.

[Seal:] *Chang Shao-p'u*
(half-relief, half-intaglio, square).

Leaf G: *"Biography of Kuo T'ai"*

SIGNATURE OF THE ARTIST: Shou tao-jen (in "small regular" script).
SEAL OF THE ARTIST: *Wan-shou* (intaglio, double seal of two small squares).

This leaf of calligraphy transcribes the life of Kuo T'ai (*tzu* Lin-tsung, 128–169), a worthy of the latter Han period,[3] in nine lines of "small regular" script.

THE COLOPHON in one line by Chang Po-ying reads:

Nei-ching's [Wan Shou-ch'i's] moral integrity is comparable to that of Kuo [T'ai] and Chiang [Hung]. Wan Shou-ch'i's transcription of the biography expresses his admiration and emulation [of these men] and thereby describes his own identity as well!

[Seal:] *Chang Shao-p'u*
(intaglio, square).

Leaf H: *"Biography of Chiang Hung"*

SIGNATURE OF THE ARTIST: Shou tao-jen (in "small regular" script).
SEAL OF THE ARTIST: *Shou* (relief, round ideogram, oval).

This leaf of calligraphy transcribes the lives of Chiang Hung (97–173) and his two brothers Chiang Chung-hai and Chiang Chi-chiang[4] in nine lines.

THE COLOPHON in two lines by Chang Po-ying reads:

The Chiang brothers [Hung, Chung-hai, and Chi-chiang] were men of lofty and pure character [who could] discourage the overambitious and encourage the fainthearted. It is a pity that none of their works are extant any longer. Even the commemorative stele carved by Liu Ts'ao [Chiang Hung's pupil and mentioned in the preceding biography] can no longer be seen.

[Seal:] *Shao-p'u* (relief, oval).

Leaf I: *"Transcription of Three Poems by the T'ang Master Lu Hung"*

SIGNATURE OF THE ARTIST: Shou tao-jen (in "small regular" script).
SEAL OF THE ARTIST: Shou-ch'i chih-yin (half-intaglio, half-relief).

Three poems by Lu Hung are transcribed in nine lines, plus one line of title inscription and signature. Lu Hung was a well-known hermit whose idyllic life in a thatched cottage inspired many pictorial representations.[5]

THE COLOPHON in two lines by Chang Po-ying reads:

Li [Kung-lin] Lung-mien's copy of the *Thatched Hut of Lu Hung* was in the T'ien-lai Hall [Hsiang Yüan-pien's] collection. Tung Ssu-weng [Ch'i-ch'ang] also had a version of the same subject. If you persuaded Nei-ching [Wan Shou-ch'i] to paint an imitation, wouldn't it be charming and wonderful!

[Seal:] *Ch'ing-yen sui-feng chih-shih* (relief, tall rectangle).

Leaf J: *"Transcription of Tu Fu's 'Mei-p'ei Lake'"* (*Mei-p'ei-hsing*)

DATED: early May of 1650 (keng-ch'en, han-shih).
SIGNATURE OF THE ARTIST: Shou tao-jen (in "small regular" script).
SEAL OF THE ARTIST: Wan-shou (relief, square).

The poem by Tu Fu (712–770)[6] is transcribed in seven lines of "small regular" script, plus three lines of title, signature, and date.

THE COLOPHON in four lines by Chang Po-ying reads:

The cyclical year *keng-ch'en* is the seventh year of the Shun-chih reign [1650]. Tao-jen [Wan Shou-ch'i] was then forty-eight. In only two years, he would pass away. The album was painted in the spring of that year, but what he painted were autumn and winter flowers, and the mood of the landscapes is lonely and sad. Whatever problems preoccupied that old gentleman we cannot know. Frustrations and depression of this sort are all harmful to one's health. I am looking at this on a cold winter's night, and involuntarily I am deeply moved by a great surge of feelings.

[Seals:] *Yü-chuang* (relief, tall rectangle), *Po-ying ssu-yin* (intaglio, square).

Leaf K: *"Transcription of Wang Wei's 'Peach Blossom Song'"* (*T'ao-yüan hsing*)

SIGNATURE OF THE ARTIST: Shou tao-jen (in "small regular" script).
SEAL OF THE ARTIST: Ch'en-shou (intaglio, square).

The poem by Wang Wei (699–759)[7] is transcribed in eleven lines of "small regular" script.

THE COLOPHON in five lines by Chang Po-ying reads:

Does the world really have a "Peach Blossom Spring"? Living in a time of chaos and separation led to this kind of imaginative creation. Wan Shou-ch'i left his land and house in Hsü-chou and went to live at Kung-lu-p'u, Kiangsu, in order to escape the upheaval and also because that place was the crossroads between north and south, so that he could be in contact with heroes and intellectuals from all over the empire. At that time [the Ch'ing government] was carrying out a purge [of Ming loyalists], so for the time being he took refuge as a monk in the Buddhist faith in order to escape his pursuers. Otherwise, how could Kung-lu-p'u even be considered a Peach Blossom Garden!

[Seal:] *Yün-lung-shan-min* (intaglio, tall rectangle).

Leaf L: *"Transcription of Tu Fu's 'On Seeing a Horse Painting by Ts'ao Pa in the House of the Recorder Wei Feng'"* (*Wei-feng lu-shih-chai kuan Ts'ao chiang-chün hua-ma-t'u*)

SIGNATURE OF THE ARTIST: Shou tao-jen (in "small regular" script).
SEAL OF THE ARTIST: Shou-ch'i (relief, square).

The poem by Tu Fu[8] is transcribed in nine lines of "small regular" script, plus one line of title and signature.

THE COLOPHON in two lines by Chang Po-ying reads:

Hu Yen-yüan [unidentified] said: "Nei-ching [Wan Shou-ch'i] once said to me: 'In my calligraphy there's nothing that I haven't learned from, but I have used two versions of the Ying-shang rubbing to understand Mi's [Fu's] method.' That's the reason there is never a dead stroke when [Wan] moves his wrist and uses ink."

[Seal:] *Yün-lung-shan-min* (intaglio, tall rectangle).

Leaf M: *"Transcription of Wei Ying-wu's 'On Observing Farm Life'"* (*Kuan t'ien-chia-shih*)

SIGNATURE OF THE ARTIST: Wan Shou (in "running" script).
SEAL OF THE ARTIST: Shou-ch'i (relief, square).

The poem by Wei Ying-wu (739–829?)[9] (in five-character "old-style" meter) is transcribed in four lines of "medium regular" script, plus one line of title. Wei Ying-wu served a long term of office under the several T'ang emperors. His nature poetry, which celebrated the joys and simplicity of farm life, was often compared to that of T'ao Ch'ien (365–427).

THE COLOPHON in two lines by Chang Po-ying reads:

Tao-jen [Wan Shou-ch'i] loved to transcribe poems about farm life and was fond of painting everything about farm life. [Now] the fires of war darken the sky, and there is no day when one can return to the fields. The present and the past share the same painful recollections.

[Seal:] *Shao-p'u* (relief, tall rectangle).

Leaf N: *"Transcription of Ch'u Kuang-hsi's 'Occasional Poem'"*

SIGNATURE OF THE ARTIST: Shou (in "small regular" script).
SEAL OF THE ARTIST: Seng-shou (relief, square).

The poem by Ch'u Kuang-hsi (707–759)[10] is transcribed in five lines of "medium regular" script, plus two lines in smaller script of title and signature. The subject of Ch'u's poem is also country life.

THE COLOPHON in two lines by Chang Po-ying reads:

The small seals in this album are all carved by Wan Shou-ch'i's own hand. In all of them one can see the subtlety of his seal cutting. It's a pity that his compilations of seals are all lost. Whenever I authenticate Tao-jen's calligraphy and painting, I always use his seals, and out of a hundred works, I have never been mistaken once!

[Seal:] *Chang Shao-p'u* (relief, tall rectangle).

Leaf O: *"Transcription of Liu Ch'un-hsü's 'Composed When Visiting East Stream upon Returning to the Lake'"* (*Shun tung-hsi huan-hu-chung tso*)

SIGNATURE OF THE ARTIST: Shou (in "small regular" script).
SEAL OF THE ARTIST: Wan-jo (intaglio, square).

The poem by Liu Ch'un-hsü[11] is transcribed in four spacious lines of "medium regular" script, plus two lines in smaller script of title and signature. Liu Ch'un-hsü was a friend of the poet Meng Hao-jan (689–740).

THE COLOPHON in four lines by Chang Po-ying reads:

Mr. Wan's retreat was called the Ts'ui-Spring Mountain Villa. It was only a few *li* from my own humble home, the Yü-chuang ["Elm Villa"]. When I was small, I received from my deceased grandfather an album of linked verse *tz'u* written at Tun-tu, in Kiangsu, and from that I learned some of the stories about Tao-jen and was drawn toward him. Now I am old! There is no way that my literary and artistic abilities can compare with my lofty fellow-countryman's. I was too poor even to keep something like this work. And I write this to record my shame.

[Seal:] *Hsü-feng-lou* (relief, square).

Leaves P and Q: *"Transcription of the 'Preface to the Orchid Pavilion'"* (Lan-t'ing-hsü)

SIGNATURE OF THE ARTIST: Shou tao-jen, lin [copied by Shou Tao-jen] (in "running" script).
SEAL OF THE ARTIST: *Wan-shou* (relief, square).

Leaf P transcribes ten lines of the poem, continuing in eight lines of "running" script on leaf Q.[12]

Leaf R: *"Copy of the Chin Master Yang Hsi's Transcription of the* T'ai-shang Huang-t'ing nei-ching yü-ching"

SIGNATURE OF THE ARTIST: Sha-men, Hui-shou, lin [copied by Hui-shou of Sha-men] (in "small regular" script).
SEAL OF THE ARTIST: *Shou-ch'i* (relief, double seal in two squares).

The text, a Taoist sutra, is transcribed in nine lines of "small regular" script, plus two lines of title and signature. The original version of Yang Hsi's text, from which Wan copied this leaf, was undoubtedly a rubbing.

COLOPHON LEAVES SS and TT contain fourteen extracts of biographical information about Wan Shou-ch'i collected by a writer who left no seal or name. Each paragraph is preceded by the title of the source from which the extract is taken.

The last line of calligraphy on leaf UU consists of a comment by Chang Po-ying:

I don't know who compiled [the preceding] information about Nei-ching [Wan Shou-ch'i]. In mid-autumn of the year *i-ch'ou* [October 2, 1925] [I], Chang Po-ying from T'ung-shan [Hsü-chou, Kiangsu], obtained this album in Peking. I suspect that Lu Ts'un-chai [Hsin-yüan,

1834–1894] compiled it [because] this album was once in the Jang-li-kuan collection [of Lu Hsin-yüan]. [Dated in the period] March 14 to April 11, 1926 [*ping-yin, erh-yüeh*].

[Seals:] *Yün-lung shan-min* (intaglio, square),
Chang Shao-p'u (relief, square).

Examples of Lu Hsin-yüan's calligraphy are rare. There is, however, a preface to his *I-ku-t'ang hsü-pa* dated 1892 and signed by him which is carved in a handwritten style, presumably his. The style of the writing is different enough to assume that the writer of these three colophon leaves and that of the *I-ku-t'ang* preface are not the same.

NOTES

1. The sources for the preceding sketch are Lo Chen-yü, *Wan Nien-shao hsien-sheng nien-p'u* (*A Chronology of Wan Shou-ch'i*) (n.p., 1919); Arthur W. Hummel, ed., *Eminent Chinese of the Ch'ing Period*, pp. 800–801; Wu Jan, "Ming i-min hua-chia Wan Nien-shao," pp. 270–74, from which the lines from Wan's poem are quoted; Chang Keng, *Kuo-ch'ao hua-cheng-lu*, pt. 1, p. 8 (appended to Tsou Chih-lin); Chiang Shao-shu, *Wu-sheng shih-shih*, pp. 79–80.
2. For further information on Hsü, see Lo Chen-yü, *Wan Nien-shao hsien-sheng nien-p'u*, under the years 1639ff.
3. See Kuo T'ai's biography in Fan Yeh (398–445), *Hou-Han-shu*, chaps. 83 and 98, translated in Homer H. Dubs, *The History of the Former Han Dynasty* (Baltimore, 1938–56), vols. 1–3.
4. See Chiang Hung's biography in the *Hou-Han-shu*, chaps. 83 and 111, translated in *ibid*.
5. For one extant interpretation, see National Palace Museum, Taipei, *Three Hundred Masterpieces*, vol. 1, pls. 5, 7, and 8; the poems represented in Wan's transcription are "Thatched Cottage" (the first poem), "Chamber of Leafy Shades" (the third poem), and "Place of Cloud-Pillows" (the fourth poem).
6. Tu Fu's poem is recorded in *Fen-lei chi-chu Tu kung-pu-shih* (*Compilation of Tu Fu's Poems by Subject*, SPTK ed., nos. 143–44), vol. 1, 4/98, translated in William Hung, *Tu Fu: China's Greatest Poet* (New York, 1952), pp. 53–54.
7. Wang Wei's poem is recorded in *Wang Yu-ch'eng-chi* (*Wang Wei's Collected Works*, SPTK ed., no. 145), 1/10, translated in Chang Yin-nan and Lewis C. Walmsley, *Poems by Wang Wei* (Rutland, Vt., 1968), pp. 157–59.
8. Tu Fu's poem is recorded in *Fen-lei chi-chu Tu kung-pu-shih*, vol. 2, 16/291, translated in David Hawkes, *A Little Primer of Tu Fu* (Oxford, 1967), pp. 145–55.
9. Wei Ying-wu's poem is recorded in Chi Yu-kung (fl. 1121–1161), ed., *T'ang-shih chi-shih* (rpt. Taipei, 1971), vol. 1, chap. 26.
10. Ch'u Kuang-hsi's poem is recorded in *T'ang-shih chi-shih*, chap. 22.
11. Liu Ch'un [or Shen]-hsü's poem is recorded in *T'ang-shih chi-shih*, chap. 25.
12. For reproductions of extant rubbings of the text, see *Shodō zenshū*, vol. 4, pls. 12–27, and the excellent discussion of the calligraphy in the accompanying text. For an examination of the authenticity of the content of the "Preface," see Kuo Mo-jo, "Yu Wang Hsieh mu-chih-te ch'u-t'u lun-tao Lan-t'ing-hsü-te chen-wei" ("The Authenticity of the Lan-t'ing-hsü in the Light of the Epitaphs of Wang Hsing-chih and Hsieh K'un"), *Wen-wu*, no. 6 (1965), pp. 1–24 (Kuo's article offers a standpoint and methodology with which we disagree); and Kao Erh-shih, "Lan-t'ing-hsü-te chen-wei shu-i," *ibid*., no. 7 (1965). The "Preface" is translated in Lin Yu-tang, *The Importance of Living* (New York, 1937), pp. 156–58; and Keng Liang, *Selected Readings Translated from Classical Chinese Prose* (Hong Kong, 1962), pp. 38–41.

X, *Landscapes, Flowers, and Calligraphy* (overleaves)

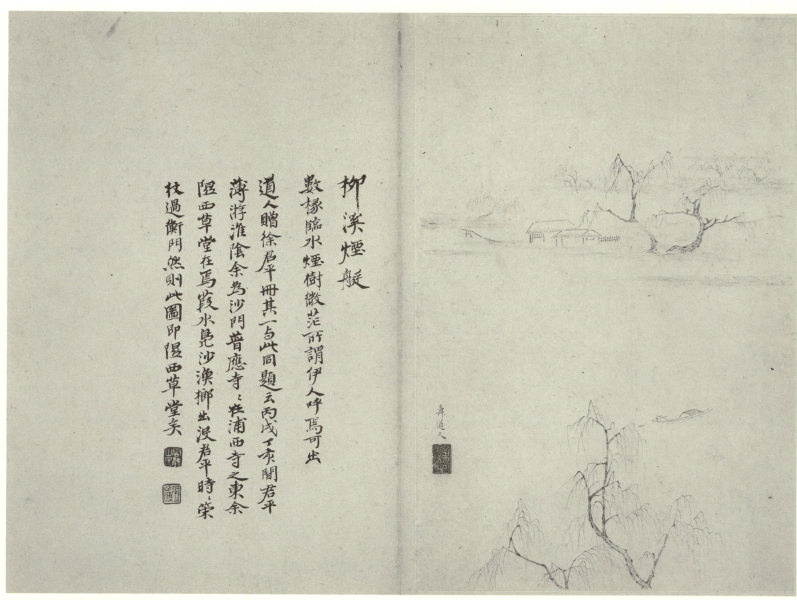

柳溪煙艇

數椽臨水煙樹微茫所謂伊人呼焉可出

道人贈徐君平冊其一与此同題云丙戌丁亥間君平
薄遊淮陰余為沙門普應寺之笠浦西寺之東余
隱西草堂在寫嵌水尾沙漁挪出没君平時榮
枝過衡門然則此圖即隱西草堂矣

Leaf A, "Misty Willow-Lined River and Boat"

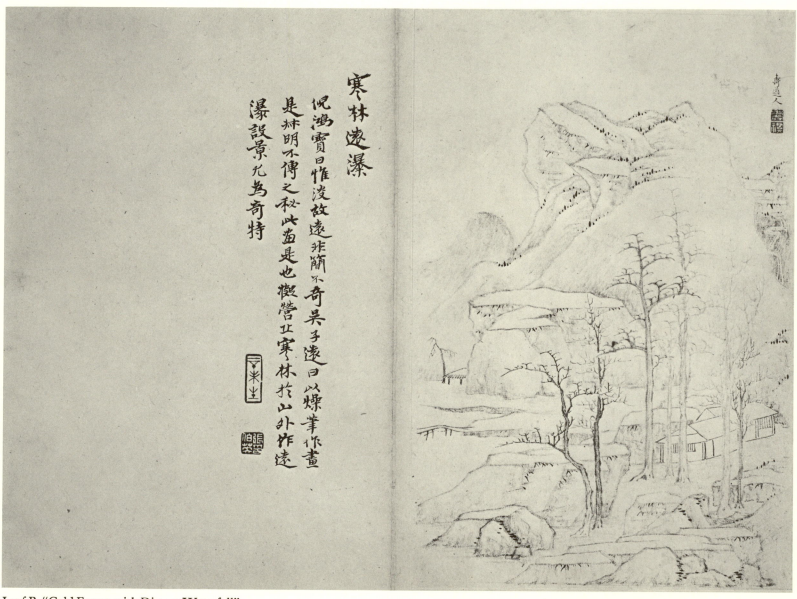

寒林遠瀑

倪鴻寶曰惟没故遠非簡不奇吳子遠曰以燥筆作畫
是林明不傳之秘此畫是也徵營丑寒林於山外作遠
瀑設景尤為奇特

Leaf B, "Cold Forest with Distant Waterfall"

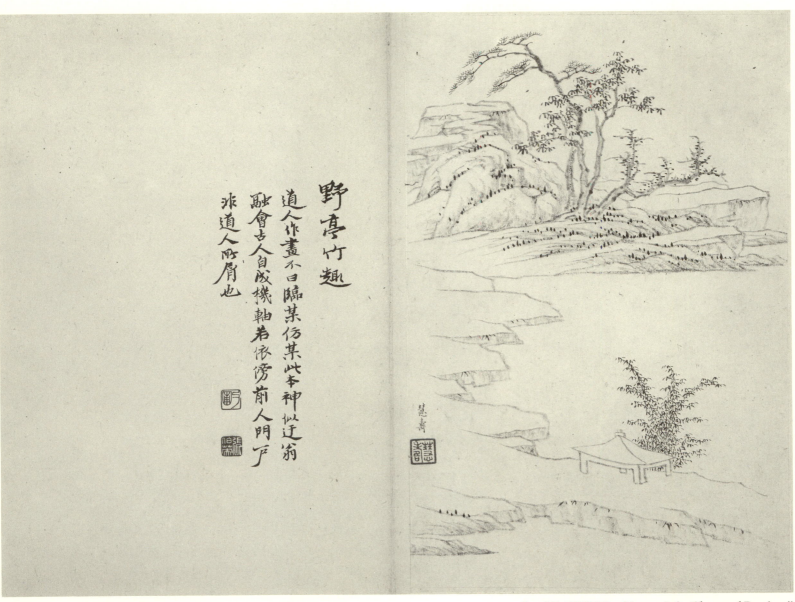

野亭竹趣

道人作畫不曰臨某倣某此本神似迂翁
融會古人自成機軸若依傍前人門戶
非道人所肎也

Leaf C, "Wild Pavilion and the Flavor of Bamboo"

秋林倚杖

曾見關仝筆如是
紙細青毛行筆有如澁滯盖以愈生愈澁
而愈靈凡滑易者不足與於此道

Leaf D, "Leaning on a Staff in an Autumn Grove"

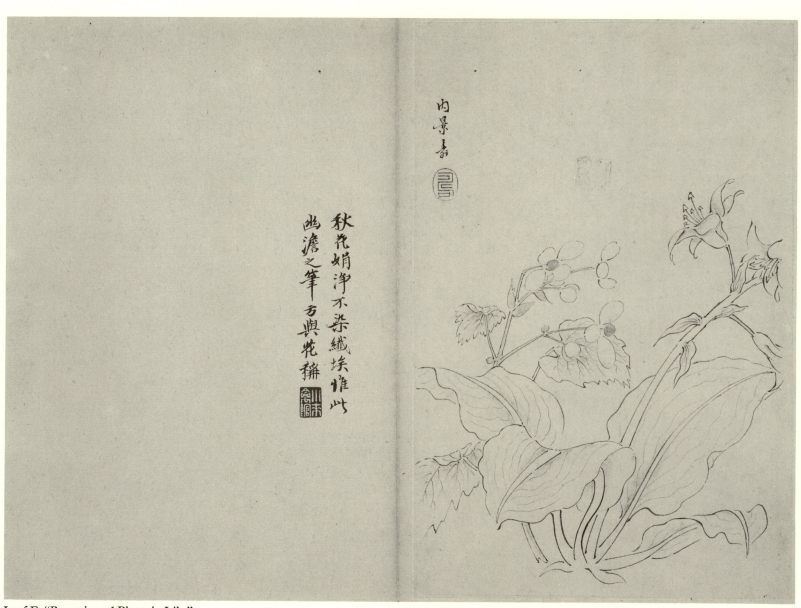

秋花娟淨不雜纖埃惟此
幽澹之筆方與芒稱

內景

Leaf E, "Begonia and Plantain Lily"

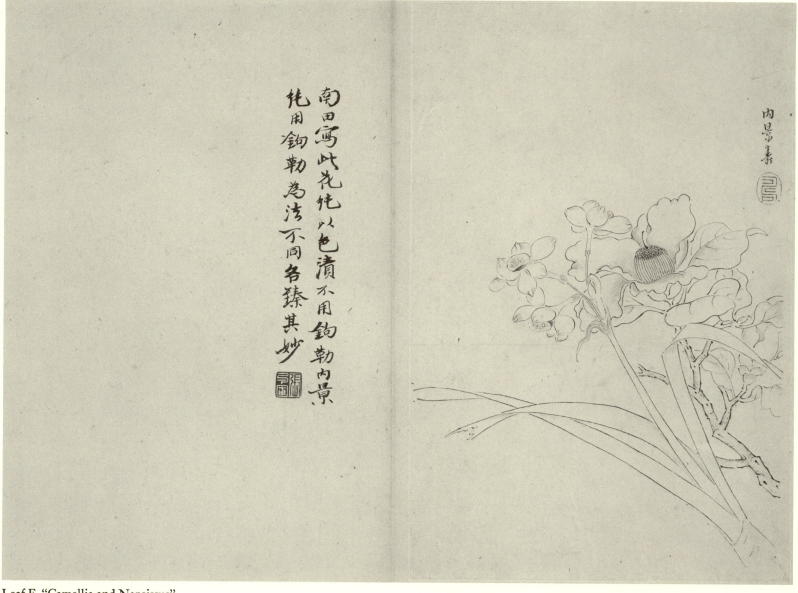

南田寫此花純以色漬不用鈎勒內景
純用鈎勒為法不同各臻其妙

內景

Leaf F, "Camellia and Narcissus"

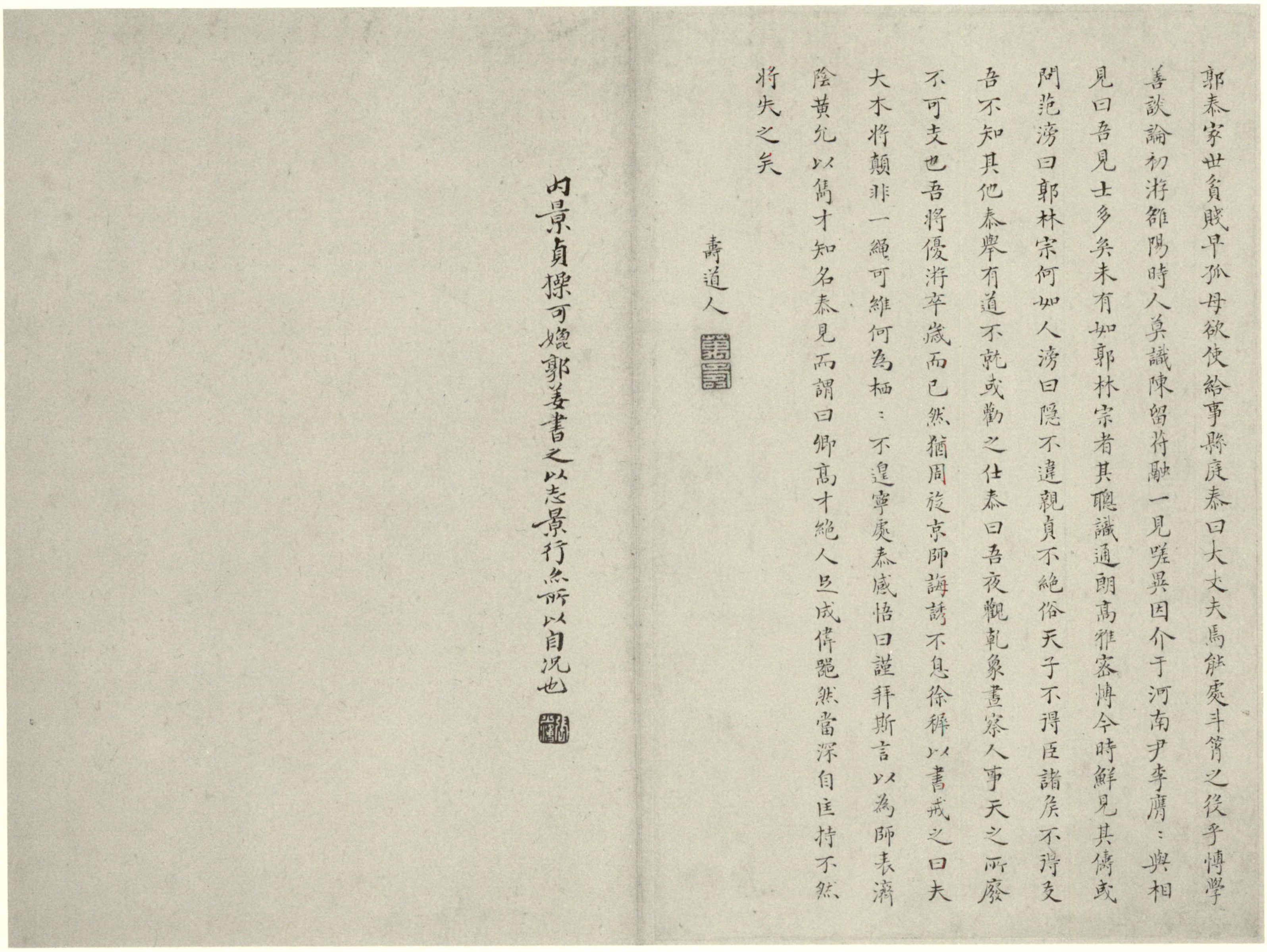

姜肱彭城廣戚士與二弟仲海季江俱孝友著聞篤愛天至肱博通五經兼明星
緯士遠來就學者三千餘人辟命皆不就肱嘗與季江入郡夜于道遇盜欲殺
之肱兄弟更相爭死賊遂兩釋但掠奪衣資而已既至郡肱終不言盜聞感悔
後乃就末見肱叩頭謝罪還所略物肱不受而遣之與徐稺等俱徵不至桓帝使
工圖其形肱臥于幽闇以被韜面工竟不得見之中常侍曹節等諷陳蕃實
武欲借寵賢遂以微肱為太守肱得詔私告其友曰吾以虛獲實遂
籍聲價明：在上稍富圖其本志況今政在閹豎夫何為哉乃遠浮海濱再以
玄纁羔書至肱使家人對曰久病就醫遂羸服間行竄伏青州賣卜給食歷
年乃還終于家弟陳留劉操追慕肱德刻石頌之

壽道人 [印]

郭泰家世貧賤早孤母欲使給事縣廷泰曰大丈夫焉能處斗筲之役乎博學
善談論初游雒陽時人莫識陳留符融一見嗟異因介于河南尹李膺：與相
見曰吾見士多矣未有如郭林宗者其聰識通朗高雅密博今時鮮見其儔或
問范滂曰郭林宗何如人滂曰隱不違親貞不絕俗天子不得臣諸侯不得友
吾不知其他泰舉有道不就或勸之仕泰曰吾夜觀乾象晝察人事天之所廢
不可支也吾將優游卒歲而已然猶周旋京師誨誘不息徐稺以書戒之曰大
大木將顛非一繩可維何為栖栖：不遑寧處泰感悟曰謹拜斯言以為師表濟
陰黃允以為才知名泰見而謂曰卿高才絕人足以成偉器然當深自匡持不然
將失之矣

壽道人 [印]

内景貞操可媲郭姜書之以志景行然所以自況也 [印]

Leaf G, "Biography of Kuo T'ai"

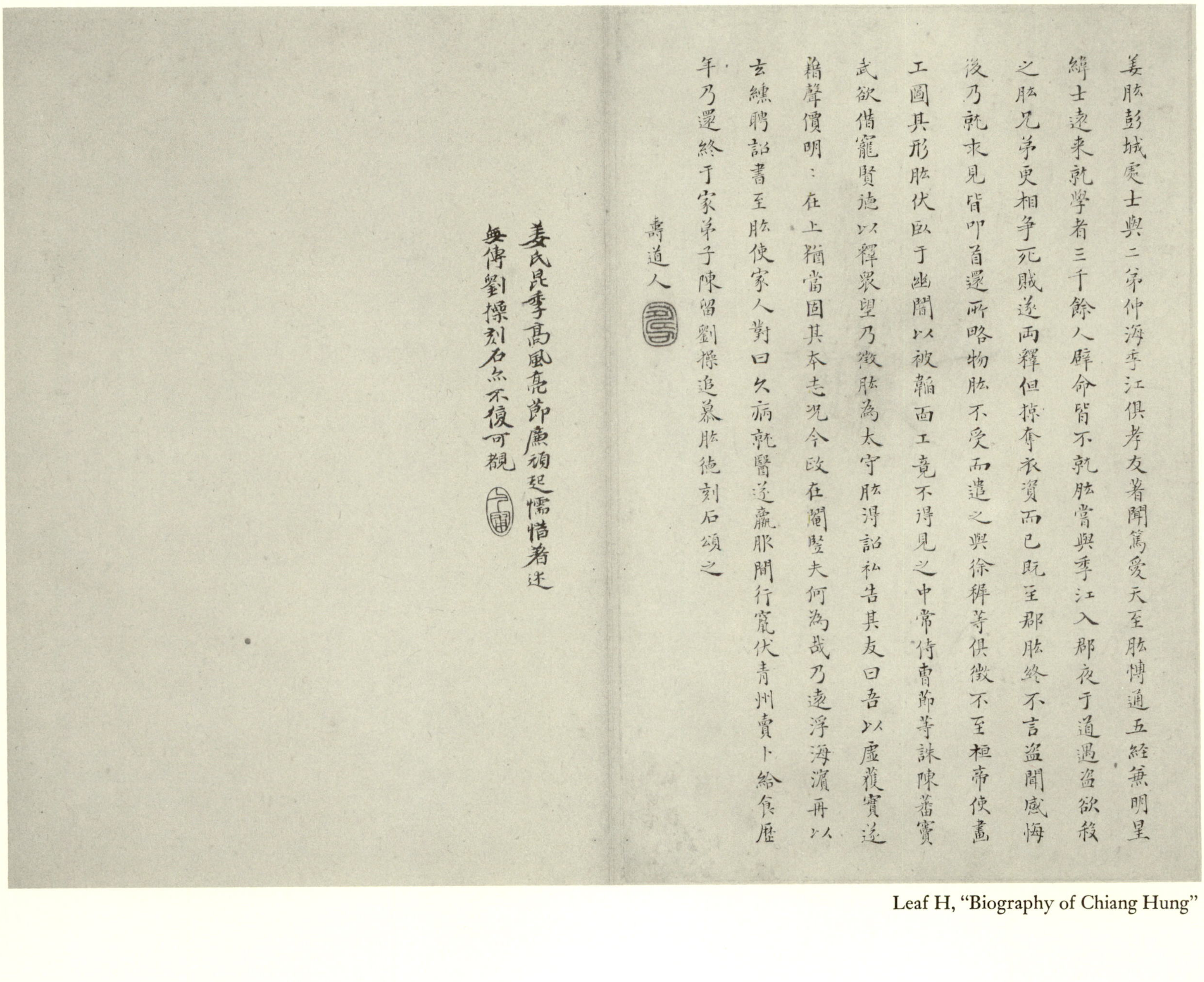

姜氏昆季高風亮節廉頑起懦情著述
無傳劉操刻石亦不復可覿 [印]

Leaf H, "Biography of Chiang Hung"

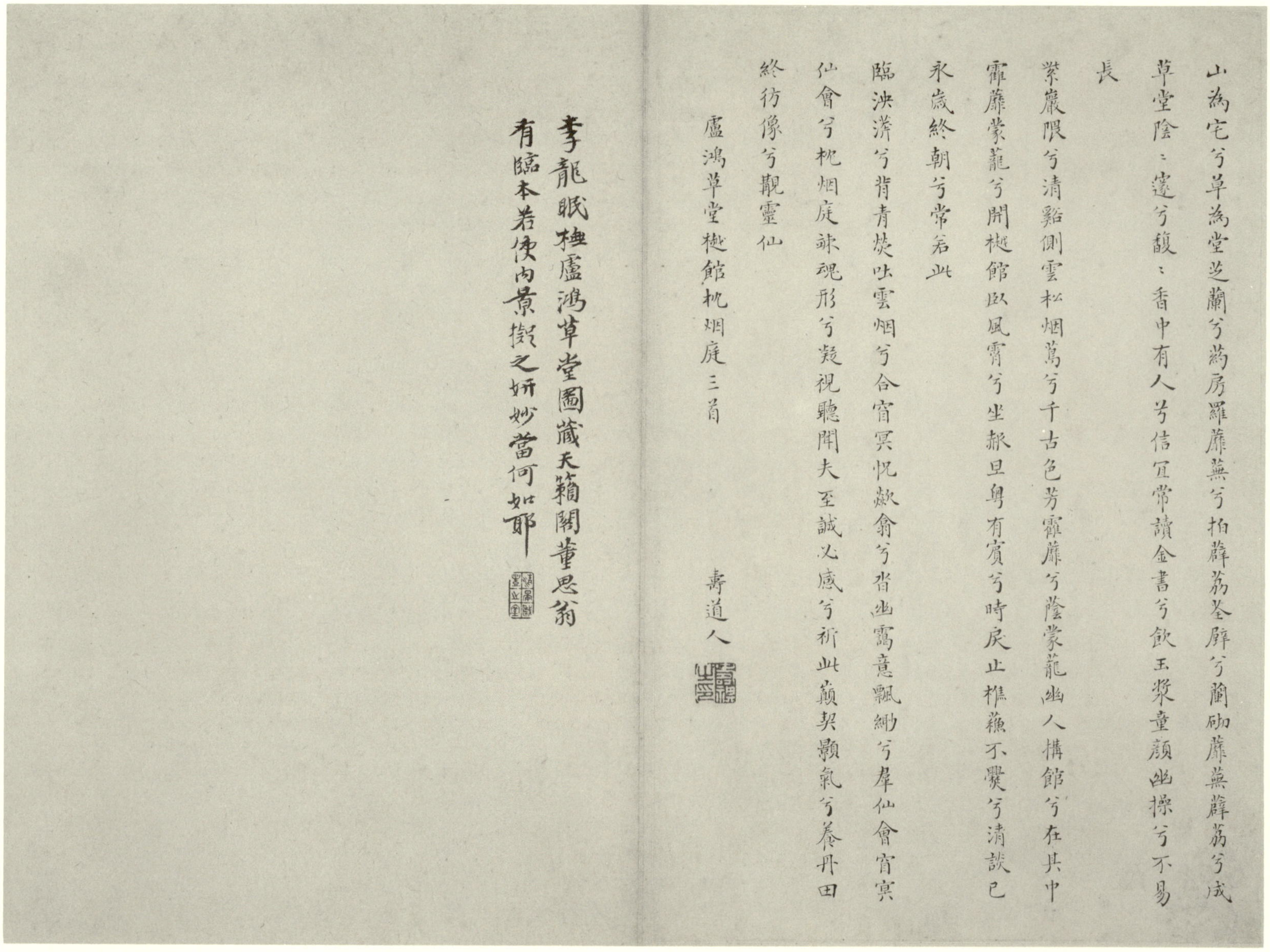

山為宅兮草為堂芝蘭兮為房羅薜荔兮拳芙蓉薜荔兮成

草堂陰兮遠兮韻兮香中有人兮芳信宜常讀金書兮飲玉漿童顏幽操兮不易

長

紫巖隈兮清谿側雲松煙蔓兮千古色芳霏靡兮陰蒙蒙蘢幽人構錦兮在其中

霏靡蒙蘢兮開榔館臥風霄兮坐郵旦旦有賓兮時戾止榷藕不饜兮清談已

永歲終朝兮常若此

終彷像兮觀靈仙

仙會兮枕煙庭眇魂形兮歆視聽開夫至誠必感兮祈此顏契顥氣兮春丹田

臨洪濛兮背青焚吐雲煙兮合窅冥忽翕歘兮沓幽意飄緲兮犀仙會窅冥

盧鴻草堂樓館枕煙庭三首

　　　　壽道人 〔印〕

李龍眠軸盧鴻草堂圖藏天籟閣董思翁

有臨本若庚內景樹之妍妙當何如耶 〔印〕

Leaf I, "Transcription of Three Poems by the T'ang Master Lu Hung"

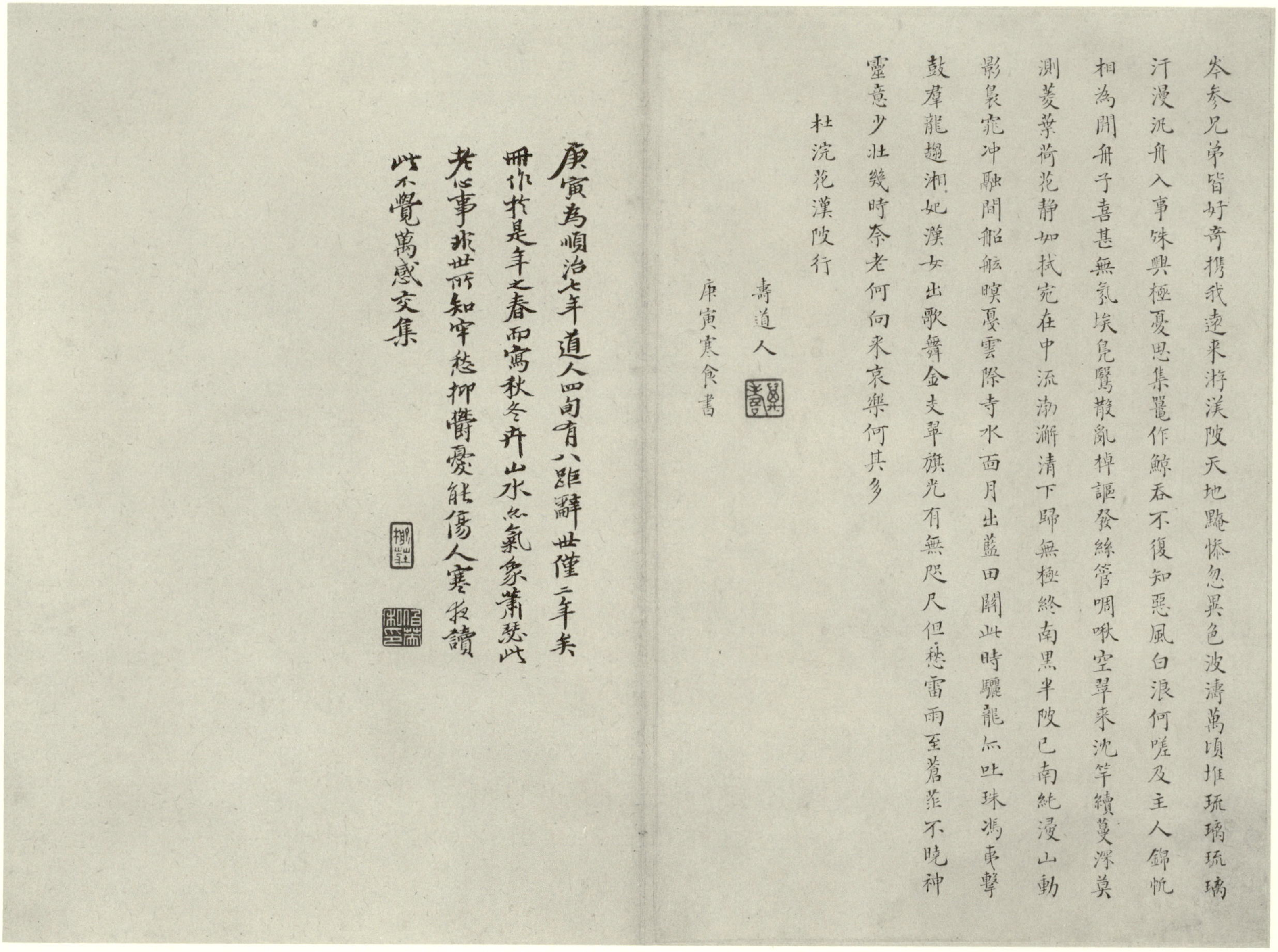

岑參兄弟皆好奇攜我遠來游渼陂天地黤慘忽異色波濤萬頃堆琉璃琉璃

汗漫沈舟入事殊興極憂集罷作鮫吞不復知惡風白浪何嗟及主人錦帆

相為開舟子喜甚無氛埃鼉鳴黿散亂棹發絲管咽啾空翠尝沈竿續蔓澤梟

測菱葉荷花靜如拭宛在中添渤澥清下歸無極終南黑半陂已南純浸山動

影裏宛冲融開船艙嘆夏雲陪寺水西月出藍田關此時驪龍兮吐珠馮夷東擊

鼓群龍趨湘妃漢女出歌舞金支草旗兒有無盡尺但愁雷雨至蒼蒼不吃神

靈意少壯幾時奈老何向來宴樂何其多

杜沈花漢陂行

　　　庚寅寒食書 〔印〕

　　壽道人 〔印〕

庚寅為順治七年道人四旬有八距辭世僅二年矣

冊作於是年之春而寫秋冬卉山水此氣象蕭楚此

老忿事求世所知審慈抑瘞憂能傷人寒荒讀

此不覺萬感交集 〔印〕〔印〕

Leaf J, "Transcription of Tu Fu's 'Mei-p'ei Lake'"

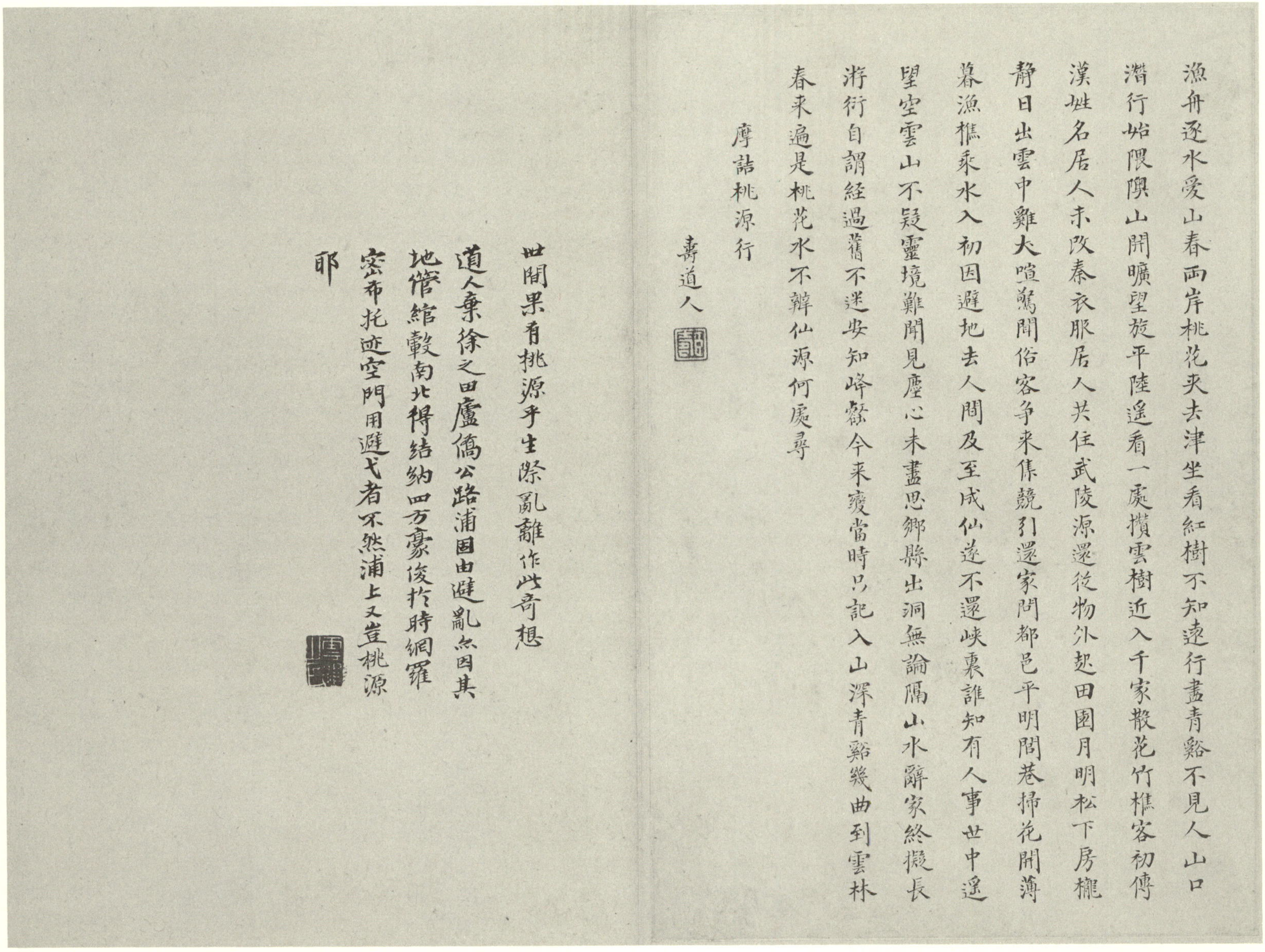

漁舟逐水愛山春兩岸桃花夾去津坐看紅樹不知遠行盡青谿不見人山口
潛行始隈隩山開曠望旋平陸遙看一處攢雲樹近入千家散花竹樵客初傳
漢姓名居人未改衣服居人共住武陵源還從物外起田園月明松下房櫳
靜日出雲中雞犬喧聞俗客爭來集引還家問都邑平明閭巷掃花開薄
暮漁樵乘水入初因避地去人間及至成仙遂不還峽裏誰知有人事世中遙
望空雲山不疑靈境難聞見塵心未盡思鄉縣出洞無論隔山水辭家終擬長
游行自謂經過舊不迷安知峰壑今來變當時只記入山深青谿幾曲到雲林
春來遍是桃花水不辨仙源何處尋

摩詰桃源行

壽道人 [印]

世間果有桃源乎生際亂離作此奇想
道人秉徐之田盧僑公路浦固由避亂為因其
地僻館轂南北得結納四方豪俊於時綢羅
密布托迹空門用避戈者不然浦上又豈桃源
耶 [印]

Leaf K, "Transcription of Wang Wei's 'Peach Blossom Song'"

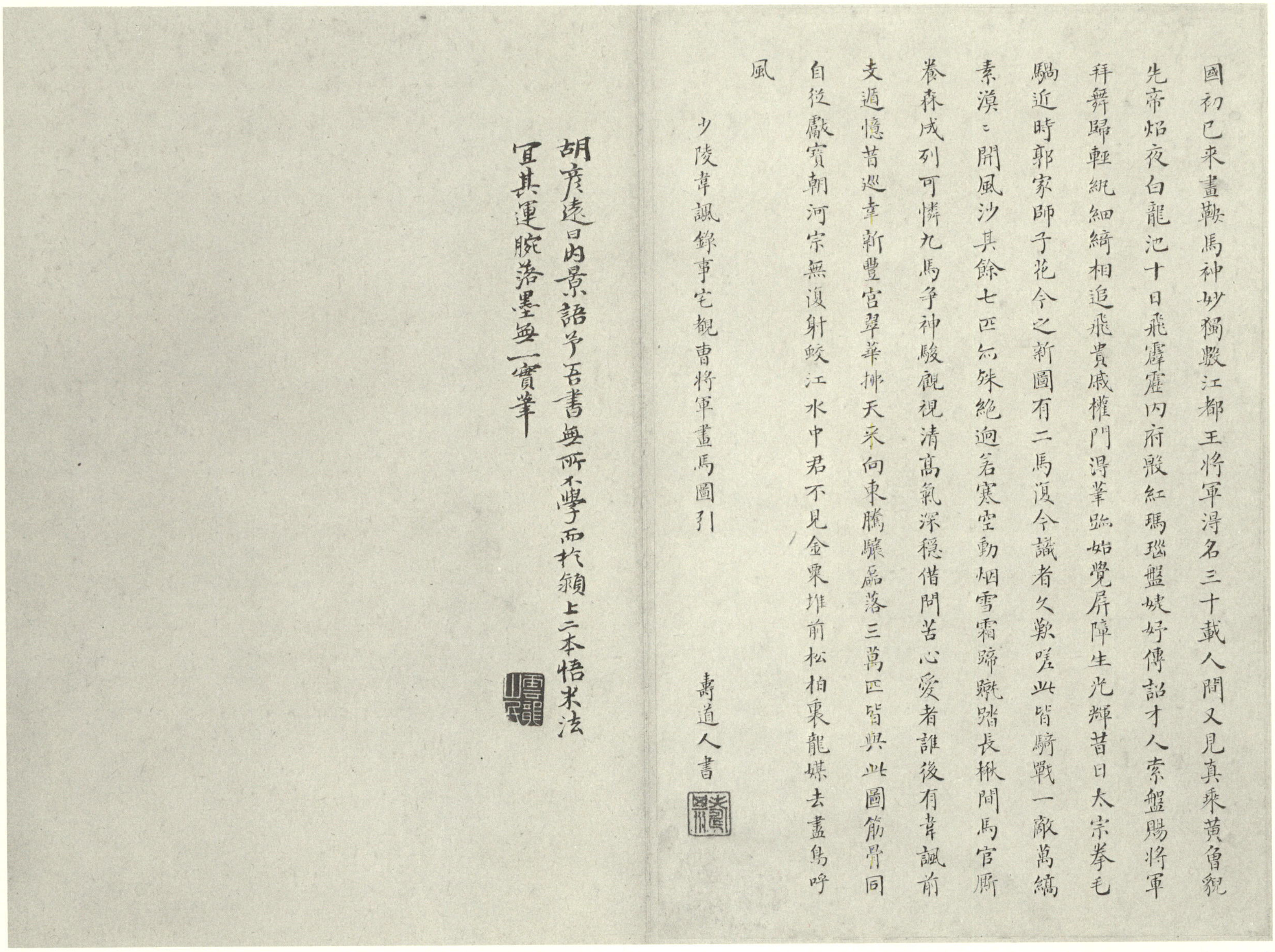

國初已來畫鞍馬神妙獨數江都王將軍得名三十載人間又見真乘黃魯親
先帝炤夜白龍池十日飛霹靂內府殷紅瑪瑙盤好傳詔才人索盤賜將軍
拜舞歸輕紈細綺相追飛貴戚權門得筆跡始覺屏障生光輝昔日太宗拳毛
騧近時郭家獅子花今之新圖有二馬復令識者久歎嗟此皆騎戰一敵萬縞
素漠漠開風沙其餘七匹亦殊絕迥若寒空動煙雪霜蹄蹴踏長楸間馬官廝
養森成列可憐九馬爭神駿顧視清高氣深穩借問苦心愛者誰後有韋諷前
支遁憶昔巡幸新豐宮翠華拂天來向東騰驤磊落三萬匹皆與此圖筋骨同
自從獻寶朝河宗無復射蛟江水中君不見金粟堆前松柏裏龍媒去盡鳥呼
風

少陵韋諷錄事宅觀曹將軍畫馬圖引

壽道人書 [印]

胡彥遠曰內景語乎吾書無所不學而於褚上二本悟米法
宜其運腕落墨無一實筆 [印]

Leaf L, "Transcription of Tu Fu's 'On Seeing a Horse Painting by Ts'ao Pa in the House of the Recorder Wei Feng'"

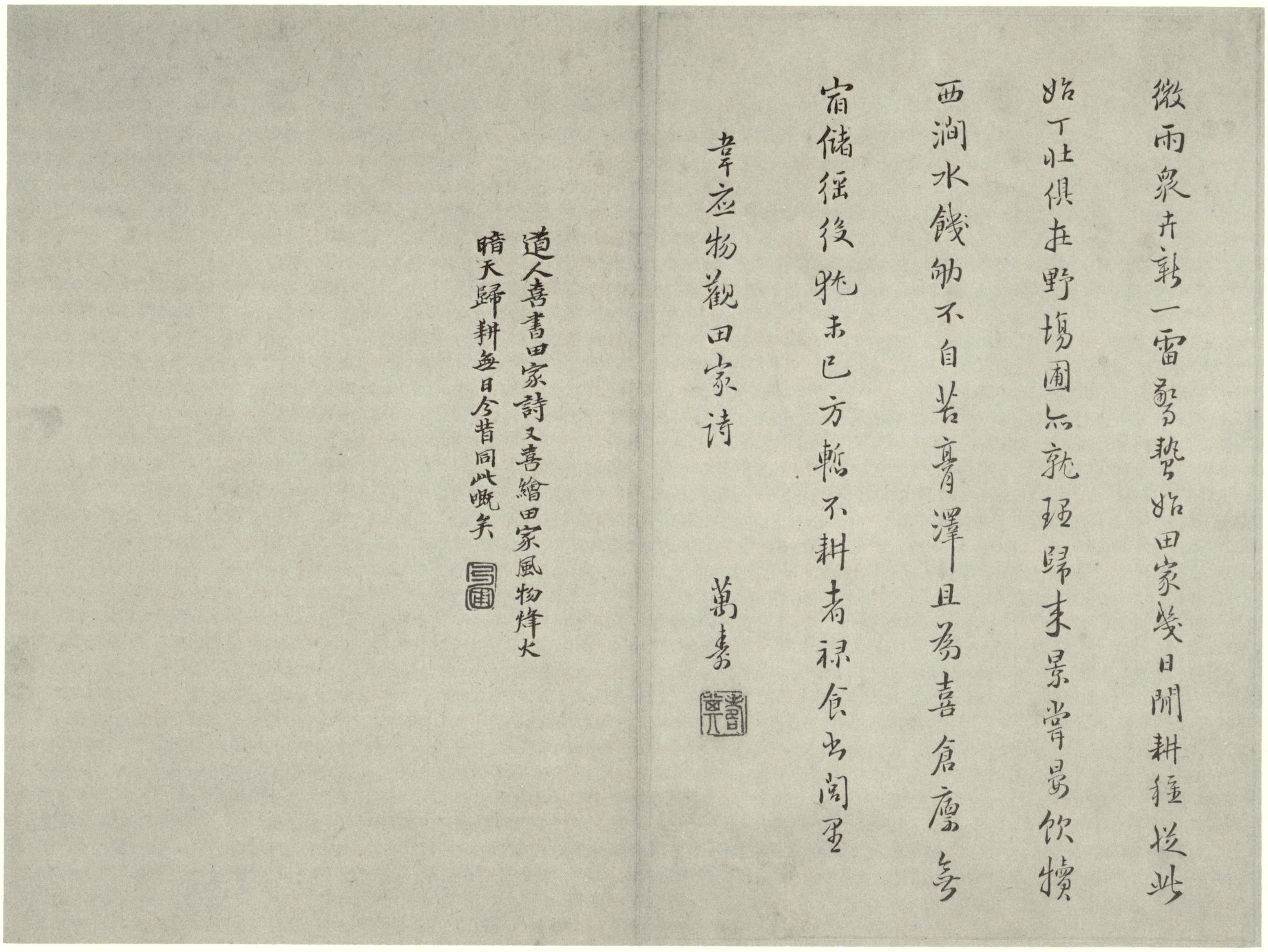

微雨眾卉新一雷驚蟄始　田家幾日閒耕種從此起
始丁壯俱在野場圃亦就理　歸來景常晏飲憊
西澗水鑱缺不自苦膏澤且為喜倉廩無
宿儲徭役猶未已方慚不耕者祿食出閭里

韋應物觀田家詩　萬壽

道人喜書田家詩又喜繪田家風物烽火
暗天歸耕無日今昔同此晚矣

Leaf M, "Transcription of Wei Ying-wu's 'On Observing Farm Life'"

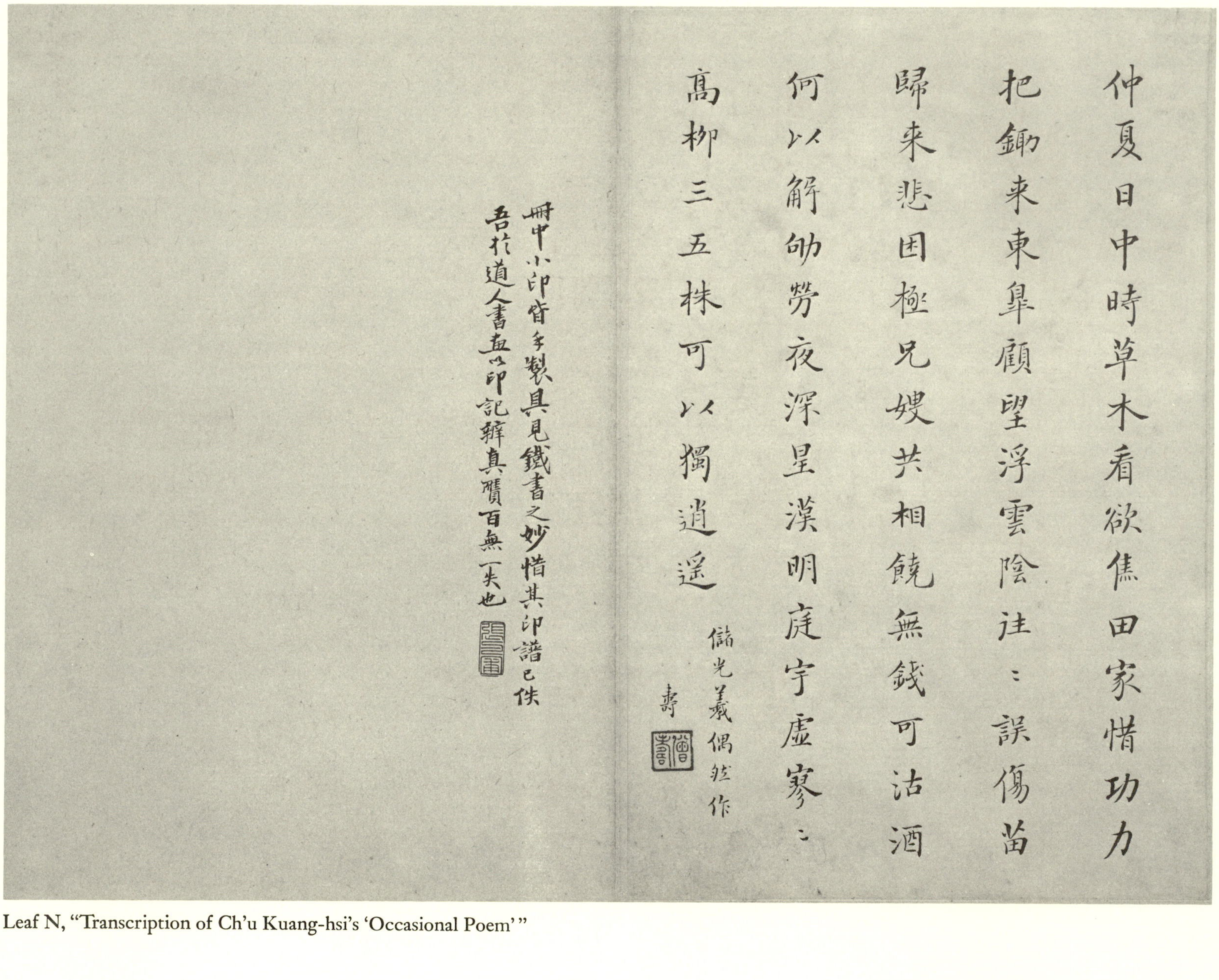

仲夏日中時草木看欲燋　田家惜功力
把鋤來東皋顧望浮雲陰注：誤傷苗
歸來悲困極兄嫂共相饒無錢可沽酒
何以解劬勞夜深星漢明庭宇虛寥：
高柳三五株可以獨逍遙　儲光羲偶然作　壽

冊中小印皆予手製具見鐵書之妙惜其印譜已佚
吾於道人書畫及印記辨真贗百無一失也

Leaf N, "Transcription of Ch'u Kuang-hsi's 'Occasional Poem'"

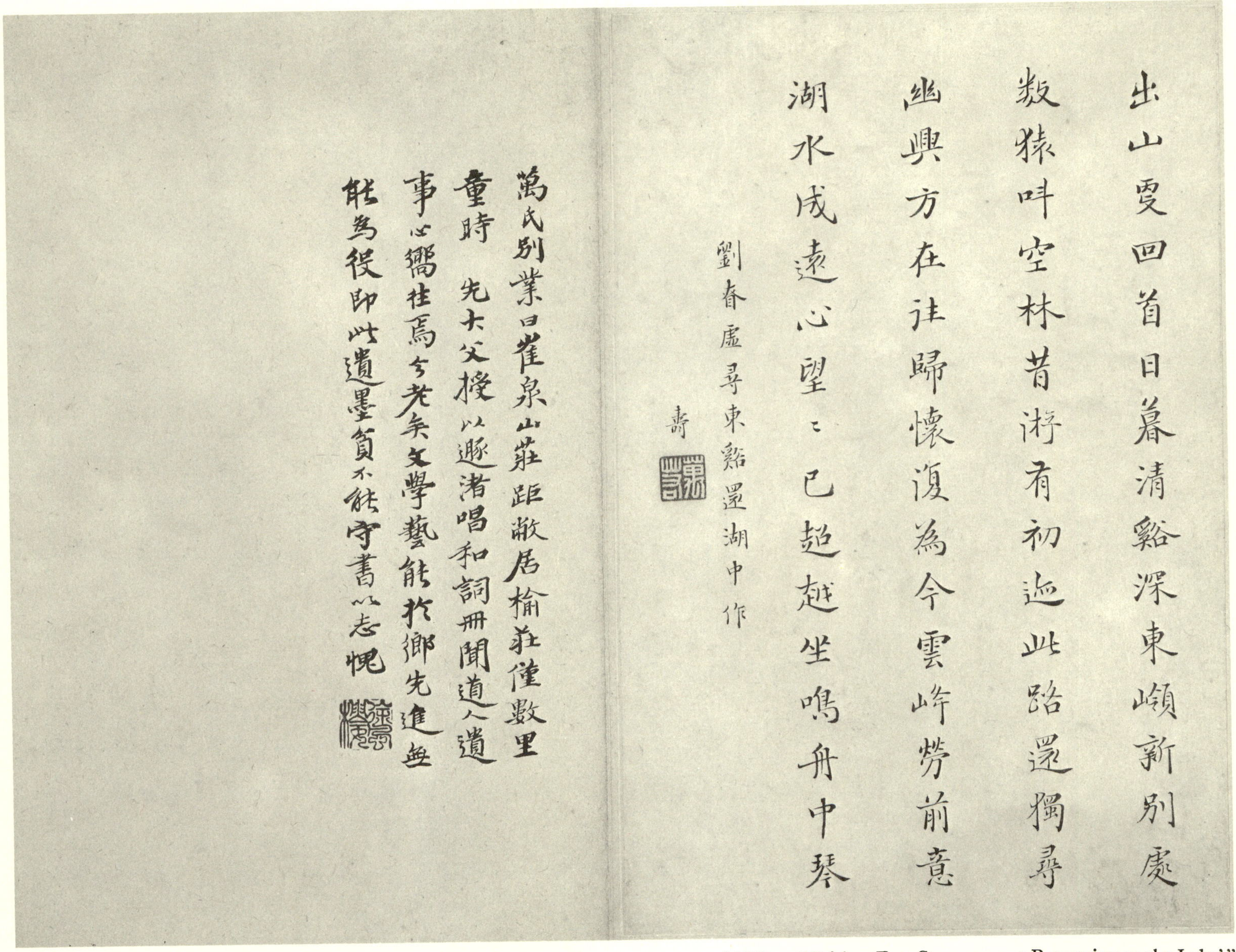

出山更回首日暮清谿深東嶺新別處

數猿叫空林昔游有初迹此路還獨尋

幽興方在往歸懷遂為今雲峰勞前意

湖水成遠心望之已超越坐嘯舟中琴

劉眘虛尋東谿還湖中作

壽

萬氏別業曰崔泉山莊距敝居榆莊僅數里

童時　先大父授以邀渚唱和詞冊聞道人遺

事心嚮往焉今老矣文學藝能於鄉先進無

能為役即此遺墨真不能守書以志愧

Leaf O, "Transcription of Liu Ch'un-hsü's 'Composed When Visiting East Stream upon Returning to the Lake'"

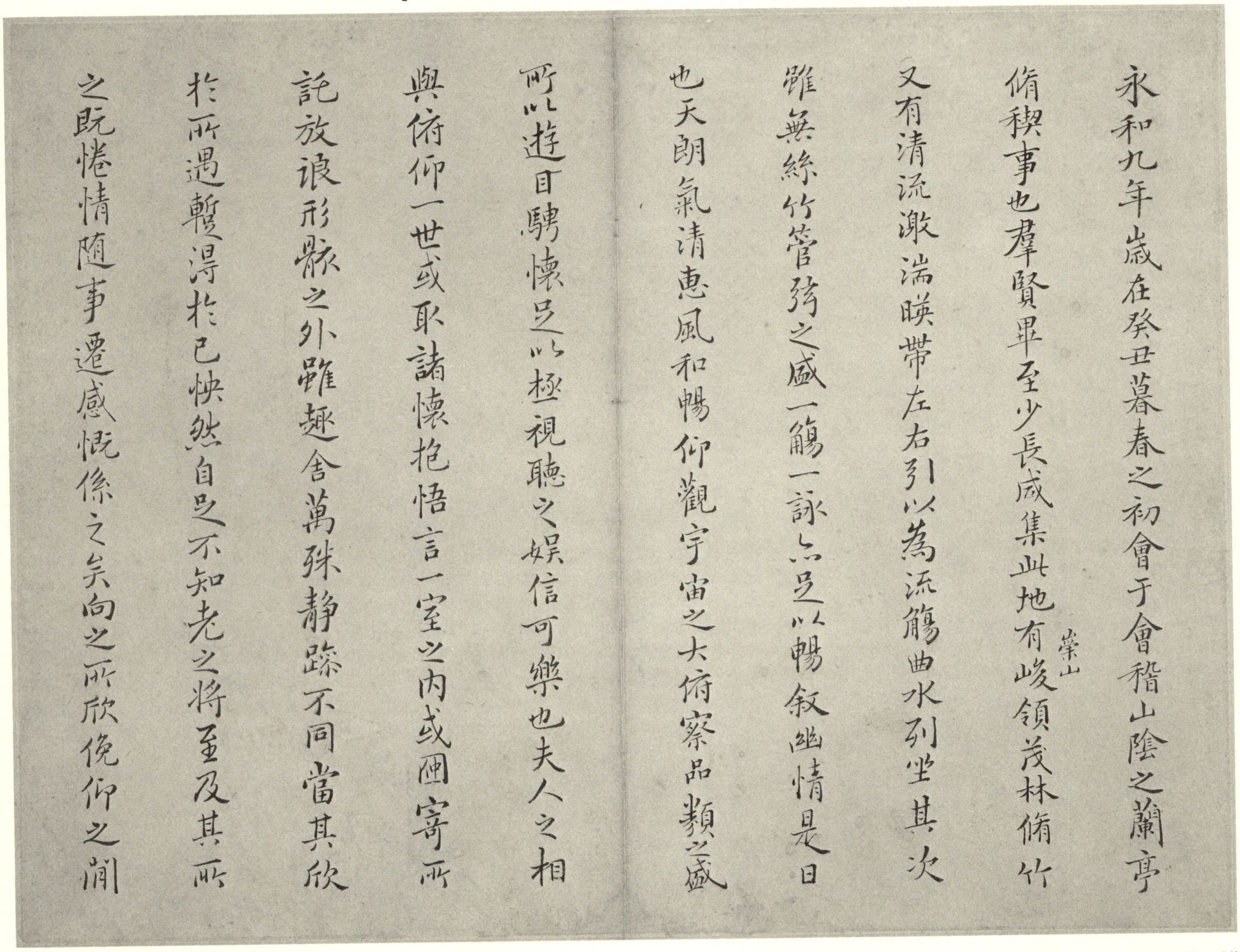

永和九年歲在癸丑暮春之初會于會稽山陰之蘭亭

修禊事也群賢畢至少長咸集此地有峻領茂林修竹

又有清流激湍暎帶左右引以為流觴曲水列坐其次

雖無絲竹管弦之盛一觴一詠亦足以暢敘幽情是日

也天朗氣清惠風和暢仰觀宇宙之大俯察品類之盛

所以遊目騁懷足以極視聽之娛信可樂也夫人之相

與俯仰一世或取諸懷抱悟言一室之內或因寄所

託放浪形骸之外雖趣舍萬殊靜躁不同當其欣

於所遇暫得於己快然自足不知老之將至及其所

之既惓情隨事遷感慨係之矣向之所欣俛仰之間

Leaf P, "Transcription of the 'Preface to the Orchid Pavilion'"

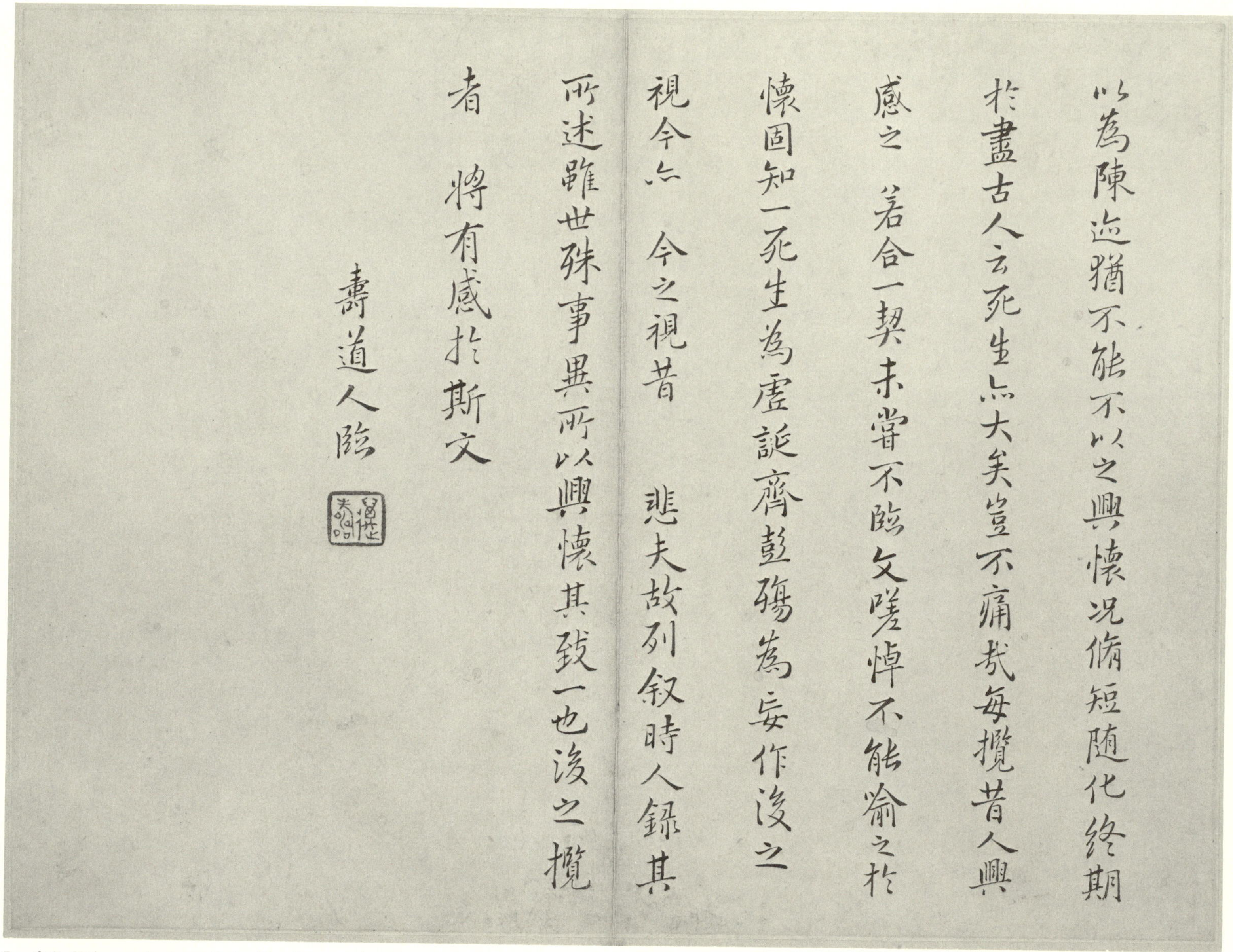

以為陳迹猶不能不以之興懷況脩短随化終期
於盡古人云死生亦大矣豈不痛哉每攬昔人興
感之由若合一契未嘗不臨文嗟悼不能喻之於
懷固知一死生為虚誕齊彭殤為妄作後之
視今亦 今之視昔 悲夫故列叙時人録其
所述雖世殊事異所以興懷其致一也後之攬
者　將有感於斯文

壽道人臨 [印]

Leaf Q, "Transcription of the 'Preface to the Orchid Pavilion'"

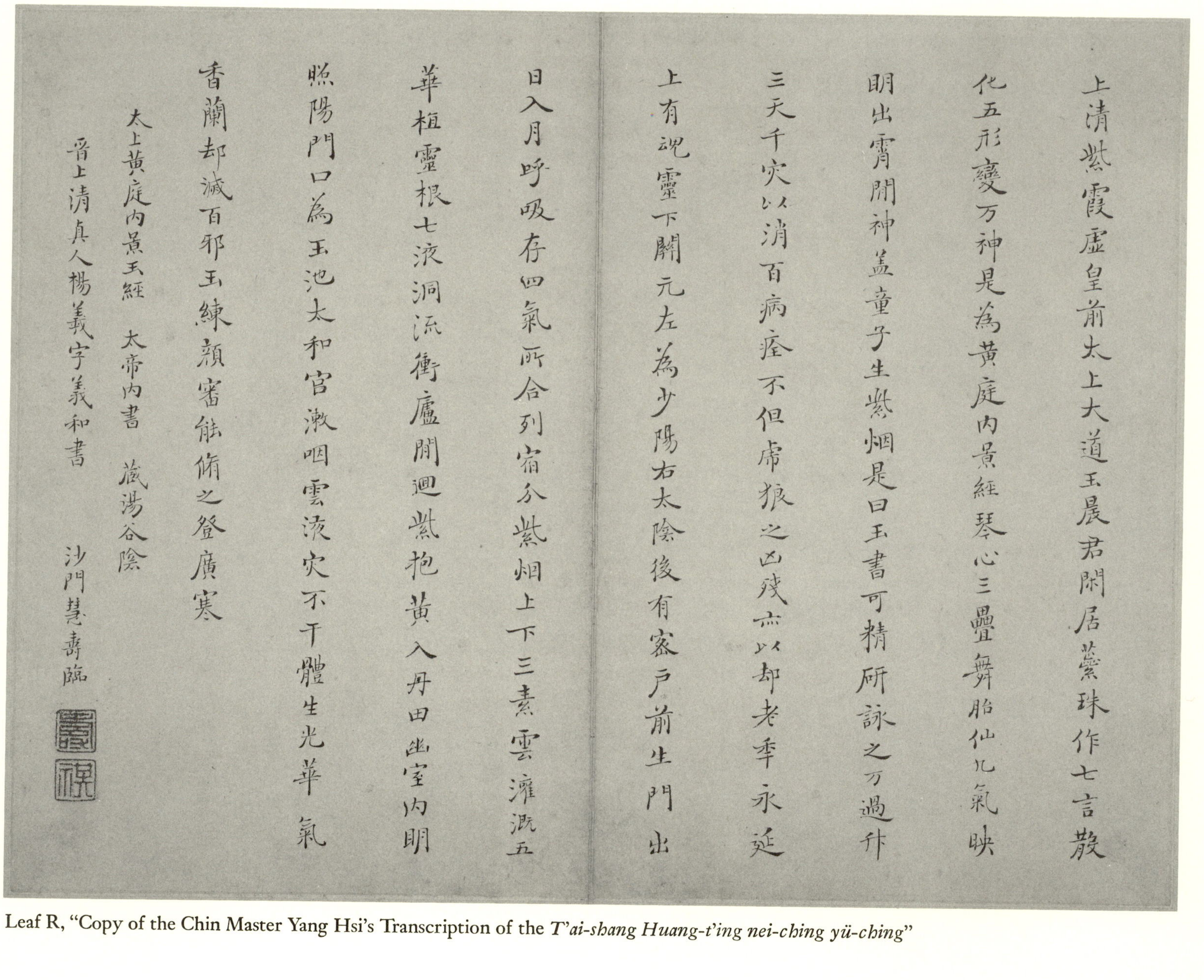

上清紫霞虚皇前太上大道玉晨君閒居蘂珠作七言散
化五形變萬神是為黄庭内景經琴心三疊舞胎仙九氣映
明出霄間神蓋童子生紫烟是曰玉書可精研詠之万過升
三天千災以消百病痊不但席挺之凶殘亦以却老季永延
上有魂靈下關元左為少陽右太陰後有密戸前生門出
日入月呼吸存四氣所合列宿分紫烟上下三素雲灌漑五
華植靈根七液洞流衝廬間迴紫抱黄入丹田幽室内明
照陽門口為玉池太和官漱咽雲液灾不干體生光華氣
香蘭却滅百邪玉練顏審能脩之登廣寒
太上黄庭内景玉經　太帝内書　崴湯谷陰
晉上清真人楊義字義和書　沙門慧壽臨 [印][印]

Leaf R, "Copy of the Chin Master Yang Hsi's Transcription of the *T'ai-shang Huang-t'ing nei-ching yü-ching*"

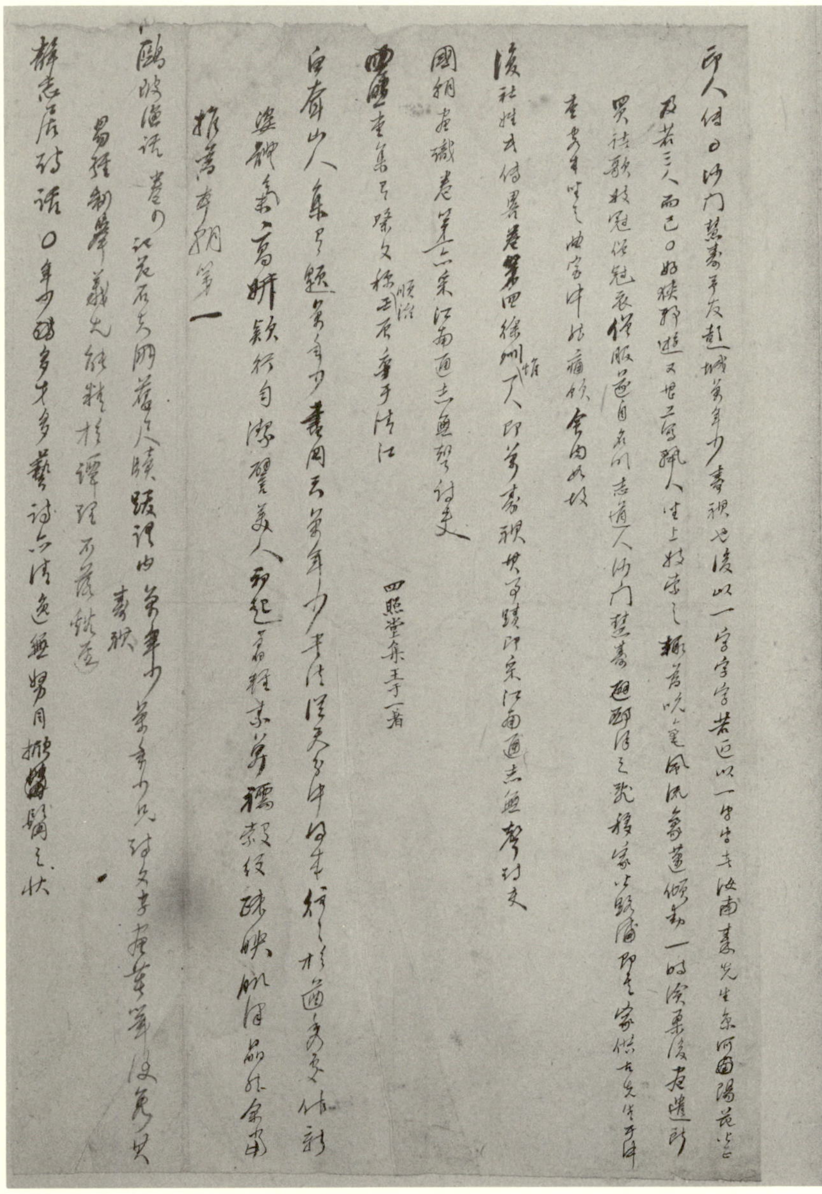

Leaf TT

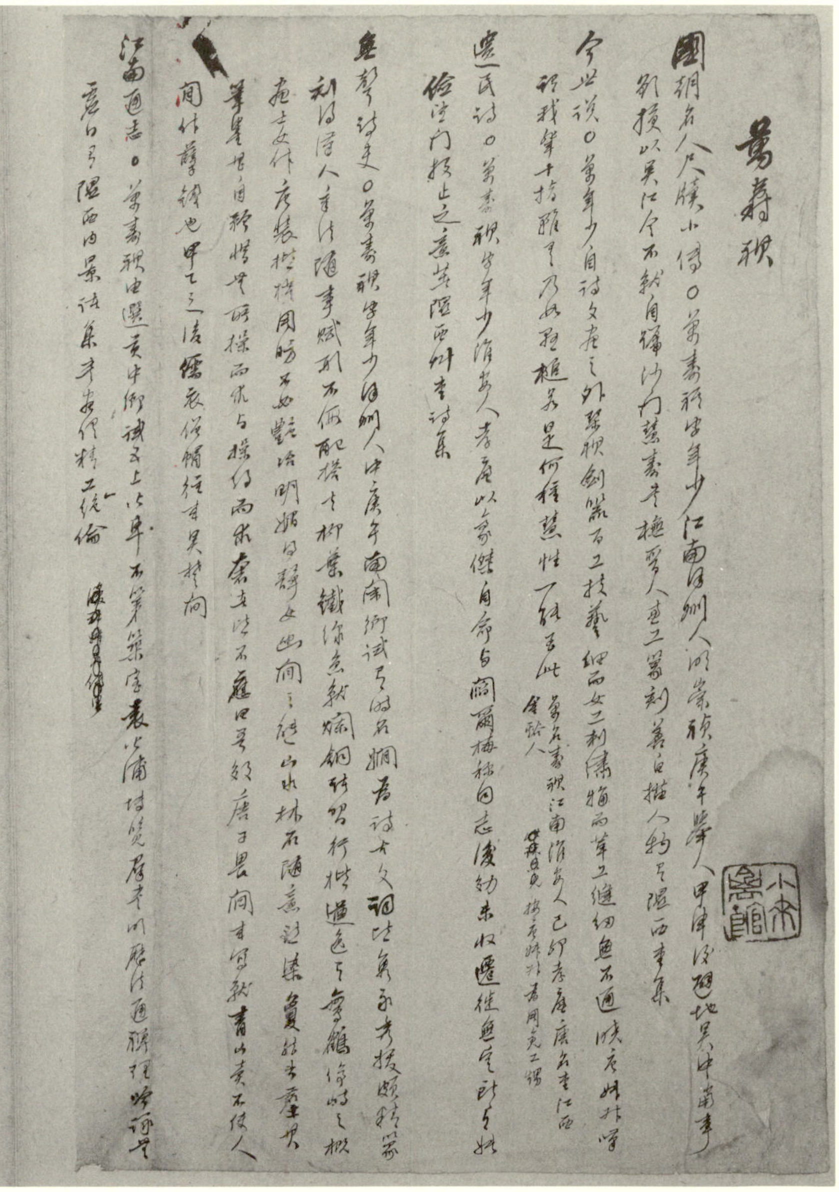

Leaf SS

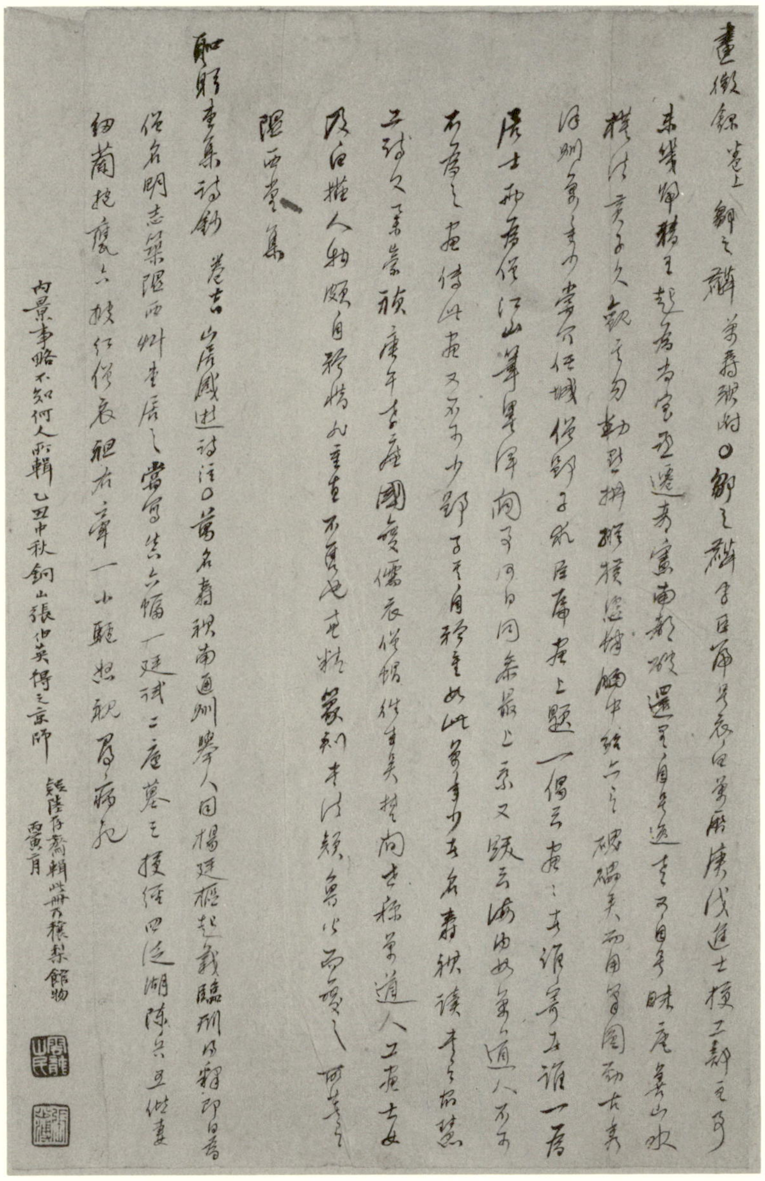

Leaf UU

XI CHANG CHI-SU (fl. ca. 1620?–1670)

P'u-chou (Yung-chi), Shansi

Snow-Capped Peaks

The Art Museum, Princeton University (67-1).

Hanging scroll. Ink and color on paper. 345.9 x 102.4 cm.

UNDATED: probably executed ca. 1660.

UNSIGNED

SEAL OF THE ARTIST: *Chang Chi-su tzu Fu-( ) hao Mo-yün* (relief, square; one character is illegible).

COLLECTOR'S SEAL: Owner unidentified; in lower left corner.

SUPERSCRIPTIONS: a single paper strip which was removed from a previous mounting and remounted above the painting proper contains two superscriptions, the first (in six characters of "running" script and eight smaller characters) by an anonymous writer and the second (in twenty-six small characters of "running" script) by Lo Chen-yü (1866–1940).

CONDITION: fair; there are heavy abrasions over the entire surface of the paper; two irregular holes of about 3–4 cm. each at the top of the painting and other smaller holes (mainly at the top) have been repaired in the remounting process.

PROVENANCE: Chang Po-chin (born 1900, Hsing-t'ang, Hopei), former ambassador to Japan from the Republic of China.

PUBLISHED: *T'ien-yin-t'ang Collection: One Hundred Masterpieces of Chinese Painting*, vol. 1, pl. 49 (illustrated and assigned to Wu Pin); *Archives of Asian Art*, vol. 22 (1968–69), p. 133 (assigned as unknown sixteenth-century artist, *Winter Landscape*); *Record of the Art Museum, Princeton University*, vol. 27, no. 1 (1968), p. 35 (assigned to Chang Chi-su after the authors' identification).

THIS IS POSSIBLY the only extant painting of the late Ming-early Ch'ing master Chang Chi-su. The landscape has in the past been attributed to various Ming masters. The painting bears no artist's signature, but there is a seal in the upper right corner (hitherto undecipherable) which can now be read as that of the painter Chang Chi-su.

Vertical and diagonal thrusts of exposed and snow-covered rock dominate this monumental landscape. The boulders project from the edges of the picture plane and recede in clearly overlapping layers which rise precipitously upward. The enormous scale of the work makes immediate reading of the various picture parts difficult, but the proportions are established in the lower half of the painting by a figure with a staff who traverses a wooden bridge. The bridge arches to an angle in the center and connects the left foreground with a group of tall, lush trees which surmount gigantic boulders in the lower right corner; it further spans a broad waterfall which descends from the middle distance in two stages, cascading downward above the head of the cloaked figure.

A huge outcropping of rock juts straight up from the middle left edge of the picture frame, as if encroaching upon the viewer's space, and soars above the treetops until it almost reaches the height of the distant peaks. This central mountain mass continues the upward ascent in serried layers to the top of the picture.

The space near the figure in the foreground is clear and crisp in feeling. Rising with the thrust of the soaring peak, layers of mist hover deep in the middle-distance pocket, half-obscuring a complex of thatched houses which are placed in the very center of the composition and are visible through the elbow of the projecting rock. A stone pass at the far right leads to them. The pass further indicates the relative scale of rocks, trees, and human habitation. From the thick mist the uppermost promontories rise and meet a sky darkened by layers of ink wash. Despite this conventional method of describing a snow scene (by negative contrast), a feeling of a white and chilly landscape is successfully established. Opaque mineral green and russet color washes are used throughout to give warmth to the craggy mountains. Touches of green and white pigment are applied in layered dabs to form mosses and shrubs and also to highlight the foliage and branches of the trees, giving the forms a decorative freshness and a three-dimensional surface quality. The brushstrokes are abrupt, coarse, and angular in their attack and strive to depict in relatively exact detail the diverse surfaces of the landscape elements.

THE MOST IMMEDIATE stylistic forebears which this scroll brings to mind are the late Ming painters Lan Ying (1585–1664-) and Wu Pin (ca. 1568–1626)—indeed, an attribution to the latter was attached to the scroll when it first entered the Sackler collection. Equally prominent, however, is its "realism"—its interest in the coherent placement of the landscape elements in space, its treatment of the solids as true massive volumes which recede logically in space, and its precise surface description of the elements—all of which relate this work to early Ch'ing dynasty style as well.

The ambitious scale of this landscape reveals Chang Chi-su to have been a supreme—even an inspired—technician of conservative temperament who undoubtedly achieved a measure of local fame. It is regrettable that no other works exist to show his stylistic range. What is of particular interest in this painting are its "transitional" features, which in retrospect link Chang stylistically and technically to painters of quite disparate spheres of influence. In *Snow-Capped Peaks* we see how the feeling for monumentality established in the Northern Sung was taken quite literally by the late Ming, reappearing in the work of this little-known master.

IN THE SUPERSCRIPTION mounted at the top of the painting two separate hands are discernible. The first inscription, in fourteen characters (see the detail, *right*), reads: "A large hanging scroll of a snow scene without signature. Acquired in the year *keng-tzu* and remounted in *jen-yin*." The writer left no signature or seal to identify him. The second superscription (see the detail, *left*) is written in small characters of fourteen even lines: "This is the best [work] of Tai Wen-chin and is harmonious with the hand of Fan [K'uan] Hua-yüan and Hsia [Kuei] Yü-yü. [Signed:] Lo Chen-yü saw and inscribed." Lo Chen-yü (1866–1940), the well-known scholar and antiquarian, also left no date, but if we postulate a close time relationship between the two inscriptions (in view of their position on the inset strip of paper), then the possible dates of acquisition and remounting may be 1840–1842 or 1900–1902.

XI, detail. Superscription in two parts: (*left*) by Lo Chen-yü (1866–1940) and (*right*) by anonymous writer.

The attribution to the middle Ming painter Tai Chin (ca. 1388–1462), chief proponent of the Che school of painting, can be dismissed, as the style of this landscape has neither the looseness of compositional structure nor the broad, oblique "axe strokes" and liberal use of flat ink wash in the rocks which are associated with Tai's works. A more recent attribution to the late Ming painter Wu Pin, who worked in Nanking, is more tenable, yet there are enough authenticated works by Wu Pin to show the difference between this Sackler scroll and his work.

On the top right-hand corner of the painting is a small square seal. This is generally not the position for a collector's seal; it is the properly prominent spot for the artist to affix his seal when he chooses not to sign his name. The impression of the seal is uneven and hard to read, but eight of the nine characters can be deciphered (the seal is reproduced actual size): "*Chang Chi-su tzu Fu-*  () *hao Mo-yün*." The following biographical information is listed for the name Chang Chi-su, which is said to be drawn from the gazetteer of the artist's home city: "Chang Chi-su. Ch'ing [dynasty], native of P'u-chou [Shansi]; he excelled in landscapes and was a pupil of Wang Han-kuang. His style achieved nuance and loftiness. His monochrome ink flowers, plants, animals, and insects were full of animation and were often extraordinary in concept."[1] P'u-chou (the present-day Yung-chi) is situated in the culturally rich Fen River valley of Shansi Province, which has long been known for its tradition of Buddhist and Taoist murals (the Taoist temple Yung-lo-kung is situated to the east in nearby Jui-ch'eng). This tradition might have exerted an important formative influence on the painters of the region.

No date other than those of the "Ch'ing dynasty" is mentioned in this account, but fortunately Chang's teacher, Wang Han-kuang (*tzu* Ho-shan, Ssu-ho), is identifiable. Wang's biography appears in several late Ming and early Ch'ing compilations. Like his pupil, he was also a native of Shansi and excelled in landscape painting. He received his *chin-shih* degree in 1631 and seems to have been relatively well known as a gentleman-painter, as he served in the Ministry of Personnel.[2] Unfortunately, no works of Wang's are extant. Although his dates are not known, we may reconstruct them on the basis of *chin-shih* dates. For example, the well-known painters Wu Wei-yeh and Sun Ch'eng-tse received their *chin-shih* degrees in 1631: Wu was born in 1609 and Sun in 1592.[3] We may guess from these birth dates that Wang Han-kuang was born about 1600. Chang Chi-su was probably about twenty years younger than his teacher; hence he may have been born about 1620. As the average lifespan of a painter was about fifty years, we may put Chang's dates at roughly 1620–1670, which would mean that he was in his maturity when the Ming dynasty fell and that he was active for about a decade in the K'ang-hsi period of the Ch'ing dynasty.

These dates seem to fit our observations of Chang's style. Some possible artistic influences on him are as follows: Wu Pin, active in Nanking; Lan Ying, active in Hang-chou and Yang-chou; Wang Han-kuang (ca. 1600?–1631-), active in P'u-chou, Shansi; Fan Ch'i (1616–1694), active in Nanking; Tai Pen-hsiao (1621–1691), active in Hsiu-ning, Anhwei; and Wang Hui (1632–1717), active in T'ai-ts'ang, Kiangsu. From this we see that Chang's teacher Wang was more or less contemporary with Wu Pin, and that Chang's birth date might have overlapped Wu's old age, with his youth probably coinciding with Lan Ying's mature years.

Stylistically, it is noteworthy that Chang's work has affinities with not only Wu Pin and Lan Ying but also such contemporaries as Fan Ch'i and Tai Pen-hsiao, who, although working in different regions, show a fondness for curving, thrusting shapes of mountains in tall

formats.[4] As noted above, before the painter's seal was deciphered, the landscape was attributed to Wu Pin. A more detailed stylistic comparison of it with the work of Lan Ying and Wu Pin reveals Chang's transitional position and also the Ch'ing elements in his style. Wu in many ways epitomizes the strongly individualist currents which gripped the late Ming (see, e.g., fig. 1). As James Cahill characterizes his work, "masses of rock rise into bizarre and mysteriously organic shapes"; the elements are rendered meticulously with a "hard edge" and are purposefully distorted in scale and spatial recession.[5] Such a visualization reveals Wu's interest in line and form as carriers of a "schematic archaism,"[6] a stylistic current which manifested itself in certain late Ming painters. His view of nature is introverted, private, and imaginative in an undeniably self-conscious sense.

1. Wu Pin, *Streams and Mountains Far from the World*, dated 1615. Hanging scroll. Ink and light color on paper. Hashimoto collection, Kyoto.

XI, detail.

XI, detail.

By contrast Chang's view of nature is direct, grandiose, and uncomplicated by archaistic references. In *Snow-Capped Peaks* the only eccentric aspect of the landscape is the exaggerated outcropping of rock. Otherwise there is a logical spatial ambiance with a minimum of linear stylization (see the detail). The rocks, trees, and buildings sit solidly in their setting, and the forms do not trick the eye with grotesqueries or dangling masses. Wu Pin's trees, on the other hand, not only are greatly reduced in scale to contrast with the rocks but also tend to be visualized in flat planes with the branches forking in even intervals and the foliage silhouetted as pattern against the masses of rock. These stylized elements indicate Wu's more personal view of nature and demonstrate tendencies more closely linked to the late Ming.

Chang's trees are full, three-dimensional forms whose foliage overlaps and covers the twisting, foreshortened branches. He works with a stiff, coarse brush, building the contours of his forms with successive broken lines; his interior modeling strokes are limited to repetitive dots or hasty, short horizontals done with a scrubbing motion. Like his contours, the modeling strokes are drawn with an oblique brushtip and are applied with a driving energy. Compositionally these elements indicate familiarity with Lan Ying's tradition of landscape (fig. 2). As in Lan's *Winter Landscape* Chang's trees are utilized as a strong foreground focus and are conceived as fully three-dimensional forms. Technically the method of dotting white pigment over mineral green became idiomatic in Lan Ying's colored landscapes and reappears in the work of his followers as well.[7]

The specific and repetitive manner of describing the surface of rocks and trees in this scroll exceeds Lan Ying's particular range, however. Certain painters in the Ch'ing stressed the increased corporeality of landscape elements and the generous use of mist to accentuate the substance of forms. They attempted by these means to restore some of the spatial atmosphere and grandeur achieved in the Northern Sung visions of landscape. While we have identified Wang Hui as a younger contemporary of Chang, such later academic masters as Yüan Chiang (fl. 1694–ca. 1744), Li Yin (fl. 1694–ca. 1702), and others[8] developed this order of depiction on a monumental scale. Their efforts are certainly prefigured in *Snow-Capped Peaks*.

There is no evidence concerning the kind of patronage that Chang Chi-su attracted. If he was mainly active in his home province, the wealthy Shansi middle class may well have paralleled that of Yang-chou in a taste for ostentation. Certainly the hall necessary to accommodate this scroll must have been of sizeable dimensions. Such a fondness for extremes seems to have increased toward the middle of the Ch'ing, especially in the north, and culminated in the taste of the Ch'ien-lung court.

NOTES

1. See *CKHCJMTT*, p. 476b, where the *P'u-chou fu-chih (Gazetteer of P'u-chou, Shansi)* is cited. We have not been able to obtain a copy of this book to verify the reference.

2. See *ibid.*, p. 44c; Chang Keng, *Kuo-ch'ao hua-cheng-lu* (preface dated 1735), pp. 21–23, where he is listed among a large group of amateur painters who held office; Lan Ying, Hsieh Pin, et al., eds., *T'u-hui pao-chien hsü-tsuan*, 2/48; and the *P'u-chou fu-chih*.

3. Kuo Wei-ch'ü, ed., *Sung-Yüan Ming-Ch'ing shu-hua-chia nien-piao*, p. 217.

4. Some representative works of Tai and Fan are shown in James Cahill, ed., *Fantastics and Eccentrics in Chinese Painting*, no. 15, p. 49, no. 21, p. 62, in the Vannoti collection, Lugano, and the A. Brundage Foundation, De Young Memorial Museum, San Francisco, respectively.

5. *Ibid.*, p. 32; see also Cahill's "Wu Pin and His Landscape Paintings."

6. See Wen Fong, "Archaism as a 'Primitive' Style."

7. Cf. James Cahill, ed., *The Restless Landscape*, pp. 136–44, which discusses such followers and contemporaries as Chiang Hung (dated works 1674–1690) and Liu Tu (fl. ca. 1636).

8. Cf. James Cahill, "Yüan Chiang and His School," pts. 1 and 2, especially the latter installment, which illustrates *Mountain Landscape with Pavilion* in the Freer Gallery of Art and *Road to Shu*, dated 1718, both by Yüan Chiang.

2. Lan Ying, *Winter Landscape*, dated 1640, detail. Hanging scroll. Ink and color on silk. Hara collection, Tokyo.

XII HUNG-JEN (1610–1664)
Hai-yang (Hsiu-ning or She-hsien), Anhwei

Feng River Landscapes

The Art Museum, Princeton University (L36.67).

Album of ten leaves. Ink on paper. 21.4 x 12.9 cm.

DATED: spring, 1660 (*keng-tzu, ch'un*), on leaf J.

SIGNATURE OF THE ARTIST: Hung-jen (on leaf J).

INSCRIPTION BY THE ARTIST: in four lines on leaf J.

SEALS OF THE ARTIST:
Chien-chiang (intaglio, square; Contag and Wang, *Seals*, no. 5, p. 85)
   leaves A and J.
Chien-chiang (intaglio, small square) leaves B, F, and H.
Hung-jen (relief, round; Contag and Wang, *Seals*, no. 3, p. 85) leaves C and D.
Hung-jen (relief, double seal in two small squares) leaf E.
Hung-jen (relief, small round) leaves G and I.

COLLECTORS' SEALS: Chang Ta-ch'ien, eleven seals, one on each leaf and two on leaf J (identified on each leaf).

CONDITION: good; there is some foxing, especially apparent on leaves A, E, F, I, and J.

PLACE OF EXECUTION: the Chieh-shih shu-wu ("Studio of the Resolute Stone"), Feng River, Anhwei.

PROVENANCE: Ta-Feng-T'ang Collection.

PUBLISHED: Contag and Wang, *Seals*, p. 85.

OTHER VERSIONS: one in ink and color on paper, recorded in *Ku-yüan ts'ui-lu* (see end of entry).

HUNG-JEN WAS the Buddhist name of Chiang T'ao.[1] He was born into one of the major families of She-hsien, Anhwei, but his father died while he was quite young. He nonetheless grew up under the auspices of a tutor and as a young man was able to earn his *hsiu-ts'ai* degree. A dutiful son, he supported his mother by transcribing the texts of old books. When Nanking fell to the Manchus in 1645, he fled with his teacher to Fukien. There he received the tonsure and entered the Buddhist faith, adopting the name Hung-jen. He spent several years in Fukien before returning to his old home in Anhwei. Some of the other names by which he was known are Liu-ch'i and especially Chien-chiang, after the Chien River, one of the tributaries of the Hsin-an River, which flowed past his home.

Most of the literary evidence of Hung-jen's artistic activity dates from the 1650's. He must have made several trips to Huang-shan with fellow painters and poets (three are recorded, in 1656, 1658, and 1660) and went also to nearby Wu-hu, Hsüan-ch'eng, Nanking (in 1657), and Hang-chou (in 1658).[2] He traveled to Wu-hu in 1658 in the company of the scholar T'ang Hsüan-i (*tzu* Yen-sheng, Yen-fu, fl. ca. 1650–1670).[3] T'ang left a record of his friendship with Hung-jen in several colophons to Hung-jen's paintings. Hung-jen also became an intimate friend of Kung Hsien through his acquaintance with the high official and collector Chou Liang-kung (1612–1672).[4] T'ang's inscriptions on Hung-jen's, Kung Hsien's, and Tao-chi's paintings document his friendship with them and are important aids to authentication. It was probably during this period that Hung-jen met other painters from Anhwei, such as Mei Ch'ing (1623–1697) and Ch'eng Sui (fl. ca. 1650–1691). From these personal and artistic exchanges, the group of Huang-shan painters

gained in stature. Hung-jen attracted a faithful following, which included his nephew, Chiang Chu. Chiang is known to have accompanied Hung-jen on one of the Huang-shan trips, and in 1697, some thirty years after Hung-jen died, Chiang visited another monk painter, Tao-chi, in Hsüan-ch'eng, thus forging another firm link between the great painters of Huang-shan vistas.[5] (In 1662 Hung-jen himself traveled to Lu-shan, Kiangsi, where Tao-chi is known to have visited that year, but there is no evidence that they met.)

Hung-jen has been associated with two Ch'an Buddhist temples. On his return to Anhwei from Fukien in the early 1650's he stayed at the T'ai-p'ing hsing-kuo temple, beneath P'i-yün-feng ("Rolling-Cloud Peak") in the western suburbs of She-hsien. He also lived at the Wu-ming temple. Hung-jen's exact burial place and date of death are known. He died on January 19, 1664, and was buried by his friend T'ang Hsüan-i and some of his pupils at the base of P'i-yün, which he had painted several times.[6]

HUNG-JEN'S ARTISTIC activity spans only about a dozen years: his reliably dated paintings range from 1651 to 1663, a relatively brief period for a Ch'ing painter. He has been well known in the West, yet primarily for a single, more monolithic aspect of his style, the "transmundane geometry of his compositions, the uplift of his astral rocks,"[7] his cool, spare vision of nature, "cleansed of all its distracting irregularities and clutter."[8]

But Hung-jen's style also had other facets which extend beyond the archetypal Huang-shan image of landscape rightfully identified with his art; the Yüan painters Wang Meng, Wu Chen, Ni Tsan, and Huang Kung-wang are also identifiable influences. In addition, many of his scenes are stark, portrait-like depictions of the famous pines of Huang-shan. Hung-jen's artistic versatility reveals itself best in the album format, where he shows not only a wide range of brush idioms but, as one would suspect from the precision and intelligence of his larger works, an impeccable sense of structure and balance in a remarkable variety of compositions. His imaginative command of formal structure far exceeds in subtlety such other late Ming masters represented in this catalogue as Lan Ying, Ch'eng Chia-sui, Cha Shih-piao, or Wan Shou-ch'i.

The importance of the Sackler ten-leaf album, therefore, lies in its demonstration of Hung-jen's artistic genius in a wider spectrum of brush and compositional styles than has been hitherto recognized. His pictorial allusions to the Yüan masters affirm his own artistic achievement and his link with the past. As in the case of Tao-chi, Hung-jen's style has many dimensions. The leaves of this Sackler album and the works discussed in connection with it exhibit a consistent visualization, and his brushwork shows a warmth, spontaneity, and liveliness, which are less apparent in his works in a larger format.

This album, dated in the spring of 1660, cannot be called a late work because Hung-jen's artistic activity was brief and the painting and calligraphic style of his works of the previous decade already offers a mature and distinct signature. Little is known about the formation of his style, but several important factors can be noted: his prolonged contact with the natural scenery of Huang-shan and its famous pines and sheer cliffs, the painting style of Ni Tsan, and the influence of his teachers, the works of one of whom, Hsiao Yün-ts'ung, are extant.

The scenery of Huang-shan was undoubtedly the crucial factor in the development of Hung-jen's style. He was able to synthesize the essence of its striking terrain into a memorable schematic image which became a stylistic trademark which was fundamental to his visualization of other views of landscape. Hung-jen was certainly conscious of his immediate contact with nature and of Huang-shan's influence on his vision, for he once said: "I confess that I have taken nature as my teacher, for I have walked alone with my staff through the myriad valleys and countless peaks."[9] This image merged with his concept of the styles of the Yüan masters, chiefly that of Ni Tsan. Hung-jen's interpretation of Ni was close to that of Wan Shou-ch'i (cf. X), but Hung-jen drew from the natural landscape a healthier, more spontaneous and monumental form. Spiritually, both Wan and Hung-jen undoubtedly identified themselves with the Yüan master and his historical circumstances.

Hung-jen's emulation of Ni Tsan was based on intimate visual contact: he is known to have collected a work or works by him. "Ni Tsan's painting[s?]," he said, "are my treasures. Every year I burn incense and make offerings to [them?] as my teacher."[10] This spiritual correspondence can be seen in the liberties Hung took with Ni Tsan's formal idioms, for he was not limited to the motifs of sparse trees, a stretch of water, and a pavilion but could reinterpret Ni Tsan's essential expression through a dense composition, tall mountains, and high waterfalls. Hung-jen was aware of the possibility of a Ni Tsan stereotype and sought not only to avoid this but to reach an expressive synthesis of his ideal of Ni's art: "Ni Tsan's style is not limited to the common image of sparseness and lightness [su-ch'ien]. In this respect we can be enlightened about the cultivated mind [or the "art of cultivation," wen-hsin], for perfection must be sought in both the simple and the complex."[11] According to Chou Liang-kung, Hung-jen's spiritual and formal link with Ni Tsan was well appreciated in his own day, and the possession of Hung's works was considered a status symbol and measure of taste and refinement by collectors in the Chiangnan area. As collectors had treasured Ni Tsan in the past, so Hung-jen's works were treasured in his own lifetime.[12]

Hung-jen's immediate stylistic sources are more obscure. Two slightly older contemporaries can be identified as his teachers. Chou Liang-kung mentions a certain Sun Tzu-hsiu (tzu Yüan-hsiu). He received his chü-jen degree in 1624 and died in 1654, so that he was probably about ten years older than Hung-jen. Known to the people of Chekiang as Hui-hsi the Monk, Sun painted plum, and Chou Liang-kung observes that the landscape elements in Hung-jen's style derive from Sun's.[13] None of Sun's works are extant to verify this relationship. One other source for which there is visual and literary evidence is Hsiao Yün-ts'ung (tzu Ch'ih-mu, 1595–1673), a native of Wu-hu, Anhwei. Hsiao was Hung-jen's senior by some fifteen years. His role as Hung's teacher is noted in a colophon which the high official and bibliophile Ts'ao Yin (1658–1712) wrote to one of Hung's paintings.[14] Their stylistic relationship was probably more

than a simple one-way exchange, for Hsiao was not only older but outlived Hung by a decade. Hsiao's works indicate that his artistic personality was not as strong as Hung-jen's. Nonetheless, the fact that he was the elder meant that in their early encounters he probably exerted the dominant influence. We may further postulate that Hung's personality soon overshadowed that of his teacher, so that in Hsiao's late years he may have been influenced by his pupil's forceful image.

In an important colophon dated 1664 (fig. 1),[15] Hsiao reveals the extent of his friendship with Hung. He also confesses a wavering of self-confidence as he views the album, some fifty leaves depicting the scenery of Huang-shan, by Hung-jen. He begins by saying that there is a kind of destiny in one's travels, for he has been to most of the famous spots—to T'ai-shan in Shantung, to Hang-chou in Chekiang, and further south across the river—but has never set foot on Huang-shan, which is nearby. He laments that he is too old now to attempt an ascent of that mountain but says that he loves to hear friends tell of the marvelous scenery. Hung-jen often described Huang-shan to him, and he always felt that to paint the unusual in nature required an inspired brush. Since Hung-jen returned to his home from Fukien, says Hsiao, he has lived just under the sheer cliffs below Huang-shan's Lotus Flower Peak, has slept and eaten amidst the cloudseas and misty mountains, and has absorbed them in his heart. Thus Hung-jen is joyous and expansive in spirit. All the wonders have been captured in this album—extraordinary rocks, old trees, contorted pines, flowing waterfalls, rivers and ponds, crimson cliffs, enormous valleys—so that one need not travel to see the special views from Heavenly Capital Peak; they are here before one's eyes. Truly the painter has grasped the secrets of painting. Hsiao closes the colophon by saying, "I am an old painter. In the art of painting, I have not yielded my claims to any predecessors. But when I see this album, I cannot help but withdraw my hand. Inscribed by the seventy-year-old Hsiao Yün-ts'ung at the Wu-men Studio on Mt. Chung beneath the plum trees."

Such generous praise from a seventy-year-old master should not be taken lightly, and it is on the basis of this inscription that we postulate the reciprocal influence which Hung-jen undoubtedly exerted on his teacher in Hsiao's late years. It is notable that Hsiao himself never visited Huang-shan, a fact which lends even greater significance to the role Huang-shan scenery played in Hung-jen's development.

1. Hsiao Yün-ts'ung, colophon dated 1664 to Hung-jen's album of fifty leaves depicting the scenery of Huang-shan. Collection unknown.

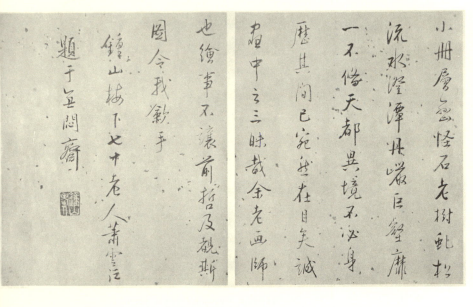
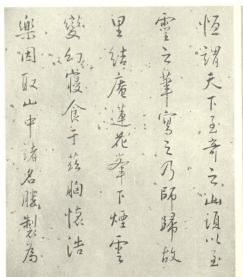
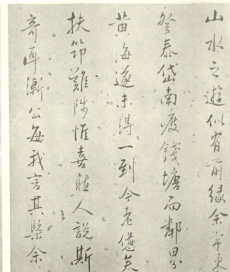

Leaf H, "Cottages below Mountainous Bluffs" (*actual size*)

Leaf A, "Old Trees by a Stream"

Leaf B, "Sheer Cliffs and Tumbling Waterfall"

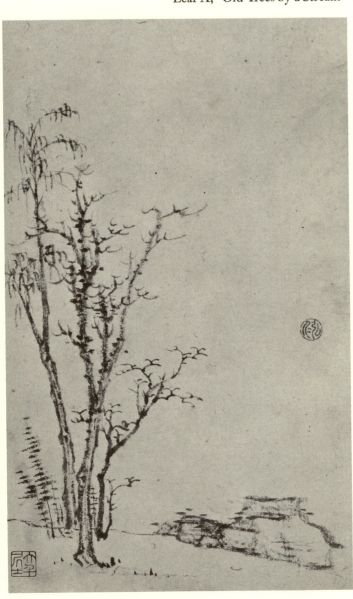

Leaf C, "Rocks and Trees"

Leaf D, "Stone Grotto and Thatched Hut"

Leaf E, "Rocky Pool and Pavilion"

Leaf F, "Cloudy Mountains and River Boats"

Leaf G, "Sparse Grove and Water Mill"

Leaf I, "Water Village"

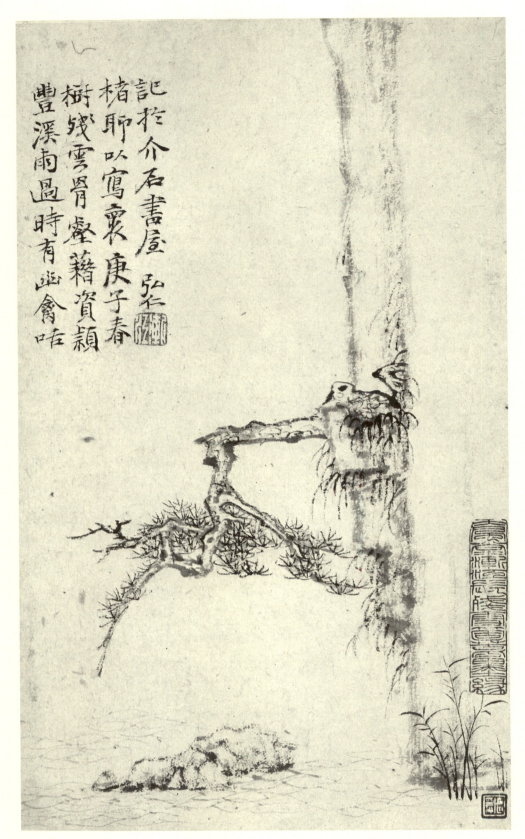

記於介石書屋 弘仁

楮耶以寫喪 庚子春

樹殘雲骨鏖藉資頛

豐溪雨過時有幽禽咭

Leaf J, "Cliff-Hanging Old Pine" (*actual size*)

Leaf A: "*Old Trees by a Stream*" (after Wu Chen)

UNSIGNED
SEAL OF THE ARTIST: *Chien-chiang* (intaglio, square) on rock in left corner.
COLLECTOR'S SEAL: *Ta-ch'ien* (relief, square) lower left corner.

A closeup view from the center of a stream to the nearby bank focuses on a single lushly foliated tree, silhouetted slightly to the left against another leafless tree close behind it. The ground mass is indicated in the lower third of the picture plane, with the very bottom foreground left blank for the water. Several registers of rocks are first lightly outlined in pale dry ink, then more conspicuously indicated in graded values of wash to establish their position in space and to stress their flat design qualities. The major tree is also enriched by layers of wash and rests firmly on the bank of rocks, which is ornamented by the same comma-dotted shrubbery as the tree itself. A rushing stream issuing from the center of the composition veers sharply to the right in a single arched curve, leaving a streak of white between the foreground slopes. A few fine, undulating ellipses drawn in the foreground and some lightly brushed reeds in dark ink enliven the frontal space.

Pictorially, the outstanding qualities of this leaf and of the album as a whole are the rich use of ink in both wet, layered gradations and dry linear outlines and the flexible, pliant rhythms of the brushlines. As the eye follows the contours of the tree trunks, foliage, and branches stretching into the air, or the filigree reeds in the foreground, one is aware of the artist's interest in both planar design and the interaction of discrete angular parts (as in the tightly meshed foreground rocks), in addition to the pulsating accents of the dark ink. There is an obvious reference to Wu Chen in these latter patterns.

Hung-jen's interpretation of Wu Chen's idiom is relatively simple in this leaf. Leaf 2 from an album of eight leaves (fig. 2)[16] shows how he could use the same motifs to create a complex structure, one which may seem more characteristic of his larger formats but which shows the same tight construction of the parts, the planes finely differentiated by graded washes, and the rich ink foliage as found in the Sackler leaf.

Leaf B: "*Sheer Cliffs and Tumbling Waterfall*"

UNSIGNED
SEAL OF THE ARTIST: *Chien-chiang* (intaglio, small square) near waterfall in lower right corner.
COLLECTOR'S SEAL: *Chang Ta-ch'ien* (relief, square) lower left corner.

From a low horizon at the very base of the picture rise several peaks dominated and enclosed by a tall, arching silhouette. The quality of ink is linear and parched; the partially dry brush moves in a strong, pulsating rhythm which penetrates the paper and coaxes the wet textures out of it. The essentially bony framework of Hung-jen's vision is striking here. His management of line is most evident in the central highest peak, where a single mobile stroke and a turning and twisting of the wrist and fingers with a vibrant power deftly separate sky from mountain. This same pulsating line appears in the slope in the left foreground. Long, wavering modeling strokes in medium ink dipped onto a partially dry brush texture the surface in a way which suggests the "hemp-fiber" strokes of Huang Kung-wang's *Dwelling in the Fu-ch'un Mountains*. At the same time the liveliness in the line is extended to the touches of shrubbery and grasses, which in the left foreground writhe with particular energy.

The way Hung-jen subdivides the form of the central peak again demonstrates his interest in and command of dense but lucidly constructed form. For example, the frontal peak is sketched in lithe interior modeling strokes, "lotus-leaf veins," while the upper boulders are contoured in shapes similar to but slightly altered from

those of the dominant peak. These interior shapes contrast with the perpendicular flat-topped plateau carved within the central silhouette. To the left the outline of the main peak is restated in reduced form but is given surface texturing by flat vertical strokes of dark ink. This pattern is balanced on the right by the slender waterfall which tumbles from a break in the mountain. The slope on the left is allowed to function as a repoussoir exaggerating the middle ground. Within this narrow, foreshortened space, Hung-jen has effectively suggested recession and the major theme of height.

Touches of shrubbery and a small grove of pines frame the waterfall at right and on the upper plateau. The marvelous touch of climbing vines and grasses lends a sense of living energy to the bones of the mountain, as do the water courses, which are defined in a few brief strokes and emphasized by dark ink.

In an album of eight leaves dated 1657,[17] a similar scene of precipitous cliffs is recorded (fig. 3). The foreground slope is replaced by shadowy mountains receding in the distance, but the same visual concept appears, in that the frontal space accentuates the height, as do the decorative touches of foliage. Small, angular rocks give the larger mass interior definition, as do the rounded "knuckles" and "dimples" in the Sackler work.

Leaf C: "*Rocks and Trees*" (after Ni Tsan)

UNSIGNED
SEAL OF THE ARTIST: *Hung-jen* (relief, round) center of right edge.
COLLECTOR'S SEAL: *Ta-ch'ien chü-shih* (relief, square) lower left corner.

A single line of slope, three different trees, a clump of bamboo placed to the far left foreground, and a small pile of fluffy, angular rocks accented with a few horizontal moss dots complete the entire composition. The space is close, with no described distance.

By the seventeenth century there were countless permutations on the Ni Tsan idiom. In this work, despite the sparseness of the elements, Hung-jen shows his feeling for the potential fullness in composition in the closeup view and in the way the landscape elements creep toward the edges of the picture. This vision differs, for example, from that of his contemporary Lan Ying, who tended to simplify and consolidate elements, placing his forms in the center and away from the edges.

Leaf D: "*Stone Grotto and Thatched Hut*"

UNSIGNED
SEAL OF THE ARTIST: *Hung-jen* (relief, round) center of right edge.
COLLECTOR'S SEAL: *Ta-ch'ien chü-shih* (intaglio, small square) lower left corner.

Two stone paths cut deep into the rock: to the left, a small thatched cottage, outlined overhead by a spiky, barren tree; to the right, a dense rock cliff with an immense interior grotto. The grotto is framed by an arching doorway and bamboo-lined path, stone steps, and terraced overhanging stone. The whole rocky assemblage has been pressed slightly slantwise into the middle ground, leaving the frontal space empty and the distance blank of any mountains. The mobile, pulsating movements penetrate deep and coax the moisture out of the partially dry brushtip. The darkest tonalities of ink have been saved for the bamboo, the spiky tree, the arching doorway, and the growths of foliage and rocky texturing at the left.

The concept of the stone grotto as a retreat from worldly cares or political tensions seems to have been a significant image among the transitional late Ming, early Ch'ing painters. It appears in Mei Ch'ing's works (there diluted of the Buddhist references seen in Ting Yün-p'eng's iconography of the Kuan-yin transformations), as well as in Tai Pen-hsiao (fig. 4);[18] probably others may be found.

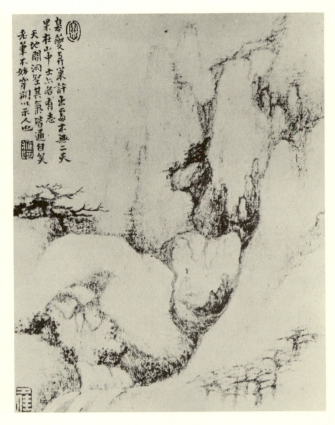

2 (*left*). Hung-jen, *Landscapes*, n.d., leaf 2. Album of eight leaves. Ink on paper. Collection unknown. 3 (*center*). Hung-jen, *Landscapes*, dated 1657, leaf 2. Album of eight leaves. Ink on paper. Collection unknown. 4 (*right*). Tai Pen-hsiao, "Man in a Cave," leaf from an album of twelve leaves. Ink on paper. Wango H. C. Weng collection. New York.

Hung-jen's portrayal here awaits the arrival of the mountain hermit, seeking immortality in the seclusion of a rocky fortress.

Leaf E: "*Rocky Pool and Pavilion*"

UNSIGNED
SEAL OF THE ARTIST: *Hung-jen* (relief, double seal in two small squares) lower left corner.
COLLECTOR'S SEAL: *Chang Ta-ch'ien* (relief, square) lower left corner at bottom.

A rock-encircled pool, with a small open pavilion on the far side, is flanked by a thin growth of trees. Clumps of reeds grow among the rocks. In the right foreground a wooden watergate separates the serene pool from the surrounding waters. To the left, a stone bridge links the scene to the outside world. The rocks are delineated in Hung-jen's characteristic partially dry, partially wet ink strokes. The darkest tones are reserved for the tree trunks, the gate, and the reeds and foliage. All are drawn with the mobile wrist motion found in the preceding leaves. This motion is especially sensitive in the lightly indicated foreground waves and the graded foliage of the trees.

This idyllic scene was one of the artist's favorite subjects. It corresponds to an actual place belonging to a friend. An undated hanging scroll (fig. 5)[19] bears an inscription by Hung-jen (*upper right*, lines 5–8) which identifies the scene: "This is the residence of Hsiang-shih, my fellow society member [*she-meng*]. There is a small gate near the rectangular pool, and you can dip up the water in your hands from deep in the pond. Old trees and low reeds grow there, heavy with dew and bowing in the wind."

right

5. Hung-jen, *Hsiang-shih's Rocky Pool*, n.d., with inscription by T'ang Hsüan-i in upper left corner. Hanging scroll. Ink on paper. Ex-Chang Ts'ung-yü collection.

Leaf F: "Cloudy Mountains and River Boats"

UNSIGNED
SEAL OF THE ARTIST: *Chien-chiang* (relief, square) lower left corner.
COLLECTOR'S SEAL: *Ta-ch'ien* (relief, square) center left edge of painting.

A dark, overcast sky and moisture-laden mountains thick with clouds in the far distance give the impression of impending rain. A clump of rocks and a sprig of foliage in the left frontal space provide an anchor for an open boat. Between lies a vast stretch of water; at the right five boats glide at full sail. Marsh and reeds accentuate the lateral movement suggested by the boats. At the base of the peaked mountains, which rise in height as they extend to the right, a forest of pines encloses the roofs of houses. The mountains and the sky are indicated by layers of wash, so that the scrolled networks of clouds stand out. The quality of the line is fluid and the ink rich and dense, a satisfying heavy contrast to the transparency of the preceding leaves.

Hung-jen can suggest an entirely different pictorial feeling using the same compositional principle. Leaf 7 from the eight-leaf album of landscapes (fig. 6)[20] shows the same stress on lateral movement, but with the composition in a more transparent skeleton than appears in the Sackler leaf. This scene may seem reminiscent of some of Tao-chi's vistas, but Tao-chi preferred to stress foreground elements, while Hung-jen invariably transfers the frontal load to the middle and far distances, which are frequently consolidated into a single mass. This treatment of space is accentuated by consistent use of a rather low horizon line, which tends to accentuate the impression of height.

Leaf G: "Sparse Grove and Water Mill"

UNSIGNED
SEAL OF THE ARTIST: *Hung-jen* (relief, round) right edge of painting.
COLLECTOR'S SEAL: *Chang Yüan yin* (intaglio, square) lower right corner.

A screen of sparsely foliated trees juts out of the corner of a neat stone enclosure on the right. Inside the enclosure are a hut and a mill which draws water from a spring. The scene is in the middle ground in the lower half of the picture plane. The trunks of the slender trees are drawn with a single stroke, and although they appear at different points in the foreshortened ground, they are evenly spaced and alternate in ink values, creating the impression of a lacy curtain. Marvelously scrolled clouds in the shape of "immortal's mushrooms" offset the foliage patterns and give potential movement to the static verticality and limited spatial depth of the scene. This subject and composition are rather unusual for Hung-jen. Although the handling of the clouds may remind us of Tao-chi (e.g., *XXXIV*), he preferred to use a slightly undulating brushline, while here the brushline is smoother and more fluid.

Leaf H: "Cottages below Mountainous Bluffs"

UNSIGNED
SEAL OF THE ARTIST: *Chien-chiang* (intaglio, square) lower left corner.
COLLECTOR'S SEAL: *Ta-ch'ien* (relief, square) lower left corner at bottom.

The themes of breadth and height, the angular and the curved, are combined in this picture. In the foreground, low slopes drawn with long "hemp-fiber" strokes lead to a stream which flows to the right. A stone hut is placed at the far right; another in the left middle ground directs the eye to the complex of high bluffs whose receding flat tops send the eye upward and dominate the entire composition. To indicate this height, a cluster of houses is set in a clearing in the forest at the base of the cliff. The angularity of this rocky promontory is accentuated by the round slopes which flank it on both sides and in the foreground. The entire composition is thus filled by tightly interlocking shapes and textures. These forms are drawn as in the preceding leaves: first a rhythmic movement of the wrist gives a dry linear outline; then greater volume is added by scrubbing movements of the brush on the edges and in the folds of the rocky forms; finally vertical and horizontal moss dots in charcoal ink are applied at strategic points to give the whole scene a feeling of growth. Despite the fullness of the composition, the fabric of the

6. Hung-jen, *Landscapes,* leaf 7. Album of eight leaves. Ink on paper. Collection unknown.

7. Hung-jen, *Landscapes,* leaf 1. Album of eight leaves. Ink on paper. Collection unknown.

elements is airy and transparent. In this sense the contouring of the individual parts has much of the feeling achieved by Huang Kung-wang in his *Dwelling in the Fu-ch'un Mountains*. Hung-jen's mobile but penetrating lines and his ability to create fused and "furry" effects with ink contribute in large measure to the power of this leaf.

Leaf I: *"Water Village"*

UNSIGNED
SEAL OF THE ARTIST: *Hung-jen* (relief, round) center of painting.
COLLECTOR'S SEAL: *Chang Yüan* (relief, square) lower left corner.

Reeds, rocks, houses, a bridge, and a distant mountain compose this simple pastoral scene. Each landscape element is stretched horizontally across the picture plane and rises, slightly slanting, in step-wise fashion to meet the horizon. In the frontal space small boulders placed in the left corner begin the progression into depth. They are generously textured in graded tones of "unraveled-hemp" strokes, which with the peppery ink dots suggest immediately Wang Meng's rocks. Delicately brushed reeds combined with a few lateral strokes of wash constitute the next step into depth. From there the elements grow denser, with a fine tree outlined in the middle ground next to a low plateau. A slender bamboo bridge links this marshy field to the water village itself, which is nestled in a thick growth of trees extending laterally to the very distant mountains. There two low humps are joined by a dip in the horizon. Atmospheric distance is suggested by contouring the mountain over moist saturated paper, which gives the edges a vague, misty silhouette. This treatment of mountains, rather unusual for Hung-jen, is emphasized by his seal, which is impressed directly between the peaks like the orb of the sun.

Hung-jen may have had Chao Meng-fu's 1302 *Water Village* in mind when he painted this; such an insistent lateral recession into depth is rarely seen in his hanging scrolls but rather (as one would expect) in his handscrolls, as a compositional coda, or, as here, in a more intimate album format. The weight of the elements is balanced on a central axis, but Hung-jen has succeeded in suggesting tranquility and limitless extension beyond the picture frame.

It is notable that the foreground rock appears in a style seldom associated with Hung-jen, that of Wang Meng. Hung-jen collected paintings by Wang Meng as well as by Ni Tsan. Painting in this manner constitutes his "finer" style, and it appears in several works of high quality such as leaf 1 of the album of landscapes (fig. 7)[21] mentioned earlier and the handscroll dated 1663 in the Boston Museum of Fine Arts.[22] In these works Hung-jen captures much of the flavor of this Yüan master in motifs and brushwork. It is worthy of note that the velvety gradations he achieved with ink were closer to the late Yüan painters than to the Ming interpretations of painters following Wen Cheng-ming's style. They adapted the linear aspect of the Wang Meng-Chao Yüan idiom to a much more meticulous extreme, de-emphasizing the rich ink textures which Hung-jen revived.

Leaf J: *"Cliff-Hanging Old Pine"*

SIGNATURE OF THE ARTIST: Hung-jen (in "regular" script) after four lines of inscription which read from left to right.
SEAL OF THE ARTIST: *Chien-chiang* (intaglio, square) after signature.
COLLECTOR'S SEALS: *Ta-feng-t'ang Chien-chiang, K'un-ts'an, Hsüeh-ko, K'u-kua mo-yüan* (relief, tall rectangle) and *Chang Yüan* (intaglio, square) right edge.
INSCRIPTION: Hung-jen's inscription in "regular" script reads:

After the rain has passed over the Feng River, secluded birds often chirp in the trees; the scattered clouds and the stark valley provide substance for my brush and paper; I casually write this out to express my feelings. Recorded at the Studio of the Resolute Stone [Chieh-shih shu-wu] by Hung-jen.

Stark geometry provides the framework for this cliff-hanging pine. It juts out horizontally and downward from a sheer vertical cliff and seems to gain strength from its precarious suspension over the Feng River. Some rocks and a clump of reeds below the cliff, along with a net of lightly indicated waves, complete this daring but tranquil design.

The Feng River was a tributary of the Hsin-an River and had its source east of Huang-shan. Its scenery appears repeatedly in Hung-jen's works. On a handscroll dated 1661 in the Sumitomo collection which depicts the river landscape, he wrote: "For these several years I have not succeeded in living in the mountains. . . . Only the Feng River scenery was uppermost in my mind."[23] It seems that Hung-jen very much wanted to settle near the river. Some time that year he had an opportunity to do so, for, according to the inscription on another handscroll dated at the end of the year, he was living at the Jen-i Ch'an temple near the river.

The calligraphy of this leaf (as well as the seals of the various leaves) can be compared with the inscriptions on three prime examples of Hung-jen's art, the 1661 handscroll *Dawn over the River*[24] (fig. 8), the well-known but undated *Coming of Autumn* in Honolulu, and the handscroll in the Sumitomo collection, also dated 1661.

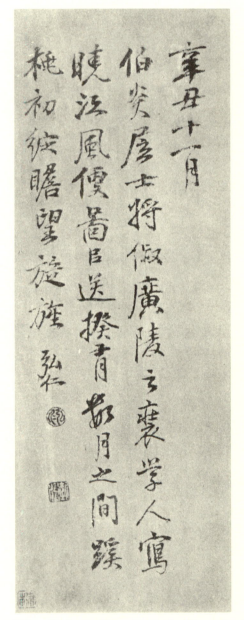

8. Hung-jen, self-inscription to *Dawn over the River*, dated 1661. Handscroll. Ink and color on paper. Collection unknown.

The skeletal framework of Hung-jen's landscapes is also reflected in his bony calligraphic style, which is based to a certain extent on Ni Tsan's calligraphy (cf. *XXIV*, fig. 2), but unlike Tao-chi or Chiang Shih-chieh (two others who also wrote in Ni's style), Hung-jen pares the forms of all fleshiness and excessive accents. The characters are mainly rectangular and elongated in configuration. Straight, angular strokes predominate over curved ones (as, for example, in the right diagonal *na* stroke, which hardly thickens and is primarily unidirectional). Hung-jen uses a stiff, stubby brush, so that the strokes vary little in thickness and pressure and are not entirely polished in form. The signature in the three works is close: in the significant movements the first character, "Hung," is tall, with the lines of the left radical written separately in "regular" or slightly cursive style. The "jen" graph is squat, with the last horizontal stroke given an unusually heavy emphasis. The spatial relationship of the two characters is also significant: the first stroke of the "jen" arches close under the left side of the first graph. Such congruence of placement and structure is maintained despite the difference in cursiveness and size (the Sackler leaves being much smaller than the two handscrolls in format and proportion).

The solitary Huang-shan pine, crusty with age and charged with an elemental vigor, was a constant theme in Hung-jen's paintings. Indeed, its portrait reappears in his works more than in those of any other Anhwei painter, including Tao-chi. As shown in this leaf, it frequently protrudes at some gravity-defying angle from cliff or promontory. The brushwork is resilient and powerful, fluctuating in width and embodying the energy of the pine's growth. Twigs, pine needles, and accompanying grasses are instilled with the vitality befitting their natural state.[25] The hardy pine tree and its roots, the delicate foreground reeds, and the filament waves offer a remarkable scope of kinesthetic feelings. Such a range of embodied energies is equaled only in a master like Tao-chi; it is not apparent in the work of painters like Lan Ying, Ch'eng Chia-sui, or Wan Shou-ch'i shown in this catalogue, despite the measure of individuality which each of them possessed. In this broad and effective command of brush repertory lies much of Hung-jen's greatness.

ANOTHER VERSION in ink and occasional color on paper is recorded in Shao Sung-nien's *Ku-yüan ts'ui-lu* (Shao's preface dated 1903).[26] It contains the same number of leaves and the same inscription and date. Each of Shao's descriptions of the leaves corresponds closely to the compositions which are found in this album except that color has been added in several leaves and two unidentified collectors' seals are found on each leaf. Although Hung-jen's self-inscription is identical in content, it is found on a leaf which corresponds to Sackler leaf G. It seems unlikely that he would have executed two albums of such similar composition in the same year with the same date and inscription. The quality of the Sackler album speaks for its originality, and on its evidence it is quite possible that the *Ku-yüan ts'ui-lu* version is a copy.

HUNG-JEN was not only included among the Four Masters of Hai-yang (see Part I, p. 9, above), but, more significant, was recognized as the fountainhead of a whole new breed of painters known as the Anhwei school. This group, active in Hsin-an, Hsüan-ch'eng, and Wu-hu, took the scenery of Mt. Huang as the focus of their art. In the early eighteenth century, for example, Chang Keng said in his *Kuo-ch'ao hua-cheng-lu* that the reason why the painters of Hsin-an all followed Ni Tsan is that Hung-jen blazed the trail.[27] But Hung's influence on the Hsin-an painters was recognized during his lifetime even among slightly older contemporaries. One of the important Anhwei painters, scholars, and collectors of antiques, Ch'eng Sui

(1605–1691), inscribed an album by Hung-jen with a long colophon in which he not only recognized him as the leading Anhwei painter but also credited him with the establishment of the province's own "orthodox tradition" (*cheng-mai*). He continues: "In recent years, people have been promoting Hung-jen's nephew Chiang Chu [*tzu* Yün-ning], who gratefully inherited his painting abilities. Now it appears that in every corner of the earth, everyone is painting in the Chiang family style and that within the empire each member has established himself firmly as a patriarch. Chien-chiang is still alive — it is as if he had never departed!"[28]

The precise nature of Hung-jen's influence on his contemporaries requires further study. It is important to ascertain more specifically, for example, the biographies and dates of two of the other Four Masters of Hai-yang, Sun I (fl. 1643–1657) and Wang Chih-jui (fl. 1649–1653; see *XIII*, fig. 3), because they may have exerted a formative influence on him. One of the rare extant works by Sun (fig. 9)

9. Sun I, *Landscape*, dated 1657. Hanging scroll. Ink on paper. Richard Edwards collection, Ann Arbor, Michigan.

is dated in the winter of the year *ting-yu*, which could be either 1597 or, more likely, 1657. In this painting the brushwork and approach to landscape form are close to Hung-jen's, and even the calligraphic style is similar.[29]

In retrospect, Hung-jen's artistic personality seems the most distinctive of all his contemporaries. He may have synthesized and refined to a more significant degree several agreeable styles (such as those of Sun, Wang, Hsiao Yün-ts'ung, and perhaps even Wan Shou-ch'i), and, if so, we would interpret his position as the peak of the development of this formal mode. The "life" of this mode did not pass with Hung-jen, but as Ch'eng Sui points out, he projected a dominant image through which his influence was disseminated until the eighteenth century. It is important to note that his work attracted not only direct followers but also a group of spiritually like-minded painters whose individualistic credo found full expression in the work of masters like Tao-chi and Chu Ta. Some of the contemporaries and later painters who fall within Hung-jen's formal lineage are listed below.

Chiang Chu (fl. 1660–1679), Hung-jen's nephew, was probably his closest disciple. There is a hanging scroll by Chiang in the Ex-Hobart collection.

Chu Ch'ang (*tzu* Shan-ch'ao, *chin-shih* degree 1649) was a contemporary of both Hung-jen and Cha Shih-piao. His extant works are rare; a handscroll in the Su-chou museum shows him to be a painter of gifts superior to Chiang Chu's.

Chiang Yüan, about whom little is known, painted an album dated 1663 for the birthday of a certain gentleman named Chung-fu; a leaf from this album is now in the Ching Yüan Chai collection, Berkeley, California.

Yao Sung (*tzu* Yü-chin, of Hsin-an, Anhwei) flourished almost a century after Hung-jen (ca. 1700), but still retained elements of Hung-jen's style. There is an album of landscapes by Yao in the Ex-Hobart collection and a hanging scroll in the Drenowatz collection, Zurich.

Chiang Shih-chieh (1647–1709, *tzu* Hsüeh-tsai, of Lai-yang, Shan-tung, later Su-chou and Yang-chou; cf. *XXXII*) was a contemporary and friend of Tao-chi; several works in the Freer Gallery of Art and the J. P. Dubosc collection well represent his style.

Ku Tsai-mei, a relatively obscure master, has a landscape album in the Liao-ning museum which reflects much of Hung-jen's style. From it one can assume that Ku was a painter of the nineteenth century.

Hung-jen's style may also be related to that of an older contemporary, Lan Ying. Art historians seldom link the two because of the sharp differences in their overall stylistic approaches and expression, but in terms of brushwork and modeling of individual landscape forms, they have much in common. For example, a comparison of details from leaf A of the Hung-jen album and leaf I of Lan's *Landscapes after Sung and Yüan Masters (VII)*, also in Wu Chen style, reveals startlingly similar notions of inking the foliage and tree branches and even of the delineation of the bank at the water's edge. Nominally imitating Wu Chen, they are really employing the same archetypal formula as it was known in the late Ming, and in this the two painters demonstrate the function of period style in the reinterpretation of an older master's image. However, there is a vast difference in temperament and expression of the same motifs: the clear, architectural mind of Hung-jen sharply contrasts with the effusive, embellishing brush of Lan Ying. Almost polar artistic personalities, their interesting but only occasional congruities of form do link them periodically as late Ming, early Ch'ing masters.

NOTES

1. Two sources (the *Hui-chou fu-chih* and the *She-hsien-chih*) give Hung-jen's *ming* as Fang, his *tzu* as Ou-meng (see Cheng Hsi-chen, *Hung-jen, K'un-ts'an*, p. 1157); the *Wu-hu hsien-chih* (Wu-hu, 1919 ed., chap. 53), Wang T'ai-cheng's *Chien-chiang-chuan*, and the *Huang-shan-chih* give his *ming* as T'ao and his *tzu* as Liu-ch'i. See Cheng, *Hung-jen, K'un-ts'an*, pp. 1151–70, for more information on Hung-jen's biography and the main sources cited in this entry.

2. Cheng, *Hung-jen, K'un-ts'an*, p. 1158. The Nanking trip was documented by an album of eight leaves, dated 1657, painted at the Hsiang-shui-an in Nanking; see *Shina nanga taisei*, vol. 11, nos. 124–31.

3. While in Wu-hu, Hung-jen and T'ang stayed at the Hsi-chun t'i-an; see *Wu-hu hsien-chih*, 53/1025.

4. See Chou Liang-kung, *Tu-hua-lu*, 2/30.

5. See Cheng Cho-lu, *Shih-t'ao yen-chiu*, pp. 13–14, which quotes a poem dated 1697 from Chiang Chu's collection, *Wan-ling-shih*, describing the visit to the Shuang-t'a-ssu ("Double Pagoda Temple") in Hsüan-ch'eng, which had been renovated by Tao-chi and Ho-t'ao.

6. Cheng, *Hung-jen, K'un-ts'an*, pp. 1158–59.

7. Gustav Ecke's beautiful characterization in *Chinese Painting in Hawaii*, vol. 1, p. 230; see also pp. 212–14.

8. James Cahill's sensible description in *Fantastics and Eccentrics in Chinese Painting*, p. 48.

9. *Hua-chieh*, quoted in Cheng, *Hung-jen, K'un-ts'an*, pp. 1165–66.

10. *Shih-kung-wen*, quoted in *ibid.*, p. 1164.

11. Quoted in *ibid.*, p. 1165. For the rendering of *wen-hsin*, see James Hightower's review of Vincent Shih's *The Literary Mind and the Carving of Dragons* (*Harvard Journal of Asian Studies*, vol. 22 [1959], pp. 280 ff.).

12. See *Tu-hua-lu*, 2/24.

13. *Lai-ku-t'ang chi*, quoted in Cheng, *Hung-jen, K'un-ts'an*, p. 1162.

14. Ts'ao felt Hung-jen had surpassed Hsiao; see the inscription on Hung-jen's *Shih-chu-chai t'u*, whereabouts unknown, quoted in *ibid.*, p. 1163. For Ts'ao Yin, see Jonathan D. Spence, *Ts'ao Yin and the K'ang-hsi Emperor*.

15. Reproduced in *Shina nanga taisei*, vol. 13, pls. 1–2.

16. Reproduced in *ibid.*, suppl. vol. 1, pl. 56.

17. Painted in the summer of 1657 at the Hsiang-shui-an in Nanking for Tsung-hsüan chü-shih; reproduced in *Shina nanga taisei*, vol. 11, pls. 124–31.

18. For Mei Ch'ing, see Chu Sheng-chai, *Chung-kuo shu-hua*, vol. 1, pl. 28; for Ting Yün-p'eng, see James Cahill, ed., *The Restless Landscape*, no. 79, p. 156.

19. Reproduced in *Yün-hui-chai ts'ang T'ang-Sung i-lai ming-hua-chi*, vol. 2, pl. 121.

20. Reproduced in *Shina nanga taisei*, suppl. vol. 1, pls. 54–61.

21. Reproduced in *ibid.*, pl. 54.

22. Reproduced in *Portfolio of Chinese Paintings in the Museum*, pls. 144–45, p. 25. For a fine, oft-neglected Wang Meng, see the hanging scroll on silk dated 1354 in the Freer Gallery of Art, reproduced in *Ta-feng-t'ang ming-chi*, vol. 1, pl. 14.

23. Reproduced in *Min-matsu san oshō*, pls. 13–15.

24. Dated in the eleventh lunar month and painted for Po-yen chü-shih, reproduced in *Shina nanga taisei*, vol. 16, pls. 46–48; a second dubious version of this scroll is in the John M. Crawford, Jr., collection, New York.

25. For other examples of paintings on this theme accompanied by perceptive commentary, see Richard M. Barnhart, *Wintry Forests, Old Trees*.

26. See 6/46a–b. The album leaves of the two versions compare as follows:

Sackler Album	Ku-yüan ts'ui-lu *Album*
A	6, ink and color
B	3, with *Chien-chiang* seal in lower left corner
C	9, ink and color, with double seal of *Hung-jen*, *Chien-chiang* on right edge
D	5
E	4
F	8, with *Hung-jen* seal in lower left corner
G	10, with identical inscription in upper left corner, also read from left to right
H	1, ink and color
I	2
J	7, ink and color, with *Hung-jen* seal in lower right corner

Shao also records an inscription dated *kuei-wei*, the tenth lunar month, which is signed with a cipher by an unidentified writer. As there is no reign date, the cyclical date may correspond to either 1703, 1763, 1823, or 1883, so it is of little help in dating the album.

27. See 2/24. Chang's opinions are representative of attitudes current at the time; see *VIII* for more on this point.

28. Reproduced in *Shina nanga taisei*, vol. 13, pl. 28, from the album of fifty landscape leaves, inscribed also by Hsiao Yün-ts'ung.

29. We are grateful to Professor Richard Edwards for allowing us to publish this fine work from his collection.

XIII CHA SHIH-PIAO (1615–1698)

Born Hai-yang (Hsiu-ning or She-hsien), Anhwei;
later active Yang-chou, Kiangsu.

River Landscape in Rain

The Art Museum, Princeton University (L300.72).

Hanging scroll. Ink on paper. 88.5 x 49.7 cm.

DATED: in the period May 11–June 10, 1687 (*ting-mao ch'ing-ho-yüeh*).

SIGNATURE OF THE ARTIST: Mei-ho lao-jen, Shih-piao
(after inscription; see below).

INSCRIPTION BY THE ARTIST (in four lines of "running" script):
"Several distant peaks are separated by rain beyond the river" is a splendid line by [Ku?] Yü-chih [unidentified poet]. This picture is close to it. [Painted in] the ch'ing-ho *[fourth lunar] month of the year* ting-mao *[1687] in the K'ang-hsi era by Mei-ho lao-jen, Shih-piao.*

SEAL OF THE ARTIST: *Cha Erh-chan* (relief, square; Contag and Wang, *Seals*, no. 12, p. 213).

NO COLLECTORS' OR APPRECIATORS' SEALS

CONDITION: fair; there is scattered wormhole damage over the surface of the painting which has been repaired and filled in lightly with gray wash.

PROVENANCE: Frank Caro, New York.

UNPUBLISHED

MOIST GRADATIONS of gray wash are employed to capture the feeling of the line "several distant peaks are separated by rain beyond the river," which the painter quotes in his inscription. Wetness is the theme, and it is expressed by simplification and abbreviation of form. The composition is an unusual one. A lateral emphasis suggests a depth of picture space and height above the picture frame. Dark accents freely drawn with a blunt brush focus the eye on spits of land, reeds, and an old tree and distinguish foreground, middle, and far distances in what would otherwise be a void. The feeling of dense atmosphere and depth suits the central theme, for the effect of driving rain is re-enacted in the inundation of ink, and the three zones of land register the idea of distance implied in the poetry.

This abbreviated brush style was one of Cha's two more or less distinct approaches to form. He could employ it with a marvelous sense of invention, as here, or in a less interesting, rather stereotyped way, as in his painting in the style of Ni Tsan of about 1690 (see *XIV*). Whatever the precise subject or theme, however, Cha's formal methods epitomize the scholar-painter's ethic: artistic freedom in composition and brushwork as an offshoot of one's discipline and accomplishment in calligraphy. Despite the extremely cursory treatment here (as in the foreground reeds and the brief undulations for the old tree), the quality of the brushline is evident and the conception is complete. It is executed with taste, authority, and a certain flair for the pictorial potential contained in the line of poetry. Cha's approach to form contrasts sharply, for example, with that of a professional painter like Sheng Mao-yeh (cf. *VI*, an album which also illustrates lines of poetry). Cha appreciated the power of understatement and refrained from the more specific kind of description in which Sheng excelled.

Cha achieved a degree of artistic breadth which has not yet been fully acknowledged by historians. Both his personal friendships and his painting styles encompassed representatives of what have be-

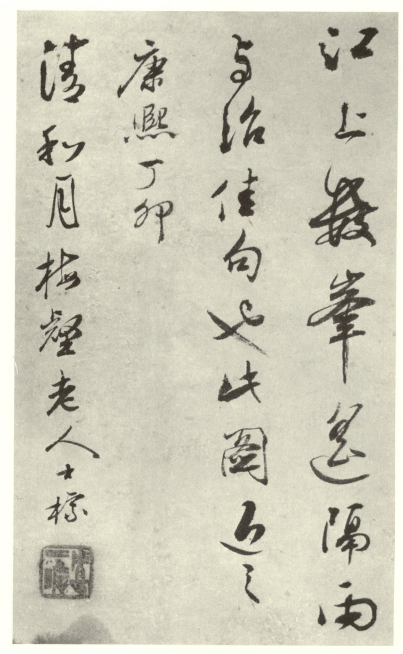

Poetic inscription in "running" script (*actual size*).

come known as the individualist and orthodox camps. He was able to keep a foot in each camp—both theoretically and expressively—and to find stylistic solutions which, in a work such as this, are clearly his own. This painting is a minor one in terms of Cha's large œuvre, but because of its maturity (it is a relatively late painting, executed twelve years before the artist's death at eighty-four), the wholeness of its conception, and perhaps the very off-handedness with which it was made, it illuminates Cha's own brand of individualism.

CHA SHIH-PIAO (*tzu* Erh-chan, *hao* Mei-ho) was born into a wealthy Anhwei family which was known for its collection of antiquities and Sung and Yüan paintings. He earned the *hsiu-ts'ai* degree but sought no further political advancement, preferring to devote his energies to literary and artistic pursuits.[1] His social contacts are significant for art historians because the various facets of his style reflect his many acquaintances. As noted above, Cha was one of the few painters who counted among his friends both the individualist masters from the Anhwei group and the orthodox

painters from Yü-shan and T'ai-ts'ang. Therefore his art-historical position, in terms of the traditional groupings, is rather an unusual one.

As a native of Anhwei, he was included in the Four Masters of Hai-yang along with Hung-jen, Sun I, and Wang Chih-jui, and was praised by Tao-chi for possessing the same qualities of "pure elusiveness" (*ch'ing-i*) as did Hung-jen (cf. *XIV* and Part IV, fig. 18, above). Thus it should come as no surprise that an identifiable "Hung-jen mode" should appear as a recurrent theme in Cha's paintings. At the same time, aspects of Tung Ch'i-ch'ang's style also appear in Cha's range of extant works.[2] The exact source of this strain in his early paintings of about 1660 is not clear. Later in his life Cha is known to have based himself in the commercial metropolis of Yang-chou, but it is not until the year 1670 that there is any evidence of a move northward and of personal contact with Yang-chou painters. From then until his death, Cha was in constant contact with painters outside the Anhwei region, especially those of Yang-chou.[3] Although his early receptiveness to Tung Ch'i-ch'ang's style may have been partly the result of artistic trends of the moment, he may actually have seen the works of Tung and related masters which wealthy merchants and collectors of Hsin-an brought back with them to Anhwei from their business trips to the Lake T'ai region.

The dual aspects of Cha's style were noted by the nineteenth-century critic Ch'in Tsu-yung in his *T'ung-yin lun-hua*,[4] but historians have not been aware of Cha's wide friendships with the members of different artistic circles. Through colophons and various other records we have assembled here some evidence of Cha's contacts and general suggestions as to how they may have influenced his painting style.

CHA SHIH-PIAO'S POSITION among intellectuals was one of esteem, as can be judged not only from the generous evaluation of his work by Chang Keng but also from Ch'in Tsu-yung's placement of him in the *i-p'in* grade within the category of "famous calligraphers and painters."[5] Ch'in comments that Cha had a "broad" style (*k'uo-pi*) and a "fine" style (*hsia-pi*). The former, he writes, could be unbridled and unrestrained, lacking in discipline and composure, the latter raw and astringent in flavor but slightly wanting in feeling. Ch'in concludes that Cha's paintings were valued largely because of his personal character.

Aside from the qualitative overtones of his account, Ch'in's categorization is useful in that its dual aspects can be verified by the paintings extant and further supplemented by what we know of Cha's development and his friends. His earliest reliably authenticated works (dated in the late 1650's and early 1660's) are fully

mature and indeed show two distinct stylistic tendencies. His "fine" style is similar to what is known of Hung-jen's style.[6] Cha was only five years younger than Hung-jen, yet he outlived him by more than thirty years. The majority of Cha's paintings postdate Hung-jen's career (which began in the 1650's and concluded in 1664; see *XII*); although relatively brief, it was recognized by contemporaries as being a seminal and truly significant visualization. These similarities, therefore, reflect Cha's admiration for Hung-jen. Two fans from the hand of each master may demonstrate the point visually (figs. 1–2).[7] The Cha fan is dated 1678, some fourteen years after Hung-jen's death. The composition and the angular geometric rocks and pathways are almost identical and are definite Hung-jen elements. Differences in the two hands are nonetheless discernible in the brushwork: Cha's overall use of ink is moister, his ink gradations darker, and his brushline much less tense and attentive to the articulation of the joints and angles of forms. He tends to use an upright brush (as opposed to Hung-jen's oblique brushhold) moving in a relatively quick and jagged rhythm (as opposed to Hung-jen's slower, more consistent and penetrating pace). These are some of the brush qualities which, magnified in his larger paintings, become Cha's "broad" style.

In view of this close relationship with Hung-jen,[8] the criticism offered by Tao-chi in his 1694 Los Angeles album (cf. Part IV, fig. 18, above) is apt. Cha was also well acquainted with one of the other Hai-yang masters, the now obscure Wang Chih-jui (fl. 1649–1653): Wang executed an album of ten landscapes on which Cha inscribed poems.[9] Although that work is no longer extant, one hanging scroll by Wang (fig. 3)[10] reveals concepts of form which are also associated with Hung-jen. To a certain extent this visual correspondence does justify the critics' description of these artists as the Four Masters of Hai-yang, a grouping which deserves further study.

There is also evidence of a relationship between Tao-chi and Cha Shih-piao. Tao-chi was some twenty-six years younger than Cha, and his esteem for the elder painter was not limited to literary encomiums; certain visual references to Cha's style can also be seen in his work. Two paintings in Ni Tsan style, one dated 1697[11] and the other 1702 (cf. Part IV, fig. 11, above), contain a rather unusual treatment of tree foliage—a very wet, free ink play done with a scrubbing motion of the brush. This is not entirely Tao-chi's own invention (nor does it appear in Ni's works) but was derived from Cha's casual and unarticulated form in such trees. This visualization can be seen in a milder form in Cha's painting of about 1690 (cf. *XIV*, tree on the far right, with *XX*, leaf E).

Cha's friendship with the prominent scholar and painter Tan Ch'ung-kuang (1623–1692)[12] forms an interesting parallel, for although Tan was a native of Tan-t'u, Kiangsu, he knew painters from

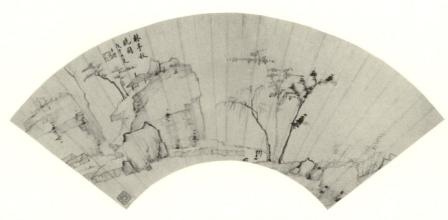

1. Cha Shih-piao, *Pavilion in Autumn*, dated 1678. Folding fan mounted as album leaf. Ink on paper. Shanghai Museum.

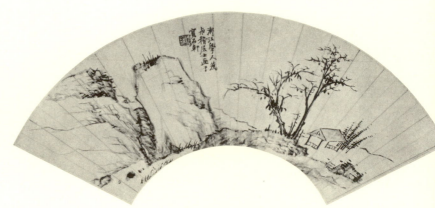

2. Hung-jen (1610–1664), *Landscape in the Style of Ni Tsan*, n.d. Folding fan mounted as album leaf. F. Vannotti collection, Lugano.

Anhwei and the Lake T'ai region. In 1670 Cha painted an album for Tan,[13] and two years later Tan asked his friend Wang Hui to "embellish" Cha's work with some moss dots and ink washes. He then invited Yün Shou-p'ing to inscribe it. The next year, 1673, Wang Hui traveled from Su-chou to Yang-chou and spent some time in Cha's company.[14] A passage in Chang Keng's biography of Cha probably relates to this visit: "Once Cha saw some paintings by Wang Hui which appealed to him and he invited Wang to his home, where he asked him to do some pictures in the manners of Ts'ao Chih-po, Ni Tsan, Huang Kung-wang, and Wu Chen, so that they could be a source of inspiration to him."[15] This passage seems to imply that Cha wished to learn from Wang Hui's works. Actually, Cha's paintings from the period of his acquaintance with Wang do not necessarily show any "influence" of this nature. Moreover, Wang was seventeen years Cha's junior. This event undoubtedly reflects Cha's high estimation of Wang Hui's paintings at a critical point in the latter's career. In that same year Wang painted an album of twelve leaves after old masters, *In Pursuit of Antiquity*, for Wang Shih-min.[16] This album is still extant and bears not only an encomium by Cha but five by Tan Ch'ung-kuang and also one by the Anhwei master Ch'eng Sui. These colophons were deliberately sought out by Wang Shih-min to enhance the album. They not only reveal Cha's, Tan's, and Ch'eng's contact with the arch-orthodoxy but the value that such men placed on their taste and judgment. Cha's praise of Wang Hui was not guarded. He wrote: "The best of painters past and present will yield to you, I would be happy to be a contemporary of someone whose reputation will last a thousand years."[17]

As the seventeenth century drew to a close, the orthodox and individualist lines became more distinct and exclusive, in the eyes of later critics. As can be seen by the colophons to Wang Hui's album of 1673 and the friendships of masters such as Cha Shih-piao and Tan Ch'ung-kuang, the actual situation was not nearly as extreme as it was later depicted. Most important, the painters did not necessarily place themselves in different ideological or mutually exclusive artistic camps. The sometimes useful grouping of painters into schools has often blinded us to what in fact may have been a free and mutual exchange of artistic values and styles, and this comment is particularly true of the late Ming and early Ch'ing. It was probably not until the eighteenth century, when critics were removed from personal contact with the painters and the artistic milieus which were the subject of their criticism, that, with their so-called critical distance, they set about classifying painters into hard-and-fast groups.

3. Wang Chih-jui (fl. 1649–1653), *Landscape*, n.d. Hanging scroll. Ink on paper. Collection unknown.

NOTES

1. See Osvald Sirén, *Chinese Painting: Leading Masters and Principles*, vol. 5, pp. 117–19, for a fair evaluation of Cha's artistic offerings. Sirén also translates Chang Keng's entry from the *Kuo-ch'ao hua-cheng-lu* (1/15), which, of all the various Chinese sources (see *ibid.*, vol. 7, p. 283), contains the most biographical material on Cha.

2. See the fine hanging scroll in ink on silk dated 1660 in the Tung Ch'i-ch'ang mode of "Mi" landscape, reproduced in *Nanju meigayen* (Tokyo, 1904), vol. 3, pl. 7.

3. In 1670 he was in Chen-chiang, Kiangsu, where he executed a work for the painter Tan Ch'ung-kuang (1623–1692) (*Hsü-chai ming-hua-lu*, 15/11ab). Extant paintings dated 1671 (in the Low Chuck Tiew collection, Hong Kong, no. 39 at the 1970 Hong Kong exhibition) and 1674 (an album in the Tokyo National Museum), a hanging scroll dated 1678 (in the J. P. Dubosc collection, listed in Sirén, *Chinese Painting*, vol. 6, no. 354), and an eight-panel series dated 1687 (in *National Fine Arts Exhibition of 1929* [Shanghai, 1929]) were all done in Yang-chou.

4. 2/12.

5. The second of four major categories, the first being "great calligraphers and painters" (which includes both Tung Ch'i-ch'ang and Tao-chi). Within each grouping Ch'in gives a *shen, miao, neng, i* ranking. Others in Cha's grouping were such painters as Ch'eng Cheng-k'uei, Hsiang Sheng-mo, Yang Pu, Hsiao Yün-ts'ung, Hung-jen, Wang Chih-jui, Kung Hsien, Hu Yü-k'un, and Tan Ch'ung-kuang.

6. As seen, for example, in the album dated 1662, reproduced in *T'ien-yin-t'ang Collection: One Hundred Masterpieces of Chinese Painting*, vol. 1, nos. 72–81.

7. The Hung-jen, an undated fan in the F. Vannotti collection, Lugano, is illustrated in *Great Chinese Painters of the Ming and Ch'ing Dynasties*, no. 69, pp. 60, 66; the Cha Shih-piao fan is in the Shanghai Museum and is illustrated in *Ming-Ch'ing shan-mien hua-hsüan-chi*, pl. 64.

8. Even Cha's early calligraphic style seems to reflect an interest in Hung-jen's skeletal forms. His late paintings in the "fine" style still retain this early orientation, while his later calligraphy is increasingly in the orthodox framework. The self-inscription to an undated scroll executed for Tan Ch'ung-kuang titled *Yü-kang chen-yin* in the Princeton Photo Archives, for example, reveals the influence of Hung-jen's rectangular and restrained hand.

9. Recorded in Fang Chün-i, *Meng-yüan shu-hua-lu*, 17/20a–b.

10. Reproduced in *Shina nanga taisei*, vol. 10, pl. 37.

11. In The Art Museum, Princeton University (acc. no. 58-122), it is illustrated and discussed in Wen Fong, "The Problem of Forgeries in Chinese Painting," figs. 15, 17, pp. 113–15.

12. Tan received his *chin-shih* degree in 1682. See his favorable biography in Ch'in Tsu-yung's *T'ung-yin lun-hua*, 2/17–18, and the references cited in Sirén, *Chinese Painting*, vol. 7, p. 402.

13. Recorded in *Hsü-chai ming-hua-lu*, 15/11ab.

14. See Wen Tsao-t'ung, *Ch'ing-ch'u liu-ta-hua-chia (The Six Great Masters of the Early Ch'ing)* (Hong Kong, 1960), under Wang Hui's chronology, p. 49.

15. Based on Sirén's translation in *Chinese Painting*, vol. 5, p. 117.

16. See Roderick Whitfield, *In Pursuit of Antiquity*, pp. 119–42.

17. Cha's inscription is found on leaf LL; Tan's inscriptions on leaves AA, BB, CC, FF, and JJ; Ch'eng's on leaf HH. See *ibid.*, pp. 119–42 (our translation differs slightly from that given there on p. 128).

Born Hai-yang (Hsiu-ning), Anhwei; later active in Yang-chou, Kiangsu

Old Man Boating on a River (*Fan-cho t'u*)

The Metropolitan Museum of Art, New York, Purchase, the Sackler Fund (69.242.7).

Hanging scroll. Ink on paper. 175.9 x 70.5 cm.

UNDATED: probably executed ca. 1690.

SIGNATURE OF THE ARTIST: Shih-piao.

INSCRIPTION BY THE ARTIST: a five-syllable poetic quatrain in three lines of "running" script.

SEALS OF THE ARTIST: *Cha Shih-piao yin* (intaglio and relief alternating, square) and *Cha Erh-chan* (relief, square; Contag and Wang, *Seals*, no. 20, p. 667), both after signature.

NO COLLECTORS' SEALS OR COLOPHONS

CONDITION: good; there is mild abrasion over the surface of the painting.

PROVENANCE: Richard Bryant Hobart collection, Cambridge, Mass., through Parke-Bernet Galleries, New York.

PUBLISHED: Sherman Lee, *Chinese Landscape Painting* (1954 ed.), no. 106, p. 156; *1000 Jahre Chinesische Malerei*, pp. 184–85 (illustrated); *1000 Years of Chinese Painting*, p. 44; Roger Goepper, *Vom Wesen Chinesischer Malerei*, figs. 82–83, pp. 60, 74–77 (illustrated); Roger Goepper, *The Essence of Chinese Painting*, figs. 82–83, pp. 60, 74–77 (illustrated); Sherman Lee, *Chinese Landscape Painting* (1962 ed.), no. 98, pp. 124, 150 (illustrated); *The Richard Bryant Hobart Collection of Chinese Ceramics and Paintings*, pp. 82–83 (illustrated); *Metropolitan Museum of Art Bulletin*, n.s., vol. 29 (October, 1970), p. 80 (illustrated); *Archives of Asian Art*, vol. 24 (1971), p. 110.

THE EXPANSIVE lake scenery and minimal motifs of this landscape are a direct reference to the composition of the Yüan master Ni Tsan, a composition which by the late Ming had become a standard, almost stereotyped formula. The large format, insistent brush movement, and generous saturations of ink (especially in the foliage of the foreground tree and moss dotting) also indicate late Ming style and spell the influence of Tung Ch'i-ch'ang's concepts of form and his emphasis on the expressive potential of ink. Cha's calligraphy likewise reveals his early study of Mi Fu through Tung's interpretive brush.

The casual attitude toward the articulation of the landscape parts and the slack linear description in this work represent an extreme of Cha's "broad" manner (*k'uo-pi*) and suggest that it may have been painted in answer to a social request. Both painting and calligraphy, the latter containing some of the fixed mannerisms of old age, point to the last stage of Cha's career, and we therefore postulate a date of ca. 1690 for the scroll. The painting in general does not show great inner conviction; nonetheless, the balance and control and the high quality of the calligraphy indicate its authenticity. It is, apart from these features, one of the "indifferent" paintings from Cha's large œuvre which, as Sirén rightfully observes, makes it often difficult to assess his artistic stature. (See *XIII* for further discussion of Cha and his painting.)

XV FAN CH'I (1616–1694-) ·

Chiang-ning (Nanking), Kiangsu

Landscapes

The Metropolitan Museum of Art, New York, Purchase, the Sackler Fund (69.242.8–15).

Album of eight leaves. Ink and color on paper. 17.0 x 20.4 cm.

DATED: in the period October 9–November 6, 1646 (*ping-hsü, ch'iu, chiu-yüeh*), on last leaf, H.

SIGNATURE OF THE ARTIST: Fan Ch'i (on last leaf, H).

INSCRIPTION BY THE ARTIST (in two lines of small "fluent regular" script preceding the signature on leaf H):
   Painted in autumn, the ninth moon of the year ping-hsü *at the Monastery of Pure Coolness.*

SEALS OF THE ARTIST: *Fan Ch'i* (intaglio, square) leaves A, B, C, D, G, and H; *Hui-kung* (relief, square) leaves A, C, E, F, and H.

NO COLLECTORS' SEALS OR COLOPHONS

CONDITION: good.

PLACE OF EXECUTION: The Ch'ing-liang ("Pure Coolness") Temple, Mt. Ch'ing-liang, Nanking.

PROVENANCE: Richard Bryant Hobart collection, Cambridge, Mass., through Parke-Bernet Galleries, New York.

PUBLISHED: Aschwin Lippe, *Kung Hsien and the Nanking School: Some Chinese Paintings of the Seventeenth Century*, no. 10, p. 7; Aschwin Lippe, "Kung Hsien and the Nanking School, II," pp. 163–65 (leaf B illustrated); Michael Sullivan, *An Introduction to Chinese Art* (London, 1961) (leaf B illustrated in color on frontispiece); Michael Sullivan, *Introduction à l'Art Chinois*, fig. 154 (leaf B illustrated); *The Richard Bryant Hobart Collection of Chinese Ceramics and Paintings*, no. 270, pp. 84–85 (leaf A illustrated); *Metropolitan Museum of Art Bulletin*, n.s., vol. 29 (October, 1970), p. 81 (acquisitions list); *Archives of Asian Art*, vol. 24 (1970–71), fig. 24, pp. 93, 110 (acquisitions list, leaf B illustrated).

THIS ALBUM DATED 1646 can be considered an early work in terms of the range of Fan's extant paintings, and the different facets of its contents help to expand our knowledge of his style. Fan's presentation of scene and control of form are precise and are conveyed by means of a tight, repetitive brush rhythm. The element of spontaneous invention in form or brushwork is almost absent (in contrast to Tao-chi's work, for example, where it was a matter of course). Landscape elements are usually wholly described with an uneven, interrupted contour of stippling, and formal omissions, when present, are calculated for their pictorial effects.

Fan prefers clear, sun-drenched air, and spatial recession is treated consistently. His interest in volume and the light cast on forms, seen not only in the clarity of his visualization but in the specific highlights, concavities, and convexities of individual objects, is characteristic of many late Ming painters. The surfaces and textures are so realistically described and the foreshortening is so accurate in some leaves that they have an almost documentary quality. Fan was also undeniably influenced by the visual innovations and Western techniques of depicting form which were imported to Nanking through prints, paintings, and other media by the Jesuit missionaries. His development of these approaches into a viable and expressive style of taste makes him a painter worthy of interest.

丙戌秋九月畫
於清涼僧舍
樊圻

Leaf H, "Promontory and View of Junks on the Horizon" (*actual size*)

Leaf A, "Thatched Cottage and Garden Rock"

Leaf B, "Crossing the Bridge in Autumn"

Leaf C, "Covered Bridge among Pines"

Leaf D, "View over Nanking"

Leaf E, "Wind-Tossed Trees and Impending Storm"

Leaf F, "Willow-Lined Bank and Pavilion"

Leaf G, "Peach-Blossom Spring"

XVI KUNG HSIEN (ca. 1618–1689)

Born K'un-shan, Kiangsu; later active Nanking, Kiangsu

Landscapes

The Metropolitan Museum of Art, New York, Purchase,
the Sackler Fund (69.242.16–21).

Album of six leaves (from an original set of twelve).
Ink on paper. 22.2 x 43.7 cm.

UNDATED: probably executed ca. 1688.

SIGNATURE OF THE ARTIST: Kung Hsien (on leaf F).

INSCRIPTIONS BY THE ARTIST: in "running" script on each leaf except leaf C.

SEALS OF THE ARTIST: *Kung Hsien yin* (square, half-relief and half-intaglio;
Contag and Wang, *Seals*, no. 11, p. 510) leaves A, C, D, E, and F; *Pan-ch'ien*
(relief, square; Contag and Wang, *Seals*, no. 12, p. 510) leaves B and F.

COLLECTOR'S SEALS: Hu Hsiao-chuo (unidentified), *Hu Hsiao-chuo ts'ang*
(relief, square) leaves A, B, C, and F and probably also *Te-i-hsüan ts'ang* (relief, square) leaf E.

CONDITION: excellent; the remaining six leaves were separated sometime in the
recent history of the album, and complete photographs are available from the
University of Michigan Asian Art Photographic Archive.

PROVENANCE: Richard Bryant Hobart collection, Cambridge, Mass.,
through Parke-Bernet Galleries, New York.

PUBLISHED: Aschwin Lippe, *Kung Hsien and the Nanking School: Some Chinese Paintings of the Seventeenth Century*, no. 8, p. 10; Osvald Sirén, "Lists,"
vol. 7, p. 370; *1000 Jahre Chinesische Malerei*, no. 124, p. 212 (one leaf from the
other group of six illustrated); Charles MacSherry, *Chinese Art* (Northamp-
ton, Mass., 1962), no. 27; Roger Goepper, *Vom Wesen Chinesischer Malerei*,
figs. 88–89, p. 225; Roger Goepper, *The Essence of Chinese Painting*, figs. 88–89,
p. 225 (one leaf from the other group of six illustrated); *The Richard Bryant
Hobart Collection of Chinese Ceramics and Paintings*, no. 273, pp. 90–91 (leaf C
illustrated); *Archives of Asian Art*, vol. 24 (1970–71), pp. 94, 100, fig. 25 (acquisitions list; leaf C illustrated). *Note:* the above publications list only six of the
original twelve leaves of this album. When it was photographed at the time of
the Parke-Bernet auction, however, twelve leaves were intact. The whereabouts of the other six leaves and the point at which the two groups of six
were separated is not clear. In addition, the 1959 Haus der Kunst catalogue
(*1000 Jahre Chinesische Malerei*) indicates the leaves as listed in John C. Ferguson, *Li-tai chu-lu hua-mu*, but we have not been able to verify this.

BOTH THE PAINTING and the calligraphy of the Sackler album are
consistent with Kung Hsien's late style, as exemplified in three dated
works, the 1688 hanging scroll in the Ching Yüan Chai collection,
the 1688 album of sixteen leaves in the ex-Chin Ch'eng collection,
and the 1689 hanging scroll in the Honolulu Academy of Arts. The
vigor of the individual calligraphic brushline dominates the depiction: in many of the scenes a bold, reinforcing contour line serves
as a focus to unify the broad, loose treatment of the landscape elements, built up, characteristically, through graded ink dots.

A certain slackening of compositional and brush tension may be
sensed in these landscapes, a feature common to many of Kung
Hsien's works in his latest years. The increased interest in the independent mobility and power of the line is paralleled in the development of his calligraphy and can be seen in works dated from
1648–49 to the year of his death, 1689. This reinforcement of fundamental stylistic characteristics in both painting and calligraphy is
an important factor in the authentication of these and other Kung
Hsien works.

Leaf A, "The 'Yellow Leaf' Village"

Leaf B, "Mountains and Clouds"

Leaf C, "Landscape"

Leaf D, "Moonlit Dream"

Leaf E, "Light-Filled Mountains"

Leaf F, "Fishing Boat in the Moonlight"

XVII TAO-CHI (1641–ca. 1710)

Born Kuei-lin, Kwangsi; active Hsüan-ch'eng, Anhwei; Nanking, Kiangsu; Peking, Hopei; and Yang-chou, Kiangsu

The Echo   (K'ung-shan hsiao-yü)

The Art Museum, Princeton University (67-20).

Album leaf mounted as hanging scroll, from a twelve-leaf album depicting the poems of Su Shih. Ink on paper. 22.1 x 29.4 cm.

UNDATED: last leaf of original album dated in the period December 24, 1677–January 23, 1678 (ting-ssu shih-erh-yüeh).

UNSIGNED

INSCRIPTION BY THE ARTIST: in two lines of "small regular" script transcribing a couplet by Su Shih (hao Tung-p'o, tzu Tzu-chan, 1036–1101):

> An echo rebounds with every whisper
> Startling, on the empty mountain, the white cloud.
> [From] Tzu-chan's poem, "Pi-lo-tung."

SEAL OF THE ARTIST: Lao-t'ao (intaglio, tall rectangle; PTC, cat. no. 50).

NO COLLECTORS' SEALS OR COLOPHONS

CONDITION: good (see also text discussion).

PROVENANCE: Ta-feng-t'ang collection.

PUBLISHED: PTC, cat. no. 44, p. 31, fig. 8 (illustrated); Record of the Art Museum, Princeton University, vol. 27, no. 1 (1968), p. 35; Archives of Asian Art, vol. 22 (1968–69), p. 134; The Selected Painting and Calligraphy of Shih-t'ao, vol. 6, pl. 124 (illustrated).

THE EXPRESSIVE POWER of this work lies in its brevity. A few strokes of the brush sweep upward from the left corner with the momentum of a billowing cloud. The dry brush twists and turns in the manner of seal-style calligraphy, charging the forms with roundness and volume. The top of the mountain is encircled by clouds drawn in pale ink. Bare twigs delineate the characteristic shape of the peak as a flattened mound. From this height the eye is thrown down to a series of earthen banks receding by progressive jumps into the distance and a small stone bridge fading into the mist. The branches of several trees stretch delicately into the air and are drawn in the same tremulous lineament as the bridge. A full corner of white paper at the right and the spare description of forms capture the feeling of stillness and echoing silence of Su Tung-p'o's lines.[1]

This leaf now is identified as part of a twelve-leaf album which has been dispersed, nine leaves of which were recently exhibited in Hong Kong.[2] The last leaf is dated in correspondence with the period late 1677–early 1678 (for convenience referred to here as 1677–78), forming valuable evidence of Tao-chi's pre-Nanking activities before the 1680's. The date makes this leaf the earliest dated Tao-chi work in a Western collection. The style and calligraphy of this leaf and of the whole album may be confidently associated with other well-known and accepted works of Tao-chi, providing us with a clearer picture of his early development.

OUR FIRST ACQUAINTANCE with this work was several years ago, before the appearance of the other nine leaves. Upon initial viewing, the two-line inscription seemed unfamiliar as Tao-chi's handwriting, which tended to place the whole work in question. After closer

study of Tao-chi's early style our doubts were dispelled. During the 1967 Tao-chi exhibition in Michigan (which we did not attend), Richard Edwards commented on this leaf as follows: "Although much admired for its sensitive touch, some opinions—particularly among Japanese scholars—saw signature and seal as interpolations. While according to this view it could well be a seventeenth century painting, it would be more just to associate it with a different artist. Ch'a [sic] Shih-piao was suggested."[3]

1. Cha Shih-piao, Landscape, dated 1671, detail. Hanging scroll. Ink on paper. Low Chuck Tiew collection, Hong Kong.

This link with Cha Shih-piao (1615–1698) was an unexpected one, mainly because our understanding of Cha's style does not fit that represented in this work (cf. fig. 1, XIII, XIV). Cha seldom employs a dry brush; he likes to use dense, wet ink, and even when he does use a dry brush it is usually with a slanted tip (ts'e-feng). Furthermore, he prefers angular mountain and rock forms, not the rounded mounds found here.[4] But to pursue this argument further, could Tai Pen-hsiao (1621–1691?) or Ch'eng Sui (1605–1691) be associated with the work? Both were contemporaries of Cha and Tao-chi (see Part IV above), and both reveal a preference for modeling "empty" volumetric forms with dry brushwork. Upon careful comparison, however, it can be seen that Tai's forms tend to be more static and his arrangements more stable (fig. 2),[5] while Ch'eng's compositions reveal a predominate dotting in dry brushwork (fig. 3).[6]

In The Echo there is a subtle tension between the compositional solids and the voids. The drift of mountain at left is set against the blank paper at right, and both are held in balance by the lopsided bridge. There is also an interplay between the large, voluminous shapes executed in softly rubbed strokes and the fine, tremulous

小語輒響答空山白雲驚　子晬碧蘚洞詩

lines in charcoal-black ink. This concept of composing a picture by juxtaposing contrasting forms to create an internal tension can be seen in three dated Tao-chi works of the Hsüan-ch'eng and Nanking periods. Although available for study only in reproduction, they give us insight into his early development from the 1670's to the 1680's: the 1667 handscroll *Sixteen Lohans* (fig. 4), the 1672 hanging scroll *Watching a Waterfall from a Stone Bridge*,[7] and the 1673 eight-leaf album of landscapes (cf. *XXXIV*, fig. 5). In these works we see, on the structural level, the formation of a feeling for spatial tensions and an interest in the developing of deep space by combining, on the level of motif, the odd shape, the tensile line, and the expressive texture of extremely moist or dry ink. These stylistic characteristics constitute the principles of Tao-chi's personal artistic vision, seen in their embryonic form here and developed and refined throughout his career.

Other than the three standard works just mentioned, stylistic affinities with other familiar and genuine works may be seen. In *Waterfall at Mt. Lu* (fig. 5), a large hanging scroll, ink and color on silk, in the Sumitomo collection,[8] differences in scale and materials should not obscure the similarity in morphological features and habits of brushwork, e.g., the modeling of the foreground masses by long undulating lines, the building up of volume in the blunted peaks by dry-moist rubbed textures, and the similar contouring of the clouds as gently vibrating ellipses in pale ink. To turn to another prime work in the Sumitomo collection, *Eight Views of Huang-shan*,[9] (especially leaves A and D, "On the Way to Streams and Mountains" and "White Dragon Pool"), we find that the modeling of the mountain is similar in these two leaves: the form of the cliffs is first outlined with a parched brush and then filled in by dragging and twisting the brush from the edges of the form inward. Further-

2. Tai Pen-hsiao (1621–1691?), *Landscape after Ni Tsan*, n.d., detail. Hanging scroll. Ink on paper. Tsi-lo Lou collection, Hong Kong.

3. Ch'eng Sui, *Landscape*, dated 1657. Album leaf mounted as hanging scroll. Ink on paper. Museum Yamato Bunkakan, Nara.

4. Tao-chi, *Sixteen Lohans*, dated 1667, detail of bare trees and modeling of the rocks by dry ink lines. Handscroll. Ink on paper. Collection unknown.

more, in *Small Album* from the Wen Fong collection[10] (especially leaves A and J, "Returning" and "Branches," figs. 6 and 7), the compositional structure of recession into deep space and the delineation of both rocks and trees closely parallel the forms in *The Echo*; also comparable is the motif of the arched stone bridge of leaf A (fig. 6).

To FURTHER CLARIFY some of the points discussed in the Tao-chi symposium, let us turn from examination of the painting to the calligraphy. One should note that the six characters of the line furthest to the left (fig. 8*a*)—*Tzu-chan Pi-lo-tung-shih*—are extremely small and are written with the few unruly hairs protruding beyond the full tip of the brush. This scratchy feeling of the line and of the parched ink and unkempt brushtip is seen in the leafless trees of the

5. Tao-chi, *Waterfall at Mt. Lu*, ca. 1697, detail of cloudy mountain. Hanging scroll. Ink and color on silk. Sumitomo collection, Oiso.

right above
6. Tao-chi, *Small Album*, ca. 1695, leaf A, "Returning." Ink on paper. Wen Fong collection, Princeton.

right below
7. Tao-chi, *Small Album*, ca. 1695, leaf J, "Branches." Ink on paper. Wen Fong collection.

landscape and is consistent with both the writing and drawing of the whole leaf. On the basis of this consistency of execution and concept, we believe the calligraphy and image to have been executed by the same hand and with the same brush and therefore that it does not represent a later addition.

Tao-chi's calligraphy is generally best known through the script styles in his later works, where an increasing formalization and ease are exhibited. With one's knowledge thus limited, one might well question the two lines of inscription in *The Echo*. But the would-be connoisseur must be cautioned against two pitfalls: being misled by something which "looks right, but isn't" (*ssu-shih erh fei*) and rejecting something which "looks wrong, but is right" (*ssu-fei erh shih*). The first case is usually a good forgery or copy where, superficially, the style seems to accord with our so-called standard image of the master, so that we accept its authenticity without closer scrutiny. In the second case, we may be the victims of our ignorance of many factors—the artist's total chronology and normative range, his mood, differences in materials of brush or paper—all of which may influence his performance. In the case of a counterfeit (i.e., a replica with intent to deceive), the clever forger will inevitably work in the most common image of the artist's style, one which is easily recognized and accepted; he will seldom choose the style which is the exception.

Some comparative observations of formal structure and brush movement will place the identification of the calligraphy of this work on firmer ground. The two-line inscription (fig. 8*a*) is rendered in a "small block" script (*hsiao-k'ai*) modeled after Chung Yu (151–230). In Tao-chi's early period, his personal variations on this script consist of elongated right and left diagonals breaking out of the rectangular framework and of extended and heavily accented "oar-like" hooks and endings. The calligraphy of the 1667 *Lohans* handscroll and the 1673 seven-leaf album, for example, also bear these structural features, even though the script itself is often of a more cursive variety (cf. Part IV, fig. 1, above).

There are two other calligraphic features of interest in *The Echo*. The ninth character, *yün* ("cloud"), is written in an archaic form with a double lower phonetic (8*a*, right line, ninth character from top). Ordinarily, this form is seldom used with *hsiao-k'ai* script, but the choice is consistent with Tao-chi's preference for mixing elements of two script styles. Instances of this form may be cited from

other genuine works dated later in his career [11] (8*e*). If the inscription had been added by another hand, the interpolator would hardly have sought out a rare form of a character. The tenth character, *ching* ("to startle"), shows an unusual stroke order and structure which is also found in other accepted works of Tao-chi (8*c* and *f*). In terms of general structure, all the characters in Tao-chi's inscription tend to slant consistently to the upper right; in the character *ching*, however, the four dots of the "horse" radical are level and extend far to the left of the whole form. Moreover, the vertical stroke of the horse radical cuts through the top of the horizontal like a skewer, and the enclosing hook stroke veers upward and shows a strongly articulated corner. Hence, the parts align to form a triangle △. As to stroke order, it seems evident that Tao-chi has habitually written the horse radical first as the character "ten" (i.e., first the horizontal stroke, then the vertical to form a cross-shape, then adding the remaining horizontals; this is not necessarily the usual stroke order). This manner of structuring a character has much to do with Tao-chi's own habits of stroke order and aesthetic balance which he developed early in his calligraphic training and which tends to differ to a significant degree from the standard formation prevailing at the time. The same forms of this character and of the others in the inscription are repeated in calligraphy throughout his career, for example, the Sumitomo Huang-shan album, leaf G (8*b*), the Fong *Small Album* (8*c* and *e*), and the Sumitomo Huang-shan handscroll (8*d* and *f*).[12]

THE FACT THAT this scroll was originally an album leaf may be seen by examination of the paper, which has a crease in the center, indicating a former butterfly-type mounting. This is of interest because of the absence of a signature: signatures and often dates are most commonly found on the last leaf of an album. The last leaf of the original album, which we examined at the Hong Kong show, does contain the signature of Tao-chi and the date, and indicates that there were originally twelve illustrations of poems by Su Shih (fig. 11). The format, seals, and painting and calligraphy style firmly link the Sackler leaf with the other nine. The small intaglio seal, *Lao-t'ao*, found on our leaf (fig. 8*a*) also adorns leaves 3 and 7. Our leaf compares pictorially with the whole album and particularly with leaves 4 and 7 (figs. 9 and 10), where mobile strokes of a dry brush model the edges of the forms and contrast with the fine delineation of the

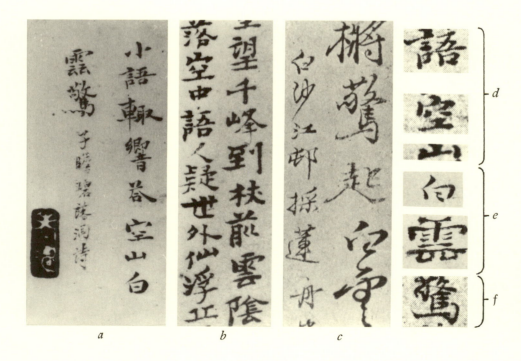

8. Tao-chi: *a*, detail of self-inscription to *The Echo*; *b*, detail of self-inscription to *Eight Views of Huang-shan*, album leaf G, Sumitomo collection; *c* and *e*, details of self-inscription to *Small Album*, leaves F, A, and K, respectively; *d* and *f*, details of self-inscription to Huang-shan handscroll, Sumitomo collection.

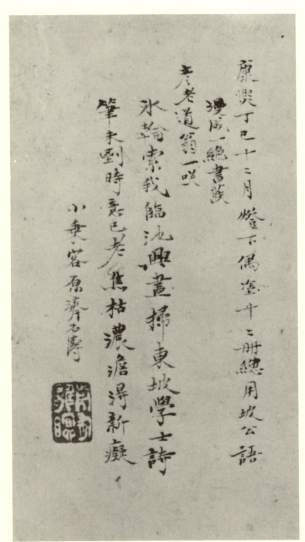

11. Tao-chi, *Album of Paintings Depicting the Poems of Su Shih*, detail of leaf 9 showing signature and date. Ink on paper. Huang Ping-chang collection.

trees in darker ink. The Sackler leaf is about one centimeter smaller in height and about one-half centimeter smaller in width than the Hong Kong leaves; this difference may be due to the manner of measuring or to trimming during a subsequent remounting.

This album is recorded in P'an Cheng-wei's *T'ing-fan-lou shu-hua-chi*,[13] where only eight leaves are mentioned. The Sackler leaf is not among them, which means that it, along with three others, had been separated from the group by 1843, when the *T'ing-fan-lou* was published. Further evidence of this is the fact that P'an's collector's seals appear on the Hong Kong album, but not on the Sackler leaf.

NOTES

1. Lines 17 and 18 from a twenty-line poem in five-character "old-style" meter. Cf. *Chi-chu fen-lei Tung-p'o hsien-sheng-shih* (SPTK ed., no. 202), vol. 1, 2/79b, where two variant characters are found. Our rendering is based on that found in *PTC*, p. 32.
2. June–July, 1970, City Museum and Art Gallery, Hong Kong, jointly presented by the Urban Council and the Min Chiu Society; see the catalogue by Chuang Shen and J. C. Y. Watt, *Exhibition of Paintings of the Ming and Ch'ing Periods*, no. 46, where leaves 1, 3, 4, 5, 6, 7, 8, and 9 are illustrated, measuring 23.5 x 30.0 cm., from the Huang Ping-chang collection, Hong Kong.
3. "Postscript to an Exhibition," p. 270.
4. Other typical and genuine examples of Cha's work are the 1671 hanging scroll in the Ex-J. D. Ch'en collection, shown in fig. 1, the 1674 ten-leaf album of landscapes in the Tokyo National Museum, and the hanging scroll in the Finlayson collection (see Shih Hsio-yen and Henry Trübner, *Individualists and Eccentrics*, pp. 10–12).
5. In the Wango H. C. Weng collection, New York, illustrated in James Cahill, ed., *Fantastics and Eccentrics in Chinese Painting*, p. 51, from an album of twelve leaves, ink on paper, 21.3 x 16.5 cm.; see also the hanging scroll in the Chih-lo-lou collection, in the Hong Kong exhibition catalogue, no. 41.
6. The album leaf is in the Museum Yamato Bunkakan, Nara, ink on paper, dated 1657, now mounted as a hanging scroll.
7. Collection unknown; illustrated in *PTC*, p. 29.
8. 212.2 x 63.0 cm.; illustrated in *Min Shin no kaiga*, nos. 81–82.
9. *PTC*, cat. no. 1, pp. 96–99.
10. *Ibid.*, cat. no. 9, pp. 111–16.
11. See also *Drunk in the Autumn Woods*, middle inscription, first line, second character, John M. Crawford, Jr., collection, New York, reproduced in *ibid.*, cat. no. 24, p. 154.
12. See also *Spring on the Min River*, eighth line from end, fourth character, Cleveland Museum of Art, *ibid.*, cat. no. 12, p. 119; *Album of Landscapes*, dated 1703, leaf L, fourth line, first character, Museum of Fine Arts, Boston, *ibid.*, cat. no. 33, p. 167.
13. Under the title "Ta-ti-tzu shan-shui-shih ts'e," 4/353–60.

9. Tao-chi, *Album of Paintings Depicting the Poems of Su Shih*, dated 1678, leaf 4. Ink on paper. Huang Ping-chang collection, Hong Kong.

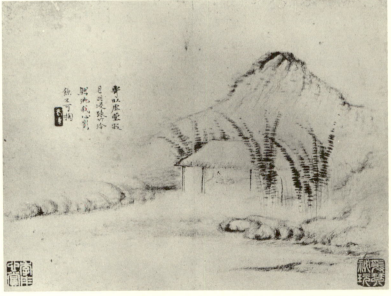

10. Tao-chi, *Album of Paintings Depicting the Poems of Su Shih*, leaf 7. Ink on paper. Huang Ping-chang collection.

XVIII TAO-CHI (1641–ca. 1710)

Searching for Plum Blossoms: Poems and Painting
(T'an-mei shih-hua t'u)

The Art Museum, Princeton University (67-3).

Handscroll. Ink and slight color on paper. 30.5 x 132.9 cm.
(The paper is continuous except for the last three lines of the
inscription, where a join is evident.)

DATED: in the period March 5–April 3, 1685 (*i-ch'ou erh-yüeh*).

UNSIGNED

INSCRIPTION BY THE ARTIST: in two parts, a nine-line prose introduction
followed by nine seven-word poems transcribed in twenty-nine continuous
lines (see text discussion).

SEAL OF THE ARTIST: *Shih-t'ao* (intaglio, square; *PTC*, cat. no. 66) after
inscription.

COLLECTOR'S SEALS: *Chang Ta-ch'ien* (born 1899), *Chang Chi-tzu*
(relief, square) right edge of painting, *Chang Yüan chih-yin-hsin* (intaglio,
square) and *Ta-ch'ien chü-shih* (relief, square) left edge of painting.

COLOPHON: by Chang Ta-ch'ien in eleven lines (see end of entry for text).

CONDITION: poor; the paper has darkened and the entire surface of the work
has been markedly damaged by insect holes; in the painting section these have
been filled in, while only random parts of the calligraphy have been retouched;
many characters remain partially obliterated.

PROVENANCE: Ta-feng-t'ang collection, through Peter Swann, Oxford.

PUBLISHED: *Ta-feng-t'ang ming-chi*, vol. 2, pl. 14 (illustrated); *PTC*, cat. no.
5, pp. 103–4 (illustrated); *Archives of Asian Art*, vol. 22 (1968–69), p. 134 (acquisitions list); *Record of the Art Museum, Princeton University*, vol. 28, no.
1 (1968), p. 35 (acquisitions list); *The Selected Painting and Calligraphy of
Shih-t'ao*, vol. 2, pl. 63 (illustrated).

INSCRIPTION: the outer label of the painting is inscribed by Chang Ta-ch'ien
in small "running" (*hsing*) script:

*Handscroll of plum blossoms by the old man Ch'ing-hsiang. Poetry, calligra-
phy, and painting—unexcelled in all three [san-chüeh]—in the possession of
Ta-feng-t'ang. Remounted in late May and early June of 1952 [jen-ch'en wu-
yüeh].* Ta-ch'ien, Yüan, of Szechuan.

OTHER VERSIONS: two inferior replicas made after this composition; one has
been acquired by the Sackler collection (see *XIX*); a comparison of these copies with the original will be found under that entry.

WILD NATURE confronts us in this work. We see not the carefully
pruned solitary branch common in plum painting, but an over-
grown tangle of old and young branches surging with vitality. The
rhythm of craggy stalks competes with rapier twigs, each providing
a foil for a spectrum of ink, the pale and dark representing recession
in depth. In the foreground, strong angular strokes in charcoal-black
ink contrast with lighter parched sweeps of the brush, which introduce a layered spatial progression of the rootless forms. Moss dots
in graded tones of ink as well as pale russet color are scattered over
vital sections of the forms.

Amid the welter of unkempt lines, the circles of multipetaled
blossoms, also outlined in double tones of pale and dark ink, appear

like fine, buoyant accents. A hillock extends to the left. Its form mocks the relentless movement of the branches at the right and conveys the curious feeling of the silent world of the cemetery.

The driving energy of the forms worked in counter-direction to each other suggests a pictorial map of Tao-chi's psychological state, a "drawing out" of his wanderings before he settled at his studio, I-chih ("One-Branch"), in Nanking, which he mentions in his introduction. This introduction in nine lines of prose acquaints us with the circumstances leading to the painting:

Since the eighth intercalary month of *keng-shen* [September 23–October 22, 1680] I have lived by myself at I-chih[ko] [his famous residence at Ch'ang-kan, Pao-en temple, south of Nanking] for six years, not going anywhere. Now it is the second month of *i-ch'ou* [March 5–April 3, 1685]; the snow having cleared and my mood being joyous, I took up my staff and went searching for plum blossoms. Traveling alone for more than a hundred *li*, I reached Ch'ing-lung [Green Dragon Mountain], T'ien-yin [Heaven's Seal Mountain], Tung-shan [East Mountain], Chung-ling [Chung mausoleum], Ling-ku [Valley of Souls], and other memorable sites, seeking all the way for mountains and valleys. Whether a country tavern, deserted village, family cottage, or monk's retreat, I sought them all out before turning back. Upon returning, there was someone who, having waited long for me, said: "The garden plum has almost come into full blossom during the evening. Would the monk please come and settle this matter?" So I followed him over to the studio, opened the shutters, and sat down in contemplation. As the midnight watch was almost complete, the solitary moon hovered above casting [the shadow of] icy branches on the ground. Taking up my brush I leave altogether the nine poems which came to me.[1] [The poems which follow are not translated here.]

This prose introduction is followed by nine seven-word poems transcribed in twenty-nine continuous lines; each poem is accompanied by a brief two-line commentary in smaller characters. The sheer length and the sustained energy with which the literary and pictorial aspects of the painting have been executed testify to the plum blossom being Tao-chi's favorite flower (see *XXXIII* for further discussion of this topic). Visually speaking, painting and calligraphy have been successfully integrated into a single unified composition.

The calligraphy is executed in a uniform "small regular" (*hsiao-k'ai*) script, one of several block scripts Tao-chi employed. Modeled after the traditional image of Chung Yu (151–230), the style expresses an archaic simplicity and inner strength, rather than fluidity and dynamic movement. The forms carry many "chancery" (*li*) brush movements which can be seen in a tendency toward a broad, squat composition, lengthened horizontals, and diagonals which extend beyond the outer "frame" of the character. There is also a purposeful choice of antique written forms of certain characters. As the ink runs thin in the brush, natural contrasts of light and dark are formed which provide a rhythmic tonal phrasing within the overall block of writing.

The excellence of this writing should place the scroll among the finest calligraphic works of Tao-chi's Nanking period. There is a consistency in both the vitality and execution of the characters which well matches the pictorial images. Each stroke-form is drawn with a slow, steady deliberateness which stresses the round, ductile strength of the line. The brush simultaneously penetrates and caresses the paper with a concentrated tension sustained from the

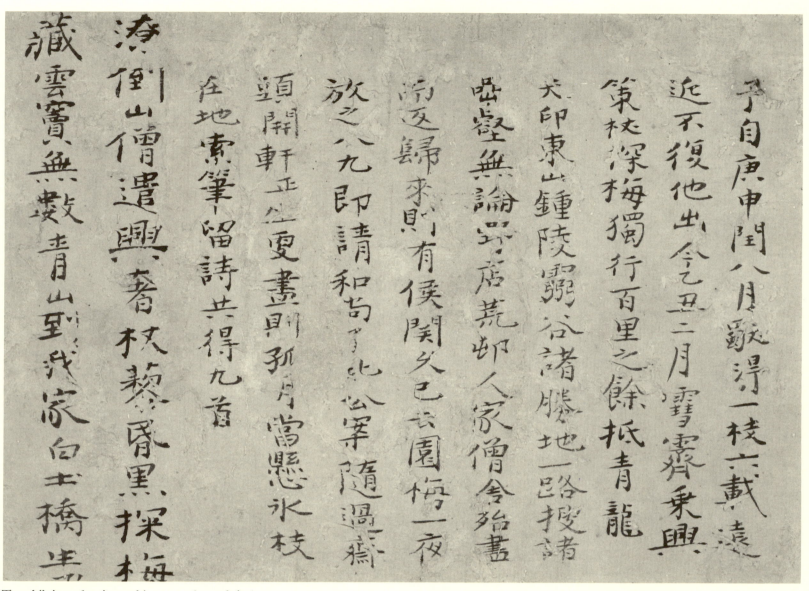

Tao-chi's introduction to his poems (*actual size*).

beginning to the end of each stroke movement. As the pressure, thickness, and speed of each stroke are under absolute control, so the same attentiveness is brought to bear on the individual configuration of strokes. Each character stands poised in balance and could be isolated as an independent design. The perfection of this design is dramatized if one compares any one character of this version with characters from the copies (see *XIX*, figs. 3–9).

One senses a striving for an ideal symmetry, along with a certain plumpness in the form and restraint in the execution. These qualities are characteristic of Tao-chi's calligraphy at this date, 1685. Finally, the feeling of heightened energy and joy in the immediate circumstances of execution ranks this work high in our estimation.

THE STYLE of the painting has a significant relationship to two other handscrolls by Tao-chi of this period, which confirm dating and style as well as quality: the ca. 1683 *Conversion of Hariti* (fig. 1) and the 1685 *Ten Thousand Ugly Inkblots* in Su-chou (fig. 2). A similar pictorial idea structures these three scrolls. Truncated verticals frame and fill a horizontal space; strong lines or projecting solids rise without a base in the foreground and form a repoussoir which plunges the eye into deep recession. In the Su-chou scroll the low hill with moss dots is rendered in the same way as the hill in the Sackler scroll but with darker, more intense use of the wet ink. In the Boston and Sackler scrolls, the motif of dark, angular branches

in the forefront reappears as a contrast to the paler forms in back, stressing tone, linear vitality, and receding depth. This concept appears in equally striking but smaller format in the Fong *Small Album* (fig. 3).[2]

An element of iconoclasm is affirmed in these three scrolls. Tao-chi's interest in bizarre and startling juxtapositions constitutes a direct flaunting of traditional methods of painting these subjects, whether they are plum branches, landscape elements, hemp-fiber texture strokes, or ink dots. The search for and the assertion of one's artistic identity in the face of potentially stifling canonical modes of expression seem to be a strong motivating factor for Tao-chi's aggressive originality. In this sense the three works, and especially the two 1685 scrolls, represent keys to the interpretation of his artistic intent and direction during this stage. That this was also a period of intense technical growth is verified by the highly disciplined and superbly poised calligraphy found on this scroll.

Searching for Plum Blossoms also holds a special place in plum genre as a whole, for the dynamic forces expressed in it seem unique in Tao-chi's own works of this subject[3] and do not appear in those of his eighteenth-century followers.[4] For example, the ca. 1705–7 *Plum Branches* album in the Sackler collection (*XXXIII*) reverts to classic, though highly subtle, variations of a single branch theme; in hanging scrolls and other works of this subject attributed to him only compositions revolving around a main stalk appear.[5]

1. Tao-chi, *The Conversion of Hariti to Buddhism,* datable ca. 1683, detail. Handscroll. Ink on paper. The Museum of Fine Arts, Boston, Marshall E. Gould Fund (56.1151).

3. Tao-chi, *Small Album,* ca. 1695, leaf I. Ink on paper. Wen Fong collection, Princeton.

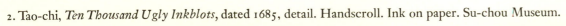

2. Tao-chi, *Ten Thousand Ugly Inkblots,* dated 1685, detail. Handscroll. Ink on paper. Su-chou Museum.

VALUABLE INSIGHT into Tao-chi's method of painting plum is given us in a self-inscription on one of his undated bamboo and plum paintings. He says: "Nowadays, people who paint plum generally fall into the 'mortar and nest' [of the ancients, i.e., stereotyped methods] [but] when I paint, I want the stems and branches to be free of both resemblance and non-resemblance. . . . According to the impulse of the brush in my hand, I judge from the [configuration of the] first stroke [*i-hua*], then follow its course to complete the design."[6] Two important ideas in this statement are illustrated in the *Plum Blossoms* handscroll: the notion of rising above "resemblance and non-resemblance" and the interaction of accident and design in actual execution. The tangle of plum Tao-chi presents does not appear this way in the natural landscape; on the contrary, it is "made up" in an insistent defiance of traditional modes. It should even strike us as "unnatural" and therefore "non-resembling." But in terms of the abstraction of the rhythms and energies of nature and of the pure pictorial elements of line, form, and ink values, this act of representation virtually simulates nature, growing from the "first stroke" with an organic integrity. Hence in synthesizing the paradoxical opposites, the work rises above both resemblance and non-resemblance.

Tao-chi's inscription also hints at the role momentary change plays in the independence and spontaneity of the composition. In submitting to the immediate inspiration of the strokes on paper after the actual realization of that initial form-giving stroke, every change acts as a foil for the succeeding movements of the design; the limitations and accidents of the medium and mood are thus anticipated and incorporated as part of the creative strategy. In addition, the execution of the plum petals and moss dots also entails an act of submission to the total impact and inspiration of the forms. The blossoms are encircled with an energy that seems self-propelled and, like the momentum of the moss dots, is almost like automatic writing.

THIS SCROLL CONTRIBUTES two points to our knowledge of Tao-chi's chronology and sympathies. First, his introduction to the nine poems fixes his geographical whereabouts for the early 1680's: by late September of 1680 he was at I-chih (Ch'ang-kan or Pao-en temple, south of Nanking), after many years of wandering, and remained there for six years; in 1685, when this painting was completed, he had roamed many of the most scenic spots in the vicinity of Nanking, seeking the plum blossoms which inspired the nine poems.[7] The second point concerns Tao-chi's loyalties. Edwards has said: "An interesting observation about the long inscription on this same scroll was that the seventh poem (line 22, character 6) has a space (for respect) before the term *jen-chu* ('Benevolent Master'). This seems to be a clear reference to [the] K'ang-hsi [Emperor] and supplies further evidence for the view that Tao-chi was in no sense a rebel against the Manchu Rule."[8] In fact, Tao-chi is known to have seen the K'ang-hsi Emperor for the first time in December of 1684, that is, three months before he executed this painting.[9] We might also call attention to the fine scroll *Spring on the Min River* in the Cleveland Museum, dated 1697,[10] which again reveals in the inscription his expression of at least formal respect for the Manchu sovereign.

The painting is followed by a single colophon by Chang Ta-ch'ien, which is one of the longest commentaries made by him on a Tao-chi work in his collection. It is interesting for the brief background it offers on Chang's particular fondness for this scroll (of all his many Tao-chi works) and on the difficulties Chinese collectors have faced, which have taken their toll of paintings:

In my lifetime I have owned more than a hundred and ten paintings by Ta-ti-tzu [Tao-chi]. I once carved a seal reading "one of a hundred Shih-[t'ao paintings] worshiped by Ta-ch'ien" because I am so fond of his works. Now, having undergone the vicissitudes of *ting-ch'ou* [1937] and *chi-ch'ou* [1949] [he is referring to the outbreak of World War II and

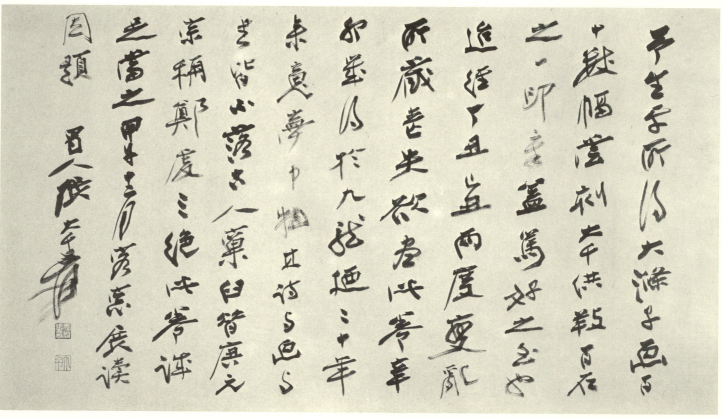

Chang Ta-ch'ien's colophon.

the takeover by the Chinese Communists], the things in my collection have almost all disappeared.

Then in 1951 in Kowloon I acquired this scroll, which for the past twenty years I had imagined only in my dreams. His painting, calligraphy, and poetry do not fall into the "mortar and nest" of the ancients. Truly, this scroll should be considered "unexcelled in all three" [*san-chüeh*], like T'ang Hsüan-tsung's praise of Cheng Ch'ien.

> Twelfth month of *chia-wu* [late December, 1954–early January, 1955], unrolled and appreciated abroad, hence inscribed. [Signed:] Ta-ch'ien, Yüan, of Szechuan. [Seals:] *Shu-chün Chang Yüan* (intaglio, square) and *Ta-ch'ien* (relief, square).

NOTES

1. We would like to acknowledge the help of Professors Shūjirō Shimada and L. S. Yang and Drs. Wai-kam Ho and Lin Shun-fu for their various interpretations of this passage, especially the somewhat enigmatic lines 6 and 7.

2. This effect was also noted by Richard Edwards in "Postscript to an Exhibition," p. 263. A similar effect of repoussoir recurs in such works as leaves E and H of the Sumitomo album, *Eight Views of Huang-shan*, leaves D and I of the Fong *Small Album*, and leaf B of the Cleveland *Reminiscences of Ch'in-huai* (see *PTC*, cat. nos. 1, 9, and 14, pp. 98–99, 112–15, 121).

3. As noted by Edwards, "Postscript to an Exhibition," p. 35.

4. For a sampling, see James Cahill, ed., *Fantastics and Eccentrics in Chinese Painting*, nos. 35, 36, and 38, the work of Li Fang-ying (1695–1754), Wang Shih-shen (1686–1759), and Chin Nung (1687–1764-), respectively.

5. E.g., the 1699 *Plum Branch*, in *Shih-t'ao hua-chi*, no. 63, or the 1700 twelve-leaf album of landscapes and flowers, in *Tao-chi hua-ts'e*, last leaf.

6. As recorded in P'an Cheng-wei's *T'ing-fan-lou shu-hua-chi*, 4/365, from a collected album.

7. Fu Pao-shih, *Shih-t'ao shang-jen nien-p'u*, p. 56; Wen Fong, "A Letter from Shih-t'ao to Pa-ta shan-jen and the Problem of Shih-t'ao's Chronology," pp. 32, 49–50, nn. 62–64; also Wu T'ung, "Tao-chi, a Chronology," in *PTC*, p. 57.

8. "Postscript to an Exhibition," p. 264.

9. According to Fu Pao-shih, *Shih-t'ao shang-jen nien-p'u*, p. 59. Cf. also Jonathan D. Spence, *Ts'ao Yin and the K'ang-hsi Emperor*, for an account of the Southern Tours, and p. 57, where he states that the Emperor was in Nanking for three days, December 7–9, 1684.

10. *PTC*, cat. no. 12, p. 119, sixth line from the end of the inscription.

Chang Ta-ch'ien's outer label (*actual size*).

XIX ARTIST UNKNOWN

Modern copy of Tao-chi's
Searching for Plum Blossoms: Poems and Painting

The Art Museum, Princeton University (68-174).

Handscroll. Ink and light color on paper. 30.5 x 205.0 cm.
(There is a join after the tenth line of the inscription.)

PROBABLE DATE OF EXECUTION: ca. 1950.

FORGED SIGNATURE OF TAO-CHI: Ch'ing-hsiang Ta-ti-tzu, Chi.

FORGED SEALS OF TAO-CHI: *K'u-kua ho-shang* (relief, tall rectangle) and *Hsia-tsun-che, Chi* (intaglio, tall rectangle) before inscription; *Shih Yüan-chi yin* (intaglio, square), *Ch'ing-hsiang* (intaglio, square), and *Ta-ti-tzu, Chi, li-weng t'u-shu* (intaglio, tall rectangle), all after inscription.

NO COLLECTORS' SEALS OR COLOPHONS

PROVENANCE: private collection, Taipei, Taiwan.

PUBLISHED: *Archives of Asian Art*, vol. 22 (1969–70), p. 85 (acquisitions list).

THIS SCROLL is a close copy (*lin-pen*) of *XVIII*. It bears the same title, date, measurements, and pictorial and calligraphic elements (with some minor departures in arrangement) as the original hand-scroll. It is evident after brief scrutiny that the brushwork of both calligraphy and image is not of the quality of Tao-chi's: the blossoms and stems are weak and listless, and the low hill has lost descriptive conviction. Moreover, five occurrences of errors and omissions in the text betray the copyist's hand (for detailed comparison, see below). The work fails to show the degree of internal integrity expected of an original, and even as a copy it indicates a hand both inept and inexperienced at forging.

It is probable that this is a modern forgery executed in the 1950's, some time before it entered the Taipei collection. Even though the

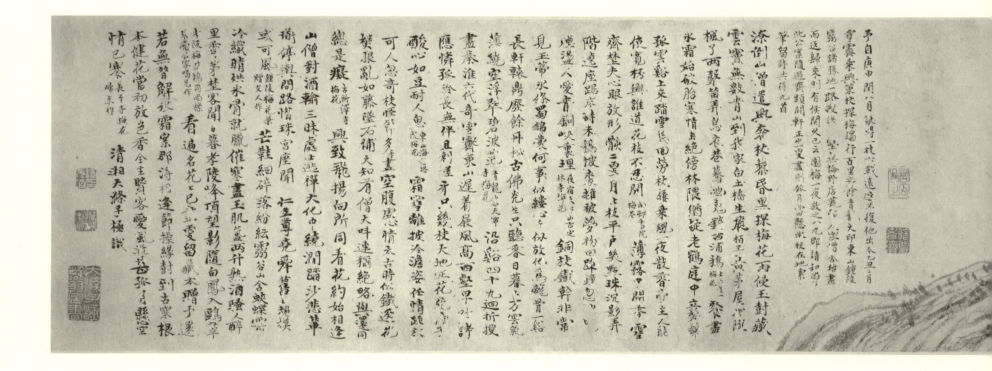

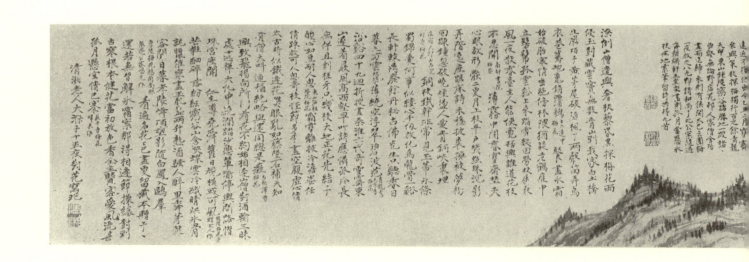

original Tao-chi scroll was once in the Chang Ta-ch'ien collection, the copy was not made by him: the technique is inferior and shows none of the sharp vigor associated with Chang's style, but most important, his aggressive temperament, which is reflected in his confident handling of the brush, is not apparent. Chang's copies usually exhibit better-cut seals, a higher degree of freedom in the forms, and more control and imagination in the execution. All five seals appearing on this scroll are complete fabrications; their prototypes are not found on any genuine Tao-chi work.

THIS VERSION is actually one of two known copies after the original handscroll *Searching for Plum Blossoms*. For convenience in the ensuing discussion, the three scrolls shall be referred to as follows: (1) Version A, the Sackler original (*XVIII*); (2) Version B[1] (fig. 1); (3) Version C, designated as cat. no. *XIX* here. We will deal first with the painting sections of the two scrolls, then the calligraphy. The primacy of Version A will be demonstrated, along with the likelihood that Version B is a late nineteenth-century free copy and

that Version C is, as the notation at the beginning of this entry indicates, a close modern copy.

Comparing Version B (fig. 1) with A and C, we find that the composition diverges from both and that, in general terms, its quality is closer to that of Version C. The prose introduction is in nine lines, as in Version A, but the poems have been copied into thirty-three rather than twenty-nine lines. The copyist could not resist adding a signature, and he did not merely enter Tao-chi's name but wrote "Ch'ing-hsiang lao-jen, Ta-ti-tzu, who faced the flowers on the eve of the fifteenth and wrote this."

Pictorially, Version B suffers from a lack of vitality in the whole, mainly because of weaknesses in both brushwork and structural concept (see the detail): the larger branches are not differentiated in shape and look like soft rubber hoses; the smaller twigs are also limp and the ink tones monotonous. The moss dots are repeated mechanically on the stalks and low hill.

In addition to quality, matters of format in the whole work and style in the calligraphy further alert us to the fact that Version B is a copy of A. In regard to format, the opening prose section should

1. Anonymous, nineteenth-century copy of Tao-chi's *Searching for Plum Blossoms: Poems and Painting*. Handscroll. Ink on paper. Collection unknown. [Version B.]

Branches and blossoms. [Version A.]

2. Wang Shih-shen (1686–1759), *Blossoming Plum.* Album leaf. Ink on paper. Moriya collection, Kyoto.

十年喜事三更夢斜日
欄干萬古心

栗林汪士慎

Branches and blossoms. [Version B.]

Branches and blossoms. [Version C.]

precede the poems as an allied introduction of circumstance; instead, in B two seals of the "artist" and a blank section of paper precede the poetry. Customarily, a seal stamped by the artist is an indication that he has finished the work. In Version B they are simply in the wrong place: the empty section between the introduction and poems wrongly implies that the poems were added separately, thereby disrupting the unity of thought explicitly claimed in the prose introduction. Significant errors which remain uncorrected in the text and the poor quality of the calligraphy further betray the ill-trained hand of the copyist.

Version B does not appear to be a modern forgery; the flabby brushwork, the particular hose-like configuration of the branches, and the mannered regularity of the moss dots presuppose the influence of a follower of Wang Shih-shen (1686–1759), one of the Eight Eccentrics of Yang-chou (fig. 2). The actual date of execution may fall in the nineteenth century.

As to Version C, our modern copy, it is a close imitation of Version A except for minor departures in format which, in this case, break up the integration of image and calligraphy so well established in the original and which reveal the forger's general tendency toward proliferation. These departures, in terms of format, are: the addition of a signature; the addition of five seals, as opposed to one in the original (two preceding the prose introduction and three following the poems); the reduction of the introduction from nine to six lines; the rendering of the poems in twenty-seven instead of twenty-nine lines; and the transfer of the whole block of calligraphy to the far left of the plum, separating image and writing into two distinct parts.

As to its quality, the most marked impression is that the brushwork fails to convey any sense of living energy. The branches lack internal tension and resemble limp ribbons blown in the wind (see the detail). Even the moss dots register the overall failure: instead of being applied with an elastic rebound of the brush as in Version A, they have been spiritlessly pressed onto the paper in careful accord with their position in the original.

The writing as well is poor. Clumsy, misshapen characters hardly succeed in emulating Tao-chi's ancient style (fig. 8). The imitation of Tao-chi's hand has involved an inevitable degree of simplification and distortion. Version C's failings, however, lie as much in the copyist's own limited literacy and calligraphic abilities as in the difficulties of imitation. Compared with the ideal symmetry of stroke

and configuration of the original, the characters from C look amateurish (figs. 5–9); the individual strokes grow excessively thick and thin and are compressed in wobbly shapes. They hardly qualify as independent brush writing and bear little resemblance to Tao-chi's model.

Some objective evidence in the form of errors and omissions in the calligraphic text further clarifies both Versions B and C and their position in this sequence of original and replicas. The following examples are errors and omissions which show that B and C were copied from A. (References to lines and characters are to the original text of each version; the illustrated figures extract these out of context, sometimes combining lines for continuity.)

First of all, there are two mistakes peculiar to the text of Version B (the text lines are the same as Version A); they are shown in figs. 3 and 4, respectively:

3. In Version A the prose introduction, line 3, characters 5ff., reads in part: "Tu-hsing pai-li-chih-yü" ("alone I have traveled more than a hundred miles"); in Version B li ("miles") has been omitted, so that the line makes no sense.

4. In Version B the second character (in the Version B text, line 4, the next to last character) is 蹝. No such character exists in any dictionary, but from the original A we can see how the B copyist made this mistake: he first transcribed the "foot" radical 足 from the preceding character lu 路 ("road"; Version A, line 4, character 13) and then accidentally omitted the right-hand part of lu and instead skipped down to copy the right-hand part of the next character, sou 搜 ("to seek"). In this way a strange hybrid was created.

The following mistakes (see figs. 5–9) are, for the most part, common to B and C:

5. In the prose introduction of Version A the character keng ("night watch"; line 8, character 6) is written in archaic clerical style, 庚. The copyist of Version B was unfamiliar with this older structure and in transcribing the character left out two strokes, making it unrecognizable. The copyist of Version C also made the same error.

6. In Version A at the end of line 17 there is a small character nien 季 ("year," written also in clerical script) which Tao-chi added when he reread the poem and noticed that he had omitted that word (the line should read "marvelous branches and strange knots ex-

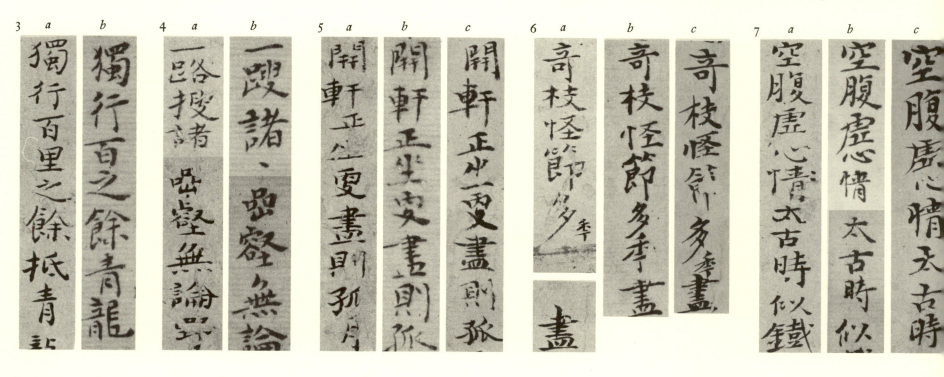

3   a   b   4   a   b   5   a   b   c   6   a   b   c   7   a   b   c

hausted for many years"); the darker ink and the fact that it is set off to one side to fit into the margin tells us this. In Version C (line 16, character 9) the omitted character has been transcribed in the same ink value as the characters before and after it and has been ambiguously placed, neither fully incorporated into the line nor honestly written to the side, showing that it was copied after Version A. Version B has fully incorporated the *nien*, proving that it was also copied from A, but that the copyist understood the emendation.

7. In Version A the character *ch'ing* 情 ("feelings"; line 18, character 6) has two small dots beside it, signifying that it is an "extra" character and should be omitted; instead of blackening it out, Tao-chi followed the custom of simply placing two dots beside it. The knowing reader will simply skip that character. Hence the line should read "K'ung-fu hsü-hsin t'ai-ku-shih" ("with an empty stomach and a vacant heart—the times are too old"). In Versions B and C (line 16, characters 11 ff.) the copyists did not understand the significance of the dots and simply omitted them. As a result the line has an extra character, making the remaining seven-character structure and rhyme scheme meaningless.

8. Version A of the poems, line 20, reads "K'an-hua pu-yüeh shih-hsiang-feng" ("to see the flowers, you must not plan to meet them"); Version C (line 8, characters 11 ff.) has omitted the *pu* negative, making the rest of the poem meaningless. Version B has not made this omission.

9. In Version A the last character of line 24 begins "Shih-li hsiang-mao yeh-k'o-wen" ("ten miles of fragrant reeds—smelled by the rustic traveler"); in both Versions B and C *shih* 十 ("ten") has been omitted, again disrupting the remaining structure and rhyme scheme of the poem.

These errors and omissions and their occasional independent occurrence in B or C testify that those versions were based directly on Version A. They also show the low level of literacy and calligraphic training of the copyists, who, moreover, were not too adept at making forgeries.

In making close copies of this kind, several difficulties of a mostly technical nature face the copyist: he must retain the original composition and ink values, while foreseeing and controlling the complexities of the design, the over- and underlapping spaces and lines of the branches and flowers. The matching of his energy and brush power to that of the original is most difficult and goes beyond mere technique.

In contrast, the painter in the process of putting down an original idea is concerned mainly with the problem of expression and the realization of the visualized idea. However vague or fleeting that idea, the technical details of its execution are a part of the total creative act, and any "accidents," whether caused by materials or moods, become incorporated into the balance of the whole composition. Every such change functions positively in the artist's subsequent movements because he, as part of his artistic experience, has learned to anticipate the limitations and potentials of his medium and responds with his entire aesthetic judgment to every stroke and its placement on the picture surface.

On the copyist's part, any accidental departures from the model have also to be accounted for in the succeeding steps, but in the hands of someone of limited abilities and imagination, the process tends to take on the aspect of a malignant growth: all alterations from the model function negatively and undermine the copyist's primary intention—to make a close copy. In the hands of an artist whose training and aesthetic judgment match that of his model, however, the inevitable changes which take place are creative in a true sense (see, for example, *XXVII*, Tao-Chi's copy after a presumable Shen Chou original). Any alterations, incidentally, may provide clues to the copyist's own personal style, which during the transference process he automatically attempts to suppress.

Generally speaking, in judging the quality of brushwork, one responds initially to a certain level of "tension" maintained throughout. This tension is a combination of different complex factors, but if the artist has attained any degree of excellence, our response to the energy infused into the brushlines is decidedly a kinesthetic one. We may not be conscious of its effects on our muscle tone, but the ultimate result is a heightening of one's psychic perceptions—the sense of visual delight in a work of art. The degree to which this energy is carried through on all levels in a work, both pictorial and calligraphic, is related to the artist's temperament and constitutes another factor in the recognition of a particular stylistic "hand."

NOTES

1. Published in Hashimoto Kansetsu, *Sekitō*, pl. 11, and in *T'ai-shan ts'an-shih-lou ts'ang-hua*, pt. 3.

8   a   b   9   a   b   c

3–9. *Searching for Plum Blossoms*, enlarged details of calligraphy: Version A, Tao-chi original; Version B, nineteenth-century copy; Version C, modern copy.

XX TAO-CHI (1641–ca. 1710)

Flowers and Figures *(Jen-wu hua-hui ts'e)*

The Art Museum, Princeton University (67-16).

Album of eight leaves, each with colophon on facing leaf.
Ink and occasional color on paper. 23.2 x 17.8 cm.

UNDATED: dated colophon facing leaf C, summer, 1695 (*i-hai, hsia-yüeh*); probably executed shortly before 1695 (see discussion at end of entry).

SIGNATURE OF THE ARTIST: on each leaf except leaf A.

INSCRIPTION BY THE ARTIST: on each leaf except leaf A.

SEALS OF THE ARTIST (on each leaf, seven in all):
K'u-kua (intaglio, tall rectangle; *PTC*, cat. no. 43, not listed) leaves A and G.
Ch'ing-hsiang Shih-t'ao (intaglio, tall rectangle; *PTC*, cat. no. 22, not listed) leaf B.
Shih Yüan-chi yin (intaglio, square; *PTC*, cat. no. 74, not listed) leaves C and F.
K'u-kua ho-shang (intaglio, square; *PTC*, cat. no. 45, not listed) leaf D.
Lao-t'ao (intaglio, tall rectangle; *PTC*, cat. no. 50, not listed) leaf E.
Yüan-chi (intaglio, square with incised border; *PTC*, cat. no. 105, not listed) leaf E.
Yüan-chi (intaglio, square without border; impression damaged, but appears close to *PTC*, cat. no. 103, not listed) leaf H.

COLOPHON WRITERS (five on eight leaves): Huang Po-shan, on leaves AA and FF; (?) Tsu-ming, on leaf BB; Wu Su-kung, on leaves CC and HH; Wang Sui-yü, on leaf DD; Li Kuo-sung, on leaf GG.

COLLECTORS' SEALS (identified on each leaf):
Huang Yen-ssu (fl. ca. 1690–1720?), three seals, painting leaf G and colophon leaf EE.
Chang Shan-tzu (Tse, 1883–1940), four seals, painting leaves A, B, C, and E only.
Chang Ta-ch'ien (Yüan, born 1899), nineteen seals, all leaves, both painting and colophon, except painting leaf C.
Lu Nan-shih (unidentified), one seal, colophon leaf GG only.

CONDITION: good, but there is minor wormhole damage to all leaves, especially painting leaf H and colophon leaf DD, where a few characters of the inscriptions have been partially obliterated; these are indicated on the individual leaves.

PROVENANCE: Ta-feng-t'ang collection.

PUBLISHED: *Ta-ti-tzu t'i-hua-shih-pa*, 3/66–69; *Ta-feng-t'ang ming-chi*, vol. 2, pls. 16–23 (illustrated); *Shih-t'ao hua-chi*, pl. 66 (leaf E illustrated); Wen Fong, "The Problem of Forgeries in Chinese Painting," fig. 25 (leaf E illustrated); Pierre Ryckmans, "Les 'Propos sur la Peinture' de Shi Tao," p. 150 (leaf E illustrated); Lin Yu-tang, *The Chinese Theory of Art*, fig. 20 (leaf E illustrated); *Record of the Art Museum, Princeton University*, vol. 27, no. 1 (1968), p. 35 (acquisitions list, leaf E illustrated); *Archives of Asian Art*, vol. 22 (1968–69), p. 134 (acquisitions list); Wen Fong, "A Chinese Album and Its Copy," pp. 74–78 (leaves A and E illustrated); *The Selected Painting and Calligraphy of Shih-t'ao*, vol. 6, pl. 111 (illustrated).

OTHER VERSIONS: a contemporary line-for-line replica, also in the Sackler collection (*XXI*).

THIS ALBUM was exhibited at length in the Princeton Art Museum galleries and was well received by both students and admirers of Chinese painting. Its appeal was partly based on its simplicity of presentation and wide variety of subject matter (orchid, bamboo, cockscomb, hibiscus, portrait figure, children, banana plant, and lotus) and partly on the interest stimulated by the display of a line-for-line copy, also in the Sackler collection (see *XXI*). With an exact replica available for direct study, the student of Chinese painting was introduced to some of the challenging stylistic problems in the field.

These leaves represent Tao-chi in a period of peak performance, ca. 1695, when his technique and conception were in perfect accord. They reveal his range and mastery of these minor genres and exhibit a certain touching and exhilarating lyric expression which he relinquished soon after the early 1700's, but which is unequaled here and in numerous other works from this period.

Leaf A: "Orchid and Plum"

Ink on paper.
UNSIGNED
SEAL OF THE ARTIST: *K'u-kua* (intaglio, tall rectangle) right edge of painting.
COLLECTORS' SEALS:
Chang Shan-tzu, *Tse* (relief, small square) lower right corner of painting.
Chang Ta-ch'ien, *Ta-feng-t'ang Chien-chiang, K'un-ts'an, Hsüeh-ko, K'u-kua mo-yüan* (relief, tall rectangle) on painting and *Chang Yüan* (intaglio, square) lower left corner of colophon leaf.
CONDITION: a small oval wormhole at upper edge, center of painting, and wormholes on colophon leaf slightly mar three characters.

A spray of orchid (*Cymbidium*) complemented by an angular branch of flowering plum (*Prunus mume*) fans outward from the right edge of the picture frame. Richly varied ink tonalities and a constantly twisting and turning brush lend a dimensional quality to the strokes and invest them with descriptive power. The energy charging the strokes extends to the tip of each leaf and petal, so that the forms seem to hover in space with a palpable resilience, making the blank parts of the paper come alive. The subtle gradations of ink suggest the weight, opacity, transparency, and movement of the orchid image. These qualities have been achieved by a control of the brush which reflects the varying pressure and rhythmic pace instinctive to the artist and his conception of the form. Thus the suffusing values of ink tell us about the painting process itself and the sequence in which the artist realized his form.

In the copy the artist has succeeded in grasping all the details of the composition, but, on a more demanding level, he has failed to capture that feeling of resilience and the subtle intermixing of wet and dry tonalities which lend such a semblance of life to the Tao-chi original. In making a close imitation, he was restrained by the composition of his model, and therefore forfeited much of the potential spontaneity and projection of his own visualization of the subject. In a copy of a painting executed in brush and ink, the interaction of the dry and wet washes with the paper or silk constitutes an integral part of the total visualization. Here we see how the tonal richness and soft blurring of ink of the orchid in the original are sadly impoverished in the copy.

In the rendering of the plum, the copyist has failed to distinguish between the textures of orchid leaf and plum branch, producing only a flat overlap of lines. The wash areas around the plum, which in the original are pale and soft to bring out the whiteness of the petals, show a careless sharp edge in the copy. Further evidence of the primacy of *XX* over *XXI* can be seen in a final detail: in *XX* the uppermost right plum blossom has been damaged by a small vertical wormhole; in *XXI* this hole has been incorporated as a blank space. Comparison with the orchids in the Fong *Small Album* and in the 1696 *Sketches of Calligraphy and Painting by Ch'ing-hsiang* (fig. 1) will confirm Tao-chi's hand in the pictorial arrangement and especially the handling of ink.

THE FACING LEAF (designated AA) bears a four-line eulogy (*tsan*) in six-character meter written in "running" script:

> *With the inner strength to withstand seasonal cold,*
> *Fragrant even without anyone to appreciate them:*
> *The two (plum and orchid) are fitting complements*
> *To be placed together in the hall of the Superior Gentleman.*

> [Signed:] Written and inscribed by Po-shan.
> [Seals:] *Po-shan* (relief, square)
> and *Huang-sheng chih-yin* (alternating intaglio, relief, square).

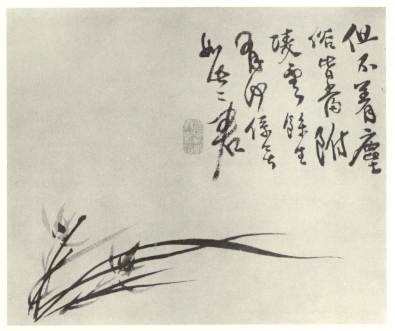

1. Tao-chi, *Sketches of Calligraphy and Painting by Ch'ing-hsiang*, dated 1696, detail of orchid. Handscroll. Ink on paper. Palace Museum, Peking.

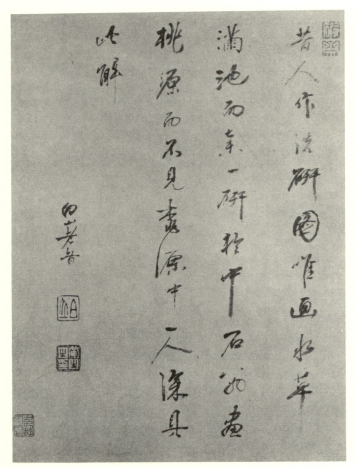

2. Huang Po-shan, colophon to leaf 1 of Tao-chi's album of twelve leaves depicting the scenery of Huang-shan, Sumitomo collection. Huang's calligraphy, signature, and seals are the same as those on *XX–AA*.

The writer did not sign his full name, but his surname appears in the first character of the second seal, Huang. Mr. Huang evidently inscribed the album three times (see leaves EE and FF), but each leaf is signed differently. By means of this second seal, which appears on leaf FF, and the identification of his calligraphy on leaf EE, we can link the three colophons to the same writer, Huang Po-shan (compare fig. 2 with *XX–AA*).

Leaf B: *"Bamboo"*

Ink on paper.
SIGNATURE OF THE ARTIST: Chi.
SEAL OF THE ARTIST: *Ch'ing-hsiang Shih-t'ao* (intaglio, tall rectangle).
COLLECTORS' SEALS:

Chang Ta-ch'ien, *Ta-ch'ien hao-meng* (relief, tall rectangle) on painting and *Chang Yüan chih-yin* (half-intaglio, half-relief) lower left corner of colophon.
Chang Shan-tzu, *Chang Tse* (intaglio, square) lower left corner of painting.
CONDITION: wormhole damage, mainly on colophon leaf, partly obliterates inscriber's seal in upper right corner and three characters of colophon in lower right corner.

Two dominant values of ink—pale wash for a single stalk and twigs and dark ink for a few leaves—combine to form a spare composition. Within this simplicity the leaves seem to create tensions which leave none of the spaces devoid of life. The comment that there are "leaves in eight directions" (*pa-mien ch'u-yeh*)[1] is quite apt here.

This leaf may be considered the most successful of the copyist's album and was most consistently mistaken for the original in student exercises. The telling differences, however, lie beyond the composition, in the actual execution of the stalks and leaves. In *XX* the tip of the brush is firmly centered, penetrating the heart of the stalk and twigs. The leaves are "written," as one would the ancient character *ko*: 个 . The movement and strength of the brush are directed from the arm and shoulder, with the pressure released gradually, allowing the hairs of the brush to gather together and the energy to carry through to the point of the leaf. The strokes produced with this centered point (*chung-feng*) are round and descriptive. In *XXI*, the brushtip has a tendency to slant to one side, producing a flat contour with one edge sharp and one edge wavering. This brush habit is characteristic of the copyist throughout this album, and here, combined with a too quick movement of the wrist, it has produced leaves with conspicuously ragged tips. Comparison with the section of bamboo from the Fong *Small Album*, as well as the works shown in *XXIX*, will help to confirm Tao-chi's hand in the details of execution, and also further pinpoint the deficiencies of the copy.

In addition to the bamboo leaves, the round brushstroke appears in the small twigs and the calligraphy of Tao-chi's five-character inscription. As in seal script, each stroke usually begins with a reverse motion, "hiding the tip," thus lending a rounded "head" to the horizontal strokes of the characters and to the small twigs. The copyist's hand undergoes a similar motion, but the tip is far from "hidden." Rather, his personal habit of slanting the brush overrides the upright brush style which he is trying to mimic, and he creates an exaggerated, unnatural line.

The inscription "kao hu Yü-k'o" ("loudly calling Yü-k'o") refers to the Northern Sung master of ink bamboo Wen T'ung (*hao* Yü-k'o, 1018–1079). Tao-chi is probably expressing satisfaction with his work by saying, "Ah, doesn't this bamboo recall Wen T'ung?" or perhaps "Say there, Wen T'ung, how do you like this bamboo of mine?"

THE COLOPHON by an unidentified writer, Tsu-ming (his surname is not known), transcribes a couplet in seven-character meter. The couplet was originally composed by the Ming painter, poet, and playwright Hsü Wei (1521–1593). The script is "fluent regular" (*hsing-k'ai*):

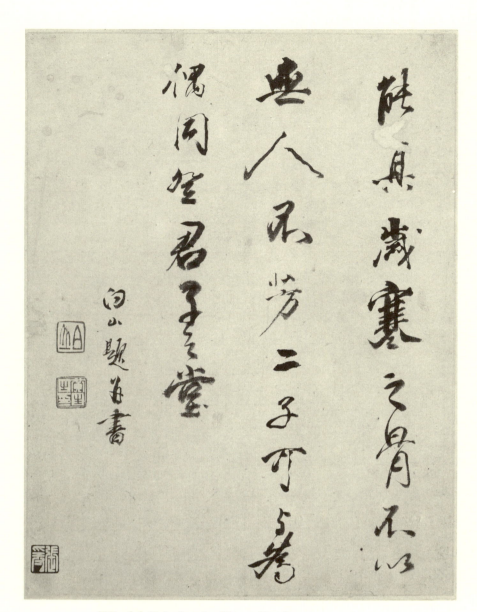

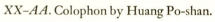
XX–AA. Colophon by Huang Po-shan.

Leaf A, "Orchid and Plum":
(*above*) Tao-chi original; (*below*) Li Jui-ch'i copy.

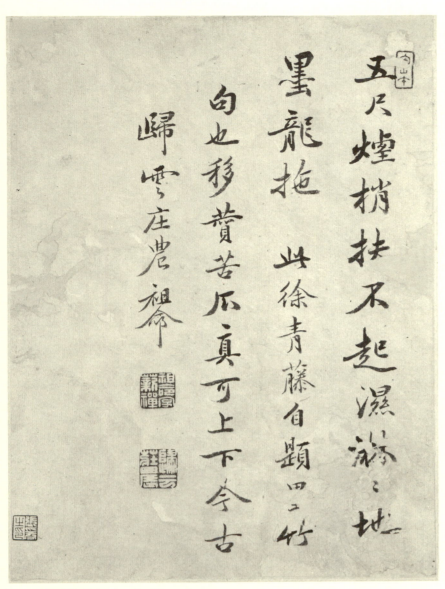

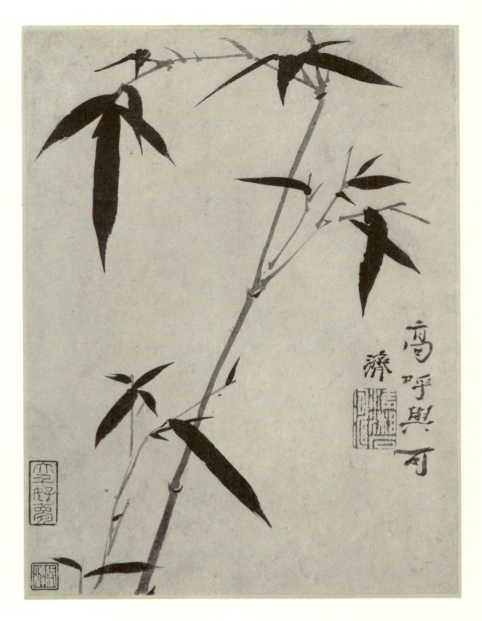

XX–BB. Colophon by Tsu-ming.

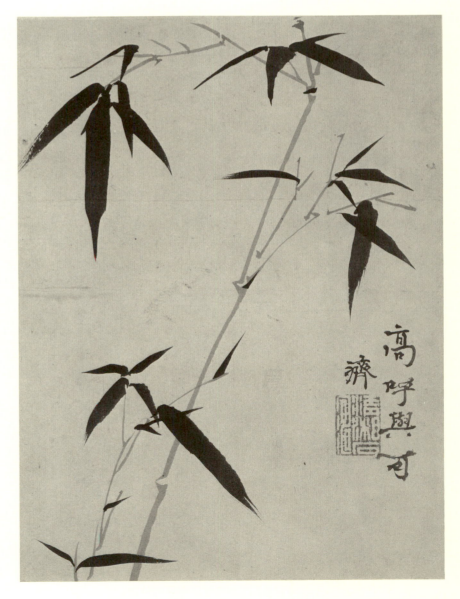

Leaf B, "Bamboo":
(*above*) Tao-chi original; (*below*) Li Jui-ch'i copy.

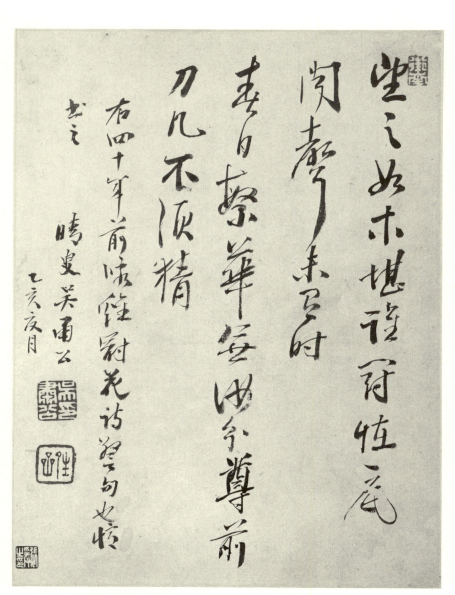

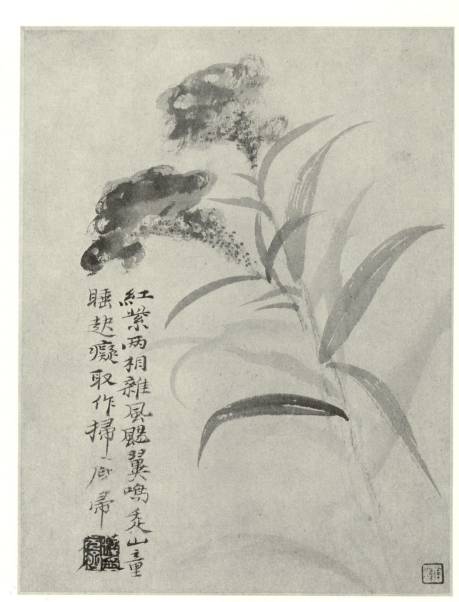

XX–CC. Colophon by Wu Su-kung, dated summer, 1695.

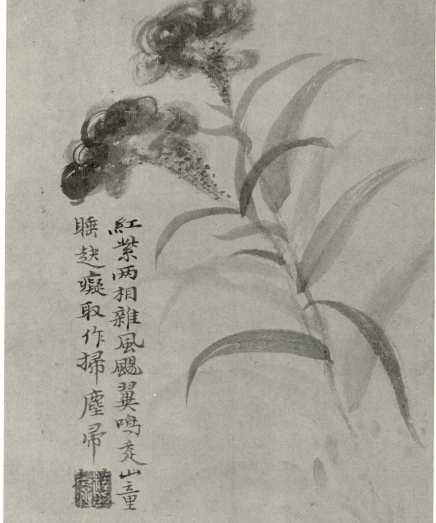

Leaf C, "Cockscomb":
(*above*) Tao-chi original; (*below*) Li Jui-ch'i copy.

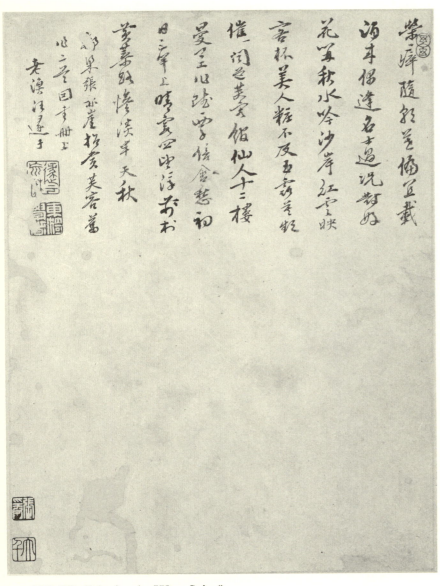

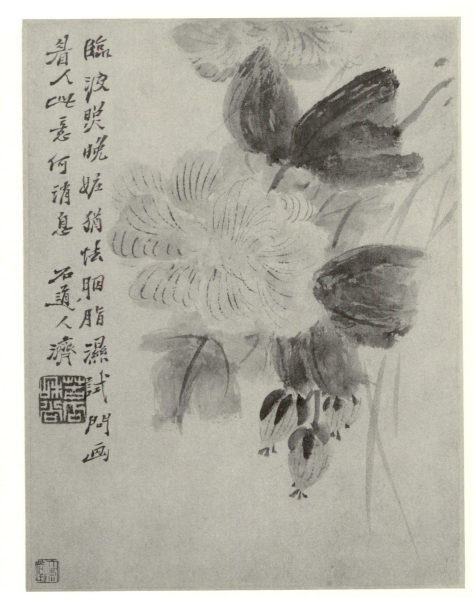

XX–DD. Colophon by Wang Sui-yü.

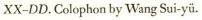

Leaf D, "Hibiscus":
(*above*) Tao-chi original; (*below*) Li Jui-ch'i copy.

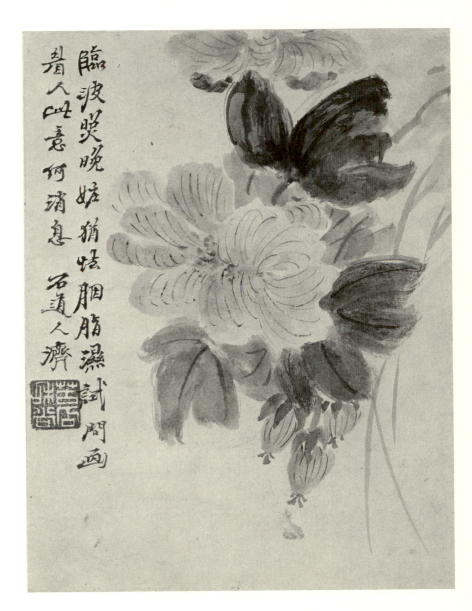

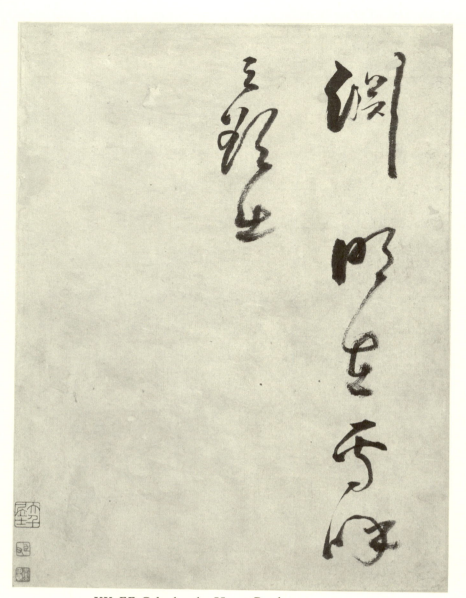

XX–EE. Colophon by Huang Po-shan.

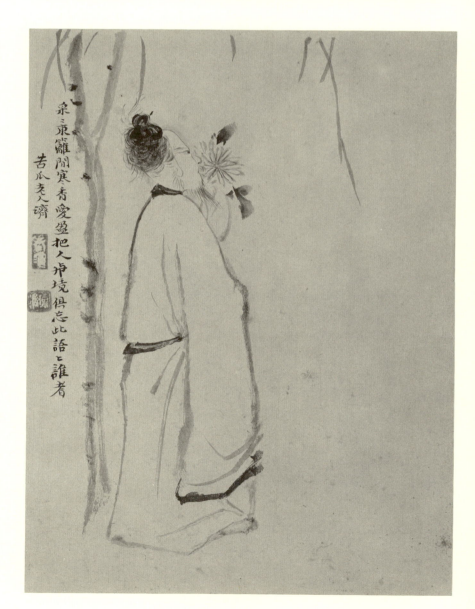

Leaf E, "Portrait of T'ao Yüan-ming":
(*above*) Tao-chi original; (*below*) Li Jui-ch'i copy.

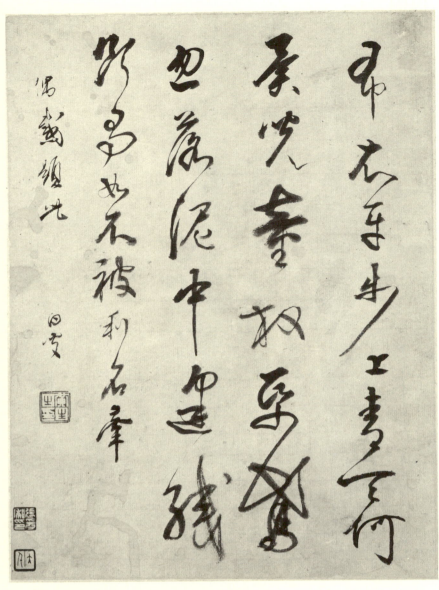

XX–FF. Colophon by Huang Po-shan.

Leaf F, "Two Children Flying a Kite":
(*above*) Tao-chi original; (*below*) Li Jui-ch'i copy.

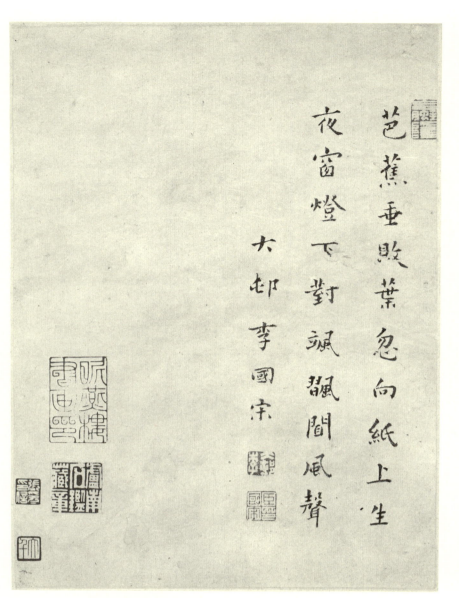

芭蕉垂敗葉忽向紙上生
夜窗燈下對颯颯聞風聲
大邨李國宋

XX–GG. Colophon by Li Kuo-sung.

Leaf G, "Banana Leaves and Pine":
(*above*) Tao-chi original; (*below*) Li Jui-ch'i copy.

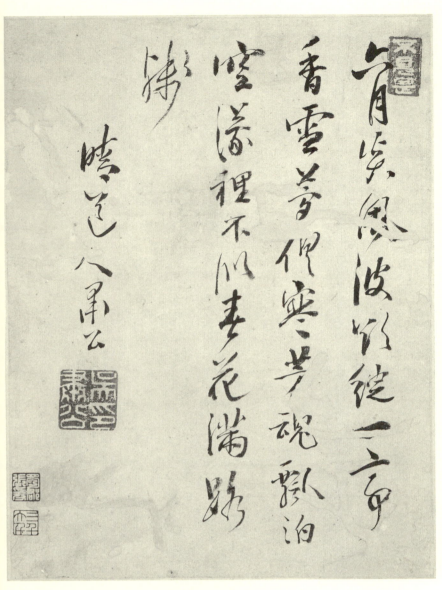

XX–HH. Colophon by Wu Su-kung.

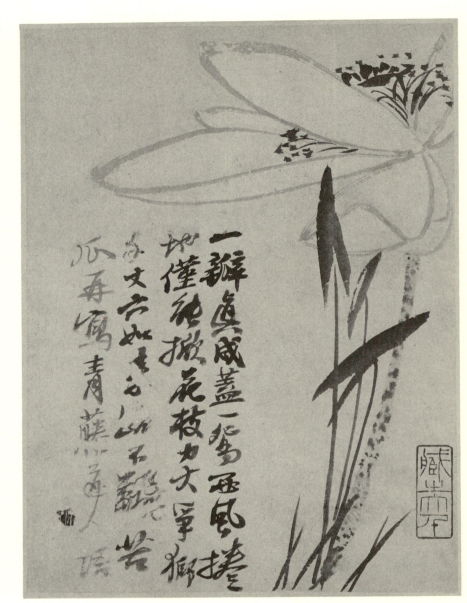

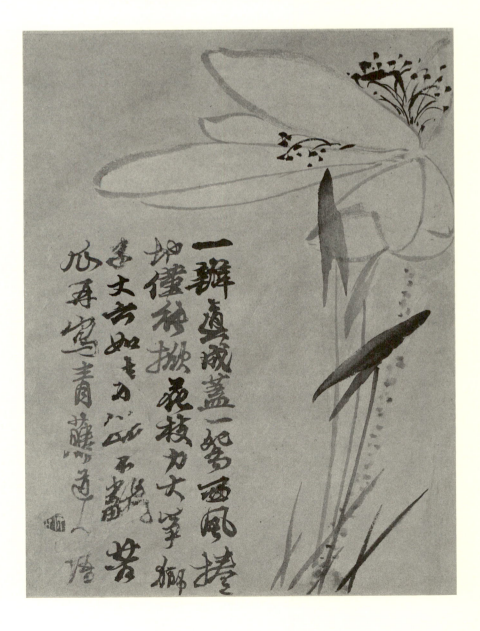

Leaf H, "Lotus":
(*above*) Tao-chi original; (*below*) Li Jui-ch'i copy.

Five feet of bamboo tips in mist can't be raised,
Dripping wet they writhe like an ink dragon.

This verse was a self-inscription on an ink bamboo painting by Hsü Ch'ing-t'eng [Wei]. I have borrowed it to praise K'u-kua [Tao-chi]. [These two painters] were truly the outstanding masters of the past and present. [Signed:] Kuei-yün chuang-nung, Tsu-ming [the farmer of the hamlet of the returning cloud]. [Seals:] (illegible)-*wu* (relief, tall rectangle) before colophon, *Tsu-ming tzu Hsin-ch'an* (intaglio, square) and *Kuei-yün chuang-nung* (intaglio, square) after signature.

Leaf C: *"Cockscomb"* (*Chi-kuan-hua*)

Ink on paper.
SIGNATURE OF THE ARTIST: K'u-kua lao-jen.
SEAL OF THE ARTIST: *Shih Yüan-chi yin* (intaglio, square).
COLLECTORS' SEALS:
Chang Shan-tzu, *Chang Tse* (relief, square) lower right corner of painting.
Chang Ta-ch'ien, *Chang Yüan chih-yin* (intaglio, square) lower left corner of colophon leaf.
CONDITION: wormhole partially obliterates second to last character of the inscription to the painting.

Two ruffled cockscombs toss their heads, their leaves waving in the breeze like plumage. The stamens are engagingly textured in dots of ink. The ink tones are graded in transparency and lead the eye upward from leaf to flower. A genuine freedom is displayed in the rendering of the cockscombs: their heads are produced with the flat of the brush in a swirling motion, first pale wash, then medium ink following quickly. The effective degree of blotting is achieved by "accidental design." The brush seems unimpeded by the knowledge of any technical precedent to limit its description of the form.

The most disturbing shortcomings of the copy are a confusion in the arrangement of the leaves and in the heavy grading of the ink tones, which are too close in value to the flowers and tend to compete with them. As to the calligraphy, the copy has succeeded in imitating the Ni Tsan style (or variation thereof) of *XX*, but, like the rendering of the leaves, the individual strokes lie on the surface of the paper, and the turns and hooks are too heavy and exaggerated.

Tao-chi has written a little quatrain in five-character meter in two lines which suggests the humor implied in the forms of the cockscombs:

Scarlet and purple blend in confusion
A gust of wind sets them flapping, crowing and scurrying,
A country boy rising muddle-headed from sleep
Takes one as his dustbroom to sweep.

Tao-chi's wonderfully free handling of ink in this leaf can be compared with the chrysanthemum leaf from the Fong *Small Album*. Cockscomb is one of Tao-chi's rarer subjects; lotus, plum, narcissus, and chrysanthemum were his most frequent. His rendering here is thus of a distinctly inventive nature, employing neither flat areas of wash nor linear outline. He lends texture and volume to the form by using the wash in a "flying-white" (*fei-pai*) manner, leaving areas of paper exposed. In this case he has improvised the means to characterize the form.

WU SU-KUNG (compare CC and fig. 3) wrote an equally amusing quatrain in seven-character meter executed in "running" script on the leaf facing this painting. Of the five writers who inscribed the eight leaves, only Wu left a date, 1695, which helps to establish the dating of Tao-chi's execution of the album. Wu's ode consists of a pun on the meaning of "cockscomb," in Chinese *chi-kuan*, which translates as "chicken's cap":

You look so wooden—who'd dare wear you as a cap?
It's no wonder I've never heard you crow!
In spring the thick blossoms don't include you.
With a wine cup or on the chopping block—it would
never occur to me that you'd be there!

This surprising verse was an ode to a cockscomb which I composed forty years ago. I was reminded of it [when I saw this leaf of Tao-chi's], so I write it here.

[Signed:] Ch'ing-sou, Wu Su-kung, in a summer month of the year 1695 (*i-hai, hsia-yüeh*). [Seals:] *Wu Su-kung-yin* (intaglio, square) and *Ch'ing-yen* (relief, square) after signature, *Hsien-nan* (intaglio, tall rectangle) before colophon.

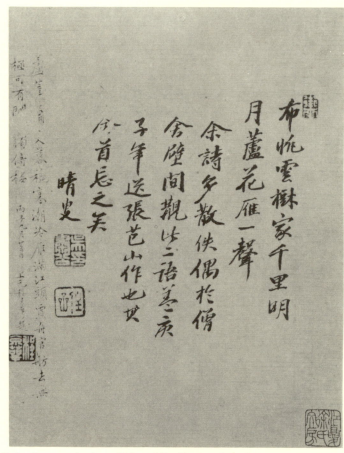

3. Colophons to leaf 5 of Tao-chi's album of twelve leaves depicting the scenery of Huang-shan, Sumitomo collection: (*left*) colophon dated 1696 by Ch'eng Ching-e; (*right*) colophon by Wu Su-kung. The writer, Wu Su-kung, and his two seals are the same as those on *XX–CC*.

Leaf D: *"Hibiscus"*

Ink and color on paper.
SIGNATURE OF THE ARTIST: Shih tao-jen, Chi.
SEAL OF THE ARTIST: *K'u-kua ho-shang* (intaglio, square).
COLLECTOR'S SEALS: Chang Ta-ch'ien, *Ta-feng-t'ang* (relief, square) lower left corner of painting, *Chang Yüan* (intaglio, square) and *Ta-ch'ien* (relief, square) lower left corner of colophon leaf.
CONDITION: there is minor wormhole damage on painting; on colophon leaf first character of third line from end and part of inscriber's seal are obliterated; the seal is still legible, however.

The "untrammeled" brushwork suggested in the preceding leaf is fully expressed in this hibiscus. With liberty of form, however, painterly discipline is not forfeited; rather, color, line, and wash function even more significantly.

The flaring petals of the hibiscus are first stained in with pale transparent pink in the "boneless method" (*mo-ku*) of description by color wash without ink outline. Then, while the wash is still moist, a partly dry brush slowly delineates the direction of the petals in space, at the same time suggesting softness and elasticity. The leaves are executed in the opposite manner: ink is applied first with the flat of a coarse brush in vigorous strokes; then generous layers of green wash over the ink. The buds and their velvety sepals are delineated by similar methods in ink first, then color, thus allowing the ink to unify and enrich the picture surface.

In this leaf Tao-chi illustrates his conception of color wash as a structural entity. Seldom in his works is the color applied in flat layers unless strongly bounded by ink lines. Rather, the colors are

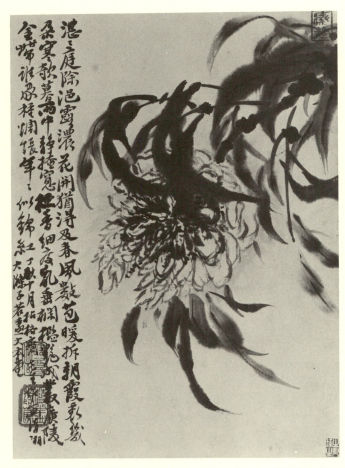

4. Tao-chi, *Ting-ch'iu Album of Flowers*, dated 1707, "White Peony." Private collection, United States.

applied to suggest curving spatial forms, in conjunction with or reinforced by ink wash or line. The fully developed effects of wash, whether color or ink, can be seen in his late 1707 *Ting-ch'iu Album of Flowers*;[2] leaf A (fig. 4), "White Peony," shows a similar drooping flower in three-quarter view balanced by a vertically placed inscription at the left. In general, one finds Tao-chi's hibiscus more frequently drawn with contour lines;[3] hence this leaf is unusual for its technique. The resultant delicacy is fittingly suggested by the color areas and the suffused ink lines.

A quatrain in five-character meter complements the sensuous tone and coloring of the painting and fills the left edge of the leaf:

> She leans over to gaze at her evening makeup
> reflected in the waves

> And fears that her rouge will get wet.
> Please ask that intimate one who paints her eyebrows
> What's this all about?

> [Seal:] *K'u-kua ho-shang* (intaglio, square).

The fragile beauty of the hibiscus is also reflected in the script style Tao-chi chose. It is a "tremulous" (*chan-pi*) and elongated version of the "fluent regular" script he used often in his earlier years (e.g., the 1673 eight-leaf album inscriptions). Here the undulating quality of the line is more expressive and reveals not only his interest in Huang T'ing-chien's brush idiom, but also his maturity as a calligrapher. The slick quality of the line which pervaded his early style is completely absent here.

In the copy the color tones are harsher, and the petals and buds are rendered as flat entities. The parallel lines of the petals reveal the temperament of the copyist, for in place of the gentle sunburst of *XX*, the brushlines thicken impulsively without relation to the curvature of the petals. The brush moves too quickly across the color wash, producing dry, monotonous lines which fail to fuse moistly in Tao-chi's characteristic manner.

In the calligraphy, we see that the copyist has mistaken the personal eccentricity of form in the original as a license for distortion. For example, the eleventh character, *shih* ("to try"), is forced and exaggerated when compared to the original.

THIS DEPICTION of hibiscus elicited the longest encomiums. Wang Sui-yü inscribed two poems in five-character regulated meter. They are written in even, continuous lines of a modest "running" and "cursive" mixture and fill the entire upper half of the paper:

> Blooming and wilting with the dawn and dusk,
> It's fitting to bring along wine.
> Occasionally poet-scholars would visit me,
> Even more so to watch pretty flowers blossoming.
> Autumn waters murmur on the sandy banks,
> Rosy clouds are reflected in the guests' cups.
> The beautiful one can't finish her makeup in time,
> Jade dew [of autumn]—please don't hurry her!

The second poem begins fifth line from the right, second character:

> I have heard there is a twelve-story Hibiscus Hall
>   for immortals,
> That the poet Man-ch'ing [unidentified] excelled at fu
>   [rhymed prose],
> And that the beauty Hsi-tzu was full of sorrow.
> The sun was high in the sky [literally, "at the height
>   of three bamboo poles"],
> And looking on all sides, clear rosy clouds were
>   floating about.
> The road to the village ahead was covered with yellow leaves,
> And autumn sadness filled half the sky.

> These are two old poems which I composed when Mr. Chang I-yai of ( ) [paper damaged] -liang invited me to view hibiscus. Therefore I inscribe them here in this album. [Signed:] Lao-yü, Wang Sui-yü. [Seals:] *Yü-yü* (relief, double circle) before colophon, *Sui-yü huang* ( ) (relief, square, with one illegible character) and *Tung-i hsüeh-che* (intaglio, square) after signature.

Leaf E: *"Portrait of T'ao Yüan-ming"*

Ink and slight color on paper.
SIGNATURE OF THE ARTIST: K'u-kua lao-jen, Chi.
SEALS OF THE ARTIST: *Lao-t'ao* (intaglio, tall rectangle) and *Yüan-chi* (intaglio, square).

A figure in a long robe, placed to the far left of the composition beneath a few strands of willow, gazes upward. He clasps a bouquet of chrysanthemum to his nostrils, and his expression is half-intense, half-preoccupied, as if lost in the fragrance of the flowers. We recognize him as the poet T'ao Ch'ien (*hao* Yüan-ming, 365–427) by his attributes of chrysanthemum and willow tree. Tao-chi's inscription in two long lines echoes the verticals of the willow tree trunk. His poetic quatrain reads:

> *Picking [chrysanthemums] by the eastern hedge,*
> *Fond of a fistful of crisp fragrance.*
> *Man and place: both forgotten—*
> *To whom can I confide these words?*

His poem offers a variation on the well-known original of T'ao Yüan-ming:

> *Thatching a hut among men*
> *Yet without horse-and-cart noise*
> *I ask you, how can it be?*
> *A heart far away: the place naturally secluded.*
>
> *Picking chrysanthemums by an eastern hedge*
> *In the distance seeing the Southern Mountains*
> *Mountain air in the evening is good*
> *Flying birds together returning*
>
> *In this there's a true thought:*
> *About to explain: already forgotten words.*[4]

The artist has omitted the mountain, but its presence is suggested by the figure's raised head and upward glance, thus realizing the pictorial dimension of the original poem.

Tao-chi has first outlined the figure with a dry brush lightly dipped in pale ink, then added a layer of partly dry, dark ink to define the volume. The brush is dragged with heavy strokes, which make penetrating contact with the paper. This procedure successfully evokes the texture and weight of the fabric and even suggests the figure's potential movement. Volume in the head is achieved with the same carefree but masterful swirls of the brush as the "heads" in the cockscomb leaf.

Portraits of single figures are rare in Tao-chi's repertoire. This is one of his finest, and its success in capturing the stance, the psychological attitude, and the sense of physical presence of the subject (see the detail) bears comparison with the well-known Southern Sung portrait of Li Po[5] (fig. 5).

The tree trunk has been rendered with coarse brushstrokes dragged across the paper in the same penetrating and purposeful manner. One branch is painted in pale blue wash. With the addition of a few overhanging streamers, we have the final attribute of the "Gentleman of the Five Willows" (*Wu-liu hsien-sheng*)—an enchanting *mise en scène*. The minimal but suggestive execution of the willow leaves in rounded strokes could well challenge Chu Ta (1626–1725), a contemporary of Tao-chi's, who also made the minimum of form speak with the maximum of effect.

This leaf most taxed the abilities of the copyist. He has sacrificed the weight and substantiality of the figure in space in trying to achieve the textured "flying-white" effect of the original, so that his brush slides and slips across the paper. More significant, the head (see the detail) has lost the sense of psychological intensity and fails to relate organically to the neck and torso. These weaknesses in the handling are repeated in the willow tree, which looks like a few strings of loose hemp.

5. Liang K'ai, *Li Po Chanting a Poem.*
Hanging scroll. Ink on paper.
Tokyo National Museum.

Tao-chi original.

Li Jui-ch'i copy.

This pair of leaves aptly demonstrates the power of line to suggest mass, weight, and volume. The discrepancy in execution allows us to isolate what is most intrinsically the artist's contribution to specific form. The copy may be spotted most easily because of the representational immediacy associated with figures: we are able to "empathize" with the human subject and instinctively perceive the relationship of its body parts. Therefore we sense more acutely (than in the rendering of flowers or other non-human subjects) the failure of the copyist to achieve a purposeful organic unity in the form.

THE INSCRIPTION on the facing leaf, EE, consists of a succinct couplet in eight characters executed in an exuberant "cursive" (ts'ao):

> T'ao Yüan-ming is there—
> Call him and he'll step out!

The lines bear no signature, but the calligraphic style can be identified with the inscriber of leaves AA and FF, Huang Po-shan (hao Po-sou; see leaf AA).

Leaf F: "Two Children Flying a Kite"

Ink on paper.
SIGNATURE OF THE ARTIST: Hsiao-ch'eng-k'o, Chi.
SEAL OF THE ARTIST: Shih Yüan-chi yin (intaglio, square).
COLLECTOR'S SEALS: Chang Ta-ch'ien, Ta-ch'ien hao-meng (relief, tall rectangle) lower left corner of painting, Chang Yüan ssu-yin (intaglio, square) and Ta-ch'ien (relief, square) lower left corner of colophon leaf.

Two children romp on an arched bridge. The younger one dances in motion, while the older one clutches the string of his treasure—a butterfly kite with long streamers. The figures and bridge have again been executed in only two tones of ink, pale and charcoal black. The children's features, hair, and clothing are defined in summary fashion, reflecting the playful spirit of the picture.

Children are a rare subject in Tao-chi's works. This rendering is quite different from that of the charming but respectful image of T'ao Yüan-ming in the preceding leaf, but the working process of double lineation in two graded tones of ink is similar. In a descriptive sense, Tao-chi shows himself quite sensitive to the unity of form and content, adjusting technique and procedure to changes in meaning. The mood here, then, like the kite in flight, is jocular, buoyant:

> How I love the heart of these two children:
> A paper kite becomes an arena for play.
> Finding joy in a moment
> When have they ever planned ahead?

The poem betrays a feeling reflected in the pictorial style of this leaf.

When we turn to the little figures of the copyist's version, we are pleasantly surprised. The modest degree of success of XXI is attributable to the formal and technical brevity of the original, which lends itself more readily to copying. In addition, swiftness and lightness are qualities also found in the copyist's own working method and brush style.

As to the calligraphy of XX, the expressive gradation of ink values can also be found in Tao-chi's inscription to the large hanging scroll Waterfall at Mt. Lu. Here, however, the script is a mixture of his freehand and formal styles and reflects the casualness of the subject. In his version the copyist has again exaggerated the nuances of habit and personal style found in the original: the hooks and turns flail outward beyond the form, and the last downward stroke of the poem, chi ("to plan"), reveals the uneven line of the brush held in his characteristic slanted position.

THE WRITER of the colophon is Huang Po-shan, who also transcribed leaves AA and EE:

> The ordinary man can reach heaven in one easy step—
> How different is this from children flying a kite?
> Suddenly it falls into the mud with broken strings—
> It's better not to be attached to fame and fortune!

> Felt on occasion and inscribed here.
> [Signed:] Po-sou.
> [Seal:] Huang-sheng chih-yin
> (alternating intaglio, relief, square).

Leaf G: "Banana Leaves and Pine"

Ink on paper.
SIGNATURE OF THE ARTIST: Shih-t'ao.
SEAL OF THE ARTIST: K'u-kua (intaglio, tall rectangle).
COLLECTORS' SEALS:
Huang Yen-ssu, Yen-lü (relief and intaglio, a double seal of a small circle and a small square) upper right corner of painting.
Chang Ta-ch'ien, Chang Ta-ch'ien (relief, small square) lower left corner of painting; Ni-yen-lou shu-hua-yin (relief, tall large rectangle), Ta-ch'ien (relief, square), and Chang Yüan yin-hsin (intaglio, square), all lower left corner of colophon.
Lu Nan-shih (unidentified), Lu Nan-shih chien-ts'ang-chang (intaglio, large square) lower left corner of colophon.

This is the most "calligraphic" of the eight leaves in the album, in the sense that the strokes delineating the banana leaves are technically close to those of seal-script calligraphy. A brush with blunted tip is held firmly upright and is turned and twisted with subtle changes of pressure and direction, giving the individual strokes a round, three-dimensional quality akin to the effect of "an iron rod writing in the sand" (ju-chui hua-sha). Such an effect is also achieved in the willow strands of leaf E.

Pictorially, the calligraphic technique also functions to create a mood of both drama and intimacy which makes this leaf outstanding among Tao-chi's minor works. Again, the procedure of pale line followed by a darker ink contour functions like the plant's skeletal structure and helps to articulate more clearly the bending and folding of the leaves in space. Characteristic of Tao-chi is the strategic staining of the leaf surfaces with layers of pale wash to create the feeling of a complex, vibrant organism. Tao-chi himself considered the ink wash like a magic spell which could bring out the living qualities of the line. He says in the accompanying inscription:

> One disgusting parched worn-out brush!
> But add fragrant ink, and the luxuriant
>   shadows hover ...

The sense of both drama and intimacy is achieved by a compositional principle which one might call "depth enclosure." Foreground elements, such as the two banana palm leaves, are placed at the very front and are partially cut off by the frame. They enclose the space and achieve a repoussoir effect, throwing the eye into deep space. Elements beyond this immediate foreground are arranged so as to suggest recession or, as here, an undefined spatial depth.

In the copy the qualities which aided the artist's rendering of the children now act as a deterrent in transcribing this composition. The copyist has neglected the multi-layering of the ink lines, resulting in a loss of depth and weight in the forms, and he has omitted all but cursory wash from the pine and banana, leaving the forms flat and the whole work spiritless.

THIS LEAF IS ACCOMPANIED by a quatrain in five-character verse. The writer is Li Kuo-sung, and the script type is "regular":

Tattered leaves of the banana palm hang
And suddenly grow on paper.
Facing it by the window under the evening lamp
One can almost hear the wind rustling through.

[Signed:] Li Kuo-sung of Ta-ts'un.
[Seals:] *Luo-yin* (intaglio, tall rectangle) before colophon, *Ta-ts'un Li* (intaglio, square) and *Ch'en yin Kuo-sung Yin* (alternating intaglio, relief, square) after signature.

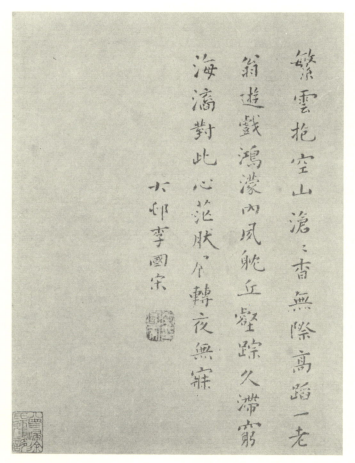

6. Li Kuo-sung, colophon to leaf 11 of Tao-chi's album of twelve leaves depicting the scenery of Huang-shan, Sumitomo collection. Li's calligraphy and signature are the same as those on XX–GG.

Leaf H: *"Lotus"*

Ink on paper.
SIGNATURE OF THE ARTIST: K'u-kua tsai-hsieh Ch'ing-t'eng tao-jen-shih.
SEAL OF THE ARTIST: *Yüan-chi.*
COLLECTOR'S SEALS: Chang Ta-ch'ien, *Ts'ang-chih Ta-ch'ien* (relief, tall rectangle) on painting, *Shu-chün Chang Yüan* (intaglio, square) and *San-ch'ien Ta-ch'ien* (relief, square) lower left corner of colophon leaf.
CONDITION: wormholes are visible on upper petal of lotus, third and fourth lines of inscription, and on Tao-chi's seal, where parts of the characters are obliterated but still legible.

This leaf announces the end of the album. With sweeping arcs of pale ink, petals are formed; with a few energetic dots and lines, stamens are added. The stem is executed in pale wash and then more dots are applied while the paper is still moist to create a mottled texture. The leaves of a trio of half-opened water plants shoot forth in the company of twin pairs of reeds which flank the group. Both leaves and reeds are drawn in velvety ink tones with rounded, seal-style strokes. A light staining of the whole ground accentuates the petals' whiteness and lends a sense of depth to the surrounding space.

The result is a fragrant water lotus, freshly emerged. Limited to only two tones of ink, a whole range is suggested, with every stroke expressing the vibrancy of the flower.

To the left, in four lines, Tao-chi has transcribed a quatrain in seven-character meter. He notes that the poem was originally composed by Hsü Wei (see colophon to leaf BB):

One petal is enough to cover one mandarin duck,
The west wind churning the ground can only lift it
a little.
The stem's great strength can struggle with a lion,
And the sixteen-foot Tathagata [ju-lai] cannot
kick it over.

Bitter-Melon [Tao-chi] again renders Ch'ing-t'eng tao-jen's [Hsü Wei's] words. [Seal:] *Yüan-chi* (intaglio, square).

Tao-chi's affinity with Hsü Wei was also commented upon by the colophon writer of leaf B. The fluency and power which characterize Tao-chi's lotus are equally evident in the calligraphy. He has employed his "freehand" (*hsing*) style to transcribe Hsü's eulogy. The solid block of writing formed also acts as a compositional balance to the strongly asymmetrical design. Hsü Wei himself often employed such structural principles in his works, aligning the pictorial elements at one side to embrace his inscription. Tao-chi repeats this principle in other works of similar subject matter, and he may have been inspired by Hsü in doing so.

In *XXI* the quality of the ink is most disappointing. The leaves and reeds have lost their lustrous feeling, and the lotus stem has been reduced to a string of dots. Although the background has been shaded in with pale ink, there is still insufficient contrast of values to suggest space effectively. Moreover, the wash is unevenly applied. The flower petals, which in the original spring forth with a sense of elasticity, are in the copy overcome by the momentum of the brushstroke and hence lose much of their descriptive effect. In the original, the two open petals are foreshortened, whereas the copyist has misunderstood the forms and connected the contours of the two petals, creating only a flat pattern.

WU SU-KUNG'S COLOPHON offers a sensuous quatrain in seven-character meter (compare HH with figs. 3 and 7):

So blazing the wind of summer (sixth month) that the pond waves
appear to crack,
One pavilion so full of snowy fragrance that all my dreams are cool.
The flowers' sweet spirit floats aimlessly in the airy mist....
How unlike spring flowers, which cover the path with their wilted
petals!

[Signed:] Ch'ing-tao-jen, Su-kung.
[Seals:] *Pu-chien-shih* (intaglio, tall rectangle) before colophon, *Wu Su-kung yin* (intaglio, square).

THE PAINTINGS themselves are undated, but the accompanying inscriptions, one of which contains a cyclical date, may offer a clue. The "summer of *i-hai*" found on leaf CC inscribed by Wu Su-kung has been interpreted as 1695 by Professor Fu Pao-shih. Unfortunately, Wu Su-kung's dates are not known. Fu states that he is a contemporary of Tao-chi, but declines to comment further;[6] however, the correctness of this 1695 date can be verified by other means.

Little is known about the other five colophon writers, but from the manner of inscription we may infer them to be contemporaries of Tao-chi. This assumption is strengthened by an album of Tao-chi's dedicated to Huang Yen-ssu (*hao* Yen-lü) in the Sumitomo collection[7] which bears accompanying inscriptions written by three of the same persons in our album: Wu Su-kung (figs. 3, 7), Huang Po-shan (fig. 2), and Li Kuo-sung (fig. 6). The calligraphy, signatures, and seals of the writers of these leaves compare favorably with the corresponding leaves by the same persons in the Sackler album. Moreover, leaf 5 of the Sumitomo album (with the colophon by Wu Su-kung [fig. 3]) also bears the dated 1696 inscription of another inscriber, Ch'eng Ching-e, who also inscribed leaf 3 of the same album. Thus this correspondence with the colophons of the Sumitomo album presents strong confirming evidence for the Sackler colophons and date.

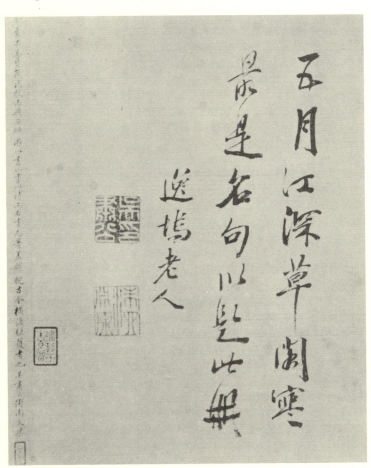

7. Wu Su-kung, colophon to leaf 9 of Tao-chi's album of twelve leaves depicting the scenery of Huang-shan, Sumitomo collection. Wu's calligraphy and intaglio seal are the same as those on *XX–HH*.

A second kind of evidence is that of the collectors' seals. Huang Yen-ssu was a fellow poet who accompanied Tao-chi on his wanderings to Mt. Huang. Tao-chi often chose Huang's poems as complements to his own paintings.[8] The tone and phraseology of the inscriptions in the Sumitomo album suggest that Tao-chi and Huang Yen-ssu were contemporaries and still living when the inscriptions were written. The link between these two persons and the albums is reinforced by the pair of small collector's seals (one round relief and one square intaglio, *Yen-lü*) found on leaf G of the Sackler album and leaf 5 of the Sumitomo album (fig. 8). Both seals belong to Huang Yen-ssu, and similar seals also appear on colophon leaf EE.

8. Seals of Huang Yen-ssu: (*left*) detail of *XX–GG*; (*right*) leaf 5 of Tao-chi's album of twelve leaves depicting the scenery of Huang-shan, Sumitomo collection.

We may infer from this evidence that the various inscribers of both the Sackler and Sumitomo albums were friends of Huang Yen-ssu (and possibly even of Tao-chi also) and had occasion to inscribe and impress their seals on both albums. If this assumption is correct, then the corresponding cyclical date falling before Tao-chi's death would be 1695, and the album would have been painted some time before the summer of that year.

NOTES

1. An observation by a Chinese critic of Tao-chi's *Bamboo and Orchid in the Wind*, in the Pao-wu-t'ang collection, New York (see *PTC*, cat. no. 25, p. 155), as reported by Richard Edwards in "Postscript to an Exhibition," p. 269.

2. In a private collection in the United States; cf. *PTC*, cat. no. 43, leaf A, p. 182.

3. E.g., the *Hibiscus and Lotus* in the Morse collection, New York (*ibid.*, cat. no. 42, p. 181); "Hibiscus," from *Album of Paintings Depicting the Poems of Su Shih*, dated 1677–78, in the collection of Huang Ping-chang (see *The Selected Painting and Calligraphy of Shih-t'ao*, vol. 6, pl. 138); or panel five of the twelve-screen *Panoramic Vista*, dated 1693–94, in the collection of Mr. and Mrs. Chang Ch'ün, Taipei (*A Garland of Chinese Painting*, vol. 4, pl. 27).

4. Tao Ch'ien's "Drinking Poem," no. 5, translated by Eric Sackheim, *The Silent Zero in Search of Sound . . . : An Anthology of Chinese Poems from the Beginning through the 6th Century* (Tokyo, 1968), p. 118.

5. In the collection of the Tokyo National Museum.

6. *Shih-t'ao shang-jen nien-p'u*, p. 77.

7. Twelve leaves depicting the scenery of Huang-shan, undated, but bearing two dated colophons, 1696 and 1699. They are reproduced fully in *Shina nanga taisei*, suppl. vol. 1, pls. 158–69. The comparison of colophon leaves follows:

Sackler Album	*Sumitomo Album*
AA. Huang Po-shan	1. Huang Po-shan (pl. 158)
BB. (?) Tsu-ming	2. Wang Yang-tu (pl. 159)
CC. Wu Su-kung, dated 1695	3. Ch'eng Ching-e (pl. 160)
DD. Wang Sui-yü	4. Ch'eng Ching-e (pl. 161)
EE. Huang Po-shan	5. Wu Su-kung and Ch'eng Ching-e, dated 1696 (pl. 162)
FF. Huang Po-shan	6. (?) Ju, dated 1699 (pl. 163)
GG. Li Kuo-sung	7. Wei Lao (pl. 164)
HH. Wu Su-kung	8. Huang Po-shan (pl. 165)
	9. Wu Su-kung (pl. 166)
	10. Sang Chih (?) (pl. 167)
	11. Li Kuo-sung (pl. 168)
	12. Hsü Shu and Chao P'ang (pl. 169)

8. Cf. his *Landscape Album Depicting the Poems of Huang Yen-ssu* (Chuang Shen and J. C. Y. Watt, *Exhibition of Paintings of the Ming and Ch'ing Periods*, no. 49), in eighteen leaves (as exhibited), and dated 1701–2.

Text for XXI begins on page 202.

XXI LI JUI-CH'I (ca. 1870–ca. 1940)

Lin-ch'uan, Kiangsi; later Shanghai, Kiangsu

Copy of Tao-chi's *Flowers and Figures*

The Art Museum, Princeton University (68-193).[1]

Album of eight leaves. Ink and occasional color on paper. 22.9 x 17.4 cm.

Approximate date of execution ca. 1920.

SEALS AND SIGNATURES OF THE ARTIST: all are precise copies after the Tao-chi originals which appear on the album leaves of the preceding entry.

NO COLLECTORS' SEALS OR COLOPHONS

FOLIO AND ALBUM COVER LABELS: by Chang Ta-ch'ien (see below).

PROVENANCE: Chang Ch'ün, Taipei.

PUBLISHED: Wen Fong, "A Chinese Album and Its Copy," pp. 74–78 (leaves A and E illustrated), 94 (acquisitions list); *Archives of Asian Art*, vol. 12 (1969–70), p. 85 (acquisitions list).

THIS IS A line-for-line replica of the original Tao-chi album, *XX*. Chang Ta-ch'ien, an old friend of Mr. Chang Ch'ün, has inscribed the label on the cover to the album (fig. 1 *right*):

An album of flowers and figures after Shih-t'ao. A close copy [*lin-pen*] by [my] teacher's brother [*shih-shu*] Yün-an, and enjoyed by Mr. Yüeh-chün [Chang Ch'ün].

> [Signed:] Yüan [Chang Ta-ch'ien].
> [Seals:] *Chang* (relief, square),
> *Yüan* (relief, square).

Chang Ta-ch'ien's inscription on the label to the outer folio (fig. 1 *left*) reads: "An album of flowers and figures after Shih-t'ao. A copy [*fu-pen*] by Mr. Yün-an." The teacher referred to is Li Jui-ch'ing (*hao* Mei-an, 1867–1920), whose younger brother, Li Jui-ch'i (*hao* Yün-an), is identified as the author of this album. Li Jui-ch'i's exact birth and death dates are not known, but it is said that he died at the beginning of World War II at age seventy[2] and that he was a gentleman of great talent but without any particular professional commitment. He occasionally liked to display his virtuosity in painting by imitating well-known works or artists. While he is not to be considered a forger per se, this album is not the only extant work of its type which he did for amusement. Unfortunately, we have been unable to obtain any further information on this artist.

The copy is of relatively high quality, as both the details of composition and, in a few leaves, a certain richness of spirit (leaf B and especially leaf F) have been transferred. This artistic level is far superior to, for example, the modern copy of Tao-chi's *Searching for Plum Blossoms* handscroll, *XIX*. The precision and technical control which this copy demanded show Li to be a painter of no

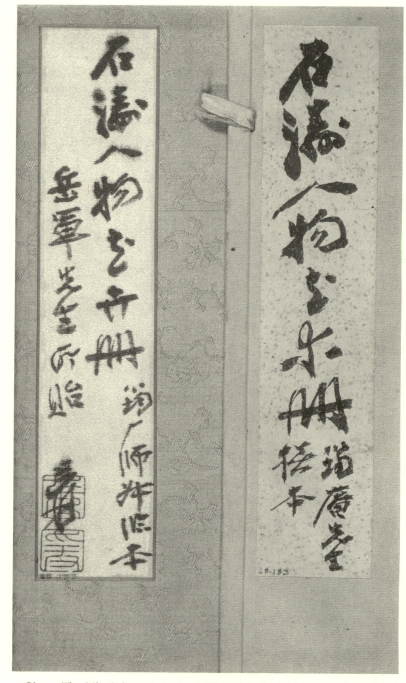

1. Chang Ta-ch'ien's inscriptions on album labels: (*left*) outer cover label; (*right*) inner cover label (*actual size*).

mean gifts. Other than a few brush mannerisms, however, little is revealed of his own artistic personality. What is quite evident is his ability to subordinate completely his own creative ideas to that of his model. In this respect, Li differs from Chang Ta-ch'ien (cf. *XXXV*), whose artistic presence can be overbearing in a copy and whose facile intellect seldom resisted creative deviations from his model.

Li Jui-ch'i seems to have possessed both taste and restraint. For example, Tao-chi's seals have been meticulously reproduced. Li was not tempted to fabricate "new" and "unknown" seals, a temptation the two copyists of *Searching for Plum Blossoms* could not resist. He also refrained from impressing a battery of prestigious collectors' seals to enhance the album's value. Such restraint and quality (as in the seal carving) is typical of educated painters of our scholar-forger category (see Part II, pp. 20–21, above). Li's level of taste is not unexpected in a man whose artistic interests and knowledge were guided by such an elder brother as Li Jui-ch'ing. The elder Li was one of the best-known calligraphers and collectors in Shanghai in the late Ch'ing and early years of the Republic. Among his pupils, Chang Ta-ch'ien has undoubtedly garnered the widest acclaim, but the elder Li's influence can still be identified in calligraphers younger than Chang. One hopes that future research will uncover other works of the younger Li.

Chang Ta-ch'ien's label inscriptions are valuable for reasons other than mere identification of the hand of the "forger." They suggest the attitude of the traditional Chinese connoisseur toward copies. In Chang's inscription to the outer folio (fig. 1 *left*) he uses the word *fu-pen*, rather than the more customary *lin-pen* or *mo-pen*, to describe the copying process. The word *fu* may mean to caress, to touch lightly, or, in this context, "to feel out"; hence it is complimentary and actually describes the sensitive, sensuous method by which the copyist proceeded. Such overtones indicate that such persons as the inscriber or the collector could appreciate the copy for its own value and as an exemplary demonstration of the art of replication. The album, therefore, is a connoisseur's copy. The cognoscenti, including those who themselves at one time or other made a copy for amusement, would peruse the album, leaf by leaf, stroke upon stroke, and pronounce judgment on the painter's successes or failures in the various scenes. We can imagine such a learned group of art lovers gathered around both the original and the copy, marveling at or frowning upon the maneuvers necessary and the triumphs achieved in solving the particularly challenging technical or expressive difficulties.

The fine quality of this copy therefore places it in an entirely different category from others in this catalogue (cf. *XIX, XXVIII*, and others cited in related comparisons). It teaches us to anticipate and to discriminate on a much finer scale the visual ramifications of the concept of "quality."

NOTES

1. Gift of Professor and Mrs. Wen Fong to The Art Museum in honor of Dr. Sackler.
2. Oral communication from Mr. Chang Ta-ch'ien.

Landscapes, Vegetables, and Flowers

The Metropolitan Museum of Art, New York, Purchase,
the Sackler Fund (1972.122.a-l).

Album of twelve leaves, ten in ink and color on paper,
two in ink only (leaves D and I). 27.6 x 21.5 cm.

UNDATED: probably executed ca. 1697.

SIGNATURE OF THE ARTIST: on each leaf except leaf E.

INSCRIPTIONS BY THE ARTIST: on each leaf.

SEALS OF THE ARTIST (on each leaf, eleven in all):
Ch'ing-hsiang lao-jen (relief, oval; PTC, cat. no. 18, not listed)
leaves E, F, and I.
Pan-ko-han (relief, tall rectangle; PTC, cat. no. 57, not listed) leaf B.
K'u-kua (intaglio, tall rectangle; PTC, cat. no. 43, not listed) leaf B.
Yu-hsi (relief, oval; PTC, cat. no. 110, not listed) leaf B.
Ch'ien yu Lung-mien, Chi (intaglio, tall rectangle; PTC, cat. no. 9, not listed)
leaves C and G.
Ch'ing-hsiang Shih-t'ao (intaglio, tall rectangle; PTC, cat. no. 22, not listed)
leaf D.
Shih Yüan-chi yin (intaglio, square; PTC, cat. no. 74, not listed) leaf A.
Hsia-tsun-che (relief, oval; PTC, cat. no. 29, not listed) leaves F and K.
Tsan-chih shih-shih-sun, A-ch'ang (relief, tall rectangle; PTC, cat. no. 95, not
listed) leaves H and L.
Lao-t'ao (intaglio, tall rectangle; PTC, cat. no. 50, not listed) leaf J.
Yüeh-shan (intaglio, square; PTC, cat. no. 108, not listed) leaf J.

PLACE OF EXECUTION: Ta-ti-t'ang, Yang-chou, Kiangsu (see leaf L).

COLLECTORS' SEALS:
Ching Ch'i-chün (tzu Chien-ch'üan, chin-shih 1852), Ching-shih chen-ts'ang
relief, square) leaf I, Chien-ch'üan chen-shang (relief, square) leaf G.
Chang Ta-ch'ien (born 1899; sixteen seals, on each leaf except I), Chang Yüan
chih-yin (intaglio, square) leaf E, Pieh-shih jung-i (relief, square) leaves A
and B, Ta-ch'ien chü-shih kung-yang pai-shih chih-i (relief, square) leaf C,
Chang Yüan (intaglio, small square) and Ta-ch'ien (relief, small square in
seal script) leaf D, Nan-pei-tung-hsi chih-yu hsiang-sui wu-pieh-li (relief,
large square) leaf A, Ti-kuo chih-fu (relief, square) leaf F, Chang Yüan
ssu-yin (intaglio, square) and Ta-ch'ien chü-shih (relief, square) leaf G, Chiu-
t'u-pao ku-jou-ch'ing (intaglio, rectangle) leaf H, Chang Yüan (intaglio,
small square with border) and Ta-ch'ien (relief, small square in oracle bone
script) leaf J, Chang Yüan (intaglio, square with border) and Ta-ch'ien po
(relief, square) leaf K, Chang Yüan (relief, square) and Ta-ch'ien chü-shih
(intaglio, square) leaf L.

CONDITION: good.

PROVENANCE: Ta-feng-t'ang collection.

PUBLISHED: Shih-t'ao hua-chi, no. 59 (leaf B only illustrated); Cheng Cho-lu,
Shih-t'ao yen-chiu, pl. 22 (leaf B only illustrated).

THIS ALBUM displays in the broadest and most impressive way Tao-chi's command of various subject matters and styles. Each leaf offers something unexpected, whether in arrangement of subject, choice of hues, or pictorial and verbal wit and subtlety. Coupled with this feast are the freshness of its condition and the brilliance of its colors, all of which could well raise questions as to the precise date of its execution. Nonetheless, studious comparisons of authentic works dated from the 1690's reveal that this very versatility of subject and approach, the bold, slightly raw color, the application of line, and the range and vigor of the calligraphy firmly place this album at the height of Tao-chi's artistic career, before the onset of the blunt pungency and evocative restraint of his style in the 1700's. This stylistic evidence, in addition to his choice of signatures and seals, suggests approximately 1697 as the date of execution. (Translation of the poems and further discussion of the album will be found in a forthcoming Metropolitan Museum publication entitled The Wilderness Colors of Tao-chi.)

Leaf A, "Moonlit Geese"

Leaf B, "Taro Root"

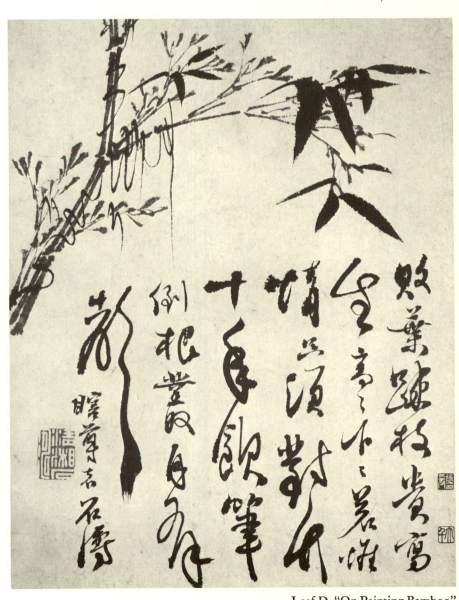

Leaf C, "River Bank of Peach Blossoms" (see Frontispiece to this volume)

Leaf D, "On Painting Bamboo"

竹光圍野色
舍影漾江流
石濤

Leaf G, "Wilderness Cottage" (*actual size*)

Leaf E, "Bird-Watching"

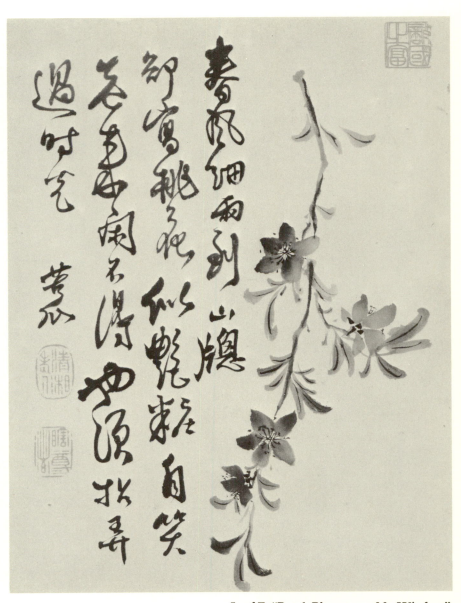

Leaf F, "Peach Blossoms at My Window"

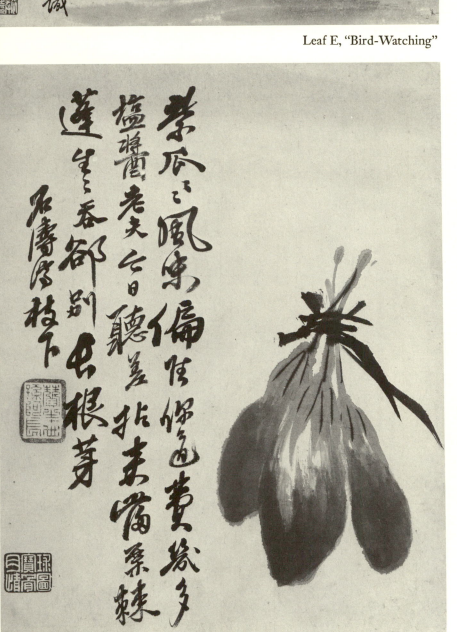

Leaf H, "Eggplants"

Leaf J, "Clouds Blocked by the Mountain"

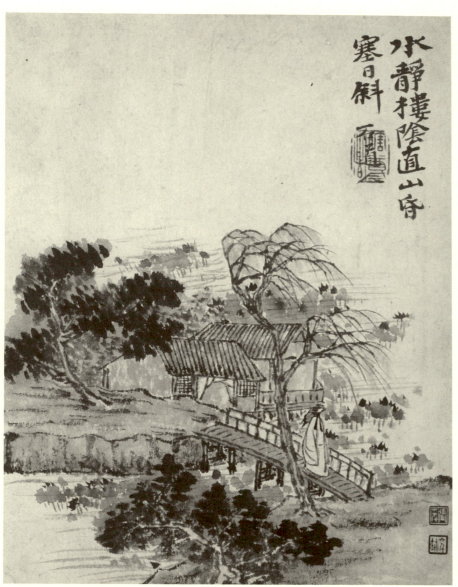

水靜樓陰直山昏
塞日斜

Leaf K, "Pavilion Reflections at Sunset"

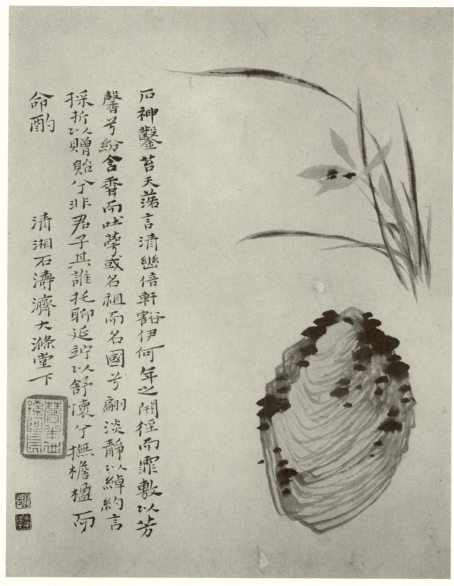

石神鑿苔夭蔿言清悠倚軒帑伊何年之開徑而羅敷以芳
馨兮紛舍香而吐蕚或名祖而名國兮嗣淡靜以綽約言
採折以贈貽兮非君子其誰托聊延䜿以舒懷兮撫檐楹而
命酌
清湘石濤濟大滌堂下

Leaf L, "Orchid and Rock"

Leaf I, "Geese by the Lake" (*actual size*)

Letter to Pa-ta shan-jen   (*Chih Pa-ta shan-jen-han*)

The Art Museum, Princeton University (68-204).

Album of six calligraphy leaves. Ink on *lo-wen* paper (unsized, with fine vertical ridges, identical with that of *XXXIII*). 18.7 x 13.0 cm.

UNDATED: probably executed ca. 1698–99.

SIGNATURE OF THE ARTIST: Chi (in "running" script on last leaf).

SEAL OF THE ARTIST: *Yen-chung chih-jen, wu-lao-i* (intaglio, large square; *PTC*, cat. no. 100) over signature on leaf 6.

COLLECTORS' SEALS:

Li Tsung-han (1769–1831, a collector and poet from Lin-ch'uan, Kiangsi),[1] *Tan-erh-yung* (relief, tall rectangle) right edge of leaf 1, *Ching-yü-chai chien-shang-chang* (relief, tall rectangle) lower right corner of leaf 1.

Liu Yün-ch'üan(?) (fl. mid-nineteenth century, from Su-chou, Kiangsu),[2] *Shen-liu tu-shu-t'ang* (intaglio, square) center left edge of leaf 6, *Hsiao-feng sui-yin* ( ) ( )-hua (relief, square; two characters illegible) left edge of leaf 6, *Hsiao-feng shen-ting* (intaglio, square) lower left corner of leaf 6. ("Hsiao-feng" is a common *hao*, but Liu Yün-ch'üan seems the most likely candidate as the collector of this letter. His father, Liu Shu [1759–1816, *hao* Jung-feng], was a collector and the friend of Wang Hsüeh-hao; cf. *XXIX*.[3])

Ou-yang Jun-sheng (fl. late nineteenth century[?], a collector from Kiangsi), *Jun-sheng kuo-yen* (relief, tall rectangle) lower left of leaf 6.

Chang Ta-ch'ien (Yüan, born 1899), *Chang Yüan* (intaglio, small square) and *Ta-ch'ien* (relief, small square), both on right edge of leaf 1; *Ta-ch'ien hao-meng* (relief, tall rectangle) bottom of leaf 3; *Ta-ch'ien kung-yang pai-Shih chih-i* (relief, large square) and *Pu-fu ku-jen kao-hou-jen* (relief, large rectangle), both on leaf 6 at left of artist's signature; *Chiu-t'u-pao ku-jou-ch'ing* (intaglio, rectangle) upper left corner of leaf 6; *Nan-pei-tung-hsi . . .* (relief, rectangular half-seal) lower left edge of leaf 6.

Owner unidentified (probably before Chang Ta-ch'ien), *Yü-t'ai hsin-shang* (relief, small square) lower right corner of leaf 1, *I-p'in* (relief, tall rectangle) lower right corner of leaf 6.

CONDITION: good, except for general foxing over all the leaves.

PLACE OF EXECUTION: Ta-ti-t'ang, Yang-chou, Kiangsu.

PROVENANCE: Li Jui-ch'ing collection, Shanghai, to Ta-feng-t'ang collection.

PUBLISHED: see end of entry.

OTHER VERSIONS: a contemporary copy by Chang Ta-ch'ien, published by Nagahara Oriharu in 1928 and 1961 (see below), ink on paper, 25.5 x 81 cm.

IN CHINA the letters or random jottings and rough drafts of poets, painters, and calligraphers have long been collected for their aesthetic value as well as their literary content. Several of Tao-chi's personal letters and one poetic manuscript survive today in their original handwritten form. Of the now extant specimens this letter to Pa-ta shan-jen is one of the more important not only for its intrinsic artistic appeal but also because it contains valuable autobiographical information, because it documents his relationship with the painter Chu Ta, and because it is a part of the evidence determining Tao-chi's birth date as 1641.

The calligraphy of this letter is an example of Tao-chi's freehand writing style—his most un-selfconscious and informal script type. In writing it he was as much concerned with content (he was undoubtedly composing as he went along) as with visual impression because it was addressed to his distant cousin, the painter Chu Ta, another exiled scion of the Ming clan. The recent history of the letter goes back to the early interest in Tao-chi. It was discovered in Shanghai in 1920 among the personal effects of the calligrapher and important collector of Tao-chi works Li Jui-ch'ing, who died in

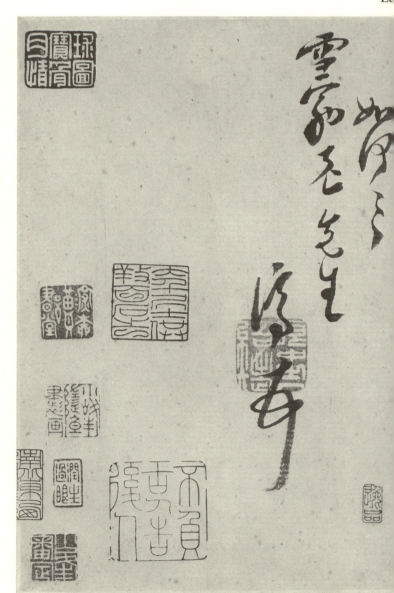

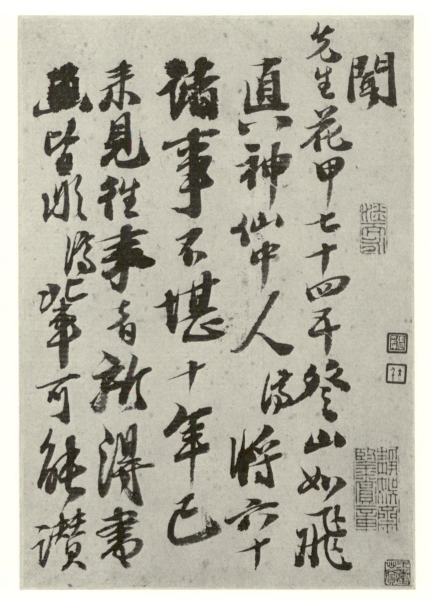

Leaf 2

Leaf 1

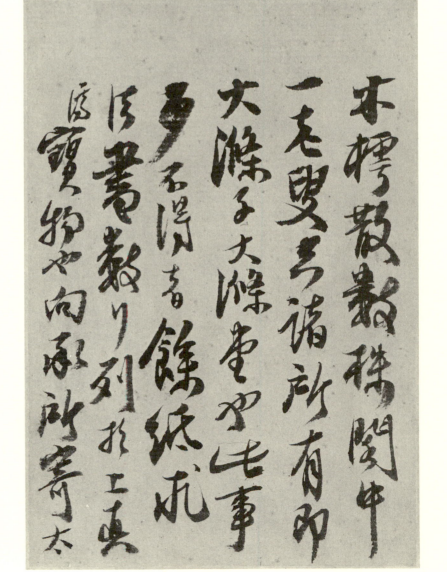

Leaf 5

Leaf 4

that year. Subsequently it found its way into the hands of Li's pupil, Chang Ta-ch'ien. In 1926 an incomplete transcription of it was published (without a photograph) by Hashimoto Kansetsu.[4] In 1928 a second letter of similar content but differing in two vital details—the ages of both painters—was also published in Japan by its owner, Nagahara Oriharu. This pair of letters stimulated a hot debate (see the end of this entry for a bibliographic summary of the controversy): it not only intensified the more scholarly interest in Tao-chi's life and works initiated by the Japanese but also ushered in what may be regarded as a new era in art-historical criticism.

A letter of quality from Tao-chi's hand constitutes a primary document. It is superior to any printed archive or record: not only can it be checked against other primary sources for internal consistency, but its physical aspect and calligraphic style can also be compared with fully authenticated works. The necessity of considering an artist's total production as an organic entity in the process of making decisions on any single work, a method stressed earlier in this volume, is of utmost importance. The problem of Tao-chi's dates could not be resolved in isolation and on the basis of literary evidence alone, nor by debating the authenticity of any one letter over another. Rather, the examination of a network of evidence involving the artist's biography and the study of his calligraphy and painting styles in other authentic works and, equally important, the styles of the possible Tao-chi forgers proved the most effective approach. This more comprehensive method, necessary here because of insufficient biographical data, also reflects the advances made in the field of art history. Not all the biographical problems have been solved; whole areas of Tao-chi's life remain obscure, but such difficulties should not deter scholars from accepting as genuine works of high quality. On the contrary, by adding to Tao-chi's corpus in a reasonable and discerning manner, the proper interpretation of these accepted works may eventually solve other problems of a biographical nature.

We will not review the contributions of previous scholars to the resolution of this issue. The interested reader is referred to Wen Fong's 1959 and 1967 studies and to Wu T'ung's articles and chronology for the most succinct interpretations of this complex subject. Here we hope to reinforce their arguments by focusing on the visual evidence and providing further analysis of Tao-chi's calligraphic style and letter-writing format, the writing style of the Nagahara forger, and the erroneous basis of the other birth date theories.

TAO-CHI COMMANDED a broad array of calligraphic styles (see Part IV above). While he used the freehand "running" style mainly in letters, this cursive form can also be found in several paintings of quality and authenticity—e.g., leaf H of the Sumitomo *Eight Views of Huang-shan*, the 1696 *Sketches of Calligraphy and Painting by Ch'ing-hsiang* (sections 5, 6, and 8–11), and the ca. 1697 *Waterfall at Mt. Lu* (epilogue in five lines). Excerpts of characters from these prime works demonstrate the absolute identity of the basic structure and of the significant brush movements between lexically similar graphs (fig. 1). The correspondence of form is remarkable, given the differences in date, medium, size, script, and intent of the inscriptions on which these works are found, but the identity of the painting style functions as the important link between them.

The significant characteristics of Tao-chi's hand[5] are a circular, roundabout, up-and-down change of brush pressure which developed out of his basic "clerical" script orientation. This fundamental rhythm governs his thick-and-thin brush modulations, creating a

writing style of lively variation in both overall impression and specific stroke movements. Modulation tends to occur within the course of a single stroke rather than between individual characters or sequences of characters. Scanning a page or even a few lines of writing in this style, one observes extreme fluctuations in size, a horizontal axis in each character which consistently slants upward to the right, and a relentless vertical momentum and tension which stretches the characters downward within the spatial confines of the column. This overall construction is confirmed in the inscription to *Waterfall at Mt. Lu* (cf. Part IV, fig. 12, above), which reveals an identical columnar structure and a tall, rectangular configuration of the individual characters, which are comfortably but closely spaced.

Several of Tao-chi's letters (figs. 2–7) and the important 1701 *Manuscript of Poems* (fig. 14) represent the same script in a slightly different format. Like the paintings we have used for comparison, these works have also been responsibly authenticated, so that they may be accepted as prime calligraphic specimens from Tao-chi's hand. In these examples and in the Sackler letter, Tao-chi shows a consistency in the structural framework of characters, as individual members and as groups, and in the format of address and personal signature. We will point out the specific nature of this consistency below.

In formal terms the Nagahara version falls short of authentic Tao-chi works not only in quality of execution but in more objective matters of format, signature, and address. The discrepancies are significant enough to put into serious question its authenticity, and therefore the reliability of its contents. We shall first discuss these points in view of the above evidence, and then present comparative materials with which to identify the forger's hand.

The writer of the Nagahara version has given what must be admitted is a virtuoso performance (fig. 8): at first glance we get the impression of a freedom and audacity which we generally associate with Tao-chi's manner. Even some of the individual characters seem extraordinarily close. We must grant this master countless hours of immersion in the original Sackler letter (which was, after all, in his collection), so that, as Fong has said, he could so skillfully play his version by ear, imitating the most salient formal characteristics and grasping the whole spirit of the writing, its dash and drive. The inconsistencies in the Nagahara text have already been pointed out by Fong.[6] Here we will show how the characteristics of each version are so distinct as to make it impossible for them to have come from the same hand. These differences become increasingly obvious upon close examination.

The Nagahara writer's brush moves not in a rhythmic up-and-down manner but in a diagonal or sideways motion, jerking from side to side across the surface of the paper. The "headlong, plunging" motion of the "action" painter[7] fittingly describes this movement of the arm and shoulder, rather than the wrist and finger motion characteristic of Tao-chi. The general impression of several lines is one of extreme variation in ink tonality and character size. Upon closer inspection, however, one can see that the variation derives not from a habitual fluctuation in the stroke rhythm; on the contrary, in the Nagahara version the strokes within a single character are surprisingly uniform in thickness. Unlike the Tao-chi work, the ink tonality follows the stroke thickness, with characters appearing either entirely dark or entirely pale. These contrasts are different from and much more exaggerated than Tao-chi's. The brush pressure is forced, self-consciously heavy or light, something quite foreign to Tao-chi's sense of rhythm. This tendency toward uniformity in the individual stroke is a characteristic of "seal" calligraphy, which we recognize as the Nagahara writer's most basic script orientation, and it accounts for the relative evenness and flatness of the strokes. In Tao-chi's "clerical" orientation, by contrast, the changes of brush pressure are relatively smooth but frequent, with the "tip" and "belly" of the brush in constant fluctuation. In terms of columnar spacing, the characters in the Nagahara letter extend wildly beyond the column. The writer's zig-zag surface movement is the source of this deviation, and his exaggerated diagonals and extended strokes suggest a centrifugal motion which tends to pull the line of characters in different directions. It is primarily these strong diagonals which give the impression of vigor and dash, when in actuality they are exaggerated mannerisms.

The Nagahara writer's basic rhythm can be seen most pointedly when two characters extracted from the Nagahara letter are examined (fig. 9, *bottom row*). The identification of the Nagahara writer can also be confirmed by comparison of the same two characters extracted from an inscription signed by him (the example is written on satin, hence the blurred edges). The top two rows of fig. 9 reproduce two characters extracted from the Sackler letter and from other genuine Tao-chi letters (shown in figs. 2–7). The two characters, *hsien-sheng* ("sir," "teacher," or a polite address), form a common phrase which is repeated several times throughout the letters. The act of repetition, like ornament in a complex design, encourages the hand, whether that of Tao-chi or a forger, to be less attentive and to betray its most basic habits.

We can see from Tao-chi's rendering of the phrase that despite changes in size several basic characteristics are present. One is the round circular loop which links the character *hsien* 先 to *sheng* 生. In "regular" script, when the two characters are not linked the last stroke of the *hsien* is an upward hook. In cursive script, Tao-chi's basic circular motion of the hand often doubles back and transforms the hook into an open loop. This motion brings the brush to the left to begin the next character, *sheng*. The horizontal strokes of this character are also joined by circular loops, which is the second basic feature of the phrase. In this respect the Sackler letter is identical with Tao-chi's letters from other sources, shown in the middle row of fig. 9. These traits do not appear in the Nagahara version, shown at the bottom of fig. 9, where the connecting lines between the strokes tend to be both angular and closed. The forger's participation in the Nagahara letter can be further demonstrated by examining the *hsien-sheng* phrase in one of his signed endorsements at the bottom left of the figure. There the strokes tend to look flat and folded, like creased ribbons, and the linking strokes assume a triangular form, which is the result of the zig-zag sideways drive of the writer's basic arm movement. We see also how the strongly horizontal axes of the characters reflect his driving diagonal brush action across the surface of the paper.

In these finer movements of the brush we can isolate what can be least well disguised by the imitative hand. We must remember that the forger is trying his utmost to suppress his own style and to imitate Tao-chi's hand. The basic characteristics of the Nagahara writer's current freehand style are a mannered spikiness which is ostensibly different from Tao-chi's (compare his frontispieces to *XVIII, XXI, XXIV,* and *XXXII*). But we must also take note of a certain conscious deception in the choice of script. The Nagahara writer has to a certain extent been influenced by Tao-chi's style over the years in which he has emulated him, and he has purposely adapted an eccentric personal style to conceal any acquired influences.

Tao-chi's form of address is another feature which the Nagahara writer failed to control. In each of the authentic letters by Tao-chi (figs. 2–7),[8] the artist employs one of the common forms of etiquette popularly called *t'ai-t'ou* ("lifting the head"); that is, when referring to the name of the person to whom the letter is addressed,

the writer respectfully leaves a space and begins a new line (which accounts for the characteristically uneven lines in Chinese personal letters). This is the most common form of courtesy to the addressee, and the Nagahara forger has complied with it. A second form, which, in this case, was also Tao-chi's consistent habit, was not only to begin a new column but also to place the reference to the addressee on a higher line. Hence in the authentic letters and the Sackler letter, all of the *hsien-sheng* forms and names are written above the top margin (cf. figs. 2–7). The Nagahara writer completely overlooked this significant personal habit.

Tao-chi's references to himself are another equally important aspect of format. He was in the habit of writing his name, "Chi," slightly smaller and placed to one side of the line, usually to the right (see fig. 10). This is a formal sign of the writer's humility and respect for the addressee. The Nagahara writer (fig. 10, *bottom row*), on the other hand, does not distinguish references to the writer, "Chi," from other characters in the line. This was the risk he took in not making an exact copy of the letter but in improvising one of his own. He was probably not accustomed to observing this form of etiquette in his own writing, and, busy trying to imitate Tao-chi's style and to suppress his own, he overlooked this detail.

One final point in this comparison concerns the form of Tao-chi's signature. In this freehand script, it appears in his abbreviated, "cursive" form (fig. 10, *top row*): the complex sequence of lines and dots from the "regular" form, 濟 has been simplified to a few fluid loops and swirls 済. Tao-chi would first make the vertical hook representing the "water" radical, then a dot and a horizontal, quickly followed by two wave-like movements, and finally a loop and circular hook. This sequence of movements was his personal graphology and was written without forethought. Therefore it appears without fail in his genuine writing. The strokes themselves may be "fatter" or "thinner," but the basic sequence of loops and waves remains constant, particularly the two wave-like movements. Although the signer of the Nagahara version (fig. 10, *bottom row*) has succeeded in capturing the overall shape, he has simplified the form and omitted the small movement of that extra wave-like stroke after the horizontal. The result is only one wave, distorting the form and even the shorthand. This oversight is of great significance and was crucial in the detection of the forgery. It appears consistently in the Nagahara letter, just as does Tao-chi's habitual but "correct" form in his writing.[9]

THE FACTUAL DIFFERENCES in the two letters are so great that on this basis alone one could only conclude that one must be spurious. The two letters are reproduced here (see fig. 8 and the detail). The comparison and translations given below are from Fong's renderings (slightly modified).[10] The line-by-line comparison of the two versions (line numbers are those of the original Chinese text) is as follows:

Sackler Letter (33 lines)	Nagahara Letter (25 lines)
lines 1–7	end of line 6–line 11
end of line 8–beginning of line 14	lines 1–6
beginning of line 14–line 33	lines 12–25

In the translated text of the Sackler version printed below, words italicized are the key phrases omitted in the Nagahara letter to suit the forger's purpose—deleting them allowed him to create the painting by Chu Ta, also in the Nagahara collection (fig. 16), which was supposedly the "answer" to Tao-chi's request. In the Nagahara version these omissions are indicated below by dots; any additions made by the forger are given in italics.

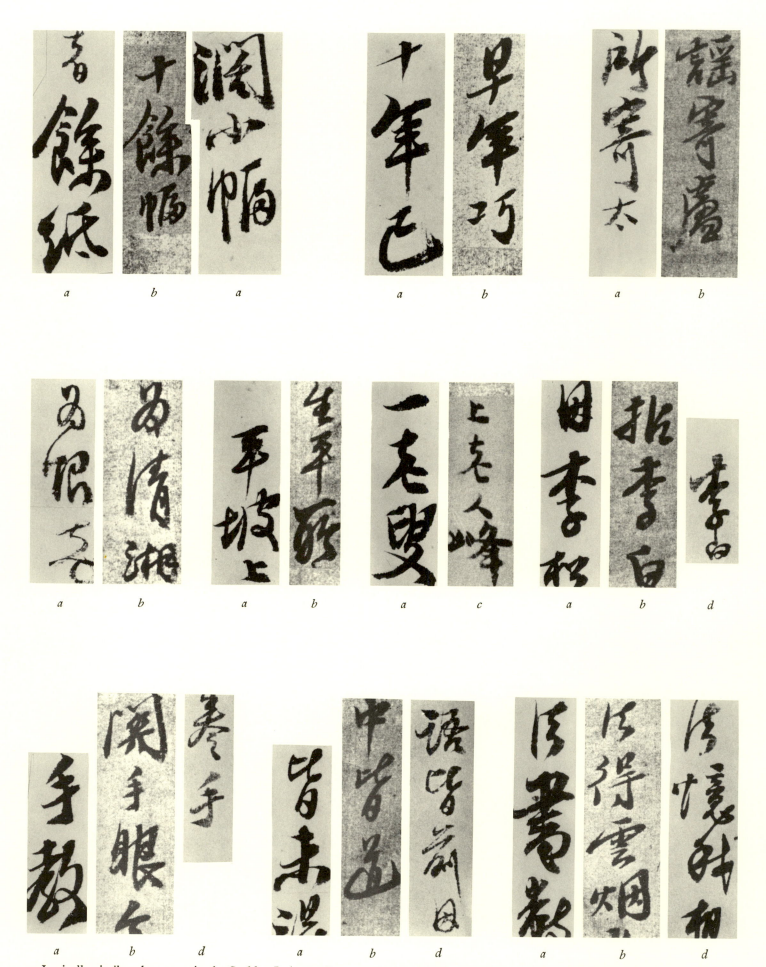

1. Lexically similar characters in the Sackler *Letter to Pa-ta* and in three prime Tao-chi works, showing identity of authorship: *a,* Sackler *Letter; b, Waterfall at Mt. Lu; c, Eight Views of Huang-shan; d, Sketches of Calligraphy and Painting by Ch'ing-hsiang.*

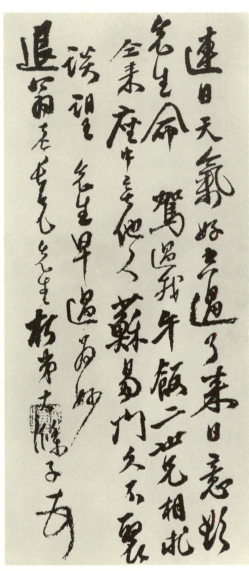
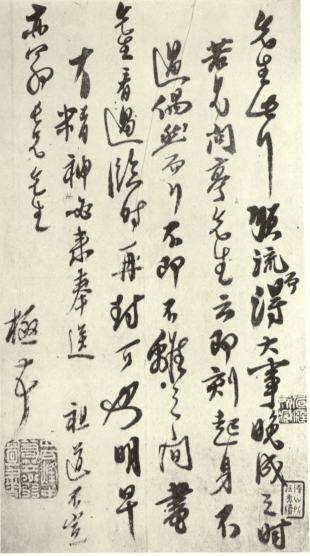
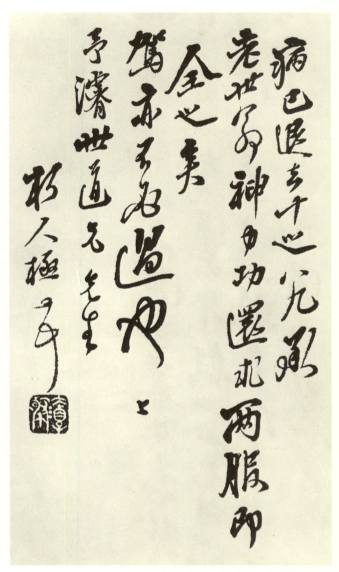

2. Tao-chi, *Letter to I-weng*. Collection unknown.

3. Tao-chi, *Letter to T'ui-weng*. Collection unknown. Photo Wang Fang-yü.

4. Tao-chi, *Letter to Yü-chün*. Collection unknown. Photo Wang Fang-yü.

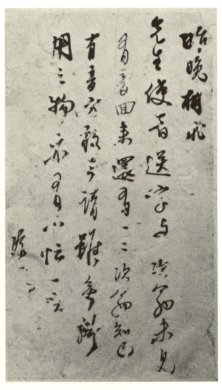
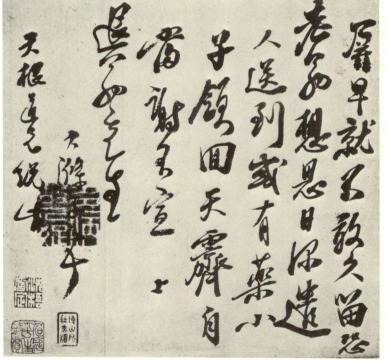

5. Tao-chi, *Letter to Shen-lao*. Anonymous loan, The Art Museum, Princeton University.

6. Tao-chi, *Letter (tso-wan)*. Anonymous loan, The Art Museum, Princeton University.

7. Tao-chi, *Letter to T'ui-weng*. Collection unknown.

Sackler Letter

I hear that you have arrived at a venerable age of seventy-*four or seventy-five,* and that you can still climb a mountain with flying speed. Truly you must be living among the immortals. I shall soon be sixty, and I already find things unbearable. In the past ten years, I have noticed specimens of your calligraphy and paintings acquired by people who came by here [*wang-lai*]. All are indeed treasured objects, certainly not to be obtained by simple offers of praises and eulogies by people like myself.

I have received several letters from you, but I have not been able to make a reply. This is because I have been troubled by illnesses and have found myself inept in entertaining and corresponding with people. I am not like this with you alone. People on all sides know about this shortcoming of mine. It makes me a laughable person.

Today, Mr. Li Sung-an is returning to Nan-chou (Nan-ch'ang), so I am sending this letter to you. I would like to beg of you a *small* hanging scroll *three feet tall and one foot wide.* [I would like to have] on a flat bank, an old house with a few rooms and a few ancient, useless trees, and in the room on the upper level *just an old man,* nothing else around. This will represent *Ta-ti-tzu in his* "Ta-ti-t'ang." I must at least have this. If there is any unused paper left, I shall beg you to do a few lines of your exemplary writing above the painting. This will truly become my most treasured object.

The picture which you were kind enough to send me some time ago was too big. My small house cannot hold it. In your inscription, I now beg you to write "Ta-ti-tzu Ta-ti-ts'ao-t'ang t'u." Please do not refer to me as a monk, for I am a man who wears a hat and keeps his hair, and who purifies (*ti*) everything from here on.

My only regret is that I cannot hurry myself to Hsi-chiang to catch a glimpse of your countenance. The sickness of old age is with me. What is to be done? What is to be done?

[Presented to:] Hsüeh-weng Old Esq.
Chi, bowing my head.

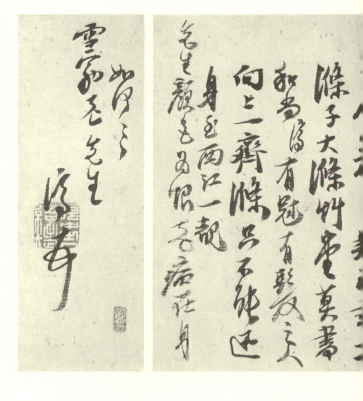

Nagahara Letter

Repeatedly I received letters from you, but I have not been able to make a reply. This is because I have been troubled by illnesses and have found myself inept in entertaining and corresponding with people. I am not like this with you alone. People on all sides know about this shortcoming of mine. It makes me a laughable person.

I hear that you are over seventy . . . years old, and that you can still climb a mountain with flying speed. Truly you must be living among the immortals! I am *barely* sixty-*four or sixty-five,* and I already find things unbearable. In the past ten years, I have noticed specimens of your calligraphy and painting, which were newly acquired by people who came by here. All are indeed treasured objects, certainly not to be obtained by my simple offering of praises and eulogies.

Today, Mr. Li Sung-an is returning to Nan-chou (Nan-ch'ang), so I am sending this letter to you. I would like to beg you to paint a . . . hanging scroll *for my hall . . .* (*t'ang*). [I would like to have] on a flat bank, an old house with a few rooms and a few ancient, useless trees, and an upper room . . . that is emptied of everything. This will represent . . . the "Ta-ti-t'ang." I must at least have this. If there is any unused paper left, I shall beg for a few lines of your exemplary writing. This will truly become my most treasured object. . . .

In your inscription, I beg you to write "Ta-ti-tzu ta-ti-ts'ao-t'ang." Please do not refer to me as a monk, for I am a man who wears a hat and keeps his hair, and who "purifies (*ti*) everything from here on *into emptiness*."

I regret that I cannot hurry myself to Hsi-chiang to catch a glimpse of your countenance. The sickness of old age is with me. What is to be done I cannot say.

Presented to: Hsüeh-weng, Esq.
Chi, bowing my head.

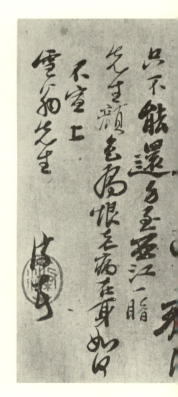

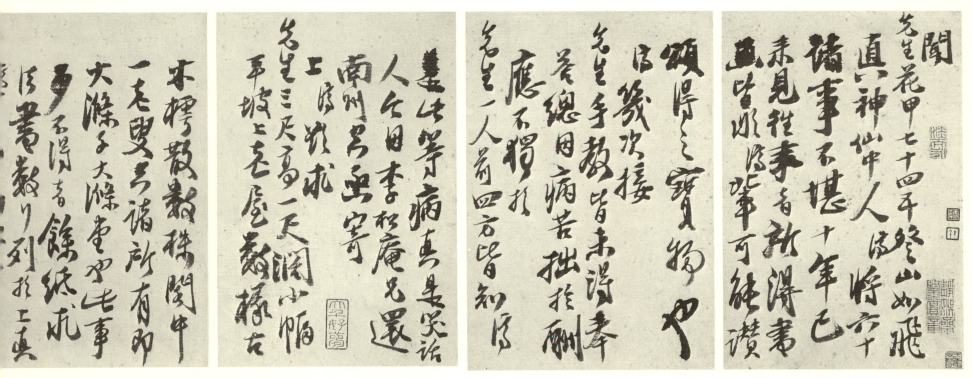

XXIII, detail. (Leaves 1-6 are shown as a unit here, reading from right to left, for easy comparison with the Nagahara version in fig. 8.)

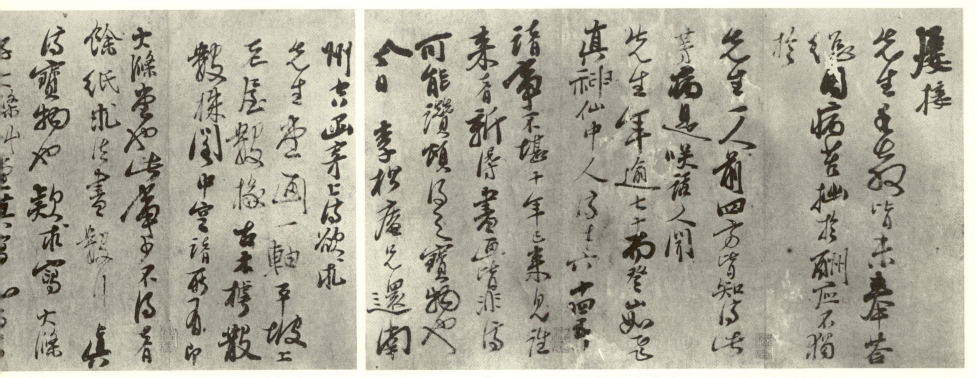

8. Chang Ta-ch'ien (born 1899), *Letter to Pa-ta shan-jen*. Six leaves mounted continuously as an album leaf. Ink on paper. Nagahara Oriharu collection.

The tone of the letter suggests a respectful friendship between Tao-chi and his distant cousin Chu Ta. Fong states that true friendship came only late in their lifetimes: "It was only in the late 1690's when Chu Ta and Tao-chi finally found peace with the world and within themselves that a satisfactory and secure relationship could grow between the two exiled Ming scions. Pa-ta made the move first by sending notes and a painting to Tao-chi." [11] On receiving the painting by Chu Ta, the *Ta-ti-ts'ao-t'ang t'u* (*Painting Depicting the Thatched Hut of Great Purity*), in the summer of 1698, Tao-chi enthusiastically wrote a long poetic colophon to the work. The painting was large and apparently there was no space for an inscription, so Tao-chi wrote his praises on a separate sheet which was set into the mounting alongside the painting. [12] In it he says that the Hsüeh-ko he once knew now calls himself Pa-ta and mentions that this large painting can "purify" his "Hall of Great Purity" (*Ta-ti-t'ang*). This colophon (fig. 11) is written in a highly disciplined and energetic hand. Each stroke is powerful and carefully formed, with a dense but well-balanced composition and columnar spacing. It compares well with inscriptions in similar script, such as leaves C, D, and G of the *Eight Views of Huang-shan* album and the 1696 *Sketches of Calligraphy and Painting by Ch'ing-hsiang*. The colophon played a key role in the dispute over the various versions of the letter to Pa-ta and itself barely escaped serious mishap in being removed from its original setting beside the painting. (Fong has provided a full translation of its seven poetic quatrains. [13])

The fact that Tao-chi specifically requested a painting with some calligraphy from Pa-ta agrees with what we know of his extremely selective and critical taste. There is no other record of his having collected the paintings of other artists or even of his requesting them of close colleagues. This entreaty for a painting which he intended to hang in his new home, and his statement that "this will truly become my most treasured object," thus appears to be a genuine and touching expression of feeling for Pa-ta's work. Inscriptions to two paintings dated 1694 and 1697, which Tao-chi wrote before this colophon—the long self-inscription on leaf E of the 1694 Los Angeles album (see Part IV, fig. 18, above) and an inscription dated 1697 to Pa-ta's painting *Narcissus* (fig. 12) [14]—reinforce this impression.

Other known details of Tao-chi's life are confirmed in this letter. He frequently complained of ill health; here it is "the sickness of old age" which is causing him pain. References to illness become more frequent in his late letters, published in 1962 by Cheng Wei. Likewise, the religious reversal which he appears to have made sometime in 1697 is here confirmed: in closing the letter he lightly admonishes Pa-ta not to refer to him as a monk, "for I am a man who wears a hat and keeps his hair." This statement is preceded by references to himself as Ta-ti-tzu ("the Greatly Purified One") and to his Ta-ti-t'ang (Hall of Great Purity). The key word *Ta-ti*, "great purification," occurs more frequently in works dating after 1697, and it has been interpreted as a significant indication of his new state of mind. The self-revelation presented here is rarely found elsewhere, although Tao-chi referred to it in the poetic colophon to the large painting given him by Pa-ta; likewise, the formulation *Ta-ti-ts'ao-t'ang* seems to appear for the first time in his colophon to Pa-ta's painting of narcissus.

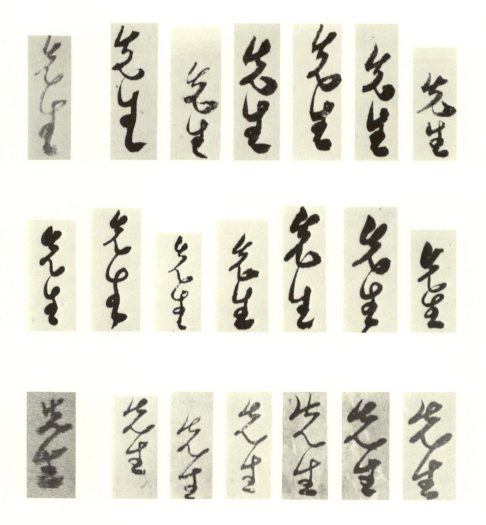

9. Comparisons of *hsien-sheng* phrase. (*Top row*) details of Sackler *Letter to Pa-ta*. (*Middle row, left to right*) details of fig. 6, fig. 4, fig. 3, fig. 3, fig. 3, fig. 2, fig. 2 (these genuine works by Tao-chi show his circular, fluctuating pressure and the round loops connecting the individual strokes and linking the two characters). (*Bottom row, left to right*) Chang Ta-ch'ien, detail of album label (on satin, cf. *XXI*); details of fig. 8 (these details show the jerky sideways movement of Chang's brush, the relatively even strokes, and the angular closed loops connecting the characters).

10. Comparisons of signatures. (*Top row, left to right*) Tao-chi's genuine signatures in "cursive" script; Tao-chi's signatures in the text of the Sackler letter, also written smaller and placed slightly to the right of the column (cf. also figs. 2–7). (*Bottom row*) signatures from the Nagahara letter, which do not differentiate size or position.

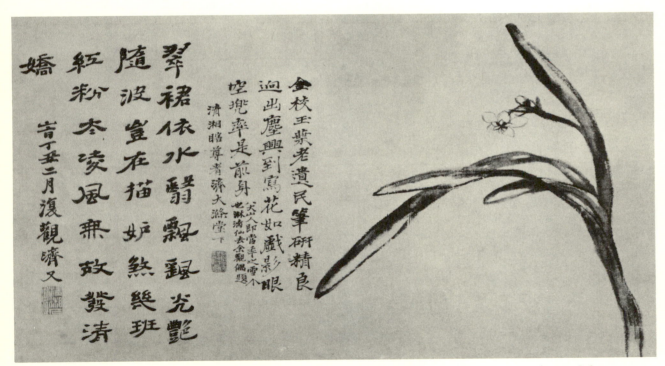

12. Chu Ta, *Narcissus*, detail from a handscroll with two inscriptions by Tao-chi, the second dated 1697. Ink on paper. Wang Fang-yü collection, Short Hills, New Jersey.

right

11. Tao-chi, colophon to Chu Ta, *Ta-ti-ts'ao-t'ang t'u*, dated 1698. Ink on paper. Ta-feng-t'ang collection. Photo Wang Fang-yü.

13. Tao-chi, *Li Sung-an's Studio*, dated 1702. Hanging scroll. Ink on paper. Li Mo-ch'ao collection.

A final word on the contents of the letter: the precise identity of the friend, Li Sung-an, to whom Tao-chi entrusted his letter (lines 14–15 of the original, which read "Chin yin Li Sung-an hsiung huan Nan-chou"), is still obscure, but we know that early in 1702 Tao-chi painted a fine landscape for him (fig. 13).[15] From Tao-chi's inscription at the upper right, it seems to be a portrait of Li in his studio. Tao-chi says that in thinking of the man in the picture he vividly remembers that he spoke with him two years ago. This comment reinforces the date given to the Sackler letter as about 1699. Although we have not seen the original, the painting appears to bear many of Tao-chi's late stylistic characteristics—a simple, bold composition with both wet and dry brushwork blended in a crusty and spontaneous manner—as seen, for example, in the Boston Museum of Fine Arts *Album of Landscapes* and *Man Walking toward a Mountain*, both dated 1703 (cf. *XXXIV*, fig. 4). The thatched cottage and the lone tree surrounded by a thick growth of bamboo also recall his depictions of his One-Branch Studio (compare *XXXIV–A, B,* and *F*). Whatever the specific reference, the addition of the figure chanting poems alone in the studio is the humanistic touch which we recognize as coming from the hand of Tao-chi.

THE SIGNIFICANCE of the Sackler letter when it first appeared in 1926 lay in the light it shed on Tao-chi's chronology relative to that of Pa-ta. Lines 2–3 of the letter read, "I hear that you have arrived at the venerable age of seventy-four or seventy-five. . . . I shall soon be sixty." There was therefore a fifteen-year difference in age between the two. Pa-ta's birth date at that time had been inferred primarily from an early Ch'ing source[16] which set it roughly at 1625. Despite this evidence, two dates, 1630 and 1636, had been given for Tao-chi, based on a series of misunderstandings and misreadings of various materials, discussed below. Wen Fong's 1641 theory, put forth in 1959, was founded on an examination of both contextual and stylistic evidence. His reasoning was confirmed in 1960, when a small portrait of Chu Ta by a friend was published. It was dated 1674 and showed him in his "forty-ninth year."[17] This established 1626 as the more accurate birth year for Chu Ta[18] and reaffirmed 1641 for Tao-chi. Fong's theory was further reinforced by the publication in 1962 of a manuscript of poems, the *Keng-ch'en ch'u-yeh shih-kao* (also known as *Meng-meng tao-jen shou-kao*), dated in accordance with February 7, 1701 (fig. 14). In this manuscript Tao-chi himself states that he has just completed his sixtieth year ("Chin chou hua-chia," line 2 of the original). The calligraphic style of this manuscript agrees on all counts with his other genuine works, and its text illuminates several aspects of his life.

The 1630 birth date theory, proposed by Fu Pao-shih in 1948 in his important *Shih-t'ao shang-jen nien-p'u*, was based on two main pieces of evidence: a poem recorded in Ch'eng Lin-sheng's *Shih-t'ao t'i-hua-lu* (1925), which ends with the words "Having enjoyed a peaceful life, I am now aged seventy. How many more poems can be added by my remaining years?" and is dated *chi-mao* (1699);[19] and a self-inscription written on a painting attributed to Tao-chi titled *Wu-jui[shui]-t'u*, in the Shinozaki Tsukasa collection (fig. 15).[20] Before the *Keng-ch'en* manuscript was published, these two works were the only ones which mentioned both the date and his age. Fu noted that three lines of the *Wu-jui-t'u* inscription were similar to those of the poem and that the date, *i-mao* (1675 or 1735), was also the same, although he had mistakenly read *chi-mao* (1699) for *i-mao*. This misreading was doubtless as much the result of working with a poor reproduction of the painting as of a desire to corroborate the date found in the poem. He therefore concluded that if Tao-chi was seventy in *chi-mao* (1699), he must have been born in 1630.

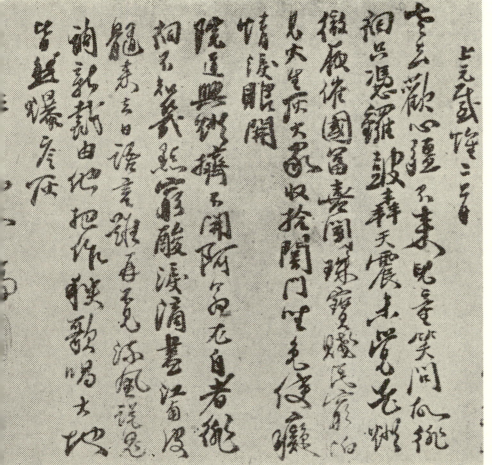 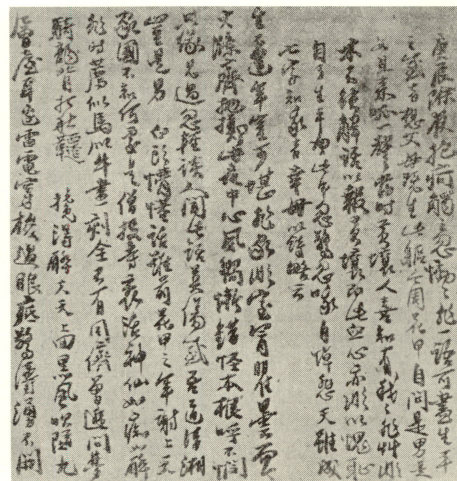

14. Tao-chi, *Keng-ch'en Manuscript of Poems*, dated in accordance with February 7, 1701, details. Ink on paper. Shanghai Museum.

The 1636 theory, proposed by Kawai Senro in 1935 and again by Cheng Wei in 1961,[21] was based on the same *Wu-jui-t'u* in the Shinozaki collection, but this time the date *i-mao* was misread as *i-yu* (1705), making Tao-chi's birth date 1636. How this happened forms an interesting lexical puzzle. The calligraphy of the *Wu-jui-t'u* inscription is a highly mannered mixture of archaic clerical and cursive scripts (fig. 15). Both Kawai and Cheng read the second character of the date as *yu* 邜, which in archaic script is close to *mao* 㘡 (without the horizontal stroke connecting the two verticals). Theirs was a correct reading but a much rarer form of the character (which usually appears as 丣 in archaic script).[22] Unfortunately, they did not take note of the fact that the writer of the Shinozaki inscription miswrote the character. His error may be demonstrated by comparing it with another character in the same poem, *liao* 聊 (i.e., a *mao* phonetic plus an "ear" radical, 耳 ; second line, eighth character from the top), which is also written incorrectly. Lexically, *liao* and *mao* bear the same phonetic and end rhyme; therefore in archaic script the phonetic should be written the same, i.e., 㘡 (without the connecting horizontal). The writer of the Shinozaki inscription has written *liao* as if it were *yu*, and no such character exists in combination with the "ear" radical. Moreover, he has also consistently miswritten what should be the *mao* phonetic 卯 as 丣. Thus although Cheng and Kawai were mistaken, they were still clearer about the formation of the character in question than the writer-forger himself, whose spelling, as we have seen, was quite poor.

As Fong pointed out in 1959, the two difficulties with these theories and their line of attack were that both the printed source on which they depended (the exact origin of which is not known, as manuscript copies and copies of copies of the original were probably in circulation long before it was published) and the painting used to "verify" this literary record were of questionable reliability. The circularity in the method is readily apparent. Printed records cannot be wholly free from error; they must be checked against other sources whose accuracy has been verified independently. In this case, the mistake introduced by the dubious choice of evidence was compounded by the misreading of a date. The content and title of the *Wu-jui-t'u* inscription as recorded by Fu, Cheng, and Kawai are close enough to those of the now-extant disreputable Shinozaki painting (fig. 15) to suggest that the recorded version may in fact have been that same painting or its prototype.

These questions can be resolved by an examination of the *Wu-jui-t'u* as it exists today. The images of the flowers, vase, and rock are dry, labored, and misshapen parodies of anything encountered in Tao-chi's work. Technically the forms are weak and incoherently conceived for such a simple subject; the brushwork is thin, tight, and listless. The lack of quality and conviction in the painting itself is compensated for in the exaggeration and distortion of the calligraphy. Comparison of this inscription with that found on any genuine Tao-chi work, such as *Waterfall at Mt. Lu*, *Sketches of Calligraphy and Painting*, or the *Keng-ch'en* manuscript, will confirm this judgment. This copyist has gone to great lengths to impress us with his dash and daring, but he has succeeded only in producing grotesque and incorrectly written characters (as evidenced by the numerous misreadings of the date). We strongly agree with Fong that the *Wu-jui-t'u* is "such a crude and careless imitation that the

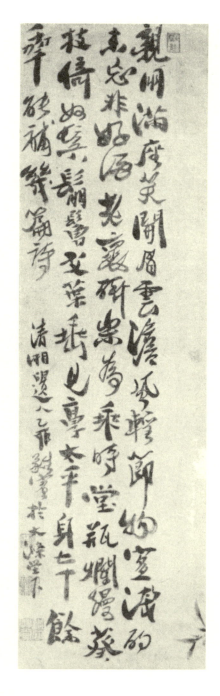

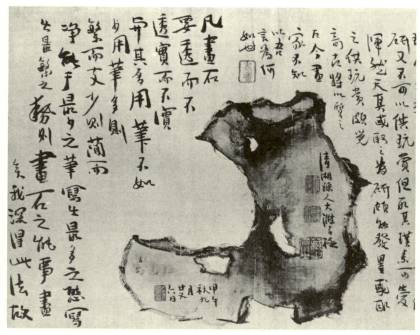

information given on it can hardly be deemed trustworthy."[23] It is probably the product of a nineteenth-century painter of the Yang-chou region several generations removed from Tao-chi but distantly influenced by him through the work of the intervening Eight Eccentrics of Yang-chou.

Two related forgeries by two different hands will be mentioned briefly in conclusion. Nagahara's publication of his version of the letter in 1928 mentions a painting which Chu Ta painted for Tao-chi. Later, in 1961, Nagahara reproduced this painting (fig. 16) and the letter,[24] along with a number of other dubious but artistically homogeneous works from his collection. Once the letter had been identified as a forgery, however, and the veracity of the Sackler version substantiated by other means, the role of this painting and the Nagahara omissions became clear. The omissions of the specific dimensions of the work requested by Tao-chi of Chu-Ta offered the forger an opportunity to produce a painting which seemed to answer Tao-chi's requirements. Thus the long 1698 encomium (fig. 11) appeared to be in response to this gift. Close study of the supposed Chu Ta work in Nagahara's collection reveals that both the landscapes and the two inscriptions (the one ascribed to Tao-chi on the left) are all by the same hand. Notice the similarity in brushwork and structure between Chu Ta's signature, "Pa-ta shan-jen," and the third and fourth characters of the inscription, also "shan-jen." Color wash has been used to fortify the impression of the masses, but, like the volumes in the forger's own paintings, they are piled one upon the other and float in mid-air with little relation to the space or water surrounding them. It is possible that the composition may derive generally from a conception of Chu Ta's; if so, it is no doubt related to the very painting for which Tao-chi wrote his long 1698 colophon, which the forger transcribed here on the painting's left edge.

Figure 17 reproduces a detail from a handscroll in ink on silk.[25] It bears the seals and signature of Tao-chi but is by the hand of yet another forger, probably a nineteenth-century painter from the Yang-chou region who knew something of Tao-chi's style through the styles of the Eccentrics. The importance of this scroll lies in its date, *chia-wu* (on the base of the rock), which, if correct, would mean that it was Tao-chi's latest dated work and would extend his chronology to that year. Unfortunately, the scroll is a disappointment in quality and overall impression and cannot be used as reliable evidence regarding Tao-chi's chronology.

PUBLISHED

This selected bibliography is intended only as a chronological summary of the controversy.

1926 Hashimoto Kansetsu, *Sekitō*, pp. 23–24; an incomplete ("Hashimoto") transcription of the Sackler letter possibly supplied by Chang Ta-ch'ien.

1928 Nagahara Oriharu, "On Shih-t'ao's Letter to Pa-ta shan-jen," *Bijutsu*, vol. 10, no. 12, pp. 56–57; includes a second ("Nagahara") version of the letter, text only, and a painting ascribed to Chu Ta, the *Ta-ti-ts'ao-t'ang t'u*, with Tao-chi's long 1698 colophon (not illustrated).

1930– Yahata Sekitarō, *Shina gaijin kenkyū (Studies on Chinese Painters)* (written 1930, published 1942), p. 152; establishes Pa-ta's chronology with the help of the Nagahara letter and proposes birth dates of 1625 for Pa-ta and 1633–34 for Tao-chi.

1935 Kawai Senrō, "On Two Problems Concerning Shih-t'ao," *Nanga kanshō*, vol. 4, no. 10, p. 14; uses the *Wu-jui-t'u* to establish Tao-chi's dates but mistakes *i-mao* for *i-yu*.

1943 Cheng Ping-shan, "Pa-ta yü Shih-t'ao," *Ku-chin pan-yüeh-k'an*, no. 32 (Oct. 1), pp. 15–17; uses the Nagahara version of letter and proposes 1630–1631 for Pa-ta's birth date.

1948 Fu Pao-shih, *Shih-t'ao shang-jen nien-p'u*; an important comprehensive chronology of Tao-chi's life with a translation of the letter from Hashimoto's incomplete transcription; proposes 1630 as date of birth. (Fu did not see the original and may have thought the transcription was the Nagahara version.)

1955 Chang Ta-ch'ien, *Ta-feng-t'ang ming-chi*, vol. 2, pls. 34–36; *Letter to Pa-ta* published for the first time in collotype. Chang presumably obtained it directly from Li Jui-ch'ing at some time between 1920 and 1926.

1956 *Niseki Hachidai* (one of three monographs reproducing the significant works in the Sumitomo Kanichi collection in collotype); articles on Tao-chi and Pa-ta by Shimada Shūjirō, Yonezawa Yoshiho, and others.

1959 Wen Fong, "A Letter from Shih-t'ao to Pa-ta shan-jen and the Problem of Shih-t'ao's Chronology"; proves the Nagahara version is a forgery and proposes 1641 birth date for Tao-chi on the basis of the Sackler letter.

1960 Li Tan, "Pa-ta shan-jen ts'ung-k'ao"; uses 1674 portrait of Pa-ta at 49 *sui* (plus additional evidence of mixed reliability) to compute his birth date as 1624.

1961 Nagahara Oriharu, *Shih-t'ao and Pa-ta*; the Nagahara letter and the Chu Ta *Ta-ti-ts'ao-t'ang t'u* in his collection are illustrated here for the first time, along with other dubious works.

Cheng Cho-lu, *Shih-t'ao yen-chiu*; a major study of Tao-chi's painting, life, seals, and influence; proposes Tao-chi's birth date as 1630 on basis of dubious *Wu-jui-t'u* but mistakes *i-mao* for *i-yu* and believes that there are three versions of the letter.

1962 Wu T'ieh-sheng, *Hua-p'u*; uses a newly discovered version of the *Hua-yü-lu* and the 1701 *Keng-ch'en Manuscript of Poems* to prove Tao-chi's birth date as 1641.

Cheng Wei, "Lun Shih-t'ao sheng-huo . . . ," pp. 43–50; a major article which uses the *Keng-ch'en Manuscript* to prove 1641 as Tao-chi's birth year and publishes some of his late letters.

I Ting, "Pa-ta shan-jen sheng-nien chih-i," pp. 280–83; corrects Li Tan's use of sources and, on the basis of the 1674 portrait, correctly proposes Chu Ta's birth date as 1626.

1965 Kohara Hironobu, "On a New Version of Shih-t'ao's *Hua-yü-lu*," pp. 5–13; concludes that the *Hua-p'u* is a forgery, accepts 1641 as birth date of Tao-chi, but believes three versions of the letter exist.

1967 Richard Edwards, Chou Ju-hsi, Sasaki Kozo, Jonathan Spence, and Wu T'ung, *The Painting of Tao-chi*; the catalogue to the first major exhibition of Tao-chi's works, which contains discussions and a broad selection of paintings, a comprehensive chronology, and a compilation of seals; the Sackler letter appears as no. 15, pp. 126–27.

A. C. Soper, "The 'Letter from Shih-t'ao to Pa-ta shan-jen'"; notes retouching of the photographic plate of Fong's 1959 article and questions whether the Sackler letter is any more reliable than the Nagahara version.

Wen Fong, "Reply to Professor Soper's Comments on Tao-chi's Letter"; refutes Soper's objections by providing evidence of Chu Ta's birth date as 1625, uses the *Keng-ch'en Manuscript* to bolster 1641 date, stresses method of content and style, and suggests identity of forger of Nagahara letter.

1968 Wu T'ung [under the pseudonym "A-wen"], eight articles in the *Central Daily News* (Taipei), first installment February 6; discusses Tao-chi's life, dates, the Sackler letter, and the Michigan exhibition and symposium of 1967.

Wang Fang-yü, "Lun Fu Pao-shih 'Shih-t'ao shang-jen nien-p'u' soting sheng-nien"; reports Chang Ta-ch'ien's admission that the Nagahara letter is his forgery.

Yonezawa Yoshiho, "Shohō-jō kara mita Sekitō ga no kijun-saku"; compares the calligraphic inscriptions on three works by Tao-chi in the Sumitomo collection — the album *Eight Views of Huang-shan, Waterfall at Mt. Lu*, and the 1699 Huang-shan handscroll — for identity of authorship.

Richard Edwards, "Postscript to an Exhibition"; reports on the Michigan symposium and summarizes prevailing stylistic arguments.

Record of the Art Museum, Princeton University, vol. 27, no. 2, p. 94 (acquisitions list); lists the letter as a gift of the Arthur M. Sackler Foundation to The Art Museum.

1969 *Archives of Asian Art*, vol. 23 (1969–70), p. 71, fig. 45; illustrates the last two leaves of the Sackler letter.

1971 Kohara Hironobu, "Sekitō to kozan hasshō gasatsu"; a short monograph on the Sumitomo *Eight Views of Huang-shan* album accompanying a portfolio of color collotypes.

Tseng Yu-ho Ecke, *Chinese Calligraphy*; illustrates the last four leaves of the Sackler letter as cat. no. 83.

NOTES

1. See Contag and Wang, *Seals*, p. 547.
2. See *CKHCJMTTT*, p. 664.
3. For Liu Shu, see Contag and Wang, *Seals*, pp. 617, 713; *CKHCJMTTT*, p. 664.
4. See Wen Fong's "Reply to Professor Soper's Comments on Tao-chi's Letter to Chu Ta," p. 353. The Hashimoto transcription later caused great confusion because it agreed with the Sackler letter in all but a single sentence, "hsiang-ch'eng suo-chi t'ai-ta, wu hsiao, fang-pu-hsia" ("the painting which you sent me was too large; my house is too small to hang it," ll. 24–25 of the original), which was omitted because of "illegibility." This led several scholars who had not seen the Sackler or Nagahara letters in reproduction to think that three versions existed. As Fong suggests, "this critical deletion surely indicates complicity on the part of the person who supplied Hashimoto with the [incomplete] tran-

script" (*ibid.*). This person was probably Chang Ta-ch'ien, who then owned the Sackler letter and who in due time produced the Nagahara letter and Chu Ta painting to lend further interest to the case. If so, the motivation behind the deletions in the Hashimoto transcript is explained.

5. See Part IV above; Fong, "A Letter from Shih-t'ao," pp. 27–28, and "Reply to Professor Soper's Comments," pp. 355–56.

6. See Fong, "A Letter from Shih-t'ao," pp. 28–29, for more detailed discussion.

7. Fong, "Reply to Professor Soper's Comments," p. 356.

8. Each of these letters has been subjected to careful scrutiny to ensure authenticity. Those collected in the *Ming-Ch'ing hua-yüan ch'ih-tu* (see figs. 2, 7) are of especial quality and interest. They came from the collection of P'an Ch'en-hou, an extremely gifted painter and connoisseur.

9. While this remains an important criterion in distinguishing the hand of the forger in the Nagahara letter, it is not necessarily true of other works after Tao-chi which the same forger may have perpetrated. There is no signature of this form in *XXXV*, for example. We are pursuing this line of investigation in another study.

10. See "A Letter from Shih-t'ao," pp. 25, 28; "Reply to Professor Soper's Comments," p. 353.

11. "Reply to Professor Soper's Comments," p. 325.

12. As first noted in *ibid.*, p. 356. Later Mr. Wang Fang-yü kindly supplied us with a photograph of this colophon. The painting on which it is found was also presumably in Chang Ta-ch'ien's collection. When Chang fled Shanghai, he is said to have hurriedly had the inscription removed from the painting, leaving the painting itself behind. Subsequent efforts to recover it from his family failed (personal communication to the authors from James Lo, Princeton).

13. "A Letter from Shih-t'ao," pp. 26–27.

14. Reproduced in *Ta-feng-t'ang ming-chi*, vol. 3, pl. 9. Tao-chi inscribed the work twice; the second inscription is dated 1697. The calligraphy is excellent and its presence on the scroll makes this charming work another important document of their friendship.

15. Reproduced in *Mo-ch'ao mi-chi ts'ang-ying*, vol. 2, pl. 13.

16. See Fong, "A Letter from Shih-t'ao," pp. 29, 38–42.

17. *Wen-wu*, vol. 7 (1960), pp. 35–41; Fong, "Reply to Professor Soper's Comments," p. 351.

18. See Wu T'ung, "Tao-chi, a Chronology," p. 59; I Ting, "Pa-ta shan-jen sheng-nien chih-i" ("Disputing Pa-ta's Birth Date"), pp. 280–83. I Ting corrects Li Tan's calculation; according to Chinese reckoning, if Pa-ta was forty-nine (*sui*) in 1674, he was born in 1626 (not 1624 or 1625). Fong also forgot to add a year at birth according to Chinese calculation ("Reply to Professor Soper's Comments," pp. 351–52), and he was not aware of I Ting's article when he quoted Li.

19. *Shih-t'ao shang-jen nien-p'u*, p. 88.

20. Reproduced in *Sō Gen Min Shin meiga taikan*, vol. 2, pl. 224.

21. Cheng Cho-lu, *Shih-t'ao yen-chiu*, p. 37.

22. These forms may be checked in such books as, for example, T'ien Yüan's *Yin-wen-hsüeh*, pt. 1, p. 65, pt. 4, p. 88.

23. Fong, "A Letter from Shih-t'ao," p. 30.

24. Nagahara Oriharu, *Shih-t'ao and Pa-ta shan-jen*, pls. 5–6.

25. Reproduced in *Sō Gen Min Shin meiga taikan*, vol. 2, pl. 225, with details in *Min-matsu san oshō*, pls. 10–11.

Thousand-Character "Eulogy of a Great Man"
(Ch'ien-tzu ta-jen sung)

The Art Museum, Princeton University (L38.67).

Handscroll of calligraphy. Ink on a single sheet of paper with vertical ruling drawn in ink. 26.9 x 99.8 cm.

UNDATED: probably executed ca. 1698.

SIGNATURE OF THE ARTIST: Ch'ing-hsiang, Pan-ko-han (as part of a three-line epilogue).

SEALS OF THE ARTIST: *Ch'ien-yu Lung-mien, Chi* (intaglio, tall rectangle; *PTC*, cat. no. 9, not listed) on painting below title in lower right corner; *T'ou-pai i-jan pu-shih-tzu* (intaglio, tall rectangle; *PTC*, cat. no. 94, not listed) and *Ch'ing-hsiang Shih-t'ao* (intaglio, tall rectangle; *PTC*, cat. no. 22, not listed), both on left side of painting after painter's epilogue.

COLLECTORS' SEALS:

Chin Ch'uan-sheng (*tzu* Lan-p'o, late Ch'ing collector from Chia-hsing, Chekiang), *Hsiu-shui Chin Lan-p'o sou-so shin-shih shu-hua* (intaglio, square; Contag and Wang, *Seals*, no. 3, p. 557) lower left corner of scroll, bottom seal.
Wu Yün (*tzu* P'ing-chai, 1811–1883, a painter and collector from Wu-hsing, Chekiang), *P'ing-chai chien-shang* (intaglio, square) lower left corner of scroll, second seal from bottom.
Wang Tsu-hsi (*hao* T'i-an, 1858–1908, a collector from Chia-hsing, Chekiang), *T'i-an chien-shang* (intaglio, square; Contag and Wang, *Seals*, no. 5, p. 531) lower right corner of scroll, bottom seal; *T'i-an ch'ing-mi* (relief, square) lower left edge of scroll, third seal from bottom.
Chang Shan-tzu (Tse, 1883–1940), *Shan-tzu shen-ting* (relief, small square) lower right corner of scroll, *Shan-tzu shin-shang* (relief, square) left side of scroll.
Chang Ta-ch'ien (Yüan, born 1899), *Ta-ch'ien hao-meng* (relief, tall rectangle) lower right edge of scroll, *Ta-ch'ien chih-pao* (relief, large square) upper left corner of scroll, *Ta-ch'ien yu-mu* (relief, oval) left edge of scroll, *Pu-fu ku-jen kao-hou-jen* (relief, large square) lower left edge of scroll.
Mr. Wang (unidentified), *Ts'eng-ts'ang Wang-shih erh-shih-pa-so-yen-chai* (relief, tall rectangle) left edge of scroll.

CONDITION: fair; there is some wormhole damage and foxing over the surface, but no characters are obliterated; originally three seals of the artist followed Tao-chi's epilogue; the traces of a tall rectangular patch, deftly woven into the fibers of the paper, are visible under a strong light in the space between his two intaglio seals. The genuine seal may have been placed on a spurious work to give it greater credence.

FRONTISPIECE: inscribed by Chang Ta-ch'ien in large "running" script precedes the work proper (see the detail):
The finest calligraphy by K'u-kua [Tao-chi] in the world: worshipped and collected at the Ta-feng-t'ang.
[Signed:] The old Yüan [Chang Ta-ch'ien].
[Seal:] *Ta-ch'ien wei-yin, Ta-nien* (relief, square).

PROVENANCE: Ta-feng-t'ang collection.

PUBLISHED: *The Selected Painting and Calligraphy of Shih-t'ao*, vol. 2, pl. 79.

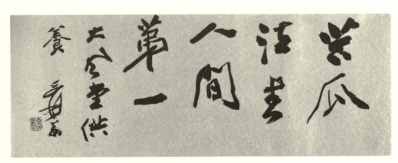

Frontispiece by Chang Ta-ch'ien.

THIS IMPRESSIVE HANDSCROLL presents a rare aspect of Tao-chi's accomplishments—calligraphy written in a diminutive and formal hand. The lengthy text was transcribed by the artist in his maturity at the peak of his physical and spiritual energies. A high degree of stamina and singlemindedness is revealed in the balanced tension and consistency of the writing. Such powers would wane soon after 1700.

Tao-chi's fame rests primarily on his paintings, of which large numbers exist. Aside from casual writing in the form of letters or folding fans, few examples of pure calligraphy by his hand are extant, and only quite recently have they begun to be appreciated and studied by Western collectors and historians. This work is important both for its intrinsic quality and its rarity; it is the only calligraphic handscroll of such content, length, format, and script in an American collection.[1]

The scroll is written in a uniform, "fluent standard" (*hsing-k'ai*) script modeled after Ni Tsan (1301–1374). It opens with a five-character title in "clerical" (*li*) script (fig. 1*b*), and the whole text, containing some fourteen hundred characters, is divided into three sections: the transcribed preface, composed by Chan Wen-te, the original author of the "Eulogy of a Great Man"; the "Eulogy" itself, in rhymed prose; and Tao-chi's own epilogue in three lines, which concludes the scroll with these words: "[I] don't know where my friend obtained [the text of] 'Eulogy of a Great Man.' [He] brought out this length of paper and asked [me], Ch'ing-hsiang Pan-ko-han, to write it. [When] I was finished [I] lifted my head and laughed: Where am I? Here is the writing, but where is the man? Isn't it strange?"

THE "EULOGY OF A GREAT MAN" is an essay in four-character rhymed parallel prose (*p'ien-t'i-wen*) composed of one thousand characters, none of which are repeated. The text, composed by Chan Wen-te (unidentified, probably a Ming scholar), is not the famous and popularly known "Thousand-Character Classic" (*Ch'ien-tzu-wen*). The traditional *Ch'ien-tzu-wen* grew out of the Liang emperor Wu's (reigned 502–549) fondness for the calligraphy of the great Eastern Chin master Wang Hsi-chih (307?–365?). Emperor Wu ordered a certain Yin T'ieh-shih (fl. 535) to assemble and trace a thousand different characters from the then extant works by the Chin master. Chou Hsing-tzu (fl. 535) was subsequently ordered to compose these thousand characters into an essay with the fitting rhymes. Chou completed the task in one night, but it had been such a grueling experience that his hair turned white. The result was the familiar text beginning "T'ien-ti hsüan-huang."

The text has been popular with calligraphers ever since, and its rendering was considered fundamental to the training of students of calligraphy. Generally, a single calligraphic specimen (*t'ieh*) chosen for emulation is too short to provide a model for all the most common characters, and single characters are invariably duplicated in a single text. With an essay such as the "Thousand-Character Classic," no two characters are repeated; hence it offers a structural model for at least a thousand basic characters.

According to the preface to the "Eulogy," Chan Wen-te was dissatisfied with the original text by Chou and discussed with his friend Hsü Yeh-chün the idea of recomposing their own version with the same thousand characters. Other scholars after Chou had also felt challenged to rewrite the text but were discouraged by problems such as the difficulty of splitting some of the common binomes (such as *p'i-p'a*, or *p'iao-yao*) which were already used in the original. In Chan Wen-te's version the same parallel syntax is retained, but he arrived at a solution in which no two characters are repeated in the same sequence or rhyme as the original. When Chan completed the task, Hsü praised him on three counts: Chou's syntax was

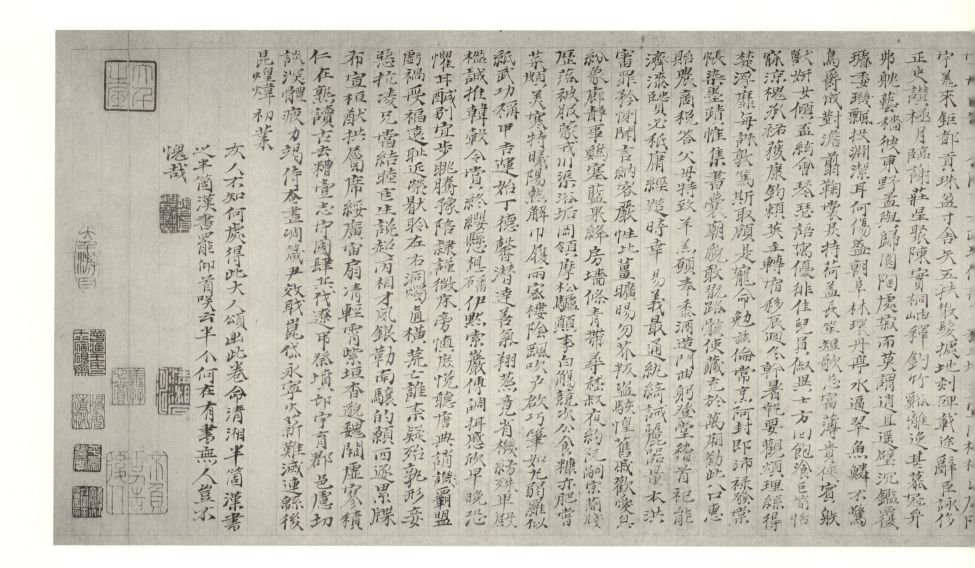

forced, while Chan's is spontaneous; Chou's content was unintegrated and discontinuous, while Chan's is unified and can be read in one breath; Chou's rhyming was uneven and random, while Chan's is symmetrical and rhythmic. Chan modestly apologized that he had taken seven days as compared to Chou's one. Hsü replied that Chou was ordered by the Emperor and under a different kind of external pressure to complete it. Besides, Chou's was the first composition using a thousand characters, and therefore he had fewer literary strictures with which to contend, while Chan, who was doing it for amusement, had to overcome Chou's precedent and seek fresh solutions. Ultimately, it is not the speed, said Hsü, but the literary quality that matters. Therefore, despite the difference in the circumstances of execution, Hsü still felt Chan's version was superior to Chou's. The preface concludes by saying that the title, "Thousand-Character 'Eulogy of a Great Man'" (*Ch'ien-tzu ta-jen sung*), was taken from the first two characters of the essay, *ta-jen* ("great man").

Those who know the older "Thousand-Character Classic" may differ with Hsü. Suffice it to say that the Chinese have considered such variations on a thousand characters as a form of intellectual word game, interest in which has been maintained sporadically even to the present. For example, P'u Ju (1887–1963, *tzu* Hsin-yü), younger brother of the last deposed Manchu emperor, was well

known for his painting and excelled in calligraphy and poetry also. He is said to have composed his own "Thousand-Character Classic," but from a completely different set of characters—certainly a feat to try one's wits in any language.

THE CALLIGRAPHY, from the standpoint of quality, consistency of presentation, and sheer length, is unrivaled among Tao-chi's works. The well-known 1696 *Sketches of Calligraphy and Painting* (fig. 3b) is comparable in excellence and has a longer text, but in it several scripts alternate with paintings, representing a different format. To our knowledge, the only other example of Tao-chi calligraphy on such a scale is the *Tao-te-ching* in Chung Yu style, in the collection of Chang Ch'ün, Taipei.[2]

The five larger characters of the title are written in "clerical" (*li*) script, in a substyle known as *T'ang-li*. Historically, the *li* script originated early in the Han dynasty; it was practiced in subsequent periods of the Six Dynasties through the T'ang, but the style gradually became more conventionalized and lost much of its earlier expressive vigor. Before the revival of *Han-li* in the middle of the Ch'ing dynasty, the *li* script of the T'ang dynasty, *T'ang-li*, was the "clerical" script more commonly practiced by such major masters as Wen Cheng-ming and Wang Shih-min.

千字大人頌

詹文德撰

因篇首有大人二字遂名大人頌。

XXIV (*above and overleaf; overleaf slightly larger than original*).

Tao-chi's *li* style was also that of *T'ang-li*. His fondness for the "clerical" script permeated his calligraphy in general, so that even his other script types contain "clerical" brush movements. This tendency is well illustrated in the first character of the title, *ch'ien* ("thousand"), which combines "clerical" brushwork with the structure of archaic "seal" (*chuan*) script, a historically older type. While the mixing of script types is unusual among other calligraphers, Tao-chi did it with frequency and imagination. He used this particular combination of clerical and seal scripts elsewhere with slight variations of brushwork, as in the 1696 *Sketches of Calligraphy and Painting by Ch'ing-hsiang*, the self-inscription to his *After Shen Chou's Bronze Peacock Inkslab (XXVII)*, of about 1698–1703, and the inscription to leaf C of his 1707 *Ting-ch'iu Album of Flowers* (fig. 1d). Tao-chi in each case has integrated the different brush movements of the clerical and seal types into a harmoniously balanced character. As for the script of the text itself, some of the characters are written with the strokes connected, as in "running" (*hsing*) script, so that the effect is more fluent than in the "formal standard" (*cheng-k'ai*), where each stroke remains separate; hence it can be identified as *hsing-k'ai*.

In general Tao-chi's "regular" scripts form two major structural groups: one has a squat composition with even, fleshy strokes which are written relatively slowly, using Chung Yu (151–230) as a model; the other, with thinner, shapelier strokes, inspired by Ch'u Sui-liang (596–658) or Ni Tsan (1301–1374). The calligraphy of this scroll strongly resembles Ni's *Jung-hsi Studio* inscription[3] (fig. 2), leading one to speculate that Tao-chi may have practiced the Yüan master's script at some time early in his training (see Part IV above for further discussion).

In contrast to Tao-chi's Chung Yu style (seen in the 1685 *Searching for Plum Blossoms* handscroll, *XVIII*), this style modeled after Ni and Ch'u stresses fluidity and contrasts of thicks and thins within the movement of a single stroke (see the detail). The composition of each character is broader and therefore allows more delicate fluctuations to emphasize expansion and contraction of the line. The characters have been written with the fine tip of a highly resilient writing brush used specifically for small characters. This brush differs from the softer and coarser painting brush with which Tao-chi customarily wrote inscriptions on his paintings. The fine point of the brush is seen in the horizontal and vertical strokes, where the tension is contracted, producing a thin, ductile line; the resiliency of the brush is seen in the diagonals and hooks, where the "head" (or opening movement) and the "tail" (or closing movement) of each stroke receive greatest pressure, producing a springy, plump form. In contrast to the inner strength and antique ideal of the Chung Yu manner, this style evinces more overt changes of pace,

寧宦政制音律陛奏表疏場脩論策粮非壇益軍閫枝梧氏慶陋

宇羌來鉅都貢珠盈寸舍矢五筷散髮攄地刻碑載途辭臣詠侈

正史讚極月臨謝莊星聚陳寶桐油釋釣竹瓠離逸甚慕冠弁

弗舭藝稍彼東野孟與歸園陶廢嶽而莫謂逍遥壁沉鑑覆

璠委璣飄投淵潔耳何傷盞朝阜林環丹得水遍翠魚鱗求驚

鳥爵成對澹前鞠裳晃持荷蓋長笙短歌忽富薄貴俠賓躬

獸妍女傾盂紈會琴瑟語瀉優徘佳兒員似異士方叵飽飱臣惷惝

寀涼槐承袿獲康釣頼茨至轉宿移辰迴今幹暑乾要觀煩理綜得

楚浮廉每誅敦篤斯取顧是寵命勉玆倫常烹阿封郎沛祿發棠

悵染墨靖帷集書囊廟覭敢骹路嶷使藏克於萬廝勤此八囗惠

貽農高税答父母特致羊羔碩奉黍酒造門曲躬登堂稽首祀能

濟漆睍兒秔庸經造時宰昜義最通絖綺誡麗囂呈童本洪

審罪矜測聞言納密嚴惟此薑曠眛勿芥叛盜駭惶舊戚歡愛貝

紛象廊静事雞塞藍果絳房墻條青帶尋茲叔夜約阮嗣宗簡戚

大人御天君子名世立千秋基興諸夏利高文起家建景閣帝二百餘
年我皇陟位河澄寶出鳳舉毛從虞雲雨旦漢日再中群黎作
又列州攸同往收故土入坐新增銘盤學湯設鼓邁禹郊因瀍規
俯欲縈矩動綠尺衡嘯合鍾呂手植四維目親九府云溫其色四後
廟斁定刑勒政過化存神姿儀豈弟陛黝藏翮池鯤躍海谷駒鳴庭
振攝流弊矯端住俗宅洛周詳營田趙獨延踐籍疏情馳真漠鬱
尊黃金膳枇素不內捕奏號外斬菀操蟬笑月悚毀譽空勞伏龍
忠貞務倡慈孝惟寫及盡閒居雅好草聖張工詩王杜妙涇渭朗
寮組悲雁止號嶽伯分佐歲精可招蓬已棄為敬身有道所求
若王不磨馬忌光孟映意指夏堅拜皋稷訓胄孔軻傳晉瞻晝接
隨用瞑眠物皆率真念匪蒲假閈賊師愚謙孤讓寢烱乎隱韜
辯乃上下老安友信并懷少者背城克賊面壁圖治禮猶節也樂則和
以稼垂霜飲蘭抽露施華實等懸根葉交資京多淑鄉縣具良牧廉
吳見知退思遺辱泰階既平禪碣將續束藁飯廳市劍駟犢姑

a   b   c   d

1. Tao-chi, details of *ch'ien* ("one thousand") character (not to scale): *a, Sketches of Calligraphy and Painting by Ch'ing-hsiang*, dated 1696, handscroll, sec. 7; *b, Eulogy of a Great Man*, title; *c, After Shen Chou's Bronze Peacock Inkslab*, ca. 1698–1703, self-inscription; *d, Ting-ch'iu Album of Flowers*, dated 1707, leaf C, self-inscription.

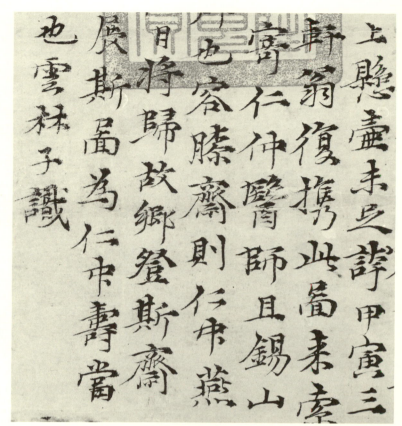

2. Ni Tsan, *Jung-hsi Studio*, dated 1372, detail of self-inscription. Hanging scroll. Ink on paper. National Palace Museum, Taipei.

pressure, and thickness and an outward formal grace. Furthermore, the small size and fineness make the characters of this scroll more challenging than larger writing because the minuteness requires a sustained tension and control: all the energy of the drives and turns must be directed within a small area. What is satisfying about the quality of this writing is the sense of tautness and pliancy maintained at such a high pitch and energy level. It is a calligraphic tour de force and certainly one of Tao-chi's most distinguished performances.

While individual sources of Tao-chi's writing styles may be recognized, they cannot be categorized strictly because he preferred to combine the various brush principles of several types into one script, in a true eclectic spirit. He loved variety and in a single album would often write one leaf in one script and a second leaf in another, and so on (the Fong *Small Album* and the Boston *Album of Landscapes* are excellent examples of this predilection). Sometimes, in a long text, the script becomes looser and more cursive toward the end, as in the 1696 *Sketches* handscroll. In the Sackler *Eulogy*, however, Tao-chi has kept to a single script and also maintained a unity and discipline which makes the work exceptional for a man of his changeable and impulsive temperament.

THE DATE OF EXECUTION, unfortunately, does not appear on the scroll, so we must rely on style and other factors. Judging from the degree of discipline and concentration needed to produce characters of this size and a text of this length, the scroll is undoubtedly a mature work. A further clue appears in the rectangular intaglio seal at the end of his own inscription: *T'ou-pai i-jan pu-shih-tzu* ("although my hair has turned white, I still can't read characters"). According to Sasaki Kozo's compilation of Tao-chi's seals, this seal

is fittingly found on works dated from about 1695 to about 1703.[4]

There are several works of calligraphy in the same script type dated within this range with which we may compare the Sackler scroll: the *View from Yü-hang* handscroll (fig. 3a);[5] the *Sketches of Calligraphy and Painting by Ch'ing-hsiang* handscroll (3b);[6] the Sumitomo collection *Huang-shan* handscroll (3d);[7] and the *Reminiscences of Nanking* (3e and XXXIV).

To determine the position of an "unknown" in a sequence of calligraphy of any one script type, we look for such formal changes as spacing of the columns (*hang-ch'i*), slant and tension in the individual strokes and in the whole configuration of the characters, length and pressure of the diagonal and hook strokes, and variations in the thickness of the stroke lines. But in order to verify the significance and consistency of the changes which enable us to date the "unknown," these observations must be closely compared with other dated and authenticated works in related and different scripts (see Part IV above, diagram of Tao-chi's calligraphy). We anticipate that the above sequence of four works can provide a summary of our findings. The structural considerations just mentioned are also qualified by the "energy level" which we sense in the work as a whole, offering a valuable key to dating beyond the purely structural level because this transmitted vitality reflects the physical powers of the calligrapher at a certain stage in life. All formal considerations, however, are still subject to the delicate variables of the immediate circumstances of execution—the mood, materials, and state of health of the master.

In the Sackler scroll, the strokes are tense and resilient regardless of thinness; the diagonals and hooks are well formed and vigorous, with a controlled emphasis given the splayed ends of the strokes. The feeling of the lines is crisp and alert. In the 1693 scroll (fig. 3a) the composition of the characters is more elongated and their inter-

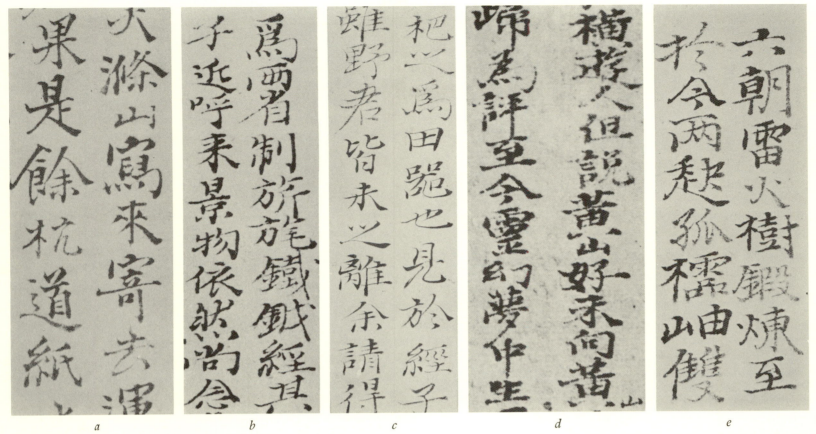

| a | b | c | d | e |

3. Tao-chi, details of calligraphy in Ch'u and Ni styles (not to scale): *a*, *View from Yü-hang*, 1693, self-inscription; *b*, *Sketches of Calligraphy and Painting by Ch'ing-hsiang*, 1696, sec. 2; *c*, *Eulogy of a Great Man*; *d*, *Huang-shan*, 1699, self-inscription on the handscroll; *e*, *Reminiscences of Nanking*, 1707, self-inscription on album leaf K.

nal structure slightly looser, with greater variation in the thickness of the strokes. In the 1696 scroll (*3b*) a similar slender grace and tense vigor indicate the same hand, but the characters have gained in compactness, and the composition is slightly squarer. The 1699 Sumitomo scroll (*3d*) bears a script which is a combination of Ni and Chung Yu; hence the configuration is even squatter. The strokes are also plumper and less well formed than in the 1696 *Sketches*, but the same basic structure and calligraphic purpose underlie the three works. The diagonals are given emphatic emphasis, and the columnar spacing is dense and unwavering. In the 1707 *Nanking* album (*3e*) the quality of the writing is still exceedingly fine, but the general physical vitality of the man has diminished. This is reflected in the loss of some of that internal tension found especially in the 1693 and 1696 works; also, the arrangement of the components is slacker, with each stroke written more slowly, and the diagonal and hook strokes lacking that energetic emphasis seen in the earlier scrolls.

Within this sequence, the *Eulogy* seems closer to the 1696 scroll and possibly earlier than the 1699 Sumitomo scroll. The total configuration of each character is compact and rectangular, as in the 1696 work; the strokes have the same tensile recoil, sharpness, and rhythmic accent, which are further enhanced by a heightened elegance and fluidity. Tao-chi was at the peak of his technical powers, and all were brought to bear in this calligraphy. In view of these comparisons, a 1698 date of execution seems fitting.

NOTES

1. The 1967 show of Tao-chi's works from European, Asian, and American collections included only one specimen of calligraphy in Tao-chi's large "regular" script, the hanging scroll *Wan-li's Porcelain Handle Brush* (*PTC*, cat. no. 24, p. 168).

2. Published in *A Garland of Chinese Calligraphy*, vol. 2, pl. 28, in album format with thirty-seven leaves, undated.

3. National Palace Museum, Taipei, *Three Hundred Masterpieces*, vol. 4, pl. 186.

4. *PTC*, p. 69.

5. *Shih-t'ao hua-chi*, no. 40.

6. *Ch'ing-hsiang shu-hua-kao-chüan*, sec. 2.

7. Self-inscription to handscroll, ink and light color on paper, Sumitomo collection, reproduced from Yonezawa Yoshiho, "Shohō-jō kara mita Sekitō ga no kijun-saku."

XXV TAO-CHI (1641–ca. 1710)

Album of Flowers and Portrait of Tao-chi

The Art Museum, Princeton University (L312.70).

Album of nine leaves, eight of painting (from an original set of ten) and one portrait leaf by an anonymous late nineteenth-century painter. Painting: 25.6 x 34.5 cm. (average); portrait: 27.5 x 35.1 cm. Ink and color on paper (four different kinds, as indicated on each leaf).

UNDATED: painting leaves probably executed ca. 1698.

UNSIGNED

INSCRIPTION BY THE ARTIST: a poetic eulogy by Tao-chi on each painting leaf.

SEALS OF THE ARTIST (on each leaf):

Yüeh-shan (intaglio, square; *PTC*, cat. no. 108, not listed) leaf A.
Pan-ko-han (intaglio, tall rectangle; *PTC*, cat. no. 57, not listed) leaves A and E.
Wo ho-chi chih-yu (intaglio, large square; this seal does not appear in *PTC*) leaf B.
K'u-kua (intaglio, tall rectangle; *PTC*, cat. no. 43, not listed) leaf C.
Yüan-chi (intaglio, small square; *PTC*, cat. no. 104, not listed) leaf C (see the discussion of leaf C for the authenticity of the two seals on this leaf).
A-ch'ang (intaglio, square; *PTC*, cat. no. 1, not listed) leaves D and E.
Yen-chung chih-jen, wu lao-i (intaglio, square; *PTC*, cat. no. 100, not listed) leaf F.
Tun-ken (intaglio, double seal in two small squares; *PTC*, cat. no. 97, not listed) leaf G.
Ping-hsüeh wu-ch'ien-shen (intaglio, tall rectangle; *PTC*, cat. no. 59, not listed) leaf H.

INSCRIPTIONS ON THE PORTRAIT LEAF: an eight-line biography of Tao-chi and a five-line eulogy and epilogue, unsigned and dated winter, 1674 (*chia-yin, tung*); see the end of the entry for discussion.

COLLECTOR'S SEALS (fourteen, all belonging to Chang Ta-ch'ien):

Ta-feng-t'ang Chien-chiang, K'un-ts'an, Hsüeh-ko, K'u-kua mo-yüan (relief, tall rectangle) leaves A, C, and portrait leaf.
Pieh-shih-jung-i (relief, square) leaf B.
Ta-ch'ien chü-shih kung-yang pai-Shih-chih-i (relief, square) leaves C and H.
Ts'ang-chih Ta-ch'ien (intaglio, square) leaf C.
Chiu-t'u-pao ku-jou-ch'ing (intaglio, rectangle) leaf D.
Chang Yüan (intaglio, square) leaf E.
Ta-ch'ien (relief, square) leaf E.
Ta-feng-t'ang (relief, large square) leaf F.
Chang Yüan (intaglio, small square) leaf G.
Nan-pei-tung-hsi chih-yu hsiang-sui wu-pieh-li (relief, square) leaf G.
Shu-chün, Chang Yüan (intaglio, small square) leaf H.
San-ch'ien Ta-ch'ien (relief, small square) leaf H.
Ta-feng-t'ang ch'ang-wu (relief, square) portrait leaf.
Ta-ch'ien wei-yin ta-nien (relief, square) mounting of portrait leaf after inscription.

CONDITION: poor; the edges of the painting leaves have suffered heavy insect damage and the top and upper sides have been skillfully repaired (see notes on condition of individual leaves below); the surface of the paper has also been heavily abraded, and at some time during the remounting and repair process the leaves were thoroughly washed, leaving the colors slightly faded. The extent of the repair is visible in the patchwork textures of the paper and in the darker and smoother ink tones. The surface of the portrait leaf has also suffered abrasion and damage from wormholes, but although the paper has been repaired, there seems to have been no extensive retouching (see also discussion of portrait leaf below).

PROVENANCE: Ta-feng-t'ang collection, which still possesses the two remaining leaves and which remounted and repaired the eight leaves shown here.

PUBLISHED: *The Selected Painting and Calligraphy of Shih-t'ao*, vol. 5, pl. 109 (leaves 1–10).

OTHER VERSIONS OF PORTRAIT LEAF: three (see the end of the entry for discussion).

Leaf A: *"Flowering Crab Apple"*

CONDITION: fair; this is one of the better-preserved leaves, as there is damage only along the top and edges of the paper, leaving the painting intact; there has been no apparent retouching in the flowers, but the wormholes in the calligraphy have been filled in, especially the characters in the lower right corner.

Two broken branches of the crab apple (*hai-t'ang*)[1] form an arc in the picture plane. This arrangement leaves the lower right-hand corner free for a seven-character quatrain, a design which was part of the painter's poetic forethought. The poem reads:

All face the east wind [of spring] and enter the land of drunkenness;
Green feeling and red sentiment are both equal.
If they were as languid as the peach blossom,
They wouldn't be as fragrant as the lotus.

The flowering crab apple, indigenous to northern China, has been much admired as an ornamental tree but is not as extensively cultivated in the Chinese garden as other flowering trees. Tao-chi's poem hints at the reason: its blossom is not as delicate as that of the peach. Russet stems and green leaves are the setting for pink blossoms with pale yellow centers. The colors are pale and moist; they almost seem to emit a sweet fragrance. The brushtip spontaneously guides the denser hues to structure the interior volumes and textures of the stems, leaves, and flowers. At the proper instant of saturation, thick lines of ink are applied to the leaves, creating a more forceful articulation and a color suffusion which, like the structural use of color, is very much Tao-chi's personal signature. The black lines of emphasis are echoed in the calligraphy, which is written in a straightforward "regular" script.

The use of ink in the calligraphy is an unusual feature in this leaf: each character is written in a sequence containing a range of dark to light. While Tao-chi loved variety, this degree of variation appears particularly unnatural. Nonetheless, the composition and brushwork are identifiable as his: the strokes are well formed, although slightly turbid, and the configuration of such characters as *feng* ("wind") and *ch'ing* ("feeling") conforms to other tendencies found in the same characters in comparable scripts (cf. the diagram of Tao-chi's calligraphy in Part IV above). The most likely explanation for the unusual appearance of the ink is that the writer was using an old worn-out brush which had not been properly washed; the glue from the old ink still adhered to the upper parts of the brush, so that only the tip absorbed the ink and became dry after a stroke or two. This would cause the thick heavy line at the beginning of the strokes in a character and the rapid fading to a dry one. (Wen Fong has suggested that the characters may have been written in winter, when the ink and brushtip were almost frozen; this explanation would hold for the calligraphy only, as the flowers here and in the remainder of the album are all quite wet.)

The lyrical spring feeling achieved in this leaf and in the album as a whole is comparable to Tao-chi's undated *Flower Album by Ch'ing-hsiang*,[2] where leaf 1 (fig. 1) is executed in a similar method of description through color and inner articulation with ink.

Leaf B: *"Orchids"*

CONDITION: the upper edge of the paper is conspicuously damaged at irregular intervals of 1 to 2 cm. in depth; these areas have been repaired and the missing parts of the characters filled in. Repair on one of the upper orchid leaves is discernible. The paper shows the finely striated watermarks of the *lo-wen* variety and is used in this leaf only (the same paper in better condition is used in XXXIII).

Three clumps of orchid (*lan-hua*) are scattered at different angles, giving the impression of floating in a free ground. Spatial depth is heightened by the strong contrast of ink and color. The ink orchid

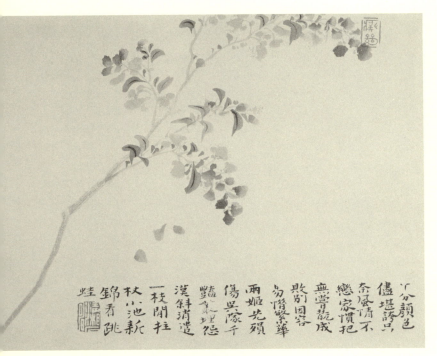

1. Tao-chi, *Flower Album by Ch'ing-hsiang*, leaf 1. Ink and color on paper. Nagano collection, Tokyo.

2. Tao-chi, *Album of Flowers and Bamboo*, dated 1701, leaf 9. Ink on paper. Collection unknown.

at the upper right has been casually conceived, the wet ink blotting freely where the leaves and flowers overlap. The two lower clumps are executed in color only, the leaves in transparent blue and the flowers in pale green with russet centers. Again moisture is suggestive of scent. The brushwork is slow, full, and round; this same feeling for form and saturation is found in the calligraphy, a semi-cursive "regular" script which fills the upper left-hand space. The seven-character quatrain reads:

The snowstorm seemed to last forever [lit., *fifty* hsün; *one* hsün *equals ten days*],
Orchids cover the ground, but their fragrance is hardly sensed [*because of the snow covering them*].
Now I [*paint them*] *together in mist and rain,*
So that they will exist gracefully and elegantly for the next four hundred years.

Orchids have a long and noble history in China's art, appearing in the poetic literature as early as the fourth century B.C. They were prized by the Chinese primarily for their delicate scent, the flowers of the Chinese *Cymbidium* varieties being small and inconspicuous. Their fragrance was associated with the exemplary character of the superior gentleman (cf. the inscription to leaf A of *XX*). In the early Yüan the Southern Sung loyalist poet Cheng Ssu-hsiao (1241–1318) became known for rootless orchids painted without a ground plane, a symbol of the land's having fallen to the Mongols. Tao-chi's orchids, also depicted without the ground, may contain a vestige of this association, an idea which may also be related to his seal, *Tun-ken* (found on leaf G), which means "blunted roots." Related to this idea is the theme of the broken branch, which recurs in the painting and poetry of his late years in more explicit form (cf. *XXXIII*, leaf A).

The composition is unusual in its freedom but is similar to that of a leaf from Tao-chi's *Album of Flowers and Bamboo*, dated 1701 (fig. 2),[3] which, according to his inscription leaf, was painted while he was drunk. Although different in expressive concept, their fundamental stylistic unity is seen in the calligraphy—the dark and light blotting of characters and the round, plump lines. (This Sackler leaf has the same drawn quality of ink found in leaf A, but it is not so marked.)

Tao-chi's seal in the lower right corner, *Wo ho-chi chih-yu*, is a pun on the meaning of his name: the *chi* character of "Tao-chi" means "to aid or succor," and here he is exclaiming rhetorically, "How could I aid anyone if I can hardly help myself?" It is one of Tao-chi's largest seals, and thus far has been found only on this leaf; it is not included in the Contag and Wang or Sasaki Kozo compilations of seals. The composition and cutting of the characters appear to be Tao-chi's and show the same spontaneous and incisive attack as found in his brushwork.

Leaf C: "Bamboo and Narcissus Bulbs"

CONDITION: poor; this leaf has suffered the most damage from insects and abrasion. As can be seen in the detail, the whole upper edge to an irregular depth of 3 to 4 cm. has been skillfully repaired (indicated by an inked line); parts of the upper leaves of the bamboo have been repainted (visible in the photograph), as have several of the topmost characters in a line. Most indicative of the deftness of the restoration are the two small seals, *K'u-kua* and *Yüan-chi*, which form part of the repair; unless carefully scrutinized, they could pass for the genuine article (see similar seals in *XX*, leaves A and E, for authentic specimens).[4] The paper of this leaf is closer to leaf A in tone but slightly looser in weave.

Opaque and transparent blues and greens color the plump and turgid leaves of the narcissus bulbs, and pale, almost iridescent tones of mat green and yellow contour the narcissus flowers (*shui-hsien-hua*). The volume and roughness of the flower bulbs have been indicated by touches of wet umber applied in a manner resembling the traditional "flying white" (*fei-pai*) technique, in which parts of the paper are revealed. Tao-chi's extension of this method to a simple round form with moist color is most inventive (cf. also his taro root, *XXII*, leaf B). The bulb on the right has been extensively retouched, hence its contrasting flatness, quite evident in the detail. The pale, listless treatment of the flowers and leaves is made more obvious by the stark length of bamboo cutting diagonally across the frame. The proportions and firmness of its stem are quite close to those of *XX*, leaf B, but here the leaves have the sharpness of a rapier. These elements convey a stiff, posed feeling, which is also evident in contemporary woodcuts by other artists. Indeed, Wen Fong feels that Tao-chi's choice of color may have been influenced by the origi-

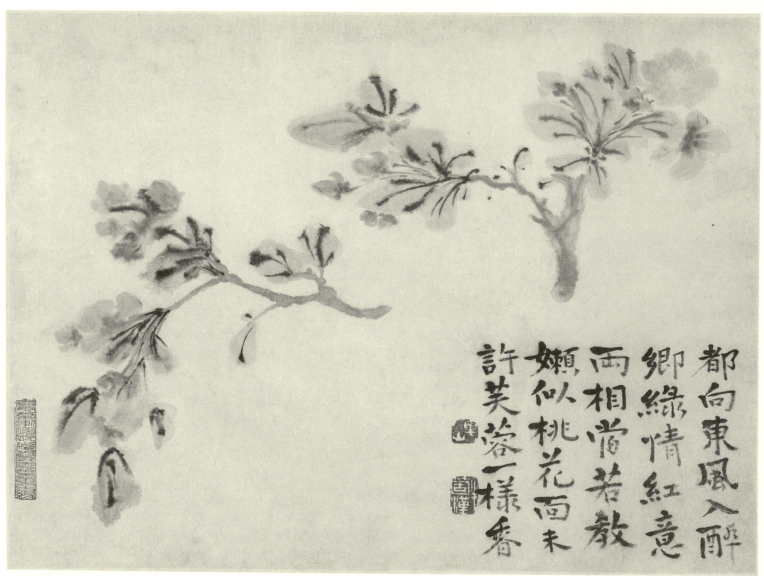

都向東風入酔
鄉綠情紅意
兩相當若教
嬾似桃花面未
許芙蓉一樣香

Leaf A, "Flowering Crab Apple"

五十餘句
風雪
連並蘭
滿地臭
難傳我將
煙雨一京
瀟灑風
流四万筆

Leaf B, "Orchids"

Leaf C, "Bamboo and Narcissus Bulbs"

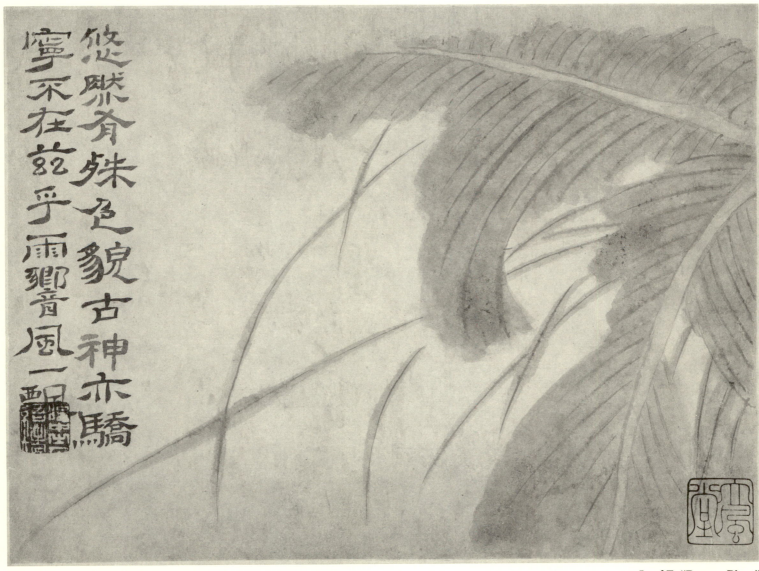

Leaf F, "Banana Plant"

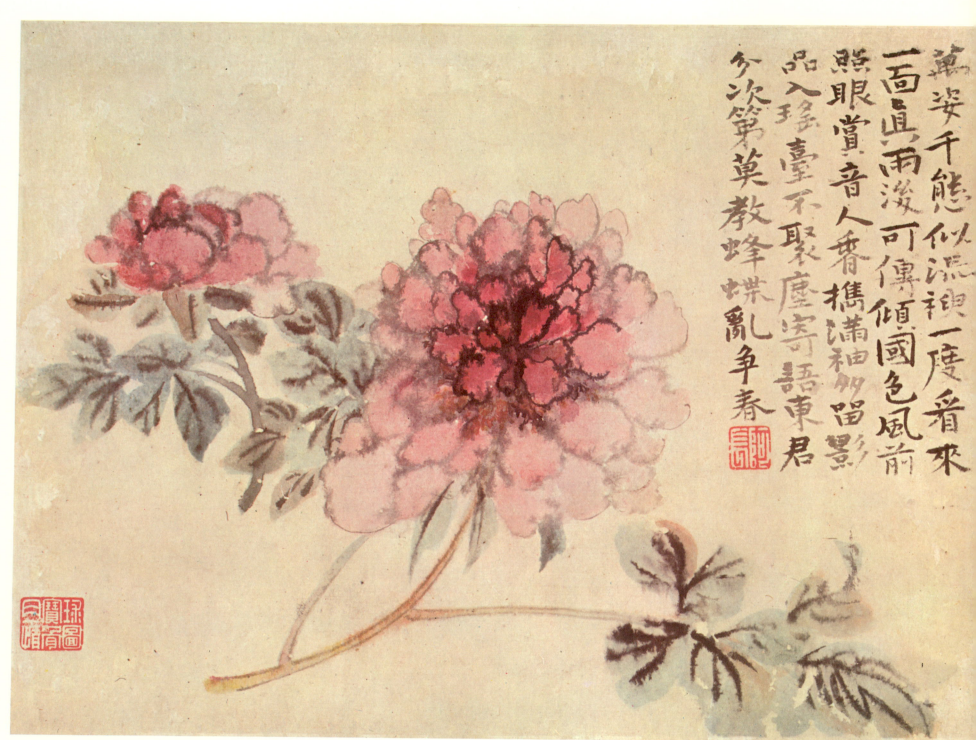

萬姿千態似濃妝 一度看來
一面真 兩後 可傳 傾國色風前
照眼賞音人香 攜滿袖留影
品入瑤 臺不聚塵寄語東君
多次第莫教蜂蝶亂爭春

Leaf D, "Peonies"

彷彿如聞
秋水香絕
芙蓉影在
蕭牆亭乙
王立蒼波
上並與清
流作興竹

Leaf E, "Lotus and Red *Polygonum*"

不學桃花色　非同柳葉黃　芳心何處着　薄暮仰斜陽

Leaf G, "Hibiscus"

那得春風十萬株　枝上照我醉模糊　暗香觸　處醒辭客　絕色開時春老夫　無以復加情欲洩　不能多得熟　還孤曉來搔首庭前看　何止人間一宿儒

Leaf H, "Plum Blossoms and Bamboo"

Leaf C, detail (hatched area indicates extent of repair).

nal edition of the *Mustard Seed Garden Manual (Chieh-tzu-yüan hua-chuan)*.[5] The early editions of this handbook (1679 and 1701) show a similar ultra-refinement and a flat, ungraded application of color; however, the extensive washing which this album underwent in the course of repair may account in part for the effect.

The seven-character quatrain, which is written in a minute and almost precious "clerical" style, is a pun on the literal meaning of "narcissus," *shui-hsien* ("water immortal") in Chinese. The poet does not mention the name of the flower but employs the words separately at the close of the poem:

In a lonely dream last night, I dropped by the river's edge
Where the icy mist and autumn waters were shimmering.
Now [I] casually play out my feelings and provoke my brush at leisure.
After [I] painted them, the spring waters became immortal.

Leaf D: *"Peonies"*

CONDITION: fair; damage to the upper edges and sides has not touched the painting; wormholes in the calligraphy and flowers are visible, but fortunately there has been no discernible retouching. The paper is the same as that of leaf A.

Peonies have been known as the most beautiful and aristocratic of China's flowers. The history of their cultivation on an extensive scale can be traced to the eighth century in the T'ang dynasty, when they were planted by the thousands in the imperial gardens of the western and eastern capitals, Ch'ang-an and Loyang. They were specially favored by emperors and empresses, were praised by poets, and were dubbed the "king of flowers" (*hua-wang*). Actually, two varieties of peonies are common in China (these were brought to the West in the late nineteenth century). The herbaceous peony (*shao-yao*) seems to have been known in ancient China and was mentioned in an early fifth century B.C. classic, *Book of Odes (Shih-ching)*. The tree peony (*mou-tan*) is the variety which later garnered imperial fame, and it is this more spectacularly blooming peony which Tao-chi portrays here. The technique reflects his awareness of the colorful history of the flower. Chromatically its range is the richest in the whole album.

Pale hues of pink and russet provide the moist color base; then deeper values of reds lightly contour the individual petals in faint undulations giving an effect of fluffiness. Reds and purples deepen in saturation as they verge toward the center. A few touches of ink accentuate the frills of the petals. Straight stems contrast in hue and texture with the flower.

The strongly graded contrast of ink and color is mirrored in the calligraphy, which moves in fine gradations from pale to dark characters. The script is the archaic and modest "regular" script of the Chung Yu type, leaving our attention focused on the ink contrasts and ravishing peonies. The seven-character verse reads:

Ten thousand stances and a thousand attitudes, as if recently made divine;
One look at them, and they are completely real.
After rain they radiate a beauty which can overthrow a city;
Before the wind they dazzle the eyes of their admirers.
Their fragrance fills your sleeves—try to catch more images.
They can enter the terrace of immortals and never gather dust there.
Send a message to the eastern god [of spring] to better distinguish the order—
And not let the bees and butterflies wildly contend with them for the season.

This album is compositionally close to another leaf from the *Flower Album by Ch'ing-hsiang* (fig. 3), executed without ink outline but with lush petals and leaves. In a work of the same subject by Chang Ta-ch'ien dated 1964 (fig. 4), the free ink play of the leaves and the basic configuration of the flowers show the influence of Tao-chi, but Chang's concept of ink is entirely different. He visualizes the leaves in a more or less single dynamic movement of the brush and each leaf in a single ink tone. As a result, his leaves are rich in ink but barely legible as descriptive forms, while Tao-chi shows a strong interest in internal articulation and in the structural value of the graded ink. This distinction is vital to the approach to form of the two painters.

Leaf E: *"Lotus and Red Polygonum"*

CONDITION: the paper is damaged at irregular intervals of 1 to 2 cm. on the upper edge and has been repaired and retouched; the paper is the same as that of leaf D.

Although it is known as the sacred flower of Buddhism, the lotus is indigenous to China and has been cultivated as an ornamental aquatic plant in private gardens quite apart from its religious associations. Tao-chi stresses its secular aspect here even though the sacred lotus was also within his repertory (cf. XX, leaf H). The flower is known by several Chinese names: *ho*, *lien*, and *fu-jung*.

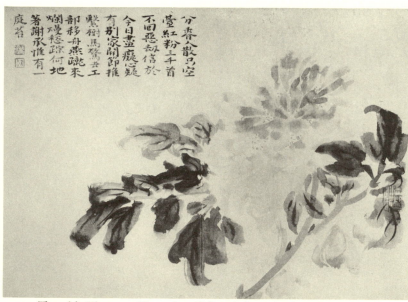

3. Tao-chi, *Flower Album by Ch'ing-hsiang*, leaf 2. Ink and color on paper. Nagano collection.

4. Chang Ta-ch'ien, *Peonies*, dated 1964. Album leaf. Ink on paper. Collection unknown.

The brushwork of the lotus in this leaf is unprecedented in Tao-chi's flower paintings. The lace-like pattern of alternating wavering and tensile lines, while meticulously executed, has a surprisingly mobile and volumetric quality which captures the heavy, moisture-filled succulence of the flower and stems. A stalk of red *Polygonum* (*hung-liao*) breaks up the more controlled parallelism of the lotus stems. The spatial rhythms, pale, refined colorism, and spontaneous ink and color fusions are both familiar and yet entirely new and sophisticated extensions of Tao-chi's style.

The frail, even strokes of the calligraphy echo the pale contours of the lotus flower, a sympathy of poetry and painting which is typical of Tao-chi. It is seen throughout this album and in other works, such as the Fong *Small Album* and the 1696 *Sketches of Calligraphy and Painting by Ch'ing-hsiang*. The seven-character quatrain reads:

> It's as if one can smell the fragrance of the autumn water;
> There are absolutely no flower shadows on the majestic wall.
> Floating gracefully on the green waves—
> You are equally pure and flowing.

Leaf F: *"Banana Plant"*

CONDITION: poor; insect damage around the edges has penetrated to a depth of 1 to 2 cm. at irregular intervals; the entire upper edge has been retouched and a layer of color wash laid over the original color areas; some of the veins have also been redrawn. The repair paper is grayer in tone than the original, which resembles that of leaf D.

Two large banana leaves (*pa-chiao-yeh*) emerge from the right edge of the picture, one fanning away from, one toward, the viewer. Pale, transparent blues and greens demarcate the shape of the leaves and set a cool, airy tone. Thin ink delineates the veins of the leaves in arched double lines, a rhythm repeated in the long, narrow palm leaves which shoot out from behind the banana. The silhouette of the leaves is not as complete and symmetrical as in nature; a deliberately irregular and broken shape has been described, one which stresses flat layers in space rather than three-dimensional volumes. This contrasting visualization can be found in Tao-chi's depiction of the same subject, *XX*, leaf H, and *XXVII*.

Damage by insects and abrasion has taken heavy toll in this leaf. It is especially difficult to tell to what extent the double lineation of the veins is a product of the retoucher's hand, although Tao-chi did often use this very technique for banana leaves. Altogether, while the leaf possesses elegance and restraint, there is a spiritlessness to the description which we suspect was accentuated by insensitive reapplication of color and ink contouring.

The five-character quatrain is written in a firm "clerical" script in primarily pale tones which blend into the overall tonality. The brushwork fits our knowledge of Tao-chi's hand and is written here with special slowness and care. The pace and paleness have affected the total energy, however; like the banana leaves it tends to be weak. The poem stresses the natural, un-selfconscious aspect of the subject, which was one of Tao-chi's favorites. The same verse appears on his *Banana Plant in Rain* painted for Po-erh-tu (see Part IV, fig. 14, above), a painting technically closer in concept than the two others mentioned above. It reads:

> It has a subtle special beauty;
> Its appearance is archaic, and its spirit proud.
> Are all of these qualities not present here—
> And the sound of rain on the leaves, and their swaying in the wind?

Leaf G: *"Hibiscus"*

CONDITION: good; this is the best-preserved leaf, especially as the painting is centered away from the edges; no retouching is apparent, although the edges of the paper have been repaired. The paper resembles that of leaf C.

Green star-shaped leaves frame a yellow hibiscus (*huang-shu-k'uei*) in full flower. The open, radiating configuration of the leaves suits the contained, circular silhouette of the retiring flower. These contrasting shapes are varied even further by the hibiscus buds: two slant slightly to the left behind the blossom, and a twig slants to the right, the pattern of its round, plump buds repeated in the moss dots on the stems and in the heart of the flower.

The colors used in this leaf are particularly vibrant. Petals were drawn in pale yellow, and, while they were still moist, the tiny pleats and wrinkles near the pistil were finely delineated in pale russet, suggesting the soft, fluffy convexity of the flowers. Deeper russet mixed with red composes the five dots of the heart. The leaves were painted in green with touches of blue and the veins then delineated with darker ink and allowed to suffuse, as in leaves A, D, E, and F. The full, almost bursting volume of the flower is the sort of visualization found in leaves D and E. The different textures, weights, and densities so beautifully achieved here are very much Tao-chi. The charm of this leaf is less arresting than that of the peony leaf; it is less splendid compositionally than the orchid, lotus, or banana leaves, but its perfection of technique and expression, coupled with its fine condition, makes it an outstanding example of Tao-chi's mastery of this art.

The five-character quatrain stresses the retiring aspect of the hibiscus, which the artist suggests in the slightly downward face of the blossom:

> *It doesn't imitate the color of peach blossoms*
> *And its yellow is not the same as the willow leaves.*
> *A fragrant heart—where can it be?*
> *At dusk it turns toward the setting sun.*

The "small clerical" script is also the most spontaneous and vigorous of all the calligraphy in this album. The ink modulates from thick to thin in a natural manner as it runs thin in the brush, and each stroke is begun and finished attentively.

Leaf H: "*Plum Blossoms and Bamboo*"

CONDITION: poor; the upper edges and part of the characters in the upper line have been retouched; wormholes scattered throughout the surface have also been filled in, which, in addition to the overall abrasion, makes the surface painting appear slightly uneven. The paper is the same as that of leaf A.

Color functions in a particularly delicate and ornamental fashion in this leaf. The stems and blossoms of the plum were first painted in pale russet and the branches outlined in pale umber. A mixture of russet and red was used to contour the flower petals, pure red for the stamens and pistils. The bamboo leaves and stalk, drawn over the flowers in thick charcoal-black ink, push the pale colors back into a misty space. Details of the execution are masterful, especially that of the plum: the tender branches turn and twist in every direction, bearing blossoms (*mei-hua*) at various stages of bloom.

The surface of the painting is particularly abraded in the area of the bamboo, and almost every leaf has been retouched, so that the overall effect of the painting is slightly dull. Nonetheless, the basic structure of the bamboo is still familiar as Tao-chi's and compares well, for example, with the *Sketches of Calligraphy and Painting by Ch'ing-hsiang* (XXIX, fig. 1); the plum blossoms may be compared with the *Searching for Plum Blossoms* handscroll (XVIII) and *Plum Branches* album (XXXIII), which convey the same buoyant feeling in the poses and angles of the blossoms and branches. The calligraphy is executed in an extremely slender "regular" script in the Ch'u Sui-liang style and is similar to that of leaf E and of the *Sketches of Calligraphy and Painting* handscroll.

In the plum Tao-chi saw much of his own life mirrored and renewed; it represented his lost youth. The four central lines of the poem tell us the underlying sentiment of this album and the reason why Tao-chi loved flowers, especially in his late years:

> *Where to find a hundred thousand [plum trees] in the spring wind?*
> *The branches shining on me make me drunk and blissful.*
> *Their hidden fragrance touches and awakes the poet—*
> *When their marvelous beauty blooms, it makes an old man feel the spring.*
> *My feelings are so full, it is almost unbearable—*
> *These passions don't come often, yet still I am lonely.*
> *At dawn I scratch my head in wonder in front of the courtyard looking [at the flowers]:*
> *How could anybody think that I am only an old useless scholar?*

THE PORTRAIT LEAF, "The Painter Supervising the Planting of Pine Trees," [6] a copy of a handscroll attributed to Tao-chi, is a well-known subject of which three versions are extant: this one, the so-called Chu Ho-nien version; a handscroll in the Lo Chia-lun collection, Taipei (fig. 5); and an album leaf in the Chang Ch'ün collection, Taipei, which accompanies Tao-chi's transcription of the *Tao-te-ching* (fig. 6). These are the only portraits of Tao-chi known to

us. The artist is seated on a large low rock, a hoe across his lap. His hair is cropped short in a brief cap, and he has a small moustache and beard. He wears a two-layered robe, a finely pleated green outer garment and an inner white one tied with a sash of ultramarine. A gray rock juts from the left foreground, and the russet ground line slopes at a sharp diagonal. At the left is a small clump of pines colored in russet and green.

The first of the two inscriptions is a transcription of Tao-chi's biography, adapted from Chang Keng's entry in his *Kuo-ch'ao hua-cheng-lu*:

The monk Tao-chi, *tzu* Shih-t'ao, also known by his *hao*, Ch'ing-hsiang lao-jen, Ch'ing-hsiang Ch'en-jen, Ta-ti-tzu, and one which he called himself, K'u-kua ho-shang. He was also called Kao-mang-tzu, and Hsia-tsun-che. . . . In painting he excelled at landscapes, orchid, and bamboo. His brush concepts were free and untrammeled and they transcended the "mortar and nest" [of conventional methods]. In his late years he wandered the [regions] of the Yangtze and Huai rivers, where persons all contended to esteem him. . . . Now today his extant works in Yang-chou are especially numerous.

The second inscription is a seven-character quatrain:

> *The monkey tags along to learn to plant pine trees;*
> *[Beneath] the "two temple banners" in his state of meditation, on which mountain peak is he concentrating?*
> *He can chant the five thousand words [of the Tao-te-ching] with fluency and ease;*
> *Clouds send the sounds of temple bells across the water from the bay.*

> Shih-t'ao's self-portrait planting pine trees. Winter, 1674 [*chia-yin tung*], inscribed under the temple banners at Chao-t'ing [Chin-t'ing-shan, Anhwei] [the paper is damaged from here to the area just above the pine trees].

Chang Ta-ch'ien has inscribed a commentary on the left mounting:

This is Master Shih[-t'ao's] painting of planting pine trees copied by Chu Ho-nien. I have also seen a copy by Lo [P'in] Liang-feng, which was mounted with Shih-t'ao's calligraphy of the *Tao-te-ching*. Master Shih's original version is in Lo [Chia-lun] Chih-hsi's collection. Yüan inscribed.

The attribution is to the Ch'ing painter Chu Ho-nien (1760–1833-).[7] The Chinese commentary to the Lo Chia-lun scroll in *A Garland of Chinese Painting*[8] confirms the existence of a Chu Ho-nien version, which it says was painted for the calligrapher I Ping-shou (1754–1815). Unfortunately, the Sackler leaf does not bear a painter's signature or seal, nor is it impressed with I Ping-shou's collector's seals. Preliminary stylistic investigation shows that Chu Ho-nien is not the author. From the extant works available to us in reproduction,[9] the brushwork of Chu's rocks, clothing, faces, and calligraphy are not comparable with this album leaf, even with due allowance made for its being a copy. In all likelihood, this version was executed in the nineteenth or early twentieth century.

The Lo Chia-lun version (fig. 5) is a handscroll, while the other two are album leaves.[10] We have not had the opportunity to examine the Lo version, but judging from the composition and the literary evidence of colophons, it seems clear that the two album leaves were executed after the handscroll (or the original version from which that itself derived). The colophons on the *Tao-te-ching* album were written by the important scholar and antiquarian Weng Fang-kang (1733–1818). In his colophon he says that the portrait accompanying the album is by Lo P'in (1733–1799), one of the major Yang-chou Eccentrics. Indeed, upon close examination of the photograph supplied us by Mr. Chang Ch'ün (fig. 6), taken from an unknown reproduction, one can see a seal of Lo P'in's on the right edge of the painting (relief, small square); Contag and Wang list the same seal.[11]

This attribution fits our knowledge of Lo P'in's style—the angular, linear rocks, the rendering of the pine trees, the contours of the tree trunks, and the touches of the grass. The fine quality of the image of the artist and his expression also support the hypothesis. Weng's late-eighteenth-century dating is also verified by the seal of the collector Yang Chi-chen (*tzu* Yu-yün, fl. ca. 1840–1857). We therefore believe that it is quite likely a genuine work by Lo P'in.

Lo P'in has not only concentrated the composition on the painter alone but has also simplified it and has replaced the clump of pine in the foreground by a protruding rock, has reduced the two pine trees in the background to one, and has eliminated a stalk of bamboo behind the rock. The Sackler leaf was evidently based on the Lo P'in version and is further simplified: the foreground also shows a protruding rock, but the background pine tree and the grasses have been eliminated and the slope made even more acute. A space at the upper left is provided for two inscriptions. They can be shown to be based on the two colophons by Weng Fang-kang which appear in the *Tao-te-ching* album. Weng borrowed the short biography from Chang Keng and then added a quatrain of his own which mentions the "five thousand words" of the *Tao-te-ching*. The copyist of the Sackler leaf was evidently not aware that Weng's colophon to the *Tao-te-ching* version was his own poem (which Weng actually adapted from Tao-chi's poem on the Lo Chia-lun handscroll) and believed it to be Tao-chi's own. Thus the mention of the five thousand words in the Sackler copy is out of place. From this literary and stylistic evidence, we can see that the Sackler or so-called Chu Ho-nien version appears to be a composite of Lo P'in's *Tao-te-ching* leaf and Weng Fang-kang's colophon to Tao-chi's *Tao-te-ching* calligraphy. It is, however, impossible to identify the painter of the Sackler leaf. The characters obliterated after the inscription may have contained his name and seal. In any event, it was executed after the Lo P'in and Weng Fang-kang versions, at some time in the nineteenth or early twentieth century.

AFTER THE ABOVE was written, a fourth version of the portrait came to our attention. It forms the opening leaf to an album of twelve landscapes dated 1699 by Tao-chi and published as *Shih-t'ao ho-shang shan-shui chi*.[12] The portrait (fig. 7) is close to the Sackler composition but bears different inscriptions. There is a five-character title in "seal" script ("a picture of Shih-t'ao planting pine trees"), followed by an inscription which reads: "Painted by myself in the winter of *chia-yin* [1674]. The winter of *wu-wu* [1798]. Chu [Ho-nien, *tzu*] Yeh-yün copied this for [I Ping-shou, *tzu*] Mo-ch'ing." In the lower right-hand corner of the painting, the artist has left his seal, *Yeh-yün* (square, relief). The first date of 1674 has been transcribed from the original Tao-chi self-portrait (it agrees with that found on the Lo Chia-lun handscroll). The second date of 1798 is that of the painting. On the far left side of the mounting, an inscription signed I Ping-shou helps to clarify the situation:

Yeh-yün [Chu Ho-nien] gave me this album. [I] had borrowed a small self-portrait by Shih-t'ao which was from the collection of the learned Mr. Weng [Fang-kang], and therefore asked [Mr. Chu] to copy it and place it at the beginning of this album. The twenty-second day, twelfth

lunar month, third year of the Chia-ch'ing era [January 27, 1799]. Mo-an, I Ping-shou recorded.

Judging from the reproduction, we believe the colophon by I Ping-shou, as well as the portrait leaf and inscription by Chu, to be genuine. This, then, is the Chu Ho-nien version painted for I Ping-shou and referred to in the discussion above.

On the far right side of the mounting appears a second colophon which reads: "Second month of the twelfth year of the Chia-ch'ing era, the year *ting-mao* [1807]. Chang Tun-( ) of Yang-ch'eng [Yang-chou] made another copy." The painter's seal has obscured the second character of his name, but the identification of the painter as Chang Tun-jen (*tzu* Ku-yü, 1754–1834) is confirmed by the intaglio seal, which contains his *tzu*. It would be tempting to conclude that the Sackler leaf is the other copy which Chang Tun-jen mentions he made, but confirmation of precise authorship must await further study.

NOTES

1. For the botanical names, a general history of horticulture in China, and an extensive botanical bibliography of the flowers found in this entry, see H. L. Li, *The Garden Flowers of China*; for an account of the transplantation of many of these flowers to Western gardens in the late nineteenth and early twentieth century, see E. H. Wilson, *China—Mother of Gardens*.

2. A seven-leaf album, in ink and light color on paper, reproduced in *Sekitō meiga fu*, no. 9 (*Ch'ing-hsiang lao-jen hua-hui ts'e*); leaves 5 and 6 are also similar in technique to this first leaf.

3. A ten-leaf album, in ink on paper, reproduced in facsimile collotype in *Shih-t'ao ho-shang lan-chu ts'e* (n.p., n.d.), collection unknown.

4. To confirm our suspicions about the repair and the addition of the seals by Chang Ta-ch'ien, the authors asked Mrs. Lucy Lo to inquire directly of Chang about the matter. He admitted that he had added these two seals, and they are therefore important material for the study of other imitations after Tao-chi by his hand; cf. *XXXV*.

5. For a study of its various editions, see Ch'iu A. K'ai-ming, "The Chieh-tzu Yüan Hua Chuan." The stylistic relationship with the *Mustard Seed Garden Manual* is strengthened by an important inscription on leaf B, "Taro Root," of the Sackler album *Landscapes, Vegetables, and Flowers (XXII)*, in which Tao-chi mentions one of the authors of the *Manual*, Wang Kai, as a good friend. The art-historical implications of this contact await further study.

6. A portrait of the artist is customarily placed at the beginning of an album, but in this case, because of its poor quality and the problem of authorship, we have decided to place it at the end and discuss it last. The presence of this leaf in the album seems gratuitous, and it was probably included with the flowers when the album entered the Ta-feng-t'ang collection.

7. Chu's dates are on the basis of dated paintings; see Kuo Wei-ch'ü, *Sung-Yüan Ming-Ch'ing shu-hua-chia nien-piao*, for the years 1760, 1828, 1830, and 1833; Hsü Pang-ta, *Li-tai liu-ch'uan shu-hua tso-p'in pien-nien-piao*, for 1799 and 1824; *CKHCJMTTT*, p. 107; Contag and Wang, *Seals*, pp. 110 and 648; Ch'in Tsu-yung, *T'ung-yin lun-hua*, pt. 3; and Osvald Sirén, *Chinese Painting: Leading Masters and Principles*, vol. 7, pp. 320–21.

8. Vol. 4, pl. 31. The Lo version, in ink and color on paper, is well known through its original publication by Sirén in *Chinese Painting*, vol. 6, pl. 388-A. See also National Palace Museum, Taipei, *Special Exhibition of Paintings*, pl. 34, cat. no. 47, p. 25.

9. Cf. Sirén, *Chinese Painting*, vol. 7, p. 321, and a portrait of Su Shih in *Su Wen-chung chi Wu-yün-t'ieh chen-chi* (Ch'ang-sha, 1938), frontispiece.

10. The version accompanying the Chang Ch'ün *Tao-te-ching* is published in *A Garland of Chinese Paintings*, vol. 3, cat. no. 28 (1–39), but with no portrait and incomplete colophons. Chang Ch'ün has kindly sent us complete photographs of his scroll.

11. *Seals*, no. 19, p. 493.

12. The publication contains a preface dated 1930 by Chang Tse. At that time the album was in the Chang family collection. We are indebted to Ch'en Jui-k'ang, New York, for making this version available to us. We knew of the landscapes but did not know that a portrait accompanied the original publication.

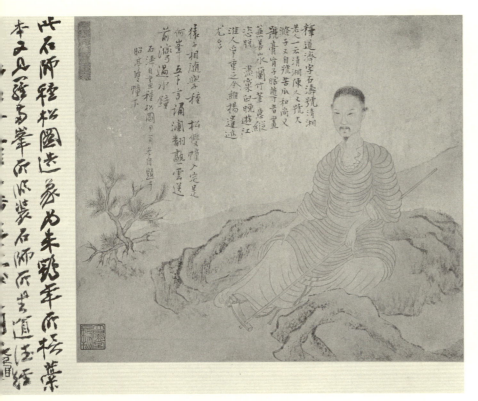

Portrait leaf: "The Painter Supervising the Planting of Pine Trees"

5. Attributed to Tao-chi, *The Painter Supervising the Planting of Pine Trees*, dated 1674. Handscroll. Ink and color on paper. Lo Chia-lun collection, Taipei.

6. Lo P'in (1733–1799), *Portrait of Tao-chi*, n.d. Album leaf. Ink and color on paper. Chang Ch'ün collection, Taipei.

7. Chu Ho-nien, *Portrait of Tao-chi*, dated 1798. Album leaf. Ink and color on paper. Ta-Feng-t'ang collection.

Album of Landscapes

The Art Museum, Princeton University (67-2).

Album of eleven leaves, ten of painting, one of calligraphy. Ink and slight color on an unsized paper of creamy tone. 24.2 x 18.7 cm.

DATED: in the period March 3–April 7, 1701 (*hsin-ssu erh-yüeh*) in the artist's inscription on the eleventh leaf, K.

SIGNATURE OF THE ARTIST: Ch'ing-hsiang Ch'en-jen, Chi (after inscription, leaf K); painting leaves unsigned.

INSCRIPTION BY THE ARTIST: on leaf K in eight lines (seven lines of "running" script, followed by two brief lines in smaller script) with signature and date (translated below).

SEALS OF THE ARTIST:
Yüan-chi (intaglio) and *K'u-kua* (relief, double seal in two squares; *PTC*, cat. no. 107) leaves A, F, I, and J.
Ch'ing-hsiang lao-jen (relief, oval; *PTC*, cat. no. 18) leaf B.
Ch'ien-yu Lung-mien, Chi (intaglio, tall rectangle; *PTC*, cat. no. 9) leaves C, D, G, and H.
Ch'ing-hsiang Shih-t'ao (intaglio, tall rectangle; *PTC*, cat. no. 22) leaf E.
K'u-kua ho-shang, Chi, hua-fa (intaglio, tall rectangle; *PTC*, cat. no. 48, not listed) inscription leaf K.

COLLECTOR'S SEALS: unidentified Chinese collector (early twentieth century?), *Wu-wei-an ts'ang-pao* (relief, tall rectangle) and *I-shou* (intaglio, square), both on mounting of inscription leaf K; *Wu-wei-an chu-jen chen-shang* (relief, square) leaf B, lower right corner, and mounting of inscription leaf K; the three seals probably belong to the same owner.

CONDITION: good; the edges of leaves B, C, G, and H have minor wormhole damage, but no retouching is apparent. On the facing inscription leaf K, four small characters on the left side have been obliterated by wormholes and three are barely legible.

FRONTISPIECE:
The outer label from a former mounting, remounted into an album leaf (see the left detail), is written on darkened paper in a Six Dynasties variation of "regular" script. It is unsigned but from the style of the calligraphy appears to be late Ch'ing or early twentieth century. It reads, "A genuine work of landscapes by the Old Man, Shih-t'ao." The right side of the detail shows the loose label indicating the album as an entry in the exhibit of Chinese paintings held in 1931 in Osaka, which is recorded in the volume *Sō Gen Min Shin meiga taikan*. At that time the album was in the collection of Sumitomo Kanichi.
A two-character encomium (detail on right) in large "running" script follows by the modern Japanese calligrapher Iriye Tamemori, who was the friend of the collector, Sumitomo Kanichi.[1] It reads, " 'Purity Transcended.' U-tei inscribed." [Seals:] *Hana-o shimu hito* (relief, tall rectangle) before inscription, *Tamemori shō* (intaglio, square) and *Dam-sui* (relief, square) after signature.

Details of frontispiece: (*left*) old outer label; (*right*) Tamemori inscription.

PROVENANCE: Sumitomo Kanichi collection, Oiso.

PUBLISHED: *Sō Gen Min Shin meiga taikan*, vol. 2, pl. 220 (leaf J illustrated); *Sekitō to Hachidai san-jin*, no. 6 (leaf F illustrated); *Un Nanden to Sekitō*, nos. 6–8 (leaves A, H, and I illustrated); *Min-matsu san oshō*, nos. 11, 12 (leaves J and K illustrated); *Niseki Hachidai*, no. 7 (leaf E illustrated); *PTC*, cat. no. 16, pp. 80, 128–32 (illustrated); *Record of the Art Museum, Princeton University*, vol. 28 (1968), p. 35 (acquisitions list); *Archives of the Chinese Art Society of America*, vol. 22 (1968–69), pp. 121, 133, fig. 50 (leaf F illustrated); *The Selected Painting and Calligraphy of Shih-t'ao*, vol. 3, pl. 93 (illustrated).

EXCEPT FOR THE first two leaves, which have heavier ink lines, the images in this album are rendered with fine tremulous line and a sense for minute and prismatic detail. Tao-chi perfected this realm of vision in the album format, especially in such works as the Huang-shan albums, the Fong *Small Album*, and others. But the lyric tenor in this series differs slightly from these earlier works, for despite the fineness of detail, the serenity and refinement are ultimately the product of the discipline and restraint of full maturity. One can sense a hard-won astringency and power underlying the appearance of lightness and freshness.

The eleventh and last leaf includes an inscription by the artist:

Literary and artistic expression can be enjoyed only by the fortunate. These past few years [my] calligraphy and painting have entered the marketplace, and "fish eyes have been mixed with pearls" [i.e., bad works have been mixed with the good], so I feel much less interested. It's not because I don't want [my works] to be hung in others' studios, but that I don't dare let this [selling of my works] become my downfall [*yeh-(chang)*].

Recently I have been free from commitments, so I happened to use this paper to make some sketches. Those who understand will treasure this as something special.

> Second lunar month of the year *hsin-ssu* [March 3–April 7, 1701] ( ) ( ) [two characters obliterated by wormholes]. I closed my door and obtained some leisure time because I was ill. I spontaneously painted what came to my mind and finished ( ) [one character missing] leaves which I here inscribe.
> [Signed:] Ch'ing [character damaged]-hsiang Ch'en-jen, Chi. [Seal of the artist:] *K'u-kua ho-shang, Chi, hua-fa* (intaglio, tall rectangle).

This inscription is valuable as a record of the exact mood and circumstance of the artist at the time of execution. It is on a paper different from the paintings, but one suitable for writing. There is no reason to question the original relationship of the inscription leaf to the whole album, as both the style of the painting and the calligraphy are comparable to other accepted works dated within this period. Hence the 1701 date in fact serves to strengthen the chronology of Tao-chi's whole range.

Initially we were cautious about the authenticity of these leaves, but careful study of both paintings and calligraphy reveals the album to be a genuine and revealing expression of the artist during a period of illness and the onset of old age (Tao-chi was sixty in 1701). As such it serves to enrich our awareness of transitory periods such as these in Tao-chi's total production.

Pictorially, the landscapes represent a summation of many themes which appeared earlier. The compositions reveal a growing interest in landscape elements as simplified and occasionally flat shapes which interact with the paper in a "solid-and-void" relationship. This interpretation of form has parallels in Tao-chi's fruit and bamboo subjects (cf. *XXIX* and *XXXI*). In addition, this album contains examples of both "coarse" and "fine" brushwork styles, providing links with works in these manners before and after 1700.

Leaf A: "*Among Peaks and Pines (Mt. Huang)*"

A low boulder in the foreground begins an abrupt progression of blunt, angular peaks which rise precipitously in the middle ground. Even taller peaks stretch upward to the right into the farthest distance. The theme of height is confidently explored by the deliberate layering of the mountains in groups of twos—one against the other—which rise ever higher into the distance. The forms are not one-dimensional planes, however; they are conceived as multifaceted prisms which can alter their faces with each change in the direction of our vision.

The motif of the pine trees functions as a secondary theme to that of height. Three angular pines with downward-hanging branches set up a counter-rhythm to the upward thrust of the peaks. Dry, textured strokes worked horizontally from the left and linear touches of foliage in dark ink enliven the surface of the forms. Discreet use of russet coloring on the figure and in the rocks provides focal points for the eye. The serene, meditative aspect of this leaf (a quality which could also describe the whole album) is concentrated in the solitary figure who sits on the cliff's edge, aloof and protected by this rocky fortress.

The depth and range of hues arrest the eye: russets, blues, and greens are used to model the mountain form sculpturally and to convey richness, despite the blunt and uncompromising charcoal-black lines in the main peak and trees. This strident quality in the linework is seldom seen in such prominence in Tao-chi's work before 1700. The rhythm of the brush and the broken impulses of pressure and release as seen in the overhanging trees on each side are movements established early in the artist's career (fig. 1)[2] but are more conspicuous here because of the simplification of the forms.

Such brushwork can be related to other Tao-chi works employing the calligraphic method of the T'ang master Yen Chen-ch'ing (705–782) to instill a more direct and incisive energy into the pictorial forms. An important work in this regard is the dated 1700 album of twelve landscapes and flowers in Peking,[3] in which such brushwork and ink appears repeatedly. In leaf F (see Part IV, fig. 5, above) Tao-chi comments directly on his brush style, saying, "This is like Lu-kung's [Yen Chen-ch'ing's] calligraphy."

The mountain shape here can be identified as Huang-shan (Mt. Huang), Anhwei, one of Tao-chi's favorite spots in his early wanderings. This characteristic peak reappears in his other works like familiar features in a series of family portraits over several generations—similar in structure, yet with each portrayal different in expression and character. Two works in this series are leaf C of the Fong *Small Album* (fig. 2) and leaf G of the Sumitomo twelve-leaf album depicting the scenery of Huang-shan (fig. 3).

2. Tao-chi, *Small Album*, leaf C, "High Peaks." Album of twelve leaves. Ink on paper. Wen Fong collection, Princeton.

3. Tao-chi, detail of leaf B. Album of twelve leaves depicting the scenery of Huang-shan. Sumitomo collection.

1. Tao-chi, *Eight Views of Huang-shan*, detail of leaf E, "Lotus Peak." Album of eight leaves. Ink and color on paper. Sumitomo collection, Oiso.

4. Tao-chi, *Album for Yü-lao*, leaf K, "Mountain Landscape" (after Mi Fu). Ink and color on paper. C. C. Wang collection, New York.

5. Tao-chi, *1700 Peking Album*, leaf G. Ink on paper. Palace Museum, Peking.

Leaf B: *"Mountain Stream"* (style of Mi Fu)

A hump of mountain in the right corner of the picture shields a stream in the foreground as it rushes down to the left. Overlooking both mountain and stream is a host of serried peaks which ascends close behind the stream. In contrast to the rocky angularity of the preceding leaf, this scene stresses rounded earth shapes. No figures or trees are present to set the scale. Stability and permanence are evoked by the complex sculptural form of the high mountain and by the strongly defined brushlines and texture dots. Conversely, mutability is implied in the vigorously flowing waters.

Paintings in the so-called Mi Fu style are generally rendered in a technique using layers of wet dots. Here, however, Tao-chi has chosen dry ink dots supplemented by colored ones to build up the forms, creating an atmosphere entirely different from the drenched cloudiness associated with earlier or contemporary Mi-style landscapes. The preliminary outlines and inner modeling of the mountains again employ the forceful and expansive line of Yen Chen-ch'ing's calligraphy: the power of the brush is communicated directly and almost bluntly onto the paper without any sense of polish or artifice. For the dotting method, russet washes and moist green dots serve as a base to the dry charcoal modeling strokes, creating a richly plastic surface and a modulated contrast of textures.

This leaf may be compared with two other Mi-style mountain-scapes by Tao-chi, leaf K of *Album for Yü-lao* (fig. 4) in the C. C. Wang collection, and leaf G of the *1700 Peking Album* (fig. 5). These three leaves all have a similar two-part composition in which one of the foreground elements functions as a source of movement which contrasts with the stable monumentality of the mountains in the near distance. In the C. C. Wang leaf wet ink dots applied over colored washes describe both the mountains and trees; the latter are tilted diagonally to create a marvelous sense of tension, which is countered by the gradually receding mountains in the far distance. Each peak is separated by parts of the paper left white to signify clouds, a deft and recurrent pictorial signature of Tao-chi. The Sackler leaf is closer to the Peking album in the round blunt strokes and dry texturing. The boatman and the slightly tilted house function as the element of movement and create the dual tension which, in the Sackler leaf, is sensed in the two contesting peaks. In all three leaves, the shape of the uppermost earthen mound is another characteristic of Tao-chi's style.

Leaf C: *"Crossing the Bridge"*

CONDITION: there are two irregular stains on the top right and left.

A path issuing diagonally from the left foreground is dotted with an occasional cottage and several trees and leads to an arched bridge in the middle distance. A small figure, having come up the path, mounts the stone bridge. In the distance low mountain peaks rise in layers and continue the diagonal progression of the path. Palest green and blue washes of controlled transparency are enlivened by touches of russet on the roof of the foreground house and the face of the figure. The pale blue-green coloring sets the ethereal mood of this scene, and the creamy tone of the paper, left in generous amounts in the right corner and throughout the landscape, suggests shifting mist.

With this leaf the tone of the whole album becomes clear. The transparent colors and acute sense of the ephemeral in the images intensify the evocative quality of the album. But this fragility is deceptive: the brushwork which created these images requires a control similar to that commanded by a dancer in leap or pirouette which seems the essence of lightness and poise, but reflects the muscular control and discipline acquired from profound study.

The impact of leaves A and B is direct; in this leaf we savor individual details—a tree trunk or its branches, groundline textures, the contour of rooftops or of the tiny figure, the toning of the colors. Each tremulous brushline can arouse delicate responses in the viewer's nerves and muscles, and, combined with the purity of the washes, the whole scene cannot but draw the fascinated viewer into its orbit.

Two other leaves from undated Tao-chi albums can be compared: leaf A of the Fong *Small Album* (*XVII*, fig. 6) and leaf F of the Osaka *Sketches after Su Tung-p'o's Poems* (fig. 6). Both exhibit a similar diagonal progression of negative and positive space culminating in a bridge in the middle ground. A third work, leaf F of the Sumitomo twelve-leaf album depicting the scenery of Huang-shan,[4] has a similar composition but with colors of greater intensity and full seasonal foliage. These three albums can be dated roughly ca. 1695, ca. 1703, and ca. 1696, respectively. Considered with this Sackler work, they reveal Tao-chi's lyrical mastery of the fragile and fleeting image.

6. Tao-chi, *Sketches after Su Tung-p'o's Poems*, leaf F, "Farewell to Spring." Ink and color on paper. Abe collection, Osaka Municipal Museum.

Leaf D: *"Cliffs"*

A precipitous cliff emerges vertically from the right side of the picture frame, its base obscured by mist. Triangular forms juxtaposed horizontally in rising layers to the left of the cliff suggest mountains in ever-receding distance. By sharply reducing the scale of these mountains against the large perpendicular cliff, the artist has achieved an awesome feeling of both height and extraordinarily deep distance. Devoid of trees, foliage, and even figures, this scene of soaring height and plunging depth—a traditional "deep-distance" scene (*shen yüan*)—restates freshly a pictorial theme reaching back to the beginnings of Chinese landscape art.

A single hue of green unites the forms. Dry tactile surfaces in the foreground are juxtaposed against distant mountains which lose in distinctness as they gain in depth, forming a true aerial perspective. Graded values of the same green wash soften the foreground textures (which reappear in leaf F). Although the incline of the cliffs seems abrupt and angular, there are no straight lines in a geometric sense. The simplicity of form is belied by the complexity of the linework: the brush moves in fine undulations and in penetrating contact with the paper. It rotates continually in its course, and the internal tension and tonal textures create a surface which reads like the craggy face of an old man.

Despite the immediacy implied by the detailed surface texturing, a deeper, almost haunting, sense of mystery pervades the scene. This underlying profundity is almost unequaled in Tao-chi's other works but may be compared with leaf B of the *Eight-Leaf Album of Landscapes* in the Abe collection (fig. 7). In it two ranges of high peaks, their bases cloaked in mist, curve around from one corner of the foreground and recede dramatically into the distance. Wet brushwork is employed to create the desolate planes of the mountains, and a combination of blank paper and wash suggest thick atmosphere. These two leaves represent the "wet" and "dry" modes, dual aspects of Tao-chi's statement on nature in some primeval state preceding man.

Leaf E: *"Lone Sailboat"*

A river bank rises diagonally to the right and cuts across the lower half of the picture frame. A cluster of rocks placed to the far right forms the foreground focus. A line of trees leaning to the left is

7. Tao-chi, *Eight-Leaf Album of Landscapes*, leaf B. Ink and color on paper. Abe collection.

silhouetted on the edge of the bank, leading the eye to the middle ground, where two rocks emerge from the water. Their shapes, one larger than the other, echo the rounded group of stones in the foreground and again lead the eye to a lone sailboat skimming along the water.

Close harmonies of like hues prevail in this glimpse of the corner of a lake. Shimmering blues, greens, and aquas model the foreground rocks with the heaviest color accent, and velvety moss dots further punctuate the forms. This emphasis on color and value pushes the remaining scene into a misty distance. Lateral movement is introduced by the gliding boat; its curved blue sail forms a diagonal progression of color from the foreground, to the middle-ground rocks, to the boat itself. The sense of movement is heightened by the screen of filigree branches which sport jade-like nuggets of leaves.

The principles of interval, balance, and color focus are here illustrated to perfection. The graded ink tones and recurrent diminishing shapes suggest movement within the subtle intervalic spacing. The leaf is remarkably close in both mood and motif, with some variation in composition, to two works, leaf A of the *Eight-Leaf Album of Landscapes* (fig. 8) and leaf E, "Skiff at Pai-sha," from the Fong *Small Album*. In the Abe work a vertical cliff and the horizontal reeds and sand bank function on the same principle as do the diagonals in the Sackler leaf; graded tones of ink and deft spacing again suggest a similar sense of depth and focus.

In all three leaves, the tranquil mood and the iconography of the single boat and figure convey a personal and intimate feeling, as if the artist were seeing himself as the wanderer in some dream-like past.

8. Tao-chi, *Eight-Leaf Album of Landscapes*, leaf A. Ink and color on paper. Abe collection.

9. Mei Ch'ing, landscape from an album depicting the scenery of Huang-shan. Ink and color on paper. Hashimoto collection.

Leaf F: "*Passing through the Gorge*"

The spatial juxtapositions in this leaf are probably the simplest and most striking of the entire album. A sampan with hatted rider floats along a milky river to an abrupt, gate-like pass in the stony mountains. The foot of the cliffs is not depicted; thick, shifting mist is suggested by leaving the lower half of the paper blank except for trees at the base of the frame. The color wash of the cliffs is carried lower on the right side, opposing the strong leftward diagonal movement of the boat and distant bank. In this way the asymmetry holds the whole composition in gentle balance. The spectator's view is high, lightly anchored by the lacy trees hovering on the foreground horizon.

As in leaf D, dry textures are modulated by soft, clear washes. Tao-chi is working here with flat planes and plain white paper; he manipulates the diagonals against the parallel and perpendicular forms of the gorge-like architectural screens. The compositional juxtaposition and dry brushwork remind one of the equally evocative landscapes of Tao-chi's contemporary and friend Mei Ch'ing (1623–1697) (fig. 9).[5] Mei Ch'ing's influence on the younger painter is evident in the composition of this leaf in particular and in the use of dry brushwork in the album in general.

Leaf G: "*Traveler on Horseback*"

CONDITION: there is a slight abrasion and small wormholes on the far right, center.

Houses nestled among the low hills and trees of a small inlet occupy the foreground and slant diagonally upward from the right edge of the frame. A line of trees shielding a rider on horseback and a servant carrying provisions are placed at the very base of the picture frame. Tao-chi has skillfully gauged the scale of figures and trees in relation to that of the houses, which diminish in size from the foreground to the far distance. By deft placement of these basic elements, he has achieved a sense of unity and sweep in which the eye moves from the small figures at the bottom upward to each of the houses, which are arranged like stepping stones receding backward into the picture space.

The color tonalities and graded ink further distinguish the receding ground plane, as successively paler ink tones, siennas, and greens are used. In the foreground the crusty charcoal accents convey a spatial immediacy which presses the unaccented forms into the distance. Similar pine tree motifs, graded color and ink tonalities, and a multi-layered visualization of forms placed in the frontal plane can also be seen in leaf H of the *Eight Views of Huang-shan* (fig. 10).

The figure of the mounted rider hunched forward beneath tall trees recalls the same motif in the Osaka *Sketches after Su Tung-p'o's Poems*, leaf B (fig. 11), as well as leaf L of *Album for Su-weng* (fig. 12).[6] In the details of the Sackler leaf one can see how in a few brief strokes Tao-chi has captured the liveliness and directed motion of the horse and rider.

Leaf H: "*Conversation on the Bridge*"

Two scholars seated in conversation on the arched stone bridge again focus attention on the lower half of the picture plane. Two trees with varied foliage and two boulders placed one slightly above the other to show recession act as the spatial frame for the bridge;

10. Tao-chi, *Eight Views of Huang-shan*, detail of leaf H, "Manjusri Temple." Ink and color on paper. Sumitomo collection.

11. Tao-chi, *Sketches after Su Tung-p'o's Poems*, detail of leaf B, "The New Year's Blizzard." Ink on color on paper. Abe collection.

12. Tao-chi, *Album for Su-weng after Poems by Sung and Yüan Masters*, detail of leaf L. Ink on paper. Collection unknown.

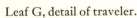

Leaf G, detail of traveler.

13. Tao-chi, *Sketches after Su Tung-p'o's Poems*, leaf G, "Fifth of the Fifth." Ink and color on paper. Abe collection.

the remainder of the scene gradually expands upward into the picture space. Two bluffs emerge from the misty middle area and curve around to enclose a cottage and a grove of pines. Generous areas of white paper suggest shifting vapor; in the far distance the same paper becomes a distant river winding its way from the far horizon back to the land and under the bridge. The forms ebb and flow into one another: line gives way to tone and hue, and form fades into river and mist.

The colors in this leaf are delineated with the precision and clarity of stained glass. One's eye is first caught by the brilliant ultramarine blue of the distant peak at the top of the painting, then by the russet thatched roof, the boulders in blue and green, then the two-toned arched bridge. The method of color wash drawing here is one which Tao-chi developed to perfection: the wet brush is loaded with color and then drawn obliquely across the dry paper surface so as to allow its tip to describe the silhouette in the richest tone and the remainder of the form to fade gradually into a pale or clear wash. Both crisp outline and suggestive volume can be achieved in a few sensitive movements, as in the winding banks or the bulbous forms of the rock.

The viewer's position is high and distant. There is the paradoxical feeling, often encountered in dreams, of acute awareness of the exquisite details of nature coupled with a feeling of the soaring, silent vastness of air and sky. The union of these delicate responses in a pictorial space shimmering with color may be the source of the evocative power which charges this leaf. Timeless, impersonal nature is contrasted with intimate human contact in the image of the two scholars on the bridge. This meeting of kindred spirits is another motif often encountered in Tao-chi's works of the 1690's and 1700's and is seen several times in the Osaka *Sketches after Su Tung-p'o's Poems* (leaves A, E, F, G, J, and K); leaf G (fig. 13) is of special interest for its similar use of the blank paper combined with complex spatial layering of the distant mountains and the strong development of the foreground focus.

Leaf I: "*Promontory and Broad River*"

In this leaf, crystalline color and soft outlines define the compositional elements as true volumes and exhibit Tao-chi's interest in the effects of both flat and volumetric space. There is a sense of dynamic progression into depth as the eye follows the boulders from the left, to the tree-topped promontory, to the sailboats, and to the rim of mountains in the far distance. As in other leaves of this album, the large areas of creamy white paper perform telling functions: in the right foreground the white acts as mist rising to engulf the tiled roofs and swaying bamboo groves; in the distance it becomes a level stretch of water tautly supporting the two skiffs between the mountains.

Color again functions significantly in defining different aspects of the forms. This mastery can be appreciated in such a seemingly minor and confined area as the remote peaks on the horizon. The textures and hues reflect and refract other portions of the landscape. The reality of the depicted space as reflective of an actual scene in nature is suggested not only by the detail of the crenelated wall (which points to Nanking) but also by the description of the varied surfaces in dry brush texture strokes, which effectively suggest plasticity and tactile value. Boats, buildings, and contours are all executed in the sensitive tremulous line found throughout this album and which began to appear frequently in the artist's works from about 1690 on.

As to compositional parallels, Tao-chi's 1695 *Graded Ink Landscapes*[7] contains a scene (*XXXV*, fig. 1) with similar spatial construction and scenery, although described from a lower viewpoint. This 1695 album presents Tao-chi in a "rougher" style, with heavy linework, dark tonalities, and liberal use of wet and dry ink. As in the Sackler album, the mood and expressive intent differ with the brushwork, but the spatial structure provides a link between them.

Leaf J: *"Mountain Retreat at Dusk"*

The final scene in this album presents a cottage nestled among cliffs and hills. The entire leaf glows with the warmth of sunset tones touched with blue. The simple mountain setting is actually the most structurally complex of this series, and the brushwork reiterates the plump, round quality found in the opening leaves. Rising cliffs piled with small rocks dissect the frontal picture plane diagonally in successive layers; in the middle ground three rising hillocks built up of clusters of stones converge around the inviting cottage perched on the boulders' edge. Pine trees on a plateau beneath the cottage bend in response to a smaller tree outlined against the valley mist. The placement of these elements leads the eye in and around the space. Jutting peaks in blue wash emerge close on the horizon. In the distant heights, a misty, pale blue range looms over all, wrapping the whole composition in a tight harmony.

As in the rest of the album, color is used with expressive significance. Spots of color in the rooftop cottage, on the rock clusters, and on the sides of cliffs intensify the integrity of the forms as elements in space. Thus the blue and russet hues not only create a sense of volume but guide the eye's movement within the spatial realm of the landscape, from the foreground path, up the promontories, to overlook the valley below and the rising peaks behind.

In addition to aiding the linear ink contours, color is also used interchangeably to build form. The pale dots enliven the surface of the forms and lend a sense of bulk; at the same time the color washes are conceived of as textures. For example, in the low mountains in the distance, the dry brush is dipped lightly in pale blue and is drawn several times across the mountain shape in a scrubbing motion to create the roughness of the mountain surface. Not only does this effect generate an extraordinary amount of interest in this usu-

ally inconspicuous spot, but these textures also echo the pale, dry surfaces of the ink in the foreground and middle-distance boulders. Thus both color dots and texture function as subtle pictorial unifiers, yet the delicate transparency which characterizes the handling of the ink and color prevents the complex composition from becoming overly heavy or uninvitingly dense. Tao-chi's genius lies in his very ability to draw the breathtaking from the commonplace and the difficult in conception. A copyist (if we were fortunate enough to have a copy of this album) would fail not in the transcription of the formal complexities of the composition but rather in the fragile handling of the colors and their interaction with the ink. In that imaginary copyist's hand, incoherence instead of lyric colorism would result.

Two scenes in this album can be identified with actual sites: leaf A with the peaks of Mt. Huang, Anhwei, and leaf I with a view near Nanking, Kiangsu. The remaining leaves are presumably associated with other scenes from Tao-chi's travels, actual or imaginary.

We know from his dated letters that in his late years Tao-chi was frequently plagued by minor ailments,[8] so that his artistic production was often uneven both in quality and quantity. Professor Shūjirō Shimada has observed that these illnesses were actually a blessing in disguise, for they released him from harassing social commitments and permitted him to paint as the mood struck him.[9] Some of the unusual aspects of this album may be the immediate fruits of such circumstances, and they speak for its exceptional quality—the attenuated images, the range of blunt and restrained ink line, the fragile coloring. Indeed, Tao-chi's comment in his inscription that he has gained some leisure because of illness was no doubt mentioned in order to differentiate this album from others of his works which he felt were of poorer quality (i.e., the "fish eyes") which were also entering the "marketplace." This album was the "genuine pearl," and, as stated in his last line, "those who understand will treasure this as something special."

The *1700 Peking Album* corroborates both the painting style and the appropriateness of the 1701 date found in the self-inscription. The coarse, decisive brushwork of the two albums reinforces the continuity of Tao-chi's development from the occasional appearance of such brush conceptions in his earlier works of around 1685 (e.g., *Searching for Plum Blossoms [XV]*, *Ten Thousand Ugly Inkblots*, and others) to this period of around 1700, and on to 1706–7, when this kind of linework dominates.

NOTES

1. We are grateful to Professor Shimada for his help in the identification of this calligrapher and the reading of his seals.

2. Earlier examples of such rhythms in Tao-chi's brushwork appear, among other works, in leaves E and H of the *Eight Views of Huang-shan* album in the Sumitomo collection, the 1685 *Searching for Plum Blossoms* handscroll in the Sackler collection (*XVIII*), and leaf E of the 1694 Los Angeles *Album of Landscapes* (*PTC*, cat. no. 7, p. 108).

3. *Tao-chi hua-ts'e*, in twelve leaves (ten landscapes, two flowers), ink and occasional color on paper, 18.5 x 26.0 cm.

4. Reproduced in color in *Sekitō to Hachidai san-jin*, no. 1.

5. Reproduced in *Min Shin no kaiga*, no. 87.

6. Cf. also Richard Edwards, "Postscript to an Exhibition," figs. 9–10, p. 266.

7. In *Ta-feng-t'ang ming-chi*, vol. 2, pls. 29–33.

8. Cheng Wei, "Lun Shih-t'ao sheng-huo, hsing-ching, ssu-hsiang ti-pien chi i-shu ch'eng-chiu," p. 47.

9. *Min-matsu san oshō*, p. 9 of text.

Leaf D, "Cliffs" (*actual size*)

Leaf A, "Among Peaks and Pines (Mt. Huang)" (*actual size*)

Leaf B, "Mountain Stream" (style of Mi Fu)

Leaf C, "Crossing the Bridge"

Leaf E, "Lone Sailboat"

Leaf F, "Passing through the Gorge"

Leaf G, "Traveler on Horseback"

Leaf I, "Promontory and Broad River"

Leaf J, "Mountain Retreat at Dusk"

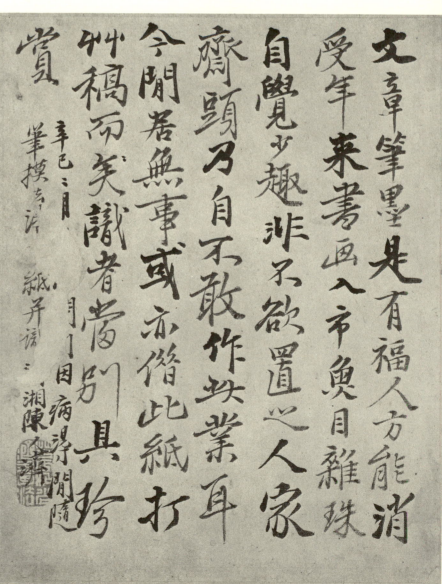

Leaf K, Artist's self-inscription

Leaf H, "Conversation on the Bridge" (*actual size*)

After Shen Chou's Bronze Peacock Inkslab
(Lin Shen Chou Mo-ch'o T'ung-ch'üeh-yen-ko t'u)

The Art Museum, Princeton University (67-21).

Hanging scroll. Ink and light color on paper. 118.5 x 41.5 cm.

UNDATED: probably executed ca. 1698–1703.

SIGNATURE OF THE ARTIST: Ch'ing-hsiang, Ta-ti-tzu (in "clerical" script after his inscription on left edge of painting).

INSCRIPTION BY THE ARTIST: a transcription of Shen Chou's original poem in song form (ko) in six lines including title (upper margin), followed by a transcription of Shen Chou's original prose epilogue in six lines (lower margin), dated summer of 1500 (Hung-chih shih-san nien, hsia wu-yüeh), both in "running" script in imitation of Shen Chou's hand; a prose inscription by Tao-chi in three lines of "clerical" script signed with the words "written again" (ch'ung-chi).

SEALS OF THE ARTIST:
Ch'i-chuang chung-cheng (relief, square; PTC, cat. no. 8, not listed, misread as Ch'i-chung chung-cheng) top edge of painting.
Ling-ting lao-jen (relief, square; PTC, cat. no. 53, not listed) after signature.
Ch'ing-hsiang Shih-t'ao (intaglio, tall rectangle; PTC, cat. no. 22, not listed) after signature.
Tsan-chih shih-shih-sun, A-ch'ang (relief, tall rectangle; PTC, cat. no. 95, not listed) after signature.

COLLECTORS' SEALS:
Ma Chi-tso (contemporary Hong Kong collector), Chi-tso shen-ting (relief, square) and Ma-shih shu-hua (intaglio, square) lower left corner of painting.
Chang Ta-ch'ien (born 1899), Ta-feng-t'ang Chien-chiang, K'un-ts'an, Hsüeh-ko, K'u-kua mo-yüan (relief, tall rectangle) left edge of painting, Pieh-shih jung-i (relief, square) and Chiu-t'u-pao ku-jou-ch'ing (intaglio, rectangle) lower left corner of painting.
Owners unidentified, Po-yüan shen-ting (relief, square) lower right corner of painting (this seal also appears on II), Ch'uan-shan chien-shang (relief, square) lower right corner of painting at bottom, Ssu-chou Yang-shih suo-ts'ang (relief, tall rectangle) lower left corner of silk mounting.

COLOPHON: by Wu Mei (unidentified), a poetic eulogy in three long lines for the collector Po-yüan (unidentified) on right side of silk mounting.

PROVENANCE: Ta-feng-t'ang collection.

PUBLISHED: Record of the Art Museum, Princeton University, vol. 27 (1968), p. 35 (acquisitions list); Archives of Asian Art, vol. 22 (1968–69), p. 134 (acquisitions list).

OTHER VERSIONS (attributed to Shen Chou): a version on paper, in a Hong Kong private collection; a version on silk, recorded in T'ao Liang (1772–1857), Hung-tou shu-kuan shu-hua-chi; a mala fide copy by a modern forger (see XXVIII for further discussion of these three versions).

THIS SCROLL is a close copy by Tao-chi of a work by the Ming master Shen Chou (1427–1509). While the original Shen Chou painting may still be extant, only replicas are known to us; one of these copies, no. XXVIII of this catalogue, will be discussed in conjunction with this work.

Two long inscriptions cover the upper half of the painting. The first, on the right, consists of a poem in five lines (plus one line of the title) and a prose commentary in six; Tao-chi has transcribed both style and content of the original inscription by Shen Chou and has also reproduced his signature. The second inscription on the far left in three lines is by Tao-chi in his own "clerical" style and indicates that he has inscribed the work twice (ch'ung-chi); thus this was intended as a bona fide copy of the original.

In the painting two gentlemen converse under the luxuriant shade of a banana grove. Behind the plants looms a large garden rockery.

On the long table at which they are seated lies a rectangular inkslab and several volumes of rare books. An attendant stands at the left grasping a long ornate sword. This scene illustrates the poem by Shen Chou transcribed above the figures, which pleads with the owner of a precious late Han tile inkslab to spare it from the blows of a guest's sword despite the fact that its owner despises the historical figure who erected the monument from which the tile was taken. A free rendering of the poem, the epilogue, and Tao-chi's comments follow:

To draw your sword and shatter this tile[1] is what a child would do.
To break and smash such a thing wouldn't mean a thing to Ts'ao Man.[2]
How would it be to pick up the pen of a grand historian
And erase his [Ts'ao's] reign from the historical records?
After Confucius, there was not another Ch'un-ch'iu [Spring and Autumn Annals];
Old Ts'ao Man has blinded the world in vain praise of Chou.
On the inkslab still is carved the era of Han;
Although full of daring, [Ts'ao Ts'ao's] heart was still timid.
I would like you to save this tile to be used for ink—
How handy it would be to mark up his face!
Those traitors of Han should be purged with Han law;
Only now does the Chang River dare to express its grudge silently.
It would be better to keep this tile as a mirror for traitorous officials;
I have never seen a good [i.e., filial] raven address a chang-jen.[3]
I say, what fault was it of the Bronze Peacock?
So I put down this poem to salvage the tile from destruction.

Mr. Liu Ts'ao-ch'uang[4] once composed a verse on the Bronze Peacock, saying: "Child, open that chest and get out that Sword—Shatter that tile and don't leave a trace!" Reading that, one learns how much he hated Ts'ao Ts'ao, letting his resentment build up and releasing it in such fierce and resolute words. I, Shen Chou, am too much of a coward, and cannot help crying out even at the sound of the breaking of a jar. So I have composed this poem not only to soften [Liu's] anger but also to have something remaining as well.

> Fifth month, summer, thirteenth year of the Hung-chih era [1500]. I was at the home of a Wang relative having wine under lamplight when he brought out some paper and asked me to paint. I couldn't respond right away to his request. Then I rummaged around and found an old work which I record here and ask for correction.
> [Signed:] Shen Chou.

Tao-chi's inscription reads:

An object can be cherished, but a poem can't be hidden. Since it was so precious in those days, why destroy it because of one's present anger? The tile does affect people, causing time to fly by [for them] like a galloping horse. But it is man who has turned the tile into an inkslab, so how can we consider it the source of our troubles? I am not moved by the tile; nor do I want to change it. And neither am I renouncing the ancients for what is more recent. [Signed:] Ch'ing-hsiang Ta-ti-tzu wrote again.[5]

SHEN CHOU'S PAINTING and the event described in the long poem are recorded in an early nineteenth-century catalogue, Hsieh Ch'eng-chün's K'uei-k'uei-chai shu-hua-chi, published in 1821–1836.[6] Hsieh appears to have seen the version in T'ao Liang's collection (see XXVIII) and gives the background of the incident as follows:

I was at the residence of the t'ai-shih T'ao Chi-hsiang [Liang, 1772–1857] and saw a painting by Shen Chou titled Chi-yen-t'u [Splitting the Inkslab]. The subject of this painting is an occasion when the venerable Wu Wen-ting [K'uan, 1435–1504] possessed a T'ung-ch'üeh tile inkslab [made from the tile of the Bronze Peacock Terrace] and brought it out

莫研銅雀硯歌

拔劍斫尾直覺美研碎於瞬莫輕何如制筆青竹中
間削其統孔子作後無春秋老瞞一世虛尊周尾狼尚剷漢正朔
其膽雖大心還盖顏留此尾仍作硯正要子墨點其西漢賊
明將漢法誅漳水無聲散流怨復留此尾鑒亂臣不見
好烏吳人鳴呼銅雀為何罪我為題詩救其碎
草窟劉先生嘗賦銅雀硯歌有云呼見開畫取長劍碎研
慎勿留其蹟讀之知先生疾操之心盖之怒氣發之於言著
其言勁且烈也周懦夫也不能不失聲拈破每故作缺詩
解其怒而顏有時存焉耳弘治十三年夏五月余手玉龍
宏對雨燃下出紙求畫一時不能應命偶獨舊作遂錄以歸
請教　　　　　　　　　　　沈周

物可斫詩不可斫跋多於當牽之手何所而今兴憤尾移此也
以牛去兮奔駿州易硯之豈燕世兴徒舉竟我拒移耶非易耶
亦非選古州而式之
　　　清波大孫學重記

to show his friends. One of the friends detested Ts'ao Man's [Ts'ao's] character and promptly drew his sword to break the slab to bits. Shih-t'ien [Shen Chou] happened to be present and later executed this painting and composed a long poem to record the incident. The poetry, calligraphy, and painting can certainly be praised as "unexcelled in all three" [san-chüeh].

AT FIRST GLANCE this painting might well be mistaken for a work by Shen Chou. The composition, figure, banana plant, rock, and even the block of calligraphy recall the image of the Ming master. It would, in fact, be difficult to associate Tao-chi's name with it had he not included his own inscription. On closer scrutiny, however, one can recognize the smaller movements of the brush, the vitality, and the expression as Tao-chi's. He has merely donned the outer guise of Shen Chou; the personality animating the forms is his own.

We have not located the Shen Chou original, but examination of several existing copies of the composition and an attributed Shen Chou of similar design suggests how close Tao-chi's general arrangement and rendering of individual elements is to its prototype. For example, schematically the banana leaves are close to those in a 1482 hanging scroll attributed to Shen Chou (cf. *XXVIII*, fig. 1). Technically, however, the leaves are visualized and completed in Tao-chi's own manner. He used double outlines of pale, dry ink in graded tones and then applied pale semi-dry washes to strategic areas as shading, giving depth and weight to the forms. While he was initially influenced by Shen Chou in both the choice and rendering of such a subject, his independent success in this mode can be seen in a leaf from his *Flowers and Figures* album (*XX*, leaf G).

The figures (see the detail) also exhibit Tao-chi's success in this, one of the rarest of his genres. The two gentlemen are animated and intense in their expression, yet serene in their attitude. The larger figure (perhaps Wu K'uan, the collector of the tile) leans over to listen to his companion (perhaps Liu Ts'ao-ch'uang, the moralist who is sensitive to historical associations, with his sword nearby). The latter speaks with both gestures and words. The expression on the listener's face is benevolent, concerned, and gracious. The profile of the guest and the set of his shoulders strongly resemble Tao-chi's portrait of T'ao Yüan-ming from the *Flowers and Figures* album (*XX*, leaf E), as well as some of the small figures on horseback which enliven many of his landscapes (cf. *XXXIV*). Modeling of the facial features in fine brushlines of graded ink is again a Tao-chi signature and makes the faces come alive as intelligent and humorous beings. The elliptical, piercing black eyes, the bulbous nose, the fine pointed whiskers, and the spherical, elongated egg shape of the head are almost identical with Tao-chi's portrait of T'ao Yüan-ming. Tao-chi has reserved the darkest ink for the eyes and for discreet details in the cap and clothing of the figures, allowing the significant expressions to dominate. The quality and subtlety of the rendering become all the more striking if we compare these figures with the Sackler forgery and the Hong Kong copy (*XXVIII* and *XXVIII*, fig. 2). There the outlines are mannered and jagged and the ink tones lack gradation.

The linework in the drapery folds of the figures is from the same hand as the linear modeling strokes (or *ts'un*—literally, "wrinkles") of the rocks. Tao-chi's "wrinkles" are invariably structured in echoing parallels of varying ink tones. The brushlines themselves may be fine and drawn mostly with the very tip (as in the clothing), or they may be bolder and drawn with a coarser blunt brush; they vary from fine undulations (as in the figures here), to more straightforward and firm lines (as in the veins of the banana leaves). Whatever their width, the brush is primarily held upright, and the fine gradations of ink, combined with telling application of washes for shading, suggest the weight and density of the material they are de-scribing. This clear differentiation of specific tactile sensations is one of Tao-chi's strong stylistic traits and is especially telling when compared with the two copies (see discussion below).

IN EXECUTING this copy, Tao-chi also remained faithful to Shen Chou's calligraphic format and style. The position of the signature and the manner of filling up the whole upper half of the painting with a block of writing is seen in a typical Shen Chou work, *Sitting Up at Night*.[7] The formation of characters and use of the brush are illustrated in such works as his excellent colophon to the handscroll *Falling Flowers: Poems and Painting* (fig. 1).[8] In this scroll we see the Ming master's most distinctive features: a tall, rectangular shape; an axis with a pronounced upward slant; strong columnar spacing; blunt angular strokes; and elongated diagonals and undulating horizontals. Typologically these features originated with the Northern Sung master Huang T'ing-ch'ien and became a part of the personal style of Shen Chou as well as Wen Cheng-ming. Occasionally Tao-chi also drew on aspects of this style (see the discussion of his calligraphy in Part IV above), so that he has captured a fairly good likeness. Like most copyists, however, he tends to exaggerate typical features of his model: he intensifies, for example, the undulating horizontal and the elongated diagonals.

But what identifies the calligraphy of this Sackler scroll as Tao-chi's and as by the same hand as the three lines of Tao-chi's own inscription despite the difference in script type and intention? As we have tried to show in our earlier discussion of Tao-chi's calligraphy, "clerical" script was his basic orientation, and the splayed diagonal strokes, squat perpendicular frame and axis, and round, plump brushstrokes further identify his hand. In the twelve lines after Shen Chou, we can see that Tao-chi was struggling to maintain a certain regularity of character slant and brush movement. Glancing back at the original Shen Chou script (fig. 1), we can see that despite an initial resemblance, Tao-chi's script habits occasionally gain supremacy. In Shen Chou's hand, the upward slant structures the entire framework of each character and of the strokes as well.

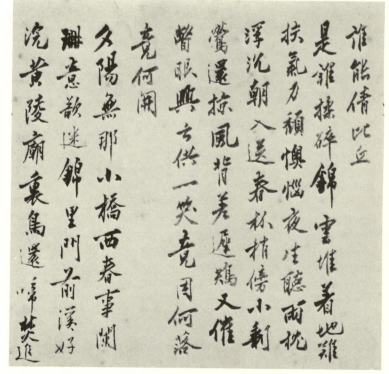

1. Shen Chou, *Falling Flowers: Poems and Painting*, before 1508, detail of colophon. Handscroll. Ink and color on paper. National Palace Museum, Taipei.

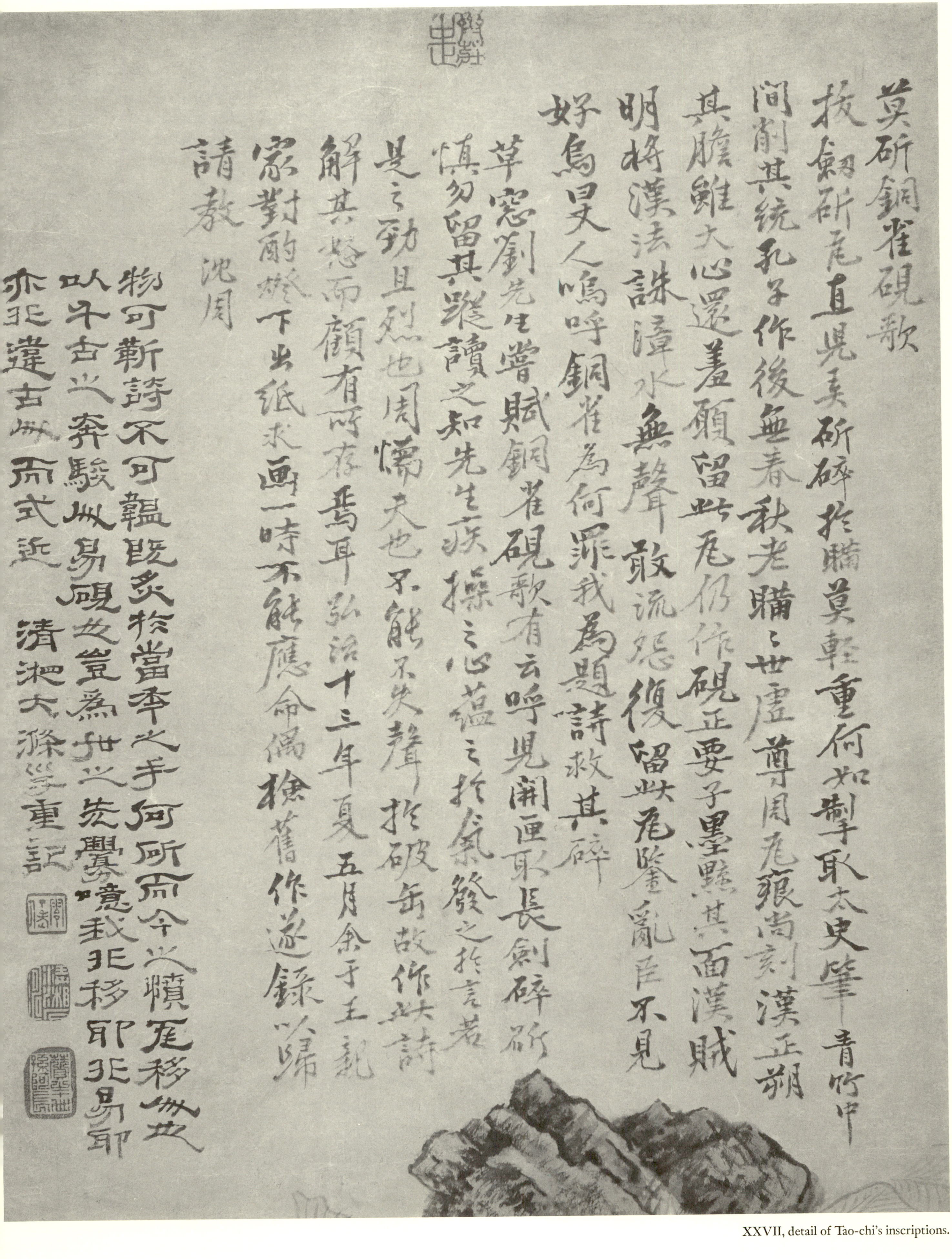

莫研銅雀硯歌

按銅研尾直視美研碎挨膽莫輕重何如擊取太史肇青竹中

間削其統孔子作後無春秋老瞞世虞尊周尾狼尚剝漢正朔

其膽雖大心還羞顏留此尾仍作硯正要子墨黥其面漢賦

明將漢法誅瞳水無聲敢流怨復留此尾鑒亂臣不見

好烏昊人鳴呼銅雀為何罪我為題詩救其碎

慎勿留其蹤讀之知先生疾操三折氣發之抒言若

草窗劉先生嘗賦銅雀硯歌有云呼兒開匣取長劍碎硯

是之勁且烈也周懍天也不能不失聲挨破岳故作此詩

解其怒而顏有可存焉耳弘治十三年夏五月余于王親

密對酌於下出紙求畫一時不能應命偶撿舊作遂錄以歸

請教　沈周

物可靳詩不可韞賤炎於當季之手阿所流今興懺尾移他址

以牛古兴奔驥城易硯女莞為世兴先舉勢意我北移耶北易耶

亦非遷古州於式近　清湘大滌學重記

XXVII, detail of Tao-chi's inscriptions.

The angle of the slant is as regular and inexorable as meter or beat in music; it was automatic and as natural for him as it was to hold his brush slightly aslant. Thus the formation of his strokes tends to be straight, angular, and oblique rather than round, curvilinear, and plump (as in Tao-chi's own free hand). Shen Chou begins the horizontals, for example, by forcefully cutting open the line with a square, exposed tip, and then drawing the brush in one unidirectional movement (rather than slightly twisting the brush to hide the tip, as Tao-chi would often do). Furthermore, Shen Chou's use of three or four undulations, a mannerism derived from Huang T'ing-chien, almost seems intended to soften the stark, angular, and decisive line which characterizes most of his strokes.

Tao-chi strains to retain Shen Chou's upward slant, but he frequently reverts to the perpendicular balance of his more habitual "clerical" script (cf. his own inscription at the left of this Sackler copy). Moreover, his diagonals are invariably plump and roundly arched (e.g., in characters 8 to 4 from the bottom of the first line, chih-ch'ü t'ai-shih-pi). These strokes curve in the same way as the chih character 之 and the horizontals in Tao-chi's own inscription. Moreover, his interpretation of the undulating horizontal also reveals his centered-tip brushhold. (Notice that they waver both at the top and the bottom of the line, in contrast to Shen Chou's, where they are straight at the top and only the bottom wavers; cf. leaf B of the Flowers and Figures album for discussion of a similar technique). From these random observations one can see that despite his primary intent to deceive, Tao-chi's calligraphic orientation remains fundamentally constant and is suppressed only with much effort.

THE DATE OF THE PAINTING falls relatively late in Tao-chi's career, possibly between 1698 and 1703, for three reasons. The brushwork of both calligraphy and painting is fully mature and shows the modulations, consistency, and control typical of his works after 1690. The signature, Ch'ing-hsiang Ta-ti-tzu, is a late one which appears most frequently on works dated after 1697 (see Tao-chi's

Letter to Pa-ta, XXIII). The square relief seal, Ch'i-chuang chung-cheng (at the very top of the painting), which he rarely used, is found on only one other work, dated 1698; two of the other seals, Ling-ting lao-jen and Tsan-chih shih-shih-sun, A-ch'ang, are even later and are found on works dated from 1701 to 1707.[9] These two seals, plus the third one after the signature, are also found on the Boston Album of Landscapes, dated 1703, and are closely comparable in condition and impression.

NOTES

1. The Bronze Peacock Inkslab was made from a tile taken from the fabulous Bronze Peacock Terrace (T'ung-ch'üeh-t'ai) erected by Ts'ao Ts'ao (133–220) in 210 A.D. on the Chang River in the Lin-chang district of Honan province.

2. Ts'ao Ts'ao's tzu was Meng-te and his hao A-man; he was a great Han general whose lesser virtues were magnified by later literary accounts, so that he became a chief antagonist in popular legend.

3. The raven was known as a filial bird who looked after its mother; chang-jen (an honorific for "old man") may refer to Ch'iao Hsüan, whose two beautiful daughters, it is said, Ts'ao hoped to woo by building the Bronze Peacock Terrace. The line is obscure, but it may mean that aspects of human nature (or of the animal world) were not altered by Ts'ao's intentions or actions.

4. Liu Pu (tzu Ts'ao-ch'uang, fl. ca. 1450–1456), of Ch'ang-chou, Kiangsu, was known as one of the Ten Talents of Ching-t'ai.

5. We are especially indebted to T'ang Hai-t'ao for his aid in elucidating the abstruse passages in these inscriptions. For further examination of the literary sources, a comparison of the various versions of Shen Chou's poems, and a brief history of the significance of the Bronze Peacock Inkslab in the tradition of inkstones, see Chuang Shen, "Ming Shen Chou 'Mo-ch'o T'ung-ch'üeh-yen-ko t'u'k'ao," especially pp. 58–59.

6. Dated according to the self-epilogue, pp. 1a–2b. The Princeton University Library has a hand-copied version from the Ex-J. D. Ch'en collection. Hsieh unfortunately did not give the exact source of his account.

7. Also called Night Vigil, reproduced in National Palace Museum, Taipei, Three Hundred Masterpieces, vol. 5, pl. 220; arch. no. 749/52 MV70.

8. The painting and poems are undated, but the fine colophon by Wen Cheng-ming is dated 1508, so the work must have been executed before that time. The painting and calligraphy do appear to be of Shen's late style. See Ku-kung shu-hua-lu, vol. 2, 4/159; arch. no. 2994 MH6 (painting), 3000 MH6i(A–E) (calligraphy). For another excellent example of Shen Chou's calligraphy, see Begging for a Beard (Hua-hsü-su), also in the National Palace Museum, Taipei, arch. no. 5256 MC4.

9. Cf. Sasaki Kozo, "Tao-chi, Seals," pp. 63, 66–69.

XXVIII   ARTIST UNKNOWN

Modern Copy of Shen Chou's Bronze Peacock Inkslab (Mo-ch'o T'ung-ch'üeh-yen-ko t'u)

The Art Museum, Princeton University (L245.70).

Hanging scroll. Ink on paper. 103.6 x 30.3 cm.

FORGED DATE: summer, 1500 (Hung-chih shih-san-nien, hsia, wu-yüeh).

FORGED SIGNATURE OF SHEN CHOU: Shen Chou.

FORGED SEALS OF SHEN CHOU: Ch'i-nan (relief, square), Pai-shih weng (intaglio, square) after signature; Yu-chu-chü (intaglio, tall rectangle) upper right corner.

FORGED INSCRIPTION OF SHEN CHOU: in thirteen lines (including title), consisting of poetry and a prose epilogue (for translation see XXVII).

PROVENANCE: Hong Kong dealer.

UNPUBLISHED

OTHER VERSIONS: see below.

THIS WORK was acquired by the Sackler collections to serve as comparative material for the painting after Shen Chou (1427–1509) by Tao-chi on the same subject. Even judged as a copy, it has small merit other than what it preserves of Shen Chou's composition.

The Shen Chou prototype can be verified by the existence of two other versions of the same composition: one on silk, entered by T'ao Liang (1772–1859) in the Hung-tou-shu-kuan shu-hua-chi, 8/17b, and one on paper (fig. 2), in a private collection in Hong Kong, published by Chuang Shen in Ming-pao, vol. 3, no. 1 (1968), p. 55. The version from Hung-tou-shu-kuan is not illustrated but is described as follows: "This picture shows two figures seated below a banana plant and rock. On the table is placed a Bronze Peacock Inkslab. To one side a tousled-haired youth grasping a sword stands at attention. The drapery folds are primarily done in tremulous strokes [chan-chih chih-pi], and appear especially antique and uncommon." (This is followed by a transcription of the Mo-ch'o T'ung-ch'üeh-yen-ko t'u.[1]) From this description we may assume that the composition and brush style of this silk version were generally close to the two paper versions now extant. Could there be a genuine Shen Chou among the three, or could all three be copies after yet another version? In publishing the Hong Kong painting, Chuang Shen studied Shen Chou's text and, after a lengthy comparison of the seals, inscription, and calligraphic styles, concluded that the silk version was

XXVII, detail of foreground figures.

a copy and the Hong Kong the original. Unfortunately, the poor quality of the Hong Kong version, which is visible even in our reproduction (fig. 2), complicates this conclusion, as does the recent appearance of the Sackler copy. As far as we know Chuang was not aware of the Tao-chi version.

The Hong Kong version is extraordinarily close to the Sackler copy and may even be of slightly higher quality, yet this very closeness indicates that one was copied from the other and that there must be yet another version somewhere which served as the model for one of the two. Whether this third version is genuine or not is impossible to say. Both the Hong Kong and Sackler copies are harsh and poorly executed: the dark ink tones in the table, chair, and rock are barely modulated; the contrast is jolting and overpowers the expression of the figures. The latter are summarily done, their expressions vacuous when compared to the Tao-chi copy. As for the brushwork in the clothing, the tremulous lines have overtaken the form and, in the hands of this copyist, have become an empty mannerism. They are meaningless as description and look more like crumpled tinfoil than like folds of fabric. Moreover, the ink tones of the brushlines hardly vary and when they do, it is with no relationship to the forms they are describing. This rather unfeeling execution of the figures in the two scrolls becomes strikingly apparent when compared with Tao-chi's sensitive and sympathetic copy.

Even the large garden rock suffers at the copyist's hands. The 1482 scroll of similar composition attributed to Shen Chou (fig. 1)[2] gives us some idea of the technique that he might have used—a free, undulating contour, varied, modeling strokes, and strongly contrasting ink tones in primarily wet textures. The liberty Tao-chi took in reinterpreting this rock reveals his personal stylistic approach: he extended it to form a larger, screen-like backdrop to fill the blank space near the banana plant on the far left and modeled the crevices and fissures with decisive strokes in blunt scrub-like textures, thereby achieving a substantial and monumental form. (Similar textural effects and execution can be seen, for example, in leaves from his *Album of Landscapes* of 1703 in Boston.) The two copyists, on the other hand, give the rock a nervous and prickly outline. Flat wash is applied in primarily a single tone to fill in the mass, and uniform stippling provides the surface texture. The result, hardly monumental, is a monotonous pattern; like the quivering drapery lines, these copies reveal a hasty and inattentive forger at work.

The calligraphy in the Sackler copy shows the same high-keyed pace. The copyist has succeeded, as in the painting itself, in capturing the general impression, and we must grant him this success. But, unlike the writing of Shen Chou (see *XXVII*, fig. 1), this inscription shows the light, nervous, and hasty hand found in the painting. To this criticism we must also add the poor quality of the supposed Shen Chou seals and also that of one of the modern collectors, Wu Hu-fan. Wu was meticulous in the choice and cutting of his seals (see the original version of the same seal in *II*); he would hardly have approved of the carving of this one.

Judging from the mediocre quality of the two extant scrolls, we do not believe that Tao-chi used either as prototypes. Indeed, it is quite likely that the Sackler forgery is modern (possibly of Wu Hu-fan's generation); it may even have been painted after the publication of the Hong Kong version.

NOTES

1. The text of Shen Chou's poem is largely the same as that of the Sackler copy and the Tao-chi version except that there are two minor variant characters in the inscription and T'ao lists three characters as illegible in the prose epilogue; also, the second of Shen Chou's seals, *Shih-t'ien*, appears instead of *Pai-shih-weng*, and four different collectors' seals are added (one of which is *Hsiang Yüan-pien*). This version in T'ao Liang's collection was apparently the one that Hsieh Ch'eng-chün saw and recorded in his *K'uei-k'uei-chai shu-hua-chi* (see *XXVII*).

2. In ink on paper, Ex-P'ang Yüan-chi collection; published in *Tō Sō Gen Min meiga taikan*, vol. 2, pl. 243.

1. Attributed to Shen Chou, *Scholar under Garden Rock*, dated 1482, detail. Hanging scroll. Ink on paper. Ex-P'ang Yüan-chi collection.

2. Attributed to Shen Chou, *Bronze Peacock Inkslab*, detail. Hanging scroll. Ink on paper. Private collection, Hong Kong.

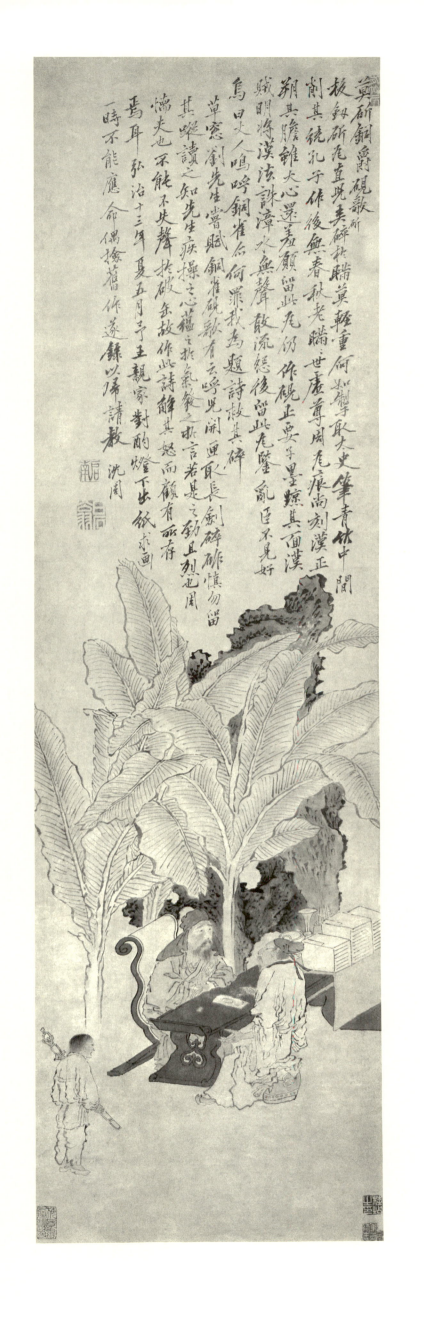

XXIX TAO-CHI (1641–ca. 1710)

Orchid, Bamboo, and Rock

The Art Museum, Princeton University (L12.67).

Hanging scroll. Ink on paper. 72.5 x 51.0 cm.

UNDATED: probably executed ca. 1700.

SIGNATURE OF THE ARTIST: Ch'ing-hsiang Ta-ti-tzu.

SEAL OF THE ARTIST: *Ho-k'o i-jih wu-tz'u-chün* (intaglio, tall rectangle; *PTC*, cat. no. 28).

NO COLLECTORS' SEALS OR COLOPHONS

CONDITION: fair; parts of the surface of the paper are moderately abraded; the lower left and right corners, which are slightly wormeaten, have been discreetly filled in.

PROVENANCE: Ta-feng-t'ang collection.

PUBLISHED: *PTC*, cat. no. 26, p. 156 (illustrated).

A CLOSEUP VIEW of a rock placed diagonally across the picture plane dominates the form of this work. One tall bamboo stalk and a few subsidiary bamboo sprays grow from its center. A clump of orchids emerges at the far left, its pale graded ink reflecting that of the taller bamboo. Two smaller rocks in dark ink are placed behind the rock to the left, and a ground of pale ink dabs signifying moss texture underlies the whole form, completing the semblance of a natural space. The proportions of the rock are almost too large for the picture and convey the artist's sense of humor. Volume is effected by a minimum of descriptive strokes—an undulating contour and a few dots and lines which intersect the bulging outline. Pictorially, we tend to read the bamboo and orchids as solid and the rock mass as void.

THE LEAVES in this work hang down in overlapping groups of twos, threes, and fours. Technically, they are drawn with the brush, as one would write the ancient character *ko* ↑. This method of painting bamboo is also seen in leaf B, "Bamboo," of the Sackler album *Flowers and Figures* (XX) and in the 1696 *Sketches of Calligraphy and Painting by Ch'ing-hsiang*, in Peking (fig. 1). In the latter work, the tonal contrast is reversed, with darker, heavier leaves placed at the top of the stalk, but the random scoring and free, "unkempt" arrangement of the leaves, as well as their plump, relatively short proportions, mark the forms as issuing from the same hand and conception.

Orchid, Bamboo, and Rock may also be compared with the large hanging scroll in the C. C. Wang collection, *Bamboo and Orchids in the Wind* (fig. 2), which, though undated, is Tao-chi's most monumental work in this genre. In that work the leaves are blown by the wind and the clusters of bamboo grow upward. But despite the differences in format and expression, these two works reveal the same working procedure and visualization of form. In the lower half of the C. C. Wang painting, one can see that Tao-chi also placed the rock on a diagonal ground. The rocks, reeds, and orchids are subsidiary to the bamboo, but compositionally they also function as dark forms against the light rock. Wet dabs of ink model the inner volume of the rock and fill in the background as grass. All together, these elements again suggest the "positive" and "negative" interchange of ground and figure. In addition, execution of individual elements is quite similar: the large stalks and small branches, the crisp bamboo leaves with long pointed tips, and the articulation of the joints.

As for the handling of ink, the major components of rock, bamboo, orchid, and grasses are drawn in Tao-chi's customary process with the brush saturated with two major ink tones, a pale and a dark, which have fused into intermediary values during the painting process. In both works the paler ink lines and dots have blurred edges. These effects of suffusion tell us several things: that the nature of the paper and its degree of absorbency were similar; that the artist was accustomed to working with this kind of paper and to loading his brush to a certain degree of saturation; and, finally, that his speed was habitual and rhythmic, so that the interaction of wet ink with paper produced comparable results. Since these technical procedures may vary slightly with the occasion and the materials used by the artist, the similarity shown in these two paintings suggests that their dates of execution are close.

In addition, the signature, "Ch'ing-hsiang Ta-ti-tzu," and seal, *Ho-k'o i-jih wu-tz'u-chün* ("how can I be one day without this gentleman?" i.e., the bamboo) (see the detail and fig. 3), are the same in the two works. This seal also appears on two other bamboo paintings, both dated 1691, executed in collaboration with Wang Hui and Wang Yüan-ch'i, respectively (cf. Part IV, figs. 15 and 16, above).

In terms of style, the Sackler design seems to be a more mature statement than these two collaborative works, however. Two other dated works related in style and subject matter may aid in ascertaining the date of execution. The 1696 *Sketches of Calligraphy and Painting by Ch'ing-hsiang* bamboo and orchid sections may be compared for similar habits of brushwork (see fig. 1 above and XX, fig. 1) to help set up a *terminus a quo*. Two paintings in the slightly different genre of vegetables and fruits, a handscroll titled *Autumn Melon and Praying Mantis*, dated 1700 (XXXI, fig. 3), and another work in the Sackler collection, *Bamboo, Vegetables, and Fruit*, dated 1705 (XXXI), are even closer in their concept and treatment of "negative" and "positive" form, light humor, and free, moist brushwork. On the basis of these dated works we would tentatively date this scroll about 1700.

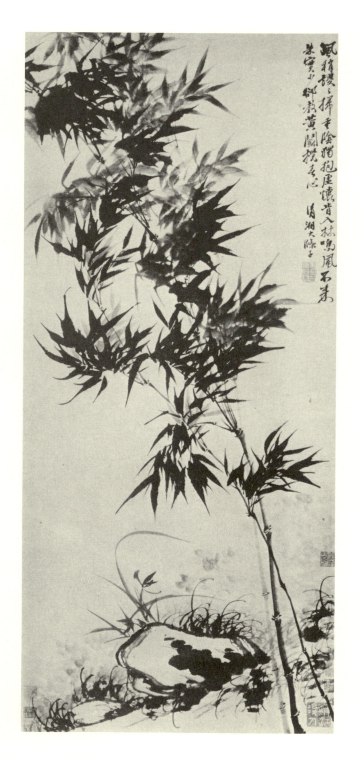

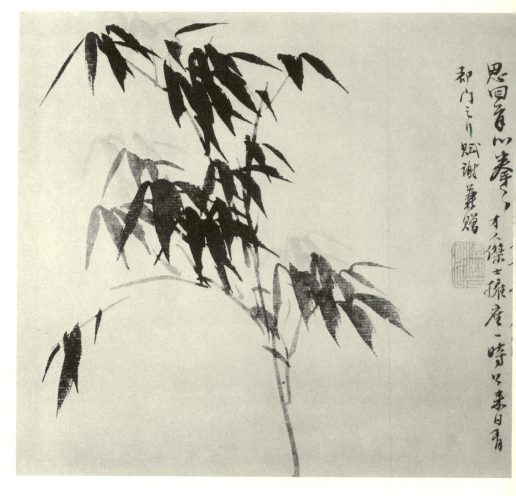

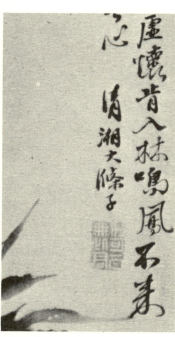

above, right

1. Tao-chi, *Sketches of Calligraphy and Painting by Ch'ing-hsiang,* dated 1696, "Bamboo," detail. Handscroll. Ink on paper. Palace Museum, Peking.

above, left

2. Tao-chi, *Bamboo and Orchids in the Wind.* Hanging scroll. Ink on paper. C. C. Wang collection, New York.

3. Details of signatures: *(left) XXIX; (right)* fig. 2.

XXIX, detail (*actual size*).

*Lo-Fu Mountains: Calligraphy and Painting
(Lo-fu-shan shu-hua ts'e)*

The Art Museum, Princeton University (67-17).

Album of eight leaves, four of painting (from a set of twelve) and four of calligraphy (each facing the painting). Painting: ink and color on creamy unsized paper; calligraphy, ink on buff-toned paper. Painting: 28.2 x 19.8 cm.; calligraphy, 28.1 x 19.6 cm.

UNDATED: probably executed 1701–1705.

UNSIGNED

SEALS OF THE ARTIST:
K'u-kua ho-shang, Chi, hua-fa (intaglio, tall rectangle; *PTC*, cat. no. 48) leaves A, B, C, and D.
Ping-hsüeh wu-ch'ien-shen (intaglio, tall rectangle; *PTC*, cat. no. 59) leaf AA.
Ch'ing-hsiang Shih-t'ao (intaglio, tall rectangle; *PTC*, cat. no. 22) leaves AA and DD.
Yüeh-shan (intaglio, small square; *PTC*, cat. no. 108) leaf BB.
Pan-ko-han (intaglio, tall rectangle; *PTC*, cat. no. 56) leaf BB.
Ch'ien-yu Lung-mien, Chi (intaglio, tall rectangle; *PTC*, cat. no. 9) leaf BB.
Te-i-jen chih-chi wu-han (intaglio, square; *PTC*, cat. no. 92) leaves CC and DD.
Hsia-tsun-che (relief, tall rectangle; *PTC*, cat. no. 29) leaf CC.
A-ch'ang (intaglio, square; *PTC*, cat. no. 1) leaf DD.

COLLECTORS' SEALS (identified on each leaf):
Chang Shan-tzu (Tse, 1883–1940), two seals, leaves C and AA.
Chang Ta-ch'ien (born 1899), thirteen seals on each leaf of painting and calligraphy.
Unidentified, one seal, leaf A.

CONDITION: good; there is minor wormhole damage at upper left of leaves B and C and upper right of leaf BB.

PROVENANCE: Ta-feng-t'ang collection.

OTHER VERSIONS: two free copies in ink and color on paper in complete sets of twelve painting leaves with twelve calligraphy leaves are in Hakone, Japan, and Cologne, Germany.[1]

PUBLISHED: *PTC*, cat. no. 37, pp. 92, 171 (leaves B and D illustrated); *Record of the Art Museum, Princeton University*, vol. 27 (1968), p. 35 (acquisitions list); *Archives of Asian Art*, vol. 22 (1968–69), p. 134 ("attributed" to Tao-chi). An album by Tao-chi under the title *Lo-Fu t'u-ts'e (Album of Illustrations of Lo-Fu)* appears in the catalogue listing to an exhibition of objects in Cantonese collections in 1940 and published in *Kuang-tung wen-wu*, p. 13; the album is not illustrated, making positive identification impossible; at the time it was in the Ch'un-lei-ko collection, which we have not been able to locate.

THIS ALBUM CONTAINS Tao-chi's landscape illustrations to descriptive texts. The texts, copied from an earlier source, are transcribed by the artist on a separate sheet of paper opposite each painting leaf. Tao-chi's inscription on the last painting leaf of the album (fig. 1) tells of the occasion which prompted this work: "I have long thought [to travel to] the Lo-Fu mountains but have never made the journey. Recently I have been glancing through these casual descriptions [*yeh-ch'eng*] and happened to execute these twelve leaves."[2] Only four genuine painting leaves of the original set of twelve are known to the authors. These four, plus four leaves of calligraphy, are shown here. Two replicas of the twelve painting leaves (plus the twelve calligraphy leaves) are extant, giving us an idea of the pictorial scope of the album and the circumstances which inspired it. The inscription quoted above is taken from one of these replicas, and the correspondence of texts and titles of the three versions speaks for the accuracy of the content of the replica.

The Lo-Fu mountains are located in Canton Province. Under the heading "famous mountains of Canton Province" in a seventeenth-century gazetteer, we find a more complete description: "The Lo-Fu mountains lie . . . in Kuang-chou . . . and Hui-chou prefectures. They measure 500 *li* in length and 3,600 *chang* in height. There are 432 peaks and promontories and 15 ranges. There are 72 valleys and caves and 919 streams, gullies, waterfalls, and the like. . . . The mountain vein of Mt. Lo originates at Ta-yü [in Kiangsi Province]. Mt. Fu is actually one of the islands of P'eng-lai; it originates in the ocean and is joined to Mt. Lo, hence the name 'Lo-Fu.'"[3] Mt. Lo-Fu was famous for its views. As Tao-chi had never been there, the illustrations to this album are largely imaginative, inspired by the descriptions he read and transcribed on the accompanying leaves, in contrast with his depictions of Mt. Lu or Mt. Huang, sites he actually visited. The accounts of these peaks (their source is not indicated) appear to be a mixture of the actual and the legendary, and their literary style is vivid enough to have aroused Tao-chi's fertile pictorial imagination. In executing these pictures Tao-chi was drawing on the scenery of his own experience and on landscape illustrations to texts familiar to him. It is noteworthy that the general compositional arrangements and certain methods of contouring and foliage dotting suggest some of the wood-block illustrations of the scenery of Huang-shan which were popular during the late Ming and early Ch'ing periods. Many of these illustrations embellished the local gazetteers, and they were often designed by painters from nearby locales.[4]

The Lo-Fu illustrations offer another opportunity to study Tao-chi's development of a landscape narrative. Like his *Peach-Blossom Spring* handscroll in the Freer Gallery of Art (cf. *XXXII*, fig. 2), the text guides his visualization of form, while he seeks to convey its spirit by adding lively and pointed details. Indeed, the fidelity to certain key geographical details of the narrative and the plausibility of the whole as landscape settings testify to the four leaves as original compositions. The brushwork is blunt and direct, in the artist's "old-age" style, yet it remains fresh and imaginative. The exemplary quality and crispness of the accompanying calligraphy suggests that both painting and writing were done in a season of good health.

The two other versions are more or less free copies of the album. In both, the painting leaves neglect the same vital points of the narrative, revealing that the forms were not inspired by the text itself but were copied from an existing model. Landscape elements and figures are either grossly simplified or eliminated. In both, the execution is loose and the total conception uninspired and incoherent. Moreover, there are misunderstandings and inconsistencies of form and space, often found in a copy, which remove them even farther from the text which they are supposed to illustrate.

1. Attributed to Tao-chi, *Lo-Fu Mountains*, leaf L, detail. Album of twelve leaves. Ink on paper. Museum für Ostasiatische Kunst, Cologne.

Further comparison of the Sackler leaves with the painting leaves of these other versions reveals that, in general, the calligraphy leaves of the copies are far superior to the paintings paired with them, especially in the case of the Cologne album. As they are also free copies, the problem of isolating distinct characteristics and effectively describing them is more challenging here than in the other cases which have been discussed. The Sackler calligraphy leaves are superior to those of the Hakone copy, but we withhold judgment on the calligraphy leaves of the Cologne version until we can examine the originals.

Leaf A: "*Mica Peak*" (*Yün-mu-feng*)

Ink and color on paper.
COLLECTORS' SEALS:
Chang Ta-ch'ien, *Chang Yüan* (relief, square), *Chang Ta-ch'ien* (intaglio, square), *Ts'ang-chih Ta-ch'ien* (intaglio, square), all in lower right corner. Owner unidentified, *Ou-an ching-yen* (relief, tall rectangle) lower left corner.

In the comparison of secondary and primary versions of a work, the differences are all-important. This leaf is superior to the Hakone and Cologne leaves (figs. 2–3) in terms of integrity of brushwork and forms within the painting and of pictorial fidelity to the text which accompanies it. Both landscape and figures inhabit a clear and believable space. The ground and rocks are solidly modeled and are set off from the horizontal stretches of water. There is a sense of the volume and surface of objects as three-dimensional forms within an illusionistic space. This sense of spatial atmosphere and formal solidity is consistent with Tao-chi's concept of form. Both the overall composition and its individual elements are vividly imagined, and each element is completely and clearly executed.

The Cologne and Hakone versions are concerned more with the movement of the brush than with the description of form. The landscape elements—trees, rocks, water—are poorly articulated as individual shapes and are indistinguishable from each other in texture. The surface of the picture seems choked with dots and lines. The ground and rocks look mushy; the figures, which sink nondescriptly into this mire of textures, are three dull, blank forms rather than the lively and individual figures of the Sackler leaf. The brushstrokes lack internal cohesiveness and lie on the surface of the paper, revealing the weak visualization of the copyist.

In the Sackler version the brush turns and twists constantly in long, sustaining rhythms with a throbbing pressure, producing a plump and firm line which suggests both its own inner vitality and the volume of the forms it describes. The dry, textured ink lines contrast with the wetter ink and color lines, which sink heartily into the highly absorbent unsized paper. The pale apple green hue softens the line and clarifies the atmosphere. Touches of blue and sienna give warmth to the generally cool tonality. In the Cologne and Hakone leaves the linework and dots are sharp and scratchy. The artist has used sized paper, so that the brush glides smoothly over the surface, causing the hairs of the point to fan out flatly; in contrast, the absorbent paper used in the Sackler leaves has a resisting surface which makes it more difficult to control the ink but prevents any tendency toward slickness.

As to the visualization, Tao-chi has attempted to base his rendition of Yün-mu-feng on key points described in the accompanying text (quoted below in full). He has conceived of the peak as a burst of cloud-like stone dominating the middle distance. Just beneath the boulders, as we can see by the changes in ink tones, the direction of texture strokes, and the accents of pale russet washes, lies the Vermilion Jade Grotto. The other two versions fail to include these details from the text.

Leaf AA: "*An Account of Mica Peak*"

Ink on paper.
COLLECTORS' SEALS:
Chang Ta-ch'ien, *Ta-feng-t'ang* (intaglio, tall rectangle) left side.
Chang Shan-tzu, *Shan-tzu shin-shang* (relief, square) lower left corner.
INSCRIPTION: in nine columns.

The facing leaf renders an account of Mica Peak in five lines of a slender freehand "running" script. The prose section reads:

Mica Peak lies above West Dragon Pond. North of the Peak is Mica Stream, which contains mica stones. The legendary immortal Madame Ho practiced alchemy with rocks like vermilion jade and swallowed her potion to attain immortality. When the rising sun casts its rays on the peak, the hill emanates a magnificent rosy glow; thus it is also called the Vermilion Jade Grotto. On the sheer side of its peak lies the Butterfly Cave. In each of the four seasons there are always butterflies resting among its flowers and trees. When a person approaches, they do not take flight, but if someone should snap off a branch and proceed to leave the grotto, they would fly back to their old home.

A poetic epilogue ascribed to the immortal Madame Ho (Ho hsien-ku) follows in three lines of smaller "running" script.

Leaf B: "*Three Peaks of the Upper Realm*" (*Shang-chieh san-feng*)

Ink and color on paper.
COLLECTOR'S SEALS: Chang Ta-ch'ien, *Ta-ch'ien hao-meng* (relief, tall rectangle) and *Ta-ch'ien chih-hsi* (intaglio, square) lower left corner.

This Sackler leaf differs in three distinct ways from the others: in the subtler complexity of the forms in space; in the contouring of the clouds into a picturesque scroll network; and in the conception of the mountain shapes in interlocking layers of depth, sculpted into a compact design. The contouring of the clouds provides a catalyst for the horizontal and vertical tensions (a marked Tao-chi trait) and subtly stresses the interweaving movements of the forms in space. Such round, plump brushlines and cloud forms appear on a monumental scale in the Sumitomo *Waterfall at Mt. Lu* and on an intimate scale in *The Echo* and *Landscape and Portrait of Hung Cheng-chih* (cf. *XVII* and *XXXII*), where the clouds function in a similar manner as space differentials between solid bodies. Bold horizontal *ts'un* strokes model each mountain peak in graded ink tones. This form of texturing is comparable to the treatment of the major peaks in the *View of Huang-shan* handscroll dated 1699 in the Sumitomo collection (fig. 4). In addition, the various hues of green, blue, cinnabar, and blue-green are used to suggest the projection of the mountain peaks in a three-dimensional space like the legs of a tripod, just as the inscription suggests.

The two other versions (figs. 5–6) lack both the engaging scrollwork and, what is more crucial, the decisive texturing, lineation, and graded ink tones. The three peaks lie in one flat plane pierced horizontally by blank streaks of paper. The "hedge" of foliage is ambiguously placed in the foreground without the encircling clouds and looks like superfluous trimming floating in empty space, unrelated to the other picture elements. It is actually made up of the tops of trees, as can clearly be seen in the Sackler leaf. This visualization is quite close to that found in the *Huang-shan* handscroll, where we also find multiple layers of treetops juxtaposed against rising mountain peaks bathed in mist.

Leaf BB: "*An Account of the Three Peaks of the Upper Realm*"

Ink on paper.

COLLECTOR'S SEAL: Chang Ta-ch'ien, *Ta-feng-t'ang Chien-chiang, K'un-ts'an, Hsüeh-ko, K'u-kua mo-yüan* (relief, tall rectangle) lower left corner.
INSCRIPTION: in twelve columns.

The account is rendered in the same format as in the preceding calligraphy leaf. The prose section in eight long lines reads in part: "There are 432 peaks in the Lo-Fu Mountains. High above the flying clouds in the west are the Three Peaks of the Upper Realm. They project upward like the three legs of a tripod. Their dense vapor, clouds, and frost prevent man from reaching the top. They connect with the Iron Bridge, and the nadir where the two mountains meet is called the Source of Spring Way." This section is followed by three shorter lines of poetry.

Leaf C: "*Solitary Azure Peak*" (*Ku-ch'ing-feng*)

Ink and color on paper.

COLLECTOR'S SEALS: Chang Ta-ch'ien, *Ta-ch'ien chih-pao* (relief, small square) and *Hsi-ch'uan Chang-pa* (relief, tall rectangle), both lower right corner.

The differences here are again significant. Even the figures speak convincingly of the originality of the Sackler leaf: a scholar leaning on a staff trudges up the stepped hill to the mountain temple, followed by his little servant bending under the weight of his provisions. Two figures ahead have already reached the temple grounds; one stands facing the temple and the looming peak behind; the other kneels in awe. Executed in a few abbreviated strokes, the figures set the scale and animate the landscape.

In the Hakone and Cologne versions (figs. 7–8) all figures but one have been eliminated, and that one limply drags himself up the pathway, staring blankly into space. Equally unsettling is the failure of this artist to differentiate the ground planes—round from flat, level from sloping—and to create a sense of depth, for where solidity is barely achieved, recession in depth can hardly be accomplished. In the Sackler leaf the spectator is drawn into the picture through the convincing solids, leading upward and culminating in the winding solitary peak placed on the horizon to dominate the scene. Each detail renders pictorial justice to the narrative text transcribed by Tao-chi on the facing leaf. The evidence for the other versions being copies goes beyond the mere presence or absence of human figures. By ignoring the steps on the path, reducing the number of trees lining it, and carelessly describing the flat terrace below the main peak, the Hakone and Cologne versions have lost all identity with the "solitary azure peak" whose title they parade.

Leaf CC: "*An Account of the Solitary Azure Peak*"

Ink on paper.

COLLECTOR'S SEAL: Chang Ta-ch'ien, *Pu-fu-ku-jen kao-hou-jen* (relief, large square) lower left corner.
INSCRIPTION: in nine columns.

The prose section is in five columns, the poetic epilogue in three. The prose account reads:

There is one peak which stands out prominently from the rest. On it pine trees grow full and luxuriant. Its light peaks of pale blackish-green look as though they were painted in one sweep or as though they were floating. This is the Solitary Azure Peak. In ancient days there was a Solitary Azure Temple; its name was later changed to the Monastery of Heavenly Glory. To the south is the Terrace of Glorious Height. Stone steps rise one after the other like fish scales. It is bordered on the right

by old trees growing hoary and thick, and there are winding pathways covered with moss. . . . Travelers passing by can all stay overnight in the mountains. Until now the peak has never been lonely because it has this!

A poem on the peak by Ts'ai Yüan-li (unidentified) follows.

It is of interest that the seal *Te-i-jen chih-chi wu-han*, which is found on calligraphy leaves CC and DD, does not, to our knowledge, appear on any other published work.

Leaf D: "*P'eng-lai Peak*" (*P'eng-lai-feng*)

Ink and color on paper.

COLLECTOR'S SEALS: Chang Ta-ch'ien, *Shu-k'o* (relief, tall rectangle) and *Ta-feng-t'ang* (relief, small square), both in lower right corner.

The composition in the Sackler leaf differs from the other two versions in several respects: it is fuller and more complex, the clouds are delineated, the buildings are raised on a plateau, and there are mountain ranges flanking both sides of the main peak. These details are confirmed in the text of the accompanying leaf.

The Hakone and Cologne works (figs. 9–10) introduce changes which weaken the composition. The stone steps leading to P'eng-lai Hall have been eliminated; the number, variety, and density of trees and foliage has been reduced; the scale of near and distant trees is hardly differentiated; finally, the wavy streaks of mist make the picture diffuse. On the other hand, in the Sackler leaf the simple tricolor tones and washes give a rich, brocaded effect.

Leaf DD: "*An Account of P'eng-lai Peak*"

Ink on paper.

COLLECTOR'S SEAL: Chang Ta-ch'ien, *Ta-ch'ien chü-shih kung-yang pai-Shih-chih-i* (relief, large square) lower left corner.
INSCRIPTION: in eleven columns.

The prose section is rendered in seven columns and reads:

P'eng-lai Peak got its name from being a part of the Sacred Islands. It is actually the third peak of Mt. Fu. It has five-toed chickens, and is also called Jade Chicken Mountain. Below the peak is the Plateau of Immortals, on which P'eng-lai Hall is found. There the sages gathered together and amused themselves. According to Taoist texts, the palaces, gates, and hall in the caves and heavenly mountains were made of gold and silver. The Taoist of the West Wall, Wang Fang-p'ing, once mounted the Yellow Chimera and soared back and forth between the two peaks of P'eng-lai and Ma-ku. From the west up to the Path of a Hundred Flowers, there is the Embroidered Brocade Peak, on which there are many extraordinary flowers and unusual grasses. In brilliant sunlight and with a gentle breeze blowing, it looks gloriously embroidered and multicolored.

In addition, the three westernmost peaks are connected and are called the Almsbowl, the Chicken Cackle, and the Tortoise Shell. Below Tortoise Shell Peak lies a pond whose water is pure and jade-like. Fantastic stones shaped like tortoise shells are scattered everywhere. In the depths of this pond lives the Sacred Tortoise; hence it is also called Tortoise Gulf.

A poetic eulogy in three long lines by an anonymous immortal of P'eng-lai Hall follows.

THE PAINTING LEAVES of the Hakone and Cologne versions are close enough to present two possibilities: that one is a copy of the other (and the two are by different hands), or that the two are by the same hand and based on a third version. Judging from the reproductions available, the Hakone version is slightly poorer in quality and more summary in execution than the Cologne. Nevertheless, the same brush techniques and visualization of form are present in both; moreover, the general level of execution is similar enough to suggest a common hand.[5]

The discrepancies in visualization and the simplification and elimination of vital details pointed out above seriously undermine the validity of both versions as illustrations to the texts. (Simplification [and its opposite, proliferation] appear to be inevitable concomitants of the copying process and in more masterful hands, of course, take on positive value as "clarification" or "reinterpretation," as one can see in Tao-chi's copy of a Shen Chou.) These discrepancies suggest that the two may not have been copied directly but may rather have been transferred from memory (*i-lin*) or painted from memory after a rough sketch (*fen-pen*) had been made. It is equally plausible, as noted above, that the two were copied from still another version unknown to us.[6]

The physical separation of the calligraphy leaves compounds the problem. The four Sackler leaves are consistent in quality, and reproductions indicate that the Hakone leaves are also a homogeneous group, as are the Cologne leaves: in other words, it seems that the three versions were not shuffled to "mix fish-eyes with pearls." Our study of all three versions indicates that the Sackler calligraphy leaves are the set which originally accompanied the paintings. The calligraphy of the Hakone leaves is visibly weaker than that of the Cologne and is quite likely to be from the same hand as the paintings which it accompanies; however, it is difficult to say whether the painting titles of the Cologne set are by the same hand as its calligraphy. The quality and freedom of this album are distinctive enough to warrant further consideration of authenticity. Tao-chi may have executed two sets of calligraphy leaves, though not necessarily two sets of painting leaves, which were later matched up by someone. If so, the calligraphy of the Hakone version was executed in imitation of the Cologne version and not after the Sackler.

One further note on the materials used in the Sackler painting leaves should be made. The surface of the paper on which the paintings are executed is relatively new, porous, and unsized. It is therefore highly absorbent, causing comparatively thick ink to bleed excessively and produce a "raw" effect. Apparently Tao-chi was not used to working with this paper, but instead of modifying the pace of his brushwork and working with greater speed, he did his best to control the bleeding and to "rub in" the contours by using a relatively dry brush. For example, the leaves "Solitary Azure Peak" and "P'eng-lai Peak" give the initial impression of scattered dots and lines, but with the deft application of colored washes, as can be seen in the subtly interacting textures of the original, the varied component parts are drawn together into a unified whole.

A rough date of execution can be obtained by comparing the four Sackler painting leaves with three dated Tao-chi works, the 1699 *Huang-shan* handscroll (fig. 4), the 1703 *Album for Liu Shih-t'ou* in Japan, and the 1706 *Landscape and Portrait of Hung Cheng-chih* (*XXXII*). One other scroll, the Freer *Peach Blossom Spring*, which we have dated ca. 1703, can be placed stylistically within the same range.

Several of the seals also suggest a date of execution after 1700. According to Sasaki Kozo's compilation, the seal *K'u-kua ho-shang, Chi, hua-fa*, which appears on the painting leaves, was used from 1694 to 1700. The seals on the calligraphy leaves are more specific: *Pan-ko-han* was used about 1706 or 1707 (it also appears on *XXIV*, *Eulogy*, which we have dated ca. 1700); *A-ch'ang* dates from 1700 to 1703.[7] In view of the landscape style in the painting leaves and its general agreement with the dates suggested by these seals, we believe the album to have been executed ca. 1701–1705.

THE FOUR CALLIGRAPHY leaves which accompany the Sackler paintings are written in a slender "running" or freehand script; the titles on the painting leaves are in a form closer to "regular" script. Careful study of the painting titles and the calligraphy leaves and their titles shows that they were all written by the same hand. Certain differences of materials should be noted. For the calligraphy Tao-chi used a thinner, less porous, sized paper and, probably, a writing brush with a finer point than the one used for painting. The more absorbent paper of the paintings produced a coarser effect of the brushline, but despite the change in script (which prescribed changes in the axis and structure of the characters), the stroke movements reveal the same basic formal tendencies.

A close comparison of extracts taken from leaf DD, "P'eng-lai Peak," will help sharpen our eye for differences in level of execution. In the Sackler version (see the detail) the columnar spacing is spacious but relatively straight (and varies slightly in spaciousness from leaves AA to DD). Two general characteristics of Tao-chi's writing, noted earlier, are a tendency for the "running" characters to be elongated and for the axis of each character to slant consistently to the upper right; these characteristics are found here. In Tao-chi's freehand script the characters vary greatly in size, and diagonals and horizontals usually break out into the columnar spaces. Nonetheless, each character is given appropriate breathing space and none is crowded. This is especially true in the line to the far left, *chin-ying suo-ch'eng, hsi-ch'eng chen-chün* ("made of gold and silver. The Taoist of the West Wall"). This kind of spacing occurs in Tao-chi's epilogue in "running" script to *Waterfall at Mt. Lu* and the *Flowers and Figures* album, which also contain lexically similar graphs.

The strongly tilted axis and the spacing around each character lend a sense of discipline to the writing despite the variations in character sizes. Close scrutiny of the strokes of each character reveals that the brush fluctuates to an extraordinary degree. In "running" script the linking of the usually separate strokes still requires articulation at each linkage and with every change of direction. The degree and attentiveness of such articulation is important in the determination of individual identity. Tao-chi's fondness for the fluctuating line and the habitual up-and-down motion of his brush are particularly evident at these points of articulation. The heads of most of his horizontal strokes, for example, usually register a slight pressure and emphasis; then they lighten in weight in their lateral course before bearing down again for the connections of the next sequential movement. His diagonal hook strokes are customarily quite thin and tensile before the brush pauses to form the hook itself, at which point it bears down and creates a hook with an emphatic upswing.

If we turn to the Hakone version (fig. 11), the columnar spacing is very different, and the characters on each side almost touch each other. Moreover, they vary less in size, the brushstrokes tend to be even in pressure and emphasis, and the ink tones are more or less uniform. In addition, the axis of each character is not consistent: some slant more strongly to the right than others, and the hooks and corners show much less attention to inner articulation.

The Cologne version (fig. 12), as noted above, is superior in quality to the Hakone, in that its ink tones are more varied and it has a greater sense of freedom. Its quality leaves something to be desired, however, compared to the Sackler version. (To reach a final judgment in such a case, it is imperative to study the original.) The strokes in the Hakone version have a tendency to be flat and more regular in width, moving in a sideways rhythm. The scattering of the forms and the axial inconsistencies are signs of a copyist.

We can imagine two forces at war in the mind of a copyist during the process of execution: he wishes to exhibit fully the style of his model, and he wishes to be free and natural—to avoid the "copied" look—while suppressing his own style. The attempt to give an impression of freedom has resulted in neglect of the stylistic particulars and small movements which count most in the identification of an artist's hand. At the same time, the attempt to convey the general

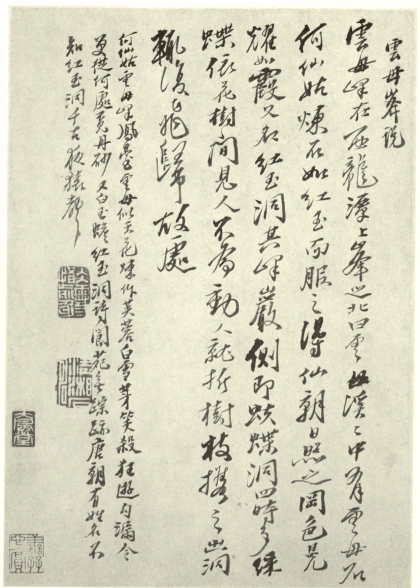

Leaf AA, "An Account of Mica Peak"

Leaf A, "Mica Peak"

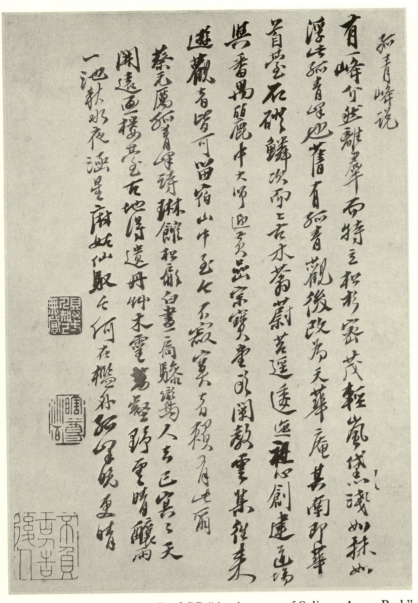

孤青峰說

有一峰介於離羣而特立於松杉密茂輕嵐黛議如挨如浮生孤青峰也舊有孤青觀後改為天華庵其南即華首臺石砌鱗次而上古木菁蔚蓬遙迤邐以創建通瑞與香馬麗中大師迎黃品宗寶書永閣敎靈集從來遠觀者晉可留宿山中至七不寂實有頹有也兩蔡元厲孤青峰詩珠璣稜稜白畫一扃臉避爲人吉已寶之天開遠逼邏丹册木雲爲聲路雲晴釀兩一池秋水夜涵是麻姑欲取名何在檻外孤峰晚更晴

Leaf CC, "An Account of Solitary Azure Peak"

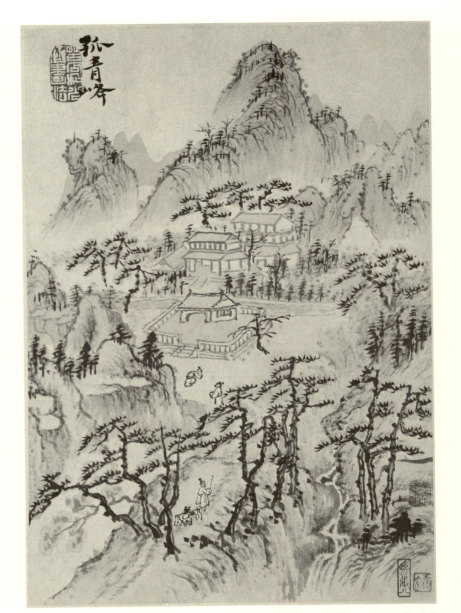

孤青峰

Leaf C, "Solitary Azure Peak"

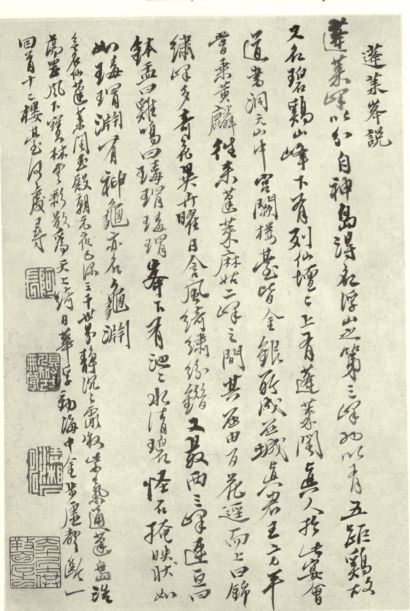

蓬萊峯說

蓬萊峯此句自神島得名浮山之第三峯而以此有五距雞林又名碧雞峰下有列仙壇已上青蓬萊閣真人於青蓁層道書洞天山牛窟關橋基臺晉金銀貝成茲城真君至之九平當兼黃麟往來蓬萊麻姑二峰之間其屋田有花遠而為石髓繡綵多奇花吳栗弄晴日含風繡綵紛鑿工最兩三峰蓬高鉢盂曰雞鳴昌璃璜峰下有泇之水清碧怪石掩映狀如山梅瑄淵有神龜承名龜淵遍嘗邢下寶林雲彩散廣爲天上將月華生勑海中遠步庵靜澱一回青十二樓臺月慶尋

Leaf DD, "An Account of P'eng-lai Peak"

蓬萊峰

Leaf D, "P'eng-lai Peak"

"look" of the model was enough to tax his full powers, leaving him no room for improvisation of a subtle or creative nature; thus the forms are generally simplified and exaggerated.

In the Sackler leaves the brush is truly free. Tao-chi is working within his own idiom, not fighting to suppress another hand, and he can attend to the expressive details of the brush—the subtle turns and twists of the tip, the changes of pace and composition in stroke and line for variety. If we follow the movement of the brushline in any character, we feel the continual twisting and turning pressure of the tip (unlike the flat, direct, and jerky movements of the other versions) which produces a round and full quality in the stroke regardless of the changes in script. The result is anything but monotonous and exaggerated. Moreover, Tao-chi was transcribing a text he enjoyed; hence the feeling is buoyant and free (quite different from the moods usually found in his letters or in his more formal writing), and he permits himself to linger over the small brush movements and to control the brush tensions.

Two Tao-chi works in a similar freehand calligraphic style may help confirm these stylistic observations and the date of execution, his *Letter to Yü-chün*, (fig. 13), published in *Ming-hsien mo-chi-ts'e* (the first line reading "Ping i t'ui-ch'ü, shih-chih pa-chiu" ["my illness has already receded almost completely"]), and the 1701 *Manuscript of Poems* (Part IV, fig. 2, and *XXIII*, fig. 14). These works exhibit a similar columnar spacing, a tendency for the ink to blot, for the right diagonal *na* stroke to bend and form a slightly angular elbow shape, and for the entering and finishing strokes to be strongly articulated. Moreover, there is a robust and candid energy which is matched in the Sackler leaves. The signature to the *Letter to Yü-chün* is a late one, Hsiu-jen, Chi ("Chi, the useless one"), which he, incidentally, used after 1700.

NOTES

1. The Hakone version (Version A) is in the Hakone Museum, Gora; its painting leaves were published in *Sekitō Rafusan zusatsu* and its calligraphy leaves in *Shohin*, no. 82 (1957), pls. 1–13. The Cologne version (Version B) is in the Museum für Ostasiatische Kunst, Cologne, Germany; its painting leaves were first published in *Ausstellung Chinesische Malerei* (Cologne, 1955), no. 68; most recently leaves 1, 7, 11, and 12 were listed in *1000 Jahre Chinesische Malerei*, cat. no. 114, p. 196. Both albums bear artist's seals which are different from the Sackler version. The Cologne seals appear to be of slightly higher quality than those on the Hakone. As we have not examined these versions in the original, we will limit our comments to the handling of composition and line and will not discuss the color of the painting leaves.

2. The rendering of *yeh-ch'eng* as "casual descriptions" was offered by Dr. Wai-kam Ho.

3. From Ku Tsu-yü (1627–1680), *Tu-shih fang-yü chi-yao*, vol. 2, 100/6a–b. The numerical estimates in this account are meant to be impressive rather than informative (3,600 *chang* would be about 1,200 kilometers—higher than Mt. Everest!). No doubt they were handed down as part of oral legends, which the content of these narratives also suggests. For further information on this locale, see *Lo-Fu-shan chih* (Gazetteer of the Lo-Fu Mountains) (Canton, preface by Ch'en Yüan-lung dated 1717), and the earlier sources cited in Edward H. Schafer, "A Fourteenth Century Gazetteer of Canton," *Oriente Poliano* (Rome, 1957), esp. pp. 74 and 88, n. 48. Schafer offers a lively translation of a gazetteer published in 1227, unavailable to us.

4. For example, Sun I (fl. late Ming) and Hsiao Ch'en (fl. ca. 1680–1710) are known to have executed such designs. This stylistic influence on Tao-chi merits further study. Cf. Kohara Hironobu, *Sekitō to Kōzan hasshō gasatsu*, pp. 5–11, 14, n. 5.

5. We identify the hand involved as that of Chang Ta-ch'ien.

6. In executing two similar copies, the copyist may have thought to deceive the gullible into thinking that if there were two, one must be genuine. In the meantime, the original version was divided neatly into groups of (presumably) four leaves each, to be offered separately. We have been unable to locate the other eight leaves of the Sackler version.

7. *PTC*, pp. 63–70.

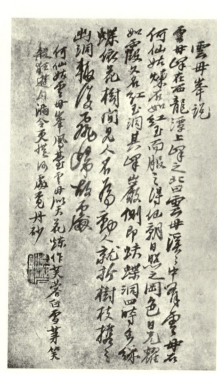

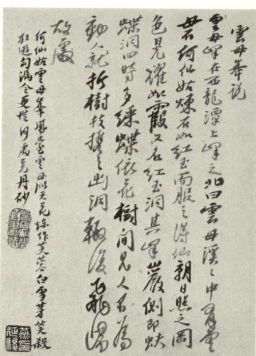

2. Attributed to Tao-chi, *Lo-Fu Mountains*, leaves A and AA: (*left*) ink on paper; (*right*) ink and color on paper. Album of twelve leaves. Hakone Museum, Gora.

3. Attributed to Tao-chi, *Lo-Fu Mountains*, leaves A and AA: (*left*) ink on paper; (*right*) ink and color on paper. Museum für Ostasiatische Kunst.

7. Attributed to Tao-chi, *Lo-Fu Mountains*, leaves C and CC:
(*left*) ink on paper; (*right*) ink and color on paper.
Hakone Museum.

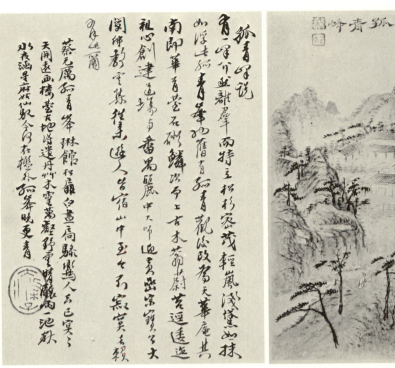

8. Attributed to Tao-chi, *Lo-Fu Mountains*, leaves C and CC:
(*left*) ink on paper; (*right*) ink and color on paper.
Museum für Ostasiatische Kunst.

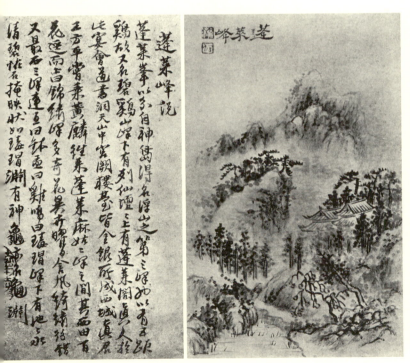

9. Attributed to Tao-chi, *Lo-Fu Mountains*, leaves D and DD:
(*left*) ink on paper; (*right*) ink and color on paper.
Hakone Museum.

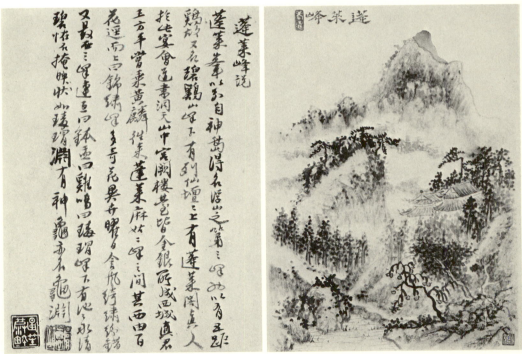

10. Attributed to Tao-chi, *Lo-Fu Mountains*, leaves D and DD:
(*left*) ink on paper; (*right*) ink and color on paper.
Museum für Ostasiatische Kunst.

4. Tao-chi, *View of Huang-shan*, dated 1699, detail. Handscroll. Ink and color on paper. Sumitomo collection, Oiso.

5. Attributed to Tao-chi, *Lo-Fu Mountains*, leaf B. Ink and color on paper. Hakone Museum.

6. Attributed to Tao-chi, *Lo-Fu Mountains*, leaf B. Ink and color on paper. Museum für Ostasiatische Kunst.

Leaf B, "Three Peaks of the Upper Realm" (*actual size*)

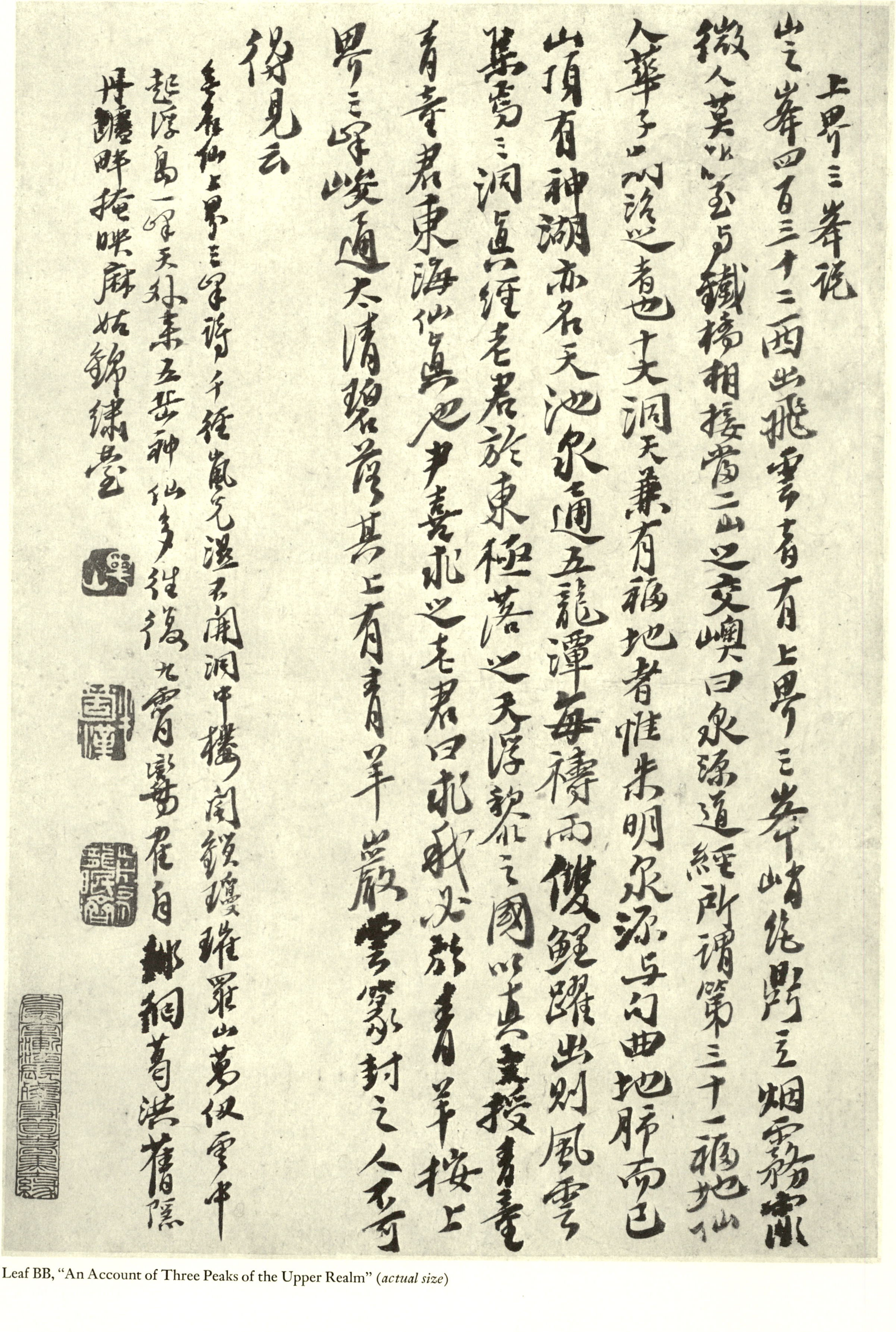

山之峯四百三十二西曰飛雲峯有上界三峯峭絕与野之烟霞霏霏
微人莫能至第与鐵橋相接霄三山之交嶼曰泉源道經所謂第三十二福地仙
人華子山以路之者也夫洞天兼有福地者惟朱明泉源与勾曲地肺而已
山頂有神湖亦名天池泉通五龍潭每禱雨傻鯉躍出則風雲
葉寫三洞真經老君旅東極落之天浮欽於之國以真書授青童
有青君東海仙真也尹喜北之老君曰我必於青羊接上
界三峯峻通太清碧彦其上有青羊嚴雲竂封之人云
得見云

毒毒仙上界三峯詳千徑嵐氣溫不開洞中橋閣鎖瓊璀羅罪山萬仞雲中
起浮島一碧天孫秦五岳神仙多往後九霄郵庭自邲桐菁洪舊隱
丹躞畔掩暎麻姑錦繍堂

上界三峯說

Leaf BB, "An Account of Three Peaks of the Upper Realm" (*actual size*)

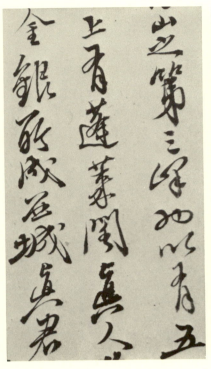

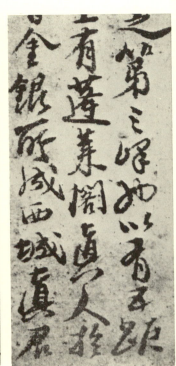

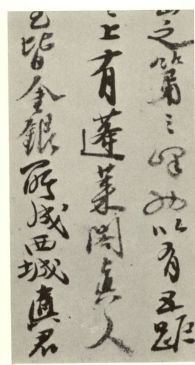

13. Tao-chi, *Letter to Yü-chün*. Ink on paper. Collection unknown. Photo Wang Fang-yü.

14. Attributed to Tao-chi, *Lo-Fu Mountains*, leaf BB, detail. Ink on paper. Hakone Museum.

15. Attributed to Tao-chi, *Lo-Fu Mountains*, leaf BB, detail. Ink on paper. Museum für Ostasiatische Kunst.

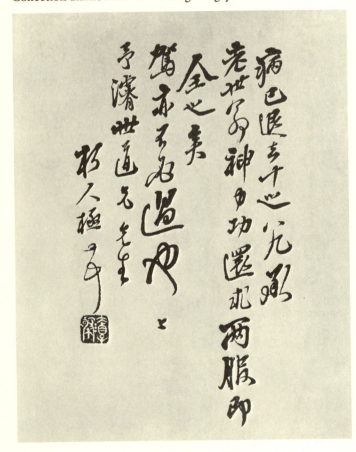

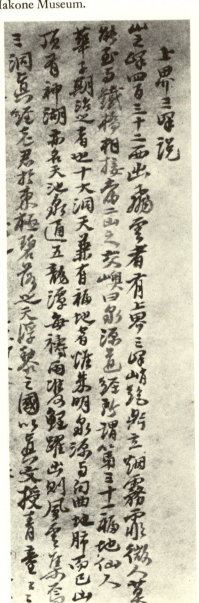

Bamboo, Vegetables, and Fruit (*Su-kuo-t'u*)

The Art Museum, Princeton University (67-22).

Hanging scroll. Ink and light color on paper. 108.4 x 45.8 cm.

DATED: September 18, 1705 (*i-yu, pa-yüeh, i-jih*).

SIGNATURE OF THE ARTIST: Ch'ing-hsiang Ta-ti-tzu (in two lines).

INSCRIPTION BY THE ARTIST: a five-line poetic eulogy (see below).

SEALS OF THE ARTIST: *Ch'ing-hsiang lao-jen* (relief, oval; *PTC*, cat. no. 18, not listed), *T'ou-pai i-jan pu-shih-tzu* (intaglio, tall rectangle; *PTC*, cat. no. 94, not listed), *Tsan-chih shih-shih-sun, A-ch'ang* (relief, tall rectangle; *PTC*, cat. no. 95, not listed).

COLLECTOR'S SEALS: Chang Ta-ch'ien, *Ta-ch'ien chü-shih kung-yang pai-Shih chih-i* (relief, square), *Ti-kuo chih-fu* (relief, square), *Nan-pei-tung-hsi chih-yu hsiang-sui wu-pieh-li* (relief, square).

CONDITION: fair; there is slight abrasion over the whole surface of the work with several creases in left and right corners of the paper, subsequently flattened in the mounting process.

PROVENANCE: Ta-feng-t'ang collection.

PUBLISHED: *The Selected Painting and Calligraphy of Shih-t'ao*, vol. 1, pl. 20 (illustrated).

BAMBOO, SEVERAL KINDS of vegetables (melon, lotus root, pumpkin, eggplant, mushroom, caltrop), and a few fruits are scattered in pleasing asymmetry. Ink and colors have a refreshing clarity. The superb brushwork and the sensitive pictorial balance of elements lift this mundane subject matter to a new level of vision. The combination of spontaneity and sensitivity presupposes a sureness of hand and concept which come only in maturity.

Above the painting a self-inscription (see the detail) is executed in a free, plump mixture of "clerical" and "cursive" (*ts'ao-li*) scripts. A poetic octet in five-character regular meter complements the pictorial image:

> *Drop by drop—with a flavor just as sour,*
> *Yellow, so yellow—much better than gold.*
> *Even immortals cannot make wine [from these fruits]*
> *[Just as] no lotus root is without an empty core.*
> *When I prepare caltrop, it's not that my feelings are less,*
> *If I give you only a melon, my sentiment can still be deep.*
> *How can anything be purer than [my] feelings*
> *When not even a bit of grime has come close!*[1]

Casually painted by Ch'ing-hsiang Ta-ti-tzu on September 18, 1705 [*i-yu pa-yüeh i-jih*], at Keng-hsin-t'ang ["Studio for Cultivating the Heart"].

The date 1705, when the artist was in his sixty-fourth year, places this work among Tao-chi's latest dated paintings. Indeed, its excellence enables us to chart more accurately the state of physical vigor and the clarity of spirit which occasionally brightened Tao-chi's late works, which were somewhat uneven in quality.

THE PERFECTION of composition and brushwork deserves closer examination. Two mobile and powerful strokes carve out the immense squash in pale dry ink. Next, the melon stalk and leaves are painted in a very wet wash with a joyous feeling. The veins of the leaves are then quickly traced over with darker ink so that the two values blot and fuse to suggest the lush, velvety texture of the leaf. Sharply contrasted with this is the charcoal black ink, which briskly delineates a central focus of bamboo leaves. At the back, the growth sections of a pumpkin are effortlessly drawn out in the same round seal-style brushlines as those of the melon and lotus root. Pale wash stained in areas around the stem suggests volume. (In much the same way Tao-chi renders banana leaves; cf. XX, leaf G).

Enclosing this group in space is a length of lotus root, its sections punctuated by dark, wet lines suggesting root hairs. The form tapers into two slender leaves which reach forward in space and lead the eye to other details of the design in the middle ground. To the right, eggplants are painted in transparent violet, dabbed directly onto the dry absorbent paper; in this way the brushtip crisply delineates the outline with a curve and twist of the wrist while simultaneously modeling and shading the interior form. A cap of sepals in strokes similar to those of the bamboo leaves tops the eggplants; these forms provide two smaller echoes to the squash. Mushrooms are colored in pale umber: one is overturned and coyly displays spikes of soft fringe—again the effect, as in the melon leaves, of "wet-on-wet." This group is reflected on the left by a quartet of three-cornered caltrop (*ling-chiao*), finely modeled in the same way by pale touches of yellow.

The black bamboo leaves placed against the white of the squash create a "negative" and "positive" interaction, the vegetables around the periphery constituting the "positive" frame for the emptiness of the squash. This conception of formal relationships, in which successive layers recede in depth, can also be seen in other Tao-chi works of similar genre, notably *Bamboo and Orchids in the Wind* (*XXIX*, fig. 2), *Autumn Melon and Praying Mantis* (fig. 3)[2] and *Orchid, Bamboo, and Rock* (*XXIX*).

The calligraphy exhibits characteristically abrupt, expressive changes of size from character to character and changes of thickness of line from stroke to stroke. There is also a tendency for the ink to blot, creating lively accents. These traits compare well with the following works (these are illustrated in comparative form in the calligraphy diagram in Part IV, pp. 63–67): the last leaf of the 1703 Boston album of landscapes, the 1705 Michigan *Wan-li's Porcelain Handle Brush*,[3] *Loquats* (fig. 4),[4] and the album leaves depicting chrysanthemum and lotus in the 1707 *Ting-ch'iu Album of Flowers*. The date of these works and their stylistic homogeneity corroborate the date and style of the scroll's calligraphy and painting.

A CLOSELY RELATED SCROLL in the C. C. Wang collection is entitled *Loquats and Melon* (fig. 1). In ink only on paper, it is similarly dated 1705, bears the same poem, and is of slightly smaller dimensions. Orchids and loquats have been added instead of bamboo and pumpkin, and all the elements have been placed against a ground of wet dots. The inscription (fig. 2) has been extended horizontally into six lines (instead of five) but is identical in poetic content, with the same date of execution, corresponding to September, 1705. A four-line dedication to one "Tung lao-nien" has been added. A close study of these two works has tested our understanding of Tao-chi's artistic scope and has allowed us to better assess the range of quality in brush performance within his œuvre.

Generally speaking, the Wang work suffers from oppressively dark ink tones. The smaller forms lack precise contours, and the elements appear to "float" against the background of gray dots. In the calligraphy (fig. 2), the composition of the characters and the sequence and articulation of the brush are all remarkably close to the Sackler work but are in no case duplicated exactly. Rather, there

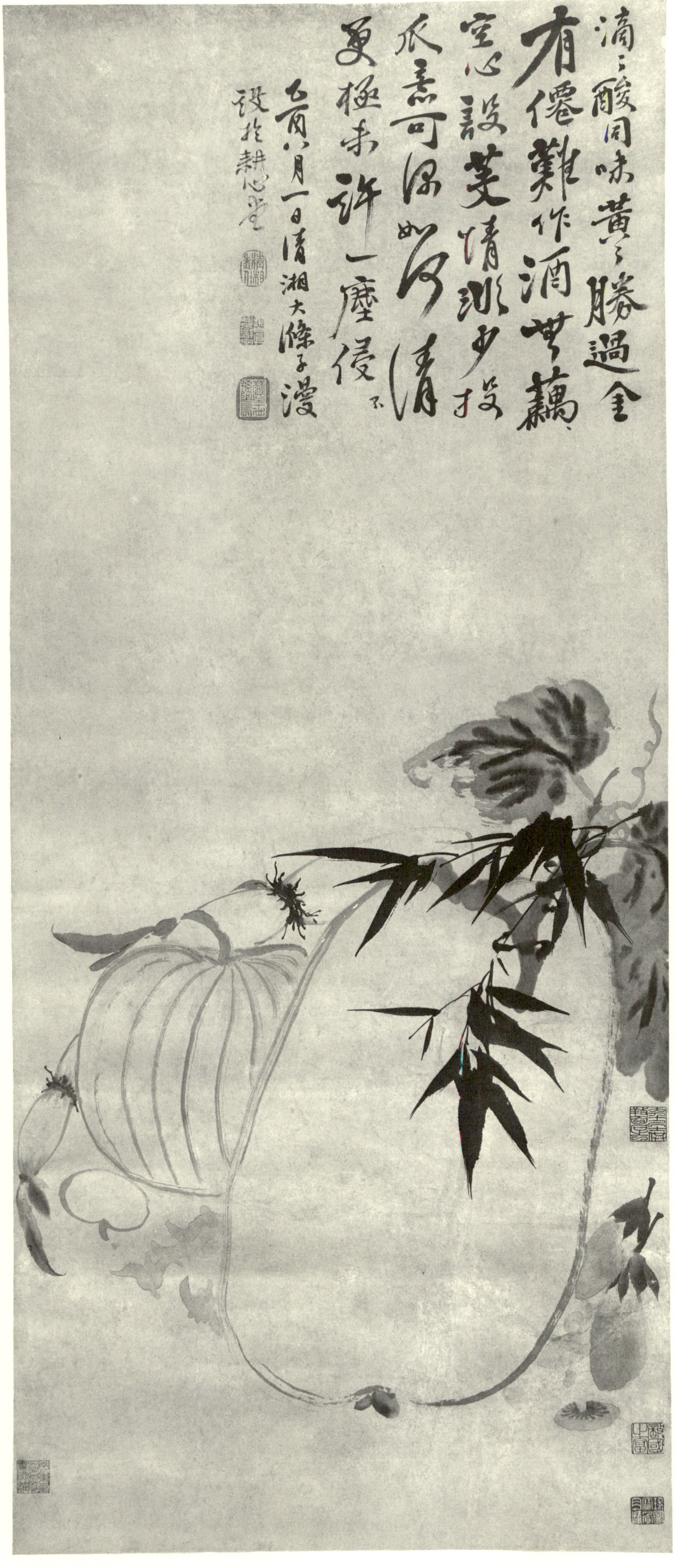

1. Tao-chi, *Loquats and Melon*, dated 1705. Hanging scroll. Ink on paper. 85.6 × 41.4 cm. C. C. Wang collection, New York.

the same rounded push-and-pull motions, and the same rhythmic flow, pace, and pressure as in the other calligraphic works by Tao-chi in this style cited above.

In the painting section, the wet dotting was intended to unify the disparate objects spatially. These dots are a feature which appear in other Tao-chi works, where they are handled with greater lightness and clarity. The *Bamboo and Orchids in the Wind*, the Sackler *Orchid, Bamboo, and Rock*, and the *Autumn Melon and Praying Mantis* scroll (fig. 3) all contain this design concept. The last work, a handscroll in ink only on paper dated 1700, is one of the most exciting in this genre. A dramatic and highly satisfying feeling of ink play is created by a similar dense "flooding" of the tones on a wet ground. This scroll also displays a comparable scattered and "floating" arrangement of forms in gradually receding layers of depth, comparable in complexity to the Sackler scroll. The foreground rock is used effectively as a repoussoir and suggests that same inner emptiness which we find in the melons of the Sackler and C. C. Wang works. In the latter work, therefore, despite the differences in quality and clarity of execution, there are actually close parallels of fundamental visualization—the working procedure of wet line on wet ground, the structural formation of depth and overlapping of shapes, and the creation of "solid" and "void" interactions of these shapes.

If, however, certain weaknesses of execution still leave doubts, one would have to take into account three aspects of the Wang works: the exceptional rendering of the loquat leaves, the dedication to "Tung lao-nien," and the purposeful calligraphic variants. The loquat leaves, which are the predominant feature of the Wang work, are executed in the same spontaneous and highly decisive manner as the exemplary Tao-chi album leaf of *Loquats* (fig. 4). Moreover, the loquats as subject are quite consistent with the content of the poem, for "yellow, so yellow" can be describing nothing but the loquats. As to the dedication, Chinese collectors in the past have as a rule disliked acquiring paintings with dedications to persons other than themselves. Hence a forger would be unlikely to "add legs to a snake" (*hua-she t'ien-tsu*) and fabricate a superfluous dedication for his copy. Lastly, few forgers have possessed either the foresight or the ingenuity to introduce calligraphic variants in such a natural manner as found in the Wang scroll.

In all likelihood, the C. C. Wang painting may even have been executed before the Sackler painting. This is suggested both by style and by the contents of the poem. The serene, almost classic sense of balance in the Sackler work seems to represent the perfected image of a design which Tao-chi had worked out earlier, while the C. C. Wang painting may be an earlier, possibly more experimental, work. As to actual time of execution, it may be close to that of the *Autumn Melon* handscroll of 1700. Tao-chi may have painted the Wang painting first, kept it, and added the 1705 inscription only upon the immediate request of the "Tung lao-nien" to whom it is dedicated. Also, the line "Yellow, so yellow—much better than gold" implies that the verse was written to complement the C. C. Wang work. It is quite common for painters to inscribe the same poem on more than one work, and there are several such occurrences among Tao-chi's extant works.[5] A process of transcription is indicated by the small dot at the end of the second line (after *ou*, "lotus root"); this dot represents the conventional sign for an omitted character, in this case *pu*, which has been written at the end of the poem in smaller script. It was added after the artist had finished rereading his inscription and found he had omitted that character. It is a perfectly acceptable "error," and speaks favorably of the work and the artist's attentiveness to both execution and meaning (Tao-chi made similar corrections in his 1685 *Searching for Plum Blossoms* handscroll, *XVIII*).

are precisely chosen variants and alterations in the sequence, form, and size of the characters which reveal purposeful deviation. For example, characters 15 and 16 (*chiu, wu*) in the C. C. Wang version have been changed to "draft" and "seal" scripts from the "running" style of the Sackler work.

From this evidence, one must ask the question whether these two works have been executed by the same hand. After lengthy study we believe that they could have been, and probably were. In the calligraphy one notices the same inner consistency of brush habits,

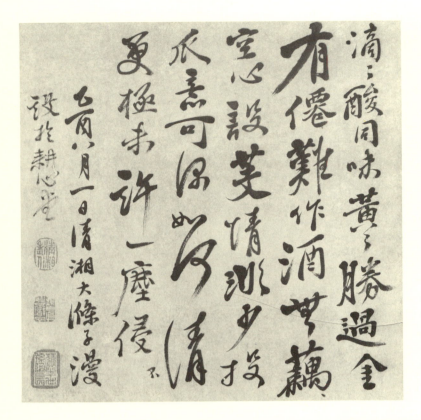

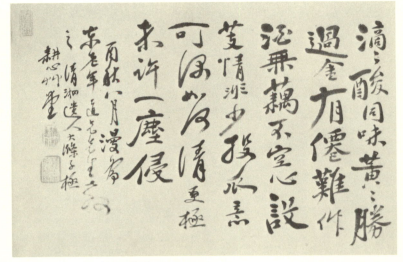

2. Fig. 1, detail of inscription.

left
XXXI, detail. Poetic eulogy, dated 1705.

below
3. Tao-chi, *Autumn Melon and Praying Mantis*, dated 1700, detail. Handscroll. Ink on paper. Collection unknown.

left
4. Tao-chi, *Loquats*. Leaf from an album. Ink and color on paper. Collection unknown.

NOTES
   1. We are grateful to Mr. and Mrs. T'ang Hai-t'ao for their aid in explicating this poem.
   2. Reproduced in *Shih-t'ao hua-chi*, pl. 50.
   3. See *PTC*, cat. no. 34, p. 168.
   4. Reproduced in Chu Sheng-chai, *Chung-kuo shu-hua*, vol. 1, p. 34.
   5. See, e.g., the Sackler collection eight-leaf album, *Plum Branches* (*XXXIII*), three poems of which appear on an earlier work.

XXXII TAO-CHI (1641–ca. 1710) and CHIANG CHI (fl. 1706–1742–)

Landscape and Portrait of Hung Cheng-chih (1674–1731–)
(Hung Kai-hua hua-hsiang)

The Art Museum, Princeton University (L13.67).

Handscroll. Ink and color on paper. 36.0 x 175.8 cm. (to the first join, which includes the first three colophons on the same sheet of paper).

DATED: winter, 1706 (*ping-hsü, tung-jih*).

SIGNATURE OF THE ARTIST: Ch'ing-hsiang I-jen, Ta-ti-tzu, Chi.

INSCRIPTION BY THE ARTIST: in four lines (see below).

SEALS OF THE ARTIST: *Ch'ih-chüeh* (relief, tall rectangle; *PTC*, cat. no. 12), *Pan-ko-han* (intaglio, tall rectangle; *PTC*, cat. no. 56), *Ta-ti-tzu, Chi* (intaglio, square; *PTC*, cat. no. 88).

COLLECTORS' SEALS:
Ho K'un-yü and Ho Yüan-yü (both early nineteenth-century Cantonese collectors), *Kao-yao Ho-shih K'un-yü Yüan-yü t'ung-huai kung-shang* (relief, square) right side of painting, *Tuan-hsi Ho Shu-tzu Yüan-yü hao chü-an kuo-yen ching-chi chin-shih shu-hua-yin-chi* (relief, tall rectangle) lower right edge of painting, *Hui-ts'un mao-wu* (intaglio, square) left corner of painting.
Chang Ta-ch'ien (Yüan, born 1899), *Chiu-t'u-pao ku-jou-ch'ing* (intaglio, rectangle) right edge of painting, *Ta-ch'ien chü-shih kung-yang pai-Shih-chih-i* (relief, square) top left corner of painting, *Nan-pei-tung-hsi chih-yu hsiang-sui wu-pieh-li* (relief, square) left edge of painting, *Pu-fu-ku-jen kao-hou-jen* (relief, rectangle) left edge of painting, *Chang Yüan, Ta-ch'ien-fu* (intaglio, square) left edge of painting, *Ta-feng-t'ang* (relief, square) left corner of painting.
Mme Chang Ta-ch'ien (*née* Hsü), *Hsü-shih hsiao-yin* (relief, square) left corner of painting, *Wen-po* (relief, tall rectangle) right corner of painting.
Owner unidentified, *Hung-pin? chang-chi* (intaglio, square) after third colophon, lower left edge of paper.

COLOPHONS: thirty-one (see end of entry).

FRONTISPIECE: eight lines written by its former owner, Chang Ta-ch'ien, in his characteristic large "standard" script.
The painted portrait of Hung Kai-hua and the inscribed mountains of Ta-ti-tzu — both worshipped and collected at the Ta-feng-t'ang. A summer day in the year chia-ch'en [1964], [exposing] the painting to sun, hence inscribing [it. Chang] Yüan.

[Seals:] *Chang Yüan ssu-yin* (intaglio, square),
Ta-ch'ien (relief, square).

CONDITION: poor; there is marked wormhole damage to edges and entire surface of painting and colophons, resulting in illegibility of several characters in the artist's inscription (see below); damaged painting areas have been filled in with parallel hatching in gray ink; parts of some characters have been redrawn where partially legible.

PROVENANCE: Ta-feng-t'ang collection.

PUBLISHED: *PTC*, cat. no. 35, p. 169 (illustrated).

AMONG TAO-CHI'S extant works, this unusual landscape and portrait is important as much for its historical information on the artist's dates and on one of his pupils as for its intrinsic artistic merit. Tao-chi's exact death date is still not known, and only recently has there been agreement on his birth date (see *XXIII* and Part IV, pp. 38–40, above). One of the key references supplying a plausible death date is an inscription dated 1720 by one of his few pupils known to us,[1] Hung Cheng-chih. The portrait subject of the scroll is this very pupil. In addition, the colophons to this painting—thirty-one in all—provide the most complete details of Hung's family and character known to us. Thus this work represents a visual and written document of Hung Cheng-chih's friendship with Tao-chi.

The portrait and landscape elements themselves are preceded by a four-line poetic inscription (see the detail, reproduced actual size) written by Tao-chi in small "standard" script in his graceful Ni Tsan style. The poem consists of three quatrains in seven-character regulated meter and may be rendered as follows:

As to Mr. Chiang, he is a distinctive and praiseworthy youth.
Grasping a vermilion brush in hand, he commands clouds and mist.
Occasionally for guests, he'll draw faces from life;
[two characters missing; the fidelity?] of the hair and bones [of his subject] makes one shiver!

As to [Hung] Kai-hua, [two characters missing] a man of breeding and style.
An antique sword girdling his waist, he gazes into the vast heavens.
With his vision extending so many miles, can it ever reach a horizon?
Looking to the past and trusting in the present, his heart is content.

As for me, I happened to unroll the painting and saw [Hung's image];
So for you I have added these soaring peaks.
Pacing back and forth, [I think to myself] might it not be worthless?
Looking at it, might someone not recognize something in it?

Ch'ing-hsiang i-jen, Ta-ti-tzu, Chi, on a
winter's day of the year *ping-hsü* [1706].

Frontispiece.

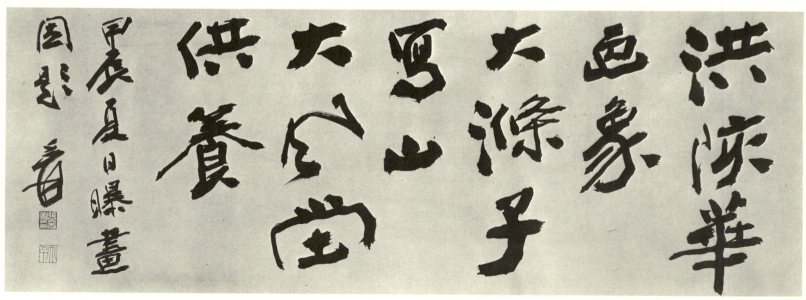

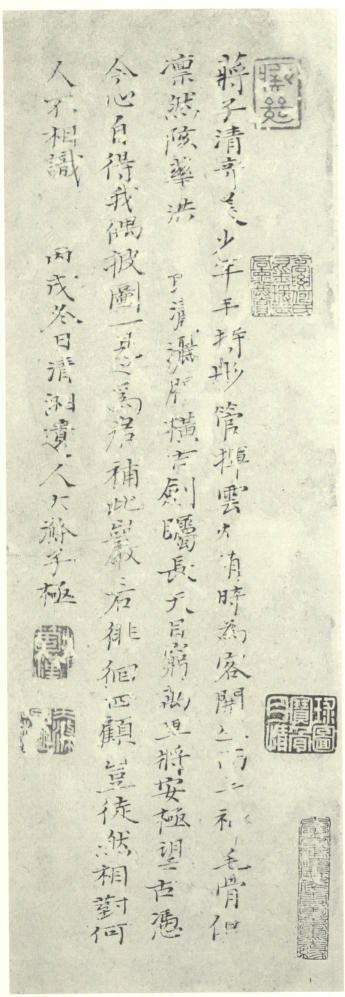

Detail of self-inscription by Tao-chi (*actual size*).

Detail of portrait (*actual size*).

The self-inscription tells us that Tao-chi contributed the land-scape and that the portrait of Hung Cheng-chih was done by a young portraitist named Chiang, not further identified.

The most remarkable feature of this painting is the design: Hung Cheng-chih's image rises from the mist like an apparition. Tao-chi has abandoned his usual respect for figures and landscape in proper scale and has chosen to obscure half of Hung's figure to heighten the sense of drama. Tao-chi muses in his poem on whether Hung's vision can ever reach a horizon, while the landscape elements present Hung's mind and ideals as literally towering and soaring limitlessly.

HUNG'S PORTRAIT (reproduced actual size in the detail) is exe-cuted in a meticulous "realistic" manner which prevailed in the late Ming as one of the ways to depict portraits from life.[2] The propor-tions of the face and figure were first outlined in pale ink and the facial features and hands then tinted in flesh-colored pigments. The bridge of the nose, the nostrils, and the areas around the eyes, chin, and contour of the face have been defined by both color wash and densely built up strokes of graded color. Such details as the eyelids and mouth have been given definition not by strict lineation but by dots and flecks of ink and color, creating a vivid sense of life. No light source is indicated, but a feeling of fullness and "shading" is achieved by the cumulative effect of modulated strokes of color. The folds of the robe have been reinforced with lines of pale blue wash to suggest the bulk of the figure beneath. Details of the sword and belt have been highlighted by lines of white pigment. The pale blue and white strokes and the saturated ultramarine hue of the cap and sword echo the high-keyed blue, green, russet, and yellow coloring of the landscape. The discrepancy between the meticulous rendering of the portrait and the landscape elements is not really as disturbing as one might think; on the contrary, it tends to intensify the relationship between the visionary character of the scene and the aspiring personality of the sitter.

The exemplary rendering of the portrait leads us to believe that the young Mr. Chiang mentioned by Tao-chi can be identified as Chiang Chi, an early eighteenth-century portraitist and author of *Ch'uan-shen mi-yao (Secrets of Portraiture)*.[3] Chiang Chi's book explains in detail the different means to achieve both a formal likeness and the spiritual vitality of the subject. The method of using both color wash and tightly built up layers of fine color lines to create the "shaded" areas agrees with Chiang's text. The preface to *Ch'uan-shen mi-yao*, written by an elder contemporary of Chiang's, is dated 1742 and refers to Chiang as still alive. The 1742 date would indicate that if Chiang is the portraitist here he would be, as Tao-chi implies, a youth (*shao-nien*), and a most talented one.

IN THE LANDSCAPE the mountains curve round in one dramatic sweep—very much the notion of "dragon vein" (*lung-mo*), that expressive unity of the masses which dominated the works of the orthodox Ch'ing masters and accounted for much of their monumentality. The verticals of the portrait figure, the waterfall, and the foreground peaks lend stability to this structure. The cloud formations and the stratified rock surfaces are totally in the character of Tao-chi: clouds in undulating linears which envelop the nearest promontories can be seen in such works as the 1673 *Eight-Leaf Album* (*XXXIV*, fig. 5) and the 1697 *Waterfall at Mt. Lu* (*XVII*, fig. 5), while similar rocks, with surface texture of wet, smudged modulations and bulky, layered placement in depth appear in such works as the 1696 *Sketches by Ch'ing-hsiang* (fig. 1) and the Freer *Peach-Blossom Spring* (fig. 2).

left

1. Tao-chi, *Sketches of Calligraphy and Painting by Ch'ing-hsiang*, dated 1696, detail of section 12. Handscroll. Ink on paper. Palace Museum, Peking.

below

2. Tao-chi, *Peach-Blossom Spring*, ca. 1703, detail of rocks. Handscroll. Ink and color on paper. Freer Gallery of Art.

XXXII, detail.

XXXII. Landscape and Portrait of Hung Cheng-chih.
Scroll reads continuously from right to left, top to bottom.

On first glance, the painting may not appear to be one of Tao-chi's most appealing works, perhaps because of its wormeaten condition or because of the materials used—a raw, unsized paper. The 1706 date places the work well toward the end of the artist's career, when an uneven quality in the brushwork tended to reflect fluctuations of energy and spirit. In this work Tao-chi had to use a relatively dry brush in order to prevent excessive bleeding of the ink on the highly absorbent paper. This restraint has created a feeling of harshness and lack of modulation between the dry, rubbed, modeling strokes in the rocks and the flat wash areas of color. Actually, the basic brushwork can be seen in two other extremely fine late Tao-chi works, the *Lo-Fu Mountains* (XXX), and the 1707 *Reminiscences of Nanking* (XXXIV), interacting on slightly different textured papers.

As Tao-chi states in his inscription, the figure was completed before he added the landscape, but the ingenious nature of the design certainly indicates some advance collaboration between portraitist, landscapist, and portrait sitter, who were undoubtedly good friends to begin with. The romantic, visionary aura of the portrait seems to be both a successful reflection of Hung Cheng-chih's self-image and a tribute to Tao-chi's fertile imagination. He probably conceived of the general idea, with Hung agreeing to it and to the choice of clothing and accessories.

The fact that Hung Cheng-chih was a pupil of Tao-chi and a native of Yang-chou, Kiangsu,[4] is verified by a contemporary of Hung's, Yüan Tun, who said: "I and Hung Kai-hua are from the same district [of Chiang-tu, or Yang-chou]. Both of us studied painting with the master [Tao-chi]."[5] Further evidence of this relationship comes from Hung Cheng-chih himself in a colophon he wrote to an album of flowers and landscapes by Tao-chi: "The venerable Ch'ing-hsiang once gave me a sixteen-leaf album of ink plum. It was perfect in every respect; therefore I mounted it, set it up in my studio, and frequently copied it. . . . the old gentleman and I lived together in the same place a long time. . . . Ninth lunar month of the year *hsin-hai* [1731] of the Yung-cheng . . . era. [Signed:] Wan-kuan chü-shih, Hung Cheng-chih, inscribed."[6] The tone of the inscription, one of affectionate respect, is found in another colophon by Hung, which also gives us information on Tao-chi's approximate date of death. In an inscription dated 1720 on a painting by Tao-chi which he acquired, Hung alludes to his master's death: "These past twenty years, my hair has turned starry-white! I think back and recall Ch'ing-hsiang [Tao-chi]—and it is just as if he were here before my eyes, yet also like a world apart."[7]

The various names by which Hung is addressed in the colophons to this scroll identify him as the man whose cognomens appear in inscriptions in other records of paintings. For example, from the signature in Hung's own inscriptions of 1720 and 1731 cited above, we can now state with certainty that Cheng-chih is his *ming* and that Kai-hua, T'ing-tso, and Wan-kuan chü-shih are his *tzu* and *hao*.

The specific facts of Hung's relationship with his teacher Tao-chi are less certain. One comment dated 1701 by a certain Huang Yün suggests that Tao-chi returned his pupil's affection and that his fondness for Hung could probably be measured by the number of paintings given him: "I have known the great teacher Shih[-t'ao] for thirty years and am most fond of his paintings, but have only been able to obtain a rare few [*chi-kuang p'ien-yü*]. Recently [he, i.e., Tao-chi] has been executing something for my friend [Hung] T'ing-tso, who must now have countless works of his!"[8]

The most complete account of Hung's life, giving his year of birth and possible death date, as well as some insight into his personality, is found in one of the longer colophons to this painting. It was written by Hung's nephew, Hung Ming, and is dated 1731. From it the following information can be gleaned (presented in chronological order, not as it appears in the colophon itself): (1) Hung Cheng-chih's great-grandfather was awarded the *chin-shih* degree in 1589 (Wan-li period, *chi-ch'ou*) and later acted as an official in the Court of Sacrificial Worship (*Feng-ch'ang*). (2) Hung's portrait in this scroll was painted in 1706 (*ping-wu*), which is the year in which Tao-chi finished the landscape sections. At this time Hung Cheng-chih was thirty-three *sui*; he was therefore born in 1674. (3) Hung Cheng-chih's eldest son, Hung Shih-mou, became a *chin-shih* in 1723 (*kuei-mao*) and was appointed a district official in Hsi-ning (either Canton or Kiangsu Province). (4) In 1731, the year the colophon was written, Shih-mou returned home from Hsi-ning; Hung was then fifty-eight. (5) His mood at this time was despondent; marriage arrangements for his children had not yet been completed, and he felt that "time was flying by and his ambitions had not been realized."

We have been able to ascertain Hung Cheng-chih's full dates from the following: the last colophon on the painting is dated 1771 (Ch'ien-lung era, *hsin-mao*), and Hung is referred to there as having passed away. From the form of the addresses to Hung in the thirty other colophons, we know that they were written while he was still alive; the latest of this group is dated in correspondence with the ninth month of 1731. The last information from Hung's own hand is an inscription corresponding to the tenth month of the same year, 1731, written on the album of landscapes and flowers by Tao-chi mentioned earlier. Thus, Hung died some time after the tenth month of 1731, but before 1771.

From Tao-chi's description of him and the expression on the face of the portrait, Hung appears to have been an idealist of possibly quixotic temperament. At thirty-three, in the prime of his intellectual and physical powers, Hung undoubtedly had hopes of gaining a *chin-shih* degree and was pursuing the arts of painting and swordsmanship. The precise significance of the sword is not known. We expect the colophon writers to give us a clue, but they do not, limiting themselves, on the whole, to comments on the portrayal (which may speak for its fidelity); they do not fail to mention the antique weapon, however. Perhaps it is an attribute symbolic of certain heroic ideals Hung held. The sword and the headdress may be a costume he frequently sported, if only in private, among his friends. Whether they represent any martial aspirations of a personal or wider political nature, or even the ideals of the *yu-hsia* ("knight-errant") of former times, is difficult to say. By 1731, when his nephew's inscription was written, almost thirty years had passed. Hung was fifty-eight, and his feelings of depression were well-founded when measured by traditional values. He was proud of his grandfather's and son's accomplishments, but his own failure to win a *chin-shih* degree must have crippled his political career and finances. If, as his nephew implies, unfulfilled ambitions lay at the root of his frustration, the sight of this early portrait must have intensified the gap between reality and his youthful visions. Indeed, as pointed out above, the research so far indicates that Hung Cheng-chih did not live far beyond the period described by his nephew.

CHIANG SHIH-CHIEH'S (1647–1709) fine colophon (see the detail) on the same sheet of paper as the painting offers strong evidence for the authenticity of this scroll and its date. Chiang's paintings and calligraphy are consistent enough to confirm the identity of his style with that of this colophon. As he was an immediate contemporary and friend of Tao-chi, the genuineness of Tao-chi's contribution to this handscroll is strengthened. The Freer Gallery of Art in Washington has in its collection a hanging scroll on ink and paper (fig. 3), dated 1707, by Chiang, and there are two fine works of his in the J. P. Dubosc collection, a landscape hanging scroll, also dated 1707,

余年子四五陪先大夫游靈巖
次日靈巖命游堯峰隨先光
勉中火往方當初年賈勇直前踏
流滂野田穿林覓路略未知遠也
茶話夜分西談甚適掲
墜壁扁舟牧景藻諸師言
於然作僧道散時時皆不葉
老來無一存者二亥十月四
日王子年四晃子梅圓招遊
堯峰千伊靈崔兒与乘登臨
村口槑紅藹密到松根靈白自鐘來
相遇遠僧談往事昔顧後盡
不勝衰

喜菴勝景

萊陽姜寔邸虔正
萊陽樓下畫

3. Chiang Shih-chieh, *Landscape in Ni Tsan Style*, dated 1707. Hanging scroll. Ink on paper. Freer Gallery of Art.

and a fan.[9] In both calligraphy and painting, all three works contain strong allusions to Ni Tsan's style.

Chiang's calligraphy (see Part III, p. 31, above) is identical in both his colophon (see the detail above) and his inscription on the Freer painting (fig. 4). Close scrutiny of both works reveals the idiosyncratic nature of his writing, such as the strongly perpendicular stance of the columns and the structure of individual characters. Furthermore, the columns in both works are rather closely spaced. The horizontal and vertical strokes in each character extend impulsively beyond the rectangular configuration of the form, and each stroke is slightly emphasized at the beginning and end. This stress may be related to an influence from *chang-ts'ao* ("draft-cursive") script. These outer accents contrast with the rest of the strokes in each character, which tend to converge tightly toward the center axis of the form.

The physical connection of Chiang's colophon with Chia Chih's colophon dated 1708 is important: the three colophons appear on the same paper; therefore Chiang must have inscribed it around the same time, or at least before 1709, the year of his death. The stylistic similarities in Chiang's extant calligraphy and painting, as described here, plus the fact that the colophons are dated close to the time of Tao-chi's execution and inscription, decidedly support the authenticity of the painting.

The remaining colophons consist of eulogies to Hung in verse and prose by his friends. The set forms a kind of social registry of his Yang-chou intellectual circle. The sequence of the colophons was evidently disrupted in the course of remounting and may at present be incomplete. The earliest is dated 1708, two years after the painting, and the latest and last 1771. Except in rare cases, little information is available about the inscribers. However, such well-known Ch'ing figures as Chu I-ts'un, Ch'en Chuan, Mei Wen-ting, Shen T'ing-fang, and Chiang Shih-chieh compose the more prominent names in the roster. The colophons offer much insight into this circle of literati and into Ch'ing cultural history in general and deserve a separate study. Due to their inordinate number, they have not been translated here.

COLOPHONS

1. Chia Chih, from Hui-t'sun, a two-part colophon dated in autumn of the year *wu-tzu* (1708), first section in eight lines, second in eighteen lines of smaller script.[10] Seals of the inscriber: *Chia Chih ssu-yin* (half-intaglio, half-relief, square), *Ch'ü-wu* (relief, square), both after signature. Chia Chih was Hung Cheng-chih's maternal uncle, which accounts for his knowledge of the details about the family revealed in his colophon. Tao-chi painted works for him, and Chia is known to have inscribed other Tao-chi paintings, notably an album of orchids dedicated to Hung Cheng-chih.[11]

2. Mei Wen-ting (1633–1721), from Wu-an (Hsüan-ch'eng), Anhwei, a seven-line colophon, undated. Mei was an astronomer and mathematician known for his calendrical studies.[12] Seals of the inscriber: *Mei Wen-ting-yin* (intaglio, square), *Ting-chiu* (relief, square), both after signature; *Wu-an* (relief, tall rectangle) before colophon.

3. Chiang Shih-chieh (1647–1709), active in Wu-hsien (Su-chou), Kiangsu, a four-line colophon, undated, signed with his studio name, Hsien-tz'u-chien ts'ao-lou. Chiang was an exact contemporary of Tao-chi and a poet, painter, and calligrapher well known in his time.[13] Seals of the inscriber: *Hsiao-tzu ssu-wei* (intaglio, square), *Chiang Shih-chieh-yin* (intaglio, square), *Hsüeh-tsai* (intaglio, square), all after signature; *Chiang Chung-tzu* (relief, square) before colophon.

First join. The three preceding colophons are written on the same paper as the painting.

4. Chu I-tsun (1629–1709), from Hsiu-shui, Chekiang, a four-line colophon written on a silk brocade insert, undated. Chu was a famous scholar, poet, and bibliophile.[14] Seals of the inscriber: *Chu I-tsun-yin* (intaglio, square), *Chu-ch'a lao-jen* (relief, square), both after signature.

Second join.

5. Chia Chao-feng, an eleven-line colophon, undated, addressed directly to Hung Cheng-shih. Seals of the inscriber: *Chia Chao-feng-yin* (intaglio, square), *T'an-ts'un* (relief, square), both after signature.

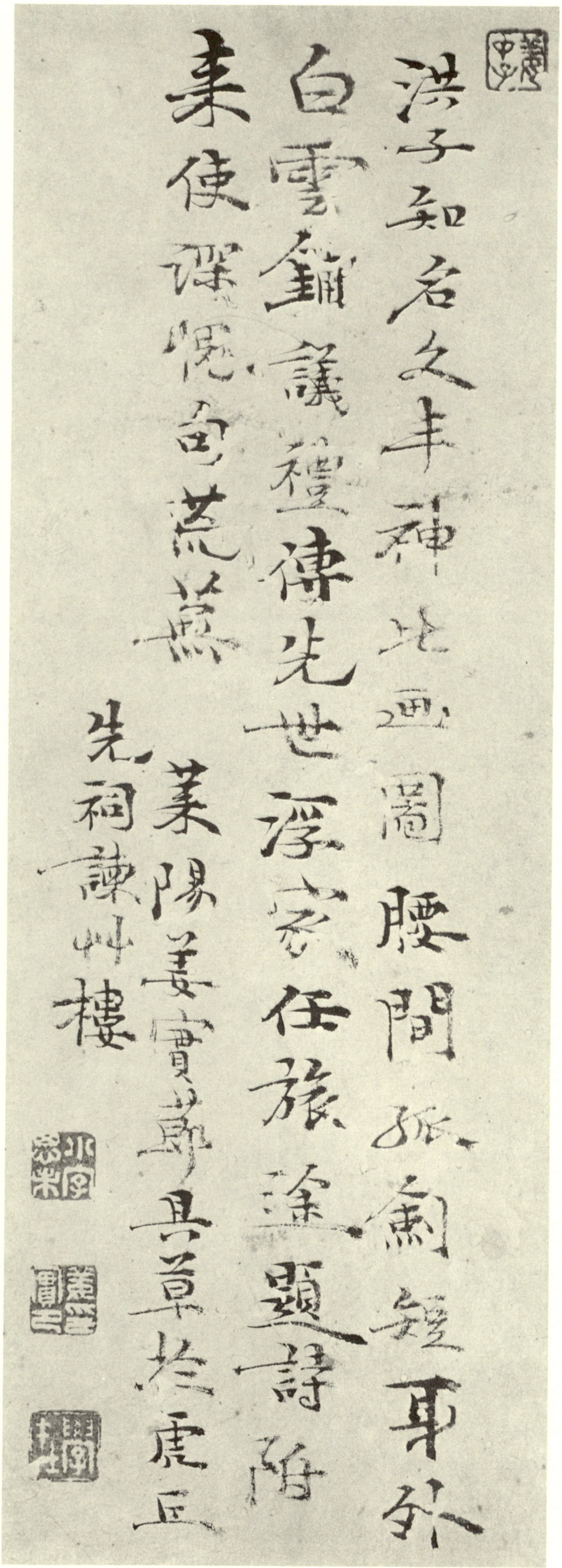

洪子知名久丰神比畫闆腰間孤劍東外

白雲鋪議禮傳先世浮家任旅途題詩附

来使深怳奇荒燕

先祠諫州樓

美陽姜實尊具草於震旦

Detail of colophon by Chiang Shih-chieh (*actual size*).

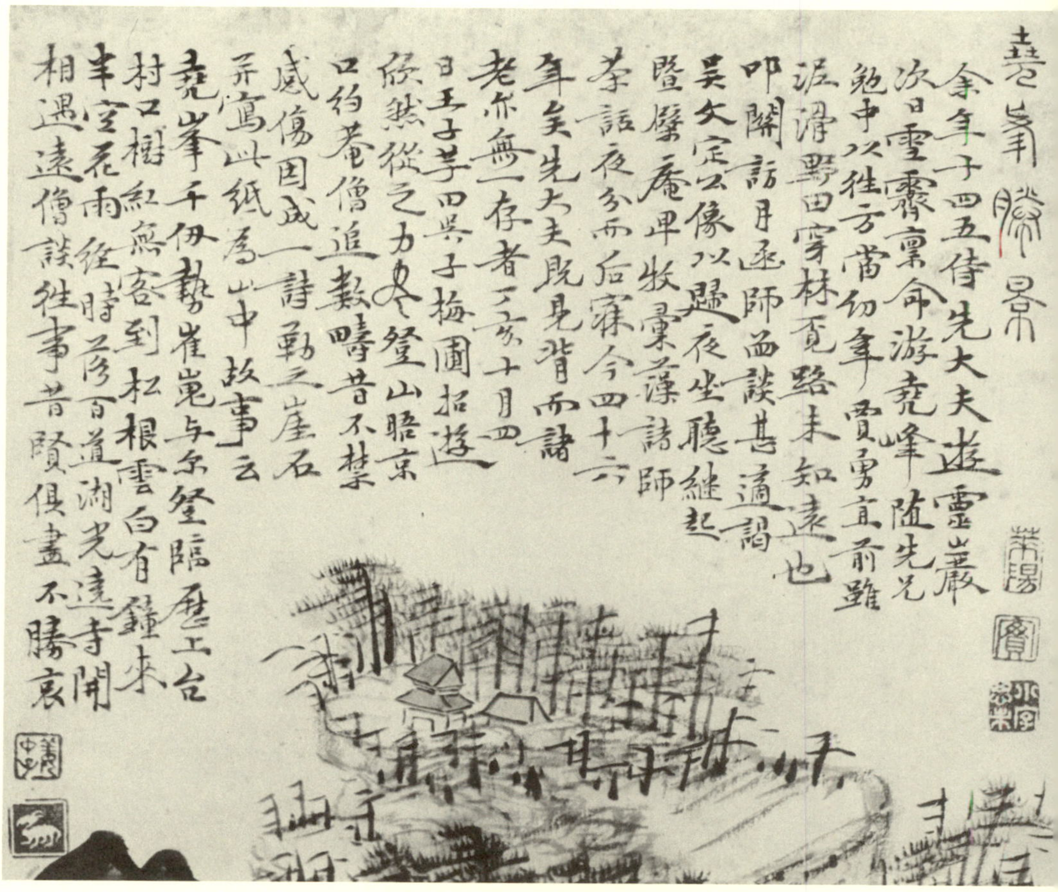

4. Chiang Shih-chieh, *Landscape in Ni Tsan Style*, detail of self-inscription.

6. Wu Shih-t'ai, a seven-line colophon, undated, addressed directly to Hung Cheng-chih. Seals of the inscriber: *Wu Shih-t'ai-yin* (intaglio, square), ()-*chi* (relief, square), both after signature; () () *pu-i* (relief, tall rectangle) before colophon.

At some time in the remounting, the order of the colophons was disrupted. The following colophons (nos. 7–13) follow no. 30 in the original chronology.

Third join.

7. Ch'u Chang-wen, from I-hsing, Anhwei, a ten-line colophon written in *kuei-mao* (1723) after Hung extended a personal invitation to inscribe the painting in *kuei-ssu* (1713). Seals of the inscriber: *Chang-wen chih-yin* (intaglio, square), *Pai-yü-fu* (half-intaglio, half-relief, square), both after signature.

8. Ch'en Chuan (fl. 1670–1740), from Hang-chou, later Yang-chou, a five-line colophon, undated. Ch'en was both a poet and a painter.[15] Seals of the inscriber: *Chuan* (relief, round), *Ling-shan* (relief, square), both after signature.

9. Shih Feng-hui, a thirteen-line colophon, dated *kuei-mao* (1723). Seals of the inscriber: *Shih Feng hui-yin* (intaglio, square), *Nan-ju-shih* (relief, square), both after signature; ()-*yung* (intaglio, tall rectangle) before colophon.

10. Chiang Ying, an eight-line colophon, dated in the *chia-ch'en* year of Yung-cheng era (1724). Seal of the inscriber: *Yen, Nan* (relief, double seal with two square faces) after signature.

11. Hsieh Chuo, a five-line colophon, undated. Seals of the inscriber: *Hsieh Chuo* (intaglio, square), *Chih-chang* (relief, square), both after signature.

12. Mr. Liang of Kuo-t'ing, a two-part colophon dated in the *hsin-hai* year of Yung-cheng era (1731), first part in five lines, second part in five lines of smaller script. Seal of the inscriber: *Hsien, Chai* (relief, single rectangular seal with two square faces) after signature.

13. Hung Ming (ca. 1730), from Yang-chou, Kiangsu, a twenty-line colophon dated mid-autumn of the year *hsin-hai* of Yung-cheng era (1731). Seals of the inscriber: *Ch'en-ming yin-hsin* (intaglio, square), ()-*chai* (relief, square), both after signature; () () (relief, tall rectangle) before colophon.

Fourth join after the seventh line of the preceding colophon with a fifth join at the end of the colophon. The following colophons, nos. 14–28, originally followed no. 6. This reconstruction is tentative, made on the basis of the available dates of the inscribers and their manner of addressing Hung.

14. Chin T'ang, a seven-line colophon, undated, addressed to Hung Cheng-chih. Seal of the inscriber: *Chin T'ang chih-yin* (intaglio, square) after signature.

15. Ch'u Ta-wen (1665–1743), from I-hsing, Anhwei, a four-line colophon, undated, addressed to Hung. Seals of the inscriber: *Ch'u Ta-wen-yin* (intaglio, square), *Liu-ya* (relief, square), both after signature.

16. Wang T'ang, a five-line colophon, undated. Seal of the inscriber: *Ming-yu* (relief, tall rectangle) after signature.

17. Ch'u Yü-wen (ca. 1720?), a three-line colophon, undated. Seals of the inscriber: *Ch'u Yü-wen-yin* (intaglio, square), *Yün*-() (relief, square), both after signature.

18. Ch'u Hsiung-wen (ca. 1720?), a three-line colophon, undated. Seal of the inscriber: *Ch'u Ssu-yün* (half-intaglio, half-relief) after signature.

19. Wang Hsien (*chü-jen*, 1794?), a three-line colophon, undated (Hummel mentions a Wang Hsien of the same name, but his dates appear to be too late, as they do not agree with the range of the rest of the inscribers on this section[16]). Seals of the inscriber: *Wang Hsien* (intaglio, square), *Mu-t'ing-shih* (relief, square), both after signature.

20. Ch'eng Shih-chuang, a three-line colophon, undated. Seals of the inscriber: *Chin-chen*(?) (relief, square), *Ch'eng Shih-chuang* (intaglio, square), both after signature; ()-*t'ing* (relief, tall rectangle) before colophon.

21. Wu Chan-t'ai, a three-line colophon, dated early autumn of *chi-ch'ou* (1709). Seals of the inscriber: *Wu-Chan t'ai-yin* (intaglio, square), *Tung-yen-shih* (relief, square), both after signature; *Keng* () () ()-*wu-tz'u-ch'ing* (relief, tall rectangle) before colophon.

22. Ch'eng Yin, a three-line colophon, dated in seventh lunar month of *chi-ch'ou* (1709). Seals of the inscriber: *Ch'en Yin* (relief, square), *K'uei-chen* (intaglio, square), both after signature, *chi-ch'ou* (relief, oval) before colophon.

23. Ch'eng Yüan-yü, a six-line colophon, dated in tenth lunar month of *chi-ch'ou* (1709). Seals of the inscriber: *Ch'eng Yüan-yü* (intaglio, square), *Hsien-ch'ü* (relief, square), both after signature; ()-*lu* (relief, tall rectangle) before colophon.

24. Chiu-ch'u-wang tao-shih, a five-line colophon, undated. Seals of the inscriber: *Chiu-ch'u* (relief, square), *Wang-sou* (intaglio, square), both after signature; *Chiu-hsiang shan-jen* (relief, tall rectangle) before colophon.

Sixth join after third line of colophon.

25. Li K'ai (1686–1755), from Peking, a five-line colophon, undated. Li was a writer and poet.[17] Seals of the inscriber: *Li K'ai ssu-yin* (intaglio, square), *Pu-wei-wu suo-ts'ai* (relief, square), both after signature; *Tan-jung-yü* (relief, oval) before colophon.

26. Hsieh Fang-ch'i, a ten-line colophon, undated. Seals of the inscriber: *Hsieh* (relief, round) before colophon; *Fang-ch'i* (relief, square), *Ying-yün* (intaglio, square), both after signature.

Seventh join.

27. Hsien Chu, from Chiang-ning, a five-line colophon, undated. Seal of the inscriber: *Hsien Chu chih-yin* (intaglio, square) after signature.

28. Hsia Liu-hsiu, a six-line colophon, dated autumn of *chi-ch'ou* (1709). Seals of the inscriber: *Liu-hsiu* (relief, square), *Chih-yüan* (intaglio, square), both after signature.

Eighth join.

29. Ku Ssu-li (1669–1722), from Ch'ang-chou, a four-line colophon, undated. Seals of the inscriber: *Ku Ssu-li-yin* (intaglio, square), *Hsia-chün* (relief, square), both after signature; *Wu-yü-hsüan* (relief, oval) before colophon.

30. Hsieh Fang-lien, inscribed twice in succession, the first in nine lines, the second in seven lines, undated. Seals of the inscriber: *Hsieh Fang-lien* (intaglio, square), *Fang-yen ts'un-chuang* (intaglio, square), both after first signature; ()-*suo* (relief, gourd-shaped) before first colophon; *Chieh* (relief, square), *Hsiang, Tsu* (relief, rectangular seal with two faces), both after second signature.

Ninth join.

31. Shen T'ing-fang (1702–1772), from Hai-ning, Chekiang, a seven-line colophon, dated in the seventh lunar month, the year *hsin-mao* of the Ch'ien-lung era (1771). Shen was a scholar, painter, and calligrapher whose maternal grandfather came from the clan of Cha Chi-tso.[18] Seals of the inscriber: *Shen T'ing-fang-yin* (half-intaglio, half-relief, square), *Ti-lin* (relief, tall rectangle), both after signature; *Yin-chuo-chai* (relief, tall rectangle) before colophon.

NOTES

1. Little information is available about Tao-chi's pupils; a few have been identified by Cheng Cho-lu in his *Shih-t'ao yen-chiu*, pp. 33–35. Cheng names Yüan Tun (see n. 5 below) of Yang-chou, Wu Yu-ho of Hsin-an, and Ch'eng Ming of Yü-yang, as well as Hung Cheng-chih.

2. See Stella Lee, "Figure Painters in the Late Ming," pp. 145–49, esp. p. 148: cat. nos. 80 and 81, also joint works by a portraitist and a landscapist, represent earlier manifestations of the same trend, combining meticulous drawing of the face with a freer landscape.

3. In the *HLTK* ed., vol. 2, pp. 856–70, the "shading" effects are called *shan-kuang*. The text also appears in the *ISTP* series, vol. 14, but without the valuable preface by Ch'eng Ssu-li (1688–1744).

4. Cheng Cho-lu, *Shih-t'ao yen-chiu*, pp. 5, 34.

5. Yüan Tun (*tzu* Chou-nan, *hao* Fan-shan-tzu; fl. ca. 1730–1758-) was also a friend of the famous poet Yüan Mei (1716–1797), who notes that he excelled at telling anecdotes (*ibid.*, p. 6, n. 1, and pp. 5, 33). See also Yüan's important colophon dated 1758 appended to *Ch'ing-hsiang lao-jen t'i-chi*, in *Hua-yüan pi-chi*, vol. 1, p. 17.

6. P'ang Yüan-chi, *Hsü-chai ming-hua-lu*, 15/17a–17b.

7. P'an Cheng-wei, *T'ing-fan-lou shu-hua-chi hsü, chüan-hsai*, p. 651. Cf. Part IV, p. 39, above.

8. Huang Yün (*tzu* Hsien-chang, *hao* Chiu-ch'ao), from T'ai-chou, Kiangsu (near Yang-chou), was known as a poet and essayist; his works are collected in his *Yu-jan-t'ang-chi* and *T'ung-yin-lou-chi*. The quote is from Cheng Cho-lu, *Shih-t'ao yen-chiu*, pp. 18–19.

9. Reproduced in Laurence Sickman and J. P. Dubosc, *Great Chinese Painters of the Ming and Ch'ing Dynasties*, pls. 72–73, pp. 67–68.

10. Numbers of lines given for colophons include the signature line.

11. *Ta-ti-tzu t'i-hua-shih-pa*, 2/40–47.

12. See Arthur W. Hummel, ed., *Eminent Chinese of the Ch'ing Period*, pp. 570, 867.

13. See *CKHCJMTT*, p. 274a.

14. See Hummel, *Eminent Chinese*, pp. 182, 606.

15. *Ibid.*, p. 85.

16. *Ibid.*, p. 822.

17. *Ibid.*, pp. 451–52.

18. *Ibid.*, p. 646.

XXXIII TAO-CHI (1641–ca. 1710)

Plum Branches: Poems and Painting (*Mei-hua-shih ts'e*)

The Art Museum, Princeton University (67-15).

Album of eight leaves. Ink on *lo-wen* paper (paper watermarked with fine striations), unsized, of creamy tone. 20.0 x 29.5 cm.

UNDATED: probably executed ca. 1705–7.

UNSIGNED

SEALS OF THE ARTIST:
Ch'ing-hsiang lao-jen (relief, oval; *PTC*, cat. no. 18, not listed) leaves A, C, and H.
Meng-tung-sheng (intaglio, square; *PTC*, cat. no. 54, not listed) leaf B.
Hsia-tsun-che (relief, tall rectangle; *PTC*, cat. no. 29, not listed) leaves D and F.
Ch'ing-hsiang Shih-t'ao (intaglio, tall rectangle; *PTC*, cat. no. 22, not listed) leaf E.
Tsan-chih shih-shih-sun, A-ch'ang (relief, tall rectangle; *PTC*, cat. no. 95, not listed) leaf G.
Kao-mang-tzu, Chi (intaglio, rectangle; *PTC*, cat. no. 41, not listed) leaf H.

COLLECTORS' SEALS (identified on each leaf):
Chang Shan-tzu (Tse, 1883–1940) leaves E and F, totaling two seals.
Chang Ta-ch'ien (Yüan, born 1899) all leaves except F, totaling fourteen seals.

CONDITION: good.

PROVENANCE: Ta-feng-t'ang collection.

PUBLISHED: *Record of the Art Museum, Princeton University*, vol. 27, no. 1 (1968), p. 35; *Archives of Asian Art*, vol. 22 (1968–69), p. 134; *The Selected Painting and Calligraphy of Shih-t'ao*, vol. 5, pl. 110 (illustrated).

PLUM BLOSSOMS were probably Tao-chi's favorite flower. They appear throughout his works, either with a solitary human figure or as a solo portrait. He thought of the plum as possessing human qualities, spoke to it through poetry, or employed it as a means to "write out" his feelings through calligraphic movements. Ultimately he identified with it, and in the process of painting its branches and flowers came to feel spiritually uplifted by its purity and its symbolic association with the recluse of noble principle. A traditional and classic subject, the ink plum had been favored by scholar- and monk-painters since the Sung dynasty because its simplicity allowed the expression of an individual manner and the conveying of personal feelings. The cultivation of the painter elevated it above any stereotyped technical convention that might be attached to its execution.[1]

In this album Tao-chi offers eight different presentations of plum in a free brush style, each matched by his poetry and calligraphy. Despite his fondness for the subject, there are proportionately few works devoted to the plum. This work in eight leaves is the only extant album of plum known to us.[2] In this small format a meditative introspection conveys an intimacy quite different from the wild branches and extroversion of his 1685 handscroll *Searching for Plum Blossoms* (*XVIII*). Almost twenty years separate these two works, and we can see how his style and attitude toward plum changed with his maturing vision. Here he reduces his presentation to a single expressive or compositional theme. While the impact is direct and immediate, it does not assault the viewer with overconfident bravura, as in his 1685 scroll. Rather, the energies are directed and sublimated in the club-like brushwork, so that the total expression is refined, quiet, and truly confident.

Branches at various stages of growth are again depicted here, but

it is the "branchwork" (in Wen Fong's word) that acts as the unifying pictorial thread. Branchwork and brushwork are identified, as are the visual and the literary: not only the writing of the poems but the painting of the plum as a pictorial extension of calligraphy are keys to understanding these leaves.

In his plan for the album Tao-chi was armed with the traditional schemata for painting plum and the consideration that each leaf must differ sequentially in design and mood. The ink suffusions and tonal gradations, together with the richly striated texture of the paper (resembling Western "laid" paper), offer a feast to which Tao-chi seemed especially sensitive in his late works. The range of compositions and moods, a few of which are of a delicate and transient nature, represents a visualization which is all the more powerful for being restricted in format and subject. It is often in a work of ostensibly limited scope that the true genius of the master is revealed to us.

Pictorially, Tao-chi's designs are also very much dictated by his awareness of the rectangular format, the spatial potential of the image on the paper surface and its interaction with the framing edge.[3] The design was drawn stroke upon stroke, branch by branch, as the plum grows—in compliance with or opposition to the borders. The kinesthetic process of growth and organic multiplication initiated in painting is entirely consistent with the artist's own description of painting plum (see *XVIII*), where the idea for any one design is governed by the configuration of the first stroke and its spontaneous pictorial growth thereafter. Coupled with the powerful broken linework (probably drawn with an old, worn-out brush, which he liked to use in these late works) and the extraordinary ink fusions, the spatial dynamics in these leaves challenge the sensitivity and taste of the viewer to savor brush and ink on Tao-chi's own terms.

At least three different styles of calligraphy are represented in the poems, reflecting the images and Tao-chi's characteristic ink phrasing. The poems are octets composed in seven-character regulated meter and are transcribed in even lines, forming a solid block, or several continuous columns. At the end of each poem Tao-chi has identified the type or locale of the plum. This identification forms the title of each leaf. The integration of poetic meaning with pictorial content was more successful in some leaves, such as A, E, G, and H, than in others, and in the former cases we have translated the poems.[4] Tao-chi probably composed the verses in advance, and the specific nature or recollection of a kind of plum may have given rise to the dominant pictorial theme. In some instances the poems were taken from earlier works, such as those on leaves B and F, which appear on a scroll dated 1699 (fig. 1), and the poem on leaf E, which is found on the last leaf of the *1700 Peking Album*.[5]

Together with *Searching for Plum Blossoms* this album mirrors the major changes in brush style which occur in Tao-chi's landscapes over this significant twenty-year period 1685–1705. His output in this minor genre of plum, like his bamboo and orchid (*XXIX*), was modest in proportion to his landscapes. Nevertheless, especially in the plum, the formal conventions of the style he established, his handling of ink, and his expressive freedom and stylistic diversity strongly influenced later artists of the Yang-chou school, such as Hua Yen (1682–1765), Li Fang-ying (1695–1754), Chin Nung (1687–after 1764), Cheng Hsieh (1693–1765), and Wang Shih-shen (1686–1759).[6]

Leaf A: *"Plum of Pao-ch'eng"* (*Pao-ch'eng mei-hua*)

COLLECTOR'S SEALS: *Ta-feng-t'ang* (relief, oval), *Ta-ch'ien chü-shih kung-yang pai-Shih-chih-i* (relief, square), *Pu-fu ku-jen kao-hou-jen* (relief, large square).

古花如見古遺民
誰遣花枝照古人
閱歷六朝惟隱逸
支離殘臘倍精神
天青地白容疏放
水擁山空任屈伸
擬欲將詩對明月
畫驅懷抱入清新
寶城梅花

Leaf A, "Plum of Pao-ch'eng"

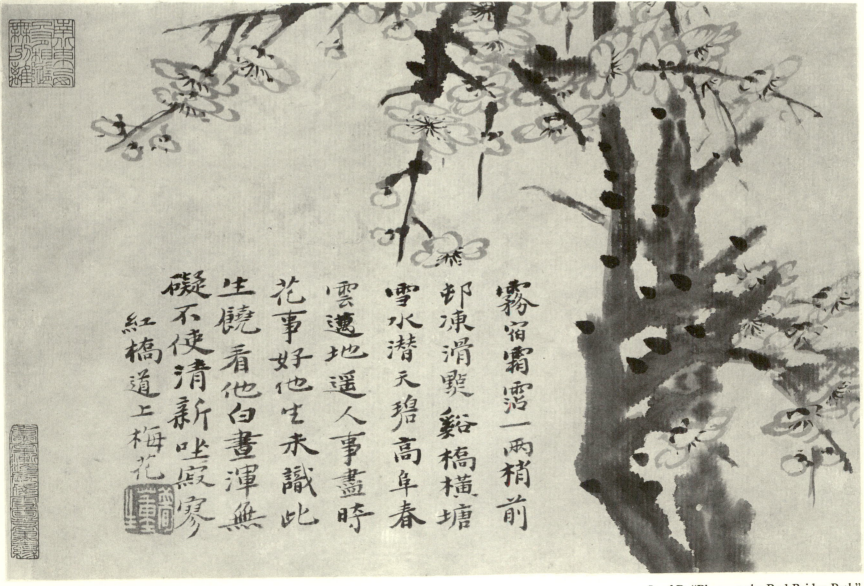

霧宿霏霏一兩梢前
邨凍滑凝谿橋橫塘
雪水潛天碧高阜春
雲邊地遙人事畫時
花事好他生未識此
生饒看他白畫渾無
礙不使清新坐寂寥
紅橋道上梅花

Leaf B, "Plum on the Red Bridge Path"

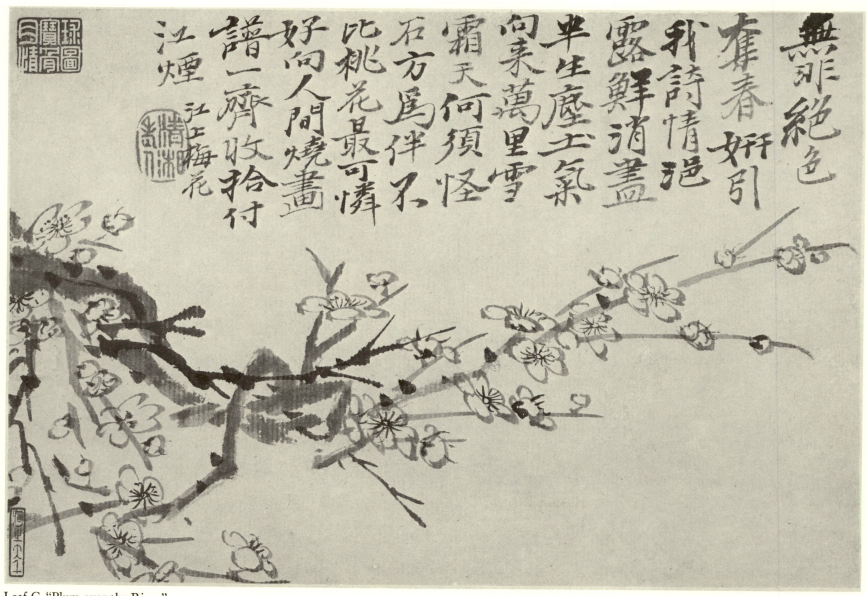

Leaf C, "Plum over the River"

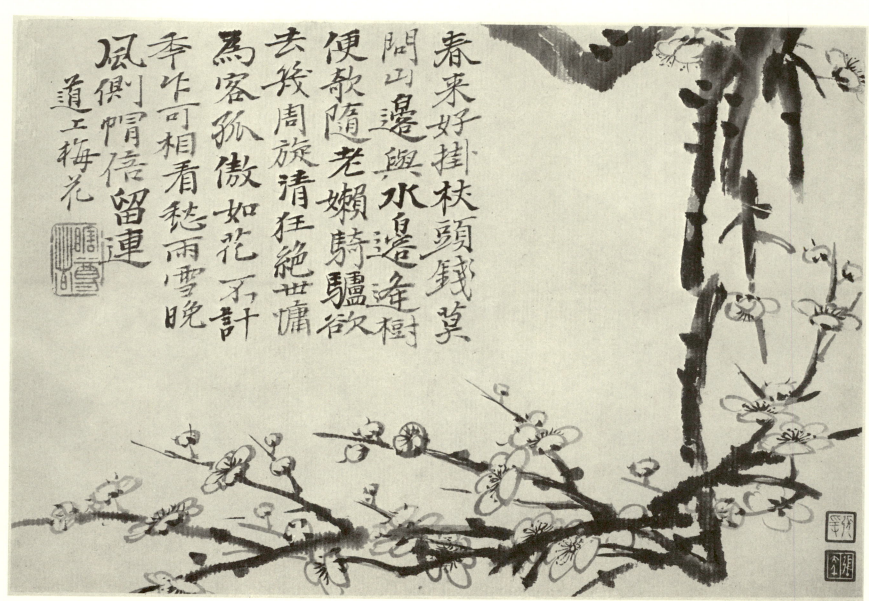

Leaf D, "Plum on the Pathway"

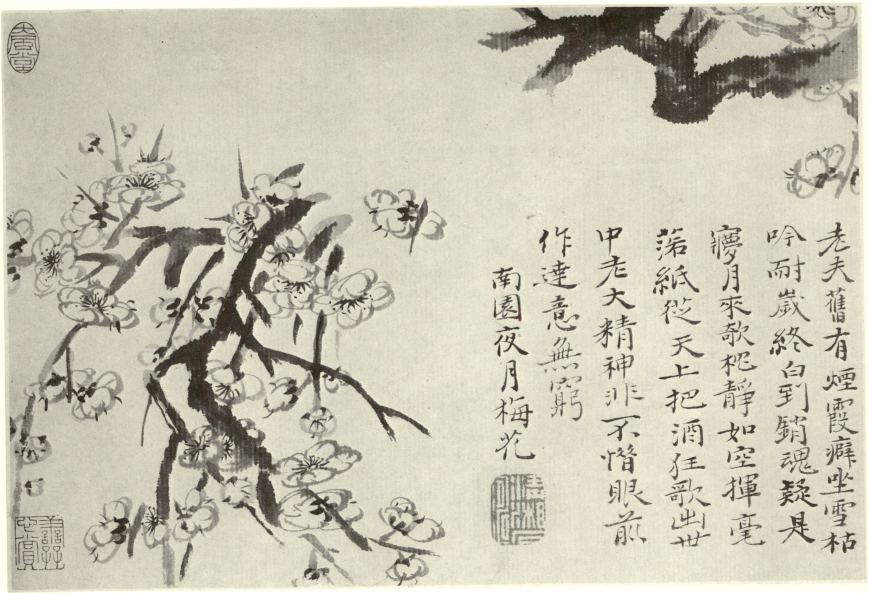

老夫舊有煙霞癖坐雪枯
吟耐歲終白到銷魂疑是
瘦月來欺枇靜如空揮毫
落紙從天上把酒狂歌出世
中老大精神非不惜眼前
作達意無窮
南園夜月梅花

Leaf E, "Moonlit Plum in the Southern Garden"

拱雲立水撐巖緊出色如非此世春幹老魁梧青玉裂香開飛幻
冒雪花新彩疑絕塞逵才子忽詩泥塗見雄神竟日抽思難畫
寫天教是牧鬪詩人
山中梅花

Leaf F, "Plum in the Mountains"

看花有底忙與花枝較短長人
盡愛花之易老花如愛我亦何妨
青山對酒春無恙白雲當風禹不翔
縱把奇思寄天上悅如仙子鶩
友人書齋梅花扶桑白子鶩

Leaf G, "Plum by the Studio of a Friend"

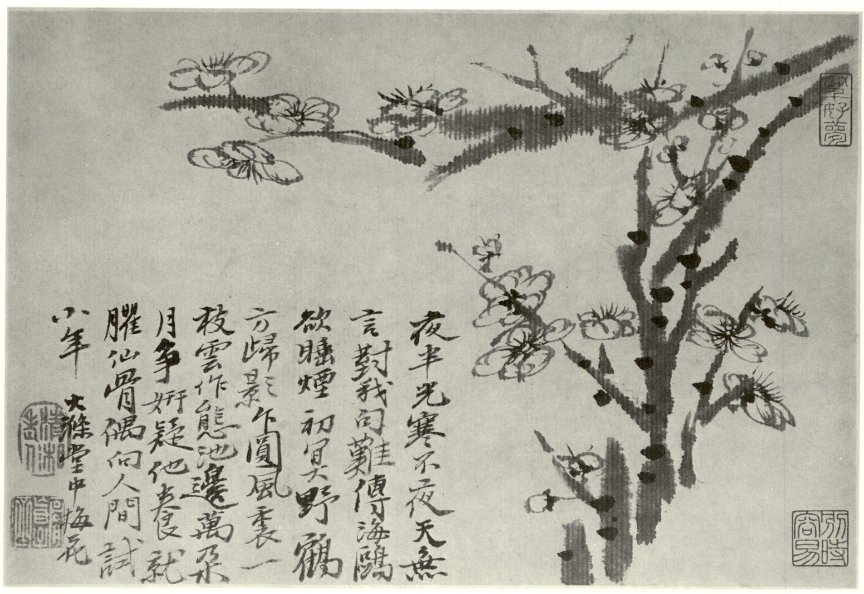

八年大雞聖中梅花
朧仙骨偶伺人間試
月爭妍疑他卷就
枝雲作態池邊萬朵
方歸景午圓風裏一
欲瞋煙初冥大野鶴
言對我向難傳海鶴
夜半光寒不夜天無

Leaf H, "Plum from Ta-ti-t'ang"

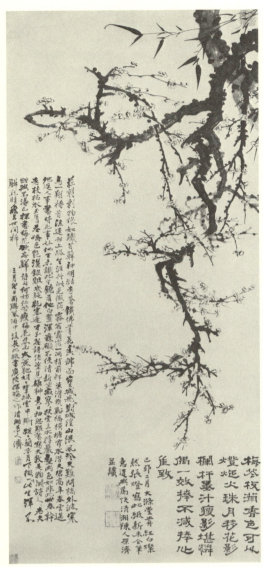

1. Tao-chi, *Plum Branch*, dated 1699. Hanging scroll. Ink on paper. Collection unknown.

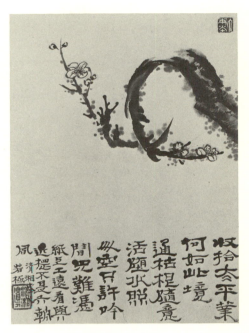

2. Tao-chi, *Ting-ch'iu Album of Flowers*, dated 1707, leaf B, "Plum Branch." Ink on paper. Private collection, United States.

A vigorous old stalk still produces blossoms on its almost broken branch. Tao-chi's accompanying poem, written in "small regular" script after Chung Yu, reflects the symbolic content of the image:

Seeing old plum is like seeing oldsters from the former dynasty—
But who ordered plum branches to reflect these ancients?
Reading through accounts of the Six Dynasties, there was only aloof re-
   tirement,
Now scattered at the year's end, [the cold] strengthens the spirit,
Blue sky and snow-white ground accommodate the flowers freely
   blooming;
A meandering river and hollow mountain accommodate their stretching.
I want to chant a poem facing the brilliant moon
To urge my spirit on and make it completely pure and fresh.

The death-defying tone of the poem transcends any political or temporal implications, and this same vigor is transmitted in the execution of the painting.

Strong diagonals project forward into the viewer's space in sharp foreshortening. This extension from flat to dimensional space is intensified by the wet, suffused ink play. First, a brush drenched in pale ink maps out the branches in a series of decisive strokes. With the idea set, dark ink is quickly applied to define the contours and smaller twigs; the texture of old bark is suggested where the ink bleeds into the wet parts. The rhythm of the brush is penetrating but brief, especially in the areas of the twigs, where spaces for the

blossoms must be left. These spaces are filled by energetic arcs of pale ink, which form the petals. Finally, a tree trunk in dilute ink at the far right serves as a backdrop, pushing the space backward while emphasizing the forward movement of the dark branches. A similar tonal layering of forms in space can be seen in earlier Tao-chi works, such as the 1682 dry-brush album,[7] leaves I and J of the Fong *Small Album* (see *XVIII*, fig. 3, *XVII*, fig. 7), and his *Searching for Plum Blossoms* handscroll (*XVIII*).

The downward-hanging broken branch is a motif which recurs in several of Tao-chi's works, such as the 1685 *Plum Blossoms* handscroll, the last leaf of the *1700 Peking Album*,[8] and leaf B of the 1707 *Ting-ch'iu Album of Flowers* (fig. 2). The 1707 album exhibits an economy of line, directness of expression, and unhindered blending of ink tones comparable to that found here.

Leaf B: *"Plum on the Red Bridge Path"* *(Hung-ch'iao tao-shang mei-hua)*

COLLECTOR'S SEALS: *Nan-pei-tung-hsi chih-yu hsiang-sui wu-pieh-li* (relief, square), *Ta-feng-t'ang Chien-chiang K'un-ts'an, Hsüeh-ko, K'u-kua mo-yüan* (relief, tall rectangle).

Two sinewy old trunks rising with vertical energy are counterbalanced by crisp young twigs projecting downward from the edge of the frame. The power of this composition lies in the twin shafts with their rich gray ink fused like a steel alloy. Their verticality accommodates the frame, while the diagonals—especially the twigs cut off at the top—resist it, and thereby accentuate the idea of framed pictorial space.

The blossoms are again of the pale, single-petaled variety, and the calligraphy repeats the restrained Chung Yu style of leaf A. Plump moss dots in darkest ink spark the branches.

Leaf C: *"Plum over the River"* *(Chiang-shang mei-hua)*

COLLECTOR'S SEALS: *Chiu-t'u-pao ku-jou-ch'ing* (intaglio, rectangle), *Ts'ang-chih Ta-ch'ien* (relief, tall narrow rectangle).

The horizontal tension of this leaf captures the idea of a branch of riverside plum found in the title. Bending low, it seems to tease its reflection on the surface of the water. The image is reminiscent of the intimate Southern Sung renderings.[9] Mirroring this coquetry is a directness in the brushwork surpassing that of the other leaves. The ink is drier and the tones more unified; this release of energy has not proceeded without some loss of clarity, however, as in the smaller branches on the far left, which are conceived rather loosely. The calligraphy is in the Ni Tsan style. A certain broadness in the structure of each character, coupled with occasional blots and tonal changes in the ink, complement the extroverted tone of this leaf.

Leaf D: *"Plum on the Pathway"* (*Tao-shang mei-hua*)

COLLECTOR'S SEALS: *Chang Yüan* (relief, small square), *Chang Ta-ch'ien* (intaglio, small square).

This design stresses simple rectangularity and repeats the shape of the frame, while combining the basic schemata of the three preceding themes in sublimated form. The verticality of leaf B, the horizontality of leaf C, and the bending, "broken" brushwork of leaf A are synthesized from the preceding movements by the bold counterforce of the perpendiculars. This synthesis offers the transmuted forms to our visual memory. The grays and blacks of the ink are more closely modulated than in previous leaves, and moss dots are again present but are closer in tone to the twigs; hence all the elements are subordinated to the direct impact of the abrupt angle of the branch. A similar composition is found in leaf D of the *Ting-ch'iu Album of Flowers* (fig. 3), where the same intense ink tonality is stressed.

Leaf E: *"Moonlit Plum in the Southern Garden"* (*Nan-yüan yeh-yüeh mei-hua*)

COLLECTORS' SEALS:
Chang Ta-ch'ien, *Ta-feng-t'ang* (relief, oval).
Chang Shan-tzu, *Shan-tzu hsin-shang* (relief, square).

The poem reads:
I have always had a weakness for mist and sunset clouds,
I wait in the snow deliberately chanting and holding out till the year's end.

The blossom's whiteness dissolves my soul—could it be a dream?
The moonlight creeps across my pillow—tranquil as nothingness.
Flourishing my brush in the air onto paper,
I grasp my wine cup and sing wildly out of this world!
It's not that I don't cherish the spirit of old age
But if I could indulge myself once in a while, my feelings would be limitless.

A branch in predominantly black ink slants diagonally forward into the viewer's space. The downward progression of the stalk from the upper right is interrupted by an empty section of paper. Is it a band of mist, or a ray of reflected moonlight? The poem gives no specific clue, but on one of Tao-chi's paintings there is an inscription written by another artist well acquainted with his work which may offer some insight (fig. 4). In this painting, the inscriber says, "The top of the man's head and the top of the boat awning have not been painted in, yet the brilliance from the moon and water can be perceived quite naturally. . . . The last two days of Double-Nine [*chia-wu*, 1954], the hermit [Chang] Ta-ch'ien recorded."[10] The power of Tao-chi's brush is even better illustrated in the depiction of the plum, for although the brushlines are quite distinctly broken, the continuous tension of the branch is clearly felt.

This evening plum has bloomed in double-petaled flowers, fat and fluffy. The linework in the petals is casually done, but it still captures the animated spirit of the branches and flower. The script combines the restraint of the Chung Yu style with the refinement of the Ni Tsan mode.

Leaf F: *"Plum in the Mountains"* (*Shan-chung mei-hua*)

COLLECTOR'S SEALS: *Shan-tzu shen-ting* (relief, small square).

The simplicity and elegance of this leaf are refreshing. Only tender young branches appear; none are old or gnarled. The growth is straight and planar, fanning outward with a single counter-movement in a slender branch. It is the only leaf to stress the visual over the literary; the spray of plum dominates the pictorial space, with the poem relegated to the far left in three lines of dilute ink.

3 (*left*). Tao-chi, *Ting-ch'iu Album of Flowers*, leaf D, "Peach Branch." Ink on paper. Private collection, United States. 4 (*right*). Tao-chi, *Graded-Ink Album of Landscapes*, dated 1695, leaf K, "Sailing Alone under a Cold Moon." Album of ten leaves, inscription on mounting by Chang Ta-ch'ien. Ink on paper. Ta-feng-t'ang collection.

The composition is the most ordinary of the group; Tao-chi's splendid ink fusions have been subdued, and there are no unusual contortions of the branches. By virtue of its commonness, this leaf quietly offsets the richness of the preceding and following compositions.

Leaf G: *"Plum by the Studio of a Friend"* (*Yu-jen shu-chai mei-hua*)

COLLECTOR'S SEALS: *Chang Yüan* (intaglio, small square), *Ta-ch'ien* (relief, small square).

The poem:

There's a limit to just looking at flowers, so I busy myself with them,
Each day I measure the growth of their branches.
Though everyone loves flowers, they grow old quickly;
[But if] the flowers love me, why should I object?
Near the blue mountain facing wine, spring still prevails;
The white snow withstands the wind and the birds don't soar.
I'd like to thrust my fantasies high into the sky
Just like the immortals riding [Time's sun-chariot of the] divine fu-sang tree.

The poem expresses a yearning and restlessness which are graphically presented in the image. Branches surge wildly in all directions across the surface of the paper. They burst beyond the confines of the rectangular frame and defy the viewer to trace their origin and direction of growth. The frenzied brush attacks the paper with an energy which infuses the smallest twig.

There is a formidable beauty in this leaf, which is the most "abstract" of the group, and in this expression Tao-chi was truly ahead of his time. Cheng Hsieh was much influenced by Tao-chi's bamboo paintings and described his working method in this way: "When Tao-chi painted bamboo, he preferred a field strategy [*yeh-chan*]; on the surface [the paintings seem] to lack laws and discipline [*chi-lü*], but, on the contrary, laws and discipline are inherent in them." [11]

This description of Tao-chi's unorthodox approach is equally applicable to his attitude toward plum painting (see *XVIII* for his own description of his method). His 1699 hanging scroll (fig. 1), which also bears two of the poems in this album, represents an expansion in larger format of the expression found in this leaf. This angular and jagged aspect of Tao-chi's brushwork seems to have been the one adopted in bamboo and orchid paintings by Cheng Hsieh (see Part IV, fig. 17) and in plum painting by Li Fang-ying.

Leaf H: *"Plum from Ta-ti-t'ang"* (*Ta-ti-t'ang-chung mei-hua*)

COLLECTOR'S SEALS: *Ta-ch'ien hao-meng* (relief, tall rectangle), *Pieh-shih jung-i* (relief, square).

Tao-chi's use of two seals and the title of the plum from his own studio, Ta-ti-t'ang, indicates that this is the last leaf. The poem, written in his free "regular" style, reads:

In the deep of night, brilliant cold doesn't darken the sky.
With [the plum flowers having] nothing to say to me, composing verses is hard.
The seagulls want sleep, as the mists begin to thicken,
The wild cranes have come home, as the shadows grow unexpectedly round.
In the wind one branch bears blossoms shaped like clouds,
Beside the pond ten thousand beauties compete with the moon.
It may be that they're taking the immortal's slimming diet,
Trying out, for once, the ordinary mortal's short-lived world.

A major horizontal and several truncated verticals compose this leaf. The ink tone is uniform: even the double-petaled blossoms are circled in the same value; only sepals, stamens, and moss dots are in velvety black. Despite the limited tone, however, there is a sense of motion in the design. The drama is focused strongly on branch design: each branch is drawn in a single decisive stroke, each longer than the other, so that the linear momentum builds up to a visual crescendo which cadences in the horizontal thrust dropping from the upper right corner. This spatial device of staggering the twigs recapitulates the foreshortened structure of leaf A and acts as a dramatic coda to the whole album. The most economical of the eight leaves, there is not a repetitious or dilatory stroke. While it ostensibly resembles leaf D, the expression is more refined and immaculate.

THE LATE SEAL on leaf G, *Tsan-chih shih-shih-sun, A-ch'ang*, is a good indication of the date of execution, and it can be found on dated works which range from 1701 to 1707; [12] the style of the album seems closer to the latter half of that range. Calligraphy and painting reveal later traits than such works as the 1703 twelve-leaf *Album of Landscapes for Liu Shih-t'ou* or the Boston *Twelve-Leaf Album of Landscapes*, dated the same year. At the end of this range, the two albums dated 1707, the *Ting-ch'iu Album of Flowers* and the Sackler *Reminiscences of Nanking*, compare favorably in style of calligraphy, painting, and format of the inscriptions. The calligraphic style, whether in the Chung Yu or Ni Tsan manner, is blunt and direct, with a perceptible lapse in the tensile vigor found in earlier works of the 1690's at the height of Tao-chi's energies. Several leaves from the *Ting-ch'iu Album* are close parallels in composition, drenched washes, and expressive inkblots, but the physical vitality seems slightly richer in this album, and we believe it to be a few years earlier. We therefore postulate about 1705 as the date of execution.

NOTES

1. For sources of intellectual attitudes in the Sung and Yüan, see Wai-kam Ho, "The Three Religions and the 'Three Friends,'" in Sherman Lee, ed., *Chinese Art under the Mongols*, pp. 96–112; also Susan Bush, "Subject Matter in the Scholarly Tradition," *The Chinese Literati on Painting* (Cambridge, 1971), pp. 97ff., 139–45. Shūjirō Shimada's "Kakō Chūnin no jo," *Hōun*, vol. 25, pp. 21–34, vol. 30, pp. 50–68; and "The Sung-chai mei-p'u," *Bunka*, vol. 20 (1956), pp. 96–118, are important inquiries into the origin of ink plum painting and its attendant issues. For literary associations attached to plum blossoms, see Hans Frankel, "The Plum Tree in Chinese Poetry," *Asiatische Studien*, vol. 6 (1952), pp. 88–115.
2. He is known to have painted a sixteen-leaf album for his pupil Hung Cheng-chih (see *XXXII*) (as recorded in Pang Yüan-chi, *Hsü-chai ming-hua-lu*, 15/17a–b); Ferguson, Sirén, and Laing do not record this or any other plum album in their lists.
3. The idea of the painter's "edge-consciousness" was sensitively pointed out by Harvey Stuppler in a graduate seminar at Princeton University in 1971.
4. We are indebted to Mr. and Mrs. T'ang Hai-t'ao for their help in the interpretation and rendering of the poems. We have tended to underestimate the possible implications of Ming loyalism and Tao-chi's imperial heritage, which surfaced in his late years. For further discussion of this point, see Marilyn Fu and Wen Fong, *The Wilderness Colors of Tao-chi*.
5. Cf. *Shih-t'ao hua-chi*, pl. 63; *Tao-chi hua-ts'e*, leaf L.
6. For a fine sampling of these masters' works, see James Cahill, ed., *Fantastics and Eccentrics in Chinese Painting*, pls. 34–38.
7. See *Ta-feng-t'ang ming-chi*, vol. 2, no. 28 (leaf I), ink on paper.
8. See *Tao-chi hua-ts'e*; it is an album of ten landscape leaves and two flower leaves. There are several of this type in ink and color on silk in the National Palace Museum, Taipei, by the Southern Sung painters Ma Yüan and Ma Lin. See two leaves illustrated in Chiang Chao-shen, "The Identity of Yang Mei-tzu and the Paintings of Ma Yüan," figs. 4–5.
10. *Ta-feng-t'ang ming-chi*, vol. 2, no. 33 (leaf K).
11. *Pan-ch'iao t'i-pa*, p. 128.
12. See PTC, p. 69.

XXXIV TAO-CHI (1641–ca. 1710)

Reminiscences of Nanking (*Chin-ling huai-ku ts'e*)

The Art Museum, Princeton University (L14.67).

Album of twelve leaves. Ink and color, six leaves; ink, six leaves; all twelve leaves executed on unsized buff paper of rough texture. 23.8 x 19.2 cm.

DATED: September 10, 1707 (*ting-hai chung-ch'iu*) on leaf J.

SIGNATURE OF THE ARTIST: on each leaf following a poetic inscription.

SEALS OF THE ARTIST:
Pan-ko-han (intaglio, tall rectangle; *PTC*, cat. no. 56) leaves A and B.
Ta-ti-tzu (relief, square; *PTC*, cat. no. 86) leaves A, D, E, and H.
Ta-pen-t'ang, Chi (intaglio, tall rectangle; *PTC*, cat. no. 82) leaves C, G, J, and L.
Ta-pen-t'ang, Jo-chi (intaglio, square; *PTC*, cat. no. 83) leaves D and K.
Ch'ing-hsiang Shih-t'ao (intaglio, tall rectangle; *PTC*, cat. no. 22) leaf F.
Ch'ing-hsiang lao-jen (relief, oval; *PTC*, cat. no. 18) leaf I.
Yüeh-shan (intaglio, square; *PTC*, cat. no. 108) leaves J and L.

COLLECTOR'S SEALS: Chang Ta-ch'ien (Yüan, born 1899) on each leaf, totaling seventeen seals.

COLOPHON: by previous owner, Yen Shih-ch'ing (*hao* P'iao-sou, ca. 1870–after 1922), on separate leaf, dated 1914.

CONDITION: good.

PROVENANCE: Ta-feng-t'ang collection.

PUBLISHED: *PTC*, cat. no. 47, pp. 44 (fig. 19, leaf L illustrated), 94; *The Selected Painting and Calligraphy of Shih-t'ao*, vol. 4, pl. 95 (illustrated); Richard M. Barnhart, *Wintry Forests, Old Trees*, cat. no. 22, p. 63 (leaf K illustrated).

THIS ALBUM REPRESENTS the latest dated landscapes by Tao-chi known to us. One senses in each leaf how the man has aged. The brushwork and forms are simplified, the colors reduced to primary hues. The brushtip he prefers is now the blunted and the worn-out, and the line it draws suggests the multidimensional possibilities of a stone carver's chisel. The coarse texture of the paper resists the brush and creates biting but pleasing tactile effects with the ink and colored washes. In both the calligraphy and painting, the fresh lyricism of such early works as *The Echo* has ripened to a pungency which extends beyond the abrupt lines of the images. One savors here not the polished skill of youth but the artless simplicity and reduced essence of expression which characterize Tao-chi's style in his old age. The simplicity of expression is part of the greater unity of pictorial impact which he sought in his latest years.

The twelve leaves offer an extraordinary inventory of landscape subjects and styles. His subjects are reinterpretations of recurring themes of an often autobiographical nature—portraits of his studio, the traveler riding on horseback or walking with his staff, the ancient tree surviving the passage of time. As for style, we see how his self-imposed limitation in the use of ink and line—such as leaves in which mainly line are used, or mainly wash, or predominantly round or slanted brushwork, and so forth—enhances the descriptive power of each theme.

The album has been traditionally known as *Views of Chin-ling* (Chin-ling being an alternative, more ancient name for Nanking), but the place of execution was undoubtedly Yang-chou, where Tao-chi had long since taken up residence. The majority of the scenes depicted can be identified as actual sites near and in Nanking. Thus

these leaves assume the form of reminiscences (*huai-ku*), or idealized projections of sites lived in and visited in the past. In addition, this album is the latest in a sequence of works which almost form a separate genre—the recording of actual scenery through memory. The Sumitomo *Eight Views of Huang-shan* album and the 1699 *Huang-shan* handscroll may be considered of this type, as may the Cleveland *Reminiscences of Ch'in-huai* and the British Museum's *Eight Views of the South*. Tao-chi's choice of nature and natural landscape (rather than the styles of the ancients) as his subject matter prompted him to turn to his memories of landscape from his actual wanderings. Moreover, the scenery of Yang-chou, the residence of his last years, seems to have been of little interest to him, so that he drew upon the inner riches of his imaginative experience.

The calligraphy found on these leaves is almost always in the Chung Yu style, with the exception of leaves H and K, two portraits of old trees which bear inscriptions in his Ni Tsan style. The small, blunt style of Chung Yu seems best suited to his temperament in old age, for it lacks all traces of ostentation. Thus the leaves in the Ni Tsan style, especially leaf K, mark an unusual appearance of his earlier preference. In each leaf Tao-chi anticipated the addition of a long poem: he reserved space for the inscription as a square block or a tall column to offset the painting and to incorporate it as part of the total composition. This is an early habit of his which he developed with sensitivity in his late works.

Leaf A: "The One-Branch Studio" (I-chih-ko)

Ink and color on paper.
SIGNATURE OF THE ARTIST: Ch'ing-hsiang Ta-ti-tzu, I-chih-ko men-yü (closing an inscription in eight lines).
COLLECTOR'S SEAL: Ta-ch'ien chü-shih kung-yang pai-Shih-chih-i (relief, large square) upper right corner.

A hump of mountain in vivid russet rises upward from the center of the page and looms starkly against a brilliant blue sky. We follow a path into a mountain pass cut below a tall tree guarding a walled retreat and are greeted by the host, who contemplates our ascent. Vivid pictorial description achieved with an economy of line is matched by the application of two hues in a direct, almost perfunctory fashion. Areas left bare to reveal the natural tone of the paper are utilized coloristically. The bottom half of the page has been left blank for a poetic inscription in five-syllable regulated meter. The mountain rises majestically from the poet's words, and the last line is followed by this signature: "Verse from the gateway of the One-Branch Studio of Ch'ing-hsiang, Ta-ti-tzu." Could the "One-Branch Studio" itself be depicted here? The storied dwelling with elevated view seems to match the description by Tao-chi's good friend, the painter Mei Ch'ing (1623–1697), who says that the studio was "a small building as high as the treetops" (*hsiao-lou ch'i-mu-ch'ao*).[1] The studio may not have been built on a hill, but the painted image may be an idealized portrait of Tao-chi's familiar retreat at the Pao-en temple in Nanking, where he spent some seven to eight years of fruitful seclusion.

Leaf B: "Cliff-Bordered Moon" (Ssu-pi k'uei-yüeh)

Ink on paper.
SIGNATURE OF THE ARTIST: Chih-hsia tz'u yu-jen, Ta-ti-tzu (after a poem in ten lines).
COLLECTOR'S SEAL: Ta-ch'ien (relief, square) lower left corner.

Steep cliffs border the path leading to a retreat. Pictorially, the composition is dense and its space tightly structured. Boulders in the foreground form an effective repoussoir to suggest a sense of depth in the middle ground. In this middle depth one stark black tree

清趣初消受寒
宵月彌圓一頁起
到骨太叔敢招憲
句冷蕭煙火腸枯
斷菜根何人知此
意欲嘆且觀吞清
湘大滌子一枝開門
語

Leaf A, "The One-Branch Studio" (*actual size*)

Leaf B, "Cliff-Bordered Moon"

Leaf C, "Walking to East Mountain"

Leaf D, "Sightseeing at Ts'ung-hsiao"

Leaf E, "Washing the Inkstone"

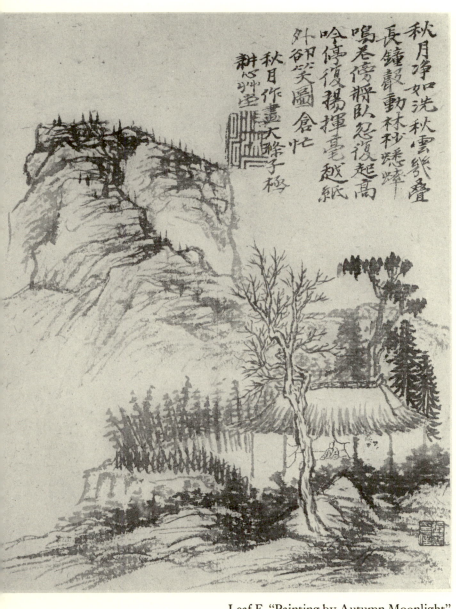

秋月淨如洗秋雲縈疊
長鐘聲動林秋猱峰
喝老傍橋臥忽復起高
吟倚復揚揮毫越紙
外卻笑圖倉忙
秋月作畫大滌子極
耕心草堂

Leaf F, "Painting by Autumn Moonlight"

山南山北延癡聾
買醉春風有甚堪
無計送春已亦遠尚
憑消息忽輕談
江城閣上送春作畫之
一清湘老人極

Leaf G, "Farewell to Spring"

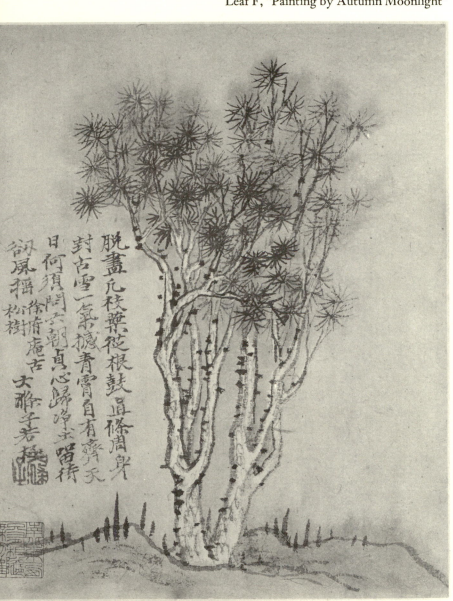

脫盡凡秩藥莜根鼓直條聳
對古雪一氣撼青霄自有齊天
日何須問本朝真心歸淳真唱紆
谽谺搖拂松樹古
徐府庵古
大滌子老人極

Leaf H, "Ancient Pine at Hsü-fu"

四袖荷衣着看短
裳拖筇竹屐屐到
橫嶺湖頭嫩
子迴青嶂山下
人家畫名陽孤
雁南來悲况遠
陳鐘初覺韻
轂長此時不用
通名姓逢着
黃昏醉晚香
歡興九首之二
指來作畫大
滌子極耕心草堂

Leaf I, "Autumn Meditation"

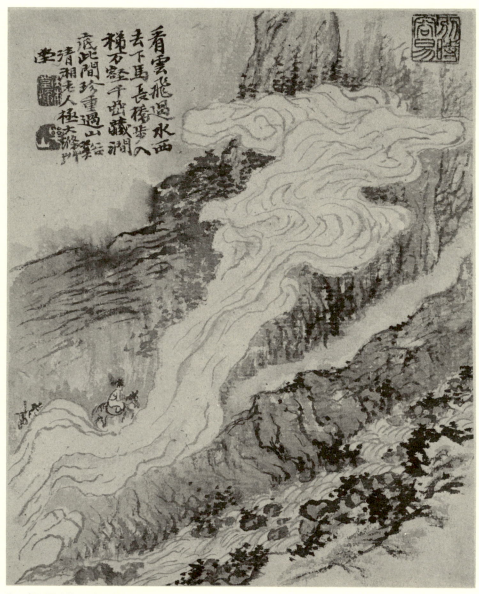

看雲飛過水西
去下馬長橋入
橫万徑千嚴藏澗
底此間珍重遇山靈
清湘老人極大滌卭

Leaf J, "Riding the Clouds"

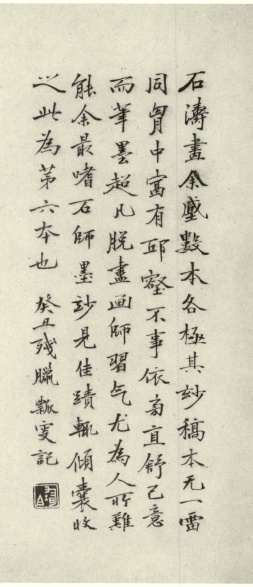

石濤畫余藏數本各極其玅稿本无一雷
同貿中富有邱壑不事依旁宜舒己意
而筆墨超凡脫盡畫師習气尤為人所難
能余最嗜石師墨玅見佳蹟輒傾囊收
之此為第六本也 癸丑殘臘瓣香愛記

Leaf M, colophon by Yen Shih-ch'ing.

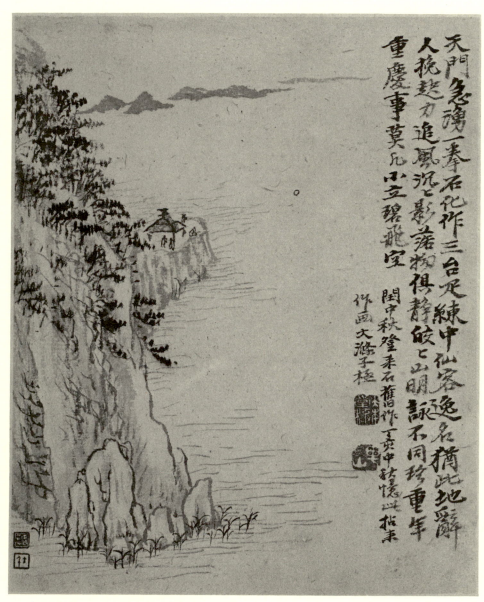

天門急湧一奉石化作三台足踏練中仙客逸名摘此地辟
人挽趢刀追風沉已影丕莽物俱靜彼己山明詠不同珍重年
重慶事莫見小立碧飛寔
閩中秋登朱石舊旧作丁亥中秋憶此松未
作画大滌子極

Leaf L, "Climbing Ts'ai-shih in Mid-Autumn"

六朝雷火樹鍛煉至
扵今兩趐孤孺山雙
分破臂琴挿天神
護力捧日露沾襟偶
向座心處撇頂間
上音杏桐

Leaf K, "Old Gingko at Mt. Ch'ing-lung" (*actual size*)

guards the gateway to the cottage. Within the wall thickets of bamboo flourish on each side. In the distance mountains enclose the cottage like a screen, and in the foreground the jutting rocks fortify the path. This secluded spot is untouched by the bustle and noise of the mortal world. Could this be another idealized portrayal of his "One-Branch Studio"? The poem reads:

> Between cliffs on all sides the moon peeks,
> The walls torn by branches of ancient trees.
> The wine-lover urges his brush on,
> The poet laments the late arrival of a letter....
>   Harmonizing to the verse of a friend,
>   Ta-ti-tzu, beneath the "Branch."

Heavy, abbreviated strokes outline the forms. Little wash is used; volume is achieved by a dry brush rubbed and dragged across the grainy paper. The paper's full absorbency can be seen in the calligraphy, where the ink bleeds, and in the right section of the mountains, where the ink dots form grainy blots. These effects are characteristic of Tao-chi's late style and appear in varying degrees of "blotchiness" according to the kind of paper chosen.[2]

This scene was one of Tao-chi's favorite subjects and may well represent an actual locale. The walled retreat guarded by a single tall tree reappears in different brush manners and slightly different compositions in the 1703 *Album for Liu Shih-t'ou*, leaf G (fig. 1),[3] and in the British Museum's *Eight Views of the South*, leaf F.[4]

Leaf C: "*Walking to East Mountain*" (*Tu-pu Tung-shan*)

Ink and color on paper.
SIGNATURE OF THE ARTIST: Ta-ti-tzu, Chi.
COLLECTOR'S SEALS: *Chang Yüan* (intaglio, square), *Ta-ch'ien* (relief, square), both lower right corner.

Poetry and painting again complement each other in every narrative detail:

> Not caring how far the secluded path takes me,
> I walk alone to East Mountain.
> Asking where the road across the autumn waters leads
> I pass through the clouds and ferry the bamboo pass.
>
> A big bridge looms across the wayside banks,
> Tall willows bend over the winding stream.
> Coming upon the distant rising peak,
> I say to myself, "I ought to settle down in this place."
>   Visiting East Mountain alone,
>   Ta-ti-tzu, Chi.

Chanting this ballad is the tiny figure with his staff—is it Tao-chi himself? He has passed through the sighing willows and is about to mount the arched bridge. East Mountain dominates the horizon, but an intimate sense of scale is achieved through the intuitively graduated size of trees, houses, boats, and figure. The whole composition seems rather ordinary, and it is just this seeming lack of effort which conveys the natural and unassertive expression of the picture.

After viewing the preceding monochrome leaf, we are struck by the riot of colors here—blues, siennas, browns, yellows, and greens—all nonchalantly smudged together. But Tao-chi's colors function structurally, and the impression of nonchalance is fundamentally that freedom gained only from complete mastery. Along with the direct energy of his brush, Tao-chi's use of color seems to have caught the spirit of the French *fauves*.

This leaf bears the same poem as the British Museum's *Eight Views of the South*, leaf A, which records a similar scene in a softer and more subdued manner,[5] but the composition and execution of the Sackler leaf are closer to the 1703 *Album for Liu Shih-t'ou*, leaf J (fig. 2).

1. Tao-chi, *Album of Landscapes for Liu Shih-t'ou*, dated 1703, leaf G. Album of twelve leaves. Ink and color on paper. Ex-Okabe Chokei collection, Tokyo.

2. Tao-chi, *Album of Landscapes for Liu Shih-t'ou*, leaf J. Ink and color on paper. Ex-Okabe Chokei collection.

Leaf D: "Sightseeing at Ts'ung-hsiao" (Yu Ts'ung-hsiao)

Ink on paper.
SIGNATURE OF THE ARTIST: Ta-ti-tzu (following inscription in three lines).
COLLECTOR'S SEALS: Chang Ta-ch'ien chih-yin (intaglio, square), Ta-ch'ien chü-shih (relief, square).

A broad view high over the waters of a lake overlooks a foreground cliff, which rises uninterrupted along the edge of the paper and stops short at a stretch of distant mountains. Two boats are placed at complementary angles on a slant, and, combined with the lightly indicated streaks of wash, give the feeling of water surface and receding depth. By maintaining a consistently reduced scale and confining description to the borders of the page in a continuous horizontal and vertical progression, Tao-chi has created an expansive and breathtaking vista. The opening words of the poem contribute yet another dimension to the scene, an aural one:

With cock's crow and the moon not yet gone down,
The sound of the temple bell drifts over the crisp, clear waters.
We formed a group to go sightseeing around Ts'ung-hsiao
And asked the boatman whether he could take us on a tour of the autumn waters....

The crenelated wall, the cluster of houses and trees, and the pagoda on the promontory identify the site as Nanking. The idea of limiting the landscape forms to the edge of the picture plane is unusual, but Tao-chi attempted it once before in a less daring manner in his 1701 Landscape Album, leaf G (XXVI). A slanted brush in gently twisting lines and cloudy, fused patches of wash add to the visual richness of this leaf.

Leaf E: "Washing the Inkstone" (Lin-hsi hsi-yen)

Ink and color on paper.
SIGNATURE OF THE ARTIST: Ch'ing-hsiang Ta-ti-tzu, Chi (after a four-line poem).
COLLECTOR'S SEAL: Chang Chi-tzu (relief, square), lower left corner.

Two small figures animate the scene. A scholar in a blue robe sits by the side of a stream and watches as his companion washes an inkstone:

Washing the inkstone and bending over the stream,
Now and then a slice of cloud drifts past.
Some fragrant tea to give you—
Beside that, what else can I offer?
By dawn there'll be thoughts of each other,
[Separated by] thousands of miles of rivers and towns.

In this leaf, colors of tapestry-like radiance are united with brushwork even stubbier than seen previously. The expressive power of the round, dimensional strokes is direct and unpremeditated and gives a satisfying tactile feeling of biting contact with the paper. The rough-textured paper, which tended to detract from the effect of smooth washes in the first leaf, here enhances the brush conception. Paper left blank between areas of color wash is again used to suggest fluffy clouds around the tops of the peaks and the foot of the mountains, and it contrasts vividly with the saturated colors, especially the deep blue mountain in the distance. The gangling pines have teeth-like foliage, another trademark of Tao-chi's hand, seen in such works as the Eight Views of Huang-shan album (cf. XXVI, figs. 1, 10).
A path which leads diagonally up the picture plane to distant mountains and focuses telescopically on figures was also a favorite composition of Tao-chi; see, for example, leaf F of the Sumitomo album depicting the scenery of Huang-shan,[6] leaf C of the 1701 Album of Landscapes (XXVI), or leaf G of the Osaka Sketches after Su Tung-p'o's Poems (cf. XXVI, fig. 13).

Leaf F: "Painting by Autumn Moonlight" (Ch'iu-yüeh tso-hua)

Ink on paper.
SIGNATURE OF THE ARTIST: Ta-ti-tzu, Chi (as part of a seven-line inscription).
COLLECTOR'S SEAL: Chang Yüan yin-hsin (intaglio, square).

Inside a thatched hut a scholar sits at his desk. Tao-chi's poem describes the scene:

The autumn moon, so clear it looks washed;
The autumn clouds, countless layers long.
A temple bell resounds through forest thickets;
Crickets chirp among the flowers.

I was about to retire, but jumped up all of a sudden—
Singing spiritedly on and off and high and low.
As I push this painting brush around, it leaps outside the paper
And makes me laugh at these funny hasty pictures.
                    Painted under the autumn moon by
                    Ta-ti-tzu, Chi, at Keng-hsin-ts'ao-t'ang
                    ["Thatched Hut of Cultivating the Heart"].

The "Thatched Hut of Cultivating the Heart" was a studio name Tao-chi used on occasion in works of the 1700's.[7] The cottage here, again guarded by a lone tree, may be a portrait of that Yang-chou abode.
The artist has employed two distinctly different brush manners in this leaf, a round, blunt line delineating the cottage and trees and an oblique stroke modeling the rocks and ground. This latter method produces sharp, flat strokes and was frequently used by Ni Tsan. Tao-chi may indeed be drawing an extended allusion to the Yüan master in both the brushwork and the compositional elements of rock formations, thatched hut, and sparse tree. Technically, the ink tonalities have been modulated with such success that broad areas of wash (usually used to unify the different parts of the composition) not only are unnecessary but have been deliberately avoided. Tao-chi has also left the top of the hut blank, suggesting the reflected bright white light of the moon.[8]

Leaf G: "Farewell to Spring" (Chiang-ch'eng-ko-shang sung-ch'un)

Ink and color on paper.
SIGNATURE OF THE ARTIST: Ch'ing-hsiang lao-jen, Chi (after a five-line inscription).
COLLECTOR'S SEALS: Chang Yüan (intaglio, square), Ta-ch'ien shu (relief, square).

This leaf is striking not only for the same forthright and rounded "seal-style" brushlines used elsewhere in this album but also for the compact construction of the elements. Two oblique triangular forms jutting from the foreground intersect horizontal and vertical shapes to create layers and pockets of deep space. The eye follows the foreground boulder and rises with the intensity of the sienna, green, and yellow hues until it reaches the foremost thrust stained in blue; then the space drops precipitously to two covered boats. A picturesque arched bridge with tile-roofed pavilion breaks the depth of the cliffs. Further engaging the viewer's eye are the patterned touches of water reeds and waves. These gossamer lines contrast sharply with the other blunt contours and attest to Tao-chi's continuing but rarely exhibited ability to execute fine linework in his old age.
The inscription at the end of the poem reads: "One of the paintings done atop the Chiang-ch'eng pavilion saying farewell to spring." Again two tiny figures lend a sense of scale and human identity to the work. The blown reeds are the last remnants of spring and seem almost overwhelmed by the intensity of the oncoming summer colors.

3. Tao-chi, *Album of Landscapes for Liu Shih-t'ou*, leaf D. Ink and color on paper. Ex-Okabe Chokei collection.

4. Tao-chi, *Man Walking toward a Mountain*, dated 1703, detail. Hanging scroll. Ink on paper. Museum of Fine Arts, Boston.

Although the composition differs, Tao-chi conveys a similar mood in leaf D from the 1703 *Album for Liu Shih-t'ou* (fig. 3). The view is closer and the cliffs even steeper; the water reeds have grown more profusely, as have the foliage and trees, which seem to be bursting with the lushness of early summer.

Leaf H: *"Ancient Pine at Hsü-fu"* (Hsü-fu-an ku-sung)

Ink on paper.
SIGNATURE OF THE ARTIST: Ta-ti-tzu, Jo-chi (after a four-line inscription).
COLLECTOR'S SEAL: *Nan-pei-tung-hsi chih-yu-hsiang-sui wu-pieh-li* (relief, square).

A solitary clump of pine stands upright against the sky. The blunt-tipped brush draws penetrating and complex intertwinings of trunk and branches in sustained, undulating strokes. Pale wash applied to the sky and ground brings out the essential plasticity of the branches and foliage, creating an impression of relief sculpture. The round configuration of pine needles (like the pinwheels of his earlier "Banana Leaves and Pine" in the *Flowers and Figures* album [XX]) is drawn in graded ink with halos of wash which convey an atmospheric dimension.

Traditionally the pine symbolizes the integrity and purity of the "superior gentleman." Here there is a strong element of self-identification with its moral qualities. Tao-chi's poem in five-character meter identifies the pine as located at the Hsü-fu-an in Kiangsu. He hints at its dating from the Six Dynasties (220–589), and ends the poem by alluding to the "steadfast heart returning to the Pure Land." Hence mixed images of immortality and the Buddhist belief in salvation are contained in the lines, enhancing the symbolic meaning of the pine and its embodiment of virtues much admired by the poet-painter.

Leaf I: *"Autumn Meditation"* (Ch'iu-hsing)

Ink and color on paper.
SIGNATURE OF THE ARTIST: Ta-ti-tzu, Chi (as part of a fourteen-line inscription).
COLLECTOR'S SEALS: *Chang Yüan* (relief, square), *Ta-ch'ien* (intaglio, square).

A rotund gentleman deep in thought clutches his staff and mounts the pathway home; a lone fisherman skims the waters near the river bank. Sunlight and air in a smattering of hues drench the simply drawn forms. A sense of security and tranquillity pervades the scene.

Pictorially, the leaf is quite ordinary. The expanse of water and land, with its curving, lateral movement from left foreground to the distant mass, is reminiscent of the plainness of the "level-distance" landscapes of the Tung Yüan and Chü-jan ideals. The drawing is carefree and summary, but each detail is felicitous, from the strongly outlined peaks in the distance, the single brushline of the boat, and the firmly positioned houses, trees, and touches of bamboo to the random but vigorous moss dots. It is Tao-chi's return to the commonplace in his old age.

This leaf is a reduction in form of a more monumental and slightly earlier work, the 1703 hanging scroll in Boston, *Man Walking Toward a Mountain*[9] (fig. 4).

5. Tao-chi, *Eight-Leaf Album of Landscapes*, dated 1673, "Riding on Horseback." Album leaf. Ink on paper. Collection unknown.

6. Tao-chi, *Sketches of Calligraphy and Painting by Ch'ing-hsiang*, dated 1696, detail. Handscroll. Ink on paper. Palace Museum, Peking.

Leaf J: *"Riding the Clouds"* (*Yün-p'ang ma-t'ou sheng*)

Ink on paper.
SIGNATURE OF THE ARTIST: Ch'ing-hsiang lao-jen, Chi, Ta-ti ts'ao-t'ang (after a four-line poem).
COLLECTOR'S SEAL: *Pieh-shih-jung-i* (relief, square).

This leaf is captivating for its movement, humor, and sense of mutability. A white cloud swoops upward from the left corner with a capricious movement, like the genie from a fairy tale. All elements of the picture are laid on the diagonal to intensify movement: the right bank, the downward-rushing rapids, the path and mountain incline. Most beguiling is the rider and his horse, and behind him, almost swallowed by the cloud, a servant boy shouldering provisions. "The mountain seems to rise up from the man, and the clouds to issue from the horse." This idea and the words actually originated in a much earlier work, Tao-chi's 1673 album in eight leaves (fig. 5).

Tao-chi's clouds are unlike those of any master we have encountered. They possess the dynamic rhythm and carefree drive of the Han whorls, but beyond that, and in this leaf especially, they also seem to embody some semi-cosmic, semi-anthropomorphic, and entirely friendly force. This cloud whirls and dances, gleefully tossing its head and stretching its limbs, urging the horse and rider onward to the top. There are no colors; rather, there are auditory effects: stream bubbling, horse clip-clopping, and cloud eddying. The brushwork is almost entirely oblique; washes and dense suffusions bring out the whiteness of the cloud. The brushwork in the swirls, if compared with the clouds of Tao-chi's earlier works, shows his age; no longer fluid, it is even scratchy in places. But what matters is the total impact and the idea, the success of which is undeniable.

Leaf K: *"Old Gingko at Mt. Ch'ing-lung"* (*Ch'ing-lung-shan ku-ying-hsing*)

Ink and color on paper.
SIGNATURE OF THE ARTIST: Ta-ti-tzu (after seven-line inscription).
COLLECTOR'S SEAL: *Ta-feng-t'ang Chien-chiang, K'un-ts'an, Hsüeh-ko, K'u-kua mo-yüan* (relief, tall rectangle).

A dramatic close-up of an ancient gingko (*ying-hsing*) recalls the portrayal of the hoary pine of leaf H. According to the artist's note and poem, this gingko grows atop Mt. Ch'ing-lung ("green dragon") in Nanking. During the Six Dynasties it was maimed by a bolt of lightning but later defied death and sprouted a new growth of leaves and branches. The subject seems not without symbolic value as a statement of Tao-chi's inner spirit and his survival into the new dynasty.

The stark visual impact of the subject is modulated by the pale hues. The dominant russet tonality is given depth by the deep blue washes and the blackening of the hollow trunk. Crisp stars of bamboo accent the rocky areas, which are further enlivened by dottings of blue and yellow foliage.

Economy is the keynote in the brushwork: round, continuous, "seal-style" strokes contrast with smooth, flat washes. Volume in the rocks is suggested by dry rubbed strokes. A polychrome complement to the preceding hoary pine, this leaf may also be compared with a closing section of the hermit in the old tree trunk from the 1696 *Sketches of Calligraphy and Painting* (fig. 6). Eleven years earlier, *Sketches* is rendered in more detail and with drier brushwork, but the long, rhythmic lines of the trunk and the method of dotting foliage are marks of the same hand, and the conception of life within the hollow trunk is also a consistent visualization.

7. Tao-chi, *Eight Views of the South*, leaf H, "Ts'ai-shih." Album leaf. Ink and color on paper. Courtesy British Museum.

The calligraphy is in Tao-chi's Ni Tsan style. This is one of his finest writings of this late date. The strokes are slightly lax, but they are formed consistently and with more care than in most of his works from this period. These traits of old age lend a special flavor to the writing.

Leaf L: "Climbing Ts'ai-shih in Mid-Autumn" (*Jun-chung-ch'iu teng Ts'ai-shih*)

Ink on paper.

SIGNATURE OF THE ARTIST: Ta-ti-tzu, Chi (following three long lines of inscription).

COLLECTOR'S SEALS: *Chang Yüan* (intaglio, square), *Ta-ch'ien* (relief, square).

This leaf captures some of the delicate imagery of Tao-chi's earlier period. We see a deep and expansive view, with a cliff and flat promontory jutting out over the waters. Description is confined to the left side of the picture. A stretch of mountains, rendered in a few supple strokes of wash, issues horizontally from the left and echoes the light lateral indications of waves on the water; the upward tilt of the distant range intensifies the feeling of spaciousness. Four minute figures and a pavilion adorn the projecting rock, establishing the scale of the scene and drawing our attention to the moon's reflection swaying on the surface of the water.

The brushwork is light, more mobile than in previous leaves; the rhythm of the brush in contact with the paper is brief but penetrating. The foliage on the cliffs, for example, is done in a pointillist manner in charcoal black, a vigorous contrast to the paler washes and twisting rock textures. Reeds in fine lines border the edges of

the water. These various touches recall motifs from previous leaves and subtly indicate the inherent unity within the set.

Ts'ai-shih ("variegated stone"), a famous site in Anhwei Province, was, like Huang-shan, one of Tao-chi's favorite places. The same scene is repeated from a different angle in leaf H of his *Eight Views of the South* in the British Museum (fig. 7).[10] As he states in his inscription to the Sackler leaf (see below), he composed the poem some years earlier during the same mid-autumn season and later painted this scene to accompany it. Note that, according to the meter and rhyme, Tao-chi has omitted a character in the next to last line of the poem.

THE INSCRIPTION on leaf L, "Climbing Ts'ai-shih," offers us another clue to Tao-chi's whereabouts and chronology: "[This poem is] an old work [written on the occasion of] climbing Ts'ai-shih [Anhwei] in the mid-autumn intercalary month [October 7, 1680]. In mid-autumn of *ting-hai* [September 10, 1707] I recalled the event and made this painting. [Signed:] Ta-ti-tzu, Chi." Thus we know that before mid-autumn, or October 7, 1680, Tao-chi was still in Anhwei Province at Ts'ai-shih, Tang-t'u prefecture. This fact agrees with the information in the artist's handscroll *Searching for Plum Blossoms* (*XVIII*), dated 1685, in which he states that he was in Nanking at I-chih after October of 1680. From this we may plot his itinerary from Anhwei to Nanking in that year; the poem on leaf J may have been written in transit between Hsüan-ch'eng, Anhwei, and Nanking, Kiangsu.

Leaf C, "Walking to East Mountain," contains a reference to Tung-shan (East Mountain): "I visited East Mountain alone." There are actually two mountains by that name which Tao-chi may have visited: Ts'ai-shih, in Anhwei, and an earthen mound located in Chiang-ning, Nanking. There seems to be no definite clue as to which is meant.

THE COLOPHON to the last leaf, in five lines of "regular" script, reads:

I have collected several scrolls by Shih-t'ao, and each has been quite wonderful. None of the designs have been repeated. His breast was replete with "hills and valleys" and he has never relied on [the compositions or designs of] others: he has always expressed his own ideas directly. His brush and ink surpass the ordinary, and he has liberated himself completely from the vulgar habits [hsi-ch'i] of common painters. Others find this truly difficult to achieve!

I like Master Shih's "ink wonders" so much that whenever I see something good by him I inevitably empty my purse to obtain it. This is the sixth work of his in my possession.

> *Kuei-ch'ou ts'an-la* [end of the twelfth
> lunar month, i.e., January, 1914].
> Recorded by P'iao Sou.
> [Seal:] *Chün-po* (intaglio square).

The writer signed only the cyclical date (*kuei-ch'ou*) and his *hao*, P'iao-sou. With no reign date to offer a clue to the century, the cycle and writer can only be tentatively identified from the style of the calligraphy as probably the late Ch'ing or early republican period. However, other signed and dated colophons with calligraphy matching that of this leaf have been discovered.

P'iao-sou can now be identified as Yen Shih-ch'ing (ca. 1870–1922-), a scholar and high official who came from a wealthy Cantonese family known for its collection of antiquities. Yen was evidently a connoisseur of superb taste, for some of the finest works of calligraphy extant today passed through his hands—Su Shih's famed *Han-shih-t'ieh* and Huang T'ing-chien's *Fu-po-shen-tz'u*, as well as Chao Meng-fu's *San-men-chi* and *Tan-pa-pei*. That Yen would rank this album by Tao-chi (one of six Tao-chi works he owned) among his treasures testifies to its quality. Yen's colophon in this instance is relatively brief; in other cases his intelligent encomiums also contribute to the knowledge of the history of the scroll.

NOTES

1. Quoted in Cheng Cho-lu, *Shih-t'ao yen-chiu*, p. 17.
2. E.g., the 1706 *Landscape and Portrait* (XXXII) and especially the 1707 *Ting-ch'iu Album of Flowers* (PTC, cat. no. 43); as Tao-chi states in the last leaf of the latter album, "the paper is new. After more than ten years it will be worth looking at" (*ibid.*, p. 94).
3. A twelve-leaf album of landscapes in the Ex-Okabe Chokei collection, Tokyo (*Sekitō meiga fu*, no. 7).
4. *PTC*, cat. no. 17, p. 135.
5. The British Museum album is not dated, but the lyric restraint of its style places it closer to a 1700 date of execution (*PTC*, cat. no. 17, p. 133).
6. *Sekitō to Hachidai san-jin*, pl. 1.
7. Cf. the Sackler *Bamboo, Vegetables, and Fruit* dated 1705 (XXXI), and the C. C. Wang painting of the same subject and date.
8. Again, a visual phenomenon translated into pictorial terms by Tao-chi in other works of his; cf. *XXXIII*, leaf E.
9. Ink on paper. Museum of Fine Arts, Boston, acc. no. 55.927, Keith McLeod Fund. It is of considerably larger dimensions (28.8 cm. in height) than the Sackler composition.
10. The remainder of the album in eight leaves (in ink and color on paper) is reproduced in *PTC*, cat. no. 17, pp. 133–36; photo courtesy British Museum.

XXXV CHANG TA-CH'IEN (born 1899)

Born Nei-chiang, Szechuan; later Shanghai, Kiangsu; São Paulo, Brazil; now Carmel, California

Tao-chi Landscapes

The Art Museum, Princeton University (68-201).

Album of six leaves. Ink and color on paper. 31.0 x 24.5 cm.

UNDATED: probably executed ca. 1920.

UNSIGNED

FORGED SEALS OF TAO-CHI:
Hsia-tsun-che (relief, tall rectangle) leaf A.
Tsan-chih shih-shih-sun, A-ch'ang (relief, tall rectangle) leaf B.
Kao-mang-tzu, Chi (intaglio, square) leaf C.
Yüan-chi, Shih-t'ao (intaglio and relief, a double seal in two small squares) leaf D.
Ch'ing-hsiang lao-jen (relief, square) leaf E.
Ta-ti-tzu (relief, oval) leaf F.

FORGED INSCRIPTIONS OF TAO-CHI: one couplet of fourteen characters on each leaf.

COLLECTORS' SEALS:
Mr. Chou (unidentified contemporary collector), *Ning-hsiang Chou-shih Meng-shui shan-fang meng-kung shen-ting chin-shih shu-hua* (relief, square) leaves C, E, and F.

Ch'in Man-ch'ing (*tzu* Keng-nien, contemporary collector), *Ch'in Man-ch'ing* (intaglio, square) on label cover after inscription.

OUTER LABEL: the inscription by Ch'in Man-ch'ing reads:
A joint album of genuine works of Hsüeh-ko [Chu Ta] and Shih-t'ao [Tao-chi]. Collected at the Hsiao-hai yüeh-an and inscribed by Keng-nien.

CONDITION: good.

PROVENANCE: Wang Fang-yü, Short Hills, New Jersey.

PUBLISHED: *Record of the Art Museum, Princeton University*, vol. 27, no. 2 (1968), p. 94; *Archives of Asian Art*, vol. 22 (1969–70), p. 85.

THESE SIX LEAVES originally composed one-half of an album, with six remaining leaves by Chu Ta. The album's cover was inscribed by one of its previous owners; it then passed into the hands of Wang Fang-yü. As Wang specialized in collecting the works of Chu Ta, he retained only the six Chu Ta leaves.

The life of the virtuoso painter, calligrapher, and collector Chang Ta-ch'ien (or Dai-chien) has all the elements of an adventure story.[1] He has been described by contemporaries as "a legend in his own time," and to some he has become a "cult"; perhaps equally tantalizing are the activities which have earned him the title the "H. van Meegeren of the East."[2] As a child Chang was taught by his mother and elder sister to read and to draw. At seventeen he was captured by bandits who had overrun his native Szechuan and, because of his beautiful cursive hand, was made their chief's personal secretary; after a hundred days he escaped. At eighteen he accompanied his elder brother Chang Tse (Shan-tzu, 1883–1940) to Japan to study textile dyeing. Two fruitless years passed before he returned to Shanghai and then, because of a disappointment in love, he entered a monastery in nearby Sung-chiang. He was a monk for another eventful hundred days, and the name Ta-ch'ien (the "great thousand") originates from this brief encounter with Buddhism and replaced his own, Yüan.

In Shanghai, in 1919, Chang (at age twenty) came under the tutelage of the famous scholar-calligraphers Tseng Hsi (*hao* Nung-jan, died 1930) and Li Jui-ch'ing (*hao* Mei-an, Ch'ing tao-jen, 1867–1920). His entrance into this exclusive circle was to be of crucial importance to his art, his reputation, and his collecting. In the next decade his fame as a painter grew and spread to the European continent. In 1933 he exhibited for the first time in Paris, where his painting of lotuses was much admired; in 1935 he had a show in London. These exhibits were paralleled by equally successful ones in Peking, Shanghai, and Chungking. In 1938, during the Sino-Japanese War, the Japanese took him prisoner in Peking; he escaped and fled to Szechuan. He spent 1940 through 1943 in the Buddhist caves of Tun-huang in Kansu, northwestern China. There he expanded his already wide repertory of subjects to include Buddhist figure painting and developed a thorough acquaintance with eighth- and ninth-century silk paintings and murals. He traced his interest in figure painting to its source in 1950, when he spent a year in India, three months of his stay at the Ajanta caves. He could not long remain untouched by the wars raging inside China, however, and in 1952 he escaped the Communists and settled for a time in São Paulo, Brazil. He later moved to Carmel, California, where he now makes his home.

Thus Chang Ta-ch'ien, alone among a number of Shanghai prodigies, has become known to the international art world. Since World War II there have been five exhibitions of his work in Paris and others in London, Brussels, Madrid, Kuala Lumpur, Hong Kong, Singapore, Taipei, New York City, and the West Coast of the United States. His subjects range from the more traditional figures, landscapes, and flowers to the ink explosions of his magnificent lotuses. In recent years he has concentrated primarily on landscapes—the vast mountain scenery of Switzerland and Taiwan, executed in bold expanses of ink, poured and splashed onto the paper in hues of brilliant jade and ultramarine. The monumentality of these mountainscapes is highly suited to the twentieth-century market and the contemporary Western concept of art as public display, but, as Basil Gray has pointed out,[3] they are inspired equally by the large and colorful murals from Tun-huang. His classical training has given Chang his extraordinary ability not merely to adapt to the present but to be in the avant garde. Younger painters not schooled in the traditional manner have been strongly influenced by his techniques of applying ink and his uninhibited concept of landscape forms.

Art historians and connoisseurs are acquainted with another facet of this painter's œuvre—the private, more discreet, but equally demanding role which has earned him the comparison with Van Meegeren, that is, that of master forger. Some know of him as an expert on Tao-chi and Chu Ta, but Chang is equally adept in other styles from the eighth to the eighteenth century. This aspect of his work is as firmly implanted in museums and private collections in China, Japan, Europe, and North and South America as are his lotuses and *bona fide* copies of the Tun-huang frescoes.

This album in the Sackler collection is a copy after several Tao-chi compositions. The prototypes for all six leaves have been located. Four are based on genuine and still extant Tao-chi works; the remaining two resemble leaves from another album attributed to Tao-chi. Chang has altered the format of the genuine Tao-chi leaves and has added a poetic couplet to each. The album is a modest, mediocre example of Chang's prowess in this field, and it reveals one aspect of his attitudes toward prototypes—they were inevitably works which he himself had collected, learned from, and admired. Imitations grew naturally out of the technical proficiency he acquired during the process of learning by copying, the age-old method of art training, but they are seldom line-for-line copies; they contain innovations and improvisations. While the force of his personality guarantees the artistic success of a copy through bravura and sheer nerve, his stylistic signature is imprinted in every brushstroke and dot. A painter of less distinction could better submerge his personality and probably would not risk improvisation but would make close or tracing copies instead. Chang never saw himself as a mere replicator, however, but as a creative artist on the same level as the master he emulated.

CHANG'S COLLECTION and those of his brother, teachers, and fellow connoisseurs in and around Shanghai during his youth had a significant influence on him. His imitations of Tao-chi, for example, seem most abundant during the 1920's and 1930's, at a time when Tao-chi was just coming into vogue among Shanghai collectors and when Chang himself was beginning to amass his collection. His fame as a collector, connoisseur, and forger kept pace with his renown as a painter, poet, and calligrapher. In the early years of the Republic, his brother Shan-tzu, sixteen years his senior, became prominent as a painter of tigers (which the affluence of his family also allowed him to raise). Chang made his debut in the Shanghai art world around the age of twenty-five at one of its habitual literary, artistic, and culinary gatherings. His poetry, calligraphy, and painting were immediately acclaimed, and this early attention helped him launch his career as a professional painter after 1925, when his family fell into financial difficulties.[4]

One amusing anecdote is told of Chang's abilities as painter, forger, and connoisseur.[5] The Shanghai real estate magnate and art lover Ch'eng Lin-sheng was once advised by the young Chang Ta-ch'ien that he should specialize in collecting the works of one or two artists whom he liked best. Chang suggested Tao-chi, since, as it happened, Ch'eng had already bought a "Tao-chi" which Chang Ta-ch'ien had produced and left at the studio of a friend. Before long Ch'eng became the unknowing possessor of no small number of "Tao-chi" works from the same hand. Ch'eng had a vast collection of paintings and antiquities, and so these acquisitions were inconspicuous among a host of excellent objects. When he died, many of his real Tao-chi works passed into Chang Ta-ch'ien's hands. On the basis of such acquisitions Chang amassed for his Ta-feng-t'ang (the "Great Wind Hall")[6] what until recently was one of the largest and finest private collections of Chinese calligraphy and painting—he owned more than a hundred and ten Tao-chi works alone (see colophon to XVIII). Many of these paintings in recent years have passed into the hands of Western collectors, who have begun an era of ownership of a different order.

A GREAT NUMBER of forgeries have been made in Tao-chi's name. While the study of his work, like that of any master, proceeds most fruitfully when based on properly authenticated objects, another useful method is to examine the styles of those identified as his forgers. An accurate identification of even one spurious hand, if made consistently, heightens our own recognition of what is genuine. Formally and expressively speaking, the degree of individuality and innovation in Tao-chi's style makes it particularly well suited to imitation, whether by professional forgers or artists famous in their own right amusing themselves with copies or ink plays after the master. Commentators from the late Ch'ing and early Republican years have noted that Tao-chi's works did not become widely popular until the early decades of this century, when the influence of the four Wangs, the lesser Four Wangs, and the followers of the orthodox school was beginning to wane.[7] The vogue for his work immediately spurred forgers to action in all the main artistic centers, Yang-chou, Canton, and Shanghai included.

As the works by Chang Ta-ch'ien have become better known, it has become fashionable, especially among less responsible students of Chinese painting, to dub any Tao-chi or earlier work which they do not "understand" such a forgery. We need not dwell on the dangers of such glibness other than to say that to attribute to this one painter any work that one cannot accept or comprehend would be endowing him with god-like powers while admitting our own failure to delve more deeply into the subject. The problem of Tao-chi forgeries, unlike those of Vermeer, are certainly more complex than the acts of one man.

To understand the role of the forger generally and of Chang Ta-ch'ien specifically, one must grasp the essential difference in the artistic personalities of the forger and his model. Decisive formal innovations and expressive changes occurred in the West in the two hundred and fifty years which separate Chang and Tao-chi and have left their imprint on Chang's style even though he was schooled in the classical Chinese manner. These traits, in addition to his temperamental divergences from Tao-chi, are too marked to be suppressed, and cannot but affect specific formal areas as well as total expression. Chang Ta-ch'ien's fame is based on superlative technique, a keen intellect, and an acute artistic intuition, and his painting and calligraphy mirror these traits.[8] His brushwork is sharp, dynamic, and aggressive, moving in angular rhythms which tend to skid across the surface of the paper rather than sinking deep into its fibers (cf. the discussion of Chang's calligraphy in XXIII). Whether working in meticulous line or splash-ink manners, he prefers light, bright, and appealing colors and compositional effects rather than astringent, blunt, or subdued tonalities. He almost never cultivates the flavor of the primitive or clumsy (cho) but prefers the sleek and striking. As a result his works occasionally suffer from a thinness, an over-brilliance, and an excessive sharpness and brittleness of line. Subtlety and restraint in artistic terms are not Chang's forte: he favors the dramatic and flamboyant.

Tao-chi, in contrast to this twentieth-century extrovert, possessed all the personal traits of the introvert. He did not lack intuitive penetration, artistic brilliance, or technical virtuosity, but they were clothed in a simpler, more unassuming guise. Like many of the monk painters, he preferred to be judged a simpleton by the world. This naive and unadorned rusticity was also in harmony with the scholarly ideals of the archaic (ku) and the primitive (cho). With Tao-chi, one feels that these traits were natural and unforced qualities of his expression, rather than self-consciously sought after. This is not to say that he could not execute technically difficult or artistically sophisticated works—on the contrary, his popularity in his later Yang-chou period was undoubtedly fed by his virtuoso displays of ink and compositional design: the late Album of Flowers (XXV) is a most urbane product, and the 1701 Album of Landscapes (XXVI) is certainly not technically flimsy. Yet his brilliant innovations were tempered by the simpler, more direct approach best exemplified in the brushwork and compositional types of Plum Branches (XXXIII) and Reminiscences of Nanking (XXXIV).

Chang Ta-ch'ien's works, whether his own compositions or his forgeries, never fail to impress with their technical mastery. What is important for Tao-chi is getting the idea on paper with a more or less spontaneous adaptation of brush and ink; what is important for Chang Ta-ch'ien is the very physical performance with brush and ink. The result is that in Chang's works the technically impressive often exceeds the conceptually expressive. Upon closer examination the surface of his paintings dissolves into an incoherent pattern of flat lines and dots. His mastery of Tao-chi therefore shows itself not in re-creating the naïve aspects of the Tao-chi style but in its sophisticated and coloristic displays, traits which come closest to his own artistic temperament. The copies which fail are of works which offer him less possibility for such identification.

Leaf A: "*Promontory*"

This leaf is an adaptation of a composition from a Tao-chi album dated 1695 (fig. 1).[9] The main difference here lies in the change from the horizontal to the vertical format, a change which reveals the forger's vastly different control and concept of space. In the original album, on coarse, unsized paper, the artist used thick ink as if it were charcoal, rubbing the almost dry brush against the paper to coax out the ink and the effects of texture. He then contrasted these effects with blunt, coarse lines in the trees and rocks; further density is suggested by a limited use of wash in the foreground boulders and distant mountain range. What succeeds pictorially is the sense of each mass receding in space, from the stark diagonal cliff at the right, to the round central boulder (almost "negative" in its effect of volume), to the square plateaus which overlook the wide curving bay. A thick flow of pine trees gradually recedes into the distance and completes the transition.

Because of his vertical format, the forger has made the mistake of merging the right-hand cliff with the rocks in the middle ground: instead of the effective repoussoir which throws the eye into the middle distance, typical of Tao-chi's concept of space, we have one continuous plane of forms. The contours and ink washes become flat patterns without depth or solidity. The slick pointed brushstrokes and the use of much wetter ink also contribute to this change, as can be seen especially in the row of pine trees. Instead of forming a dense mass as in the original, they line up as a thin screen. The color, blues and russets, is indiscriminately applied and, like the ink wash, flattens rather than enhancing the form. The couplet reads:

The rocks emerge when the Ch'in-huai River water descends,
The bright moon stays, as the T'ien-yin peaks are so high.

We need not press the forger for an exact rendering of "rocks" and "moon"; by adding the couplet, he has made the viewer search for its specific relationship to the painting, an analogy which Tao-chi did not force.

The calligraphy is in Tao-chi's "running" style. Like the brushwork in the landscape, the line is sharp and brittle. Most revealing are the arbitrary fluctuations in the strokes of a single character—one thin, one thick, all drawn with Chang's customary exposed tip and with few of the internal finger movements which lend the plump roundness to the Tao-chi writing. A comparison of two characters, *ch'u* ("to emerge," the seventh) and *t'ien* ("sky," the eighth), with similar characters from the calligraphy diagram in Part IV above will show these discrepancies: for example, the composition of *t'ien* is lopsided, and the right diagonal *na* stroke is poorly formed in comparison with Tao-chi's. (For further discussion see *XXIII*.)

Leaf B: "*Rice Fields*"

A pine tree, cottage, and path between rice fields pay tribute to a subject and compositional arrangement favored by Tao-chi, but on closer examination one is repelled by the parched and scratchy dots which relentlessly fill the page. The purpose of moss dots is to unify and enliven the disparate elements of a painting, but here they are only irrelevant surface adornments. Most disturbing is the composition itself: the strongly tilted ground rises up the picture surface, leaving no breathing space among the congested forms. This lack of differentiation is seen in the forms; clumps of ink bamboo surrounding the house and tree are lost among the scattering of dots and the haphazardly placed rocks. The couplet in one line on the left reads:

A rainbow scatters showers over the deep pine valley;
White egrets fly over rice fields of jade-green pools.

The lines and dots of the calligraphy have the same shrill quality as the dots on the fields and the pattern of the bamboo. As in leaf A, the color washes fail to describe form, and nowhere in the choice or application of colors is there a hint of Tao-chi's discriminating palette. This composition is close to a leaf in an undated album of landscapes ascribed to Tao-chi.[10] It is quite likely that Chang Ta-ch'ien based his composition on this or one close to it. The poem on the album is not the same as this one.

Leaf C: "*T'ao Yüan-ming under a Pine Tree*"

This leaf, like the first one, has been adapted after a composition in the 1695 Tao-chi album (fig. 2). To make up for the simplification in format and reduction of garden elements, the forger has shown the figure in greater detail, modifying it after leaf E, "Portrait of T'ao Yüan-ming," in the *Flowers and Figures* album (XX), which was also in Chang Ta-ch'ien's collection. The change of emphasis is felicitous, and the two lines of poetry have been appropriately adapted from T'ao's "Homecoming" ode (cf. *XX*, leaf E):

The lofty scholar's three rows of chrysanthemums lay uncultivated for
*   a long time,*
The useless [painter] finds a resting place on the branch of an old tree.

As in the preceding leaves, the flattening of space is evidence of a twentieth-century origin. Not only have the various levels of depth in the ground plane been eliminated but the rocks have been pressed into one large shape, whereas in the Tao-chi leaf the graded saturations of wash clearly differentiate two large boulders. In the background of the Tao-chi original, ink wash has been applied to moist paper, and the ensuing effect of a mountain range in atmospheric perspective serves as a compositional unifier. Chang Ta-ch'ien's "mountain" looks more like a flat curtain hung over the washline. Both technique and intent differ in this case; Chang's changes betray his increased awareness of the flatness of the picture space.

Leaf D: "*View from Tall Peaks of Lo-Fu*"

A deep valley filled with bamboo and a large tree slant diagonally up the picture plane. A scholar accompanied by his attendant stands high up, gazing into space. Tall peaks in thick ink fill the right-hand corner. This leaf, like leaf B, is similar to one from an undated album. What is most disturbing about this interpretation are the ubiquitous dots, which seem to overwhelm the forms and make them chaotic. There is definite spatial confusion in the foreground: the tall tree seems plastered against the rising mountain, and the bamboo grove floats aimlessly in a sea of multicolored dots. The couplet may be rendered:

The moon—in front of Mt. Lo-Fu's four hundred peaks;
The wind—under your wrist high on the Red Stone Cliff.

No doubt the forger had in mind the famous leaf from the *Album for Yü-lao*,[11] where the shimmering watercolor dabs hover in space among the mountains, or the monochromatic *Ten Thousand Ugly Inkblots* (cf. *XVIII*, fig. 2). These crab-like dots fail mainly because of the brittle brush and exposed tip which is typical of Chang Ta-ch'ien's execution. Moreover, the colors appear drab and soiled. This leaf is probably the least successful of the whole group; it is also closest to Chang Ta-ch'ien's early style.

Leaf E: "*Fortification Deep in the Mountains*"

The twentieth-century origins of this album are most marked here. Tao-chi and other Ch'ing dynasty artists still adhered to the concept of solids placed in three more or less distinct distances, near, middle, and far. Here that scheme is abandoned, and the forms are manipulated with utter disregard for their relative position in the compositional space. This work is a pastiche of two leaves from the original Tao-chi album: the foreground boulder and cottage of "City Wall by a River" (fig. 4), and the distant mountains and blurred ink wash range of "Icy Rains" (fig. 3). But Chang need not have had a prototype, for the arrangement strongly suggests some of his own landscape explorations in color over the past few decades. His taste for uncontrolled space or "wandering" ink wash is seen in embryonic form here. Oceans of ink swimming in ink (or color) distinguish much of his most recent landscapes, such as *Summer Cottage in the Hills* (fig. 5). Unlike the Tao-chi originals, where the white paper functions distinctly as river or sky and the washes describe volume or suggest texture, Chang's spaces and washes are flat and replace mass rather than describing it. They are liberated from the three-dimensional object and exist in their own right as pure color or space, or as brush action over the paper surface. Chang Ta-ch'ien thus reveals his debt to Tao-chi while demonstrating his own stylistic advances.

The calligraphy imitates a form of Tao-chi's "clerical" script, and the couplet is reminiscent of Tu Fu:

Over the wall, horns and drums rise with the sad wind;
From the frontier, the smoke of war dies away with the brave soldiers.

Leaf F: *"A View of Fu-ch'un"*

This final leaf is a close rendering of "A Segment of Fu-ch'un" (fig. 6), another original Tao-chi leaf. The rock forms with their flat tops pay homage to the Yüan master Huang Kung-wang and the formal types he established in his handscroll of 1350, *Dwelling in the Fu-ch'un Mountains*. Here the forger has added two figures in boats (who look back at a flight of birds hardly distinguishable from the mountains) to fill the space which resulted from the change to a vertical format. The basically architectonic shapes of the original have aided his usually flat concept of form, especially in the background mountains, and in this sense, the scene is one of the more successful leaves in the album. The mountains still suffer from thinness and a tendency to be "blank," however, a quality which is especially apparent in the left and right foreground. In order to correct

this, rocks have been added along the right edge and the pointed mound filled in with some texture strokes. The latter are especially odd; they appear to be mere surface decoration rather than adding the desired bulk. The couplet in two lines of "running" script reads:

The boats on the lake make the blue mountains turn round;
All the houses below the mountains are set aglow by the sunset.

NOTES

1. Biographical information cited in this account has been taken from the various chronologies which appear at the end of *Recent Paintings by Chang Dai-chien* and other exhibition catalogues of the 1950's and 1960's, as well as from Hsieh Chia-hsiao, *Chang Ta-ch'ien-te shih-chieh*. The most comprehensive catalogue is the recent *Chang Dai-chien: A Retrospective*, which contains a charming autobiographical preface (pp. 8–13) and a brief introduction by René-Yvon Lefebre d'Argencé (pp. 14–17).

2. For Wen Fong's description of him as a "living legend" and Lin Yutang's account of the "cult," see the introductions in *Recent Paintings by Chang Dai-chien*; for the "H. van Meegeren of the East," see Chu Sheng-chai, *Chung-kuo shu-hua*, p. 47. For an account of the Van Meegeren case, see Frank Arnau, *Three Thousand Years of Deception in Art and Antiquities* (London, 1961).

3. As found in Gray's brief preface to *Exhibition of Paintings by Chang Dai-chien*.

4. See Hsieh Chia-hsiao, *Chang Ta-ch'ien-te shih-chieh*, pp. 42–45.

5. Ch'en Ting-shan, a painter, poet, and calligrapher now residing in Taichung, tells the story in his memoirs, *Ch'un-shen chiu-wen*; it is recounted by Chu Sheng-chai in *Chung-kuo shu-hua*, p. 46.

6. A portion of his collection was published in 1955 in a four-volume catalogue, *Ta-feng-t'ang ming-chi*, in fine collotype; a preliminary catalogue (no illustrations) of his early collection was published as *Ta-feng-t'ang shu-hua-lu*.

7. As observed, for example, by Yeh Kung-cho, *Hsia-an t'an-i-lu*, p. 6.

8. Illustrations of Chang's paintings have been published intermittently. Some of the more accessible sources are *Chang Dai-chien's Paintings*, which reproduces 130 works dated from 1944 to 1966; *Tchang Ta-ts'ien, peintre chinois*, which contains twenty-six works executed before 1956; the various small catalogues to his recent exhibitions in New York, Carmel, Chicago, Boston, and Taipei; and *Chang Dai-chien: A Retrospective*, which reproduces fifty-four works dating from 1928 to 1970. Of great interest in this latter catalogue are the early paintings dated 1928, 1930, 1933, and 1935, all of which are "in the manner of Shih-t'ao" and document his study of the master at that time.

9. The ten-leaf album in ink on paper, entitled *Graded Ink Landscapes* (*p'o-mo shan-shui*), is reproduced in *Ta-feng-t'ang ming-chi*, vol. 2, pls. 29–33 passim.

10. Cf. *Shih-t'ao shan-shui hua-p'u* (*Sekitō sansui gafu*) (n.p., n.d.), leaf 7; the eight-leaf album is followed by a colophon by Ho Shao-chi dated 1853. We are grateful to Nora Liu (Shih Ling-yün) of the University of Michigan for obtaining photographs for us from this publication. It may be a close copy or an early work, possibly from the late 1670's or early 1680's.

11. In the C. C. Wang collection, illustrated in color in James Cahill, *Chinese Painting*, p. 180.

Leaf A, "Promontory"

Leaf B, "Ricefields"

1. Tao-chi, *Graded Ink Landscapes* (*P'o-mo shan-shui-ts'e*), dated 1695, leaf 9, "Gazing from an Eminence." Ink on paper. Ta-feng-t'ang collection.

三徑久芸高士菊不
材老樹一枝安

Leaf C, "T'ao Yüan-ming under a Pine Tree"

羅浮
四百
山峰巖
月赤
石磯
頭腕
玉風

Leaf D, "View from Tall Peaks"

Tao-chi, *Graded Ink Landscapes*, leaf 6, "Composing a Verse under a Tall Pine."
k on paper. Ta-feng-t'ang collection.

城頭鼓角悲風寨
士煙豆起之峯牡十休

Leaf E, "Fortifications Deep in the Mountains"

5. Chang Ta-ch'ien, *Summer Cottage in the Hills*, ca. 1960. Hanging scroll. Ink on paper. Ta-feng-t'ang collection.

3. Tao-chi, *Graded Ink Landscapes*, leaf 7, "Icy Rains." Ink on paper. Ta-feng-t'ang collection.

4. Tao-chi, *Graded Ink Landscapes*, leaf 5, "City Wall by a River." Ink on paper. Ta-feng-t'ang collection.

湖頭艇子廻青峯山下人家畫夕陽

Leaf F, "A View of Fu-ch'un"

6. Tao-chi, *Graded Ink Landscapes*, leaf 8, "A Segment of Fu-ch'un." Ink on paper. Ta-feng-t'ang collection.

XXXVI HUA YEN (1682–1765–)

Lin-ting, Fukien; later Yang-chou, Kiangsu

Cloudsea at Mt. T'ai (*T'ai-tai yün-hai-t'u*)

The Art Museum, Princeton University (69-75).

Hanging scroll. Ink on paper. 179.0 x 67.6 cm.

DATED: September 14, 1730 (*keng-hsü, pa-yüeh, san-jih*).

SIGNATURE OF THE ARTIST: Nan-yang-shan-chung ch'iao-k'o, Yen.

INSCRIPTION BY THE ARTIST: a five-character title in seal script and an eleven-line prose inscription (see below).

SEALS OF THE ARTIST:
Hsin-lo shan-jen (intaglio, square; Contag and Wang, *Seals*, no. 17, p. 381) lower right corner.
Nai-ho (intaglio, tall rectangle) before inscription.
Hua Yen (intaglio, square; Contag and Wang, *Seals*, no. 5, p. 381) after signature.
Ch'iu-yüeh (intaglio, square) after signature.

COLLECTORS' SEALS: owners unidentified, *Wei-ch'ing chien-ts'ang* (relief, square); *Hai-yang Huang-shih chia-ts'ang* (relief, tall rectangle), seal of Mr. Huang; *Chin-ch'uan-*() (intaglio, square), seal of Mr. Chin; undecipherable, extremely faint seal (relief, square); all in lower left corner.

CONDITION: good.

PROVENANCE: Frank Caro, New York.

PUBLISHED: *Art Journal*, vol. 29 (1969–70), p. 214; *Record of the Art Museum, Princeton University*, vol. 29 (1970), p. 18, fig. 2 (illustrated); *Archives of Asian Art*, vol. 24 (1970–71), p. 100, fig. 43, p. 113 (illustrated).

HUA YEN (*tzu* Ch'iu-yüeh, *hao* Hsin-lo shan-jen, etc.) was originally from Lin-ting, Fukien; some sources are in disagreement about this fact, but Hua Yen's own sobriquet, Hsin-lo, is another name for Lin-ting, Fukien. In 1703, when he was in his twenties, he moved to Hang-chou, but, like many painters of this period, he traveled about and was soon attracted to the metropolis, Yang-chou. He is identified only occasionally as one of the Eight Eccentrics of Yang-chou, but his painting activities and stylistic tendencies certainly qualify him for membership in that convenient grouping. He painted a variety of subjects, and his style is notable for the witty sense of movement and life with which he endowed his forms, whether landscapes and large trees, human figures, birds and animals, rocks, or, as here, clouds and mountains. His collected poetic works are found in *Hsin-lo shan-jen Li-kou-chi*.[1]

The subject of this hanging scroll is the sea of clouds around T'ai-tai, or Mt. T'ai, the tallest mountain in Shantung Province and one of five venerated mountain ranges where state sacrifices were conducted. Mountains and clouds have been reduced to their most basic pictorial elements—velvety black peaks enveloped by swirling white clouds—allowing formal shape, brushline, and tonal gradation direct expression.

Movement and stability are juxtaposed here to create "a duality of protean cloud and herculean mountain,"[2] a force which seems to strain the borders of the frame. The cloud rising from the left encases the block of the artist's inscription as an integral part of the compositional balance. Like the five-line title written to the right, the text of the inscription stresses the importance of certain ancient symbolic and literary values contained in the picture. Such paint-

ings with a single powerful image executed in coarse brushwork and in a monumental format are rare among Hua Yen's works, but the style and subject matter can be firmly related to the other paintings in his range.

On the lower right side of the painting, the artist has written a five-character title, *T'ai-tai yün-hai-t'u* ("Cloudsea at Mt. T'ai"), in slender "great-seal" (*ta-chuan*) script. At the lower left side of the painting a long inscription in prose followed by a poetic quatrain is written in eleven lines of "running" script. In it the artist relates the occasion of the painting:

My friend said: "Ting Nan-yü [Yün-p'eng, 1580–1621] painted the *Cloudsea of Mt. Huang* [Anhwei] and Yün Nan-t'ien [Shou-p'ing, 1633–1690] the *Cloudsea of Mt. T'ien-mu* [Chekiang]. Mt. Huang is a marvel of precipitousness, while Mt. T'ien-mu is brooding and mysterious. When clouds and vapors gather, there are endless transformations. The two gentlemen [Ting and Yün] have exercised their imagination, and each has grasped a secret flavor [of the mountains]."
I once traveled in the T'ai mountains (T'ai-an district, Shantung province) and saw the clouds issuing from between the Lotus and Sun-sight Peaks. In their beginning, they were like dragons, like horses, like a phoenix soaring or a monstrous bird taking flight. They seemed to rumble thunderously like circling chariots. In an instant, they filled the emptiness with succeeding billows which spread into a vast sea.[3]
Now the three cloudseas which Ting and Yün painted and the one I have seen are all unique experiences. What difficulty should I have in releasing this expansive force in my breast, completely purifying this vision of the mountain's soul?

Inscribed on September 14, 1730
[*keng-hsü, pa-yüeh, san-jih*].

I suddenly marvel at the mountain chilled to the bone,
Its myriad fissures awash with billowing crests.
Playfully patterning myself after Lieh-tzu,
I ride on nothing but emptiness and the whistling wind.

[Signed:] The traveler-woodsman
of Nan-yang Mountain, [Hua] Yen.

Line contrasts with tone in these two distinct images of the transient and the immovable. The massive quality of the mountains is suggested in the dominant group by the heavy application with the side of the brush of graded layers of wet dots on a wet ground. This technique of "wet on wet" is derived from Tao-chi's interpretation of the so-called Mi Fu style of using ink dots to depict a mountain in clouds (cf. *XXVI*, fig. 4), but this painting, like Tao-chi's work, is now far removed in its animating concept and degree of bulk from its Sung, Yüan, or even Ming counterparts. The artist is not concerned with depth or distance: on the contrary, two peaks in a middle gray tonality deny any further exploration into space and unite the forms in a generic configuration recalling the ancient pictograph for mountain, 山 . The idea of the pictograph and the symbolic order of the image extends to the clouds as well. The ideogram is a whorl, 回 (seen in the third character of the title), which becomes embodied on an expanded scale, like the cloudsea itself. The volume and tension of the shifting mass is suggested only by the energy and the varying thickness of the line, which has been traced over in several layers of ink for tonal depth. The forms undulate in a compelling manner as they envelop the mountains, and the quality of "cloud-ness," its smoky volatility, seems to rise from the very depths of the picture.

The symbolic content of the painting is further enhanced by the ancient belief, recorded in such Han texts as the *Lun-heng* and *Ch'un-ch'iu Commentary*, that the clouds around Mt. T'ai supplied rain to the whole empire.[4] The final allusion in the artist's inscription to the legendary Taoist sage Lieh-tzu asserts the imaginative and philosophical values implied in both description and image.

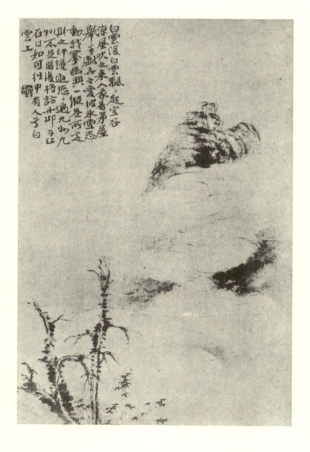

IN HUA YEN'S œuvre there are few works which are conceived on such an impressive scale, but *Giant Bird* in the Sumitomo collection (fig. 1) contains comparable execution and imagery. The Sumitomo painting[5] shows a giant roc soaring above the clouds, again a Taoist reference to ultimate freedom.[6] Simplicity of line and tone function here with a directness similar to that in the Sackler work. The feathers of the bird are built up by the interaction of dry and wet brushwork, which creates both linear definition and three-dimensional volume; it is a method usually found in Hua Yen's rocks. The rendering of the clouds is technically close to that of the Sackler painting, but with a change in mood: layers of wash, moist dabbing, and round, undulating lines now suggest murky depths and changing vapors. The artist's inscription on the right is briefer and in a larger script, but it is also written in a block to one side. The simplicity, intensity, and profundity of execution are equal to those in the Sackler *Cloudsea*.

While these two paintings are unusual, they can be closely linked to other Hua Yen works in both subject matter and style. An album of landscapes in twelve leaves dated 1729 contains two leaves which again contain the round, fluctuating line and the reduced graphic representation of the mountain surrounded by dense clouds[7] (fig. 2). This leaf is executed with the drier brushwork found in *Giant Bird*. A lovely colored landscape fan in the Boston Museum[8] (fig. 3) also presents the same subject, but rendered instead in an archaistic "blue-and-green" mode of landscape painting. The mood of the Boston fan is lyrical and intimate, and with the addition of color, the cloudy mountain seems drenched with sunlight. Technically, the heavy hues tend to flatten the mountain forms, a feature which is actually in accord with the archaistic intent, but the filigree waves, the cloud and mountain shape, and the whole conception of forms are from the same hand as the Sumitomo and Sackler works. Even the inscription on the Boston work testifies to this relationship. It contains excerpts from the longer inscription on the Sackler painting and shows what a favored subject the cloudsea at Mt. T'ai, in all its moods and transformations, was for Hua Yen.

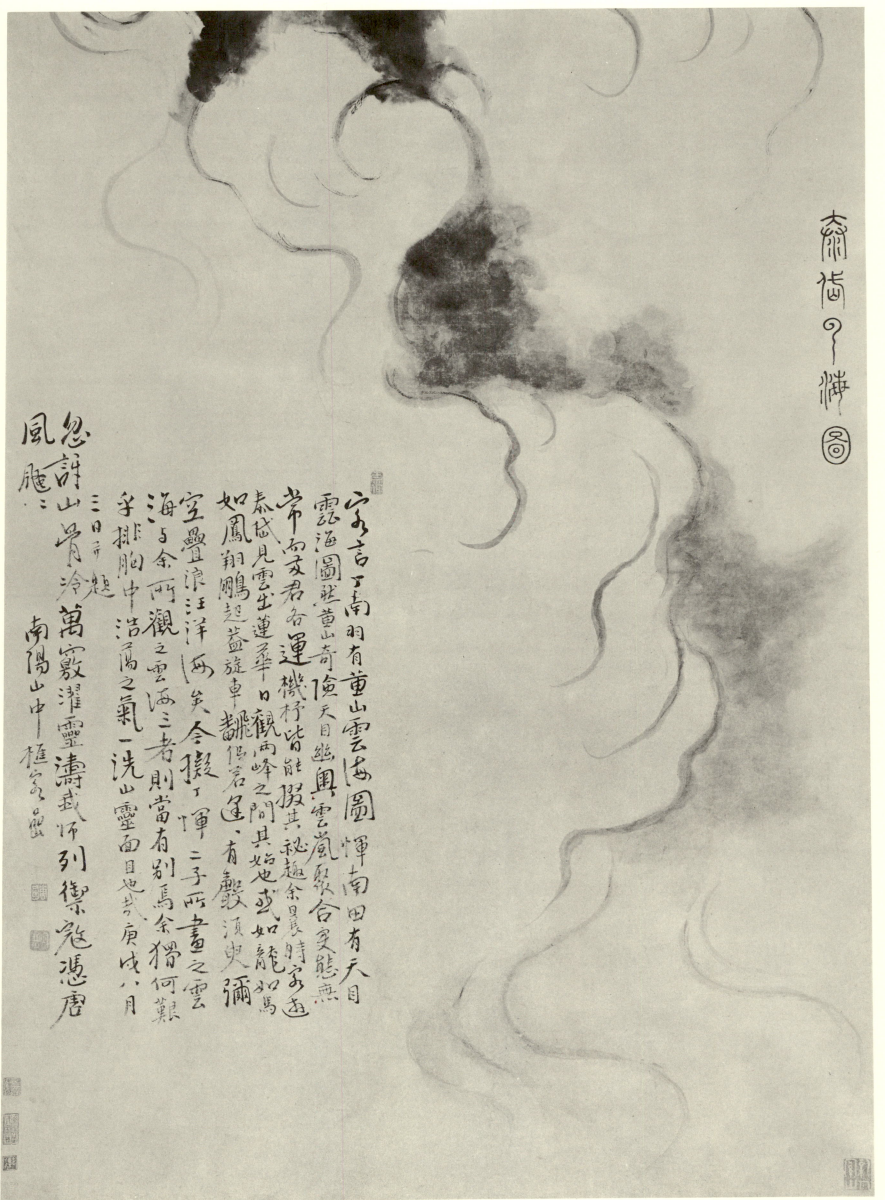

忽許山骨冷　萬竅洩靈濤武師列儒憑唐
風颾颾　南陽山中樵雲昜識
三日示趣

宗言丁南羽有黃山雲海圖惲南田有天目
雲海圖詆黃山奇險天目幽奧雲嵐變態合兩態無
常而文君各運機杼皆能擷其祕趣余晨時家遊
泰岱見雲出蓮子峯日觀兩峯之間其始也武如龍如馬
如鳳翔鶡起蓋旋車駝信君連有縠須臾彌
空疊浪汪洋海英今擬丁惲二子兩畫之雲
海子余所觀之雲海三者則當有別焉余猶何難
乎排胸中浩浩陽之氣一洗山靈面目也歲庚戌八月

XXXVI, detail of inscription.

A true individualist, Hua drew from stylistic traditions which were formally quite different and often thought to be mutually exclusive. For example, like other Yang-chou masters he was influenced by Tao-chi, yet Hua's style also contains features derived from Yün Shou-p'ing and Chu Ta. This admixture shows how, a century later, a creative master could synthesize different stylistic trends of the seventeenth century in a distinctive and fresh way.

Chu Ta's influence on Hua Yen can be seen in both calligraphy and image. Hua Yen's versatile use of the round stroke with the brush held in a firm upright position is basically a calligrapher's brush-hold, and for Tao-chi (cf. XXVI, leaves A and B) and other painters who mastered its potential, it allows the line to suggest volume, creating the illusion of a third, volumetric dimension. The five-character title shows the line in the original calligraphic state—that is, in the "seal script" from which the brushline evolved historically; the cloud swirls show the line in its pictorial transformation.

Hua's ordinary calligraphic style is usually a free mixture of "running" and "cursive" scripts. As seen in the inscription, his characters vary spontaneously in size and depth of ink from one to another. The columns are often close together, and one of the more distinctive features of his hand is that the axis of each character tends to slant in a different direction, creating a tangled effect. He handles his brush with a firmly centered tip, irrespective of the abrupt tilts in the axis, and it is this feature which links him with Chu Ta (fig. 4).[9] Chu Ta's columns are more spacious and his characters more regular in size, but in him we recognize a source of Hua Yen's rod-like energy and succinct forms.

The fluidity in the calligraphy, as in the lengthened diagonal strokes and the graceful cloud forms, shows an equally strong influence from Yün Shou-p'ing (1633–1690), indicating an appreciation of this orthodox master unusual for Hua's time. Hua himself mentioned his emulation of Yün in his inscription. Neither Yün Shou-p'ing nor Ting Yün-p'eng's depictions of cloudseas are available for specific comparison, but Yün's general influence may be further identified in Hua's landscapes, for example, the 1732 *Conversation in Autumn* in Cleveland[10] or the 1755 *Autumn Music and Poetic Thoughts* in Osaka (fig. 5).[11] Yün's inimitable sense of nuance and his feeling for movement in the brushline is reinterpreted with wit and humor in Hua's forms—the swaying trees and the extended and stretching shapes of the rocks, which suggest an animated life within, much like the moving figures of dancers whose bodies are shrouded. A colored handscroll dated 1671[12] attributed to Yün (fig. 6) shows how closely, in fact, Hua pursued Yün's ideal in both the linear and the coloristic realms. We have not seen this work in the original, but if it is a reliable indication of Yün Shou-p'ing's style, his influence on Hua Yen has been underestimated.

The expressive tone and structure of Hua Yen's later works are set by these undulating rhythms—the depiction of forms slightly off balance, either moving or imbued with potential movement. His more personal brush idiom emerges in the dry and sooty network of textures which he employs to model rocks, or, as in the Sumitomo work, the giant roc. These drier areas frequently contrast with more buoyant touches of foliage dotted in wet ink or color. His fluffy, charcoal effects recall the works of such earlier painters as Ch'eng Sui (1605–1691; cf. XVII, fig. 3) or Tai Pen-hsiao (1615–1698; cf. XVII, fig. 2). This preference for dry textures is unusual in a period when wet brushwork dominated, for by the Ch'ien-lung era the wet, blunt, and rather limited brush style of the major Yang-chou Eccentrics held sway.

NOTES

1. For biographical information see the preface (dated 1889) by Lo Chia-chieh to Hua Yen's collected poems, *Hsin-lo shan-jen Li-kou-chi*, in five *chüan*, and the postscript, dated 1835, by Hua Yen's grandnephew, Hua Shih-chung. The poems are arranged in roughly chronological order. Cf. also the evaluations given in such sources as *CKHCJMTTT*, p. 519b; Chang Keng, *Kuo-ch'ao hua-cheng-lu* (preface dated 1739, *HSTS* ed.), pt. 2, p. 102; Osvald Sirén, *Chinese Painting: Leading Masters and Principles*, vol. 5, pp. 235–37, 247–49; Sherman Lee, *Chinese Landscape Painting* (1962 ed.), pp. 126–27, 150–51; James Cahill, ed., *Fantastics and Eccentrics in Chinese Painting*, p. 94.

2. This phrase, some of the descriptive ideas, and part of the translation of the artist's inscription (see below) are taken from a label written by John Hay.

3. The translation of this paragraph is by John Hay.

4. For one source of these allusions, see Wang Ch'ung (A.D. 27–ca. 97), *Lun-heng (Disquisitions)* (*SPTK* ed., nos. 98–99), 11/2 (on the sun) and 15/3 (on the clouds); also A. Forke, trans., *Lun-heng* (New York, 1907), vol. 1, pp. 276–77, vol. 2, p. 330. We are grateful to Ulysses B. Li for calling our attention to this source.

5. This hanging scroll, ink and light color on paper, measures 173.2 x 85.5 cm. and is undated (*Min Shin no kaiga*, no. 137). The poem inscribed on the right side by Hua Yen is recorded in his *Hsin-lo shan-jen Li-kou-chi*, 2/2a; it is found between other poems dated from 1730 to 1738. In view of the stylistic development seen in other dated paintings by Hua, we would tend to place this work slightly later than the Sackler painting.

6. Referring to the *p'eng* bird in *Chuang-tzu*, chap. 1, "Hsiao-yao-yu" ("The Happy Excursion"). Cf. Fung Yu-lan, trans., *Chuang-tzu* (New York, 1933), pp. 27ff.

7. *Shina nanga taisei*, vol. 12, nos. 48–59; see nos. 59 and 55, respectively.

8. Museum of Fine Arts, Boston, acc. no. 14.79, part of a ten-leaf album; see *Portfolio of Chinese Paintings in the Museum*, pl. 118 (in color).

9. Cf. Chu Ta's three albums of painting and calligraphy after various ancient masters in *Ta-feng-t'ang ming-chi*, vol. 3, pls. 20–23, 28–30, 31–40. These works are worthy of attention because they not only "imitate," and therefore reveal his admiration for, past masters of the Chin and Sung but also present Chu Ta in a highly disciplined mood and hand.

10. Reproduced in a color detail in Cahill, *Fantastics and Eccentrics*, p. 89, no. 33, p. 95.

11. Ink and light color on paper; *Min Shin no kaiga*, no. 136.

12. Ink and light color on paper; *ibid.*, nos. 106–7.

5. Hua Yen, *Autumn Music and Poetic Thoughts*, dated 1755. Hanging scroll. Ink and color on paper. Osaka Municipal Museum.

4. Chu Ta (1626–1730), leaf from an album of painting and calligraphy after ancient masters. Ink on paper. Ta-feng-t'ang collection.

6. Yün Shou-p'ing, landscape, dated 1671. Handscroll. Ink and color on paper. Kyoto National Museum.

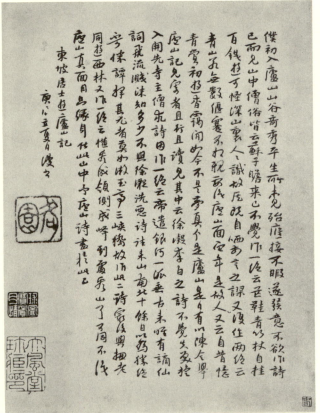

XXXVII HUNG-LI (1711-1799)

The Ch'ien-lung Emperor, Ch'ing Kao-tsung (reigned 1736–1796)

Eight Fragrant Summer Flowers (Hsia-hui pa-hsiang t'u)

The Art Museum, Princeton University (68-225).

Handscroll. Ink on sized paper. 28.9 x 97.8 cm.

DATED: intercalary summer, 1759 (*i-mao jen-hsia*).

SIGNATURE OF THE ARTIST: Yü-pi ("imperial brush") after prose inscription.

INSCRIPTIONS BY THE ARTIST (in "running" script): a frontispiece in four large characters, 20.4 x 72.4 cm.; eight poetic quatrains (*chüeh-chü*) written above each of the eight flowers; and a prose epilogue in four long lines at end of scroll.

SEALS OF THE ARTIST (totaling nineteen imperial seals):
Ch'ien-lung ch'en-han (relief, large square) on frontispiece.
Ch'un-ou-chai (relief, large square) on silk mounting preceding painting.
T'ai-shang huang-ti chih-pao (relief, large square) on silk mounting preceding painting.
I-tsai pi-chien (relief, oval; Contag and Wang, *Seals*, p. 587, no. 124) lower right corner of painting.
Ch'ih-tsao wei-ch'un (intaglio, square; Contag and Wang, *Seals*, p. 588, no. 147) lower right corner of painting.
Chi-hsia i-ch'ing (intaglio, square; Contag and Wang, *Seals*, p. 586, no. 71) after first poem.
Te-chia-ch'ü (intaglio, square; Contag and Wang, *Seals*, p. 586, no. 72) after first poem.
Shih-ch'ü pao-chi suo-ts'ang (relief, square; Contag and Wang, *Seals*, p. 583, no. 54) upper edge of painting.
Ch'en-han (intaglio, oval; Contag and Wang, *Seals*, p. 588, no. 153) after third poem.
Chung-ho (relief, oval; Contag and Wang, *Seals*, p. 683, no. 198) after fourth poem.
Ch'ien-lung ch'en-han (relief, small square; Contag and Wang, *Seals*, p. 581, no. 5) after fourth poem.
Hui-hsin pu-yüan (intaglio, square; Contag and Wang, *Seals*, p. 586, no. 73) after fifth poem.
Te-ch'ung-fu (relief, square; Contag and Wang, *Seals*, p. 586, no. 74) after fifth poem.

Hsieh-sheng (relief, tall rectangle; Contag and Wang, *Seals*, p. 588, no. 155) after sixth poem.
P'o-mo (relief, oval; Contag and Wang, *Seals*, p. 587, no. 120) after seventh poem.
K'an-yün (relief, tall rectangle; Contag and Wang, *Seals*, p. 588, no. 156) after eighth poem.
Ch'ien (relief, round; Contag and Wang, *Seals*, p. 683, no. 201) after epilogue.
Lung (relief, square; Contag and Wang, *Seals*, p. 683, no. 202) after epilogue.
Chi-hsia lin-ch'ih (intaglio, square) after epilogue.

NO COLLECTORS' SEALS OR COLOPHONS

CONDITION: poor; the imperial Ch'ing dynasty mounting is still intact, but the painting itself is extremely brittle and has more than a dozen severe vertical cracks; these cracks were crudely repaired with plastic and cloth tape on the reverse side of the mounting before entering the collection.

FRONTISPIECE: written by the Emperor in his characteristic "running" script in four large characters: "Scenes of the flower garden intermingle" (*I-p'u chiao-fen*).

PROVENANCE: Frank Caro, New York.

PUBLISHED: Wang Chieh and others, *SCPC hsü-pien* (1791–93) (in the "Western Garden" [*hsi-yüan*] section), 36/10b; *Record of the Art Museum, Princeton University*, vol. 27 (1968), p. 94 (acquisitions list); *Archives of Asian Art*, vol. 22 (1969–70), p. 85 (acquisitions list).

EIGHT DIFFERENT SUMMER FLOWERS are drawn in monochromatic ink line (*pai-miao*) style. The flowers have been arranged on a plain ground to give the impression of casual placement, some springing rootless from the immediate foreground, some overlapping. Foreshortening is used sparingly in the leaves and in the larger flowers to indicate changing spatial directions; otherwise, most of the flowers are shown in profile. Graded wash is also employed in the leaves, stems, and sepal, but weight, texture, and degrees of opacity have not been distinguished. The poetic quatrains characterize each flower, and although the depiction is simplified, the relative proportions and distinguishing botanical characteristics have been preserved. The Chinese names of the flowers have been identified in the imperial catalogue. Reading from right to left, they are *lan* (*Cymbidium* orchid), *yeh-lai-hsiang* ("night-fragrant flower"—

Frontispiece.

a species of *Telosma*), *wan-hsiang-yü* (tuberose), *mo-li-hua* (jasmine), *chen-chu-lan* ("pearl orchid"—an aromatic species of *Chloranthus*), *ho-hua* (Indian lotus), *chih-tzu* (gardenia), and *yü-tsan* (plantain lily).[1]

The Emperor's own prose at the end of the scroll sets the tone and describes the circumstances inspiring the painting and poems:

The summer rain had just stopped, causing the flowers by the footpaths to emit such a wondrous fragrance that it was as if I had entered the Land of Fragrance itself. Eight hundred noses are needed to inhale their unimaginable potency. So I have painted these summer flowers of eight fragrances and composed brief verses for each. Color, scent, flavor, and touch—all participate in "non-conforming detachment" [*pu-chi-li chien*]. I feel as though my Studio of Painting and Ch'an [Hua-Ch'an-shih] had been enriched by another fine episode. The intercalary summer of 1759.

[Signed:] The imperial brush.

Paintings from Kao-tsung's hand are rarely found outside the imperial collection. As far as we know, this scroll may be the only such painting in a private collection. For many viewers, its importance may lie more in the person who painted it than in its quality or artistic appeal. This scroll represents but one aspect of a complex spectrum of activities in which the Emperor engaged.[2] His prolix calligraphic encomiums and enormous seals found on works of calligraphy and painting which passed into the imperial collection give evidence of his untiring enthusiasm for art.[3] Exercising the imperial prerogative on a hitherto unprecedented scale, he amassed the largest collection of art in existence—and by that act made inaccessible many of the greatest masterpieces of the ancients, thus cutting off from succeeding generations of artists one of the most vital sources of artistic renewal of the Great Tradition. In this sense, Kao-tsung's role as a collector is crucial, and the history of art after him is written quite differently because of it (see Part I, pp. 11–12, above).

ART HISTORIANS' interest in the Emperor has stemmed primarily from the quality and quantity of this vast art collection. His attitude and his taste determined its character, in large part, and molded that of the era as well. The interpretation that the Manchus undertook "systematic Sinicization and Confucianization" as a conscious policy[4] can be confirmed in Kao-tsung's general attitude toward art, and even in this one work. His emulation in artistic terms of the Chinese scholar-painters' taste and interests can be said to have exceeded that of the most model Confucian, not only in enthusiasm but in scope.

The stamp of his taste, as expressed in imperial patronage of items for court consumption, can be traced from the most minor craft—the smallest jade hairpin, snuffbox or cricket cage—to the painting and calligraphy of the great masters, jades, bronzes, porcelains, lacquers, Buddhist ritual implements, furniture, brushes, ink, inkstones, paper, and bibelots (such as miniature treasure boxes with hidden compartments), as well as rare books, calligraphic rubbings, and vast catalogues and encyclopedias of extant literature such as the *Ssu-k'u ch'üan-shu (Complete Library in Four Branches of Literature)*,[5] which included the catalogue of the imperial art collection itself. All these endeavors were in principle modeled after Sung or Ming precedents, but they far exceeded them in scope, and in the course of compilation must have sapped their authors of intellectual energy. One can say without reservation that, artistically, an encyclopedic excess—a penchant for extremes of size and detail—and an ornate extravagance characterize the taste of the Ch'ien-lung era.

Such extremism has been suppressed in this handscroll; on the whole, it is relatively austere and simple. Only a slight tendency

to crowd the composition with the accompanying poems and the presence of enormous and freely impressed seals remind us of the omnipresence of Kao-tsung's eulogies on the works in his collection. What is equally notable about the subject and style of this scroll, however, is its eschewing of the methods of painting flowers

1. Hung-li (the Ch'ien-lung Emperor), *Rainy Scene*, dated 1762, with second self-inscription dated 1790. Hanging scroll. Ink on paper. Palace Museum, Peking.

used by previous Chinese emperors, like Hui-tsung of the Sung or Hsüan-te of the Ming. Kao-tsung deliberately chose a style associated since the Sung primarily with the amateurism of scholar painting.

That this choice was a conscious one can also be seen in paintings of other subjects, such as landscapes (fig. 1),[6] where he boldly emulated the loose, broad style by which one "wrote out the idea" (*hsieh-i*) of one's subject. Such a stylistic pose could camouflage certain technical deficiencies, yet fall completely within the amateur ideal. In *Eight Fragrant Summer Flowers*, however, such deficiencies are readily apparent. The composition was first lightly sketched in with charcoal, undoubtedly by one of the court painters. The Emperor himself then retraced the outline with brush and ink, making impromptu changes as he saw fit (the faint charcoal indications, or *pentimenti*, which lie outside the final ink lines indicate his changes). This ink outline technique customarily assumes great command of the brush achieved by training in calligraphy and a sensitivity to the expressive and descriptive potential of the line; the spectator's attention is focused less on the subject matter (except as it suitably complements the style) than on the expressive energies

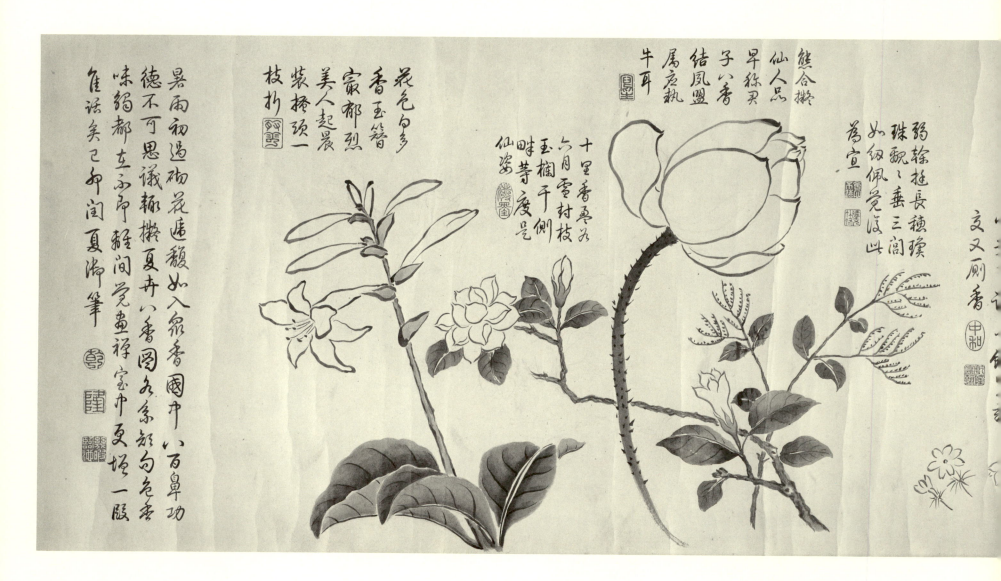

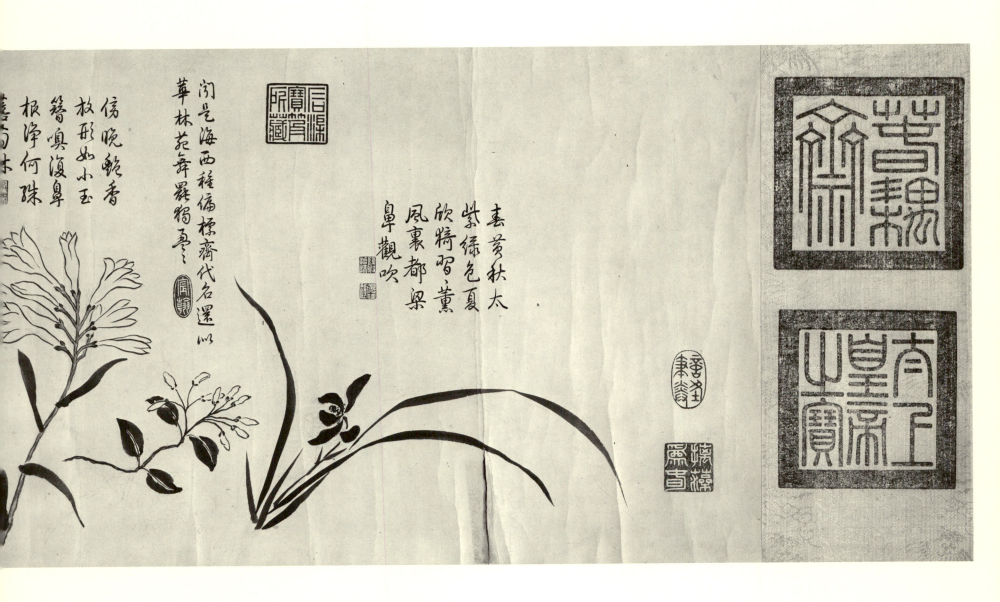

and tensions of the line itself, as these inevitably reflect the artistic sensibilities of the author. Here the conception and execution fail to convey a forceful sense of linear tension. The artist seems unaware of the descriptive potential of the line.

Kao-tsung was, however, a diligent student of the calligraphic masterworks of Wang Hsi-chih, Chao Meng-fu, Wen Cheng-ming, and Tung Ch'i-ch'ang in his collection. His copies bear a superficial resemblance to their models and are still of interest to art historians.[7] His passion for the *K'uai-hsüeh shih-ch'ing (Sudden Clearing after a Lively Snowfall,* in the National Palace Museum, Taipei), a brief letter attributed to the Chin master Wang Hsi-chih,[8] is attested by the awesome number of colophons which blanket the four lines of this specimen, as well as by the general stylistic resemblance of his own hand to this single example of Wang's style.

Although the Emperor's calligraphy may confidently be judged superior to his painting simply because he spent more time practicing it, his writing suffers from the same shortcomings as his painting—a general lassitude in the line and a want of decisive articulation in the total form. The calligraphy lacks modulation, and the brush-line has a soft, languid feeling; the pace and pressure are quite uniform, and the links between strokes assume an importance equal to the stroke components themselves, giving a rather monotonous impression. In his painting, the low level of energy in the lines tells us much about his technique. One may imagine that the whole work was cautiously traced out at a slow, steady, but determined pace. He paused frequently, perhaps looking up for encouragement and correction from his retinue of courtiers and scholars, and no doubt reflected carefully on the placement of this petal or that bud, seeking praise and support before continuing a passage. This work thus reflects an aspect of a psychology whose salient characteristics were patience, diligence, and persistence.

The execution of the painting—from choice of subject matter and first traced outlines to composition of the poems and transcription of them into final form—must easily have occupied an entire day. If the attention the Emperor gave this single scroll is considered in terms of the number of extant paintings, calligraphy, colophons, and individual projects in the classics and other arts which he undertook during his sixty-year reign,[9] the sheer weight and quantity of his output is astounding. Still, we must remember that artistic and literary activities were peripheral to his main business of running the empire and maintaining peace within its borders. That he could devote such time to these secondary pursuits suggests great leisure and affluence, a strong desire to emulate and personify the quintessential pastimes of the Confucian scholar, and a dwindling interest in the challenges of government.

Ch'ien-lung's interest in art seems to have been derived from that of his grandfather, the K'ang-hsi Emperor, and from the collection maintained in the palace during his youth. In a self-inscription he states that he learned to paint at the age of nineteen, at which time he loved bird and flower subjects most and brought all the works by famous masters on that subject from the palace collection to his studio to study and enjoy. He mentions that he copied works by such painters as Lin Ch'un, Hsü Hsi, Pien Luan, and Huang Ch'üan, and that, although he achieved some resemblance to his models, he lacked that elusive *ch'i-yün.* It was not until he was able to observe nature that he understood the works of the ancients, he writes.[10]

From extant paintings we see that, indeed, his interests eventually extended to all subjects, from flowers and animals to landscapes. We must also not underestimate the degree of influence on him from court painters. Unlike his calligraphy, which is written in a characteristic and consistent hand, his painting style was heavily dependent on the design and correction of court painters who practiced both the amateur and orthodox modes.[11] Meticulously rendered

landscapes and animals in color with Western shading have traditionally been included within his range, but judging from his potential as a painter, the more complex or technically difficult the work, the less likely it is to have come entirely from Ch'ien-lung's hand. Simpler paintings, such as this Sackler handscroll, the 1762 landscape shown in fig. 1, or his copy after Chao Meng-fu's orchids, are more characteristic and are consistent with his calligraphic style as well. Whereas a large or detailed work could well occupy weeks, these minor works were certainly within his scope. His artistic gifts were not exceptional: what he did achieve was attained through constant application and magnified by his enthusiasm.

Politically and culturally, Kao-tsung profited from the prosperous and well-administered reigns of his father, the Yung-cheng Emperor, and his grandfather, the K'ang-hsi Emperor. During his sixty years on the throne the country had an air of prosperity sufficient to impress the Western world of his supreme position as a "philosopher-emperor."[12] Indeed, by its very length, his reign could be said to be as illustrious as his grandfather's. The quality of the collection he amassed[13] is rivaled only by that of the Sung emperor Hui-tsung (reigned 1110–1125), whose own calligraphy and painting remains unchallenged among his royal peers.

Despite the high quality of the antique works he collected, however, Kao-tsung's personal preferences remained relatively commonplace and untutored. His passion for collecting painting and calligraphy should not be seen as an isolated phenomenon but as part of a contemporary interest in the acquisition of material goods, both for reasons of status and as a reflection of the wealth of the times. It spread to the lower ranks of courtiers, high officials, and wealthy merchant-princes like a contagious disease,[14] and was indeed a kind of "personified monumentalism."[15] In artistic and cultural terms one might see this addiction to accumulation as reflecting a spiritual emptiness—a society surfeited with the "good life" and showing symptoms of the onset of an inner decay.

NOTES

1. We are indebted to Shui-ying Hu of the Arnold Arboretum, Harvard University, and Wesley Wong, Brandeis University, for their aid in identifying the common and botanical names of flowers in this and entry *XI.*

2. Excellent studies of the Emperor and his era have appeared in recent years. See, for example, Harold L. Kahn, *Monarchy in the Emperor's Eyes* (Cambridge, Mass., 1971), the definitive presentation of several of his earlier articles; Fang Chao-ying's concise study in Arthur W. Hummel, ed., *Eminent Chinese of the Ch'ing Period,* pp. 369–73; Frederick Wakeman, Jr., "High Ch'ing: 1683–1839," in James B. Crowley, ed., *Modern East Asia: Essays in Interpretation* (New York, 1970), a dramatic characterization of the institutions and political tendencies of the period; Ho Ping-ti, "The Significance of the Ch'ing Period in Chinese History," *Journal of Asian Studies,* vol. 26 (1967), pp. 189–95; and David Nivison, "Ho-shen and His Accusers: Ideology and Political Behavior in the 18th Century," in A. Wright and D. Nivison, eds., *Confucianism in Action* (Stanford, Calif., 1959). (We are grateful to Christian F. Murck for his bibliographical aid in this regard.) See also Beatrice S. Bartlett, "Imperial Notations on Ch'ing Official Documents in the Ch'ien-lung (1736–1795) and Chia-ch'ing (1796–1820) Reigns," *National Palace Museum Bulletin,* vol. 7 (1972), which discusses several fundamental aspects of the primary materials found only in the National Palace Museum, Taipei.

3. The exact number of eulogies which Ch'ien-lung wrote on ancient works in the imperial collection has not yet been determined (we do not even know how many works were in the collection). Even if all the colophons to the works recorded in the three editions of the imperial catalogue, *Shih-ch'ü-pao-chi,* were counted, there would still be vast omissions, as the first two editions, *SCPC ch'u-pien* (1744–45) and *SCPC hsü-pien* (1791–93), would not record colophons written by the Emperor subsequent to the cataloguing. A low estimate of the number of the Emperor's eulogies would be in the tens of thousands. As to the number of his seals, one can only offer a minimum count; Contag and Wang list 216; the four unrecorded seals on this Sackler scroll would make the total 220. There are, of course, other unrecorded seals on other paintings which must be added to this estimate.

4. Ho Ping-ti, "The Significance of the Ch'ing Period," pp. 191–93.

5. This listing is based on the authors' acquaintance with the objects from Kao-tsung's collection still extant in the National Palace Museum, Taipei. For a description and bibliography on the *Ssu-k'u ch'üan-shu,* see Fang Chao-

ying's discussion in Hummel, *Eminent Chinese*, pp. 120–23 (*s.v.* "Chi Yün," chief editor); L. C. Goodrich, *The Literary Inquisition of Ch'ien-lung* (Baltimore, 1935), pp. 30–64.

6. Reproduced in *Ku-kung shu-hua-chi*, vol. 19, dated 1762. In the "broad style," it is a fine specimen of his art. It bears four of the same seals (the round and square seals *Ch'ien-lung* following the colophons and the oval and square seals preceding the painting) as does the Sackler scroll. It is recorded in *SCPC san-pien* under the title *Hua chi-ching shih-i*, vol. 3, p. 1153. Two other authentic examples in a "finer" style accompany the famous Wang Hsi-chih scroll, *K'uai-hsüeh shih-ch'ing* (see no. 7 below), both dated 1746.

7. See, for example, the copy of Chao Meng-fu's *Orchid*, with its inscription, in *Shodō zenshū*, vol. 17, p. 14, fig. 21.

8. Recorded in *Ku-kung shu-hua-lu*, vol. 1, 3/1–4; it bears seventy colophons by the Emperor, one of which mentions that he avidly copied its few lines whenever he had time and that even though he had copied it "several hundred times" (*shu-shih-pai-pien*) he never tired of it. It is reproduced in full in *Chin Wang Hsi-chih mo-chi* (reprint Taipei, n.d.; Ku-kung fa-shu series, no. 1), pp. 1–12. The colophons are embellished by two paintings dated 1646, one in the style of Ni Tsan, the other showing Wang Hsi-chih watching geese. See also *Shodō zenshū*, vol. 4, for a discussion of extant works attributed to Wang.

9. A count of this sort has not yet been made. To give some idea of the extent of his activity, however, the listing of the titles of the Emperor's own paintings and calligraphic works which appears in *SCPS san-pien* (1793–1817) extends for some seventy-four pages in the original Palace edition (thirty-seven pages in the Taipei reprint); it contains some 1,120 titles and, of course, does not include works which appeared in the two earlier editions of the catalogue (cf. no. 3 above).

10. Quoted in Sugimura Yuzō, *Ken ryū kōtei* (*The Ch'ien-lung Emperor*), p. 27. No reference is cited, and we have been unable to locate the painting which bears this inscription in any of the three editions of *SCPC*.

11. For information on some of these court painters, see *ibid.*, pp. 179–83, where both Chinese and Westerners at the court are mentioned; Osvald Sirén, *Chinese Painting: Leading Masters and Principles*, vol. 5, pp. 225–34.

12. See, for example, the account of Simon Harcourt-Smith, "The Emperor Ch'ien-lung," *History Today* (March, 1955), pp. 164–73.

13. The story of how the various art objects entered the imperial collection forms a separate study in itself. In brief, they were acquired in three ways: as forms of tribute (from ministers and high officials on special festivals and birthdays); through confiscation or what was euphemistically called "requisition"; and through purchase (rarest of all). For a detailed discussion of the matter and of the various editions of the *SCPC*, see Chuang Yen, "Ku-kung po-wu-yüan chen-ts'ang ch'ien-jen fa-shu kai-kuan" ("The Preservation of Calligraphy in the National Palace Museum").

14. The description of Ho Ping-ti in *The Ladder of Success in Imperial China*, pp. 154–55; see also his *Studies on the Population of China*, p. 216.

15. From Wakeman, "High Ch'ing: 1683–1839," p. 11.

XXXVIII CH'IEN TU (1763–1844)

Ch'ien-t'ang, Chekiang

Contemplating Poetry by a Snowy River
(Hsüeh-hsi shih-ssu)

The Art Museum, Princeton University (68-221).

Folding fan mounted as album leaf. Ink and light color on paper. 17.6 x 52.1 cm.

DATED: autumn, 1816 (*ping-tzu ch'iu-chung*).

SIGNATURE OF THE ARTIST: Ch'ien Shu-mei.

SEALS OF THE ARTIST: *Ch'ien Tu* (intaglio, square), *Shu-mei* (relief, square; similar to Contag and Wang, *Seals*, nos. 1–2, p. 464).

INSCRIPTION BY THE ARTIST: in four lines.

NO COLLECTORS' SEALS OR COLOPHONS

CONDITION: fair; one oval-shaped tear in upper right corner.

PROVENANCE: Frank Caro, New York.

PUBLISHED: *Record of the Art Museum, Princeton University*, vol. 27 (1968), p. 94; *Archives of Asian Art*, vol. 22 (1968–69), p. 85.

THE STANDARD SOURCES characterize Ch'ien Tu (*tzu* Shu-mei, *hao* Sung-hu, etc.; his early name was Ch'ien Yü) as retiring and aloof by nature and of uncommon cultivation. He loved to travel and did so frequently and widely. He excelled in poetry, and his literary collections, *Sung-hu hua-i* and *Sung-hu hua-ao*, also include astute comments on the calligraphy and painting which he saw.[1]

Forms built up of lines of a hair's breadth and pale tones of white, cinnabar, russet, and mineral green combine in a winter's scene of utmost delicacy. Extremely fine in width, the brushlines still turn and twist with a ductile strength, yet the artist has achieved such lightness that we feel that the brush barely touches the surface of the paper.

Ch'ien Tu's brief inscription in four lines of "running" script reads: "Imitating Chü Shang-ku, contemplating poetry over a snowy river. *Ping-tzu* [1816], *ch'iu-chung* [autumn], Ch'ien Shu-mei." Chü Shang-ku is Chü Chieh (1531–1585), one of Wen Cheng-ming's (1470–1559) pupils in landscape painting. Chü once was called "the delicate Wen" (*hsi*-Wen), a reference to the fact that his style was even more delicate than his teacher's. The reference is apt in that it also calls attention to his stylistic predecessors in the Ming. The formal roots of his style can be traced even further to the Yüan, however, for the undulating modeling lines of the landscape forms allude to Wang Meng and his "unraveled-hemp" stroke, but here the figuration is conceived of entirely in Ch'ing terms. The tone of elegance and refinement points to Yün Shou-p'ing (1633–1690) as the most immediate stylistic influence in both a formal and spiritual sense. In successfully integrating the salient features of the two great

masters Wen Cheng-ming and Yün Shou-p'ing, Ch'ien's work bridges two stylistic schools, the Ming Wu and the early Ch'ing orthodox.

THE PICTORIAL VOCABULARY of this fetching snow scene is typical of its period: a renewed interest in surface description of three-dimensional solids, an almost complete ascendance of the brushlines, which pulsate rhythmically through the rock forms, and a very precise buildup of the shapes by lines. Ch'ien's fragile vision and "miniaturist"[2] view of nature is well suited to the small album format of this work. The delicate moon face of the figure, the finely dotted trees, and the thready linework convey a sense of the withdrawn and sensitive personality of the poet.[3] This work was painted in 1816, when the artist was fifty-four, in the middle of his career, but it shows the tendency toward increasing lightness in the forms and dryness in the brushwork. A fine work by Ch'ien dated one year earlier (fig. 1) reveals similar features, coupled with the same preference for transparent colored washes.

A scroll dated 1813, *Cottage at Lu-shan* (fig. 2),[4] demonstrates more graphically the transformation of Ch'ien's modeling strokes in the rock forms from their archetype in Wang Meng into an exaggerated and self-conscious brush mannerism which came to characterize many of the later Ming and Ch'ing reworkings of earlier masters. The identifying "hemp" stroke has here literally overwhelmed the form of the rocks with a kind of nervous energy. Earlier Yün Shou-p'ing adopted this same basic schemata to build form

with great elegance. For example, he did not allow the line itself to dominate the form completely, and the quality of his brushwork conveys a greater sense of fullness and repose. Yün's works in smaller format, such as a landscape after Ni Tsan (fig. 3), suggest a more immediate prototype in composition, formation of the rocks, angular branchwork, and dotting manner in the trees. The elongation and slenderness of Yün's calligraphy can also be seen as the formal and expressive model for Ch'ien's writing. Like his painting style, however, Ch'ien's strokes are thinner, drier, and less rhythmic.

Ch'ien Tu's style was distinctive enough to admit followers, a direct one being Ch'eng Ting-lu (1797–1859). A fine album leaf in ink monochrome (fig. 4), dated 1827, is strongly reminiscent of Ch'ien's linework, while Ch'eng's stylistic individuality is seen in the more compact composition, the softly rubbed modeling strokes, and the lighter emphasis on the movement of the lines themselves. The inscription states that he also is imitating Chü Chieh.

NOTES
1. Sheng Ta-shih, *Hsi-shan wo-yu-lu* (preface dated 1822, *HSTS* ed.), vol. 9, 3/46. *Sung-hu hua-i* and *Sung-hu hua-ao* can be found in the *ISTP* series, vol. 16.
2. Sherman Lee's descriptive term (*Chinese Landscape Painting*, 1962 ed., p. 132). Cf. his figs. 107 and 108, dated 1826 and 1828, respectively.
3. The styles of such of his contemporaries as Kai Ch'i (1774–1829) and Fei Tan-hsü (1802–1850) evoke a similar tone of sheltered introspection, well characterized by Lee in *ibid.*, p. 132.
4. Reproduced from *Sōraikan kinshō*, vol. 1, pt. 3, pl. 69.

1. Ch'ien Tu, *Boat Returning Home*, dated 1815, detail. Hanging scroll. Ink and light color on paper. The Art Museum, Princeton University. Anonymous loan.

2. Ch'ien Tu, *Cottage at Lu-Shan*, dated 1813, detail. Hanging scroll. Ink and light color on paper. Abe collection, Osaka Municipal Museum.

3. Yün Shou-p'ing (1633–1690), *Landscape after Ni Tsan*, detail. Album leaf. Ink and light color on paper. Princeton Photo Archives. Collection unknown.

4. Ch'eng Ting-lu, *Teahouse and Garden*, dated 1827. Album leaf. Ink on paper. Ex-Richard Bryant Hobart collection.

3

4

1

2

XXXIX WANG HSÜEH-HAO (1754–1832)

K'un-shan, Kiangsu

Landscape after Wang Fu

The Art Museum, Princeton University (68–222).

Folding fan mounted as album leaf. Ink on paper. 17.0 x 52.0 cm.

DATED: summer, 1831 (*hsin-mao hsia-wu*).

SIGNATURE OF THE ARTIST: Hao.

SEALS OF THE ARTIST: *Wang Hsüeh-hao yin* (intaglio, square), *Chiao-hsi* (relief, square), both accompanying signature; *Hsiang* [?]-*shih* (relief, tall rectangle) before inscription (none listed in Contag and Wang, *Seals*).

INSCRIPTION BY THE ARTIST: seven lines of "running" script reading:
The fifth month, summer of the year hsin-mao [*1831*]. *Imitating the feeling of Chiu-lung shan-jen* [*Wang Fu*] *at Shan-nan lao-nung's* [*my*] *studio, I-hua-hsüan.* [*Painted for*] *my "third brother," Hsiang-lin* [*unidentified*].
[Signed:] *The seventy-nine-year-old man, Hao.*

NO COLLECTORS' SEALS OR COLOPHONS

CONDITION: good.

PROVENANCE: Frank Caro, New York.

PUBLISHED: *Record of the Art Museum, Princeton University*, vol. 27 (1968), p. 94; *Archives of Asian Art*, vol. 22 (1968–69), p. 85.

THIS PAINTING is by a third-generation painting descendant of Wang Yüan-ch'i (1642–1715), who is sometimes counted among the Lesser Four Wangs.[1] The landscape was executed one year before Wang Hsüeh-hao's death. It is a well-worked-out, cogent, and mature pictorial statement of a painter completely at home in the orthodox idiom of the Four Wangs. A fair degree of monumentality has been achieved within the confines of the fan format. The major mass is built up of three connected groups. Short, energetic verticals of tree trunks file through the smaller rectangular forms, lending surface interest to the compact mountain. The softly rubbed outlines of the rocks in gray wash contrast with the crisp charcoal blacks of the trees, cottages, and occasional moss dots. Throughout, one has the feeling that the plain white paper played a positive structural role in the execution of the larger design and the diversity of the textures and shapes.

WANG HSÜEH-HAO's (*tzu* Chiao-hsi, *hao* Meng-yang, Shan-nan lao-nung) sensitivity to the interaction of paper surface with landscape structure may remind us of the youngest of the Four Wangs, Wang Yüan-ch'i: indeed, the standard biographical sources state that Wang's landscape style descends from the orthodox line of the youngest of the Four, in that Hsüeh-hao's first teacher was Li Yü-te, and Li's father was Li Hsien, who was the maternal nephew of Wang Yüan-ch'i.[2] Like other painters on the periphery of the orthodox school, Wang Hsüeh-hao's individual statement and subtlety have not received sufficient attention today, but his talents were

duly recognized in his time. A contemporary of Wang's, Ch'ien Yung (1759–1844), described Wang's activity in the Su-chou area: "He excelled in landscapes [which had the appearance of being] messy and coarsely rendered, but which were rationally achieved in every aspect [*yu li-ch'ü*]. In his late years he adopted Shen Chou's style. Recently the painters around Su-chou all acknowledge Chiao-hsi [Wang Hsüeh-hao] as being foremost."[3]

Wang was aware of his artistic position as a scholar-painter and sought to maintain its ideals. Thus he articulated the process which he felt constituted painting by the literary man (*shih-ta-fu hua*):

There are six styles [of calligraphy], but only one Way [*Tao*]. It is enough to [watch a man] write to perceive it: the writer must have his meaning foremost [in his mind] before the brush [touches the paper]. Then he need only pursue what he perceives, and although [the work may have the appearance of] disheveled hair and coarse clothing, the flavor of the meaning will naturally be full, exceedingly precise and entrancing, and it will convey the vitality and flavor of antique refinement. This is painting by the literary man! Otherwise how could it be distinguished from vulgar craftwork?[4]

From this we know that Wang was not a blind follower of formal canons and that he was alert to the dangers of perpetuating empty brush formulas devoid of a personal conception.

The inscription on this painting states that he is imitating Chiu-lung shan-jen, the early Ming master Wang Fu (1362–1416). By the Ming and Ch'ing dynasties, the concept of "imitate" (*fang*) had acquired associations which could have deep philosophical implications, depending on the individual master, but it had at least a primary surface meaning of "emulate the spirit." A specific work of the master who was being imitated would sometimes be mentioned as an "in-group" reference, and the formal allusions would inevitably be multileveled and often several times removed from their nominal inspiration. Hence in this fan if one were to insist on tracing the reference to Wang Fu, it would more likely be Wang's style as interpreted through the images of other Yüan masters, such as Huang Kung-wang or Ni Tsan, and as further interpreted by Shen Chou, Tung Ch'i-ch'ang, and Wang Yüan-ch'i.

In a slightly earlier work, dated 1827 (fig. 1),[5] Wang Hsüeh-hao reveals the same ability to integrate landscape and foliage masses successfully and to leave judicious areas of white paper to suggest bulging space or volume. In this landscape and in the Sackler fan shapes are built up by flat, oblique brushlines, deftly stroked onto the paper in several layers for a soft effect. These oblique strokes and the sense of abstract design may also be related to Lu Chih (1496–1576) in the Ming, but the sense of density and rounded, three-dimensional volume still derives most significantly from Wang Yüan-ch'i and, ultimately, from the stylistic redirection given seventeenth-century painting by Tung Ch'i-ch'ang.

In the terms of his own orthodox branch, Wang Hsüeh-hao's subtleties were not capricious, and they earned him a respectable place in that artistic line. The degree of his success, however minor it may seem in retrospect, testifies to the strength of that tradition and its coninued challenge to artists of Wang's sensitivity and abilities in the nineteenth century.

1. Wang Hsüeh-hao, *Landscape after Chü-jan and Wu Chen*, dated 1827. Hanging scroll. Ink on paper. Collection unknown.

NOTES

1. The other three being Wang Ch'en (1720–1797), the great grandson of Wang Yüan-ch'i; Wang Su (fl. 1760–1766), the great-grandson of Wang Shih-min; and Wang Yü (1662–1722), who was the pupil of Wang Yüan-ch'i. Cf. Ch'en Ting-shan's listing in *Ting-shan lun-hua ch'i-chung*, pp. 54–56, where the Lesser Four Wangs are included under the "Lou-tung" school. Contag and Wang list Wang Chiu (ca. 1768), the great-grandson of Wang Hui, instead of Wang Hsüeh-hao (*Seals*, p. xvi).
2. *CKHCJMTTT*, p. 57.
3. *Lü-yüan hua-hsüeh*, p. 190.
4. *CKHCJMTTT*, p. 57.
5. *Tōan-zō shōgafu*, 4/67.

XL CH'EN CHAO (ca. 1835–1884-)

Yang-chou, Kiangsu

Landscape

The Art Museum, Princeton University (68-223).

Folding fan mounted as album leaf. Ink and light color on silk. 17.2 x 52.1 cm.

UNDATED: probably executed ca. 1865–1870.

SIGNATURE OF THE ARTIST: Ch'ung-kuang, Ch'en Chao (after inscription).

INSCRIPTION BY THE ARTIST (three lines in "running" script):
[Painted] at the elegant request of my second elder brother Meng-hsiang. Please correct it.

SEAL OF THE ARTIST: Ch'ung-kuang-fu (intaglio, tall rectangle).

NO COLLECTORS' SEALS OR COLOPHONS

CONDITION: poor; the fan had seen much wear when mounted on its folding frame; heavy creases on each of the folds are evident, and in some places the silk is split completely; on the right side, the silk of the entire third rib has been replaced and painted in; minor repairs and repainting on the second rib of the left side are visible; the edges of the fan were trimmed at the time of the most recent remounting.

PROVENANCE: Frank Caro, New York.

PUBLISHED: Record of the Art Museum, Princeton University, vol. 27 (1968), p. 94; Archives of Asian Art, vol. 22 (1968–69), p. 85.

THIS COLORED FAN is a minor work of a painter and poet who gained local fame in Yang-chou for his flowers and landscapes. Today Ch'en's name has fallen into obscurity, and even though he lived in the nineteenth century, his extant works are quite rare. This painting is the only Ch'en Chao known to us in a Western collection.

The landscape scene fills the whole fan to its borders, and the brush has a tendency to move in a quick, short rhythm in contact with the silk. No striking artistic personality has yet emerged. The style is strongly derivative, and we sense most prominently the influence of Wang Shih-min (1592–1680) as well as that of a few closely related contemporaries, such as Huang I (1744–1801), Hsi Kang (1746–1803), and Ku Yün (1835–1896; cf. XLI). It shows quite clearly the persistence of the orthodox tradition among minor painters in areas distant from Sung-chiang and T'ai-ts'ang, where the Four Wangs worked. Although Ch'en is a minor figure in terms of art history, knowledge of his activities fills in the gaps between the major personalities and innovators of the Ch'ing period.

CH'EN CHAO (tzu Ch'ung-kuang, Jo-mu, hao Le-sheng, etc.) has received little notice in the standard biographical sources. Material presented here is culled primarily from observations by the modern painter and theorist Huang Pin-hung (1864–1955), who was Ch'en's younger contemporary. We have attempted to establish Ch'en's birth and death dates, which hitherto have not been determined, and to introduce some of his aesthetic ideals. Ch'en's interests were broad and almost modern in that his personal taste was not confined to any particular school, albeit this work shows distinct derivations from the orthodox line.

Huang Pin-hung bears witness to Ch'en's fame in his Lun-hua ch'ang-hsin (Long Letters on Painting), published in 1954: "I recall when I was more than twenty years of age, I went to Yang-chou for the first time. . . . I heard that there were over seven hundred professional painters and close to three thousand scholars and intellectuals. But Ch'en Jo-mu [Chao] had gained the most fame for his flower paintings in outline style [shuang-kou]. As he was already deranged, he did not paint very much, and [his works] commanded the highest price. After him there was Wu Jang-chih [tzu T'ing-yang, 1799–1870]."[1] It is significant that Huang places Ch'en's reputation higher than that of the archeologist and painter Wu Jang-chih, who was renowned for his studies in bronze and stone inscriptions at the time. Tribute was paid to Ch'en's reputation in another way, according to Huang: "At that time there was competition to make forgeries of Ch'en's works. Even today [ca. 1910], there are those who make a living by such a practice."[2]

Huang offers more background information on Ch'en in his Chin shu-shih-nien hua-che-p'ing (Critique of Painters of Recent Decades), published in 1930: "Ch'en Jo-mu, T. Ch'ung-kuang, paints flowers and plants in the outline method, and comes exceedingly close to the way of the ancients. As for his figures and landscapes, they are all of the finest subtlety. He lived in Anhwei for a time as a guest of the Ching family and was able to see original works of the Sung and Yüan masters. Therefore his works have a monumental and weighty quality to them."[3] In the Yang-chou area where Ch'en was active, the influence of the Eight Eccentrics was preeminent. Collectors' taste for landscapes ranked second to that for bird and flower paintings, subjects the Eccentrics had made popular, which accounts for Huang's stress on Ch'en's achievement in flower painting. Ch'en's popularity in Yang-chou is also notable because it shows that the patrons of this metropolis also supported painters of a more conservative style.

Ch'en's poetry survives in a collection titled I-ou yin-kuan hsüan-chi.[4] The most common subjects of his poems are memories of travel or inscriptions to his paintings. They provide not only rare biographical material but insight into his circle of friends and artistic ideals. For example, one elegy titled "Weeping for Wu Jang-chih" witnesses the close personal friendship of the two men. This poem strengthens Ch'en's chronology, since we know from it that he was still alive in 1870, when Wu died. The inscriptions from this collection are all the more valuable because so few paintings by Ch'en are extant today to offer concrete evidence of his style.

A poetic quatrain on a painting imitating the style of Tung Ch'i-ch'ang (1555–1636) reads:

Greatly expand on "Ch'an-shih" [i.e., Tung Ch'i-ch'ang] in order to "transmit the candleflame";
The "orthodox" and the "plain" represent the Uppermost Vehicle.
One need not share the "mantle and almsbowl" of the many [Four] Wangs;
For only the monk Shih-t'ao has attained divinity.

An inscription on another painting reads:

Who could attain the immortal realm of Ni [Tsan] and Huang [Kung-wang]?
It is difficult enough to capture [the secrets of] Tung Hua-t'ing [Ch'i-ch'ang].

In the first poem, "Ch'an-shih" refers to Tung Ch'i-ch'ang, by allusion to his studio, Hua-Ch'an-shih. Thus in the two poems Ch'en considered both Tung Ch'i-ch'ang and Tao-chi as worthy painting ideals. As to the Four Wangs, Ch'en still held them in lower esteem even though he himself owed them a stylistic debt.

From the title of the paintings in Ch'en's poetic collection, we can infer that although he was known for his flower paintings a large proportion of his works were landscapes. Of these a majority were in direct "imitation" of (lin) or "in the style" of (fang) such Yüan masters as Ni Tsan, Wu Chen, and even the early Ch'ing monk

K'un-ts'an (fl. 1657–1686). Ch'en seems to have lacked innovative spirit and, like other late Ch'ing painters, to have succumbed to a stifling over-reliance on the formal prescriptions of earlier masters. Nevertheless, he was still a painter of broad and selective tastes who not only had high expressive goals but also could respond to the artistic genius of both orthodox and individualist masters such as Tung Ch'i-ch'ang and Tao-chi.

We know little about Chen's personal history. When he was forty-eight, however, the serious illness of his second wife caused him to become moody, and according to Huang Pin-hung, when he was about fifty he suffered an emotional collapse, which must have affected his painting.[5] We might reconstruct Ch'en's rough dates on this basis: if Huang Pin-hung, born in 1864, went to Yang-chou when he was over twenty (i.e., probably between 1884 and 1892) and Ch'en was already ill, it would mean Ch'en was already past fifty. Therefore he was probably born about 1838 and died after about 1884. This calculation would agree with the observation mentioned above, that his death occurred after that of his contemporary Wu Jang-chih in 1880.

Ch'en's work has been divided into three periods recently by a Hong Kong writer, Ch'iu Wen: (1) early period, when Ch'en signed his paintings primarily as "Ch'ung-kuang, Ch'en Chao," and his style showed a heavy reliance on imitating older painters; (2) middle period, when his signatures were variations of his several *tzu*, such as "Jo-mu, Ch'en Ch'ung-kuang," "Jo-mu chü-shih," or simply "Jo-mu," in cursive script—in this period he seemed to show more artistic independence and gradually developed his own style; (3) later period, works which were produced when he was forty to fifty years of age and usually signed "Le-sheng, Ch'en Jo-mu." This last was perhaps his greatest period of achievement.[6]

If we were to adhere to Ch'iu Wen's outline of Ch'en's style, the signature on the Sackler fan would indicate that this is a work of Ch'en's early period, when he was still strongly influenced by his training. This interpretation would agree with the rough dates we have set, for it would mean that the painting was executed around 1865, when Ch'en was only thirty years of age.

NOTES

1. As quoted by Ch'iu Wen in "Huang Pin-hung yü Ch'en Jo-mu," p. 276.
2. *Ibid*.
3. As quoted by Ch'iu Wen in *ibid*.
4. In two *chüan*, published in 1909 in Canton; quoted in *ibid*., p. 280.
5. *Ibid*., p. 276.
6. *Ibid*., pp. 276–77.

XLI KU YÜN (1835–1896)

Su-chou, Kiangsu

Landscape at Dusk

The Art Museum, Princeton University (68-224).

Folding fan mounted as album leaf.
Ink and light color on gold-flecked paper. 18.4 x 52.5 cm.

UNDATED

SIGNATURE OF THE ARTIST: Jo-po, Ku Yün.

SEAL OF THE ARTIST: *Jo-po* (relief, square; not listed in Contag and Wang, *Seals*).

NO COLLECTORS' SEALS OR COLOPHONS

CONDITION: fair; the paper is worn considerably at the edges of the folds of each of the ribs, leaving heavy crease marks; three conspicuously abraded areas on the left side of the fan and also along the top edge no longer carry any gold flecks.

PROVENANCE: Frank Caro, New York.

PUBLISHED: *Record of the Art Museum, Princeton University*, vol. 27 (1968), p. 94; *Archives of Asian Art*, vol. 22 (1968–69), p. 85.

KU YÜN WAS KNOWN for his landscapes in the style of the Four Wangs, Wu Li, and Yün Shou-p'ing, showing again the persistent influence of those styles in the Wu area. Ku was included among the Nine Friends of Painting active in Su-chou in the late nineteenth century.[1]

The artist's brief poetic inscription is written to the far right in two lines of "running" script:

> *Blown mist rises from the treetops,*
> *Evening vapor presses upon the mountains.*

The painting presents a familiar natural scene: evening mist settling over houses and trees. Dark ink dotted alternately with a transparent green hue in the foliage establishes the key tonality, while pale wash delineates the rock and mountain shapes. The blank areas of the gold-flecked paper around the trees and at the base of the mountains suggest descending twilight vapor and, together with the touches of green, lend a glimmering quality to the scene. The composition fills the borders of the fan without any prominent foreground or far distant elements. The feeling conveyed is serene and intimate.

KU YÜN WAS a contemporary of Ch'en Chao (see *XL*), but his artistic fate was not as unfortunate as Ch'en's. A considerable number of Ku's works survive today, and reproductions of a large majority were printed and bound soon after his death. For example,

the edition published in 1927, entitled *Ku Jo-po shan-shui chi-ts'e* (*Landscape Album by Ku Yün*), offers a broad range of his works with which to compare this fan. Very close in style is a landscape after Wang Shih-min (1592–1680) (fig. 1). Dated 1895, a year before his death, this album was executed for a fellow Su-chou painter, Chin Lan (1841–1909), who inscribed the work as follows: "Among the finest [in this album] are those paintings in the style of Lien-chou [Wang Chien], Yen-k'o [Wang Shih-min], Lu-t'ai [Wang Yüan-ch'i], and Ching-yen [Wang Hui]. Indeed, these are the most accomplished works of his entire œuvre."[2] This seemingly innocuous comment is indicative of the state of painting in the late nineteenth century and the models that painters in the Wu area revered at this time. Since the Four Wangs, the Lesser Four Wangs had also risen in influence, and Chin's own style was considered to be close to Wang Ch'en, one of the Lesser Wangs. In contrast to the late seventeenth century, when the Four Wangs flourished, models for imitation at this time were not T'ang or Sung masters but their close predecessors from the Ch'ing. For example, Ku made a spirited and faithful copy of an album by Wang Hui after Sung and Yüan masters (fig. 2), now in the Morse collection.[3] It is signed and dated 1884, and its inscription pays homage to this major formative influence.

Ku Yün did not confine himself to inspiration from the orthodox school, however. His artistic interests and eye for quality, like those of his contemporary Ch'en Chao, were attracted by the individualist Tao-chi. A copy by Ku of a composition by the monk painter[4] (fig. 3) testifies to the catholicity which later nineteenth-century paint-

1. Ku Yün, landscape after the brush method of Wang Shih-min, dated 1895, leaf A. Album of twelve leaves. Collection unknown.

2. Ku Yün, signed copy of a leaf from an album by Wang Hui (1632–1717). Ink on paper. Collection unknown.

3. Ku Yün, signed copy of a composition by Tao-chi. Hanging scroll. Ink on paper. Collection unknown.

ers had cultivated. The spirit of their forerunners was very much alive to them. Thus Chin Lan's criticism of Ku as a peer is worthy of note for the substantial changes in artistic ideals which it represents. The towering image of perfection attained by the Four Wangs and other early Ch'ing individualists made it difficult for any follower in the tradition to step beyond their shadow and proceed further into the past.

Later masters such as Ku Yün turned to the Four Wangs even for criticism of painting. In an inscription on one of his paintings, Ku writes that Wang Ching-yen (Hui) once said: "Someone asked me what is scholar painting [*shih-ta-fu-hua*]. I answered: 'There's only one word to describe it completely: calligraphy.'" Wang's reply "hits the mark," Ku wrote, "for as soon as one becomes involved in tracing [*miao-hua*] one has descended to common craftsmanship!"[5] Ku's statement reminds one of Wang Hsüeh-hao's observation of a similar nature (cf. *XXXIX*). Both comments indicate that these painters were constantly aware of calligraphy as the fundamental basis of the tradition of scholar painting of which they were a part, and they point to the motivating force underlying the strength of the orthodox line almost three hundred years after its inception with Tung Ch'i-ch'ang. The Four Wangs and the early subscribers to Tung's theories were able to study the great private collections of antique paintings before the large majority of them entered the Imperial Palace during Ch'ien-lung's reign. This firsthand acquaintance with early works gave them an aesthetic wellspring which proved to be an inexhaustible source of cultivation—the *ta-ch'eng*, or "great synthesis," as articulated by Tung Ch'i-ch'ang. By the mid-eighteenth century and the time of the Lesser Four Wangs, the quality of this artistic milieu was denied them, and these original works were less easily accessible. Subsequent artists in this tradition, further limited in their breadth of exposure to genuine antique models, were left only a choice of variations on artistic themes now several times removed from their original antique impulse.

Given the untimely "entrance" (in George Kubler's words) which fates certain artists to become followers rather than innovators of any tradition, the fact that Ku Yün was able to maintain such a degree of artistic quality and that he carved out a corner of posterity is due in part to such factors as his artistic persistence, the refinement of his personal taste and cultivation, and his eye for quality, but, in the main, it is due to his training in and understanding of calligraphy as the theoretical and practical basis of painting.

NOTES

1. Others of the Nine were Wu Ta-cheng (1835–1902), Lu Hui (1851–1920), Ku Lin-shih (fl. 1896–1916), Jen Yü (1853–1901), Ni T'ien (1855–1919), Chin Lan (1841–1909), Hu Hsi-kuei (fl. 1882), and Wu Ku-hsiang (1848–1903); see Ch'en Ting-shan, *Ting-shan lun-hua ch'i-chung*, pp. 56, 73, 117. We are indebted to David Sensabaugh for this reference. He reports that landscapes by Lu Hui and Ku Lin-shih are in the Chia-an collection in Palo Alto, California.
2. (Shanghai, 1927). Chin Lan's colophon is found on leaf thirteen after Ku's own self-inscription.
3. The Morse album is dated 1673. See Roderick Whitfield, *In Pursuit of Antiquity*, pp. 119–42. The copy by Ku Yün contains only eight leaves and is published in successive issues of *Shoen*, vol. 1 (1937), nos. 1–9. Leaves A, C, G, I, and J of the Morse album are missing from Ku's copy, and another leaf not found in the Wang Hui version has made its way into Ku's otherwise faithful replica (*Shoen*, no. 4).
4. Published in *Ku Jo-po shan-shui-ts'e* (Shanghai, 1926), last page.
5. Illustrated in *Shina nanga taisei*, vol. 12, p. 230.

Bibliography

NOTE: *entries are listed by title or by author's or editor's name, according to their citation in the text references.*

Ackerman, James S., and Carpenter, Rhys. *Art and Archaeology.* Englewood Cliffs, N.J., 1963.

Barnhart, Richard M. *"Marriage of the Lord of the River": A Lost Landscape by Tung Yüan.* Ascona, 1970.

_____ . *Wintry Forests, Old Trees: Some Landscape Themes in Chinese Painting.* New York, 1972.

Berenson, Bernard. *Aesthetics and History.* New York, 1948.

_____ . *Drawings of the Florentine Painters.* Vol. 1. Chicago, 1938.

_____ . "The Rudiments of Connoisseurship." In *The Study and Criticism of Italian Art.* 2d ser. London, 1902.

Bush, Susan. *The Chinese Literati on Painting: Su Shih (1037–1101) to Tung Ch'i-ch'ang (1555–1636).* Cambridge, Mass., 1971.

Cahill, James. *Chinese Painting.* Lausanne, 1960.

_____ . "The Early Styles of Kung Hsien." *Oriental Art,* vol. 16 (1970), pp. 51–71.

_____ , ed. *Fantastics and Eccentrics in Chinese Painting.* New York, 1967.

_____ , ed. *The Restless Landscape.* Berkeley, Calif., 1971.

_____ . "Wu Pin and His Landscape Paintings." *See* National Palace Museum, Taipei, *Proceedings of the International Symposium on Chinese Painting.*

_____ . "Yüan Chiang and His School." *Ars Orientalis,* vol. 5 (1963), pp. 259–72; vol. 6 (1966), pp. 191–212.

Chang Dai-chien: A Retrospective, edited by René-Yvon Lefebre d'Argencé. San Francisco, Calif., 1972.

Chang Dai-chien's Paintings. Hong Kong, 1967.

Chang Heng. "Tsen-yang chien-ting shu-hua" ("How To Authenticate Ancient Paintings and Calligraphy"). *Wen-wu,* no. 4 (1964), pp. 3–23.

Chang Keng. *Kuo-ch'ao hua-cheng-lu* (self-preface dated 1735) and *Kuo-ch'ao hua-cheng hsü-lu.* HSTS ed., vol. 2, pt. 5.

Chang Ta-ch'ien. *Ta-ch'ien chü-shih chi-ch'ou i-hou so-yung-yin (Seals of Chang Ta-ch'ien Used after 1949),* edited by Li Shun-hua. Taipei, 1967.

Chang Yen-yüan. *Li-tai ming-hua-chi* (self-preface traditionally dated 847). ISTP ed., vol. 8.

Chao Pu-chih. *Wu-chiu t'i-pa (Colophons of Chao Pu-chih).* ISTP ed., vol. 22.

Ch'en Jen-t'ao [J. D. Chen]. *Chin-k'uei ts'ang-hua p'ing-shih (Notes and Comments on the Paintings in the King Kwei Collection).* 3 vols. Hong Kong, 1956.

Ch'en Ting-shan. *Ting-shan lun-hua ch'i-chung (Miscellaneous Comments on Painting).* Taipei, 1969.

Cheng Chen-to, ed. *Yün-hui-chai-ts'ang Tang-Sung-i-lai ming-hua-chi (Paintings in the Collection of Chang Heng).* Shanghai, 1947.

Cheng Cho-lu. *Shih-t'ao yen-chiu (A Study of Shih-t'ao).* Peking, 1961.

Cheng Hsi-chen. *Hung-jen, K'un-ts'an.* Shanghai, 1963; rpt. Hong Kong, 1970.

Cheng Hsieh. *Pan-ch'iao t'i-pa (Colophons of Cheng Hsieh).* ISTP ed., vol. 26.

Cheng Wei. "Lun Shih-t'ao sheng-huo, hsing-ching, ssu-hsiang ti-pien chi i-shu ch'eng-chiu" ("On Shih-t'ao's Life, Intellectual Development, and Artistic Achievements"). *Wen-wu,* no. 12 (1962), pp. 6–7, 43–50.

Cheng Wu-min. "Shih-t'ao shu-chi pa" ("Colophons to Shih-t'ao's Calligraphy"). *I-lin ts'ung-lu.* Hong Kong, 1961–66. Vol. 4, pp. 169–74.

Chia Tsu-chang and Chia Tsu-shan, eds. *Chung-kuo chih-wu t'u-tien (Illustrated Dictionary of Chinese Plants).* Peking, 1958.

Chiang Chao-shen. "The Identity of Yang Mei-tzu and the Paintings of Ma Yüan." *National Palace Museum Bulletin,* vol. 2, nos. 2–3 (1967), pp. 1–15, 8–14.

_____ . "The Life of Wen Cheng-ming and the School of Su-chou Painting in the Middle and Late Ming" ("Wen Cheng-ming hsing-i yü Ming chung-yeh-i-hou chih Su-chou hua-t'an"). *National Palace Museum Quarterly,* vol. 4 (1971), pp. 27–30 (English summary and chronology for 1470–1508), 39–88 (Chinese text and chronology for 1470–1499).

_____ . "A Study of T'ang Yin" ("Liu-ju chü-shih chih shen-shih"). *National Palace Museum Quarterly,* vol. 2, no. 4 (1967–68), pp. 15–32; vol. 3, nos. 1–3 (1968–69), pp. 33–60, 31–71, 35–79, respectively.

_____ . "Wang Yüan-ch'i: Notes on a Special Exhibition." *National Palace Museum Bulletin,* vol. 2 (1967), pp. 10–15.

Chiang I-han. "K'u-kua ho-shang Hua-yü-lu" yen-chiu (A Study of Tao-chi's "Hua-yü-lu"). Taipei, 1965. Offprint with paging 397–546.

Chiang Liang-fu. *Li-tai ming-jen nien-li pei-chuan tsung-piao (A Chronology of Prominent Chinese throughout History).* Shanghai, 1937.

Chiang Shao-shu. *Wu-sheng shih-shih (A History of Voiceless Poems)* (n.d.; self-preface indicates inclusion of painters to 1643). HSTS ed., vol. 4.

Ch'ien Yung. *Lü-yüan hua-hsüeh (Lü-yüan's Comments on Painters and Paintings).* ISTP ed., vol. 16.

Chin-k'uei ts'ang-hua-chi (Masterpieces of Chinese Painting from the King Kwei Collection), edited by J. D. Chen. 2 vols. Tokyo, 1956.

Ch'in Tsu-yung. *T'ung-yin lun-hua (Evaluation of Painters of the Late Ming and Ch'ing Periods)* (self-preface dated 1864). ISTP ed., vol. 16.

Chinese Art Treasures. Lausanne, 1961.

Ch'ing-hsiang lao-jen t'i-chi (Record of Inscriptions by the Old Man Ch'ing-hsiang), edited by Wang Yün. In *Hua-yüan pi-chi,* edited by Wu P'i-chiang. Su-chou, 1939. Vol. 1, pp. 1–21.

Ch'ing-hsiang shu-hua-kao-chüan (Sketches of Calligraphy and Painting by Ch'ing-hsiang). Peking, 1961.

Ch'iu A. K'ai-ming. "The Chieh-tzu Yüan Hua Chuan." *Archives of the Chinese Art Society of America,* vol. 5 (1951), pp. 55–69.

Ch'iu Wen. "Huang Pin-hung yü Ch'en Jo-mu" ("On the Painters Huang Pin-hung and Ch'en Chao"). *I-lin ts'ung-lu.* Hong Kong, 1966. Vol. 6, pp. 274–81.

Chou Ju-hsi. "A Note on the 'Verdant Hills and Red Maples' by Lu Chih." *Allen Memorial Art Museum* [Oberlin College] *Bulletin,* spring, 1971, pp. 163–75.

_____ . "In Quest of the Primordial Line: The Genesis and Content of Tao-chi's *Hua-yü-lu.*" Ph.D. dissertation, Princeton University, 1969.

Chou Liang-kung. *Tu-hua-lu (Record of Painters and Paintings)* (epilogue dated 1673). HSTS ed., vol. 9.

Chu Sheng-chai. *Chung-kuo shu-hua (Chinese Painting and Calligra-*

phy). Hong Kong, 1961. Vol. 1.

_____. *Sheng-chai tu-hua-chi* (*Chu's Notes on Painting*). Hong Kong, [1951].

Chu Ts'un-li. *T'ieh-wang shan-hu shu-hua-p'in*. N.p., epilogue dated 1600.

Chuang Shen. "Ming Shen Chou Mo-ch'o T'ung-ch'üeh-yen-ko t'u k'ao" ("A Study of Shen Chou's Painting 'Bronze Peacock Inkslab' "). *Ming-pao*, vol. 3 (1968), pp. 53–65.

_____, and Watt, J. C. Y. *Exhibition of Paintings of the Ming and Ch'ing Periods*. Hong Kong [City Museum and Art Gallery], 1970.

Chuang Yen. "Ku-kung po-wu-yüan chen-ts'ang ch'ien-jen fa-shu kai-kuan" ("The Preservation of Calligraphy in the National Palace Museum"). *National Palace Museum Quarterly*, vol. 3 (1969), pp. 5–15.

Chung-hua min-kuo jen-shih-lu (*Notes on the Chinese of the Republican Period*). Taipei, 1953.

Chung-kuo ming-hua-chi (*Famous Chinese Paintings*), edited by Ti P'ing-tzu. 2 vols. Shanghai, 1939.

Chung-kuo ming-hua-chia ts'ung-shu (*A Collection of Famous Painters in Chinese History*). 2 vols. Shanghai, 1959; rpt. Hong Kong, 1970.

CKHCJMTTT: *Chung-kuo hua-chia jen-ming ta-tz'u-tien* (*A Biographical Dictionary of Prominent Chinese Painters*), edited by Sun Ta-kung. Taipei, 1959.

CKHLLP: *Chung-kuo hua-lun lei-pien* (*Classified Remarks on Chinese Painting*), edited by Yü Chien-hua. 2 vols. Peking, 1957.

CKJMTTT: *Chung-kuo jen-ming ta-tz'u-tien* (*A Biographical Dictionary of Prominent Chinese*). Hong Kong, 1959.

Collingwood, R. G. *The Idea of History*. New York, 1956.

Contag, Victoria. *Chinese Masters of the 17th Century*, translated by Michael Bullock. Tokyo, 1969–70.

_____. *Zwei Meister chinesischer Landschaftsmalerei*. Baden-Baden, [1955].

_____, and Wang, C. C. *Seals of Chinese Painters and Collectors of the Ming and Ch'ing Periods*. Hong Kong, 1966. (Contag and Wang, *Seals*, in text references.)

De Bary, W. T., ed. *Self and Society in Ming Thought*. New York, 1970.

Draft Ming Biographies. *See* Ming Biographical History Project.

Ecke, Gustav. *Chinese Painting in Hawaii*. 3 vols. Honolulu, 1965.

Ecke, Tseng Yu-ho. *Chinese Calligraphy*. Philadelphia, 1971.

Edwards, Richard. *The Field of Stones*. Washington, D.C., 1962.

_____. "The Painting of Tao-chi: Postscript to an Exhibition." *Oriental Art*, vol. 14 (1968), pp. 261–70.

_____. "Tao-chi the Painter." *See The Painting of Tao-chi*, pp. 21–52.

Exhibition of Paintings by Chang Dai-chien. Carmel, Calif., 1967.

Fang Chün-i. *Meng-yüan shu-hua-lu* (*Record of Calligraphy and Painting*). N.p., self-preface dated 1877.

Ferguson, John C. *Li-tai chu-lu hua-mu* (*Index of Recorded Chinese Paintings in All Periods*). 2 vols. Peking, 1934; rpt. Taipei, 1968.

Fong, Wen. "A Chinese Album and Its Copy." *Record of the Art Museum, Princeton University*, vol. 28 (1968), pp. 74–78.

_____. "Chinese Painting: A Statement of Method." *Oriental Art*, vol. 9 (1963), pp. 72–78.

_____. "Archaism as a 'Primitive' Style." In *Artists and Traditions: The Uses of the Past in Chinese Culture*, edited by Christian F. Murck. Princeton, N.J. Forthcoming.

_____. "A Letter from Shih-t'ao to Pa-ta shan-jen and the Problem of Shih-t'ao's Chronology." *Archives of the Chinese Art Society of America*, vol. 13 (1959), pp. 22–53.

_____. *The Lohans and a Bridge to Heaven*. Washington, D.C., 1958.

_____. "The Problem of Ch'ien Hsüan." *Art Bulletin*, vol. 42 (1960), pp. 173–89.

_____. "The Problem of Forgeries in Chinese Painting." *Artibus Asiae*, vol. 25 (1962), pp. 95–119.

_____. "Reply to Professor Soper's Comments on Tao-chi's Letter to Chu Ta." *Artibus Asiae*, vol. 29 (1967), pp. 351–57.

_____. "Towards a Structural Analysis of Chinese Landscape Painting." *Art Journal*, vol. 28 (1969), pp. 388–97.

_____. "Tung Ch'i-ch'ang and the Orthodox Theory of Painting." *National Palace Museum Quarterly*, vol. 2 (1967–68), pp. 1–26.

_____. "Wang Hui: The Great Synthesis." *National Palace Museum Quarterly*, vol. 3 (1968–69), pp. 5–10.

Friedländer, Max J. *On Art and Connoisseurship*, translated by T. Borenius. New York, 1932.

Fu, Marilyn, and Fong, Wen. *The Wilderness Colors of Tao-chi*. New York: Metropolitan Museum of Art, 1973.

Fu Pao-shih. *Ming-mo min-tsu i-jen-chuan* (*Biographies of Ming Loyalist Artists*). Ch'ang-sha, 1939.

_____. *Shih-t'ao shang-jen nien-p'u* (*Chronology of Shih-t'ao*). Shanghai, 1948.

Fu, Shen C. Y. "Notes on Chiang Shen." *National Palace Museum Bulletin*, vol. 1 (1966), pp. 1–10.

_____. "A Preliminary Study to the Extant Works of Chü-jan." *National Palace Museum Quarterly*, vol. 2 (1967), pp. 11–24, 51–79.

_____. "A Study of the Authorship of the So-Called 'Hua-shuo' Painting Treatise." *See* National Palace Museum, Taipei, *Proceedings of the International Symposium on Chinese Painting*.

_____. "Two Anonymous Sung Dynasty Paintings and the Lu-shan Landscape: The Problem of Their Stylistic Origins." *National Palace Museum Bulletin*, vol. 2 (1968), p. 1016; vol. 3 (1969), pp. 6–10.

A Garland of Chinese Calligraphy (*I-yüan i-chen*), edited by Wang Shih-chieh, Na Chih-liang, and Chang Wan-li. 2 vols. Hong Kong, 1967.

A Garland of Chinese Paintings (*I-yüan i-chen*), edited by Wang Shih-chieh, Na Chih-liang, and Chang Wan-li. 5 vols. Hong Kong, 1967.

Goepper, Roger. *The Essence of Chinese Painting*, translated by Michael Bullock. London, 1963.

_____. *Vom Wesen Chinesischer Malerei*. Munich, 1962.

Gombrich, Ernst H. *Art and Illusion*. London, 1960.

_____. *Meditations on a Hobby Horse*. London, 1963.

_____. "A Plea for Pluralism." *American Art Journal*, vol. 3 (1971), pp. 83–87.

_____. *In Search of Cultural History*. Oxford, 1969.

_____. "Style." *International Encyclopedia of Social Sciences*. New York, 1968.

_____. "The Tradition of General Knowledge." In *A Critical Approach to Science and Philosophy*, edited by M. Bunge. New York, 1964.

Hashimoto Kansetsu. *Sekitō*. Tokyo, 1926.

Hay, John. "Along the River during Winter's First Snow." *Burlington Magazine*, vol. 114 (1972), pp. 294–304.

HLTK: *Hua-lun ts'ung-k'an* (*A Selection of Critical Essays on Art*), edited by Yü An-lan. 2 vols. Peking, 1960.

Ho Ping-ti. *The Ladder of Success in Imperial China: Aspects of Social Mobility, 1368–1911*. New York, 1962.

_____. "The Salt Merchants of Yang-chou: A Study of Commercial Capitalism in Eighteenth Century China." *Harvard Journal of Asiatic Studies*, vol. 17 (1954), pp. 130–68.

_____. *Studies on the Population of China*. Cambridge, 1967.

Ho, Wai-kam. "Chinese under the Mongols." In Sherman Lee and Wai-kam Ho, *Chinese Art under the Mongols: The Yüan Dynasty (1279–1368)*. Cleveland, O., 1968. Pp. 73–112.

_____. "Tung Ch'i-ch'ang's New Orthodoxy and the Southern School Theory." In *Artists and Traditions: The Uses of the Past in Chinese Culture*, edited by Christian F. Murck. Princeton, N.J. Forthcoming.

Hsieh Ch'eng-chün. *K'uei-k'uei-chai shu-hua-chi* (*Record of Paintings and Calligraphy from the K'uei-k'uei Studio*). N.p., preface dated 1838.

Hsieh Chia-hsiao. *Chang Ta-ch'ien-te shih-chieh* (*The World of Chang Ta-ch'ien*). Taipei, 1968.

HSTS: *Hua-shih ts'ung-shu* (*Encyclopedia of the History of Painting*), edited by Yü Hai-yen. 9 vols. Shanghai, 1963.

Hsü Ch'in. *Ming-hua-lu* (*An Account of Ming Painters*). N.p., n.d. HSTS ed., vol. 5.

Hsü Pang-ta. *Li-tai liu-ch'uan shu-hua tso-p'in pien-nien-piao* (*Chronology of Extant Painting and Calligraphy of All Periods*). Peking, 1963.

Hsüan-ho hua-p'u (*Imperial Catalogue of Painting Compiled during the Hsüan-ho Era*) (preface traditionally dated 1120). ISTP ed., vol. 9.

Hu Shui-ying. "The Orchidaceae of China." *Quarterly Journal of the Taiwan Museum*, vol. 24 (1971), pp. 67–103.

Hua Yen. *Hsin-lo shan-jen Li-kou-chi* (*Collected Poetical Works of Hua Yen*). N.p., postscript dated 1835.

Hua-yüan pi-chi (*A Collection of Commentaries on Chinese Paintings*), edited by Wu P'i-chiang. 3 vols. Su-chou, 1939–40?.

Hua-yüan to-ying (Gems of Chinese Painting), edited by Hsü Shen-yü. 3 vols. Shanghai, 1955.

Huang T'ing-chien. *Shan-ku t'i-pa (Colophons of Huang T'ing-chien)*. *ISTP* ed., vol. 22.

Huang Yung-ch'üan. *Ch'en Hung-shou*. Shanghai, 1958; rpt. Hong Kong, 1968. Vol. 2, pp. 1051–94.

———. *Ch'en Hung-shou nien-p'u (Chronology of Ch'en Hung-shou)*. Peking, 1960.

Huizinga, Johan. "A Definition of the Concept of History." In *Philosophy and History: Essays Presented to Ernst Cassirer*, edited by Raymond Klibansky and H. J. Paton. Oxford, 1936. Pp. 1–10.

Hummel, Arthur W., ed. *Eminent Chinese of the Ch'ing Period*. 2 vols. Washington, D.C., 1943; rpt. in 1 vol. Taipei, 1967.

I-lin ts'ung-lu (Groves of Art). 6 vols. Hong Kong, 1961–66.

I Ting. "Pa-ta shan-jen sheng-nien chih-i" ("Disputing Pa-ta's Birth Date"). *I-lin ts'ung-lu*. Hong Kong, 1961–66. Vol. 2, pp. 280–83.

International Symposium on Chinese Painting, Taipei, 1970. *See* National Palace Museum, Taipei, *Proceedings of the International Symposium on Chinese Painting*.

ISTP: I-shu ts'ung-pien (Encyclopedia of Chinese Art), edited by Yang Chia-lo. 36 vols. Taipei, 1962.

Jun-ka kaku-jō, edited by Fujiwara Sosui. 11 vols. Tokyo, 1960.

Kao Erh-shih. "Lan-t'ing-hsü-te chen-wei po-i" ("On the Dispute over the Authentication of the Lan-t'ing-hsü"). *Wen-wu*, no. 7 (1965), supplement.

Kohara Hironobu. "On a New Version of Shih-t'ao's *Hua-yü-lu*" ("Sekitō gagoroku no ihon ni tsuite"). *Kokka*, 876 (March, 1965), pp. 5–14.

———. "Sekitō to Kōzan hasshō gasatsu" ("Shih-t'ao and the Album of Eight Scenic Views of Huang-shan"). N.p., n.d. [Kyoto, 1971?]. [An explanatory booklet of 81 pages accompanying a color portfolio of the Sumitomo album.]

Kokka. Tokyo, 1889–. [An illustrated monthly of the arts of the Far East.]

Ku Tsu-yü. *Tu-shih fang-yü chi-yao*. 3 vols. N.p., preface dated 1879.

Kuan Mien-chün. *San-ch'iu-ko shu-hua-lu (A Catalogue of Calligraphy and Painting from the Hall of Three Autumns)*. N.p., self-preface dated 1928.

Kuang-tung wen-wu (Cultural Relics of Canton). 4 vols. Hong Kong, 1931.

Kubler, George. *The Shape of Time*. New Haven, Conn., 1962.

Ku-kung po-wu-yüan ts'ang-hua-niao hua-hsüan (A Selection of Bird and Flower Paintings from the Collection of the Peking Palace Museum). Peking, 1965.

Ku-kung shu-hua-chi (A Collection of Painting and Calligraphy from the Palace Museum). 43 parts in 5 vols. Peking, 1931–34.

Ku-kung shu-hua-lu. *See* National Palace Museum, Taipei.

Kuo Hsi. *Lin-ch'üan kao-chih (An Essay on Landscape Painting)*. *ISTP* ed., vol. 10.

Kuo Jo-hsü. *Tu-hua chien-wen-chih* (self-preface dated 1074). *ISTP* ed., vol. 10.

Kuo Mo-jo. "Yu Wang Hsieh mu-chih-te ch'u-t'u lun-tao Lan-t'ing hsü-te chen-wei" ("The Authenticity of the Lan-t'ing-hsü in the Light of the Epitaphs of Wang Hsing-chih and Hsieh K'un"). *Wen Wu*, no. 6 (1965), pp. 1–24.

Kuo Shao-yü. *Chung-kuo wen-hsüeh p'i-p'ing-shih (A History of Chinese Literary Criticism)*. Rpt. Taipei, 1969.

Kuo Wei-ch'ü, ed. *Sung-Yüan Ming-Ch'ing shu-hua-chia nien-piao (A Chronology of Calligraphers and Painters of the Sung, Yüan, and Ming Periods)*. Peking, 1958.

Laing, Ellen. *Chinese Paintings in Chinese Publications, 1956–68: An Annotated Bibliography and an Index to the Paintings*. Ann Arbor, Mich., 1969.

Lan Ying, Hsieh Pin, et al., eds. *T'u-hui pao-chien hsü-tsuan*. *HSTS* ed., vol. 4.

Lawton, Thomas. "The Mo-yüan Hui-kuan by An Ch'i." *National Palace Museum Quarterly Special Issue No. 1, Symposium in Honor of Dr. Chiang Fu-ts'ung on His 70th Birthday*. Taipei, 1969. Pp. 13–35.

———. "Notes on Five Paintings from a Ch'ing Dynasty Collection." *Ars Orientalis*, vol. 8 (1970), pp. 191–215.

———. "Scholars and Servants." *National Palace Museum Bulletin*, vol. 1 (1966), pp. 8–11.

Ledderhose, Lothar. "An Approach to Chinese Calligraphy." *National Palace Museum Bulletin*, vol. 7 (1972), pp. 1–14.

———. *Die Siegelschrift (Chuan-shu) in der Ch'ingzeit: Ein Beitrag zur Geschichte der Chinesischen Schriftkunst*. Wiesbaden, 1970.

Lee, Sherman. *Chinese Landscape Painting*. Cleveland, O., 1954.

———. *Chinese Landscape Painting*. Cleveland, O., 1962.

———. "Literati and Professionals: Four Ming Painters." *Cleveland Museum of Art Bulletin*, vol. 53 (1966), pp. 3–25.

———, and Fong, Wen. *Streams and Mountains without End*. Ascona, 1955.

———, and Ho, Wai-kam. *Chinese Art under the Mongols: The Yüan Dynasty (1279–1368)*. Cleveland, O., 1968.

Lee, Stella. "Figure Painters in the Late Ming." In *The Restless Landscape*, edited by J. Cahill. Pp. 145–60.

Li, Chu-tsing. *Autumn Colors on the Ch'iao and Hua Mountains*. Ascona, 1965.

———. "The Development of Painting in Soochow during the Yüan Dynasty." *See* National Palace Museum, Taipei, *Proceedings of the International Symposium on Chinese Painting*.

———. "The Freer Sheep and Goat and Chao Meng-fu's Horse Paintings." *Artibus Asiae*, vol. 30 (1968), pp. 279–326.

———. "Rocks and Trees and the Art of Ts'ao Chih-po." *Artibus Asiae*, vol. 23 (1960), pp. 153–92.

———. "Stages of Development in Yüan Dynasty Landscape Painting." *National Palace Museum Bulletin*, vol. 4, nos. 2 and 3 (May and August, 1969), pp. 1–10, 1–12.

Li, H. L. *The Garden Flowers of China*. New York, 1959.

Li Tan. "Pa-ta shan-jen ts'ung-k'ao" ("A Study of Pa-ta shan-jen"). *Wen Wu*, no. 7 (1960), pp. 35–42.

Li Tou. *Yang-chou hua-fang-lu (A Descriptive Account of Yang-chou's "Decorated Boats")* (preface dated 1795). Rpt. Peking, 1960.

Liao-ning po-wu-kuan ts'ang-hua-chi (A Collection of Paintings from the Liao-ning Museum). 2 vols. Peking, 1962.

Lin Yu-tang. *The Chinese Theory of Art: Translation from the Masters of Chinese Art*. New York, 1967.

Lippe, Aschwin. "Kung Hsien and the Nanking School." *Oriental Art*, vol. 2 (1956), pp. 21–29; vol. 4 (1958), pp. 159–70.

———. *Kung Hsien and the Nanking School: Some Chinese Paintings of the Seventeenth Century*. New York, 1955.

Liu Kang-chi. *Kung Hsien*. Shanghai, 1962; rpt. Hong Kong, 1970.

Lo Chen-yü. *Wan Nien-shao hsien-sheng nien-p'u (A Chronology of Wan Shou-ch'i)*. N.p., 1919.

Loehr, Max. "The Question of Individualism in Chinese Art." *Journal of the History of Ideas*, no. 2 (1961), pp. 147–58.

———. Review of Chu-tsing Li, *Autumn Colors on the Ch'iao and Hua Mountains*. *Harvard Journal of Asiatic Studies*, vol. 26 (1963), pp. 271–73.

———. "Some Fundamental Issues in the History of Chinese Painting." *Journal of Asian Studies*, vol. 23 (1964), pp. 185–93.

Lovell, Hin-cheung. "Wang Hui's 'Dwelling in the Fu-ch'un Mountains.'" *Ars Orientalis*, vol. 8 (1970), pp. 217–42.

Lu Hsin-yüan. *Jang-li-kuan kuo-yen-lu (Appreciative Notes on Painting and Calligraphy)*. N.p., self-preface dated 1892.

Maeda, Robert J. "The Chao Ta-nien Tradition." *Ars Orientalis*, vol. 8 (1970), pp. 243–53.

Mei Ch'ing. *Mei Ch'ü-shan hua-chi (Paintings of Mei Ch'ing)*. Shanghai, 1959.

Mi Fu. *Pao-chin ying-kuang-chi*. T'u-shu chi-ch'eng ch'u-pien ed. Shanghai, 1934.

Ming Biographical History Project, Columbia University, edited by L. Carrington Goodrich. Forthcoming.

Ming-Ch'ing hua-yüan ch'ih-tu (Letters of Painters of the Ming and Ch'ing), edited by P'an Ch'en-hou. 6 vols. N.p.; preface dated 1943.

Ming-Ch'ing shan-mien hua-hsüan-chi (A Selection of Fan Paintings of the Ming and Ch'ing). Shanghai, 1959.

Ming-Ch'ing ts'ang shu-chia ch'ih-tu (*Letters of Calligraphers Collected from the Ming and Ch'ing*), edited by P'an Ch'en-hou. 4 vols. N.p., 1943?.

Ming-hsien mo-chi-ts'e (*Album of Calligraphic Works by Ming Masters*). N.p., n.d.

Ming-jen chuan-chi tzu-liao so-yin. 2 vols. Taipei, 1966.

Min-matsu san oshō (*Three Monks of the Late Ming*), edited by Sumitomo Kanichi. Tokyo, 1954.

Min Shin no kaiga (*Paintings from the Ming and Ch'ing Dynasties*). Tokyo, 1964.

Mo-ch'ao mi-chi ts'ang-ying, edited by Li Mo-ch'ao. 3 vols. Shanghai, 1935–38.

Morohashi Tetsuji, ed. *Dai Kanwa jiten.* 13 vols. Tokyo, 1958.

Mote, Frederick W. "The Arts and the 'Theorizing Mode' of the Civilization." In *Artists and Traditions: The Uses of the Past in Chinese Culture,* edited by Christian F. Murck. Princeton, N.J. Forthcoming.

———. "Confucian Eremitism in the Yüan Period." In *The Confucian Persuasion,* edited by A. F. Wright. Stanford, Calif., 1960. Pp. 202–40.

———. *The Intellectual Foundations of China.* New York, 1971.

———. *The Poet Kao Ch'i (1336–1374).* Princeton, N.J., 1962.

Mu-fei ts'ang-hua k'ao-p'ing (*Paintings in the Cheng Te-k'un Collection*), edited by Ch'eng Hsi. Hong Kong, 1965.

Museum of Fine Arts, Boston. *Portfolio of Chinese Paintings in the Museum: Yüan to Ch'ing Periods,* edited by Kojiro Tomita and Hsien-ch'i Tseng. Boston, 1961.

Nagahara Oriharu. *Shih-t'ao and Pa-ta shan-jen.* Tokyo, 1961.

The National Fine Arts Exhibition of 1929. 2 vols. Shanghai, 1929.

National Palace Museum, Taipei. *Catalogue of Wang Hui's Paintings in the National Palace Museum* (*Wang Hui hua-lu*). Taipei, 1970.

———. *Ku-kung shu-hua-lu* (*A Descriptive Catalogue of the Painting and Calligraphy in the National Palace and Central Museums*). 4 vols. Taipei, 1965.

———. *National Palace Museum Bulletin* (*Ku-kung t'ung-hsün*). Taipei, 1966–.

———. *National Palace Museum Quarterly* (*Ku-kung chi-k'an*). Taipei, 1966–.

———. *Proceedings of the International Symposium on Chinese Painting* (*Chung-kuo ku-hua t'ao-lun-hui*). Taipei, 1972.

———. *Special Exhibition of Paintings from the Ming and Ch'ing Dynasties* (*Ming-Ch'ing chih-chi ming-hua t'e-chan*). Taipei, 1970.

———. *Three Hundred Masterpieces of Chinese Painting in the Palace Museum* (*Ku-kung ming-hua san-pai-chung*). 6 vols. Taipei, 1959.

Niseki Hachidai (*The Two Stones and Pa-ta*), edited by Sumitomo Kanichi. Oiso, 1956.

Offner, Richard. *A Critical and Historical Corpus of Florentine Painting, 1933–1947,* New York, 1931–47. Sec. 3, vols. 1 and 3.

1000 Jahre Chinesische Malerei. Munich [Haus der Kunst], 1959.

1000 Years of Chinese Painting. The Hague [Haags Gemeentemuseum], 1960.

The Pageant of Chinese Painting (*Chūgoku meiga hōkan*), edited by Kinjiro Harada. Tokyo, 1936.

The Painting of Tao-chi: Catalogue of an Exhibition, August 13–September 17, 1967. Held at the Museum of Art, University of Michigan, edited by Richard Edwards. Ann Arbor, 1967.

P'an Cheng-wei. *T'ing-fan-lou shu-hua-chi* (*Record of Painting and Calligraphy from P'an's Collection*) and supplement (*hsü*) (self-preface dated 1843). *ISTP* ed., vol. 20.

P'ang Yüan-chi. *Hsü-chai ming-hua-lu* (*Catalogue of Paintings in P'ang's Collection*) (self-preface dated 1909). 16 vols. N.p.

———. *Ming-pi chi-sheng* (*Masterpieces of Chinese Painting*). Shanghai, 1940.

Panofsky, Erwin. *Meaning in the Visual Arts.* New York, 1955.

Pei Ch'iung. *Ch'ing-chiang Pei hsien-sheng-chi* (*Pei Ch'iung's Collected Works*). *SPTK* ed., no. 319.

Pien Yung-yü. *Shih-ku-t'ang shu-hua hui-k'ao.* 4 vols. Rpt. Taipei, 1921.

Portfolio of Chinese Paintings in the Museum: Yüan to Ch'ing Periods, edited by Kojiro Tomita and Hsien-ch'i Tseng. Boston, 1961.

PTC. See The Painting of Tao-chi.

Recent Paintings by Chang Dai-chien. Taipei, 1968.

The Richard Bryant Hobart Collection of Chinese Ceramics and Paintings. New York [Parke-Bernet Galleries], 1969. Pt. 2.

Rosenberg, Jakob. *On Quality in Art: Criteria of Excellence, Past and Present.* Princeton, N.J., 1967.

Ryckmans, Pierre. "Les 'Propos sur la Peinture' de Shi Tao: Traduction et Commentaire." *Arts Asiatiques,* vol. 14 (1966), pp. 79–150.

———. "Les 'Propos sur la Peinture' de Shi Tao (Traduction et Commentaire pour Servir de Contribuer à l'Étude Terminologique et Esthétique des Théories Chinoises de la Peinture)." *Mélanges Chinois et Bouddhiques* [Brussels], vol. 15 (1968–69).

Sasaki Kozo. "Tao-chi, Seals." *See The Painting of Tao-chi,* pp. 63–70.

SCPC: Shih-ch'ü pao-chi ch'u-pien (1744–45), *SCPC hsü-pien* (1791–93), *SCPC san-pien* (1793–1817).

Schapiro, Meyer. "Style," in *Anthropology Today,* edited by A. L. Kroeber. Chicago, 1953. Pp. 287–312.

Seian hirin (*Monument Collection in Hsi-an, Shensi*), edited by Nishikawa Yasushi et al. Tokyo, 1966.

Sekitō meiga fu (*Portfolio of Famous Paintings by Shih-t'ao*). Tokyo, 1937.

Sekitō Rafusan zusatsu (*An Album of Mt. Lo-Fu by Shih-t'ao*). Tokyo, 1953.

Sekitō to Hachidai san-jin (*Shih-t'ao and Pa-ta shan-jen*), edited by Sumitomo Kanichi. Oiso, 1952.

The Selected Painting and Calligraphy of Shih-t'ao (*Shih-t'ao shu-hua chi*), edited by Chang Wan-li and Hu Jen-mou. 6 vols. Hong Kong, 1969.

Shang Ch'eng-tsu and Huang Hua, eds. *Chung-kuo li-tai shu-hua-chuan-k'o-chia tzu-hao suo-yin* (*Index of the "Tzu" and "Hao" of Chinese Calligraphers, Painters, and Seal Carvers in Successive Periods*). 2 vols. Peking, 1960.

Shanghai po-wu-kuan ts'ang-hua (*Paintings in the Collection of the Shanghai Museum*). Shanghai, 1959.

Sheng Ta-shih. *Hsi-shan wo-yu-lu.* HSTS ed., vol. 9.

Shih Hsio-yen, and Trübner, Henry. *Individualists and Eccentrics.* Toronto, 1963.

Shih-t'ao ho-shang, Pa-ta shan-jen shan-shui ching-p'in. N.p. [Peking?], 1936.

Shih-t'ao hua-chi (*A Collection of Shih-t'ao's Paintings*), edited by Hsieh Chih-liu. Peking, 1960.

Shih-t'ao shan-shui-chi (*A Collection of Shih-t'ao's Landscapes*). Shanghai, 1930.

Shimada, Shūjirō. "Concerning the 'I-p'in' Style of Painting" ("I-p'in gafu ni tsuite"), translated by James Cahill. *Oriental Art,* vol. 7 (1961), pp. 66–74; vol. 8 (1962), pp. 130–37; vol. 10 (1964), pp. 3–10. Originally published in *Bijutsu kenkyū,* vol. 161, pp. 264–90.

———, and Yoshiho, Yonezawa. *Painting of the Sung and Yüan Dynasties.* Tokyo, 1952.

Shina nanga taisei (*Compendium of Chinese Painting of the Southern School*). Tokyo, 1935–37. Vol. 1 in 16 parts; vol. 2 (supplement) in 6 parts.

Shinchō shoga fu, edited by Naitō Torajiro. 2 vols. Osaka, 1916–26.

Shodō zenshū (*Collection of Famous Calligraphy*). Ser. 1, 25 vols. Tokyo, 1930–32. Ser. 2, 25 vols. Tokyo, 1958–65.

Shoen (*A Garland of Calligraphy*). Ser. 1 and 2. Tokyo, 1911–20, 1937–43.

Shohin (*Journal of Calligraphy*). Tokyo, 1949–.

Shoseki meihin sōkan (*Masterpieces of Chinese Calligraphy*). 200 vols. Tokyo, 1964–.

Sickman, Laurence, ed. *Chinese Calligraphy and Painting in the Collection of John M. Crawford, Jr.* New York, 1962.

———, and Dubosc, J. P. *Great Chinese Painters of the Ming and Ch'ing Dynasties.* New York [Wildenstein Galleries], 1949.

Sirén, Osvald. *The Chinese on the Art of Painting.* Peking, 1937.

———. *Chinese Painting: Leading Masters and Principles.* 7 vols. New York, 1956–58.

———. *A History of Later Chinese Painting.* 2 vols. London, 1938.

———. "Lists." *See Chinese Painting: Leading Masters and Principles,* vols. 2, 7.

———. "Shih-t'ao, Painter, Poet and Theoretician." *Bulletin of the*

[Stockholm] Museum of Far Eastern Antiquities, vol. 21 (1949), pp. 31–62.

Sō Gen Min Shin meiga taikan (A Catalogue of Famous Paintings of the Sung, Yüan, Ming, and Ch'ing Periods). 2 vols. Tokyo, 1931.

Sō Gen no kaiga (Painting of the Sung and Yüan). Tokyo, 1962.

Soper, Alexander C. "The 'Letter from Shih-t'ao to Pa-ta shan-jen.'" Artibus Asiae, vol. 29 (1967), pp. 67–69.

Sōraikan kinshō, edited by Abe Fusajiro. 2 vols. in 6 parts. Osaka, 1930–39.

Spence, Jonathan D. "Tao-chi, an Historical Introduction." See The Painting of Tao-chi, pp. 11–20.

_____ . Ts'ao Yin and the K'ang-hsi Emperor, Bond-servant and Master. New Haven, Conn., 1966.

SPTK: Ssu-pu ts'ung-k'an ch'u-pien suo-pen. 440 vols. Rpt. Taipei, 1965.

Su Shih. Chi-chu fen-lei Tung-p'o hsien-sheng-shih (Collected Poems of Su Shih, Arranged by Subject), edited by Wang Shih-p'eng. SPTK ed., vols. 202–3.

_____ . Tung-p'o t'i-pa (Colophons of Su Shih), edited by Mao Chin. ISTP ed., vol. 22.

Su-chou po-wu-kuan ts'ang-hua-chi (Paintings in the Collection of the Su-chou Museum). Peking, 1963.

Sugimura Yuzō. Ken-ryū kōtei (The Ch'ien-lung Emperor). Tokyo, 1961.

Sullivan, Michael. Introduction à l'Art Chinois. Paris, 1968.

_____ . "Some Possible Sources of European Influence on Late Ming and Early Ch'ing Painting." See National Palace Museum, Taipei, Proceedings of the International Symposium on Chinese Painting.

Suzuki Kei. Mindai kaigashi no kenkyū: Seppa (A Study of Ming Painting: The Che School). Tokyo, 1968.

Ta-feng-t'ang ming-chi (Masterpieces of Chinese Painting from the Great Wind Hall Collection), edited by Chang Ta-ch'ien. 4 vols. Kyoto, 1955–56.

Ta-feng-t'ang shu-hua-lu (Record of Calligraphy and Painting in the Great Wind Hall). Chengtu, 1943.

T'ai-shan ts'an-shih-lou ts'ang-hua, edited by Kao Yung. 4 vols. N.p., 1926–29.

T'ao Liang (1772–1857). Hung-tou shu-kuan shu-hua-chi. N.p., n.d.

Tao-chi. Hua-p'u (preface by Hu Ch'i dated 1710; epilogue by Wu T'ieh-sheng). Shanghai, 1962.

_____ . Tao-chi hua-ts'e (Album by Tao-chi Dated 1700). Peking, 1960.

_____ . Ta-ti-tzu t'i-hua-shih-pa (Tao-chi's Poetic Colophons), edited by Wang I-ch'en. ISTP ed., vol. 25.

Tchang Ta-ts'ien, Peintre Chinois. Paris, 1956.

T'ien-chin-shih i-shu po-wu-kuan ts'ang-hua-chi (Collection of Paintings from the Tsientsin Municipal Museum). 1 vol. and supplement. Peking, 1963.

T'ien-yin-t'ang Collection: One Hundred Masterpieces of Chinese Painting, edited by Chang Po-chin. 2 vols. Tokyo, 1963.

T'ien Yüan. Yin-wen-hsüeh. 4 vols. Taipei, 1957.

Tietze, Hans. Genuine and False: Copies, Imitations, Forgeries. New York, 1948.

Ting Fu-pao, ed. Ssu-pu tsung-lu i-shu-pien. 2 vols. Shanghai, 1956.

Tōan-zō shōgafu, edited by Saitō Etsuzō. 4 vols. Osaka, 1928.

Tō Sō Gen Min meiga taikan (A Catalogue of Famous Paintings of the T'ang, Sung, Yüan, and Ming Dynasties. 2 vols. Tokyo, 1929.

Tō Sō Gen Min meiga tengo (Exhibition of Great Paintings from the T'ang, Sung, and Ming). Tokyo, 1928.

Tu Fu. Fen-lei chi-chu Tu kung-pu-shih (Compilation of Tu Fu's Poems by Subject). SPTK ed., vols. 143–44.

_____ . Tu-shih Ch'ien-chu (Ch'ien's Commentary to Tu Fu's Poems), edited by Ch'ien Ch'ien-i. N.p., n.d. Rpt. Taipei, 1969.

Tu Mu. T'ieh-wang shan-hu. N.p., preface dated 1758.

Tu Wei-ming. "'Inner Experience'—The Basis of Creativity in Neo-Confucian Thinking." In Artists and Traditions: The Uses of the Past in Chinese Culture, edited by Christian F. Murck. Princeton, N.J. Forthcoming.

Tung Ch'i-ch'ang. Hua-ch'an-shih sui-pi, edited by Yang Pu (preface dated 1720, compiled before 1657). ISTP ed., vol. 28.

_____ . Jung-t'ai pieh-chi, edited by Yeh Yu-sheng (Fukien, between 1630 and 1639). Taipei [Chung-yang t'u-shu-kuan ed.], 1968. Vol. 4 of Jung-t'ai-chi.

_____ . Tung Hua-t'ing shu-hua-lu (Tung's Comments on Painting and Calligraphy), Ch'ing-fou shan-jen ed. N.d. ISTP ed., vol. 25.

Un Nanden to Sekitō (Yün Nan-t'ien and Shih-t'ao), edited by Sumitomo Kanichi. Oiso, 1953.

Van Gulik, R. H. Chinese Pictorial Art as Viewed by the Connoisseur. Rome, 1958.

Wang Fang-yü. "Lun Fu Pao-shih 'Shih-t'ao shang-jen nien-p'u' suo-ting sheng-nien" ("On the Birth Date Given by Fu Pao-shih in His Chronology of Shih-t'ao"). The Central Daily News [Taipei], October 21, 1968.

Wang Hui. Catalogue of Wang Hui's Paintings in the Collection of the National Palace Museum. Taipei, 1970.

Wang K'o-yü. Shan-hu-wang (preface dated 1916).

Wang Shu. Ch'un-hua mi-ko fa-t'ieh k'ao-cheng (An Investigation into the Ch'un-hua mi-ko Collection of Ink Rubbings) (preface dated 1730). Rpt. Taipei, 1971.

Wenley, Archibald. "A Breath of Spring by Tsou Fu-lei." Ars Orientalis, vol. 2 (1957), pp. 458–69.

Wen Wu (Cultural Relics). Peking, 1950–66, 1972–.

Whitfield, Roderick. In Pursuit of Antiquity. Princeton, N.J., 1969.

Wilson, E. H. China—Mother of Gardens. Boston, 1929.

Wilson, Marc F. Kung Hsien: Theorist and Technician in Painting. Kansas City, Mo., 1969.

Wind, Edgar. "Some Points of Contact between History and Natural Science." In Philosophy and History: Essays Presented to Ernst Cassirer, edited by Raymond Klibansky and H. J. Paton. Pp. 255–64.

Wölfflin, Heinrich. Principles of Art History, translated by M. D. Hottinger. New York, 1932.

Wu Hsiu. Ch'ing-hsia-kuan lun-hua chüeh-chü i-pai-shou (One Hundred Quatrains Praising Painting) (self-preface dated 1824). ISTP ed., vol. 16.

Wu Jan. "Ming i-min hua-chia Wan Nien-shao" ("The Ming Loyalist Painter Wan Shou-ch'i"). I-lin ts'ung-lu, vol. 6, pp. 270–74.

Wu, Nelson I. "The Evolution of Tung Ch'i-ch'ang's Landscape Style as Revealed by His Works in the National Palace Museum." See National Palace Museum, Taipei, Proceedings of the International Symposium on Chinese Painting.

_____ . "The Toleration of Eccentrics." Art News, vol. 56 (1957), pp. 26–29, 52–54.

_____ . "Tung Ch'i-ch'ang (1555–1636): Apathy in Government and Fervor in Art." In Confucian Personalities, edited by A. F. Wright and D. Twitchett. Stanford, Calif., 1962. Pp. 260–93.

Wu T'ieh-sheng. "Hou-chi" ("Afterword"). See Tao-chi. Hua-p'u, pp. 53–62.

Wu T'ung. "Tao-chi, a Chronology." See The Painting of Tao-chi, pp. 53–61.

"A-wen" [Wu T'ung]. "An Na-pao Shih-t'ao ta-chan chui-chi" ("The Shih-t'ao Exhibit at Ann Arbor in Retrospect"). Central Daily News [Taipei], February 6, 1968, in 8 installments.

Wu, William. "Kung Hsien's Style and His Sketchbooks." Oriental Art, vol. 16 (1970), pp. 72–80.

Yang En-shou. Yen-fu-pien (self-preface dated 1831). 4 vols. Rpt. Taipei, 1971.

Yang Lien-sheng. Money and Credit in China. Cambridge, Mass., 1952.

_____ . Studies in Institutional History. Cambridge, Mass., 1961.

Yeh Kung-cho. Hsia-an t'an-i-lu (Conversations on Art). N.p., n.d.

Yonezawa Yoshiho. "Shoho-jo kara mita Sekitō ga no kijun-saku" ("Some Standard Works of Shih-t'ao Seen from the Viewpoint of Calligraphy"). Kokka, 913 (April, 1968), pp. 5–17.

Young, Martie, ed. The Eccentric Painters of China. Ithaca, N.Y., 1965.

Yü Chien-hua, ed. Shih-t'ao Hua-yü-lu (On Shih-t'ao's Hua-yü-lu). Peking, 1962.

Yü Feng-ch'ing. Shu-hua t'i-pa-chi (Record of Colophons of Calligraphy and Painting) (self-colophon dated 1634). Rpt. Taipei, 1970.

Yü Shao-sung. Shu-hua shu-lu chien-t'i (Commentaries on Calligraphy and Painting Documents). Peking, 1932.

Chinese and Japanese Names and Terms

An Lu-shan 安禄山
PT. I

Aoki Masaru 青木正兒
PT. I

A-ch'ang (PTC 1) 阿長
XXV, LEAVES D AND E, XXX, LEAF DD

A-wen. *See* Wu T'ung 阿問

Bordu. *See* Po-erh-tu 博爾都

Cha Erh-chan 查二瞻
XIII, XIV

Cha Shih-piao 查士標
PT. I; PT. IV; VI, XII, XVII

Cha Shih-piao yin 查士標印
XIV

chan-ch'e chih-pi 顫掣之筆
XXVIII

chan-pi 戰筆
XX, LEAF D

Chan-te-yü-chi k'uai-jan tzu-tsu 覲得於己快然自足
I

Chan Wen-te 詹文德
XXIV

Chang Chi-su 張積素
PT. I; XI

Chang Chi-su tzu Fu-( ) hao Mo-yün 張積素字府口號墨雲
XI

Chang Chi-tzu 張季子
XVIII, XXXIV, LEAF E

Chang Ch'in 張欽
III

Chang Chih-ho 張志和
PT. IV

Chang Chih-wan 張之萬
III

Chang Chung 張中
PT. I

Chang Ch'ün 張羣
XXI, XXII

Chang Fu 張復
PT. I

Chang Heng (*tzu* Ts'ung-yü) 張珩 (字葱玉)
I

Chang Heng ssu-yin 張珩私印
I

Chang Hsiung (*tzu* Tzu-hsiang) 張熊 (字子祥)
IX

Chang Hsü 張旭
PT. I

Chang Hsüeh-tseng 張學曾
PT. I

Chang Hung 張宏
PT. I; VIII, IX

Chang Jui-t'u 張瑞圖
PT. IV

Chang Keng 張庚
VIII, XII, XIII, XXV

Chang Lu 張路
PT. I

Chang Po-chin 張伯謹
IX, XI

Chang Po-ying (*tzu* Shao-p'u) 張伯英 (字勺圃)
X

Chang Po-ying ssu-yin 張伯英私印
X, LEAF J

Chang Po-ying-yin 張伯英印
X, LEAF B

Chang Seng-yu 張僧繇
PT. I; PT. IV

Chang Shan-tzu (*ming* Tse) 張善孖 (名澤)
PT. I

Chang Shao-p'u 張少溥
X, LEAVES A, G, UU

Chang Shao-p'u 張勺圃
X, LEAVES F AND N

Chang-shih chi-ts'ang shu-hua chih-chang (owner unidentified) 張氏庋藏書畫之章
I

Chang-shih T'ung-po Ch'ien-piao 張氏通波阡表
I

Chang Ta-ch'ien (ming Yüan) 張大千 (名爰)
PT. I; PT. II; PT. III; V, XXI, XXIII, XXXV

Chang Ta-ch'ien (relief, small square; seal script with heavy border) 張大千
XII, LEAF B

Chang Ta-ch'ien (relief, small square; ancient seal script with central line and heavy border) 張大千
XII, LEAF E

Chang Ta-ch'ien (relief, small square; ancient seal script) 張大千
XX, LEAF G

Chang Ta-ch'ien (intaglio, square; ancient seal script with heavy border) 張大千 (以上諸印皆不同)
XXX, LEAF A

chang-ts'ao 章草
I

Chang Tse (tzu Shan-tzu) 張澤 (字善孖)
PT. I

Chang Tse (intaglio, square) 張澤 (陰文方印)
XX, LEAF B

Chang Tse (relief, square; ancient seal script) 張澤 (陽文)
XX, LEAF C

Chang Tun-jen (tzu Ku-yü) 張敦仁 (字古愚或古餘)
XXV, PORTRAIT LEAF

Chang-wen chih-yin 掌文之印
XXXII, COLOPHON 7

Chang Yüan. See Chang Ta-ch'ien 張爰 (大千)

Chang Yüan (intaglio, small square with border) XII, LEAF J 張爰

Chang Yüan (intaglio, medium square) 張爰
XX, LEAF AA

Chang Yüan (intaglio, medium-small square) 張爰
XX, LEAF DD, XXV, LEAF E

Chang Yüan (intaglio, small square with border) 張爰
XXII, LEAF K, XXXIV, LEAF G

Chang Yüan (intaglio, small square) 張爰
XXV, LEAF G

Chang Yüan (intaglio, small square with border) 張爰
XXXIV, LEAF G

Chang Yüan (intaglio, small square with border) 張爰
XXII, LEAF J, XXIII, LEAF I, XXXIII, LEAF G, XXXIV, LEAF L

Chang Yüan (relief, small square) 張爰
XII, LEAF I, XXII, LEAF L

Chang, Yüan (relief, double seal in two squares; thin seal script) 張爰 (連珠)
XXI, LABEL

Chang Yüan (relief, small square with heavy border) 張爰
XXX, LEAF A, XXXIII, LEAF D

Chang Yüan (relief, small square) 張爰 (以上諸印皆不同)
XXXIV, LEAF I

Chang Yüan chih-yin (half-intaglio, half-relief, square) 張爰之印
XX, LEAF BB

Chang Yüan chih-yin (intaglio, small square) 張爰之印
XX, LEAF CC, XXII, LEAF E, XXXIV, LEAF D

Chang Yüan chih-yin-hsin 張爰之印信
XVIII

Chang Yüan ssu-yin (intaglio, small square) 張爰私印 (小)
XX, LEAF FF, XXII, LEAF G, XXXII, FRONTISPIECE

Chang Yüan ssu-yin (intaglio, large square) 張爰私印 (大)
V

Chang Yüan Ta-ch'ien fu 張爰大千父
XXXII

Chang Yüan yin (intaglio, small square) 張爰印
XII, LEAF G, XXII, LEAF D

Chang Yüan yin (intaglio, small square with border) 張爰印
XXII, LEAF J

Chang Yüan yin-hsin (intaglio, square) 張爰印信
XX, LEAF GG, XXXIV, LEAF F

Ch'ang-kan-ssu 長干寺
PT. IV

Chao Chih-ch'ien 趙之謙
PT. I

Chao Kan 趙幹
I

Chao Lin 趙麟
PT. I

Chao Ling-jang 趙令穰
VII

Chao Meng-fu 趙孟頫
PT. I; PT. IV; I, III, XII

Chao Yüan 趙原
PT. I

Chao Yung 趙雍
PT. I

Chao-(?)-fei ts'ang 趙口非藏
VIII

Ch'ao-chi 超濟
PT. IV

Ch'ao-jan hsin-shang 超然心賞
II

Che (school) 浙 (派)
PT. I; VIII

chen-chu-lan 珍珠蘭
XXXVII

chen mien-mu 真面目
PT. IV

Chen-ts'ang (relief, double-gourd; owner unidentified) 珍藏
I

Chen-yin 真印
IX

Ch'en Chao 陳焰
PT. I; XL

Ch'en Chi 陳繼
PT. I

Ch'en Chi-ju 陳繼儒
PT. I; III, VIII

Ch'en Chi-ju yin 陳繼儒印
III

Ch'en Chuan 陳撰
XXXII, COLOPHON 8

Ch'en-fu 臣父
XX, LEAF EE

Ch'en-han 宸翰
XXXVII

Ch'en Huan 陳煥
PT. I

Ch'en Hung-shou 陳洪綬
PT. I; VII, IX, X

Ch'en Ju-yen (tzu Wei-yün) 陳汝言
PT. I; I

Ch'en Kuo-sung yin 臣國宋印
XX, LEAF GG

Ch'en Ming 臣銘
XXXII, COLOPHON 13

Ch'en Ming yin-hsin 臣銘印信
XXXII, COLOPHON 13

Ch'en-shou 臣壽
X, LEAF K

Ch'en Shu 陳舒
PT. I; PT. IV

Ch'en Shun 陳淳
PT. I; II, IX

Ch'en Tu 臣杜
XXXVIII

Cheng Cho-lu 鄭拙廬
XXIII

Cheng-chung 徵仲
II

Cheng Hsieh (tzu Pan-ch'iao) 鄭燮 (字板橋)
PT. IV

cheng-k'ai 正楷
XXIV

cheng-mai 正脈
XII

Cheng Ping-shan 鄭秉珊
XXIII

Cheng Ssu-hsiao 鄭思肖
XXV, LEAF B

Cheng Wei 鄭為
XXIII

Ch'eng Cheng-k'uei 程正揆
PT. I; PT. IV

Ch'eng Chia-sui 程嘉燧
PT. I; PT. IV; XII

ch'eng-hsin-t'ang (chih) 澄心堂 (紙)
PT. IV

Ch'eng Lin-sheng 程霖生
PT. I; XXIII, XXXV

Ch'eng Ming 程鳴
XXXII, N. I

Ch'eng Shang-fu 程尚甫
III

Ch'eng Shih-chuang 程式莊
XXXII, COLOPHON 20

Ch'eng Sui 程邃
PT. IV; XII, XIII, XVII, XXXVI

Ch'eng Yin 程釜
XXXII, COLOPHON 22

Ch'eng Yüan-yü 程元愈
XXXII, COLOPHON 23

chi-ch'ou 己丑
XXXII, COLOPHON 22

Chi-hsia i-ch'ing 幾暇怡情
XXXVII

Chi-hsia lin-ch'ih 幾暇臨池
XXXVII

chi-kuan-hua 雞冠花
XX, LEAF C

chi-kuang p'ien-yü 吉光片羽
V, XXXII

chi-lü 計律
XXXIII, LEAF G

chi-mao (1699) 己卯
XXIII

chi-ta-ch'eng 集大成
PT. I; PT. IV

Chi-tso shen-ting 積祚審定
XXVII

Chi-tso 積祚
II

Chi-yen-t'u 擊硯圖
XXVII

ch'i 氣
PT. II

Ch'i-chuang chung-cheng (PTC 8) 齊莊中正
XXVII

ch'i-k'o ch'uan-che tzu-ch'eng i-chia 其可傳者自成一家
PT. IV

Ch'i Pai-shih 齊白石
PT. I

ch'i-yün 氣韻
PT. II; XXXVII

ch'i-yün sheng-tung 氣韻生動
PT. II

Chia Chao-feng 賈兆鳳
XXXII, COLOPHON 5

Chia Chao-feng-yin 賈兆鳳印
XXXII, COLOPHON 5

Chia Chih 嘉植
XXXII, COLOPHON I

Chia Chih ssu-yin 嘉植私印
XXXII, COLOPHON I

Chia-hui 嘉會
II

chia-shan 假山
PT. I

Chiang Chi 蔣驥
PT. I; XXXII

Chiang Chi-chiang 姜季江
X, LEAF H

Chiang Chu 江注
XII

Chiang Chung-hai 姜仲海
X, LEAF H

Chiang Chung-tzu 姜中子
XXXII, COLOPHON 3

Chiang Hung (97-173) 姜肱
X, LEAVES G AND H

Chiang Hung (fl. ca. 1674-1690) 姜泓
VII

Chiang-nan 江南
PT. I

Chiang Shao-shu (tzu Erh-yu) 姜紹書 (字二酉)
VII

Chiang Shih-chieh 姜實節
PT. III; XII, XXXII, COLOPHON 3

Chiang Shih-chieh-yin 姜實節印
XXXII, COLOPHON 3

Chiang Sung 蔣嵩
PT. I

Chiang T'ao 江韜
XII

Chiang Ying 江㶁
XXXII, COLOPHON IO

Chiang Yüan 江遠
XII

Chiao-hsi 茶畦
XXXIX

ch'iao 巧
XXXV

Ch'iao-hsiu yu-chü-t'u 喬岫幽居圖
I

Chieh 偕
XXXII, COLOPHON 30

chieh-ku k'ai-chin 借古開今
PT. IV

Chien-chiang (intaglio, square) 漸江
X, LEAVES A AND J

Chien-chiang (intaglio, small square) 漸江 (小方印)
X, LEAVES B, F, H

Chien-ch'üan chen-shang 劍泉珍賞
XXII, LEAF G

Chien-ch'üan p'ing-sheng p'i-tz'u 劍泉平生癖此
III

chien-kuo 監國
PT. IV

chien-shang-chia 鑑賞家
PT. II

"Chien-tzu" 兼字
PT. IV

Ch'ien trigram and tripod within a square 鼎形乾卦方印
(relief; unidentified seal)
IV

Ch'ien 乾
XXXVII

Ch'ien Ch'ien-i 錢謙益
PT. IV; V, XXIII

Ch'ien Hsüan 錢選
PT. I

Ch'ien Ku 錢穀
PT. I; IV

Ch'ien-lung 乾隆
PT. I; XXXVII

Ch'ien-lung ch'en-han (relief, small square) 乾隆宸翰 (小方印)
XXXVII

Ch'ien-lung ch'en-han (relief, large square) 乾隆宸翰 (大方印)
XXXVII

Ch'ien T'ien-shu 錢天樹
III

Ch'ien T'ien-shu yin 錢天樹印
III

Ch'ien Tu 錢杜
PT. I; XXXVIII

Ch'ien T'ung-ai 錢同愛
III

Ch'ien-tzu-wen 千字文
XXIV

Ch'ien-yu Lung-mien, Chi (PTC 9) 前有龍眠濟
XXII, LEAVES C AND G, XXIV, XXVI, LEAVES C, D, G, H, XXX, LEAF BB

Ch'ien Yung, *Lü-yüan hua-hsüeh* 錢 泳履園畫學
XXXIX

Ch'ien Yü 錢 榆
XXXVIII

Ch'ien-yüan chien-shang 潛園鑑賞
III

Ch'ien-yüan shu-hua chih-yin 潛園書畫之印
III

Chih-chang 直章
XXXII, COLOPHON 11

chih-ch'ü t'ai-shih-pi (should read *ch'e-ch'ü t'ai-shih-pi*) 掣取太史筆
XXVII

Chih-feng shen-ting (should read *I-feng shen-ting*) 執風審定
III

Chih Pa-ta shan-jen-han 致八大山人函
PT. III; XXIII

chih-tzu 梔子
XXXVII

chih-yin (che) 知音者
PT. II

Ch'ih-chüeh (PTC 12) 癡絶
XXXII

Chih-yüan (should read *Ch'i-yüan*) 企園
XXXII, COLOPHON 28

Chin-chen? 瑾闔?
XXXII, COLOPHON 20

Chin Ch'eng 金城
XVI

chin chou hua-chia 今周花甲
XXIII

Chin Ch'uan-( ) (owner unidentified) 金傳□
XXXVI

Chin Ch'uan-sheng 金傳聲
XXIV

Chin Fu-t'ing 金黻廷
III

Chin Fu-t'ing shou-hsien-shih k'ao-ts'ang 金黻廷瘦仙氏考藏
III

Chin Lan 金彰
XLI

Chin-ling huai-ku ts'e 金陵懷古冊
XXXIV

chin-shih (degree) 進士
PT. I

chin t'ien-hsia hua-shih 今天下畫士
PT. IV

Chin T'ang 金湯
XXXII, COLOPHON 14

Chin T'ang chih-yin 金湯之印
XXXII, COLOPHON 14

Ch'in Man-ch'ing (*tzu* Keng-nien) 秦曼青 (字更年)
XXXV, LABEL

Ch'in Man-ch'ing 秦曼青
XXXV, LABEL

Ch'in Tsu-yung 秦祖永
XIII

Ching Ch'i-chün (*tzu* Chien-ch'üan) 景其濬 (字劍泉)
III, XXII, LEAVES G AND I

Ching-chai hsin-shang (owner unidentified) 儆齋心賞
II

Ching-shih 景氏
III

Ching-shih chen-ts'ang 景氏珍藏
XXII, LEAF I

Ching-t'ing-shan 敬亭山
PT. IV

Ching-yü-chai chien-shang-chang 靜娛齋鑒賞章
XXIII

Ching Yüan Chai 景元齋
XII, XVI

ch'ing 情
PT. IV

Ch'ing-chiang-chi 清江集
I

Ch'ing-hsiang 清湘
PT. IV

Ch'ing-hsiang (forged seal) 清湘 (偽印)
XIX

Ch'ing-hsiang Ch'en-jen 清湘陳人
PT. IV

Ch'ing-hsiang lao-jen 清湘老人
PT. IV

Ch'ing-hsiang lao-jen (PTC 18) 清湘老人 (印)
XXII, LEAVES E, F, I, XXVI, LEAF B, XXXI,
XXXIII, LEAVES A, C, H, XXXIV, LEAF I

Ch'ing-hsiang lao-jen (forged seal) 清湘老人 (偽印)
XXXV, LEAF E

Ch'ing-hsiang Shih-t'ao (PTC 22) 清湘石濤
XX, LEAF B, XXII, LEAF D, XXIV, XXVI, LEAF E, XXVII,
XXX, LEAVES AA AND DD, XXXIII, LEAF E, XXXIV, LEAF F

ch'ing-i 清逸
PT. IV; XIII

Ch'ing-lien ts'ao-ko 青蓮草閣
PT. IV

Ch'ing-mi-ko 清閟閣
PT. IV

Ch'ing-yen 晴嵒
XX, LEAF CC

Ch'ing-yen sui-feng chih-shih 清晏歲豐之室
X, LEAF I

Chiu-ch'u 九初
XXXII, COLOPHON 24

Chiu-ch'u-wang tao-shih 九初望道士
XXXII, COLOPHON 24

Chiu-hsiang shan-jen 酒香山人
XXXII, COLOPHON 24

Chiu-t'u-pao ku-jou-ch'ing 球圖寶骨肉情
XXII, LEAF H, XXIII, XXV, LEAF D, XXVII,
XXXII, XXXIII, LEAF C (should read Ch'iu-t'u-pao ku-jou-ch'ing)

Ch'iu-lin t'ing-tzu-t'u 秋林亭子圖
V

Ch'iu Wen 裘溫
XL

Ch'iu Ying 仇英
PT. I; PT. IV; III

Ch'iu-yüeh 秋岳
XXXVI

cho 拙
XXXV

Cho-cheng-yüan 拙政園
PT. I

Cho Erh-k'an 卓爾堪
PT. IV

Chou (Mr. Chou, unidentified) 周
XXXV

Chou Ch'en 周臣
PT. I; III

Chou Fang 周昉
PT. IV

Chou Hsing-tz'u (should read Chou Hsing-ssu) 周興嗣
XXIV

Chou Ju-hsi 周汝式
XXIII

Chou Liang-kung 周亮工
PT. I; PT. IV; V, XII

Chou Wen-chü 周文矩
PT. I; PT. IV

Chu-ch'a lao-jen 竹垞老人
XXXII, COLOPHON 4

Chu Ch'ang 祝昌
XII

chu-chiao 助教
I

Chu Chih-fan 朱之蕃
III

Chu Chih-fan yin 朱之蕃印
III

Chu Heng-chia 朱亨嘉
PT. IV

Chu Ho-nien 朱鶴年
XXII

Chu-hsiang (relief, square) 竹香（方印）
III

Chu-hsiang (relief, double seal in two small squares) 竹香（連珠印）
III

Chu-hsiang-an 竹香盦
III

Chu I-tsun 朱彝尊
XXXII, COLOPHON 4

Chu I-tsun-yin 朱彝尊印
XXXII, COLOPHON 4

Chu Liang-yü 朱良育
III

Chu Shou-ch'ien 朱守謙
PT. IV

Chu Ta 朱耷
PT. I; PT. IV; VII, IX, X, XXXVI

Chu Te-jun 朱德潤
PT. I

Chu Tsan-i 朱贊儀
PT. IV

Chu Ts'un-li (tzu Hsing-fu) 朱存理
PT. I; III

Chu Tuan 朱端
PT. I

Chu Yün-ming 祝允明
III

Ch'u Chang-wen 儲掌文
XXXII, COLOPHON 7

Ch'u Hsiung-wen 儲雄文
XXXII, COLOPHON 18

Ch'u Kuang-hsi 儲光羲
X, LEAF N

Ch'u Sui-liang 褚遂良
PT. IV; XXIV

Ch'u Ssu-yün 儲汇雲
XXXII, COLOPHON 18

Ch'u Ta-wen 儲大文
XXXII, COLOPHON 15

Ch'u Ta-wen yin 儲大文印
XXXII, COLOPHON 15

Ch'u Yü-wen 儲郁文
XXXII, COLOPHON 17

Ch'u Yü-wen yin 儲郁文印
XXXII, COLOPHON 17

Chü Chieh 居節
PT. I; XXXVIII

Chü-jan 巨然
PT. I

chü-jen (degree) 舉人
X, XII

chü-ku i-hua 具古以化
PT. IV

Ch'ü Weng-shan 屈翁山

Ch'ü-wu 去蕪
XXXII, COLOPHON I

chuan (shu) 篆（書）
PT. IV; XXIV

Chuan 撰
XXXII, COLOPHON 8

ch'uan-chu ku-chin, tzu-ch'eng i-chia 傳諸古今.自成一家
PT. IV

Ch'uan-shan chien-shang (owner unidentified) 傳山鑑賞
XXVII

Ch'uan-shen mi-yao 傳神秘要
XXXII

Ch'un-lei-ko 春雷閣
XXX

Ch'un-ou-chai 春藕齋
XXXVII

Ch'un-shan lou-ch'uan-t'u 春山樓船圖
I

Ch'un-hua ko-t'ieh 淳化閣帖
PT. IV

Chün-yen chih-yin 俊參之印
III

Chuang Shen 莊申
XXVIII

Chuang-yüan tsung-po 狀元宗伯
III

chung-feng 中鋒
VIII, XX, LEAF B

Chung-ho 中和
XXXVII

Chung Tzu-ch'i 鍾子期
PT. II

Chung Yu 鍾繇
PT. IV; XVIII

Ch'ung-kuang-fu 崇光父
XL

Dam-sui 淡水 （日語發音）
XXVI, FRONTISPIECE

Elie Tamemori 入江為守
XXVI, FRONTISPIECE

erh-shih 耳食
PT. II

fa-tu 法度
PT. IV

Fan Ch'i 樊圻
PT. I; XI

Fan Ch'i 樊圻
XV, LEAVES A, B, C, D, G, H

Fan-cho-t'u 泛棹圖
XIV

Fan K'uan 范寬
PT. II; PT. IV; VII, XI

Fan Yün-lin 范允臨
VIII

fang 倣
PT. IV; XXXIX

Fang Chün-i, *Meng-yüan shu-hua-lu* 方濬頤夢園書畫錄
XII

Fang Heng-hsien 方亨咸
VII

Fang Sung-Yüan shan-shui ts'e 仿宋元山水冊
VII

Fang Ts'ung-i 方從義
PT. I

Fang-yen ts'un-chuang 方硯村莊
XXXII, COLOPHON 30

Fang Yin 房瀛
VIII

fei-pai 飛白
XX, LEAF C, XXV, LEAF C

Feng Ch'ao-jan 馮超然
II

fu-jung 芙蓉
XX, LEAF D, XXV, LEAF E

Fu Pao-shih 傅抱石
XXIII

fu-pen 撫本
XXI

Fu Shan 傅山
PT. IV

Fu Shen (*tzu* Chün-yüeh) 傅申（字君約）

Fu-she 復社
PT. I; X, XV

hai-t'ang 海棠
XXV, LEAF A

Hai-yang Huang-shih chia-ts'ang 海陽黃氏家藏
XXXVI

Hai-yang ssu-ta-chia 海陽四大家
PT. IV; XII, XIII

Han-li 漢隸
PT. IV; XXIV

Han Wu, "Su-yü-shih" 韓偓 疎雨詩
IV

Hana-o shimu hito 惜花人 (日語發音)
XXVI, FRONTISPIECE

hang-ch'i 行氣
XXIV

hao (sobriquet) 號
PT. IV

hao-fang 豪放
PT. IV

Hashimoto Kansetsu 橋本關雪
XXIII

Heng-shan 衡山
II

ho-hua 荷花
XX, LEAF H, XXV, LEAF E, XXXVII

Ho-k'o i-jih wu-tz'u-chün (PTC 28) 何可一日無此君
XXIX

Ho K'un-yü 何昆玉
XXXII

Ho Liang-chün 何良俊
PT. I

Ho-t'ao 喝濤
PT. IV

Ho Yüan-yü 何瑗玉
XXXII

hsi-ch'i 習氣
PT. IV

Hsi-ch'uan Chang-pa 西川張八
XXX, LEAF C

Hsi-hsi ts'ao-t'ang 隰西草堂
PT. X

Hsi Kang 奚岡
XL

Hsia Ch'ang 夏㫤
PT. I

Hsia-chün 俠君
XXXII, COLOPHON 29

Hsia-hui pa-hsiang t'u 夏卉八香圖
XXXVII

Hsia Kuei 夏珪
PT. I; XI

Hsia Liu-hsiu 夏六修
XXXII, COLOPHON 27

Hsia Shih-tse 夏世澤
PT. I

hsia-pi 狹筆
XIII

Hsiang[?]-shih 鄉士
XXXIX

Hsiang, Tsu 香祖
XXXII

Hsia-tsun-che 瞎尊者
PT. IV

Hsia-tsun-che (PTC 29) 瞎尊者（印）
XXII, LEAVES F AND K, XXXIII, LEAVES D AND F, XXX, LEAF CC

Hsia-tsun-che (forged seal) 瞎尊者（偽印）
XXXV, LEAF A

Hsia-tsun-che, Chi (forged seal) 瞎尊者濟（偽印）
XIX

Hsiang Yüan-pien 項元汴
I

Hsiang Yüan-pien yin 項元汴印
I

Hsiao-chung hsien-ta 小中現大
PT. II

Hsiao-feng shen-ting 小峯審定
XXIII

Hsiao-feng sui-yin ( ) ( )-hua 小峯隨隱□□畫
XXIII

Hsiao-lai-ch'in-kuan 小來禽館
X, LEAVES E AND S

hsiao-lou ch'i-mu-ch'ao (should read *hsiao-lou ch'i-mu-miao*) 小樓齊木杪
XXXIV

Hsiao Shih-wei 蕭士瑋
PT. IV

Hsiao-tzu ssu-wei 小字思未
XXXII, COLOPHON 3

Hsiao Yün-ts'ung 蕭雲從
PT. I; XII

Hsieh Ch'eng-chün 謝誠鈞
XXVII

Hsieh Chin 謝縉
I

Hsieh Chuo 解擢
XXXII, COLOPHON I I

Hsieh Fang-ch'i 謝方琦
XXXII, COLOPHON 26

Hsieh Fang-lien 謝芳連
XXXII, COLOPHON 30

Hsieh Ho 謝赫
PT. I

hsieh-i 寫意
I

Hsieh-nan Hang-fu Ts'ao-shih kuo-yün-lou chien-ts'ang chin-shih shu-hua-yin 歙南杭阜曹氏過雲樓鑑藏金石書畫印
III

Hsieh Pin 謝彬
VIII

Hsieh shan-shui-chüeh 寫山水訣
PT. IV

Hsieh-sheng 寫生
XXXVII

Hsien, Chai 咸齋
XXXII, COLOPHON 12

Hsien Chu 先箸
XXXII, COLOPHON 27

Hsien Chu chih-yin 先箸之印
XXXII, COLOPHON 27

Hsien-ch'ü 儇矔
XXXII, COLOPHON 23

Hsien-nan 衙南
XVII, LEAF CC, XX, LEAF CC

Hsien-yü Shu 鮮于樞
PT. I

hsin 心
PT. IV

hsin-chiang 心匠
PT. IV

Hsin-lo shan-jen 新羅山人
XXXVI

Hsin-wei-sheng 辛未生
X, LEAF B

hsin-yen 心眼
PT. IV

hsing 興
PT. IV

Hsing-ch'eng chien-ts'ang 杏城鑑藏
III

hsing-k'ai 行楷
XX, LEAF B, XXIV

Hsing Shen 邢參
III

Hsing-t'ang Chang-shih Huan-an 行唐張氏還庵鑑賞印
chien-shang-yin
IX

hsing-ts'ao 行草
PT. IV

Hsiu-jen, Chi 朽人極
PT. IV

Hsiu-shui Chin Lan-p'o sou-suo 秀水金蘭坡搜索金石書畫
chin-shih shu-hua
XXIV

hsiu-ts'ai (degree) 秀才
XII, XIII

Hsü Chen-ch'ing 徐禎卿
III

Hsü Chin 徐縉
II

Hsü Ch'in 徐沁
VIII

Hsü-feng-lou 徐風樓
X, LEAF O

Hsü Hsi 徐熙
PT. I

Hsü Hung-tsu (hao Hsia-k'o) 徐宏祖（䚟霞客）
PT. I

Hsü Pen 徐賁
PT. I

Hsü Ping-heng (tzu Chün-p'ing) 徐秉衡（字君平）
X, LEAF A

Hsü-shih hsiao-yin 徐氏小印
XXXII

Hsü-t'ang chien-ting 照堂鑑定
III

Hsü Wei 徐渭
PT. I; IX, XX, LEAF H

Hsü Wen-min-kung chi 徐文敏公集
II

Hsü Yeh-chün 徐野君
XXIV

Hsüan-ch'ing-shih hua-yin 懸磬室畫印
IV

Hsüan-yeh 玄燁
PT. I

Hsüeh-hsi shih-ssu t'u 雪溪詩思圖
XXXVIII

Hsüeh-shang tao-che 雪山道者
III

Hsüeh-tsai 學在
XXXII, COLOPHON 3

Hu Ch'i 胡琪
PT. IV

Hu-chou Lu-shih so-ts'ang 潮州陸氏所藏
III

Hu Hsiao-chuo-ts'ang 胡小琢藏
XVI, LEAVES A, B, C, F

Hu Yen-yüan 胡彥遠
X, LEAF L

hua 化
PT. IV

Hua-Ch'an-shih 畫禪室
XXXVII, XL

hua-she t'ien-tsu 畫蛇添足
PT. IV; XXXI

Hua-p'u 畫譜
PT. IV; XXIII

Hua Yen 華嵒
PT. I; XXXVI

Hua-yü-lu 畫語錄
PT. IV; XXIII

Huang Chao 黃照
III

Huang Ch'üan 黄筌
PT. I

Huang I 黄易
XL

Huang Kung-wang 黄公望
PT. I; I, VII, VIII, XII

Huang Pin-hung 黄賓虹
XL

Huang Po-hou 黄伯厚
VI

Huang Po-shan 黄白山
XX, LEAVES AA AND FF

Huang Po-ssu 黄伯思
PT. IV

Huang-shan (Mt. Huang) 黄山
PT. I; PT. IV; XII, XXX

Huang-sheng chih-yin 黄生之印
(alternating intaglio-relief, square)
XX, LEAVES AA AND FF

huang-shu-k'uei 黄蜀葵
XX, LEAF G

Huang Tao-chou 黄道周
PT. I

Huang T'ing-chien 黄庭堅
PT. I; PT. IV

Huang Yen-ssu 黄燕思
XX

Huang Yün 黄雲
XXXII

Hui-hsin pu-yüan 會心不遠
XXXVII

Hui-kung 會公
XV, LEAVES A, C, E, F, H

Hui-shou 慈壽
X, LEAVES C AND D

Hui-ts'un mao-wu 匯邨茅屋
XXXII

Hung Cheng-chih 洪正治
PT. IV; XXXII

Hung-jen 弘仁
PT. I; PT. III; X

Hung-jen (relief, round) 弘仁 (陽文圓印)
XII, LEAVES C, D

Hung-jen (relief, double seal in two small squares) 弘仁 (連珠)
XII, LEAF E

Hung-jen (relief, small round) 弘仁 (陽文小圓印)
XII, LEAVES G AND I

Hung Kai-hua hua-hsiang 洪陔華畫像
XXXII

Hung-li 弘曆
PT. I; XXXVII

hung-liao 紅蓼
XXV, LEAF E

Hung Ming 洪銘
XXXII, COLOPHON 13

Hung-pin? chang-chi (owner unidentified) 鴻嬪?掌記
XXXII

Hung Shih-mou 洪時懋
XXXII

Hung-tou-shu-kuan shu-hua-chi 紅豆樹館書畫記
XXVIII

huo-ch'i 火氣
X

I-chih-ko 一枝閣
XXXIV, LEAF A

i-hua 一畫
XVIII

i-jen chih-yung 一人之用
PT. IV

I-ku-t'ang hsü-pa 儀顧堂續跋
X

i-lin 意臨
XXX

i-mao (1675 or 1735) 乙卯 (乙邜)
XXIII

i-min 遺民
PT. I; X

I-p'in (owner unidentified) 逸品 (印)
XXIII

i-p'in 逸品
XIII

I Ping-shou 伊秉綬
XXV, PORTRAIT LEAF

I-shou (owner unidentified) 頤壽
XXVI, LEAF K

I Ting 一丁
XXIII

I-tsai pi-chien 意在筆尖
XXXVII

i-yu (1705) 乙酉 (乙酉或乙邜)
XXIII

Jen-wu hua-hui ts'e 人物花卉冊
XX

Jo-chi 若極
PT. IV

Jo-mu 若木
XL

Jo-po 若波
XLI

ju-chui hua-sha 如錐畫沙
XX, LEAF G

Jun-sheng kuo-yen 潤生過眼
XXIII

Kai-hua 陔華
XXXII

k'ai-(shu) 楷書
PT. IV; VIII

kan-shou 乾瘦
PT. IV

k'an-pu-ju 看不入
PT. IV

K'an-yün 看雲
XXXVII

K'ang-hsi 康熙
PT. I

kao-jen 高人
PT. IV

kao-ku 高古
PT. IV

Kao K'o-kung 高克恭
PT. I; VII

Kao-mang-tzu (forged seal) 瞽盲子（偽印）
XXXV, LEAF C

Kao-mang-tzu, Chi (PTC 41) 瞽盲子濟
XXXIII, LEAF H

Kao-yao Ho-shih K'un-yü, 高要何氏昆玉
Yüan-yü t'ung-huai kung-shang 暖玉同懷共賞
XXXII

Kawai Senrō 河井荃廬
XXIII

Keng Chao-chung 耿昭忠
PT. IV

Keng-ch'en ch'u-yeh shih-kao 庚辰除夜詩稿
PT. IV; XXIII

Keng ( )( )( )-wu-tz'u-ch'ing 耕□□□無此情
XXXII

Keng-hsin (ts'ao)-t'ang 耕心草堂
PT. IV; XXXI, XXXIV, LEAF F

keng-yin 庚寅
PT. IV

ko-t'ieh 閣帖
PT. IV; X

Kohara Hironobu 古原宏伸
XXIII

Ku Cheng-i 顧正誼
PT. I

ku-i 古意
I

Ku K'ai-chih 顧愷之
PT. I

Ku Ssu-li 顧嗣立
XXXII, COLOPHON 20

Ku Ssu-li-yin 顧嗣立印
XXXII, COLOPHON 20

Ku Tsai-mei 顧在湄
XII

Ku Ying 顧瑛
PT. I

Ku-yüan ts'ui-lu 古緣萃錄
XII

Ku Yün 顧澐
PT. I; XL, L

K'u-kua (PTC 43) 苦瓜
XX, LEAVES A AND G, XXII, LEAF B, XXV, LEAF C

K'u-kua ho-shang 苦瓜和尚
PT. IV

K'u-kua ho-shang (PTC 45) 苦瓜和尚
XX, LEAF D

K'u-kua ho-shang (forged seal) 苦瓜和尚（偽印）
XIX

K'u-kua ho-shang, Chi hua-fa (PTC 48) 苦瓜和尚濟畫法
XXVI, LEAF K, XXX, LEAVES A, B, C, D

K'uai-chi Yang Wei-chen yin 會稽楊維楨印
I

K'uai-hsüeh shih-ch'ing 快雪時晴
XXXVII

Kuan-yüan-chi 灌園集
I

k'uang Ch'an 狂禪
PT. IV

Kuei-an Lu Hsin-yüan, tzu Kang-fu yin 歸安陸心源字剛父印
III

Kuei-yün chuang-nung 歸雲莊農
XX, LEAF BB

K'uei-chen 夔震
XXXII, COLOPHON 22

K'un-ts'an 髡殘
PT. I; PT. IV; X

Kung Chin 龔瑾
I

Kung Hsien 龔賢
PT. I; PT. IV; X, XII, XVI

Kung Hsien yin 龔賢印
XVI, LEAVES A, C, D, E, F

Kung Hsiu 龔璓
I

Kung-ya-shih 公雅氏
III

K'ung I 孔毅
VI

K'ung I shen-ting 孔毅審定
VI

K'ung I so-ts'ang 孔毅所藏
VI

K'ung-shan hsiao-yü 空山小語
XVII

K'ung Shang-jen 孔尚任
PT. IV

Kuo Hsi 郭熙
PT. IV

Kuo Pi 郭畀
PT. I

Kuo T'ai 郭泰
X, LEAF G

Kuo-tzu-chien 國子監
I

k'uo-pi 闊筆
XIII, XIV

lan-hua 蘭花
XXV, LEAF B, XXXVII

Lan Meng 藍孟
VII, IX

Lan Shen 藍深
VII, IX

Lan T'ao 藍濤
VII

Lan T'ing-hsü 蘭亭序
X, LEAVES P AND Q

Lan Ying 藍瑛
PT. I; PT. IV; V, VI, VII, VIII, XI, XII

Lan Ying chih-yin 藍瑛之印
IX

Lan Ying, T'ien-shu-shih 藍瑛田叔氏
VII

Lao-t'ao (PTC 50) 老濤
XVII, XX, LEAF E, XXII, LEAF J

Le-sheng 檪生
XL

li 理
PT. IV

li-(shu) 隸(書)
PT. IV; XXIV

Li Ch'eng 李成
PT. IV; VII

Li Chih 李鷹
III

Li Hsien 李憲
XXXIX

Li Jui-ch'i (hao Yün-an) 李瑞奇 (號筠厂)
PT. I; PT. II; XXI

Li Jui-ch'ing (hao Mei-an, Ch'ing tao-jen) 李瑞清(號梅盦清道人)
PT. I; XXI, XXIII, XXXV

Li K'ai 李鍇
XXXII, COLOPHON 25

Li K'ai ssu-yin 李鍇私印
XXXII, COLOPHON 25

Li Kung-lin 李公麟
PT. I; III, X, LEAF I

Li Kuo-sung 李國宋
XX, LEAF GG

Li Liu-fang 李流芳
PT. I; PT. IV; V, XIII

Li Po 李白
PT. IV

Li Sung-an 李松庵
XXIII

Li Tan 李旦
XXIII

Li-tsao wei-ch'un 摛藻為春
XXXVII

Li Tsung-ch'eng 李宗成
PT. IV

Li Tsung-han 李宗瀚
XXIII

li-tu chien-wu 離堵間物
PT. IV

Li Yen-kua 李延适
III

Li Yin 李寅
XI

Li Yü 李煜
PT. I

Liang (Mr. Liang, unidentified) 亮 (名亮、不知姓氏)
XXXII, COLOPHON 12

liao-fa 了法
PT. IV

Lin-ch'i (should read Lin-chi) 臨濟
PT. IV

Lin-ch'üan kao-chih 林泉高致
PT. IV

lin-li, ch'i-ku 淋漓奇古
PT. IV

Lin Liang 林良
IX

lin-mo tsui-i, shen-hui nan-ch'uan 臨摹最易,神會難傳
PT. IV

lin-pen 臨本
PT. II; XIX, XXI

Lin-su lao-jen 鄰蘇老人
III

ling-chiao 菱角
XXXI

360 / Glossary

Ling-shan (should read Leng-shan) 稜山
XXXII

Ling-ting lao-jen (PTC 53) 零丁老人
XXVII

Liu-ch'i 六奇
XII

Liu Ch'un-hsü 劉眷虛
X, LEAF O

Liu Chüeh 劉玨
I

liu-fa 六法
PT. II

Liu-hsiu 六修
XXXII, COLOPHON 27

Liu Pen-chung 劉本中
I

Liu P'u 劉溥
XXVII

Liu Ts'ao 劉燥
X, LEAF H

Liu Ts'ao-ch'uang 劉草窓
XXVII

Liu Tu 劉度
VII

Liu-ya 六雅
XXXII, COLOPHON 15

Liu Yün-ch'üan 劉運銓
XXIII

Lo Chen-yü 羅振玉
XI

Lo Chia-lun 羅家倫
XXV, PORTRAIT LEAF

Lo P'in 羅聘
XXV, PORTRAIT LEAF

lo-wen-chih 羅紋紙
XXIII, XXV, LEAF B

Lu Chi 陸機
PT. I

Lu Chih 陸治
IX, XXXIX

Lu Hsin-yüan 陸心源
III, X

Lu Hung 盧鴻
X, LEAF I

Lu Kuang 陸廣
PT. I

Lu Nan-shih 盧南石
XX

Lu Nan-shih chien-ts'ang-chang 盧南石鑑藏章
XX, LEAF GG

Lu-shan (Mt. Lu) 廬山
PT. I; XXX

Lu T'an-wei 陸探微
PT. I

Lu-tun-sheng 魯鈍生
I

Lu-tun-sheng 魯鈍生 (印)
I

Lü-an Pen-yüeh 旅菴本月
PT. IV

Lü Chi 呂紀
IX

Lung 隆
XXXVII

lung-mo 龍脈
XXXII

Luo-yin 贏隱
XX, LEAF GG

Ma Chi-tso 馬積祚
II, XXVII

Ma-shih shu-hua 馬氏書畫
XXVII

Ma Wan 馬琬
PT. I; I

Ma Wan chang 馬琬章
I

Ma Wan, Wen-pi yin-chang 馬琬文璧印章
I

Mao Ch'i-ling 毛奇齡
IX

Mei-an 梅盦
XXI

Mei Ch'ing 梅清
PT. I; PT. IV; XII, XXVI

Mei-ho 梅壑
XIII

Mei-hua-shih ts'e 梅花詩冊
XXXIII

Mei Keng 梅庚
PT. I; PT. IV

Mei-kung 眉公
III

Mei Wen-ting 梅文鼎
XXXII, COLOPHON 2

Mei Wen-ting-yin 梅文鼎印
XXXII, COLOPHON 2

Mei-ying shu-wu pi-chi 梅影書屋秘笈
II

Meng Hao-jan 孟浩然
X, LEAF O

Meng-meng tao-jen shou-kao 夢夢道人手稿
XXIII

Meng-tung-sheng (PTC 54) 夢董生
XXXIII, LEAF B

Meng-yang 盂陽
V

Mi Fu 米芾
PT. I; PT. II; PT. IV; VII, XIV

mi-tien 米點
PT. IV

Miao Ch'üan-sun 繆荃孫
III

miao-hua 描畫
XLI

Ming-pao 明報
XXVIII

Ming-yu 名友
XXXII, COLOPHON 16

mo-chi 墨蹟
X

mo-ku 沒骨
XX, LEAF D

mo-ku-fa 沒骨法
PT. IV

mo-li-hua 茉莉花
XXXVII

Mo-lin mi-wan 墨林秘玩
I

mo-pen 摹本
PT. II; XXI

Mo Shih-lung 莫是龍
PT. I

mou-tan 牡丹
XXV, LEAF D

Mu-ch'en Tao-min 木陳道忞
PT. IV

Mu-ch'i 牧谿
PT. I

Mu-lü-t'u 摹驢圖
III

Mu-t'ing-shih 牧庭氏
XXXII, COLOPHON 19

na (stroke) 捺
XXXV

Na Yen 衲彥
III

Nagahara Oriharu 永原織治
XXIII

Nai-ho 奈何
XXXVI

Nan-ju-shih 南如氏
XXXII, COLOPHON 9

Nan-pei-tung-hsi chih-yu 南北東西只有相隨無別離
hsiang-sui wu-pieh-li
XXII, LEAF A, XXIII, XXV, LEAF G, XXXI, XXXII, XXXIII, LEAF B, XXXIV, LEAF H

Ni Tsan 倪瓚
PT. I; PT. IV; V, VII, X, XII

Ni-yen-lou shu hua-yin 眠燕樓書畫印
XX, LEAF GG

Ni Yüan-lu (tzu Hung-pao) 倪元璐 (字鴻寶)
X, LEAF B

Nien-shao 年少 (萬壽祺)
X

Ning-hsiang Chou-shih Meng-shui shan-fang 寧鄉周氏夢水山房
meng-kung shen-ting chin-shih shu-hua 夢公審定金石書畫
(owner unidentified)
XXXV, LEAVES C, E, F

Okabe Chokei 岡部長景
XXXIV

Ou-an ching-yen (owner unidentified) 耦庵經眼
XXX, LEAF A

Ou-yang Hsiu 歐陽修
PT. I

Ou-yang Hsün 歐陽詢
X

Ou-yang Jun-sheng 歐陽潤生
XXIII

pa-chiao-yeh 芭蕉葉
XXV, LEAF F

pa-fen-(shu) 八分
PT. IV

pa-mien ch'u-yeh 八面出葉
XX, LEAF B

pai-miao 白描
III, XXXVII

Pan-ch'ien 半千
XVI, LEAVES B AND F

Pan-ko-han (PTC 56) 半簡漢 (陰文)
XXX, LEAF BB, XXXII, XXXIV, LEAVES A AND B

Pan-ko-han (PTC 57) 半簡漢 (陽文)
XXII, LEAF B, XXV, LEAVES A AND E

P'an Cheng-wei 潘正煒
XVII

P'ang Yüan-chi 龐元濟
VIII

Pao-en-ssu 報恩寺
PT. IV

Pao Hu-ch'en 包虎臣
IV

Pao Hu-ch'en ts'ang 包虎臣藏
IV

Pao-lun-t'ang-chi 寶綸堂集
IX

Pei Ch'iung 貝瓊
I

pei-lin 背臨
XXX

P'eng-ch'eng Chang-lao 彭城張老
X, LEAF D

pi-i 筆意
PT. IV; IV

p'i-ma-ts'un 披麻皴
PT. IV; I

Pieh-shih jung-i 別時容易
XXII, LEAVES A AND B, XXV, LEAF B, XXVII, XXXIV, LEAF J

pien 變
PT. IV

pien-e 扁額
PT. I

"Pien-hua" 變化
PT. IV

Pien Wen-chin 邊文進
IX

Pien Wen-yü 卞文瑜
PT. I

Pien Yung-yü 卞永譽
I

P'ien-shih shan-fang 片石山房
PT. I

P'ien-p'ang pien-cheng 偏旁辨正
I

p'ien-t'i-wen 駢體文
XXIV

Ping-hsüeh wu-ch'ien-shen (PTC 59) 冰雪悟前身
XXV, LEAF H, XXX, LEAF AA

P'ing-chai chien-shang 平齋鑑賞
XXIV

P'ing-shan-t'ang 平山堂
PT. I; VII

Po-erh-tu 博爾都
PT. IV

Po-shan 白山
XX, LEAF AA

Po-ya 伯牙
PT. II

Po-ying ssu-yin 伯奬私印
X, LEAF J

Po-yüan shen-ting (owner unidentified) 伯元審定
II; XXVII

P'o-mo 潑墨
XXXVII

p'o-mo-fa 破墨法
PT. IV

pu-chi-li chien 不即離間
XXXVII

Pu-chien-shih 不見是
XX, LEAF HH

Pu-fu-ku-jen kao-hou-jen 不負古人告後人
XXIII, XXIV, XXX, LEAF CC, XXXII, XXXIII, LEAF A

Pu-wei-wu so-ts'ai 不為物所裁
XXXII, COLOPHON 25

P'u Ju (tzu Hsin-yü) 溥儒（字心畬）
XXIV

P'u-men (Monk) （釋）普門
PT. I

Ricci, Matteo (Li Ma-tou) 利瑪竇
PT. I

San-ch'ien Ta-ch'ien 三千大千
XX, LEAF HH, XXV, LEAF H

san-chüeh 三絕
XXVII

Sasaki Kozo 佐佐木剛三
XXIII

Sekitō 石濤（日語發音）
PT. IV

seng 僧
PT. IV

Seng-shou 僧壽
X, LEAF N

"Shan-ch'uan" 山川（章）
PT. IV

shan-ch'uan t'uo-t'ai yü-wo 山川脫胎於我
PT. IV

Shan-hu mu-nan 珊瑚木難
III

Shan-hu-wang 珊瑚網
I

shan-shui 山水
PT. I

Shan-tzu hsin-shang 善孖心賞
XX, LEAF E, XXIV, XXX, LEAF AA, XXXIII, LEAF E

Shan-tzu shen-ting 善孖審定
XXIV, XXX, LEAF C, XXXIII, LEAF F

Shang-ch'ih-chai Chi-shih chen-ts'ang 尚䂖齋李氏珍藏
IV

Shao Mi 邵彌
PT. I; PT. IV

Shao-p'u 勺圃
X, LEAVES C, H, M

Shao Sung-nien 邵松年
XII

She-meng 社盟
XII, LEAF E

Shen Chen 沈貞
PT. I

Shen Ch'eng 沈澄
PT. I

Shen Chou 沈周
PT. I; PT. II; PT. IV; II, III, IX, XXVII, XXVIII

Shen Chou 'Mo-ch'o T'ung-ch'üeh-yen-ko' t'u 沈周莫斫銅爵硯歌圖
XXVII, XXVIII

Shen Heng 沈恒
PT. I

shen-hui 神會
PT. IV

Shen Hung-tu 沈弘度
III

Shen-liu tu-shu-t'ang 深柳讀書堂
XXIII

Shen Pin 沈邠
III

Shen-p'in 神品
I

Shen-p'ing-hsing 生平行
PT. IV

Shen Shu-yung 沈樹鏞
III

Shen T'ing-fang 沈廷芳
XXXII, COLOPHON 31

Shen T'ing-fang-yin 沈廷芳印
XXXII, COLOPHON 31

shen-yüan 深遠
XXVI, LEAF D

Shen Yün-ch'u chen-ts'ang-yin 沈韻初珍藏印
III

Sheng Mao-yeh 盛茂燁
VI, XIII

shih-ch'i 士氣
IV

Shih-ch'ü pao-chi so-ts'ang 石渠寶笈所藏
XXXVII

Shih Feng-hui 史鳳輝
XXXII, COLOPHON 9

Shih Feng-hui-yin 史鳳輝印
XXXII, COLOPHON 9

Shih-fu 實父
III

shih-hsin 師心
PT. IV

Shih-ku-t'ang shu-hua hui-k'ao 式古堂書畫彙考
I

shih-mu 師目
PT. IV

shih-pi 士筆
IV

shih-shu 師叔
XXI

shih-ta-fu-hua 士大夫畫
XXXIX, XLI

Shih-t'ao. See Tao-chi 石濤（道濟）
PT. IV

Shih-t'ao (PTC 66) 石濤（印）
XVIII

Shih-t'ao nien-piao 石濤年表
PT. IV

Shih-t'ao shang-jen nien-p'u 石濤上人年譜
XXIII

Shih-t'ao t'i-hua-lu 石濤題畫錄
XXIII

Shih-tzu-lin 獅子林
PT. I

shih-wo wei-mou-chia-i 是我為某家役
PT. IV

shih-yen 詩眼
PT. I

Shih Yüan-chi yin (PTC 74) 釋元濟印
XX, LEAVES C AND F, XXII, LEAF A

Shih Yüan-chi yin (forged seal) 釋元濟印（偽印）
XIX

Shimada, Shūjirō 島田修二郎
XXVI, XXIII

Shinozaki Tsukasa 篠崎都香佐
XXIII

Shou 壽
X, LEAVES E, F, H

Shou-ch'i 壽祺
X, LEAVES B, L, M, R

Shou-ch'i chih-yin 壽祺之印
X, LEAF I

shou-fa pu-pien, ch'i-wei shu-chia-nu-erh 守法不變其為書家奴耳
PT. IV

shou-yen 手眼
PT. IV

shou-ying-fa 瘦硬法
PT. IV

Shu-chün Chang Yüan 蜀郡張爰
XVIII, XX, LEAF HH, XXV, LEAF H

Shu-hua t'i-pa-chi 書畫題跋記
I

Shu-k'o 蜀客
XXX, LEAF D

Shu-mei 叔美
XXXVIII

shuang-kou 雙鉤
XL

shui-hsien-hua 水仙花
XXV, LEAF C

Ssu-chou Yang-shih so-ts'ang 泗州楊氏所藏
XXVII

ssu 似
PT. IV

ssu-fei chih-chien 似非之間
PT. IV; XVIII

Ssu-k'u ch'üan-shu 四庫全書
XXXVII

ssu-shih erh fei, ssu-fei erh shih 似是而非，似非而是
XVII

Su-an 疏菴
III

su-ch'ien 疏淺
XII

Su-kuo-t'u 蔬果圖
XXXI

Su Shih (tzu Tzu-chan, hao Tung-p'o) 蘇軾（字子瞻號東坡）
PT. I; PT. IV; III, XVII

Sui-yü huang () 遂于荒□
XX, LEAF DD

Sumitomo Kanichi 住友寬一
XXVI

Sun Ch'eng-tse 孫承澤
XI

Sun Ch'ien-li 孫虔禮
PT. I

Sun I 孫逸
PT. I; XII, XIII

Sun K'o-hung 孫克弘
PT. I; VIII

Sun Tzu-hsiu 孫自修
XII

Sung Hsü 宋旭
VIII

ta-ch'eng 大成
XLI

Ta-ch'ien (relief, small square; seal script) 大千（以下諸印皆不同）
XII, LEAF A, XX, LEAF DD, XXV, LEAF E

Ta-ch'ien (relief, medium square; ancient seal script with heavy border) 大千
XII, LEAF F, XXXIV, LEAF B

Ta-ch'ien (relief, small square; ancient seal script) 大千
XII, LEAF H

Ta-ch'ien (relief, medium square; thin seal script) 大千
XVIII, COLOPHON

Ta-ch'ien (relief, square; ancient seal script with heavy border and center line) 大千
XX, LEAF FF

Ta-ch'ien (relief, square; seal script with heavy border) 大千
XX, LEAF GG

Ta-ch'ien (relief, large square; thin seal script) 大千
XXXII, FRONTISPIECE

Ta-ch'ien chih-hsi 大千之鉨
XXX, LEAF B

Ta-ch'ien chih-pao 大千之寶
XXIV, XXX, LEAF C

Ta-ch'ien chü-shih (intaglio, small square; heavy border and center line) 大千居士（陰文小）
XII, LEAF D, XXII, LEAF L

Ta-ch'ien chü-shih (relief, medium square; seal script) 大千居士（陽文中）
XII, LEAF C

Ta-ch'ien chü-shih (relief, large square; seal script) 大千居士（陽文大）
XVIII

Ta-ch'ien chü-shih (intaglio, square) 大千居士（陰文）
XX, LEAF EE

Ta-ch'ien chü-shih (relief, small square; seal script) 大千居士（陽文小）
XXII, LEAF G, XXXIV, LEAF D

Ta-ch'ien chü-shih kung-yang pai-Shih chih-i 大千居士供養百石之一
XXII, LEAF C, XXIII, XXV, LEAVES C AND H, XXX, LEAF DD
XXXI, XXXII, XXXIII, LEAF A, XXXIV, LEAF A

Ta-ch'ien fu-ch'ang ta-chi 大千富昌大吉
V

Ta-ch'ien hao-meng 大千好夢
XX, LEAF B, XXIV, XXX, LEAF B, XXXIII, LEAF H

Ta-ch'ien-hsi 大千鉨
XXII, LEAF K, XXXIV, LEAF G

Ta-ch'ien wei-yin ta-nien 大千唯印大年
XXV, PORTRAIT LEAF

Ta-ch'ien yu-mu 大千游目
XXIV

ta-chuan 大篆
XXXVI

Ta-feng-t'ang (relief, square) 大風堂（陽文方印）
XX, LEAF D, XXX, LEAF D

Ta-feng-t'ang 大風堂（陰文長方）
XXX, LEAF AA

Ta-feng-t'ang (relief, large square) 大風堂（陽文大印）
XXXII

Ta-feng-t'ang (relief, oval) 大風堂（陽文腰圓印）
XXXIII, LEAF A

Ta-feng-t'ang (relief, wide oval) 大風堂（陽文短腰圓印）
XXXIII, LEAF E

Ta-feng-t'ang ch'ang-wu 大風堂長物
XXV, PORTRAIT LEAF

Ta-feng-t'ang Chien-chiang, K'un-ts'an, Hsüeh-ko, K'u-kua mo-yüan 大風堂漸江蜣殘雪箇苦瓜墨緣
XII, LEAF J, XX, LEAF A, XXV, LEAVES A, C, PORTRAIT, XXVII, XXX, LEAF BB, XXXIII, LEAF B, XXXIV, LEAF K

Ta-pen-t'ang 大本堂
PT. IV

Ta-pen-t'ang, Chi (PTC 82) 大本堂極
XXXIV, LEAVES C, G, J, L

Ta-pen-t'ang, Jo-chi (PTC 83) 大本堂若極
XXXIV, LEAVES D AND K

Ta-ti-shan (Mt. Ta-ti) 大滌山
PT. IV

Ta-ti-t'ang 大滌堂
PT. IV

Ta-ti-ts'ao-t'ang t'u 大滌草堂圖
XXIII

Ta-ti-tzu 大滌子
PT. IV

Ta-ti-tzu (PTC 86) 大滌子 (印)
XXXIV, LEAVES A, D, E, H

Ta-ti-tzu (forged seal) 大滌子 (偽印)
XXXV, LEAF F

Ta-ti-tzu, Chi (PTC 88) 大滌子極
XXXII

Ta-ti-tzu, Chi, li-weng t'u-shu (forged seal) 大滌子極笠翁圖書
XIX

Ta-ti-tzu t'i-hua shih-pa 大滌子題畫詩跋
PT. IV

Ta-ts'un Li 大邨李
XX, LEAF GG

Ta-wu? 大污 ?
IX

Ta-yin chin-men 大隱金門
III

Tai Chin 戴進
PT. I; VIII, XI

Tai Pen-hsiao 戴本孝
PT. I; PT. IV; XI, XII, XVII, XXXVI

tai-pi 代筆
PT. IV

T'ai-hu (Lake T'ai) 太湖
PT. I

t'ai-hu stones 太湖石
PT. I

T'ai-shang huang-ti chih-pao 太上皇帝之寶
XXXVII

T'ai-tai Yün-hai-t'u 泰岱雲海圖
XXXVI

t'ai-t'ou 檯頭
XXIII

Tamemori shō 為守章 (日語發音)
XXVI, FRONTISPIECE

Tan Ch'ung-kuang (should read Ta Ch'ung-kuang) 笪重光
XIII

Tan-erh-yung 淡而永
XXIII

Tan Hsün 單恂
III

Tan-jung-yü 澹容與
XXXII, COLOPHON 25

T'an-mei shih-hua-t'u 探梅詩畫圖
XVIII

T'an-ts'un 檀村
XXXII, COLOPHON 5

T'ang Hsüan-i (tzu Yen-sheng) 湯玄翼 (字燕生)
PT. IV; XII

T'ang-li (shu) 唐隸 (書)
PT. IV; XXIV

T'ang Yin 唐寅
PT. I; PT. IV; III

Tao-chi 道濟
PT. I; PT. II; PT. III; PT. IV; X, XVII–XXXV, XL

Tao-hsiang ts'ao-lu ts'ang-pao 稻香草廬藏寶
VI

tao-yen 道眼
PT. IV

T'ao Ch'ien (tzu Yüan-ming) 陶潛 (字淵明)
X, LEAF M, XX, LEAF E

T'ao Liang 陶樑
XXVII

T'ao Yüan-ming. See T'ao Ch'ien 陶淵明

Te-ch'ung-fu 德充符
XXXVII

Te-chia-ch'ü 得佳趣
XXXVII

Te-i-hsüan ts'ang 得一軒藏
XVI, LEAF E

Te-i-jen chih-chi wu-han (PTC 92) 得一人知己無憾
XXX, LEAVES CC AND DD

Ti-kuo chih-fu 敵國之富
XXII, LEAF F, XXXI

Ti-lin 荻林
XXXII, COLOPHON 31

Tieh-sou 蜨叟
VIII

T'i-an chien-shang 惕安鑑賞
XXIV

T'i-an ch'ing-mi 惕安清秘
XXIV

t'ieh 帖
XX

T'ieh-hsin tao-jen 鐵心道人
I

T'ieh-ti tao-jen 鐵邃道人
I

T'ieh-yai 鐵厓
I

tien-ching 點睛
PT. IV

T'ien-shu (relief, oval) 田叔 （腰圓印）
VIII

T'ien-shu (relief, square) 田叔 （方印）
IX

Ting-chiu 定九
XXXII, COLOPHON 2

T'ing-fan-lou shu-hua-chi 聽颿樓書畫記
XVII

ting-hai 丁亥
PT. IV

ting-yu 丁酉
PT. IV

Ting Yün-p'eng 丁雲鵬
PT. I; XXXVI

T'ing-chü 廷琚
I

T'ing-tso 廷佐
XXXII

t'ou-kuan shou-yen 透關手眼
PT. IV

T'ou-pai i-jan pu-shih-tzu (PTC 94) 頭白依然不識字
XXIV, XXXI

Tsan-chih shih-shih-sun, A-ch'ang (PTC 95) 贊之十世孫阿長
PT. I; XXII, LEAVES H AND L, XXVII, XXXI, XXXIII, LEAF G, XXXV, LEAF B

Tsan-chih shih-shih-sun, A-ch'ang (forged seal) 贊之十世孫阿長 （偽印）
XXXV, LEAF B

ts'an-keng 殘羹
PT. IV

Ts'ang-chih Ta-ch'ien (intaglio, square) 藏之大千 （陰文方印）
XX, LEAF E, XXV, LEAF C, XXX, LEAF A, XXXIII, LEAF C

Ts'ang-chih Ta-ch'ien (relief, large tall rectangle) 藏之大千 （陽文）
XX, LEAF H

Ts'ao Chih-po 曹知白
PT. I; VII

ts'ao-li 草隸
XXXI

Ts'ao Pa 曹霸
X, LEAF L

Ts'ao Pu-hsing 曹不興
PT. I

Ts'ao Ts'ao (tzu Meng-te, hao A-man) 曹操 （字孟德號阿瞞）
XXVII

Ts'ao Yin 曹寅
XII

Tse 澤 （張善孖）
XX, LEAF A

ts'e-feng 側鋒
XVII

Tseng Ching 曾鯨
PT. I

Tseng Hsi (tzu Tzu-chi, hao Nung-jan) 曾熙 （號農髯）
PT. I; XXXV

Tseng Yu-ho 曾幼荷
XXIII

Ts'eng-ts'ang Ch'ien Meng-lu-chia 曾藏錢夢廬家
III

Ts'eng-ts'ang Wang-shih erh-shih-pa-so-yen-chai 曾藏王氏二十八宿硯齋
XXIV

(?)Tsu-ming 口祖命
XX, LEAF BB

Tsu-ming tzu Hsin-ch'an 祖命字薪禪
XX, LEAF BB

Ts'ui Tzu-chung 崔子忠
PT. I

"Tsun-shou" 尊受
PT. IV

ts'un 皴
PT. IV; XXVII

Ts'un-chai yu-ch'eng Ch'ien-yüan 存齋又稱潛園
III

Tu Ch'iung 杜瓊
PT. I

Tu Fu 杜甫
X, LEAVES J AND L

Tu Wan 杜綰
PT. I

Tuan-hsi Ho Shu-tzu Yüan-yü hao chü-an kuo-yen ching-chi chin-shih shu-hua-yin-chi 端溪何叔子瑗玉號遽盦過眼經籍金石書畫印記
XXXII

T'ui-mi 退密
I

Tun-ken (PTC 97) 鈍根
XXV, LEAF G

Tung Ch'i-ch'ang 董其昌
PT. I; PT. IV; V, VII, XIV, XL

Tung-i hsüeh-che 東漪學者
XX, LEAF DD

Tung Sung 董淞
III

Tung-t'ing-shan (Mt. Tung-t'ing) 洞庭山
PT. I

Tung-yen-shih 東巖氏
XXXII, COLOPHON 2 I

Tung Yüan 董源
PT. I

T'ung-yin lun-hua 桐蔭論畫
XIII

t'uo-t'ai 脫胎
PT. IV

tzu (style name) 字

tzu-ch'eng i-chia 自成一家
PT. IV

Tzu-ch'ing so-chien 子清所見
III

Tzu-jung 子容
II

Tzu-sun yung-pao 子孫永保
I

tzu-yü-hua-che, ch'i-chü liang-tuan, 字與畫者其具兩端
ch'i kung i-t'i 其功一體
PT. IV

U-tei 雨亭 (入江為守之號)
XXVI, FRONTISPIECE

Wa-ying-hsüan 窪盈軒
PT. I

wai-shih tsao-hua, chung te hsin-yüan 外師造化中得心源
PT. IV

wan-hsiang-yü 晚香玉
XXXVII

Wan-jo 萬若
X, LEAF O

Wan-kuan chü-shih 晚盥居士
XXXII

Wan-shih-yüan 萬石園
PT. I

Wan-shou 萬壽
X, LEAVES A, G, Q

Wan Shou-ch'i 萬壽祺
PT. I; V, X, XII

Wang (Mr. Wang, unidentified) 王 (氏)
XXIV

Wang Chien 王鑑
PT. I; V, XLI

Wang Chih-jui 汪之瑞
PT. I; XIII

Wang Fang-yü (Fred Wang) 王方宇
XXIII, XXXV

Wang Fu 王紱
PT. I; I

Wang Han-kuang 王含光
XI

Wang Hsi-chih 王羲之
PT. I; PT. II; XX

Wang Hsien 汪誠
XXXII, COLOPHON 19

Wang Hsien-chih 王獻之
PT. II

Wang Hsüeh-hao-yin 王學浩印
XXXIX

Wang Hui 王翬
PT. I; PT. II; PT. IV; XI, XIII, XLI

Wang Kai 王槩
PT. IV; XXII, LEAF B

Wang K'o-yü 汪珂玉
I

Wang Lü 王履
PT. IV

Wang Meng 王蒙
PT. I; II, VII, XII, XXXVIII

Wang Shih-min 王時敏
PT. I; PT. II; V, XIII, XL

Wang Shih-shen 汪士慎
XIX

Wang Sui-yü 汪遂于
XX, LEAF DD

Wang-sou 望叟
XXXII, COLOPHON 24

Wang T'ang 王棠
XXXII, COLOPHON 16

Wang To 王鐸
PT. IV

Wang Tsu-hsi (hao T'i-an) 王祖錫 (號惕安)
XXIV

Wang Wei 王維
X, LEAF K

Wang Yüan 王淵
PT. I

Wang Yüan-ch'i 王原祁
PT. I; PT. IV; XXXIX, XLI

Wei-ch'ing chien-ts'ang (owner unidentified) 渭卿鑑藏
XXXVI

Wei Chiu-ting 衛九鼎
PT. I

wei-hsin-lun 唯心論
PT. IV

(Monk) Wei-tse (僧) 維則
PT. I

Wei Ying-wu 韋應物
X, LEAF M

Wen Cheng-ming 文徵明
PT. I; II, III, XXXVIII

Wen Cheng-ming yin 文徵明印
II

Wen Chia 文嘉
III

wen-fang ssu-pao 文房四寶
PT. I

Wen Fong (Fang Wen) 方聞
PT. IV; XXIII

wen-hsin 文心
XII

wen-jang ku-fa (should read *yün-jang ku-fa*) 醞釀古法
PT. IV

Wen-pi 文璧
I

Weng Fang-kang 翁方綱
XXII, XXV, PORTRAIT LEAF

wo-fa 我法
PT. IV

Wo ho-chi chih-yu (not in *PTC*) 我何濟之有
XXV, LEAF B

wo-tzu-yung wo-fa 我自用我法
PT. IV

Wu-an 勿盦
XXXII, COLOPHON 2

Wu Chan-t'ai 吳瞻泰
XXXII, COLOPHON 2 I

Wu Chan-t'ai-yin 吳瞻泰印
XXXII, COLOPHON 2 I

Wu Ch'ang-shih 吳昌碩（倉石）
PT. I

Wu Chen 吳鎮
PT. I; PT. IV; II, VII, XII

Wu-ch'eng Li Yen-kua, Ch'ü-chi-fu so-chien so-ts'ang chin-shih shu-hua-chi 烏城李延适去疾父所見所藏金石書畫記
III

Wu Ch'i-yüan 吳期遠
X, LEAF B

Wu-chung ssu-ts'ai-tzu 吳中四才子
III

Wu Hu-fan 吳湖帆
II, XXIII

Wu Jang-chih 吳讓之
XL

Wu-jui[shui]-t'u 五瑞圖
XXIII

Wu K'uan 吳寬
XXVII

Wu Li 吳歷
PT. I

Wu-liu hsien-sheng 五柳先生
XX, LEAF E

Wu Mei 吳梅
XXVII

Wu Pin 吳彬
PT. I; PT. IV; XI

Wu Shang-chung 吳尚忠
III

Wu Shang-chung yin 吳尚忠印
III

Wu Shih-t'ai 吳世泰
XXXII, COLOPHON 6

Wu Shih-t'ai-yin 吳世泰印
XXXII, COLOPHON 6

Wu Su-kung 吳蕭公
XX, LEAVES CC AND HH

Wu Su-kung-yin (intaglio, square) 吳蕭公印
XX, LEAF CC

Wu Su-kung-yin (intaglio, large square) 吳蕭公印（大方印）
XX, LEAF HH

Wu T'ieh-sheng 吳鐵聲
XXIII

Wu T'ing 吳廷
PT. I

Wu T'ung (Tom Wu) 吳同
XXIII

Wu Wei 吳偉
PT. I

Wu-wei-an ts'ang-pao 無為庵藏寶
XXVI, LEAF K

Wu-wei-an chu-jen chen-shang 無為庵主人真賞
XXVI, LEAVES B AND K

Wu Wei-yeh 吳偉業
V, XI

Wu Yu-ho 吳又和
XXXII, N.I

Wu-yü-hsüan 梧語軒
XXXII

Wu Yün 吳雲
XXIV

Yahata Sekitarō 八幡關太郎
XXIII

Yang Chi-chen 楊繼振
XXV, PORTRAIT LEAF

Yang En-shou 楊恩壽
VIII

Yang Hsi 楊羲
X, LEAF R

Yang Mei 楊美
III

Yang Shou-ching 楊守敬
III

Yang Shou-ching yin 楊守敬印
III

Yang Wei-chen PT. I; I	楊維楨	Ying X, LEAF D	英
Yang Wen-ts'ung PT. I; V, VIII, IX	楊文驄	Ying-hai-t'u I	瀛海圖
Yao-nung p'ing-sheng chen-shang VIII	藥農平生真賞	Ying, T'ien-shu VII	瑛、田叔（連珠印）
Yao Shou PT. I	姚綬	Ying-yün XXXII, COLOPHON 26	應雲
Yao Sung XII	姚宋	Yonezawa Yoshiho PT. IV; XXIII	米澤嘉圃
yeh-chan XXXIII, LEAF G	野戰	Yu-hsi (PTC 110?) XXII, LEAF B	游戲
yeh-chang XXVI	業障	yu-hsia XXXII	游俠
yeh-ch'eng XXX	野乘	Yu-hsin ch'iu-ho VI	游心丘壑
Yeh Chieh III	葉玠	yu li-ch'ü XXXIX	有理趣
Yeh-lai-hsiang XXXVII	夜來香	Yü Chien-hua PT. IV	俞劍華
Yeh-yün XXV, PORTRAIT LEAF	野雲	Yü-chuang X, LEAF J	榆莊
Yen Chen-ch'ing (hao Lu-kung) PT. IV; I, III, XXVI	顏真卿（魯公）	Yü Feng-ch'ing I	郁逢慶
Yen-chung chih-jen, wu-lao-i (PTC 100) XXIII, XXV, LEAF F	眼中之人吾老矣	Yü-hua VI	與華
Yen-hsi II	崦西	Yü Jung VIII	郁榕
Yen-lü XX, LEAF G	研旅	Yü-pei Huang-shih Po-hou chen-ts'ang VI	禺北黃氏伯厚珍藏
Yen, Nan XXXII, COLOPHON 10	硯南	Yü-shan ts'ao-t'ang PT. IV	玉山草堂
yen-po-ching PT. IV	煙波景	Yü-t'ai hsin-shang XXIII	玉臺心賞
Yen Shih-ch'ing (hao P'iao-sou) XXXIV, COLOPHON	顏世清（號瓢叟）	yü-tsan X, LEAF E, XXXVII	玉簪
Yen-ssu XX, LEAF EE	燕思	Yü-tzu-wo-ming I	鸞字窩銘
Yin-chin XXXII, COLOPHON 30	吟堇	Yü-yü XX, LEAF DD	予予
Yin-cho-chai XXXII, COLOPHON 31	隱拙齋	Yüan XXI	爰（張大千）
Yin-chü-t'u I	隱居圖	Yüan-chi PT. IV	原濟
Yin T'ieh-shih XXIV	殷鐵石	Yüan-chi (PTC 105) XX, LEAF E, XVII, LEAF H(?)	原濟
"Yin-yün" PT. IV	絪緼	Yüan-chi (PTC 104) XXV, LEAF C	原濟
Ying VII	瑛	Yüan-chi, K'u-kua (PTC 107) XXVI, LEAVES A, F, I, J	元濟、苦瓜

Yüan-chi, Shih-t'ao (forged seal)　原濟石濤（偽印）
　XXXV, LEAF D

Yüan Chiang　袁江
　XI

Yüan Tun　員燉
　PT. IV; XXXII

Yüeh-shan (PTC 108)　粤山
　XXII, LEAF J, XXV, LEAF A, XXX,
　LEAF BB, XXXIV, LEAVES J AND L

Yüeh-yü-fu　曰粤父
　XXXII, COLOPHON 7

Yün-( )　允□
　XXXII, COLOPHON 17

Yün-an　筠厂
　XXI

Yün-hui-chai yin　韞輝齋印
　I

Yün-lung-shan-min　雲龍山民
　X, LEAVES A, K, L, UU

Yün Shou-p'ing　惲壽平
　PT. I; XXXVI, XXXVIII

Undecipherable seals: (relief, square, fourth seal, lower left corner of painting)　沈?□□□
　XXXVI

( )-*chai*　□齋
　XXXII, COLOPHON 13

( )-*chi*　□吉
　XXXII, COLOPHON 6

( )-*lu*　□廬
　XXXII, COLOPHON 23

( ) ( ) *pu-i*　□□布衣
　XXXII, COLOPHON 6

( )-*suo*　□所
　XXXII, COLOPHON 30

( )-*t'ing*　□亭
　XXXII, COLOPHON 20

( )-*wu*　□午
　XX, LEAF BB

( )-*yung*　□詠
　XXXII, COLOPHON 9

Note: References to illustrations are printed in *italic* type. Catalogue entries are referred to by roman numerals. Seals may be found under "Chinese and Japanese Names and Terms."

Abe coll., Osaka Municipal Museum, 84, 247, 249, 335
Academy school, 114
Amateur painting. *See* Scholar painting
An Lu-shan, 6
Anhwei, as producer of calligraphy implements, 9
Aoki Masaru, 11
Archaistic style. *See* Painting, styles of
Archeological material, as basis for authentication, 18, 20, 21, 24, 26 n. 38, 30
Art theory, Chinese: 16–17, 18, 20–21
Artistic personality, 16, 20, 23; as related to brushwork, 59–62, 119, 212–13, 258, 260, 282, 316; as related to forger and model, 174, 181, 203, 239, 268–71, 315. *See also* "Identities," artistic; Individualist tradition
Attribution. *See* Connoisseurship; "Identities," artistic
A-wen. *See* Wu T'ung

Berenson, Bernard, 16, 19, 20
Book of Odes, 239
Bordu. *See* Po-erh-tu
British Museum, London, 307
Brushwork: "axe-cut" stroke, 112, 136; blunt, 244–45, 262, 268–69, 294, 299, 302, 308–12 passim; "boneless method" (*mo-ku fa*), 46, 197; "broken," 309; "brush concepts," 46, 47; "centered point" (*chung-feng*), 187; "coarse," 244; "dragon-vein" (*lung-mo*), 286; effects produced by, 53, 54; "fine," 244; "flying white" (*fei-pai*), 85, 196, 198, 233; "hemp-fiber" strokes (*p'i-ma ts'un*), 46, 50, 72, 75, 146, 148, 149, 334, 335; "hiding the tip," 187; "iron rod writing in sand" (*ju-chui hua-sha*), 199; kinesthetic response to, 20, 150, 185, 246, 294; "lotus-leaf veins," 146; "oblique" strokes (*ts'e-feng*), 85, 112, 136, 139, 309, 311, 337; "plump" mode, 41, 227; related to calligraphy script, 58, 199, 226–27, 230–31; "seal style," 309, 311; "slender" mode, 41, 227; "untrammeled," 196; wrist movement, 58, 85. *See also* Artistic personality; Calligraphy; "Energy level"; Painting, terms of; Quality, artistic
Buddhism: as shelter for Ming loyalists, 4, 9, 36, 119, 121; renunciation of, by Tao-chi, 37; influence of, 140. *See also* Ch'an Buddhism

Calligraphy: as basis for authentication of paintings, 30–31, 39, 59–67; as related to painting, 58, 85, 92, 175, 342; *chan-pi* ("tremulous"), 43, 197; diagram, 59, 62, 63–67; "eight principles of," 58; errors in, 184–85, 282; establishing developmental sequence of, 60–62, 230–31; imitating models of, 40–43, 52, 119; of Ch'u Sui-liang, 40–45 passim; of Chung Yu, 40–45 passim; of Huang T'ing-chien, *41*, 43, 197; of

Ni Tsan, 40–45 passim; of Tao-chi, *41*, 40–45, 59–67, 172, 175–76, 184–85, 212–23, 225–31, 280, 282; of Yen Chen-ch'ing, *44*, 43; "old-age" style, 42, 301, 312, 315
SCRIPT TYPES: *chang-ts'ao* ("draft cursive"), 43, 78, 80, 282, 291; *chuan-shu* ("seal"), 41–45 passim, 58, 168, 199, 212–13, 227, 242, 280, 282, 326 [*ta-chuan* ("great seal"), 322]; *chung-k'ai* ("medium regular"), 122, 123 [*hsing-k'ai* ("fluent, regular or standard"), 187–97, 225]; *hsing-shu* ("running," "freehand"), 41–45 passim, 58, 61, 62, 82, 121, 122, 123, 187, 196, 200, 210, 212, 227, 271, 316, 317, 322, 326, 334; *k'ai-shu* ("regular," "model," "block," "standard"), 41–45 passim, 58, 61, 62, 78, 92, 112, 119, 199, 213, 227, 232, 233, 239, 241, 271 [*cheng-k'ai* ("formal standard"), 227; *hsiao-k'ai* ("small block, standard or regular"), 42, 78, 87, 121–22, 123, 172, 175, 284, 299]; *li-shu* ("clerical," "official," or "Chancery"), 41–45 passim, 58, 61, 62, 78, 212, 213, 221, 226–27, 239, 256, 258, 260 [*Han-li*, 226; *pa-fen*, 42; *T'ang-li*, 41, 42, 226, 227]; *ts'ao-shu* ("cursive"), 41–45 passim, 58, 61, 78, 114, 199, 213, 219, 221, 326
TECHNIQUES: *na* stroke, 78, 150, 256, 316; *ko*, 187. *See also* Artistic personality; Brushwork; Quality, artistic
Caro, Frank, New York, 72, 82, 86, 96, 98, 118, 152, 322, 328, 334, 336, 338, 340
Cha Shih-piao, 5, 9, 10, 36, 37, 45, 53, 101, 102, 140, 173 n. 4; *Landscape*, *168*; *Old Man Boating on a River (XIV)*, *157*, 156–57; *Pavilion in Autumn*, *154*; *River Landscape in Rain (XIII)*, *152*, *153*, 152–55
Chan Wen-te: "Eulogy of a Great Man," 225, 226
Ch'an Buddhism: influence on painters of, 36, 56, 57; Lin-chi sect of, 36, 51; temples of, 5, 9, 140. *See also* Buddhism
Chang Chi-su, 10; *Snow-Capped Peaks (XI)*, *134*, *135*, *137*, *138*, 30, 134–39
Chang Chih-ho, 46
Chang Ch'in, 87
Chang Ch'ün, 202, 226, 241; coll. of, Taipei, 243
Chang Chung, 7
Chang Fu, 8
Chang Hsü, 5
Chang Hsüeh-seng, 7
Chang Hung, 9; *Bird, Rock, and Camellias* (with Lan Ying and Yang Wen-ts'ung) *117*
Chang Jui-t'u, 45
Chang Jung, 55
Chang Keng, 154, 155; *Kuo-ch'ao hua-cheng-lu*, 112, 113, 150, 241
Chang Lu, 10
Chang Po-chin coll., Taipei, 114, 134
Chang Po-ying, 119, 120, 121, 122, 123
Chang Seng-yu, 5, 46
Chang Shih-ch'eng, 7
Chang Ta-ch'ien, 11, 23, 29, 178, 181, 202, 203, 212, 224 n. 4, 224 n. 12, 225, 241, 242 n. 4, 274 n. 5, 300; forgery of *Ta-ti-ts'ao-t'ang t'u* (Chu Ta), *222*, 213,

223; label and colophon to Tao-chi *Searching for Plum Blossoms*, *178*, *179*; label to copy of Tao-chi *Flowers and Figures*, *202*, 218; *Letter to Pa-ta shan-jen*, *217*, *218*, 29, 212, 213, 218 (translation of, 216); *Peonies*, *240*, 239; *Summer Cottage in the Hills*, *320*, 317; *Tao-chi Landscapes (XXXV)*, *318–21*, 33, 314–21
Chang Tsao, 5, 58
Chang Tse, 11, 314, 315
Chang Ts'ung-yü coll., 147
Chang Tun-jen, 242
Chang Yüan, see Chang Ta-chien
Chao Chih-ch'ien, 8
Chao Kan: *Early Snow on the River*, 75
Chao Lin, 6
Chao Ling-jang, 106
Chao Meng-chien, 85
Chao Meng-fu, 5, 6, 7, 34, 49, 58, 69 n. 61, 75, 76, 85, 90, 91, 93 n. 9, 332; *San-men-chi*, 313; *Tan-pa-pei*, 313; *Autumn Colors on the Ch'iao and Hua Mountains*, 75; *East Tung-t'ing Mountain*, *74*, 75; *Horse and Groom*, 90; *Water Village*, 75, 149
Chao Po-chü: and Chao Po-hsiao, 91
Chao Pu-chih, 57
Chao Tso, 68 n. 28
Chao Yüan, 6, 9, 76, 149
Chao Yung, 6, 76
Che school, 5, 10, 112, 114, 136
Ch'en Chao, 11, 12, 49; *I-ou yin-kuan hsüan-chi*, 338; *Ku Jo-po shan-sui chi-ts'e*, 341; *Landscape (XL)*, *339*, 30, 338–39
Ch'en Chi, 7
Ch'en Chi-ju, 7, 92, 113
Ch'en Chuan, 291, 293
Ch'en Hsüan, 112
Ch'en Huan, 8
Ch'en Hung-shou, 8, 9, 10, 45, 106, 114, 116, 117 n. 5; *Pao-lun-t'ang-chi*, 117; *Birds and Flowers*, 116
Ch'en Ju-yen, 6, 7, 76
Ch'en Lin, 7
Ch'en Shu, 10, 36, 53; *Old Tree by Waterfall*, 53
Ch'en Shun, 8, 45, 114; *Chrysanthemum and Pine*, *84*, 85
Ch'en Ting-shan, 317
Cheng Ch'ien, 179
Cheng Cho-lu, 40
Cheng Hsieh, 294, 300; *Bamboo*, *51*, 301
Cheng Ssu-hsiao, 233
Cheng Wei, 218, 221
Ch'eng Cheng-k'uei, 10, 53
Ch'eng Chia-sui, 7, 49, 98, 117, 119, 140, 150; *Landscape in the Style of Ni Tsan*, *100*, 101; *Landscapes after Old Masters*, *100*, 101; *Pavilion in an Autumn Grove (V)*, *99*, 98–101
Ch'eng Ching-e, *196* (colophon), 201
Ch'eng Hao, 57
Ch'eng Lin-sheng, 11, 315; *Shih-t'ao t'i-hua-lu*, 220
Ch'eng Ming, 293 n. 1

Ch'eng Shih-chuang, 293
Ch'eng Sui, 36, 140, 150, 151, 155, 168, 326; *Landscape, 170*, 53, 168
Ch'eng Ting-lu: *Teahouse and Garden, 335*
Ch'eng Yin, 293
Ch'eng Yüan-yü, 293
Chi (as signature), 87, 210. *See also* Tao-chi, signatures of
Ch'i Pai-shih, 8
Chia Chao-feng, 291
Chia Chih, 291
Chiang Chi: *Ch'uan-shen mi-yao*, 8, 286; *Landscape and Portrait of Hung Cheng-chih* (with Tao-chi) *(XXXII), 284, 285, 287, 288–89, 292*, 284–93
Chiang Chi-chiang, 121
Chiang Chu, 140, 150, 151
Chiang hung-hai, 121
Chiang Hung (97–173), 119, 121
Chiang Hung (1674–1690), 106
Chiang K'uei: *Lan-t'ing-k'ao*, 34
Chiang-nan area: cultural importance of, 4, 7, 8–9; gardens in, 4
Chiang Shao-shu, 112; *Wu-sheng shih-shih*, 106–13; *Yun-shih-chai pi-t'an*, 106
Chiang Shih-chieh, 150, 151; *Landscape and Portrait of Hung Cheng-chih, 292*, 31, 290, 291; *Landscape in Ni Tsan Style, 291, 292*, 31, 43, 290, 293
Chiang Sung, 10
Chiang Ying, 293
Chiang Yüan, 151
Chih-hsia tz'u yu-jen, Ta-ti-tzu (as signature), 302. *See also* Tao-chi, signatures of
Ch'ien Ch'ien-i, 38, 98
Ch'ien Hsüan, 6
Ch'ien Ku, 8; *Gathering at the Orchid Pavilion, 96; Scholar under Banana Plant (IV), 97*, 31, 96–97
Ch'ien-lung (Ch'ing emperor). *See* Hung-li
Ch'ien Tu, 8, 9, 12; *Sung-hu hua-i, 334; Sung-hu hua-ao, 334; Boat Returning Home, 335; Contemplating Poetry by a Snowy River (XXXVIII), 334*, 31, 334–35; *Cottage at Lu-Shan, 335*
Ch'ien T'ung-ai, 87, 93 n. 4
Ch'ien Yung, 337
Chin Lan, 341, 342 n. 1
Chin Nung, 294
Chin T'ang, 293
Ch'in *Tsu-yung*, 154, 155 n. 5; *T'ung-yin lun-hua*, 154
Ching Hao, 55, 69 n. 61
Ch'ing dynasty, 4, 7, 8, 10, 12, 30, 43, 45, 49, 51, 52, 54, 58, 134, 136, 139, 146, 155, 286, 291, 316, 334, 335, 337, 338; Six Great Masters of, 5, 7
Ch'ing-hsiang Ch'en-jen, Chi (as signature), 244. *See also* Tao-chi, signatures of
Ch'ing-hsiang I-jen, Ta-ti-tzu, Chi (as signature), 284. *See also* Tao-chi, signatures of
Ch'ing-hsiang lao-jen, Chi (as signature), 309. *See also* Tao-chi, signatures of
Ch'ing-hsiang lao-jen, Chi, Ta-ti ts'ao-t'ang (as signature), 311. *See also* Tao-chi, signatures of
Ch'ing-hsiang, Pan-ko-han (as signature), 225. *See also* Tao-chi, signatures of
Ch'ing-hsiang, Ta-ti-tzu (as signature), 256, 260, 264, 280. *See also* Tao-chi, signatures of
Ch'ing-hsiang Ta-ti-tzu, Chi (as signature), 309. *See also* Tao-chi, signatures of
Ch'ing-hsiang Ta-ti-tzu, I-chih-ko (as signature), 302. *See also* Tao-chi, signatures of
Ch'ing Kao-tsung. *See* Hung-li
Chiu-ch'u-wang tao-shih (colophon), 293
Ch'iu Wen, 339
Ch'iu Ying, 5, 8, 9, 38, 117 n. 5; signature, *92; A Donkey for Mr. Chu* (with Hsü Chen-ch'ing) *(III), 89, 90, 91, 94, 95*, 86–95; *Hundred Beauties Competing in Loveliness*, 49
Cho Erh-k'an, 37

Chou Ch'en, 90, 91
Chou Fang: *One Hundred Beauties*, 49
Chou Hsing-tzu, 225, 226
Chou Liang-kung, 49, 98, 140, 141
Chou Wen-chü, 6, 46
Chu Chang-wen, 293
Chu Ch'ang, 151
Chu Chih-fan, *86*, 92
Chu Heng-chia, 36
Chu Ho-nien: *Portrait of Tao-chi, 243*, 241, 242
Chu Hsing-fu, 87, 91
Chu I-ts'un, 291
Chu Liang-yü, 87
Chu Shou-ch'ien, 36, 68 n. 2
Chu Ta, 5, 8, 45, 53, 68 n. 19, 106, 118, 151, 198, 210–24, 314, 326, 326 n.9; leaf of calligraphy, *327*, 326; *Birds, 116; Narcissus, 219*, 218; *Ta-ti-ts'ao-t'ang t'u, 219*, 213, 218, 222, 223
Chu Te-jun, 9
Chu Tsan-i, 36
Chu Ts'un-li, 8; *Shan-hu mu-nan*, 87; as depicted by Ch'iu Ying, *88*, 87–92 passim
Chu Tuan, 10
Chu Wen-cheng, 68 n. 2
Chu Yüan-chang, 68 n. 2
Chu Yün-ming, 45, 87, 93 n. 4
Ch'u Hsiung-wen, 293
Ch'u Kuang-hsi, 122
Ch'u Sui-liang, 40–45 passim, 119, 227, 241
Ch'u Ta-wen, 293
Ch'u Yü-wen, 293
Chü Chieh, 8, 335
Chü-jan, 5, 6, 7, 75, 310
Chü Shang-ku (Chü Chieh), 334
Chuang Shen: *Ming-pao*, 260, 262
Ch'un-hua ko-t'ieh. See Ko-t'ieh
Chung Yu, 40–45 passim, 68 n. 44, 69 n. 49, 172, 175, 226, 227, 231, 239, 299, 300, 301, 302
Collingwood, R. G., 18
Connoisseurship: issues of, 16–26; methods of, 19, 172, 212; terms of, 45. *See also* Quality, artistic; "Energy levels"; Art theory, Chinese
Copies: *bona fide*, 33, 256; connoisseur's, 203; *fen-pen* ("rough sketch"), 271; *fu-pen* or *mo-pen*, 203; *i-lin* ("memory copy"), 271; *lin-mo* or *lin-pen* ("close copy"), 45, 203; "line-for-line," 20–25 passim, 29, 33; *mala fide*, 33; of ancient works, for technical training, 12, 45, 52, 54, 55, 68 n. 44, 106, 111, 113, 314, 329, 337, 339, 342; study value of, 21, 23, 24, 25, 121, 180–85, 186–203, 260–63, 268–80, 314–21. *See also* Artistic personality; Forgery; "Identities," artistic; Quality, artistic

Eastern Chin period, 5
Edwards coll., Ann Arbor, Mich., 150
Eight Eccentrics of Yang-chou, 8, 11, 12, 51, 184, 223, 241, 294, 322, 326, 338
"Energy level": as related to artistic quality, 20–21, 178, 230–31, 290, 300, 301. *See also* Brushwork; Quality, artistic; Artistic personality
"Eye" (*yen*): as concept, 4, 47, 54–55. *See also* "Eye area"
"Eye area," 4, 6, 9, 10, 11, 12

Fan Ch'i, 10, 136; Western influence on, 158; *Landscapes (XV), 159–63*, 158–63
Fan K'uan, 46, 47, 57, 106, 134; *Travelers in Mountains and Streams*, 22
Fan Yü-lin, 113
Fang Heng-hsien, 106, 112
Fei Tan-hsü, 335 n. 3
Feng Shih, 112
Five Dynasties, 5, 6, 7, 9, 75
Flowers, as subjects in painting. *See* Painting, subjects in

Fong, Wen, 18, 21, 24, 38, 39, 212, 213, 218, 220, 221, 232, 233; coll. of, Princeton, 171, 177, 245
Forgery, 98, *172*, 180, 212–24 passim, 271, 282, 314–21 passim; assimilation of style for, 59; detecting of, 28, 29, 40–41, 59; disguised by fine mountings, 32–33; obvious, 33, 184–85; of "typical" work, 31, 172; quality in, 202–3. *See also* Artistic personality; Copies; "Identities," artistic; Nagahara forger; Quality, artistic; Scholar-forger
Freer Gallery, Washington, D.C., 286, 291
Friedländer, Max, 19, 20, 21
Fu Pao-shih: *Shih-t'ao shang-jen nien-p'u*, 220, 221
Fu Shan, 45
Fu-she ("Restoration" Society), 10, 118

Gardens, private: as sign of cultivated taste, 4; as depicted in painting, 8–9
Gombrich, E. H., 20, 25 n. 20
Grand Canal: as link between north and south, 4, 5, 11
"Great synthesis": of Tao-chi, 58; of Tung Ch'i-ch'ang, 7, 12, 342

Hai-yang, Four Masters of, 9, 150, 154
Hakone Museum, Gora, 274, 275, 276, 279
Han Wu, 96 n. 1
Hang-chou: cultural and political importance of, 5, 10
Hao, defined, 36
Hara coll., Tokyo, 139
Hashimoto coll., Osaka, 120, 136, 248
Hashimoto Kansetsu, 11, 212
Historian, vs. connoisseur, 18. *See also* Archeological material; Connoisseurship
Ho Liang-chün, 7; *Ssu-yu-chia hua-lun*, 6
Hobart coll., Cambridge, Mass., 102, 106, 156, 158, 164, 335
Hong Kong exhibition (1970), 33, 168, 172, 173 n. 2
Ho-t'ao, 36, 37
Hsi Kang, 338
Hsia Ch'ang, 7
Hsia Kuei, 10, 134
Hsia Liu-hsiu, 293
Hsia Shih-tse, 6
Hsiang River: relation of, to Tao-chi, 36
Hsiang-shih, 147
Hsiang Yüan-pien, 122
Hsiao Ch'en, 274 n. 4
Hsiao-ch'eng-k'o, Chi (as signature), 199. *See also* Tao-chi, signatures of
Hsiao Yün-ts'ung, 10, 140, 141, 151; colophon, *141*
Hsieh Ch'eng-chün: *K'uei-k'uei-chai shu-hua-chi*, 256
Hsieh Chin, 76
Hsieh Chuo, 293
Hsieh Fang-ch'i, 293
Hsieh Fang-lien, 293
Hsieh Ho, 5; "six principles" of, 20, 58
Hsieh Pin, 113
Hsien Chu, 293
Hsien-yü Shu, 6
Hsin-yen ("eye of the heart"), 46. *See also* "Eye," as concept
Hsing Shen, 87, 93 n. 4
Hsü Chen-ch'ing: *A Donkey for Mr. Chu* (with Ch'iu Ying) *(III), 89, 90, 91, 94, 95*, 86–95
Hsü Chin, 82, 85 n. 1
Hsü Ch'in: *Ming-hua-lu*, 112, 113
Hsü Hsi, 6, 332
Hsü Pen, 6, 9
Hsü P'ing-heng, 120
Hsü Wei, 8, 45, 53, 114, 187, 196, 197, 200
Hsü Yeh-chün, 225, 226
Hsüan-ch'eng, site of Tao-chi's painting, 36
Hsüan-te (Ming emperor), 12, 329

Hsüan-tsung (T'ang emperor), 6, 12, 179
Hsuan-yeh (Ch'ing emperor K'ang-hsi), 11–12, 37, 178, 332
Hu Ch'i, 40
Hu Hsi-kuei, 342 n. 1
Hu Yen-yüan, 122
Hu Yü-k'un, 53
Hua-p'u, 40
Hua Shih-chung, 326 n. 1
Hua Yen, 11, 294; *Hsin-lo shan-jen Li-kou-chi,* 322; *Autumn Music and Poetic Thoughts, 327, 326; Cloudsea, 324; Cloudsea at Mt. T'ai (XXXVI), 323, 325, 322–27; Cloudsea at Mt. T'ai* (Boston), *324; Conversation in Autumn, 326; Giant Bird, 324*
Hua-yü-lu, 40, 51, 52, 55–58 passim
Huang coll., Hong Kong, 173
Huang Ch'üan, 6, 332
Huang I, 338
Huang Kung-wang, 5, 6, 106, 111, 112, 113, 113 n. 1, 140, 155, 337, 338; *Hsieh Shan-shui-chüeh* (Secrets of Landscape Painting), 58; *Dwelling in the Fu-ch'un Mountains,* 6, 76, 113, 113 n. 11, 146, 149, 317
Huang Pin-hung, 339; *Chin shu-shih-nien hua-che-p'ing,* 338; *Lun-hua ch'ang-hsin,* 338
Huang Po-shan (colophons), *187, 188, 192, 193, 186, 187, 199, 201*
Huang Po-ssu, 68 n. 44
Huang-shan. *See* Mt. Huang
Huang Shan-ku, 92
Huang Tao-chou, 45
Huang T'ing-chien, 5, 40, 43, 55, 57, 69 n. 51, 197, 258, 260; *Fu-po-shen-tz'u,* 313
Huang Yen-ssu, *201* (seals), 200
Huang Yün, 290, 293 n. 8
Hui-tsung (Sung emperor), 12, 329, 332
Hung Cheng-chih, 8, 39–40, 68 n. 35, 284–93, 301 n. 2
Hung-jen, 5, 9, 10, 12, 36, 40, 45, 53, 118, 119, 140, 149, 154, 155 n. 8; *Coming of Autumn,* 149; *Dawn over the River, 149; Feng River Landscapes (XII), 141–45, 140–51* (copy of, 29, 150, 151 n. 26); *Hsiang-shih's Rocky Pool, 147; Landscape in the Style of Ni Tsan, 154; Landscapes* (4), *147, 148, 146, 149*
Hung-li (Ch'ien-lung emperor Ch'ing Kao-tsung), 342; as collector, 11–12; *Eight Fragrant Summer Flowers (XXXVII), 328, 330–31, 328–33; Rainy Scene, 329, 332*
Hung Ming, 290, 293
Hung Shih-mou, 290, 291
Hung Tu, 112
Hung-wu emperor, 72

I Ping-shou, 241, 242
"Identities," artistic: typical, 31; unusual, 31–32; early, 32; late, 32; altered, 32–33; forged, 33. *See also* Artistic personality; Copies; Forgery
I-hua: as "first stroke" in painting, 178, 294; as fundamental concept, 52
Imperial collecting, 11, 12, 329
Individualist tradition, 5, 12, 38, 45, 49, 52, 55, 56, 116, 136, 152, 155, 326, 339, 341

Jen Yü, 342 n. 1

Kai Ch'i, 335 n. 3
K'ang-hsi (Ch'ing emperor). *See* Hsuan-yeh
Kao K'o-kung, 7, 69 n. 61, 106
Kao-tsung (Ch'ing emperor). *See* Hung-li
Kawai Senrō, 221
Keng Chao-chung, 49
Ko-t'ieh tradition, 40, 41, 42, 68 n. 44, 119
Ku Cheng-i, 7
Ku Hsing, 112
Ku K'ai-chih, 5
Ku Lin-shih, 342 n. 1
Ku Ssu-li, 293

Ku Tsai-mei, 151
Ku Ying, 6
Ku-yüan ts'ui-lu album: comparison with cat. no. XII, 151 n. 26
Ku Yün, 11, 12, 49, 338; copy of Tao-chi, *341;* copy of Wang Hui, *341;* landscape after Wang Shih-min, *341; Landscape at Dusk (XLI), 340,* 31, 340–42
Kuan T'ung, 69 n. 61, 121
Kuan-yin, transformations of, 146
Kubler, George, 21, 22
K'un-ts'an, 5, 10, 37, 45, 53, 118, 339
Kung Chin, 31, 78, 80, 81
Kung Hsien, 5, 9, 10, 37, 45, 68 n. 12, 69 n. 61, 118, 140; *Landscapes (XVI), 165–67, 164–67;* other works mentioned, 164
Kung Hsiu, 80
K'u-kua [tsai-hsieh Ch'ing-t'eng tao-jen-shih] (as signature), 200. *See also* Tao-chi, signatures of
K'u-kua lao-jen (as signature), 196. *See also* Tao-chi, signatures of
K'u-kua lao-jen, Chi (as signature), 197. *See also* Tao-chi, signatures of
K'ung Shang-jen, 37
Kuo Hsi, 47, 49; *Lin-ch'üan kao-chih,* 55, 58
Kuo Jo-hsü, 20
Kuo T'ai, 119, 121
Kyoto National Museum, 327

Lake T'ai: as cultural center, 4, 5, 10, 12, 31, 72, 75
Lan Meng, 106, 117
Lan Shen, 106, 117
Lan T'ao, 106
Lan Ying, 10, 11, 12, 30, 31, 45, 101, 119, 134, 136, 140, 146, 150, 151; album dedicated to Fang Heng-hsien, 106, 112; *Bird on a Willow Branch (IX), 115, 116,* 31, 114–17; *Bird, Rock, and Camellias* (with Yang Wen-ts'ung and Chang Hung), *117; Bluejay on a Branch, 114; Landscape in the Style of Huang Kung-wang (VIII), 111,* 31, 111–13; *Landscapes after Four Masters, 111; Landscapes after Sung and Yüan Masters (VII), 107–10,* 10, 11, 31, 106–10, 112, 151; *Winter Landscape, 139*
Li Ch'eng, 47, 57, 106, 120
Li Chih, 56
Li Fang-ying, 294, 301
Li Hsien, 336
Li Jui-ch'i, 11, 23; copy of Tao-chi's *Flowers and Figures (XXI), 188–95, 198,* 29, 186, 187, 199, 202–3
Li Jui-ch'ing, 11, 202, 203, 210, 212, 314
Li K'ai, 293
Li Kung-lin, 8, 122; *Five Tribute Horses, 88,* 90, 91, 93 n. 8
Li Kuo-sung (colophon), *194, 200,* 199–200, 201
Li Liu-fang, 7, 49, 98, 117; *Thin Forest and Distant Mountains, 100,* 101
Li Mo-ch'ao coll., 220
Li Pao-hsün, 92
Li Po, 40, 47
Li Sung-an, 216, 220
Li T'ang, 91, 113 n. 5
Li Tsung-ch'eng, 46
Li Yin, 139
Li Yü (Southern T'ang emperor), 6
Li Yü-te, 336
Liang-huai: importance of, in salt trade, 11
Liang K'ai: *Li Po Chanting a Poem, 198*
Liang, Mr., of Kuo-t'ing, 293
Lieh-tzu, 322
Lin Ch'un, 332
Lin Liang, 114
Literati tradition. *See* Scholar painting
Liu Chüeh, 7, 76
Liu Ch'un-hsü, 122–23
Liu Sung-nien, 69 n. 61, 91
Liu Ts'ao, 121

Liu Ts'ao-ch'uang (Liu Pu), 256, 258, 260 n. 4
Liu Tu, 106
Lo Chen-yü, 134
Lo Chia-chieh, 326 n. 1
Lo Chia-lun coll., Taipei, 243
Lo-Fu Mountains, 268–80
Lo P'in: *Portrait of Tao-chi, 243,* 241, 242
Loehr, Max, 19
Los Angeles County Museum of Art, 53, 154
Low coll., Hong Kong, 168
Loyalist painters, see Ming dynasty, loyalists
Lu Chi, 5
Lu Chih, 114, 337
Lu Hsiang-shan, 57
Lu Hsin-yüan: *I-ku-t'ang hsü-pa,* 123
Lu Hui, 342 n. 1
Lu Hung, 119, 122
Lu Kuang, 6
Lu T'an-wei, 5
Lü-an Pen-yüeh (monk), 36
Lü Chi, 114

Ma Lin, 301 n. 9
Ma Wan, 5, 6, 7; forgeries of, 81 n. 9; signatures of, 79, 78; *Kuan-yüan-chi, 76; Pien-p'ang pien-cheng, 76; Yin-chü-t'u, 76; The Ocean, 81; Spring Hills after Rain, 74, 76, 79, 72; Spring Landscape (I), 73, 77, 79, 80, 6, 31, 72–81*
Ma Yüan, 10, 113 n. 5, 301 n. 9
Manchu rule, 4, 118, 140, 178, 329
Mao Ch'i-ling, 116, 117
Mei Ch'ing, 5, 9, 36, 37, 45, 53, 140, 146, 248, 302; album depicting the scenery of Huang-shan, *248*
Mei Keng, 9, 36, 53
Mei Wen-ting, 291
Meng Hao-jan, 123
Methodology of connoisseur, 19–21. *See also* Artistic personality; Brushwork; Connoisseurship, issues of; "Energy level"
Mi Fu, 5, 9, 23, 46, 55, 57, 68 n. 44, 75, 106, 156, 246, 322; "*mi-tien,*" see Painting, terms in
Michigan exhibition, 1967 (Tao-chi), 168
Ming dynasty, 4, 6, 7, 8, 9, 12, 36, 37, 43, 45, 49, 51, 52, 54–58 passim, 72, 76, 80, 87, 90, 92, 96, 98, 102, 106, 111, 114, 119, 134, 136, 139, 146, 149, 155, 156, 158, 285, 334, 337; Four Masters of, 5; loyalists, 4, 9, 10, 118, 119, 122
Mo Shih-lung, 7
Mongol domination, 6, 72, 119, 233
Moriya coll., Kyoto, 182
Morse coll., New York, 96, 341
Mt. Huang: as subject in painting, 4, 5, 9, 10, 36, 140–41, 150, 245, 250, 268. *See also* Cha Shih-piao; Hung-jen; Mei Ch'ing; Tao-chi
Mt. Lu, as depicted by Tao-chi, 268
Mu-ch'en Tao-min (monk), 36
Mu-ch'i (monk), 7
Museum für Ostasiatische Kunst, Cologne, 268, 274, 275, 279
Museum of Fine Arts, Boston, 44, 45, 52, 54, 57, 58, 177, 310, 324
Museum Yamato Bunkakan, Nara, 170
Mustard Seed Garden Manual, 239

Na Yen, 92
Nagahara forger, 29, 39, 212, 213, 216–21 passim, 223
Nagahara Oriharu, 212; coll. of, 217, 222
Nagano coll., Tokyo, 233, 240
Nanking: as artistic center, 10, 37, 302
National Palace Museum, Taipei, 50, 74, 76, 100, 116, 231, 258
Ni Hung-pao, 120
Ni T'ien, 342 n. 1
Ni Tsan, 5, 6, 7, 9, 40–45 passim, 47, 85, 98, 106, 119, 121, 140, 141, 146, 149, 150, 152, 154, 155, 156, 196,

225, 227, 231, 284, 291, 300, 301, 302, 309, 312, 335, 337, 338; *Jung-hsi Studio, 230* (detail), 227–30
Ni Yüan-lu, 45
Nine Friends of Painting, 7, 98, 113, 117, 340
Northern Wei barbarians, 5

Offner, Richard, 19, 20
Okabe Chokei coll., 308, 310
Orthodox tradition, 5, 7, 9, 10, 12, 38, 41, 43, 47, 49, 52, 98, 101, 106, 150, 152, 155, 315, 326, 332, 336, 337, 338, 339, 341, 342. *See also* Six Masters; Tung Ch'i-ch'ang; Wangs, Four
Osaka Municipal Museum. *See* Abe coll.
Ou-yang Hsiu, 11, 55
Ou-yang Hsün, 119

Pa-ta shan-jen. *See* Chu Ta
Painting: as document in social history, 87; as related to calligraphy, 39, 119, 164, 175, 187, 294, 322; as related to poetry, 119, 175, 294, 299; interaction of ink with paper in, 186, 264, 271, 280, 308, 309; portrait, 87, 284–86, 290; symbolic content in, 119, 175, 233, 294, 299, 310, 311
STYLES OF: archaistic, 8, 40, 136, 315, 324; "blue-green," 111, 324; "broad," 154, 156; "fine," 154; "garden," 91; monochrome, 87, 91, 328; "outline," 338; *pai-miao* ("plain-line drawing"), 8, 12, 87, 91; "palace," 8, 9, 87, 91; "wet on wet" (suffused style), 280, 299, 301, 322. *See also* Individualist tradition; Orthodox tradition; Professional painter; Scholar painting; Tao-chi, painting of; Tung-chü tradition
SUBJECTS IN: bamboo, *50–51, 83, 84, 104, 125, 189, 205, 235, 238, 265–67, 281,* 82, 120, 187, 233, 241, 264, 280; banana plant, *50, 97, 194, 235, 257, 261–63,* 96, 199, 240; begonia, *126,* 121; birds, *114, 115, 116, 117, 205, 207, 209, 324;* camellia, *117, 126,* 121; children, *193,* 199; chloranthus *(chen-chu-lan), 330,* 329; chrysanthemum, *83–84, 115, 192,* 82, 114, 198; cockscomb *(chi-kuan-hua), 190,* 196; crab apple *(hai-t'ang), 234,* 232; eggplant, 207; figures, *88–89, 192,* 87–88, 198–99; gardenia *(chih-tzu), 330,* 329; gingko *(ying-hsing), 307,* 311; hibiscus *(huang-shu-k'uei), 191, 238,* 196–97, 240–41; jasmine *(mo-li-hua), 330,* 329; lotus *(ho-hua, lien, fu-jung), 195, 237, 330,* 200, 239–40, 329; narcissus *(shui-hsien), 126, 219, 235,* 121, 233; orchid *(lan), 115, 187, 188, 208, 233, 234, 265–66, 331,* 114, 186, 232–33, 264, 328; peach blossom *(t'ao-hua), 163, 205, 207;* peony *(mou-tan), 197, 236, 240, 239;* pine, *84, 108, 110, 120, 145, 161, 194, 243, 252, 305, 319,* 149, 199, 310, 316; plantain lily *(yü-tsan), 126, 330,* 121, 329; plum blossom *(mei-hua), 174, 175, 180–83, 188, 238, 295–99,* 28, 37, 42, *174–79,* 180–85, 186, 241, 294–301; polygonum *(hung-liao), 237,* 239–40; rock *(t'ai-hu), 83–84, 115, 117, 160, 208, 222, 265,* 8–9, 82, 264; taro, 205; telosma *(yeh-lai-hsiang), 331,* 328–29; tuberose *(wan-hsiang-yü), 330,* 329; vegetables (misc.), *281–83,* 280; willow, *84, 115, 124, 162, 192,* 114, 119, 198. *See also* Huang-shan; Huang Kung-wang, Ni Tsan, Wang Meng, Wu Chen
TERMS IN: "accident and design," 178; *ch'i-ku* ("rare antiquity"), 53; *ch'ing-i* ("pure elusiveness"), 53; *fang* ("to imitate"), 47; *fei-pai* ("flying white"), 233; *hao-fang* ("untrammeled expressiveness"), 53; *hsieh-i* ("to write out ideas and feelings"), 75, 85, 175, 178, 329; *hua* ("transcendence"), 52, 58; *i-hua* ("first stroke"), 52, 178, 294; intuitive faculties, 47, 54, 55, 56, 57; *kan-shou* ("parched leanness"), 53; *kao-ku* ("lofty antiquity"), 53; *ku-pen* ("only extant work"), 28, 30; *lin-li* ("drenched moistness"), 53; *mi-tien,* 46; *mo-ku-fa* ("boneless method"), 46, 197; *pien* ("transformation"), 52; *p'i-ma-ts'un,* 46, 50, 72, 75, 149, 334; *p'o-mo-fa* ("graded ink method"), 46; "resemblance and non-resemblance," 46, 47, 178; "rough sketch,"

271; *shen-hui* ("spiritual correspondence"), 52; *shou-ying-fa,* 46; "six principles," 20, 58; "solid-void" or "negative-positive" relationships, 244, 280; "spirit of antiquity," 75; "transferred from memory," 271; "transformation of models," 52, 55; *ts'un* ("wrinkles" or modeling strokes), 258; workshop painter, 38, 59, 68 n. 28; *yen-po-ching,* 46. *See also* Brushwork; Calligraphy
Palace Museum, Peking, 44, 187, 246, 266, 285, 311, 329
Panofsky, Erwin, 17, 18, 20, 25
P'an Cheng-wei: *T'ing-fan-lou shu-hua-chi,* 173
P'ang Yüan-chi coll., 262
Pei Ch'iung, 72; *Ch'ing-chiang chi,* 76
Peking: as artistic center, 37; Tao-chi in, 37, 47–48, 49–51
Period style: as means of authentication, 29, 33; importance of, in copying old masters, 151; problems of, 21, 22. *See also* Connoisseurship; Tao-chi, painting of (by style)
P'iao-sou. *See* Yen Shih-ch'ing
Pien Luan, 332
Pien Wen-yü, 7
Pien Yung-yü: *Shih-ku-t'ang shu-hua hui-k'ao,* 81
P'ien-shih-shan-fang ("Sliver of Stone Retreat"), 11
P'ing-shan-t'ang (historic site), 11, 106, 112
Po-erh-tu, 37, 49, 50; *Landscape with Self-Inscription, 48,* 49
Professional painter, 102; inferior status of, 11, 38, 93 n. 3, 112
P'u Ju, 226
P'u-men (monk), 9

Quality, artistic, 20–21, 24; as evidenced in copies and forgeries, 180–81, 184–85, 186–87, 196–200, 202–3, 212–13, 221, 223, 270–71, 316–17; in calligraphy, 39, 40–41, 59–60, 175–76, 225–26; in painting, 32, 313

"Resemblance and non-resemblance," as conceptual process in painting, 178
Ricci, Matteo, 10
Rubbings, antique. *See* Ko-t'ieh tradition

Schapiro, Meyer, 24
Scholar painting, 5–8 passim, 10, 11, 12, 31, 38, 49, 58, 72, 76, 82, 85, 87, 90, 92, 96, 98, 102, 112, 114, 152, 294, 329, 332, 337, 341
Scholar-forger, 23, 202–3, 314–15
Seal-carving: of Tao-chi, 41–42; of Wan Shou-ch'i, 119, 121, 122
Seals: for determining date of work, 24; identification of authorship through, 30. *See also* Tao-chi, seals of
Shanghai: as artistic center, 11, 314
Shanghai Museum, 39, 74, 114, 154, 221
Shansi: as business center, 10
Shao Mi, 7, 45, 53, 117
Shao Sung-nien: *Ku-yüan ts'ui-lu,* 150
She-hsien: as cultural city, 10
Shen Chen, 7
Shen Ch'eng, 7
Shen Chou, 5, 7, 8, 10, 23, 40, 43, 57, 69 n. 61, 82, 85, 96, 114, 256, 258, 260, 337; *Mo-ch'o T'ung-ch'üeh-yen-ko t'u,* 260; *Cock and Chrysanthemum, 84, 85; Falling Flowers,* 258; *Sitting up at Night,* 258; *Bronze Peacock Inkslab* (attributed to), *262,* 260 (copy of, *263,* 31, 33, 256, 258, 260–63); *Scholar under Garden Rock* (attributed to), *262, 258*
Shen Heng, 7
Shen Hung-tu, 92
Shen Pin, 87
Shen Shih-ch'ung, 68 n. 28
Shen T'ing-fang, 291, 293
Shen Ts'an, 81 n. 16
Shen Tu, 81 n. 16
Sheng Mao-yeh, 152; *Landscapes after T'ang Poems,*

103–5, 102–5
Shih Feng-hui, 293
Shih-t'ao (as signature), 199. *See also* Tao-chi, signatures of
Shih tao-jen, Chi (as signature), 196. *See also* Tao-chi, signatures of
Shih-yen ("eye of poem"), 4. *See also* "Eye"
Shinozaki coll., 222
Shou-yen ("eye of the hand"), 47, 55. *See also* "Eye"
Shu (Szechuan), 6, 314
Six Masters (of the Ch'ing), 12, 106. *See also* Wangs, Four; Wang Chien; Wang Hui; Wang Shih-min; Wang Yüan-ch'i; Wu Li; Yün Shou-p'ing
"Six principles" (of Hsieh Ho), 20, 58
Soper, A. C., 223
Spiritual correspondence *(shen-hui),* 52
Ssu-kuang-ssu ("Temple of Merciful Brilliance"), 9
Su-chou: as center of artistic activity, 7–8, 87; Museum, 44, 177
Su Shih, 5, 33, 40, 43, 55, 57, 58, 92, 168, 172, 313; *Han-shih-t'ieh,* 313
Su Tung-p'o. *See* Su Shih
Sui dynasty, 5
Sumitomo coll., 39, 48, 149, 171, 187, 196, 200, 201, 222, 244, 245, 249, 276, 324
Sun Ch'eng-tse, 136
Sun Ch'ien-li, 5
Sun I, 9, 10, 150–51, 154, 274 n. 4; *Landscape, 150*
Sun K'o-hung, 7, 9, 112, 113
Sun Tzu-hsiu, 141
Sung-chiang, 6–7
Sung dynasty, 5–12 passim, 19, 20, 22, 23, 43, 44, 47, 55, 56, 58, 75, 91, 92, 106, 134, 139, 300
Sung Hsü, 113
Sung K'o, 81 n. 16
Sung Sui, 81 n. 16

Ta-ti-tzu (as signature), 40, 49, 218, 309, 311. *See also* Tao-chi, signatures of
Ta-ti-tzu, Chi (as signature), 308, 309, 310, 312. *See also* Tao-chi, signatures of
Ta-ti-tzu, Jo-chi (as signatures), 310. *See also* Tao-chi, signatures of
Ta-feng-t'ang coll., 44, 48, 50, 54, 140, 168, 174, 186, 204, 210, 225, 232, 243, 256, 264, 268, 280, 284, 294, 300, 302, 315, 320, 327
Tai Chin, 10, 30, 112, 134, 136
Tai Pen-hsiao, 10, 37, 136, 326; *Landscape after Ni Tsan, 170,* 53, 168; "Man in a Cave," *147,* 146
Tai Wen-chin, 114
T'ai-chou school, 57
T'ai-shang Huang-t'ing nei-ching yü-ching (Taoist sutra), 123
T'ai-tsu (Sung emperor), 6
T'ai-tsung (Sung emperor), 68 n. 44
Tan Ch'ung-kuang, 154, 155
T'ang dynasty, 5, 6, 7, 9, 55, 58
T'ang Hsüan-i, 70 n. 107, 140
T'ang Yin, 5, 7, 8, 34, 38, 87, 92, 93 n. 4
Tao-chi, 5, 7–12 passim, 68 n. 12, 68 n. 31, 70 n. 107, 118, 140, 148, 150, 151, 158, 326, 338, 339, 341; art theories of, 45–49, 51–58; color, use of, in painting by, 232–33, 239–41 passim, 245–50 passim, 269, 280, 286, 302, 308–11 passim; copies of, 180–85; copies of, by Chang Ta-ch'ien, 314–17; copies of, by Li Jui-chi, 186–203; dates of, 38, 284; gardens of, 11; "great synthesis" of, 58; *Hua-yü-lu,* 40, 51, 52, 55–58 passim; I-chih-ko (studio of), 37, 175, 178, 302, 308; imperial heritage of, 36, 37, 178, 218; in Hsüan-ch'eng (1660s–1680), 36–37, 168; in Nanking (1680–1686), 10, 37, 174–75; in Peking (1689–1692), 37, 47–48, 49–51; in Yang-chou (1687–1689, 1693–ca. 1710), 10, 37–38, 290–91, 294, 302, 315; life of, 36–40; Michigan exhibition of (1967), 168; portrait of, by anonymous painter, *243,* 232, 241–42; portrait of,

by Chu Ho-nien, *243*; portrait of, by Lo P'in, *243*; renunciation of Buddhism by, 37, 218; seals of, 68 n. 46, 260, 264, 301, 271, 353; self-inscriptions of, *36, 39, 44, 48, 56*, 57, *172*, 219, 230, 231, 266, 283, 285; self-portrait of, *243*, 241–42; "Shen-p'ing-hsing," 37; Taoism, influence of, on, 51; Ta-ti-t'ang (studio of), 37; *Ta-ti-tzu t'i-hua shih-pa*, 40
CALLIGRAPHY OF: *41*, 63–67, *184*, 218, 219, 230, 231, 40–45, 59–67, *172*, 175–76, 184–85, 212–23, 225–31, 280, 282; (by title): *Keng-ch'en Manuscript of Poems, 39*, 221, 38, 212, 220, 221, 274; *Letter (tso-wan)*, *215*, 212, 213; *Letter to I-weng*, *215*, 212, 213; *Letter to Pa-ta shan-jen (XXIII)*, 210–11, *214, 216, 217, 218, 219*, 29, 38, 39, 41, 43, 68 n. 19, 210–24 (translation of, 216); *Letter to Shen-lao*, *215*, 212, 213; *Letter to T'ui-weng*, *215*, 212, 213; *Letter to Yü-chün*, *215, 279*, 212, 213, 274; *Ta-ti-ts'ao-t'ang t'u* (colophon of), *219*, 218, 223; *Thousand-Character "Eulogy of a Great Man" (XXIV)*, 226–29, 41, 42, 225–31; *Wan-li's Porcelain Handle Brush*, 280
PAINTING OF (BY STYLE): "early style" paintings of, *169*, 174–75, 32, 170, 176; figure painting by, *192, 193, 243, 249*, 198–99, 241–42, 248, 258; "mature style" paintings of, *188–95, 205–9, 234–38, 265–66*, 50, 186, 204, 232–33, 239–41, 264, 280–82; "old-age style" paintings of, *272–73, 277, 295–99, 303–7*, 38, 244, 250, 268–71, 294, 299–301, 302, 308–12
PAINTING OF (BY TITLE): *After Shen Chou's Bronze Peacock Inkslab (XXVII), 257, 259, 261*, 31, 32, 33, 42, 185, 227, 230, 256–60; *Album for Liu Shih-t'ou, 308, 310*, 271; *Album for Su-weng after Poems by Sung and Yuan Masters, 249*, 248; *Album for Yü-lao, 246*, 316; *Album of Flowers and Bamboo, 233*; *Album of Flowers and Portrait of Tao-chi (XXV), 234–38, 243*, 49, 232–43, 315; *Album of Landscapes (XXVI), 251–55*, 38, 43, 244–55, 315; *Album of Landscapes (Boston)*, 220, 230, 262, 280; *Album of Landscapes (Sakuragi coll.), 52; Album of Landscapes for Liu Shih-t'ou, 308, 310; Album of Landscapes in Six Leaves, 46; Album of Paintings Depicting the Poems of Su Shih, 173, 172*; album of twelve leaves depicting the scenery of Huang-shan, *187, 245*, 196, 200, 201, 201 n. 7, 244, 246; *Autumn Melon and Praying Mantis, 283*, 49, 264, 280, 282; *Bamboo and Orchids in the Wind, 266*, 264, 280, 282; *Bamboo in Wind* (with Wang Yüan-ch'i), *50*, 49; *Bamboo, Orchid, and Rock* (with Wang Hui), *50*, 49; *Bamboo, Vegetables, and Fruit (XXXI), 281*, 8, 29–30, 41, 43, 49, 264, 280–83; *Banana Plant in Rain, 50*, 49, 240; *Conversion of Hariti to Buddhism, 177*, 176; *The Echo (XVII), 169*, 32, 33, 168–73; *Eight-Leaf Album of Landscapes* (dated 1673), *311*, 170; *Eight-Leaf Album of Landscapes* (Abe coll.), *247*, 248; *Eight Views of Huang-shan, 245, 249*, 170, 179 n. 2, 212, 214, 218, 230–31, 244, 248, 302; *Eight Views of the South, 312*, 302, 308; *Flower Album by Ch'ing-hsiang, 233, 240*, 232, 239; *Flowers and Figures (XX), 188–95, 198*, 8, 29, 43, 49, 186–201, 202–3, 258, 260, 316; *Flowers and Rocks* (nineteenth-century forgery of), *222*, 40, 223; *Graded Ink Landscapes, 318, 319, 320, 321*, 250, 316, 317; *Landscape after Chou Wen-chü, 47*, 46; *Landscape after Fan K'uan, 47; Landscape and Portrait of Hung-chih (XXXII)* (with Chiang Chi), *284, 285, 287, 288–89, 292*, 31, 32, 40, 43, 271, 284–93; *Landscape in Ni Tsan Style, 48*, 47, 154; *Landscapes, Vegetables, and Flowers (XXII), 205–9*, 204–9; *Li Sung-an's Studio, 220; Lo-Fu Mountains (XXX), 272, 273*, 274–76, 277, 278, 29, 43, 268–79; *Lo-Fu Mountains* (Cologne), *268, 274, 275, 276, 279*, 29, 269, 270, 271; *Lo-Fu Mountains* (Hakone), *274, 275, 276, 279*, 29, 269, 270, 271; *Loquats, 283*, 280, 282; *Loquats and Melon, 282*, 280; *Man Walking toward a Mountain, 310*, 220; *Old Trees for Ming-liu, 53*, 52, 154, 218; *The Painter Supervising*

the Planting of Pine Trees, 243, 241, 242; *The Painter Supervising the Planting of Pine Trees* (Lo Chia-lun coll.), *243*, 241, 242; *Orchid, Bamboo, and Rock (XXIX), 265, 267*, 8, 187, 264–67, 280, 282; *Panoramic Vista*, 38, 50; *Peach Blossom Spring, 286*, 271; *Plum Branch, 299*, 294, 301; *Plum Branches (XXXIII), 295–98*, 42, 43, 176, 241, 294–301, 315; *Reminiscences of Ch'in-huai*, 179 n. 2, 302; *Reminiscences of Nanking (XXXIV), 303–7*, 32, 230–31, 302–13, 315; *Searching for Plum Blossoms (XVIII), 174, 175, 176, 178, 179, 182*, 28, 37, 41, 42, 174–79, 180–85, 241, 294, 299 [modern copy of *(XIX)*, *180–81, 183*, 28, 180–85, 202, 203; nineteenth-century copy of, *180–81, 183*, 28, 29, 180–85, 203]; *1700 Peking Album*, 44, 246, 43, 245, 250, 294, 299; *Sixteen Lohans, 170*, 36, 172; *Sketches after Su Tung-p'o's Poems, 247, 249*, 246, 248; *Sketches of Calligraphy and Painting by Ch'ing-hsiang, 187*, 266, 286, *311*, 41, 186, 212, 214, 218, 221, 226, 227, 230, 231, 240, 241, 264; *Small Album* (Fong coll.), *171, 177, 245*, 43, 172, 176, 186, 187, 196, 230, 240, 244, 246, 247, 299; *Splash-Ink Album of Landscapes*, 300; *Spring on the Min River*, 178; *Ten-Leaf Album of Landscapes, 44*, 45; *Ten Thousand Ugly Inkblots, 44, 177*, 46, 176, 316; *Ting-ch'iu Album of Flowers, 197, 299*, 300, 39, 40, 227, 230, 280, 299; *Twelve-Leaf Album of Landscapes* (Boston), *44*, 57, 45, 52, 54, 56, 58; *View from Yü-hang*, 230, 231; *View of Huang-shan* (dated 1667), *56*, 55; *View of Huang-shan* (Sumitomo coll.), *276*, 39, 269, 271, 302; *Village among Green Willows*, *54*; *Watching a Waterfall from a Stone Bridge*, 170; *Waterfall at Mt. Lu, 48, 171*, 39, 47, 170, 172, 199, 212, 214, 221; *Wu-jui-t'u* (nineteenth-century copy of), *222*, 220, 221
SIGNATURES OF: *218–19*, 266, 37–38, 40, 49, 59, 68 n. 30, 181, 187, 196, 197, 199, 200, 210, 212–13, 218, 225, 233, 244, 256, 260, 264, 280, 284, 302, 308–12 passim
T'ao Ch'ien, *192, 198*, 119, 197–99, 258
T'ao Liang: *Hung-tou-shu-kuan shu-hua-chi*, 256, 260
Tao-yen ("eye of understanding"), 54–55. *See also* "Eye"
T'ao Yüan-ming. *See* T'ao Ch'ien
Tao-te-ching (Chang Ch'ün coll.), 226, 241, 242
"Thousand-Character Classic," 225, 226; of P'u Ju, 226
Three Kingdoms period, 5
Ting Yün-p'eng, 8, 9, 326; iconography of Kuan-yin transformations, 146
Tokyo National Museum, 198
Ts'ai Yüan-li, 270
Ts'ao Chih-po, 6, 106, 155
Ts'ao P'u-hsing, 5
Ts'ao Ts'ao, 256, 258, 260 n. 1, 260 n. 2
Ts'ao Yin, 141
Tseng Hsi, 314
Ts'eng Ching, 8
Tsi-lo Lou coll., Hong Kong, 50, 170
Tsou Fu-lei: *Breath of Spring*, 78
Tsu-ming (colophon), *189*, 187
Ts'ui Tzu-chung, 8
Tu Ch'iung, 7
Tu Wan, 9
T'u-hui-pao-chien hsü-tsuan, 96, 113
Tuan Fang, 92
Tung Ch'i-ch'ang, 6, 7, 10, 12, 37, 43–45, 52, 54, 55, 56, 58, 68 n. 28, 70 n. 120, 98, 106, 112, 113, 117, 119, 122, 154, 156, 332, 337, 338, 339, 342; "great synthesis" of, 7, 12, 342
Tung-Chü tradition, 6, 75, 76. *See also* Chü-jan; Tung Yüan
Tung Sung, 87
Tung Yüan, 5, 6, 7, 46, 57, 75, 113 n. 1, 310
Tzu, defined, 36

Tzu-ch'eng i-chia ("to establish one's own style"). *See* Individualist tradition

Vannotti coll., Lugano, 154

Wan-shih-yüan ("Garden of Ten Thousand Stones"), 11
Wan Shou-ch'i, 8, 10, 98, 119, 121, 122, 140, 141, 150, 151; *Landscapes, Flowers, and Calligraphy (X), 118*, 124–33, 9, 118–33; *Lofty Pine and Secluded Dwelling, 120*
Wang, Chi-ch'ien, coll., New York, 246, 266, 282
Wang Ch'en, 337 n. 1, 341
Wang Chien, 5, 6, 7, 98, 101 n. 6, 341
Wang Chih-jui, 9, 10, 150, 151, 154; *Landscape, 155*, 154
Wang Chiu, 337 n. 1
Wang Ch'ung, 45, 87
Wang Fang-p'ing, 270
Wang Fang-yü, *314*; coll. of, Short Hills, N.J., 219
Wang Fu, 7, 76, 337
Wang Han-kuang, 136
Wang Hsi-chih, 5, 23, 24, 68 n. 44, 225; *K'uai-hsüeh shih-ch'ing*, 332
Wang Hsien, 293
Wang Hsien-chih, 23, 68 n. 44
Wang Hsüeh-hao, 12, 341; *Landscape after Chü-jan and Wu Chen*, 337; *Landscape after Wang Fu (XXXIX), 336*, 31, 336–37
Wang Huan, 112
Wang Hui, 5, 7, 12, 22, 37, 38, 58, 136, 139, 264, 337 n. 1, 341; *Bamboo, Orchid, and Rock* (with Tao-chi), *50*, 49, 51; *Dwelling in the Fu-ch'un Mountains, 113*; *In Pursuit of Antiquity*, 155
Wang Kai, 37
Wang K'o-yü: *Shan-hu-wang*, 81
Wang Lü, 57
Wang Meng, 5, 6, 7, 50, 85, 106, 113 n. 1, 120, 140, 149, 334, 335
Wang Shih-min, 5, 7, 45, 98, 155, 226, 337 n. 1, 338, 341; *Hsiao-chung hsien-ta* album, 22
Wang Shih-shen, 294; *Blossoming Plum, 182*, 184
Wang Su, 337 n. 1
Wang Sui-yü (colophon), *191*, 197
Wang T'ang, 293
Wang To, 45
Wang Wei, 7, 122
Wang Ya-i, 92
Wang Yang-ming, 57
Wang Yü, 337 n. 1
Wang Yüan, 7
Wang Yüan-ch'i, 5, 7, 12, 264, 336, 337, 337 n. 1, 341; *Bamboo in Wind* (with Tao-chi), *50*, 49, 51
Wangs, Four, 30, 51, 98, 101, 315, 336, 338, 340, 341, 342. *See also* Wang Chien; Wang Hui; Wang Shih-min; Wang Yüan-ch'i
Wangs, Lesser Four, 315, 336, 337 n. 1, 341, 342
Wangs, Two, 55. *See also* Wang Hsi-chih; Wang Hsien-chih
Wei Chiu-ting, 76
Wei-tse (monk), 9
Wei Ying-wu, 122
Wen school, 8. *See also* Wen Cheng-ming
Wen Cheng-ming, 5, 7–10 passim, 32, 43–45, 87, 96, 114, 149, 226, 258, 260 n. 8, 332, 334, 335; *Chrysanthemum, Bamboo, and Rock* (1512), *84*, 82, 85; *Chrysanthemum, Bamboo, and Rock* (1535) *(II), 83*, 82–85; *Cypress and Weathered Rocks*, 82; *Old Pine Tree*, 82
Wen Chia, 92
Wen T'ung, 55, 187
Weng coll., New York, 147
Weng Fang-kang, 241, 242
West Lake, gardens around, 5. *See also* Gardens; Hang-chou

Wölfflin, Heinrich, 21
Wu (Liang emperor), 225, 226
"Wu" school, 5, 7, 9, 10, 82, 96, 102, 112, 117, 335. *See also* Shen Chou; Wen Cheng-ming; "Wen" school
Wu Chan-t'ai, 293
Wu Ch'ang-shih, 8, 34
Wu Chen, 5, 6, 7, 38, 69 n. 61, 85, 106, 113 n. 1, 140, 146, 151, 155, 338; *Hermit Fisherman at Tung-t'ing, 74, 76*
Wu Ch'i-yüan, 120
Wu Hu-fan, 262
Wu Jang-chih, 338, 339
Wu Ku-hsiang, 342 n. 1
Wu K'uan, 256, 258
Wu Li, 5, 7, 340
Wu Pin, 5, 9, 10, 30, 45; *Streams and Mountains Far from the World, 136,* 134, 139
Wu Su-kung (colophons), *190, 195, 196, 201, 200*
Wu Ta-cheng, 342 n. 1
Wu T'ing, 10

Wu T'ung, 212
Wu Wei, 10
Wu Wei-yeh, 98, 136
Wu-yueh kingdom, 5
Wu Yu-ho, 293 n. 1

Yang (Sui emperor), 5
Yang-chou: as artistic center, 10–11, 37. *See also* Eight Eccentrics of Yang-chou; Tao-chi, in Yang-chou
Yang Hsi, 123
Yang Mei, 87
Yang Shou-ching, 92
Yang Wei-chen, 6, 7, 31, 72, 76; *Chang-shih T'ung-po Ch'ien-piao,* 78; *Essay on the Den of Selling One's Writings, 80,* 78, 81; inscription on *Spring Landscape (I), 72, 80,* 78–81 passim
Yang Wen-ts'ung, 7, 98, 101, 113; *Bird, Rock, and Camellias* (with Lan Ying and Chang Hung), *117*
Yangtze River, 11

Yao Shou, 7
Yao Sung, 9, 151
Yeh Chieh, 87
Yen. See "Eye"
Yen Chen-ch'ing, 24, 43, 78, 92, 119, 245, 246
Yen Shih-ch'ing, 306 (colophon), 313
Yin T'ieh-shih, 225
Yonezawa Yoshiho, 39, 60
Yü Chien-hua: *Shih-t'ao nien-piao,* 40
Yü Feng-ch'ing: *Shu-hua t'i-pa-chi,* 81
Yüan Chiang, 139
Yüan dynasty, 4, 6, 7, 9, 12, 23, 31, 58, 72, 75, 76, 80, 85, 98, 106, 111, 119, 149, 334; Four Great Masters of, 5, 6, 7, 112, 140
Yüan Hung-tao, 56
Yüan Mei, 293 n. 5
Yüan Tun, 36, 290, 293 n. 1, 293 n. 5
Yün Shou-p'ing, 5, 7, 8, 121, 155, 334, 335, 340; landscape, *327, 326; Landscape after Ni Tsan, 335,* 334
Yung-cheng (Ch'ing emperor), 332